foliage
plant
production

Jasper N. Joiner, Editor

Department of Ornamental Horticulture
Institute of Food and Agricultural Sciences
University of Florida

foliage
plant
production

Prentice-Hall, Inc., Englewood Cliffs, N.J. 07632

Library of Congress Cataloging in Publication Data

Main entry under title:

FOLIAGE PLANT PRODUCTION.

    Includes bibliographies and index.
      1.-Foliage plants. I.-Joiner, Jasper N.
SB431.F64   635.9'75   80-21797
ISBN 0-13-322867-3

Printed in the United States of America

10 9 8 7 6 5 4 3

Editorial production/supervision
and interior design by Ellen W. Caughey
Editorial assistant: Susan Pintner
Cover design by Edsal Enterprises
Manufacturing buyer: John B. Hall

Prentice-Hall International, Inc., *London*
Prentice-Hall of Australia Pty. Limited, *Sydney*
Prentice-Hall of Canada, Ltd., *Toronto*
Prentice-Hall of India Private Limited, *New Delhi*
Prentice-Hall of Japan, Inc., *Tokyo*
Prentice-Hall of Southeast Asia Pte. Ltd., *Singapore*
Whitehall Books Limited, Wellington, *New Zealand*

contributors

S. A. Alfieri, Jr., Ph.D.
Assistant Director, Division of Plant Industry
State Department of Agriculture
Gainesville, Florida

R. L. Biamonte, Ph.D.
Supervisor of Applied Research
Tara-Lite and Peters Products
W. R. Grace and Company
Traveler's Rest, South Carolina

G. G. Blalock
Products and Operations Manager
Oakdell, Inc., a Division of Weyerhauser, Inc.
Apopka, Florida

C. A. Conover, Ph.D.
Professor of Ornamental Horticulture
Center Director, Institute of Food and Agricultural Sciences (IFAS)
Agricultural Research Center
Apopka, Florida

D. W. Dickson, Ph.D.
Associate Professor, Nematology Extension
IFAS, University of Florida
Gainesville, Florida

A. Donnan, Jr., Ph.D.
Tissue Culture and Research Manager
Oakdell, Inc., a Division of Weyerhauser, Inc.
Apopka, Florida

R. A. Hamlen, Ph.D.
Assistant Professor of Entomology
IFAS, Agricultural Research Center
Apopka, Florida

R. W. Henley, Ph.D.
Associate Professor of Ornamental Horticulture
IFAS, Agricultural Research Center
Apopka, Florida

R. J. Henny, Ph.D.
Assistant Professor of Ornamental Horticulture
IFAS, Agricultural Research Center
Apopka, Florida

J. N. Joiner, Ph.D.
Professor of Ornamental Horticulture
IFAS, University of Florida
Gainesville, Florida

J. F. Knauss, Ph.D.
Associate Professor of Plant Pathology
IFAS, Agricultural Research Center
Apopka, Florida

R. B. Marlatt, Ph.D.
Professor of Plant Pathology
IFAS, Agricultural Research and Education Center
Homestead, Florida

D. B. McConnell, Ph.D.
Associate Professor of Ornamental Horticulture
IFAS, University of Florida
Gainesville, Florida

P. L. Neel, Ph.D.
Southern Ornamental Plant, Inc.
Lantana, Florida

R. T. Poole, Ph.D.
Professor of Plant Physiology
IFAS, Agricultural Research Center
Apopka, Florida

E. F. Scarborough, B.S.A.
Marketing Specialist
Florida Department of Agriculture and Consumer Services
Winter Park, Florida

M. R. Sheehan, M. S.
Assistant Professor of Ornamental Horticulture
IFAS, University of Florida
Gainesville, Florida

T. J. Sheehan, Ph.D.
Professor of Ornamental Horticulture
IFAS, University of Florida
Gainesville, Florida

D. E. Short, Ph.D.
Associate Professor of Entomology Extension
IFAS, University of Florida
Gainesville, Florida

C. N. Smith, Ph.D.
Professor of Food and Resource Economics Marketing
IFAS, University of Florida
Gainesville, Florida

D. Stokes, Ph.D.
Assistant Professor of Nematology
IFAS, University of Florida
Gainesville, Florida

W. E. Waters, Ph.D.
Professor and Center Director
IFAS, Agricultural Research and Education Center
Bradenton, Florida

G. J. Wilfret, Ph.D.
Associate Professor of Genetics
IFAS, Agricultural Research and Education Center
Bradenton, Florida

F. W. Zettler, Ph.D.
Professor of Virology
IFAS, University of Florida
Gainesville, Florida

contents

two

greenhouses, related structures,
and environmental control   40
Will E. Waters and Charles A. Conover

three

mechanization   72
Charles A. Conover and Glenn G. Blalock

four

plant classification and structure   102
D. B. McConnell and M. R. Sheehan

five

development of new foliage plant cultivars   126
Gary J. Wilfret and T. J. Sheehan

six

seven

eight

nine

ten

eleven

twelve

thirteen

fourteen

fifteen

sixteen

seventeen

eighteen

preface

This will be the only book published that covers all aspects of foliage plant production throughout the world. It is uniquely adaptable for use as a college textbook and as a practical production guide for professional foliage plant producers. Each chapter of the book is written by specialists who are highly trained and have technical and practical experience.

Information for this book was obtained from all parts of the world. Several of the authors have consulted for and visited foliage operations in every major production area of the world and, thus, are especially competent in writing for an international audience.

Foliage Plant Production intensively covers every aspect of plant production and cultural techniques, marketing, problem diagnoses, species identification, and plant use and acclimatization.

A history of the foliage plant industry—production and marketing—worldwide is given, as well as the current status of the production and marketing situations. Marketing systems and problems are outlined and discussed in detail.

Diagrams and flow charts of sample nursery designs and layouts are presented with complete discussions of potentials for mechanization to reduce labor costs and improve production efficiency. A potential grower could completely design a new operation from this information and current growers can improve their operational efficiency. Plans, charts, and pictures are also presented relative to greenhouses, related structures, and environmental control mechanisms. There are detailed discussions on the operation of greenhouses and related structures and on controlling the environment in relationship to plant physiology.

Breeding techniques for the genetic production of new cultivars are described and potentials for future new crops given. Step-by-step instructions for establishing a tissue culture laboratory for production of virus-free plants are given along with formulas for culture media for different crops. Tissue culture also is currently being used to obtain the largest number of plants from the minimum amount of stock area in the shortest period of time. Regular vegetative, spore, and seed propagational techniques are discussed with drawings showing the most common techniques used in foliage plant production.

Foliage plant nutrition and fertilization is completely covered in terms of nutritional interactions with environmental factors, fertilizer sources, availability and leachability in the media, instructions for developing fertilizer formulas, tables on suggested application levels and frequencies, tables on mixing desired concentrations of fertilizer materials, and tables on taking and interpreting soluble salt readings. The information given will allow the development of a complete fertilizer program for any type of operation.

Water use and application, plus light and temperature relationships are discussed singly and as interacting factors. Charts on best light intensities for specific crops are presented for production and interior holding and use.

Pictures of primary insects and disease pests are included with specific control materials and application techniques. Tables give mixing instructions for various pesticides and application techniques.

Perhaps the most valuable, practical information in the text is a detailed chart guide to diagnosing plant disorders (pages 330–339). A grower seeing any disorder in his or her operation can find the symptomology in the diagnostic chart and will be given the causal agent and corrective procedure. The chart is an easy-to-use, simple outline of all problem areas.

Pictures and tables give instruction on plant identification, how to acclimatize plants for low light stress conditions, and how to use foliage plants in interior locations.

Acknowledgments

The original idea for the development of this book on foliage plant production came from Dr. Charles A. Conover, Center Director, Agricultural Research Center, Apopka, Florida. He saw the need and initiated the process that resulted in this text. Drs. Dennis B. McConnell and Richard W. Henley joined forces with Dr. Conover to develop the content of the book and obtain the most expert authors for the information to be covered. It was at this point that I assumed responsibility.

The authors were very cooperative in submitting their materials on the time schedules requested and exceedingly patient with the editing necessary to produce the end product. The authors are to be highly commended in agreeing to allow all royalties from this book to go to a graduate assistantship(s) at the Institute of Food and Agricultural Sciences, University of Florida.

The authors gratefully acknowledge Lynda Eads Chandler, under the expert supervision of Marion Ruff Sheehan, for providing some of the line drawings for this text.

Jasper N. Joiner

one

Cecil N. Smith
Elmo F. Scarborough

status and development of foliage plant industries

A host of close relationships between people and plants has been exhibited as tropical foliage plants were transported to temperate zones for growth and use in orangeries, stove houses, conservatories, lath houses, greenhouses, homes, offices, shopping centers, and elsewhere. These relationships included the adventure of seeking and finding new cultivars in tropic jungles, the romance of transporting them by sailing ships over huge distances, and the joy of learning to grow them in protected structures and environments. They also include, especially in the past thirty years, the experiences of financial opportunities perceived and entrepreneurial risks taken in growing and marketing plants.

Another prominent group in developing the foliage plant industry is the consumers who enjoy having plants in their surroundings and whose demand for foliage plants and their associated services has grown greatly. A leading expert in interior design has expressed the idea that a primal feeling deep within all people makes them not fully content unless they are in close association with the plant world [7]. This relationship goes back to the beginning when all animals, including humans, lived in open association with plants. Indeed plants made—and still make—it possible for animals to exist! This concept is especially noteworthy of consideration by people in the western world. Western people tend to have an interior culture: they spend most of their lives indoors. Thus it is natural to recognize this latent desire related to primal association—the relationship between all animals, including humans, and plants made it possible for them to exist and bring the out of doors indoors. This is interior ecology [7].

Important contributions to the development of the foliage industry have been made by many pioneers of the nineteenth and past centuries. In this century, and especially since World War II, many contributions of a different nature have been added by those growers, brokers, wholesalers, retailers, plant specialists, and others whose bright visions of the future provided the base for the tremendous expansion of the production and marketing of foliage plants, much of which has occurred in the 1970s. A debt of gratitude is owed to those pioneers who made their mark on the huge and complex industry that supplies the green plants that fulfill the needs of today's consumer.

Some of the events and personalities that contributed to the development of the modern foliage industry are recorded here.[1] Following a discussion of the status of the foliage industry in the United States, developments in Europe and different sectors of the United States are covered. A brief discussion pertains to major managerial and technological innovations that have had important impact on the tropical foliage industry.

Current Status in the United States

The tropical foliage plant industry in the United States reached a sales level valued at wholesale of more than $13 million by 1949 from the early small beginnings. Marketings continued an upward trend throughout the 1950s, with annual sales of $32 million reached by 1959 [38]. Foliage sales leveled off during the 1960s, probably owing to competition from artificial foliage.

Growth during the 1970s increased geometrically, with net sales by growers of foliage plants reaching $299 million by 1978 [39]. Many leaders in the foliage industry believed this figure underestimated the true value of plants marketed by growers.

Values from net foliage plants sales and areas in production in 1970 and 1978 in ten major producing states are shown in Table 1-1. Growth in sales and production area occurred in all ten states. Even with a 90 percent rise in the Index of Producer Prices during this period, a vast expansion in the U.S. tropical foliage plant industries took place.

The increase of net sales of foliage plants in the United States is

---

[1]Appreciation is expressed to the many persons who, through correspondence, personal interviews, and telephone conversations, provided valuable information about the earlier years of foliage industry development.

TABLE 1-1 Net sales of foliage plants and area in production, selected states, 1970 and 1978 [39]

	Net sales					Area in production				
	1970		1978	Change		U.S. units (acres)		Metric (hectares)		Change (%)
	Actual (1,000s)	Adjusted[a] (1,000s)		Actual (%)	Adjusted[a] (%)	1970	1978	1970	1978	
Florida	15,938	30,242	124,135	679	310	621.8	1,814.3	251.7	734.5	192
California	3,657	6,939	86,125	2,255	1,141	43.4	496.8	17.6	201.1	1,045
Texas	1,156	2,194	20,284	1,655	825	33.8	149.9	13.7	60.7	342
Ohio	1,431	2,715	12,969	806	378	9.8	45.0	4.0	18.2	359
Pennsylvania	1,121	2,127	7,420	562	249	7.1	28.7	2.9	11.6	304
Michigan	683	1,296	7,392	1,026	470	3.9	38.3	1.6	15.5	882
New York	715	1,357	6,571	819	384	8.2	35.0	3.3	14.2	327
Illinois	412	781	6,015	1,360	670	1.1	26.0	0.4	10.5	2,264
New Jersey	384	729	5,810	1,413	697	3.4	18.8	1.4	7.6	453
Massachusetts	529	1,004	4,970	840	395	2.8	21.3	1.1	8.6	659
United States[b]	27,692	52,546	298,998	980	469	748.9	2,812.7	303.2	1,138.7	276

[a]1970 sales data adjusted by the Index of Producer Prices (all commodities) with 1978 = 100. This was formerly known as the Index of Whole sale Prices.

[b]Twenty-three states in 1970 and sixteen states in 1977. Production and sales were minimal in the states dropped from the U.S. Department of Agriculture report.

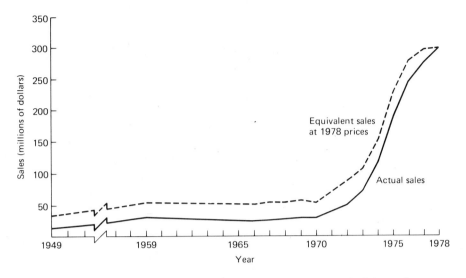

Figure 1-1.   Estimated net sales of foliage plants in the United States for the years 1949, 1959, and annually from 1966 to 1978.

illustrated in Figure 1-1. The bottom solid line represents sales at actual prices in order to make a rough approximation of what sales would have been had there been no change in the level of prices. The annual net sales volume was divided by the Index of Producer Prices; thus the upper line relates to adjusted prices with 1978 as a base. Essentially, the same pattern of movement is depicted, but since the 1978 price level was higher than that in any previous year, the sales trend in adjusted prices is at a higher level.

Plants and Institutions

Institutions such as public conservatories, botanical gardens, and private estates open to the public undoubtedly did much to foster public interest in foliage plants. Many conservatories and botanical gardens have educational programs designed to inform interested persons about various aspects of foliage and other plants. A partial list of such institutions in the United States includes the Brooklyn (New York) and St. Louis botanical gardens, the Los Angeles Arboretum, Garfield Park in Chicago, the Phipps Conservatory in Pittsburgh, and Longwood Gardens—the Du Pont estate—near Wilmington, Delaware [11].

Similar institutions in Europe have also done much to educate the public about foliage plants. Included in this group are Kew Gardens in

England and three German institutions, Palm Gardens in Frankfurt and the Hamburg and Munich conservatories.

There has been an increased use of foliage plants in interior design, not only for houses and apartments, but also for office buildings, shopping centers, and other structures during the past decade [13]. These expanding demands have added tremendously to the traditional demand for foliage plants. Although much of this may be associated with the move to suburbia, there has also been a renaissance in many cities in building and remodeling apartment units and office buildings. Many of these used professional interior designers in planning the use of tropical foliage plants. A considerable number of foliage plants, mostly of larger size, are used in shopping centers and offices to create a better environment. The use of plants in these spaces, frequented not only by the people who worked there but also by others who saw them, has probably been a major factor in encouraging people to utilize foliage plants in their own homes.

Another institution, the plant broker, has acted to bring buyers and sellers together. Although most plant brokers in the United States are located in terminal market areas, many also operate in growing regions. Brokers, for example, have performed an important role in selling plants from Florida, Texas, and elsewhere to northern greenhouse operators as well as to other outlets. Many had faith in the future of the foliage industry and on their own did much to promote its development. Some brokers were involved in introducing new plants to the trade.

The marketing system for foliage plants has experienced change from the situation several generations ago, in which conservatories and estates were the main users, to the situation today where almost every household in the western world is a current or potential buyer and user of foliage plants. In the past thirty-five years, and especially in the last ten, there has been a vast expansion in consumer demand. Plants are now sold not only at florist shops, garden centers, retail nurseries, and outlets such as variety, grocery, and other mass-market stores, which have now become traditional, but also at new types of outlets, such as specialized plant stores. Plant care and rental firms have come upon the scene, and in addition to selling and caring for plants in malls, office buildings, hotels, and similar institutions, they also market and care for plants in private households.

The primal association between people and green plants that has become increasingly evident since World War II can be expected to continue. Thus the institutions involved in producing and marketing these products can expect further change. This change, however, will likely be at a slower pace than that which characterized the 1970s.

Origin of the Foliage Industry[2]

Humans have cultivated and imported unusual plants from earliest times. Stone carvings show that plants were grown in containers during the ancient empires of the Sumerians and the Egyptians some 3,500 years ago. A classic example of growing plants in stone vessels was in the Hanging Gardens of Babylon constructed by Nebuchadnezzar II in the sixth century B.C. Records from China, Greece, and Rome indicate an interest in ornamental horticulture by people in those civilizations. The ruins of Pompeii also show definite proof that plants were grown in decorative containers, some of which were works of art.

Wealthy merchants of Venice, Florence, and Genoa became involved in plant introductions from the East into Europe in the early years of the fifteenth century. Dealers in Holland and Belgium have imported plants from Asia Minor and the East Indies from the time of the Crusaders. A desire for exotic flowering plants and trees developed among the aristocracy of France and England by the middle of the sixteenth century. Many wealthy persons in Europe constructed orangeries and conservatories in the seventeenth century. By the following century, an estimated 5,000 species of exotic plants had been brought into Europe.

Alfred B. Graf [14] felt that the eighteenth and early nineteenth centuries were the greatest botanical era—a time when plants from India, the Americas, Africa, and Australia were collected, imported, and brought into cultivation in European countries. Commercial nurseries began operating on a large scale with increased numbers of plants being grown, making them available in large quantities to plant lovers [15]. House plants became very popular in Europe as a result of these and other factors.

Plant enthusiasm spread to North America about the middle of the nineteenth century when private estates boasted many conservatories, which competed with one another to have the best "winter garden." Catalogs of nurseries and early greenhouse ranges listed collections of "stove plants" equal to those in Europe. The Julius Roehrs Co. of New Jersey imported shiploads of decorative plants and palms, dormant flowering plants, and bulbs from Europe. This firm also had a large collection of orchids from South America and Southeast Asia to supply its "exotic nurseries."

Relatively few big estates with skilled gardeners, conservatories, and plant collections remain, but an increasing number of people have living plants in and around their homes. Many exotic plants are grown in

[2]This section is adapted from [8].

6

glassed-in porches or small greenhouses. Many persons grow plants for a hobby or use them to decorate homes or apartments. More plants are also being used in offices, hotel lobbies, shopping centers, and other structures, since architects and interior designers are recommending use of containerized foliage and flowering plants to improve interior decor.

Sources of Tropical Plants

Most of the foliage plants in the trade are native to the tropics, a 3,200-mile strip with varied climatic conditions and light intensities.[3] Some also originated in subtropical zones 300 to 700 miles on the northern and southern borders of the tropics. Most tropical areas tend to have relatively uniform temperatures throughout the year, differing from the large temperature variations between summer and winter in temperate zones of the world.

A large number of foliage plants are now being produced in the United States and elsewhere, and others are constantly being introduced into the trade from the tropics by individual growers or by professional plant breeders. Approximately 500 species and cultivars of foliage plants are now grown for sale, compared with 300 five years ago, indicating the tremendous change in products produced that has occurred in the foliage industry.

Nursery workers and greenhouse operators adjacent to U.S. population centers, primarily in the Northeast and Midwest, were the primary sources of supply for foliage plants for many years. However, sales were limited mostly to florists and conservatories on large estates. Common hardy plants were grown and sold to the general public for window box and porch plantings. A shift in the location of the industry and a changed price structure finally resulted in a wider usage of tropical foliage plants.

Development of Foliage Plants in Europe[4]

Interest in growing tropical and subtropical fruits in Northern Europe gave birth to the orangeries of the sixteenth and seventeenth centuries. These were originally only built as shelter houses with heating facilities

---

[3]Many tropical foliage plants have low light intensity requirements in their native habitat.

[4]Except for the quotation later in this section, the material on European foliage development is largely adapted from (20).

used during cold months, but often more emphasis was placed on fancy or classical architecture than giving plants good winter conditions.

Growing grapes, oranges, and other subtropical fruit became a hobby among the wealthy people. However, this declined in the late part of the seventeenth century, and instead a growing interest occurred in decorative plants. Many orangeries became "laurel and myrtle" houses since the first plants in this "Age of Grace" were Mediterranean plants.

Early plant hunters brought back large numbers of plants from overseas, and as the conditions of the orangeries were not satisfactory, a gradual change took place from orangery to conservatory and the English term greenhouse originated. Later the heated house was called a stove, a result of the gradual change from subtropical to tropical plants.

The eighteenth century was a period of great interest in science and especially in botany. A multitude of plants were brought in from the colonies and "greenhouse coteries"—groups of noblemen, scientists, planthunters, and gardeners originated, and the building of spacious, impressive conservatories became a fashion (Figure 1-2). The most popular plants were palms, evergreen rain forest trees, and exotic climbers. Seed and tubers could be imported, but the tender plants could not withstand the long, rough sea journey. However, in the 1830s the Wardian case, a closed glass cabinet, developed by the Londoner Dr. Nathaniel Ward, revolutionized the transport of exotics from all parts of the world.

Figure 1-2.   An old "Orangery" of Europe which was a precursor to the modern greenhouse.

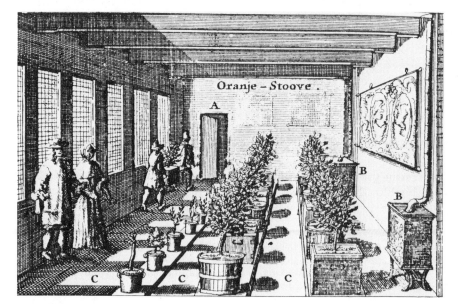

Growing tropical plants was for a small upper class and took place primarily at court houses, estates, and big mansions. Around 1830, commercial nurseries began and soon replaced botanical gardens as major producers of tropical plants. Some nurseries even had their own collectors. In England, names such as C. Loddiges, Stuart Low, Knight and Perry, and John G. Veitch became famous. Van Houtte in Belgium and his nursery in Ghent became an important station on the way from the tropics to nurseries in Europe.

The Victorian period in England made conservatories very popular. Among them, the Chatsworth Conservatory was a wonder of grace and new architecture. It was designed by the famous gardner Joseph Paxton in 1836 to 1840 and ranked among the wonders of England. In 1846 a total of 48,000 Londoners came to this large greenhouse, which was 24 feet high and covered 30,000 square feet (2,790 square meters).

Living rooms with plants became popular in the Victorian period. This interest also spread to poorer classes of society. Restaurants were called winter gardens or palm gardens, and a large production of howea, phoenix, and other palms took place. Araucaria, *Ficus elastica,* pandanus, aspidistra, aechmea, dieffenbachia, philodendron, cordyline, euonymus, callistemon, begonia, aralia, laurels, ferns, and palms were the most popular plants in the latter nineteenth century up to World War I.

Mea Allan had this to say about the culture of tropical plants in the early and mid nineteenth century [1]:

> The stage was set for an upsurge of energy in all directions. Industry boomed and a new class of society rose amid the ugliness of belching smoke and thunder and clatter of machinery—the wealthy lords of industry who, having created it all, looked around for relief from it, for quiet beauty on which to rest their eyes. Horticulture was the answer, especially the raising of fabulous exotic flowers in conservatories where they could wander and forget the din. . . .
>
> If the first half of the nineteenth century had seen astounding progress in horticulture, a flood of new plants from every quarter of the globe to be grown in temperatures equal to their native own, the flood was now a deluge. Plant-hunting expeditions found no lack of financial support; and competition was fierce not only between collectors but among their employers. To subscribe to these expeditions was not only fashionable but ground on which the new aristocracy could challenge the old. In 1837 the Duke of Devonshire had built at Chatsworth the biggest conservatory in the world, designed by his gardener Joseph Paxton, whom he was proud to call his friend, and soon conservatories were springing up everywhere around the fringe of factories. With collectors sending back seeds and plants by every boat spreading homeward-bound sails and with heated glasshouses ready to receive them, England stood on the threshold of the greatest era of flower-culture ever known.

In the 1920s interest shifted from foliage to flower plants. The export of large indoor plants from Belgium and England decreased.

During the 1930s the new indoor style called functionalism made many houses in Europe somewhat roomier, with large windows giving better light conditions in living rooms. A certain "bareness feeling" of the new style gave renewed interest for "plant curtains" and indoor greenery.

Plants from botanical gardens were brought into production. *Monstera* and *Ficus* species started the new era around 1940 and were followed by climbers such as *Cissus antarctica* and *C. rhombifolia*. Since then the list of plants has been enlarged from year to year, with Denmark leading in introductions. Some 400 plants, of which more than 50 percent are foliage plants, are offered in cooperative auction catalogs in Denmark.

There has been a growing interest in having large plant containers in offices, schools, restaurants, and shops since 1965. Special firms plant and maintain these tubs. Many tubs are based on hydroponics and use Haydite, Leca, or Stonewool as growing media.

The desire for large plants has brought about an increased demand for pregrown large plants, but as greenhouse space in northern Europe is costly, many plants are now shipped to northern Europe from Italy, Spain, the Canary Islands, the Ivory Coast, and Central America. These plants are often replanted in inert media and adapted to indoor climate before final sale.

The use of plants in window shelves has long been a tradition in Scandinavia, Germany, Holland, and northern France, but not in England. Householders use a number of foliage plants, and flowering species also are bought regularly to add color to the setting. Plants must be tolerant to the indoor climate, about 18°C air.

Production from seed of tropical origin is very popular now, since juvenile stages of evergreen trees such as dizygotheca, schefflera, aralia, pseudopanax, monstera, philodendron, and grevillea are easy to produce. They are well adapted to indoor climates. Cacti and succulents are also sold in great quantities, with the tendency toward large *Euphorbia*, *Kleinia*, and *Cereus*. Variegated and colored plants also enjoy great interest.

The oil crisis has forced north European nurseries to make better production planning to get higher production per week per unit of production area. Movable benches have increased the production in glasshouses by some 20 percent. Labor costs have been reduced 40 percent by carbon dioxide application up to 1000 to 2000 ppm and also capillary watering and machine potting. The pot plant industry is expanding at a high rate.

The two leading pot plant groups in Holland are Bromeliaceae and succulents. In Belgium production of large specimens of plants like *Dracaena, Araucaria,* bromiliads, laurel, Marantaceae, and palms is characteristic.

Germany produces a great quantity of foliage plants, but not sufficient for internal demand. Large quantities are shipped in from Holland and Denmark as well as from overseas sources.

The development of foliage plant production in England has been slow, partly due to the lack of trade connections, but some efficient firms like Rochford's have pushed the frontier forward, and chain stores are offering numerous varieties of such plants.

A rapid increase in demand has taken place in France in recent years. This area is now a potential field for larger production and import.

Israel is building up a trade in pot plant production of precultivated materials to ship to northern Europe for final production processes.

The Development of Rochford's in England[5]

The most popular indoor plant in England during the middle of the last century was *Ficus elastica,* the India-rubber tree. Other foliage plants included dracaenas, maidenhair fern, and other ferns. Solanums were grown in the winter.

An example of changing commodity production over time in greenhouses is exhibited by Rochford's, currently the largest producer of foliage plants in the British Isles. The firm was started by Michael Rochford, a gardener and steward who was an Irish immigrant. He built two glasshouses at Tottenham in the late 1850s and went into business on his own as a forcer of grapes. After making many technical improvements, the Rochfords found in the 1870s that ornamental plants such as maidenhair ferns and dracaenas paid higher revenues than forced grapes. The firm grew a combination of grapes, green plants, and flowers in its 3 acres (1.2 hectares) of greenhouses. By the turn of the century the Rochford brothers owned 86 acres (34.8 hectares) of glass in the Lea Valley.

Tom Rochford moved his operations to Turnford in the 1880s and built a palm house of 18,000 square feet (1,674 square meters). He grew orchids, ferns, foliage plants, and a variety of other showy species. His exhibitions at various shows and expositions won many medals and awards. The business, now Thomas Rochford and Sons Limited, con-

[5]Adapted from [1].

tinued to grow, and at the end of World War II Thomas Rochford III decided to turn the nursery over to the greatest extent possible to pot plants and concentrate on hydrangeas, ferns, cyclamen, crotons, heaths, and geraniums, rather than growing smaller numbers of a larger variety of plants. However, the mainstay remained tomatoes, and sales of ornamental items, despite a growing market demand, stayed at a relatively low level.

Tom Rochford began marketing "green plants" in 1951 and found demand outstripping supply. He decided in 1952 to specialize in the culture of hydrangeas, cyclamen, azaleas, ferns, liliums, and "house plants." From that time the names of "house plants" essentially became synonymous with the name "Rochford's."

Despite much publicity for foliage plants and a growing demand for them, the Covent Garden Market scorned them because of their lasting quality. Market dealers forecast doom while admitting the present popularity of house plants. However, they did not understand that more people were becoming apartment dwellers; they missed the greenery of gardens and felt nostalgia for the country. In short, a vast new demand for house plants, as in the United States, was taking place.

Rochford's has continued to publicize house plants through leaflets and brochures, participation in exhibitions, on television and radio, and in other media. Today the 30 acres (12.1 hectares) of glass at Rochford's contains one of the largest house plant nurseries in the world.

Developments in the United States

Early commercial production levels and the history and development of the foliage plant industry in major areas of the United States are treated in the pages that follow. Key persons and organizations contributing to the early history of foliage are delineated. In addition, major forces or events, to the extent they could be identified, are presented.

Early Commercial Production Levels

The major foliage plant production growth since World War II has taken place in Florida and California. Florida's primary business in the year 1949 was in unpotted plants,[6] with fifty-three growers having sales valued at $1,453,000 [38]. Nevertheless, of the total of $13 million in foliage plants marketed by producers in the United States, growers of

---

[6]Unpotted plants include rooted cuttings, bare-root mature specimens, divisions, cane sections, and the like.

unpotted plants sold only about $3.3 million. By 1959 Florida had supplanted California as the leading source of foliage plants. Florida sold less than $400,000 worth of potted plants in 1949, but by 1959 the value had risen to over $7 million, a figure higher than the total value of such sales in California and Pennsylvania, the next two states leading in the production of tropical foliage plants.

In other commercial foliage plant producing states, substantial quantities of unpotted plants were sold. However, nearly all states, except Illinois and Florida, showed decreases in the value of sales of unpotted plants.

California[7]

Early years   The first commercial foliage plant grower in California was H. Plath and Sons of San Francisco [10]. Other firms that entered the industry at an early date were Lawndale, A. A. Schneirow of Los Angeles, and Smith and Walker of El Cajon (now Jamacha Nurseries) [14].[8]

During the 1920s the potted palm *Kentia forsteriana* came into vogue as a background decoration for weddings, funerals, head tables at banquets, and other arrangements. Virtually all were grown in California by the Roy F. Wilcox Co. and Bassett and Washburn Nurseries and shipped as finished plants to major U.S. cities.

Roy F. Wilcox had a large greenhouse area of probably 5 acres (2 hectares) devoted to foliage plants in Montebello, a suburb of Los Angeles. The *Pothos aureus* 'Wilcoxi' was named for the founder of this establishment. The Roy F. Wilcox Co. (succeeded by the Keeline-Wilcox Co. of East Irvine, California) was especially known for Kentia palms, which were grown from seed to 6-inch (15.4-centimeter) pot or large wooden tub size. The company moved its Kentia palm and azalea operation to Santa Barbara, California, directly on the ocean when the smog in the Los Angeles basin became too injurious to the palm leaves.

Sizable stocks of *Philodendron pertusum, P. scandens oxycardium (cordatum), Araucaria* and other foliate plants were also marketed by the Roy Wilcox Co. (Fig. 1-3). They traveled by rail to eastern cities.

Robert Weidner began Buena Park Greenhouses in the late 1940s to specialize in growing pathogen-free *Philodendron pertusum.* Cane was hot-water treated, propagated, and sold to other nurseries in small sizes

---

[7]Largely adapted from [22] and [35].
[8]Information provided by Dr. A. B. Graf.

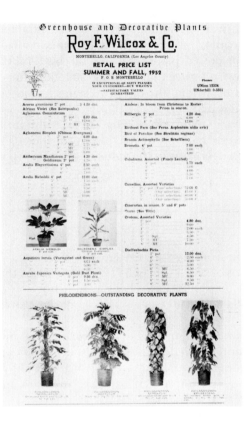

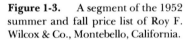

Figure 1-3. A segment of the 1952 summer and fall price list of Roy F. Wilcox & Co., Montebello, California.

to "finish off." This business was so successful that he grew and propagated several hundred pathogen-free foliage plants in a similar manner. Weidman moved from Buena Park to La Habra, California, in order to expand his greenhouse area. Before retiring in the early 1970s he made a concerted effort to bring hanging baskets back into the trade. He was the industry leader in trying both old and new plants as hanging baskets, for which wide consumer acceptance has evolved.

The early centers of foliage plant culture in southern California included Montebello, Lawndale, the San Fernando Valley, and La Habra. Population pressure forced companies in these areas to move to Encinitas, Ventura, Santa Barbara, and elsewhere. Foliage plant centers in northern California were located in San Francisco, South San Francisco, and Hayward.

Current status The foliage enterprise is currently scattered in many areas of California. Perhaps the major center is in San Diego County, with a large number of the some sixty growers there being located in the vicinity of Encinitas. Another specialized area is in San Mateo County, with much acreage near Half Moon Bay, about 25 miles south of San Francisco. Other concentrations of growers are in the Salinas Valley and in the upper San Joaquin Valley, with centers of production at Lodi and Sacramento.

Relatively few growers in California have produced foliage plants for any substantial length of time. Due to the tremendous rise in demand for foliage plants and the potential for earning higher profits than with other crops, growers of related products have entered the foliage industry. Many growers of chrysanthemums, carnations, and other cut flowers in the Salinas, San Mateo County, and San Diego County areas transformed a portion of all of their production facilities from cut flowers to foliage. This shift took place largely because of the decline in the profitability of cut flower items. As South American producers moved very rapidly to expand their production and gained an increasing share of the market, prices of these flowers, despite rises in the general price level, have risen very slightly over the last 5 years. Profits of domestic growers fell, with many growers operating at a loss. Hence many domestic growers of cut flowers turned to foliage and other products.

Other new California foliage producers are the woody ornamental field and landscape nurseries, which, with the decline in the volume of building and the subsequent fall in demand for landscape nursery items, have shifted a portion or all of their productive resources to growing hanging baskets and potted plants. This situation appears to have been most prevalent in the southern California area but is also characteristic of the northern sector of the state.

Perhaps a unique type of operator entering the foliage industry is the benchgrafter. In recent years there was an overplanting of grapes, which has resulted in a drop in the demand for propagated grape vines. Many of the production facilities of benchgrafters are easily adaptable to foliage plants. Benchgrafters in the Sonoma-Napa County area north of San Francisco and elsewhere in northern California, plus others in the southern portion of the state, have entered the foliage business. Some of these operators had technical problems in transforming their operations to foliage. Many of them have had marketing problems as their output has increased, and they have found it necessary to devote substantial attention to this phase of their operations.

A limited number of poultry farmers have gone into the foliage business in California. At least one operator removed the roofs on his poultry houses and replaced them with fiberglass, thereby permitting sufficient light to reach his plants. Former vegetable growers have also made entry into the foliage and other facets of the flower and plant business.

Some growers have entered the industry with no previous experience in growing ornamentals. Much of the financing of the new growers, as well as established operations and those who have transformed their operations from other sectors of the ornamental industry, has come from various types of investors or silent partners who have opted to invest in this area. The foliage industry in California, along with the industries in Florida and elsewhere, is attracting investors who formerly were placing their funds in fed cattle and other business opportunities.

Marketing   Southern California is perhaps characterized by more effective marketing of foliage and cut flowers by supermarkets and other mass market stores than through such outlets in almost any other sector of the country. This area is characterized by a very large population with high levels of disposable income. The Alpha Beta chain has had very aggressive leadership in charting the way; other competitors have followed them in the marketing and merchandising of foliage and cut flowers.

As in other sections of the country, many specialized plant stores, usually small in size, have sprung up throughout California. The volume of plants such stores or boutiques handle is substantial. Florists have also remained important outlets in the retail marketing of foliage plants. Growth of consumer purchases in these and other channels has been in response to a vast rise in the demand for foliage plants. A phase of the demand pattern has been the growing consumer preference for hanging baskets, which for a number of years have been popular in Canada, England, and other countries. A large group of truckers, owning their own vehicles, purchase plants from growers and other entities in the foliage industry and sell them to plant stores and other outlets.

A number of foliage growers make most of their sales directly to supermarket chains and other mass market outlets. Several of the larger growers have salespeople who make contacts with supermarkets, wholesale and retail florists, and other buyers. Still other growers run delivery trucks to make plant deliveries to buyers in California and other areas. Many small growers cater solely to plant stores and retail florists and make sales directly to them. Certain large growers market flowers and foliage plants not only for themselves, but also for other producers.

Other major outlets include wholesalers, jobbers, and distributors located in the major cities of California. The major market to which wholesale operators in the Los Angeles floral market sell are supermarket chains.

Because of the concentration of California's population in the Los Angeles and San Diego metropolitan areas, it appears that a high proportion of foliage plants produced in southern California is marketed in these areas, with the remainder going to markets elsewhere. On the other hand, growers in the Salinas Valley, the San Francisco metropolitan area, and other producing sections in nothern California not only cater to the metropolitan areas north of the Tehachapis, but also are shipping a large amount of their output to markets in the Pacific Northwest and other points in the West and Midwest. Some California growers also send general foliage items on an increasingly large scale to Chicago and other Midwest points. Specialized products are marketed throughout the country, including Florida and New York.

Transportation   With the rapid expansion of the California foliage industry, growers have had to search for markets outside of the Pacific Coast and other nearby states. Truckers responded with specialized equipment and organized routes to the Midwest and other distant market destinations.

Freight rates to most points in the Midwest and East are higher than those from Florida and Texas. The structure of rates, which is far from static, is expected to continue to favor Florida over California in shipments made to most areas of the nation. Nevertheless, California foliage growers can be expected to market an increasing amount of their plants in areas where Florida growers have formerly had a minimal amount of serious competition.

Central Florida (Apopka) Area

Boston fern, the forerunner of Central Florida (Apopka) foliage[9]   The plant that paved the way for the Central Florida foliage industry was the Boston fern (*Nephrolepis exaltata* 'Bostoniensis'). A Mr. Powell, sales manager of a Springfield, Ohio, floral company, conceived the idea in 1912 of producing Boston fern, then very expensive to produce in northern locations, outdoors in Florida. He and Harry Ustler, a clerk in the company, calculated that Boston ferns could be grown for 10 to 20 percent of their cost in Ohio.

Harry Ustler came to Florida, but Powell was unable to do so. Problems also evolved in financing the venture. Ustler became acquainted with W. P. Newell, who put up the capital for the two to organize the first Boston fern operation in a lath shed near Lake Eola in Orlando in an area formerly used for growing pineapples. The fern operation was moved to Apopka in 1917 and was followed by the entry into the business of other operators. At the first Foliage Hall of Fame

---

[9]Largely adapted from [36].

banquet in 1978, Harry Ustler was honored as the Father of the Indoor Foliage Industry. Some writers believed that the presence of two well-known horticulturists, Theodore Mead and Henry Nehrling, may have contributed to the beginning of the fern and other ornamental industries in central Florida.

During the formative years most ferneries were small units, generally backyard operations ranging between ¼ to 1 acre (0.1 to 0.4 hectares) in size. There were over 100 ferneries at one time [5]. Many families that started producing Boston ferns in the 1920s have continued in the ornamental plant business.

Early foliage plant production   The first recorded "attempt" to produce foliage plants commercially in Central Florida occurred in 1928. W. W. Walters visited the D. S. Geddis greenhouse in St. Louis and noticed *Philodendron scandens oxycardium (cordatum)*[10] plants growing there. He requested some of the material to try in his fernery at Apopka, but two years after starting, he destroyed the test plantings. It was reported that the rank growth occurring with vine growth on a trellis impressed no one favorably.

Robert Mitchell was the first person to grow cordatum commercially in Orange County [24]. A stepson of Henry Nehrling, he studied at Washington University in St. Louis, Missouri, and worked at the Missouri Botanical Gardens for several years. He returned to Orange County in 1929 and started the Shore Acres Nursery in the southern portion of Orlando.

While in St. Louis, Mitchell had studied under Alex Laurie who, after retiring as a professor of floriculture at Ohio State University, came to Florida in the early 1950s to manage the Whistling Pines foliage operation at Eustis.

The 1930s have been described as the depression years for ferns. Growers had relied primarily on Boston ferns as their primary source of income, and there had been little incentive for diversification to other products. As the number of ferneries increased, their output rose, resulting in lower prices and sales values.

Markets, the key for foliage   The apparent key to Robert Mitchell's success in producing cordatum was that of finding a market. Wade Walters, who had earlier grown this item, apparently had been

[10]Cordatum, as the plant is commonly known, was first introduced into the St. Louis area from its substation in Bogotá, Colombia, by the Missouri Botanical Gardens in St. Louis. The identification and naming of this new plant introduction was done by Jesse Greenman, a taxonomist with the Gardens [23]. The leaf of the plant was cordate or heart shaped, hence the name "cordatum."

unable to attract buyers. Mitchell's success in marketing probably resulted from contacts he had established while a student at Washington University and while working at the Missouri Botanical Gardens and in the nearby florists' industry. His key contact was Glen Turner, then head of the National School of Floral Design, who had encouraged him to produce cordatum. Mitchell acquired a supply of plants from Frank Sherloff and Company of St. Louis and produced the plant commercially in 1930. Turner agreed to promote use of heart-leaf philodendron over the country and to urge potential customers to contact Mitchell for supplies, since Florida was considered a better place to grow such plants than the St. Louis area. Thus much credit for developing a wide market for cordatum should go to Glen Turner and the activities of his National School of Floral Design.

Following his success, Mitchell introduced another plant, Chinese evergreen (*Aglaonema modestum*), to Florida. Again his contacts with the Missouri Botanical Gardens played an important role. The initial canes of Chinese evergreen came by way of a liaison established through the U.S. consul at Shanghai, China, in the early 1930s.

Another early cordatum grower was J. W. Smith of Apopka. He started growing the plant in the 1930s and reportedly did well with it [6].

John Masek began buying and selling foliage plants and ferns from local growers, following the demise of the Apopka Fern Growers Association of which he had been executive secretary, during the 1930s. Later he established a marketing firm around which he built his own nursery, John's. Masek, honored along with Harry Ustler, Raymond Hogshead, and Alex Laurie as pioneers at the first Foliage Hall of Fame banquet in 1978, has been widely credited as the moving force in shifting the fern business in Orange County into Florida's giant foliage industry of today. He established mail order and other techniques utilized in developing mass markets for foliage plants. Masek, who spent summers studying at the University of Chicago and earning a doctorate in business there, is known as the "Henry Ford" of the foliage industry because his pioneering efforts helped other growers as well as himself.

Many new plants for indoor use were introduced in the 1930s. In addition to *Aglaonema* and *Pothos*, others included *Sansevieria zeylanica, S. laurentii, Ficus elastica, Euphorbia actea* and *Peperomia* spp.

An outstanding pioneer foliage plant hybridizer was Robert H. (Bob) McColly of Bamboo Gardens. In the mid 1950s, McColly's first successful philodendron, Florida, was made available to the trade. Several years later he released Emerald Queen and Burgundy, two other hybrids well accepted by the trade. In later years the many hybrids McColly continued to breed were patented.

Markets gained have sometimes turned out to be markets lost.

Sansevieria was exported to Europe during the 1950s by growers in both central and south Florida [10]. Many of these shipments were arranged for by brokers. However, the European market was soured by the poor quality of plants sent by many shippers. The ensuing result was that German growers went to the Canary Islands to arrange for the production of their own supply. Currently, German operators are producing large numbers of foliage plants in the Canary Islands and in their own greenhouses. At present, European growers are attempting to enter the U.S. market with their foliage plants.

Greenhouses Freezes during the 1940s destroyed a large number of Central Florida foliage crops. These, along with memories of the severe 1934 freeze, convinced growers that greenhouses were necessary for the future development of commercial foliage production in Central Florida [5]. The first large commercial greenhouses for growing plants in Central Florida were constructed by George Smith[11] of Winter Garden and Ustler Brothers of Apopka around 1929. These structures were of great help in reducing severe plant losses and ensuring a uniform supply, even when Florida was subjected to hard freezes.

Many changes have taken place in the last 25 years in the structures used for foliage production in the Apopka area. The first large-scale tests of polyethylene film to provide cold protection in slat houses around Apopka (Figure 1-4) were made in 1957. Heat was retained in the houses covered by the film, but other sheds had plants freeze right up to the heaters. The following year most growers put plastic underneath or on top of their slat sheds. Originally, this was done for cold protection, but it also resulted in a large increase in production and quality.

Alex Laurie did much to show the value of bringing plants indoors by growing quality plants [21]. Certainly, his example encouraged the "glass boom." A large expansion occurred in the construction of fiberglass greenhouses in the 1960s and 1970s. The first Dutch glass and steel greenhouses were built in the late 1960s, with still more constructed in the 1970s. The free space design in many greenhouses permits the use of various types of machinery within the structure. Such innovations contribute to higher productivity and better quality.

---

[11]His son, Harry Smith, was a leading foliage grower and industry and civic leader. The Boyd brothers, who initially grew *Sansevieria zeylanica* brought in from New Orleans, were wiped out financially, following which George Smith, a banker, assumed control of the firm [10]. The operation, now named the Winter Garden Ornamental Nursery, grew woody ornamentals and later shifted to foliage.

Figure 1-4. An old lath house used in the early days of foliage stock plant production in Apopka, Florida.

Industry boom   The Crop Reporting Board of the U.S. Department of Agriculture showed 207 commercial foliage growers in the Apopka area during 1978 [39]. These included operators in Orange, Seminole, Lake, and surrounding counties with sales of $10,000 or more of foliage and other floricultural crops. In Orange County alone it is estimated that there are currently some 850 growers, most of them small, of foliage plants.

The foliage boom of the 1970s has not only attracted more growers, but many other changes have taken place. These comprise modernization of facilities, including shifts to glass greenhouses, more efficient handling of inputs and finished foliage, and the growing of higher quality plants. Several large conglomerates have also entered the industry. The Green Thumb Corporation, a subsidiary of Stratford of Texas, was formed when the organization purchased a number of producing firms, updated them, and also expanded its physical plant. The Ralston Purina Company purchased Green Thumb in 1978. Another acquisition was that of Oakdell, Inc., by the Weyerhaeuser Company.

Additional service firms to care for providing production inputs and to assist in marketing have sprung up in the Apopka area. These include the development of a large supply cooperative, Apopka Growers Supply, which was purchased several years ago by Vaughan-Jacklin. Trucking firms now have service units in the area. A large Dutch greenhouse construction firm has located a warehouse in the Apopka area. Laboratories offer soil and leaf analyses to growers. Additional local brokers have entered the business of marketing.

Foliage research   A major event of the past 15 years was approval and construction of the University of Florida Agricultural Experiment Station concerned with problems relating to foliage plants produced and marketed by Florida growers. The research station was constructed, following legislative funding, and officially dedicated as the Ridge Ornamental Laboratory of the University of Florida Agricultural Experiment Stations. The station, now designated as the University of Florida Agricultural Research Center, Apopka, has a worldwide reputation for its research in foliage plant production, nutrition, handling, and insect and disease control.

Although most research on foliage done by the University of Florida Agricultural Experiment Stations is concentrated at Apopka, small amounts are done by scientists at the Agricultural Research Center at Ft. Lauderdale, the Agricultural Research and Education Center at Homestead, and the main station on the University of Florida campus in Gainesville.

South Florida

South Florida, which experienced killing frosts less often then Central Florida, became an important source of foliage production. It led the Central Florida, or Apopka, area in the value of foliage plants produced in the 1940s and 1950s.

Early operations   One of the earliest foliage operations in South Florida was that of the Soar Brothers, who operated at Little River, north of Miami, from 1897 to 1909. They grew citrus trees and ornamental plants, including ferns and native plants found in the Everglades and on nearby islands, for use in greenhouses and homes.

John Soar in 1909 began operating the Little River Nursery, which specialized in small potted plants, shipped mostly bare root [37]. F. M. Soar formed the F. M. Soar Nursery in which he propagated ferns, *Pandanus veitchii*, and sansevieria; he also grew several varieties of palms, used as landscape items, in open fields. The ferns, pandanus, and sansevieria were all grown in lath houses built of rough-sawed cypress lumber. Initially, shipments to the east coast and other distant markets were made by ship, but with the advent of the railroad to Miami about the time the Soar nursery was begun, shipping to inland cities became much more convenient.

The F. M. Soar Nursery began growing *Monstera deliciosa* and several cultivars of ferns in the late 1920s and early 1930s [37]. Included among its customers were Julius Roehrs, Robert Craig, Roy Wilcox, Louis Hahn, and Fred Oechslin. Brokers through which the nursery marketed its plants embraced Louis Dank, Fred Gloeckner, William Nieman, and S. S. Skidelsky.

The Robert Craig Co. introduced sansevieria into the United States [26]. Roger Spicer started growing it in Stuart, Florida, about the time of World War I. Shipments were generally made by sea transport.

Duncan Macaw was another early sansevieria grower. He purchased land in Dade County in 1926 and used it for growing sansevieria and pandanus [41]. The Florida unit was used to supply material for his Pennsylvania greenhouses.

Fabian Oskierko, who at one time served in a position of high responsibility in the czar's court at St. Petersburg, came to the United States in 1899 [26]. He later opened his own greenhouse firm in Middle Village, Queens, New York. Oskierko purchased land in the Homestead area in 1926 and, after having it scarified,[12] began growing sansevieria, *Dracaena massangeana* and pandanus. After leaving Cornell University, Fabian Oskierko's eldest son, Paul, came to Florida in the 1930s to continue the business. The business became known as Horticultural Plant Farms. At one time some 30 acres of land, located adjacent to the present site of Homestead Air Force Base, were in sansevieria. Ruth Perkins, Paul Oskierko's widow, cultivated as much as 85 acres of land in sansevieria and other foliage plants. She later sold the operation to Green Thumb Corporation.

Sansevierias marketed in the late 1920s and early 1930s sold for a dollar a leaf for a bare-root three-leaf plant [3]. In early 1979 growers were selling similar plants for 17 cents or less.

Another early firm in South Florida was Jones and Scully of Miami. Robert M. Scully, a former student of Alex Laurie, was not only a foliage plant grower but an accomplished hybridizer of orchids. He was in partnership with Walter Jones.

Some growers who later produced foliage in South Florida initially began by harvesting bromeliads, or "swamp orchids," from the

---

[12]The process, using specialized equipment, of breaking up and compacting the marl soils that characterize much of the Homestead area.

Everglades and selling them primarily to variety and other chain stores
[17]. Other growers who went into foliage plant production had experience in landscape nursery operations; others migrated to Florida from
northern locations in the 1940s and succeeding years.

Boston fern   The Boston fern, which has played an important
part in the tropical foliage industry, has an interesting history. David
Fairchild reported that John Soar, who came to south Florida before
Miami was in the planning stage, scoured the wildernesses of the area
and discovered on the Keys some pretty ferns with immensely long
fronds [12]. Soar brought a selection of them to his nursery, grew them,
and sent a selection to some friends in Boston. The famous "Boston,"
really a Florida fern, has since become one of the more popular foliage
plants and is now a major item utilized in hanging baskets.

Growing structures and shipping supplies   In the
early years of the Florida foliage industry, many waste materials from
other industries were acquired free or at minimal cost to use for constructing growing structures [4]. For example, slabs of cypress were obtained free from nearby sawmills and old telephone poles were used as
supports for lath houses. Later, saran and other plastics were used as
they became available, and other more specialized items were adapted
for use in the foliage industry.

A variety of cartons was used for shipping plants in the developmental years of the Florida foliage industry [4]. Initially, growers used
old apple, lettuce, celery, and other crates and cut them to size for
foliage plants. Later, as the foliage industry grew, boxes in which pots of
various sizes would fit readily were fabricated by the cardboard industry.
However, problems arose in shipping, as it was often impossible, owing
to the wide variety of cartons, to utilize completely the shipping space in
trucks. Many improvements have been made in the last few years to solve
some of these problems.

Truckers, brokers, and growers   The first plant trucker
for the Dade and Apopka areas was Paul Oskierko [4]. Johnny Brown,
who trucked eggs from Wisconsin and Minnesota to Florida, started
hauling plants to Bachman's in Minneapolis as well as receivers in
Chicago and Madison in order to get return loads. Currently, Brown's is
the largest firm engaged in hauling Florida foliage. Other trucking firms
are also involved.

More plants were moved through brokers than any other market
outlet before Woolworth and other chain stores entered the plant busi-

ness on a large scale. Brokers had sales forces in the field covering major cities, the buying offices of large stores, and many nurseries.

By the 1940s, Dade County nursery workers included not only the Oskierkos (Horticultural Plant Farms), but also Dan Greer, Hugh Lalor, Oscar Nelson, Jim Vosters, Macaws, and Raymond Hogshead. In the 1950s, Lou Super, Lex Ritter, and Arvida joined the group.

The first very large foliage operation in Florida was Arvida Greenhouses. A nursery purchased by Arthur Vining Davis, retired aluminum magnate who had moved to Dade County, was modernized and expanded during the 1950s. Each week five trailer loads of 3-inch potted plants, mostly pothos and *Philodendron scandens oxycardium (cordatum)*, were usually shipped, primarily to northern greenhouses and thence to variety stores such as Woolworth and Kresge [9]. The Arvida operation also sent regular shipments of foliage plants by air to Woolworth in Havana, Cuba, during the 1950s. Hurricane Donna in September 1960 destroyed the 300 acres of saran in the huge Arvida operation [41].

The only foliage grower to have been elected president of the Society of American Florists was Jim Vosters of Miami, who served in this capacity in 1975 and 1976. Vosters came to Miami from Pennsylvania to start a foliage operation, with initial specialization in *Ficus elastica* 'Decora.' He makes periodic trips to various areas of the world to locate new or unusual cultivars or species of foliage plants. He then follows the practice of growing large supplies of such items to take maximum advantage of market demand.

Large plants   Plants and tropical trees of large sizes used for decorating malls, offices, and other areas are produced by various operators in South Florida. It takes up to 12 years to grow a ficus tree to a height of 24 feet. A limited number of firms are engaged in conditioning these plants to be placed in environments with minimal leaf loss by keeping them for specified periods of time in areas with reduced light. The wholesale price f.o.b. South Florida of four ficus trees, 24 feet high, in 200-gallon containers early in 1979 was $12,000.

With much of its production consisting of large plants used primarily for decorating the interiors of commercial buildings and malls, foliage operators in South Florida have catered to buyers in somewhat more exotic realms. These include such sales as those made to the White House in Washington, a Boeing 747 plane load of plants to Saudi Arabia, ten smaller plane loads sent to the Rockefeller estates in the Virgin Islands, and a combination of large foliage plants for decorating the yacht of Aristotle Onassis [19]. Nearly all such plants are now conditioned prior to sale by placing them under partial shade in which they receive only a given amount of sunlight. Operations engaged in conditioning plants contain areas covered with shade cloth that permits only a given proportion of sunlight to enter. One firm has a section equipped to condition plants with heights up to 36 feet.

Recent trends   The foliage industry in South Florida expanded after World War II from Dade to Broward and Palm Beach counties. The industry is tending to specialize in plants with pot sizes of 6 inches (15.4 centimeters) and above. Various operators are also growing ficus, schefflera, dieffenbachia, and other large items for use in the interior decor of malls, office buildings, and other structures.

The foliage enterprise in South Florida during the 1970s has spread from its area of concentration in the three "Gold Coast" counties of Dade, Broward, and Palm Beach to Martin in the north and Lee in the west. One such operation is Yoder Brothers, Inc., located at Fort Myers.

Various national firms are involved in the South Florida foliage industry. They include United Brands, Green Thumb, and Florafax. Foliage wholesale and service firms in the Northeast and Midwest have integrated growing and conditioning operations in Palm Beach County.

Tissue culture or meristemming laboratories are now being operated by several South Florida foliage firms. Similar laboratories have also opened in the Apopka area, California, and elsewhere.

Gulf Coast Area

New Orleans, Louisiana, was another area in which foliage was grown outdoors and under lath and glass as early as 1900 [2]. Louisiana growers produced mostly *Ficus elastica* propagated in mossed layers. These were sent by ship to ports along the eastern seaboard and then hauled inland by Railway Express. New Orleans growers also produced *Microcoelum widdellianum, Phoenix roebelinii,* and *Aspidistra.* Producers included Lawrence Gerlinger, Herman Doescher, and Henry Kraak.

A Pittsburgh grower, Sylvan Hahn, expanded his production area for various foliage plants to Long Beach, Mississippi, near Biloxi on the Gulf Coast, during the 1930s. He introduced several varieties of sansevieria, one of which is known as *Sansevieria trifasciata* 'Hahnii,' a sport of *S. trifasciata laurentii* found at New Orleans in 1939 [16]. Hahn bought an existing nursery, including the special type of sansevieria that he patented as *Sansevieria* 'Hahnii.'

Another firm that moved early to a warm climate for foliage plant production was that of Arthur James, a greenhouse operator near Pittsburgh, Pennsylvania. Just before World War I he purchased 40 acres (16.2 hectares) of land at Oneco, on the Gulf Coast of Florida between Bradenton and Sarasota, with the idea of growing plants and shipping them north. Leonard J. Seiger, who worked with James and helped build a lath house, recalls the growing of *Dracaena godseffiana, D. sanderiana, Ficus lyrata,* Boston ferns and *Sanseveria trifasciata* [34]. After James moved to Florida, his business consisted more of shipping cut foliage than live plants.

Foliage operations in Texas, another state on the Gulf Coast, are treated later.

Hawaii[13]

The commercial foliage industry is a relative newcomer to Hawaii but has shown a steady and healthy growth rate during the past 8 to 10 years. Estimates by the Hawaii Department of Agriculture on potted foliage production in Hawaii are shown in Table 1-2.

The Crop Reporting Board of the U.S. Department of Agriculture included Hawaii in its crop report on tropical foliage plants for the first time in 1977. The twenty-three growers enumerated in that year were reported as having sales of $2,262,000 on the 1,743,000 square feet (161,989 centares) or 40.3 acres (16.2 hectares) devoted to the culture of foliage plants in Hawaii [39]. The number of growers rose to forty-one in 1978, and they grew foliage plants on 2,720,000 square feet (252,788 centares) or 62.4 acres (25.3 hectares) with a sales value of $3,215,000.

The export foliage industry started about 1973 when Evergreen Nurseries, Inc., a major supplier of plant material for the local market, started shipping liners of dwarf brassaia (*Schefflera arboricola*) to the mainland. This was followed shortly thereafter by the establishment, with its output destined primarily for the export market, of the 87-acre

TABLE 1-2   Potted foliage production in Hawaii

Year	Wholesale value ($1,000)	Out of state shipment value ($1,000)
1972	171	28
1973	249	47
1974	284	78
1975	540	484
1976	1,550	800
1977	2,450	1,375

[13]The main source for the information on Hawaii is [29].

Kohala Nursery on the island of Hawaii. Another large operation, the AmFac Nursery, was established in 1976, with major production facilities under cover on Oahu for producing cuttings, liners, and finished plants and extensive field plantings on the island of Hawaii to supply propagation material. Other nurseries producing foliage are located on Maui, as well as on Oahu and Hawaii.

Another developing trend is for mainland firms, primarily from California and Arizona, to develop branch growing areas in Hawaii to supply all or a portion of their requirements of plant material. Figures from the Hawaii Department of Agriculture show 116 certified nurseries in 1979.

The primary market for Hawaiian foliage is the West Coast of the United States and Canada. However, some shipments go as far as the East Coast. Currently, very little, if any, potted foliage is being shipped to Europe and Japan. Although much material goes by air, an increasing amount moves to the West Coast by sea in climate-controlled containers. The plant items, which range from rooted and unrooted cuttings to specimen 6- to 8-inch (15.4 to 20.5 centimeters) pots, are marketed mainly through brokers.

Northeast and Midwest

Three firms were major producers in the early commercial history of the tropical foliage industry in the United States. These included the Robert Craig Company of Norwood, Pennsylvania, founded about 1878, the Julius Roehrs Company in 1869 at Rutherford, New Jersey, and, across the street from the Julius Roehrs Company, Bobbink and Atkins, founded in 1897 [7, 40]. Bobbink and Atkins by 1910 was probably the largest importer of "stove plants" from Belgium, Holland, and other European sources. These three firms were the major entities in the green plant market in the eastern part of the nation.

Early in this century, shiploads of plants came to the United States from Belgium, Holland, and England [32]. They were packed in large wooden cases (Figure 1-5), unloaded from the ships, and trucked by horse-drawn wagons to greenhouses for finishing and sale.

The smaller firm of W. A. Manda, founded in 1885, of Livingston, New Jersey, introduced more varieties than Roehrs and Craig [2]. Specimens of several plants sent to Puerto Rico by the Manda operation made possible the future export of large quantities of these plants to the United States and Europe over the period since 1953 [10].

The largest strictly foliage operation in the northern United States was that of Klugman and Schneirow of Brooklyn, New York [2]. This firm, established around 1910, originally brought palms and foliage

Figure 1-5.   Plant tubs and boxes used for growing and shipping foliage plants in the early 1900s.

from Europe. The firm had about 110,000 square feet (10,230 square meters) of foliage production in comparison with the some 75,000 square feet (6,975 square meters) grown by Julius Roehrs. The Joseph Heacock Co. of Wyncote, Pennsylvania, was almost as large as Klugman and Schneirow and equally famous. This firm grew *Kentia* palms on the ground and *Cibotium schiedei* suspended in baskets above.

The only major producer of tropical foliage plants (plus cacti and succulents) in the New England area for many years was the F. I. Carter and Sons Co. of Tewksbury, Massachusetts [27]. Still a regional leader, Carter's pioneered the push toward growing small-sized plants for mass merchandising outlets in the early 1940s. It shipped 2¼- and 3-inch (5.8- and 7.7-centimeter) pots over much of the United States and also into Canada. In the early days most plant material was brought in bare root from Florida for finishing.

Sylvan Hahn of Pittsburgh was characterized as an outstanding plant grower [32]. He was the pioneer in growing brassaia (*Schefflera actinophylla*) as an indoor item in addition to the plants listed later in the section on marketing. He brought small plants from Florida, collected seed there, and grew the plants to larger sizes in Pittsburgh and also in Mississippi.

Hahn was the first to raise and grow dracaena cane upright in random lengths as a group or multihead planting. It took almost 10 years for the upright cane to gain acceptance other than in Pittsburgh, where Hahn pushed this product. Hahn also grew various types of English ivies and secured the first patents for foliage plants.

The Oechslin Co. of Chicago was the major early producer in the Midwest. It, along with Craig, Roehers, and Bobbink and Atkins, was one of the four giants in the industry as producers and also as introducers of new plants. For example, *Dracaena deremensis* 'Janet Craig' was named after Robert Craig's daughter Janet and *Dieffenbachia maculata* 'Rudolph Roehrs' was named after a son of Julius Roehrs, Sr.

Frank Oeschlin pioneered the concept of operating exclusively as a wholesale plant grower [25]. His entire production was marketed through retail florists' shops to which he offered a comprehensive set of plants representing the combination of plants then in general usage.

Foliage growers have learned to cultivate certain plants by accident. Fred Gloeckner, who developed a very large brokerage and supply business, is reported to have secured plants of *Philodendron scandens oxycardium (cordatum)* from the Missouri Botanical Garden in 1926 [2]. He interested Henry I. Faust of Merion, Pennsylvania, in growing them. Cultural instructions from the Missouri Botanical Garden stated that cordatum was an epiphyte and was to be grown in chopped osmunda fiber. Henry Frentzen, grower for the Faust nursery, could not see possibilities for this plant. After working with it for a short time, he requested Gloeckner to dispose of his large stock. Other operators tried growing the plant and had essentially the same experience. Somewhere along the line, a worker misunderstood the instructions to pot the plants in osmunda and planted them in regular soil. They grew well and demonstrated the feasibility of producing this plant in various types of growing media.

Marketing   S. Kahn, a grower on Staten Island, New York, was one of the first, if not the first, persons in the foliage business to develop the idea of doing business with the chain stores. He developed such markets in the late 1920s or early 1930s [10].

Another pioneer mass marketer in the Northeast was Sylvan Hahn of Louis Hahn and Son in Pittsburgh. About 1935 he and Arthur Hirt of Strongville, Ohio, grew plants for and planted dish gardens and terrariums in large volume. A variety of these items was sold in farmers' markets and other nonflorist outlets. These dish gardens, terrariums, and colored sand gardens helped develop the first widespread market in foliage plants.

A new trend to mass merchandising began in the latter part of the

Great Depression of the 1930s and resulted in much of the expanding demand for foliage in the late 1940s and into the 1950s. The great expansion of foliage production in the 1970s was in response to expanded demand in most segments of earlier market outlets, plus large increases in the interior design market.

Much credit for development of mass marketing of cut flowers and potted plants must be given to Larry Heinl of Toledo, Ohio, when he began selling to chain stores [13]. This marketing effort drew threats from retail florists to boycott growers and wholesale florists who sold products to mass market stores. Heinl started selling to the chain stores, of which Woolworth was the first, in the late 1930s [18]. He began with plants in 1¾-inch (4.5-centimeter) clay pots, shipping the material by Railway Express in corrugated boxes. The number of pots per box was 100. Later, following trips to contact buyers, sales were made to other chains.

Truck distribution directly to individual stores was begun in the late 1940s. Truck drivers also served as plant salespeople. The line of products has expanded from 1¾-inch (4.5-centimeter) material to sizes as large as 6 inches (15.4 centimeters). At the height of distribution in the 1960s, store-door deliveries were made from terminals in Toledo, Detroit, Cleveland, Chicago, Minneapolis, Jacksonville, Illinois (also serving the St. Louis area), Philadelphia, and Baltimore. The distribution operation was sold in 1970 to the Green Thumb Corporation, then controlled by the conglomerate Stratford of Texas.

The Heinl operation developed the first almost completely mechanized facilities for large-scale production of foliage plants. Later, production in the Northeast and Midwest declined as the mass production of foliage plants in the South replaced them and the popularity of larger plants increased.

A new outlet evolved for foliage plants, that of plant care and rental firms, during the 1970s. Such firms contract to furnish, and often care for, plants of certain types for use in offices, shopping centers, hotels, and other commercial buildings. Most major metropolitan areas have a number of such firms in existence.

Puerto Rico

Frederick Moses Pennock, who came to Puerto Rico in 1899 from the Philadelphia area, is generally regarded as the father of ornamental horticulture in Puerto Rico [28]. Pennock was a graduate in the first agricultural class at Cornell University and was the founding dean, School of Agriculture, University of Puerto Rico. He started a nursery in Sabana Llana called North South Nursery Co. in 1906, which is still in operation as Pennock Gardens. In its early days the firm grew caladiums, *Dracaena* cane, palm seed, and other plants, which were shipped to U.S. markets; for many years it was the sole supplier of caladium tubers [2]. Recently, a new company, Cerro Gordo Nursery, was formed to take over the exporting done originally by North South Nursery Co.

Charles F. Pennock, the oldest son of F. M. Pennock, earned recognition as primary developer of the ornamental horticulture industry in Puerto Rico. He introduced sixty-five plants into the local industry for export markets and local use. His early designs for the construction of shade houses were copied in South Florida as well as Puerto Rico. He has achieved professional recognition elsewhere by his peers and was elected an honorary member of the American Horticultural Society.

Other early Puerto Rican operations include the Robert Craig Co. of Norwood, Pennsylvania, which located there in the early 1900s, Jardines Selles (now operating as Jardines Dorado), Holger Fog, S. R. Capifali, and Pedro Iglesias.

Puerto Rico was a source of stock material prior to Florida's entrance into the foliage plant industry [33]. Growers there took advantage of its tropical location and political association with the United States to grow items more economically than could be done by mainland growers.

The Andre Nursery in Trinidad pioneered the hybridizing of *Dracaenas* and established the remarkable record of developing more than forty varieties, comprising the finer cultivars now in use. Some old nurseries that began growing *Dracaenas* in Puerto Rico have stock plantings of many old and fine Andre varieties generally unknown to the trade today [2].

McHutchison and Co. began importing Andre's cane in 1905. Bare cane of *Dracaena massangeana* from Trinidad sold in those days for $1 per foot, with hybrids bringing up to $5 per foot.

The North South Nursery Co. in Puerto Rico began cultivating *Philodendron scandens oxycardium* about 1933 [2]. Five years later it had 3 acres (1.2 hectares) of stock producing propagating vines, with customers assured of nine eyes per vine not including the tip. The sale price f.o.b. New York was $25 per 1,000 vines. These and other plants were shipped by sea to New York and thence by Railway Express to final destinations.

Acquisition of stock plants of cultivars in short supply was often fraught with intrigue and adventure. This was the case in getting a supply of Chinese evergreen (*Aglaonema*) canes from Canton, China, to Puerto Rico in the late 1930s [10]. Louis Dank had foreseen the possible end of trade with China owing to its invasion by Japan and acquired a supply of Chinese evergreens in Canton. He made arrangements with a group of growers in Puerto Rico, who were in a latitude about 5 degrees south of Canton to grow and market plants propagated from these. Thus, when the Sino-Japanese war was at its peak, a supply of Chinese evergreens was en route to Puerto Rico.

During World War II, shipments of foliage plants by sea became unreliable. Puerto Rico thus lost its major customer of *Philodendron scandens oxycardium,* and the growing business moved to Florida. The first major production of vines and rooted cuttings in Florida was established by 1945 [2].

Louis Dank, a broker, was a pioneer in air shipments of foliage plants and made many contributions to the development of the foliage industry. At the end of World War II there was a large demand for foliage cuttings by northern greenhouse operators. Despite a large supply of cuttings in Puerto Rico, the available means of transportation were insufficient to get them to New York and other markets. Dank arranged to have air shipments of *Dracaena sanderiana* cane from Puerto Rico to Miami [10]. Later, air freight became an established function of commercial passenger airlines, and as freight-carrying airlines entered the field, shipment of foliage plants by air increased.

The Puerto Rico Department of Agriculture certified forty-six nurseries for commercial export shipments of live plants in 1979. The majority of such shipments consists of foliage plants. The value of sales at wholesale of ornamental horticultural products from Puerto Rico was more than $13 million in 1979 [28].

Puerto Rican growers have entered into the finished plant business in addition to cuttings. Approximately 125 trailer loads of potted plant materials were shipped from Puerto Rico by sea to various U.S. destinations in 1978. They were transported by SeaLand, which has the same freight rate to all eastern seaboard destinations. Such plants are grown in media that permit them to enter the United States. The predominant size was 6-inch (15.4-centimeter) pots, but ranged from 4 to 10 inches (10.3 to 25.6 centimeters). Large quantities of cuttings as well as finished plants also move by air.

Texas

The commercial production of foliage plants in Texas received its major emphasis following World War II [11]. The primary production areas developed along the Rio Grande owing to its warm climate. This area was adjacent to Mexico, and many amateur horticulturists and growers of various crops in the Rio Grande Valley made frequent trips to Mexico to bring back specimens of "new" and little known species from the wealth of tropical foliage abounding in Mexico.

Probably the pioneer producer in the area was Carl Klinger, located in Pharr. His major production facilities were outdoors and under lath, where he grew small plants for sale to outlets such as variety stores and fruit and vegetable markets. Later Klinger, like most other Rio Grande Valley foliage operators, replaced his lath houses with greenhouses.

The earliest collector of plants and seeds from Mexico was Morris Clint of Brownsville. Several large organizations in the Rio Grande Valley are now involved in the importation of seeds of tropical plants.

Pothos, including much large-leaf pothos, was the major plant grown in the early days of the Rio Grande Valley foliage industry [31]. Other major crops included *Ficus, Peperomia, Philodendron,* and cacti and other succulents. The crop mix in recent years has expanded to include a wide variety of cultivars.

Neal Robinson of Brownsville, who developed the miniruffled fern and grew it in large volumes, started the firm in 1953 that is now the largest foliage operation in Texas [8, 31]. The Robinson firm pioneered in selling foliage by telephone to mass market outlets.

In addition to foliage nurseries in Brownsville and Pharr, others are located in Weslaco. Growers in the Rio Grande Valley generally use natural gas for heating their greenhouses.

Waxahatchie, located approximately 25 miles south of Dallas, is another foliage center. The operation there was begun in the 1940s when Harry Smith of the Winter Garden Ornamental Nursery in Florida opened a greenhouse where cane stock shipped in was grown to marketable sizes [9]. Smith also used Waxahatchie as a distribution center for other plants, which he either shipped in or grew there. Additional nurseries also began producing foliage plants. The 1970 Census showed that Harris County, in which Waxahatchie is located, ranked third among Texas counties in the production of finished foliage plants [36]. The two leading counties were in the Rio Grande Valley.

Recent Economic and Technical Developments

Market Expansion

Tremendous expansion in the demand for foliage plants occurred during the 1970s throughout the world. Some increased sales value was occasioned by inflationary forces, but still more was due to the vast increase in demand for tropical foliage plants (Figure 1-1). Outlets that formerly handled plants have expanded their volume of sales; new types of outlets marketing foliage plants have appeared on the scene.

A number of reasons have been propounded as causes for the large expansion in consumer demand. These include the ecology movement with its emphasis on living things, a trend to apartment living with little or no opportunity to grow gardens or outdoor plants, the substitution of plants for pets, the increased availability of foliage plants in an increased variety of retail outlets, and the rising use of plants in magazine and television pictures and scenes.

Entry of Conglomerates

A number of large conglomerate firms have entered the U.S. foliage plant industry, mostly in Florida, during the past 15 years. Others have investigated the possibilities of doing so; many made offers to purchase going firms. Conglomerate firms have purchased efficient, large, operating, growing concerns rather than planning and starting new ones.

Foliage firms operated by conglomerates are organized as separate corporations or as divisions of the parent companies. Innovations in marketing have often evolved as a result of management and other policies, encouraged by knowledge of diverse operations with respect to other commodities. Several large foliage firms owned by conglomerates have integrated production operations for foliage cuttings in Latin America and the Caribbean.

Overseas Production of Cuttings

Aside from that in Puerto Rico, the initial production of foliage plant cuttings in the tropics for importation into the United States was begun in Cuba by Lex Ritter in 1955. He discontinued his business there after the rise to power of Fidel Castro. Ritter then started propagating plants in Honduras and later sold his operation to United Brands, previously the United Fruit Company. Currently, his firm, Far West Botanicals, is one of the largest overseas foliage operators, producing cuttings in Costa Rica, Honduras, and Puerto Rico. Other large overseas operations include the Green Thumb Corporation (now a subsidiary of Ralston Purina Company) and United Brands.

Since plants rooted in soil cannot be imported into the United States, overseas foliage ventures have generally produced unrooted cuttings, which can be brought in. Reduced labor costs and high productivity year round without heat were primary reasons for initiating this enterprise, which has far outstretched the expectations of industry leaders. Now more than 2,000 acres (810 hectares) are devoted to foliage culture in various Latin American and Caribbean countries [30]. Still others are produced in Puerto Rico. Shipments go not only to the United States, but also to Europe and elsewhere.

Overseas foliage operations expanded rapidly in the 1960s and 1970s. The second firm to enter the business was comprised of a group of five Central Florida indoor decorative foliage growers who purchased a large tract of land in Guatemala and began growing a portion of their propagating plant needs in 1963. Other U.S. growers and entrepreneurs in tropical lands have followed. Some firms have operations in more than one country and may have two or more growing areas in the same country at different elevations to maximize growing efficiency for various plants, some of which do best at low and others at high elevations. Such conditions may readily be found in most tropical countries.

The bulk of the tropical foliage cuttings in Central America and the Caribbean is grown by integrated units of U.S. foliage producing firms. In addition to the firms listed, which operate in Costa Rica, Guatemala, Honduras, Jamaica, and Puerto Rico, others also have foliage cuttings businesses there. Additional firms are located in Colombia, the Dominican Republic, Hawaii, Mexico, and elsewhere. The Ivory Coast in West Africa also produces foliage cuttings, most of which are sent to Europe.

Technological Developments

Successful foliage growers have used management skills to utilize or adapt to changed technology over the past 30 years. Through aggressive entrepreneurship, many growers have attained high degrees of efficiency in production and marketing operations. Many growers with management skills less well honed than those of the more successful have nevertheless tended to remain in the profit column for many years owing to the expanding nature of market demand over much of the 30-year period.

Technological developments that have affected the production and marketing of foliage plants are as follows:

1. Development and fabrication of plastic pots, which replaced clay pots; they are cheaper in original cost and to transport.
2. Plastic plants, which are believed to have been responsible for doldrums in this foliage industry's development in the late 1950s and early 1960s.

3. Acceptance and use of sanitary cultural techniques; chemical and steam soil sterilization kills weed seed, insects, disease pathogens, and nematodes and results in higher productivity.

4. Tissue culture, which permits rapid, disease-free propagation of certain plant cultivars.

5. Pesticide, fungicide, and nematicide availability, which contributes to increased productivity, especially nematicides and soil drenches to control root rotting.

6. Advances in greenhouse design; free space design permits improved materials handling, and cooling systems have been improved.

7. Automatic controls for watering.

8. Plant conditioning, which controls or minimizes leaf drop and other maladies of plants moved from one light environment to another.

9. Increased availability and use of technical information from experiment stations, commercial firms, and other growers.

10. Interstate highway system, which permits rapid transportation to market destinations.

Acknowledgments

In addition to individuals cited in the references, the authors wish to express their appreciation to the following persons for the helpful comments made when they reviewed an earlier draft of this chapter: Dr. Arthur Bing, Cornell University, Riverhead, New York; Dr. C. D. Brickell, Royal Horticultural Society, Wisley, Woking, Surrey, England; Dr. Charles A. Conover, University of Florida, Apopka, Florida; Prof. Ralph Dickey, University of Florida (Emeritus), Gainesville, Florida; Dr. Wesley M. Davidson, Rutgers University (Emeritus), New Brunswick, New Jersey; Dr. Alvan Donnan, Jr., Apopka, Florida; M. Truman Fossum, Washington, D.C.; Paul G. Faircloth, Apopka, Florida; Walter Gammel, Sr., Perrine, Florida; Dr. Raymond F. Hasek, University of California, Davis, California; Bunny Hogshead, Apopka, Florida; Dr. Harry Kohl, University of California, Davis, California; M. James Leider, Prairie View, Illinois; Dr. Conrad B. Link, University of Maryland, College Park, Maryland; Dr. Dennis B. McConnell, University of Florida, Gainesville, Florida; Dr. E. W. McElwee, University of Florida (Emeritus), Gainesville, Florida; Dr. John Mastalerz, Pennsylvania State University, University Park, Pennsylvania; Dr. Neil W. Stuart, U.S. Department of Agriculture (Ret.), Silver Spring, Maryland; Dr. Thomas

Weiler, Purdue University, West Lafayette, Indiana; and Dr. K. Zimmer, Technical University of Hanover, Hanover, West Germany.

REFERENCES

[1] Allan, Mea. 1970. *Tom's weeds—The story of Rochford's and their house plants.* London: Faber & Faber, Ltd., p. 220.

[2] Bliss, Calvin, Woodcliff Lake, N.J. Letter dated November 8, 1978.

[3] Blue, Fabia, Homestead, Fla. Interview, February 12, 1979.

[4] Brown, Theodore, South Miami Heights, Fla. Memorandum of December 1978.

[5] Buck, Verne. 1960. "The Growth and Development of the Foliage Plant Industry in Florida," *Proceedings of the Florida State Horticultural Society* 73: 342–344.

[6] ———, Apopka, Fla. Memorandum dated November 1978.

[7] Conklin, Everett, Montvale, N.J. Letter dated October 30, 1978.

[8] Cook, Charlie, Dallas, Tex. Telephone interview, February 1979.

[9] Criley, Art, Homestead, Fla. Interview, February 13, 1979.

[10] Dank, Louis, Hollywood, Fla. Interview, February 14, 1979.

[11] DeWerth, A. F., Texas A&M University (Emeritus), College Station, Tex. Memorandum, Spring 1978.

[12] Fairchild, David. 1947. *The world grows round my door.* New York: Charles Scribner's Sons, p. 347.

[13] Gartner, John B., University of Illinois (Emeritus), Urbana, Ill. Letter dated November 12, 1978.

[14] Graf, A. B., East Rutherford, N.J. Letter dated May 30, 1979.

[15] Graf, Alfred Byrd. 1970. *Exotica* 3, Vol. I. East Rutherford, N.J.: Roehrs Company, p. 840.

[16] ———. 1970. *Exotic plant manual.* East Rutherford, N.J.: Roehrs Company, p. 840.

[17] Greer, Dan J., Miami, Fla. Interview, November 1975.

[18] Heinl, Harry, Miami, Fla. Interview, February 12, 1979.

[19] Hoffman, Bill, and Tommy Hoffman, Hollywood, Fla. Interview, February 13, 1979.

[20] Klogart, Asger, Royal Veterinary and Agricultural University, Copenhagen Denmark. Memorandum dated December 1978.

[21] Knauss, James, University of Florida, Apopka, Fla. Notes for talk at Hall of Fame banquet, 1978.

[22] Kofranek, Anton M., University of California, Davis, Calif. Memorandum dated December 19, 1978.

[23] Marchman, Lamont, Apopka, Fla. Letter dated November 9, 1978.

[24] Mitchell, Robert, Orlando, Fla. Telephone conversation, February 1979.

[25] Oechslin, Ernest, Jr., Lake Worth, Fla. Letter dated November 20, 1978.

[26] Oskierko, Fabian, Homestead, Fla. Telephone conversation, February 13, 1979.

[27] Patch, F. Wallace, Framingham Centre, Mass. Letter dated November 12, 1978.

[28] Pennock, Charles F., San Juan, Puerto Rico. Letter and memorandum dated May 4, 1979.

[29] Rauch, Fred D., University of Hawaii, Honolulu, Hawaii. Letter dated February 21, 1979.

[30] Ritter, Lex, Miami, Fla. Interview, February 13, 1979.

[31] Robinson, Don, Brownsville, Tex. Telephone conversation, February 1979.

[32] Roehrs, Julius E., East Irvine, Calif. Letter dated October 26, 1978.

[33] **Scarborough, Elmo F., and Cecil N. Smith. 1976. "Tropical foliage production in Latin America and the Caribbean,"** *Proceedings of the Tropical Region, American Society for Horticulture Science* 24: 455–467.

[34] Seiger, Leonard J., Ocean City, N.J. Letter dated November 20, 1978.

[35] Smith, Cecil N. 1976. "Increasing competition from California foliage," *Florida Foliage Horn of Plenty Report* 2: 3, pp. 3–5.

[36] Swanson, Henry. 1975. *Countdown for agriculture.* Orlando, Fla.: Henry F. Swanson, pp. 169–196.

[37] Soar, Frank D., Hollywood, Fla. Letter dated November 24, 1978.

[38] **U.S. Bureau of the Census.** 1952, 1962, 1974. *U.S. Census of Agriculture 1949, 1959* and *1969, Vol. V., Special Reports, Part 1* (1949 and 1959) and *part 10* (1969). Washington, D.C.: U.S. Government Printing Office.

[39] U.S. Statistical Reporting Service. 1969 to 1979. *Flowers and foliage plants—Production and sales in selected states, 1956–68,* and annually through 1978. U.S. Department of Agriculture Statistical Bulletin 442 and related SpCr reports. Washington, D.C.: U.S. Government Printing Office.

[40] Vosters, James, Miami, Fla. Interview, Summer 1978.

[41] ———. Letter to Jim Knauss dated September 28, 1977.

two

Will E. Waters
Charles A. Conover

greenhouses, related structures, and environmental control

The greenhouse design chosen for foliage plant production will exert a major influence upon the success or failure of the business. Greenhouse designs have undergone revolutionary changes in covering materials, superstructures, and heating facilities since the advent of plastics in 1938. Prior to the plastics age, greenhouses were primarily constructed from wood or steel with glass covers. This chapter describes the various options in greenhouse location, structures, framing, covers, heating and cooling, shading, irrigation, internal designs and economic considerations that should be examined in constructing and renovating greenhouses for foliage plant production.

Greenhouse Design and Construction

Location

Location of a commercial foliage plant growing range is an important and essentially nonreversible decision for foliage producers to make. The following points should be considered individually and collectively for one structure or an entire range for maximum economic advantage [5, 26, 32, 38, 46, 48].

Local building and zoning codes are first items to consider in greenhouse location prior to land purchase. These regulations vary from state to state or from county to county or city to city within a state. Greenhouse construction codes may be similar to commercial structures in some areas, whereas in others they may be classified as agricultural buildings or even temporary structures with simpler requirements. Code requirements will determine to a considerable extent construction costs.

Availability and initial cost of land constitute a large percentage of structure cost and savings may be realized by purchasing well-drained, poor-quality soils less suitable for agriculture and real estate development. Such land is usually more available than choice real estate.

Land characteristics to consider are local accessibility, elevation, topography, and drainage. Ideally, greenhouse and nursery land should be accessible without expensive road construction, fairly level to avoid ponding, have southerly or southeasterly exposures, and be well drained [46]. Tile drainage prior to construction should be evaluated in poorly drained soils since it will be more expensive to install later.

Irrigation sources depend on availability, legal constraints on usage, chemical and biological quality of irrigation water, and surface water control and should be investigated prior to land purchase or structural development. Chemical analysis should include total soluble salts, boron, fluoride, iron, sodium, chloride, and natural dissolved solids that could be detrimental to plant growth and/or appearance [25, 46].

Temperature maxima and minima and *wind patterns* are influenced significantly by land elevation, topography, slope exposure, and wind current. These factors may strongly influence high or low temperatures, potential wind damage, and energy cost for heating and cooling.

House orientation, where practical, should be north to south for uniform and maximum light, with headhouse or solid structures on the north end.

Availability of labor is a key factor for consideration since ornamental plant production is a labor-intensive commodity. New operations should avoid, if possible, locations with highly competitive labor markets, such as heavy manufacturing, construction, and tourist centers. Location of production houses in less developed areas of a given community should help assure labor supplies.

Transportation facilities, such as commercial transportation, airports, and adequate highway systems, are critical factors in the shipment of ornamental plant materials.

Accessibility to technical information, equipment dealers, maintenance services, horticultural supply sources, and utility services is important in the operation and maintenance of greenhouse ranges. Location in close proximity to urban centers should enhance sales for operations specializing in local wholesale and retail markets.

Types of Structures

Increased costs of energy and building materials necessitate efficient and effective structural design. Distinctive types of greenhouse designs have evolved over the years and have been used successfully to grow foliage plants. These can be classified by structural design: open structure, ridge-and-gutter (ridge-and-furrow), lean-to, quonset (vault type), sawtooth, and inflatable.

Open structures   These are usually supported with treated posts of 4- by 4-inch lumber spaced on 12- to 16-foot centers (Figure 2-1) [46], although concrete and steel posts are used also. The roof is supported by wooden stringers, galvanized cable, or heavy galvanized wire mounted to the post from 7 to 12 feet above the soil. The covering usually consists of polypropylene or saran shade cloth fastened to stringers by metal S hooks, nylon cord, or wood lath mounted to 1- by 6-inch or 2- by 4-inch wooden stringers. These structures have the advantages of being relatively inexpensive and easy to construct with normal farm labor. They may be designed to permit easy operation of tractor-drawn equipment inside the range, may be covered with perforated polyethylene for winter protection, and offer a rapid means of expan-

Figure 2-1.   Open polypropylene shade structure common to tropical and subtropical climates.

Figure 2-2. A ridge and gutter greenhouse, also referred to as a "free-standing greenhouse."

sion. Their estimated cost of construction is about one tenth that of conventional domestic glasshouses.

Open structures have the disadvantages of being difficult and expensive to heat in winter and are best suited to warm areas (California, Florida, Texas). They have limited climatic or environmental control characteristics, are subject to wind and hail damage, and the shade cloth coverings must be replaced every 6 to 10 years, with winter plastic replaced yearly.

Ridge and gutter greenhouses   These are the most common structural design used for foliage plants (Figure 2-2) [5, 44, 48]. They usually have a ridge in the middle of the structure with even-span roofs. When several units are arranged so the inside walls are omitted and gutters placed on top of posts, the cluster is referred to as a ridge-and-furrow house (Figure 2-3). Recently, the "Dutch-type" greenhouse (Figure 2-4) has appeared on the American market; it differs from the standard ridge-and-furrow house primarily in the width of individual houses, length of rafters, and glazing with single panes of glass running from ridge to eaves and sometimes to the ground. The roof pitch of the rigid-gutter type can be broadly classified as low pitch (1 to 2 feet per 12-foot span), medium pitch (4 to 6 feet per 12-foot span), or high pitch

Figure 2-3.   Fiberglass ridge-and-furrow greenhouse showing two units joined by a common gutter.

Figure 2-4.   Glass ridge-and-furrow Dutch-type greenhouse.

(6 to 7 feet per 12-foot span). Factors to consider in figuring appropriate pitch are side wall height, snow, rainfall, wind loads, and construction materials available. High pitch is most functional in northern latitudes, the medium pitch is satisfactory in southern states, and the low pitch is satisfactory in subtropical and tropical areas providing side walls are high enough (7 feet minimum) to ensure proper ventilation.

Rigid designs have many advantages since they can be easily covered with film or rigid coverings, interior supports may be held to a minimum to permit mechanization, they have long structural life, can be mass produced, are easily constructed, and are relatively maintenance free. The main disadvantage is in their high initial costs.

Quonset or vault design greenhouses These greenhouses (Figure 2-5) are commonly constructed of steel or bowed galvanized pipe; however, a variety of other materials, including heavy-mesh steel wire, wooden strips, or even PVC pipe, may be used for less permanent structures. These houses usually range from 8 to 15 feet in height and from 12 to 35 feet in width per bow. Quonset houses may be mounted on concrete walls raised 2 or 3 feet above the ground or by properly bending the pipe mounted directly in the ground, thus allowing more light to enter under side benches and aid in side ventilation. Side walls may be omitted, gutter added, and several units connected together as with ridge and gutter structures. For this type of construc-

Figure 2-5.   Quonset design greenhouse. Uneven painting due to use of polypropylene shade cloth inside just above fans.

tion at least 1-inch-diameter, high-tensile-strength galvanized steel pipes are suggested for the bows. These structures are relatively low in initial cost, permanent, can be mass prefabricated, are relatively easy to erect with farm labor, are fairly versatile, and may be covered with polyethylene or fiberglass. Unfortunately, they have no roof ventilation, cooling and heating frequently present problems, and when built from low-strength materials they are subject to wind damage.

   Sawtooth structures   These are constructed with 4- by 4-inch posts or smaller galvanized steel frames usually on 12- to 20-foot centers (Figure 2-6). The roof is designed in a sawtooth configuration with a series of roof spans sloped in the same direction; such structures are adaptable for continuous coverage of large areas. A 2- to 4-foot vertical opening designed for ventilation is left between each roof level. Ventilators are installed in the vertical roof openings for cool climates; in tropical areas they are often left open. This design and several modifications are used extensively in the subtropical and tropical regions of the world.
   Sawtooth designs are useful for large areas for ground or bench culture, relatively easy to cool, relatively inexpensive, and can be constructed with semiskilled labor. Disadvantages include internal posts that can interfere with mechanical equipment and nonsuitability for northern climates because of low roof slope and winter heating problems.

Figure 2-6.   Sawtooth fiberglass greenhouse with vented openings.

Other structures   An array of temporary structures have come on the market in recent years, including air-supported inflatables, PVC pipe structures, and low-cost plastic houses. These structures should be evaluated carefully to determine life expectancy and suitability before making an investment.

Framing Materials

The superstructure frame is an important part of modern growing houses since it determines life span and maintenance requirements. Framing materials normally used in growing structures include aluminum, steel, concrete, wood, galvanized pipe and PVC [32, 34, 44, 49].

Prefabricated aluminum alloy extrusions are commonly utilized today to build free-span commercial greenhouses since they have long life expectancy, are corrosion resistant, are lightweight, are prefabricated for relatively fast erection, and have excellent strength to support glass and withstand high winds. They are rigid with straight side walls, free span inside, have low maintenance cost, may be permanently glazed, are suitable for any type of covering, and may be glassed to the ground. Aluminum framing has high initial cost and requires experienced personnel to erect.

Precast steel, wrought and malleable iron are commonly utilized for greenhouse structures; when utilized, a hot-dip galvanized coating is recommended to protect against rusting from corrosive fertilizer salts utilized inside the structure. Galvanized metals have structural strength, long life expectancy, low maintenance cost, free-span options, will support permanent glazed glass, and are prefabricated for relatively fast erection. They have high initial cost, are heavy for shipping and handling, and require experienced personnel to erect.

Prestressed and poured concrete materials are used less commonly than metals for framing but are satisfactory for side walls and center posts in shade house ranges or sawtooth houses. Wood or metal roof supports may be satisfactorily combined with masonry foundation structure. Concrete is recommended for foundations and setting of posts regardless of the type of structure used.

Galvanized pipe may be utilized for any of the structures discussed. Lightweight and standard galvanized water pipes can be used. Heavier weight pipes have increased structural strength and life expectancy, and require less maintenance. Pipes can be prefabricated for easy construction and are moderately inexpensive, free span, corrosive resistant, and easy to construct, but they have less overall structural strength.

Wood is a common framing material utilized in low-cost greenhouse and shade house designs. Careful selection of the wood species will increase the structure life. The inside environments of growing structures are maintained at high levels of humidity; therefore, precautions must be taken to protect wood from rotting or rot-resistant species must be used. Tree woods fairly resistant to rotting include black locust, red cedar, redwood, heart cypress, western cedar, and heart pitch pine. Heartwood of most species is the most rot resistant and durable. Soft surface or sapwood should be avoided. Wood that touches the ground or comes in frequent contact with water should be treated with a good wood preservative to increase the life of the structure.

Commercial pressure-treated lumber is preferred over custom soaking or surface brush applications because preservative salts penetrate into the wood by use of a vacuum pressure process.

Some wood preservatives are not satisfactory for treating greenhouse lumber because their vapors may be toxic to plants for several years, such as the oil-based preservatives creosote and penta (pentachlorophenol) compounds. Materials satisfactory for treating greenhouse lumber include copper naphthenate (10 percent) in oil and waterborne metallic salts of copper and zinc [14, 16, 48].

Lumber, except pressure-treated materials, should be air dried prior to construction and the superstructure painted with a high-quality water-based paint for appearance and uniformity of light distribution. Oil-based paints are less desirable because they may blister, peel, and interfere with moisture vapor transfer from the wood. Painting should not be substituted for wood treatment since this rarely adds to the life of the house. The use of proper wood treatment can add 10 or more years of life expectancy to the structure.

Wood frames are available and easy to purchase, may be cut to suit any size and design structure, are less expensive than metals, can be free spans by use of trusses, and are relatively easy to construct with routine farm labor. They do have high maintenance cost. Wood needs to be treated, it is flammable, and it has less structural strength and more internal shadings than metals.

Temporary frames of PVC pipe, mesh and welded wire, bamboo mesh, cables, wire, and several other materials are used as semipermanent or temporary frames. These structures are usually temporary, susceptible to wind damage, and require high maintenance, but they are inexpensive, may give winter protection in southern climates, and afford a grower with limited capital some protection for plants.

Greenhouse Coverings

A variety of materials is available to cover greenhouse structures, ranging from woven fabrics and wooden lath for open structures to a variety of films, rigid plastics, and glass for enclosed structures [15, 29, 30, 35, 43, 47, 48, 49]. See Table 2-1.

Several woven fabrics of saran and polypropylene providing a range of 6 to 100 percent shade are available for covering open structures and cost from 6 to 20 cents per square foot according to quality and percent of shade. Polypropylene flame-retardant-type material appears superior presently because of safety, low shrinkage factor, life expectancy, and strength. These fabrics should be taken down during winter months in areas where ice and snow loads are expected. Nylon cord should be used in hurricane zones to tie on the cloth, but both should be removed if hurricane force winds are forecast.

When lath coverings are used to cover open areas, special precautions should be taken to use rot-resistant or pressure-treated woods. These structures can be covered with perforated poly-film material for

TABLE 2-1 Estimated characteristics of single-layer greenhouse coverings, 1976 [15, 30, 35, 37, 43]

Material	Initial cost/sq ft	Thickness suggested	Life expectancy
Regular polyethylene, 4 mil (single layer)	1×	4–6 mils	3–8 months
Polyethylene, ultraviolet resistant	2×	4–6 mils	12–24 months
Vinyls	4×	8–12 mils	2–5 years
Regular clear fiberglass	10 to 15×	4–5 oz per sq ft	5–10 years
Clear fiberglass (Tedlar® coated)	20 to 25×	5–6 oz per sq ft	15–20 years
Glass (double strength)	20 to 25×	28 oz per sq ft	25–30+ years

Material	Approximate solar light transmittance (%)	Thermal (heat) transmittance (%)	Relative maintenance requirements
Regular polyethylene, 4 mil (single layer)	88–94	70–75	Very high
Polyethylene, ultraviolet resistant	74–92	70–75	High
Vinyls	86–91	16.2	Medium
Regular clear fiberglass	78–95	1.0	Low
Clear fiberglass (Tedlar® coated)	78–92	1.0	Low
Glass (double strength)	86–90	4.4	Low

winter months if they are designed to allow attachment of the poly-film and the interior space heated.

Plastic films of several types are used for greenhouse covers, including polyethylene with and without ultraviolet inhibitors. Polyethylene without UV inhibitors is not recommended because the film rapidly deteriorates photochemically. It will last for 4 to 6 months as a temporary open structure cover in warm climates if obtained in 4-mil thickness.

Major advantages of polyethylene UV-resistant films for greenhouse coverings include low initial cost compared to glass or fiberglass, light weight, availability in sizes to cover entire greenhouses, and high light transmittance; it permits double layering, provides an airtight house, is easy to apply, and is satisfactory for temporary coverings. It has a relatively short life, may split along folds, transmits thermal radiations, which allows the house to cool rapidly, and has relatively high labor requirements for maintenance and replacement.

Vinyl films are more resistant to photochemical breakdown than polyethylene and may last 2 to 5 years, although the initial cost is significantly higher. Vinyls are usually 8 mils or more in thickness, heat seamed in 5- to 7-foot bands, are soft and pliable and are somewhat electrostatic, which necessitates periodic cleaning.

Polyvinyl fluoride (Tedlar[1]) is not used extensively as greenhouse film owing to its costs, but it is sometimes used as bonded surface coating to prolong the life of fiberglass because of its high UV resistance and life expectancy.

Polyester resin, rigid fiberglasses are available in various compositions, forms, weights, and colors. Originally, fiberglass panels were composed of basic polyester resins with strands of fiberglass, but improved formulations include the addition of about 15 percent acrylic additive (Plexiglas[2]) to retard weathering and coating with polyvinyl fluoride (Tedlar) to retard discoloration of photooxidation by UV radiation. Actual test data are unavailable, but there are indications that fiberglass panels with acrylic and Tedlar additives may transmit 90 to 95 percent of their original light transmission after 10 to 20 years of continuous exposure, depending upon the latitude and climate where used.

Fiberglass panels are formulated in flat and corrugated design, in weights ranging from 4 to 8 ounces per square foot, in widths of 26 to 52 inches, which cover 24 and 48 inches, and in multiple lengths up to 30 feet or more. Different colors of commercial fiberglass are available, but

[1]Tedlar is a trade name registered by E. I. Du Pont de Nemours & Co., Wilmington, Delaware.

[2]Plexiglas is a trade name registered by Rohm and Haas Co., Philadelphia, Pennsylvania.

only clear or frosted panels are suggested for commercial greenhouse covers because different colors will filter out desirable wavelengths from the visible spectrum. Generally, 4.5- to 5-ounce acrylic modified-Tedlar coated fiberglass is suggested if long sections of fiberglass are desired. This cover has relatively high light transmittance, long life expectancy, and low thermal radiation properties (less heating and cooling problems), is easy to install, is readily available, requires little cleaning if Tedlar coated, is low in maintenance requirements, and has more resistance to impact than glass. However, initial cost is high, it burns rapidly, requires care in sealing and fastening laps and joints, may lose transmittance properties with age, is not hail tolerant, and frequently comes with nebulous guarantees.

Glass at one time was the most common covering used for greenhouses and is still recognized as the choice greenhouse covering where initial cost is not prohibitive. Types of U.S. glass commonly used are A or B grades with both grades made in two weights or thicknesses referred to as single-strength, weighing approximately 20 ounces per square foot, or double strength, weighing approximately 28 ounces per square foot. A wide range of sizes for individual pieces or "lights" is available, but the standard side lights generally used are 16 inches wide and 18 to 24 inches long. Dutch-manufactured glass has appeared on the market recently and is of high quality. It is available in sizes up to 24 by 48 inches and larger. Plateglass is not normally used in greenhouse construction because of excessive cost, so double-strength glass is recommended. Glass coverings have long life expectancy, relatively low maintenance costs, high light transmittance, relatively low thermal heat transfer, and good weather resistance; however, they have high initial cost, require skilled labor for construction and service, and break upon impact.

Greenhouse Heating

Greenhouse heating systems should supply adequate and dependable heat to handle the coldest nights, circulate uniform temperatures throughout the house, produce no harmful fumes, and maintain appropriate humidity control. Principles of greenhouse heating are essentially the same as those of other buildings and dwellings, except that heat loss at night and radiation during the day are more rapid through greenhouse coverings. Several methods of supplying heat to greenhouses are currently used and may be broadly grouped into steam, hot water, forced-air furnaces, direct forced-air unit heaters, and solar systems [2, 4, 5, 6, 11, 16, 27, 31, 32, 39, 47, 48].

Steam

Steam systems are used in many old greenhouse ranges and in ranges of an acre or more. Steam systems essentially consist of boiler, delivery pipes to heating coils or radiating surfaces of various types, where the steam condenses or gives up "latent" heat, and pipes to return water back to the boiler. Specific needs as to boiler capacity, pipe sizes, and condensing systems will vary according to the size of the range, geographical location, specific environmental factors, and crops to be grown; therefore, individual grower needs should be evaluated by qualified greenhouse engineers familiar with specific crops and geographical areas. Steam systems are less costly, require fewer pipes than hot-water systems, are clean, have relatively low maintenance cost, may be used in soil sterilization and cleaning operations, and steam may be forced long distances. They have high initial cost, require trained maintenance personnel, and are dangerous if not maintained properly.

Hot Water

Hot-water systems heat water to temperatures slightly less than boiling, which then flows through pipes under greenhouse benches or around walls and gives up heat by radiation. Hot-water systems consist of a boiler, flow pipes, radiation pipes to dissipate heat, and return pipes to the boiler. Hot-water systems furnish a constant, uniform heat, are more flexible than steam, require less maintenance and labor to operate, are safer than steam, are satisfactory for ranges under one acre in size, and will hold heat for long periods of time if the heat source fails.

Forced Air Systems

Direct-forced-air-unit heaters are the most common type of heating system being installed in new greenhouses. The combustion and heater unit are mounted directly in the greenhouse with an electrical blower to deliver a jet stream of heat, and insulated vent stacks are used to exhaust fumes to the outside atmosphere. Distribution of heat can be facilitated by the use of polyethylene delivery tubes attached directly to the blower system or to a special fan-jet system mounted in front of the heater. The need for additional fan-jet blower systems is determined by individual heat demands within greenhouses. Direct forced-air unit heaters are fired by natural gas, bottled propane, or fuel oil. They are relatively inexpensive, readily available, have low maintenance requirements, respond rapidly to temperature demands, can be tailored to any need, and are easy to install. They have the hazardous potential of gas leakage, can possibly damage crops, and are expensive to operate owing to high cost of fuel.

Solar Heat

Solar heat for greenhouses is of considerable interest owing to increases in fuel cost, limited energy supplies, and pollution problems. A hydronic solar heating system consists of a solar collector, heat-storage vessel, heat-distribution system (usually some type of radiator), and mechanical equipment to direct water flow (Figure 2-7). Water is the vehicle currently recommended for storing and delivering the heat, but current research indicates that the moderate temperature hot-air system with graded rock or gravel as the storage component and air as the heat-delivery vehicle may have potential for greenhouse heating in certain parts of the world [3, 4, 24, 27, 28].

Solar heat systems use available free sun energy, and some may be built or installed by individuals with limited plumbing knowledge; they have long life expectancy, provide clean, fume-free heat, and require limited mechanical equipment, but some are complex and difficult to maintain. The systems have high initial cost with present-day equipment, require relatively large storage areas for heat storage, entire winter heat requirements cannot be stored in advance, and they are less satisfactory for northern climates or areas with extended overcast atmosphere during the winter.

Heating requirements for solar energy may be calculated by fuel

Figure 2-7.   Schematic diagram of a greenhouse solar heating system.

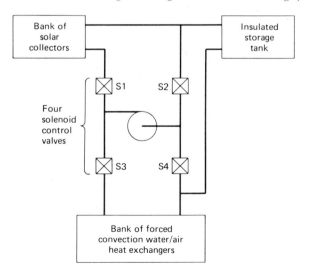

TABLE 2-2   BTU Equivalence of various
fuels used in greenhouse
heating [20, 24]

	Btu's per unit
Fuel oil	143,924/gal
Kerosene	135,143/gal
Coal	11,800/lb
Natural gas	1,000–1,700/cu ft
Propane	2,300/cu ft
Electricity	3,413/kW-hr

consumption history of the range or by the greenhouse heat loss method [24]. Greenhouse heat requirements are influenced by several factors, including local climatic and environmental conditions, size of greenhouse, structural design, type of covering, number of layers of glazing, and temperature requirements of the crop. Equipment manufacturers and universities have developed extensive tables and charts to aid in calculating heating needs [2, 45]. Individuals should consult these publications, qualified greenhouse engineers, and their state Cooperative Extension Service before purchase and installation of solar heat systems.

Fuel

Fuel sources commonly used in greenhouse heating are coal, natural gas, propane gas, fuel oil, kerosene, and electricity. Each energy source varies in Btu capacity (Table 2-2), and various types of heating systems generally operate at 70 to 80 percent efficiency.

Prices of fuel vary throughout the country, and the economics of heat cost should be determined locally. Initial equipment, operation and maintenance cost, and heating efficiencies must be considered in a complete economic analysis of heating alternatives.

Greenhouse Cooling

Increased demand for quality foliage plants and the need for higher yields has resulted in large investments in greenhouse cooling systems throughout the United States. Cooling for foliage production is less expensive than for flower crops because greenhouse coverings are usually heavily shaded to produce a cooling effect, and temperatures lower than 80°F are not desired. Regular ridge and side ventilation may be adequate in areas where extremely high temperatures and humidity are not experienced, but under other conditions additional facilities must be employed [2, 7, 8, 10, 13, 19, 22, 37, 40].

Ventilators

Ventilators provide efficient natural cooling, especially when double ridge ventilators are combined with side ventilators. Ridge ventilators are satisfactory in large ridge-and-furrow ranges. Cooling occurs when warm air rises through the ridge ventilator and is replaced by cool air from side ventilators or air that enters from the ridge. A single ridge ventilator on the leeward side of each ridge is usually adequate in areas where prevailing winds are from one direction. Research in the United Kingdom indicates that ventilator areas should equal 20 to 25 percent of the square footage of the unit [29], but in the United States ventilator area is rarely greater than 10 to 15 percent and, therefore, is less efficient in rapid heat transmission. Ventilators require less energy to operate and have lower maintenance costs than fan and pad systems, but the initial investment is about the same.

Fan and Pad Systems

Fans and pads have become the standard and expected system of cooling where extreme summer temperatures occur. Cooling results when heat in the house is utilized as energy in the evaporation of water [19, 22, 40]. The basic system uses fans to pull hot outside air through moist pads where it is cooled as the water evaporates; the air is then pulled through the greenhouse and out through the fans. The system works best in areas where or when humidity is low (i.e., arid or semiarid regions) and during the day since it is based on the dry bulb-wet bulb differential.

The system is simple in design and reliable, but the following design parameters must be met for the system to operate efficiently:

1. Increased number of fans (but not capacity) will improve air movement and allow staging of fans to reduce energy requirements when full cooling capacity is not required.
2. Fans should not be positioned so they exhaust into other fans, pads on adjacent greenhouses, or against walls closer than 20 feet because of increased back pressure and/or increased temperature and humidity of exhausted air on pads.
3. Fans should not be positioned to exhaust into prevailing winds. Fan capacity and pad size must be carefully chosen for each greenhouse

TABLE 2-3 Steps necessary to determine air volume requirements as cubic feet per minute for cooling of greenhouses with required pad area [2]

Step	Description	Example
1.	Establish the specifications for the system.	
	a. Permissible temperature variation from pad to fan.	5°F
	b. Placement of fan and pads; therefore, distance from fans to pads.	80 ft
	c. Elevation above sea level of greenhouse.	1,500 ft
	d. Maximum light intensity in greenhouse.	5,000 fc
	e. Size of greenhouses to be cooled by each system.	25 × 80 ft
2.	Calculate floor or ground area of greenhouse.	25 × 80 = 2,000 ft²
3.	Calculate basic airflow rate by multiplying floor area by 7 cubic feet per minute.	2,000 × 7 = 14,000 ft³
4.	Variation in temperature from pad to fan correction applied by increasing airflow obtained in step 3 by 14% for each degree in temperature below 7°F.	7°F − 5°F = 2 14,000 × 0.28 = 3,920 14,000 + 3,920 = 17,920
5.	Correct for distance from fan to pad by increasing airflow obtained in step 4 by 14% for each 15 feet of distance less than 100 feet.	100 ft − 80 ft = 20 17,920 × 0.14 = 2,509 17,920 + 2,509 = 20,429
6.	Correct for air density by increasing air volume calculated in step 5 by 4% for each 1,000 feet of elevation above sea level.	20,429 × 0.04 = 817 20,429 + 817 = 21,246
7.	Correct for light intensity by adding 10% of the result of step 6 for each 500 fc of light over 4,500 fc to the result of step 6.	5 000 fc − 4,500 fc = 500 21,246 × 0.10 = 2,125 21,246 + 2,125 = 23,371
8.	Air volume required to meet specification in step 1.	23,371 ft³ per min
9.	Pad area required in square feet is obtained by dividing cubic feet per minute obtained in steps 7 and 8 by 150 (aspen pads).	23,371 ÷ 150 = 155.8 ft² of pad area

to be cooled. Table 2-3 provides a summary of important factors, but complete details will be found in [2].

Recently, several new pad materials have been manufactured as replacements for aspen fiber, which was the standard pad material used for many years. These materials include pads made of hog bristles, aluminum, excelsior, cement, and coated cardboard. Only the coated cardboard in the form of Kool Cel® or Cool Dek® has an efficiency better than aspen [10]. The cost of coated cardboard is considerably above that of aspen, but the pad area needed is about 25 percent less, and its life-span is estimated at 3 to 5 years rather than 1 year. When labor of annual replacement is calculated into the cost, the newer coated cardboard materials appear to be a good choice. Another system of pad construction recently suggested is made of wire and washed river rock [22].

Maintenance costs of fans and pads are high, primarily due to pad replacement costs and electrical energy costs that range between 3 and 5 cents per square foot per year [13].

Fog Systems

High-pressure mist (fog system) utilizes water at approximately 600 pounds per square inch ejected through mist nozzles spaced uniformly throughout the top of the greenhouse [6, 9]. This system, like the fan and pad system, depends on evaporation to cool the air. With low humidity, evaporation lowers the greenhouse air temperature without moisture touching plant leaf surfaces. With high humidity conditions, little cooling results and moisture may reach the foliage, increasing foliar disease problems. This system works best in climates where the relative humidity is below 90 percent.

Components of this system include a high-pressure pump, distribution lines capable of withstanding high pressure, a control system to automate the system, and nozzles capable of distributing high pressure water at approximately ½ gallon per minute. Water used in the system must be of high purity because dissolved minerals clog nozzles and appear as residues on plant foliage. Several methods can be used to treat unsatisfactory water. These include methods used in ice plants to produce clear ice (mixing liquid sodium aluminate and hydrated lime with water in a tank and using the clear water in the system), use of a standard water softener (provided water has less than ten grains of hardness) and use of a deionizer. The best system is the use of a deionizer, but it is also the most expensive. Water usage is low in the fog system, and total costs of operation are not much different than other systems listed.

Control units should be set for mist durations of about 30 seconds, alternated with similar periods of no mist. Best success is obtained with control units that incorporate a humidistat and a thermometer. Continuous air movement within the greenhouse improves efficiency of the system; therefore, ventilators should be open during its operation and, where possible, air circulation fans also should be in operation.

Water distribution lines are usually copper or schedule 80 PVC,

Figure 2-8.   High pressure mist being used to cool a multicrop greenhouse. (Courtesy Mee Industries, Inc.)

since they reduce introduction of rust and other impurities into nozzles, which are stainless steel, oil-burner type. Nozzles are usually spaced 5 feet on center lines about 20 feet apart. This system is most effective when lines are 10 feet above the soil (Figure 2-8).

Ground Irrigation

Ground irrigation is an old but effective method of reducing temperatures within greenhouses by wetting walks and under benches. This method also depends on evaporation and is dependent on humidity within the greenhouse. Temperatures drop several degrees soon after wetting occurs, but rise as surfaces dry. Some producers have installed mist lines beneath benches that operate on temperature and humidistat controls or time clocks to maintain moisture on the ground. This system is low cost, but algae buildup on walks may be a problem, and where concrete walks are not present, aisles can turn to mud, presenting problems to employee morale. This method of cooling can be used in vented greenhouses or in those with fans and pads to increase efficiency.

Forced Air

Forced-air systems are based on the principle of forcing cool air into a greenhouse with a fan and allowing warm air to escape at another point, or forcing hot air out and allowing cool air to enter. This system is designed for winter use, although it has found some application in foliage production where temperatures as high as 95°F are acceptable for some crops.

The best application of the system is use of a fan jet to evenly distribute cool, outside air throughout the greenhouse while expelling warm air out through a gravity or motorized shutter. The system is not very efficient unless outside air is considerably cooler than inside air (20°F); therefore, it has excellent winter application but is of less use during summer.

Producers in tropical and subtropical areas often use large fans on the south end of the greenhouse and open the north end. Foliage greenhouses are often shaded to allow only 32 kilolux (klx) or less inside, and such structures often remain at or only several degrees above outside temperature. The same fans can be used to cool during the winter if shutters are incorporated into the north wall.

Shade Sources

Most foliage plants should be grown under various degrees of shade to properly acclimatize them prior to sale for interior use. Materials most commonly used are paints, fabric shade cloths, and preshaded fiberglass.

Paints, both oil based and water based, can be used on glass surfaces, but water-based ones are best on fiberglass surfaces and soft plastics like Mylar or polyethylene. Oil-based paints are more dangerous to apply, since they must be thinned with highly volatile solvents to permit application with a sprayer and may be phytotoxic. Most greenhouse supply houses sell quality water-based paints for painting glass, fiberglass, and other plastics. Paints from other than greenhouse supply sources may contain harmful solvents [36]. Thin to a 1 : 4 to 1 : 5 paint to water ratio and apply to a clean dry surface on a windless day. Apply a thin coat, allow to dry, and check the shade level before applying another coat. Most paints last for several years if glass or other surfaces are clean at time of application. If new paint is applied over old, scaling, chipping paint, a poor job will result. Glass can be cleaned with a solution of muriatic acid prior to painting. The acid solution should not be allowed to come into contact with live tissue, plant or animal.

Fabrics are commonly used as shading material; polypropylene is the most popular. It can be used as the sole source on shade houses, or over or beneath glass, fiberglass, or polyethylene. Polypropylene lasts up to 10 years when attached if only limited movement occurs and rubbing on wires or supports is eliminated. It can be obtained in most sizes and shade levels necessary for growing quality foliage plants.

Use of shade cloth over greenhouses has not been satisfactory because dirt collects between the shade cloth and structural surfaces and further decreases light intensity. Attaching shade cloth to the outside of greenhouses is difficult, and it restricts air movement through vents. There are advantages to using shade cloth inside greenhouses, including longer fabric life, ability to adjust intensity by opening or double layering cloth, decreased heating requirement in winter, and more efficient summer cooling. When selecting shade cloth, the right choice of shade level must be made the first time since it is difficult and expensive to change. Several factors to consider in choosing shade fabrics are the following:

1. Some shade cloth is listed in percent of "actual shade," while others are listed as "calculated shade." Measurements made beneath shade cloths of the same percentage, but different designations, when the sun is directly overhead indicate that less shade is obtained from "calculated shade." Differences between actual and calculated shade increase as shade level increases, being off 2 to 3 percent at 50 percent, but 5 to 8 percent at 73 percent, depending on the manufacturer.

2. Cost of shade cloth sold as "actual" or "calculated" is approximately equal when considered in relation to percent of light reduction.

3. Calculations for selection of proper-percent shade cloth should be made in relation to shade provided by the greenhouse itself.

4. Light intensity in summer is greater than in winter; thus use of a two-layer system is beneficial so that one layer can be moved back during low light periods.

To calculate the percent shade cloth needed, base the percentage of reduction of light on the light remaining beneath the bottom layer as shown in Figure 2-9 [12].

Automatic and manual shade cloth moving devices are commonly used in Europe, but are just becoming available in the United States. Shade cloth can be attached to systems originally designed to cover and

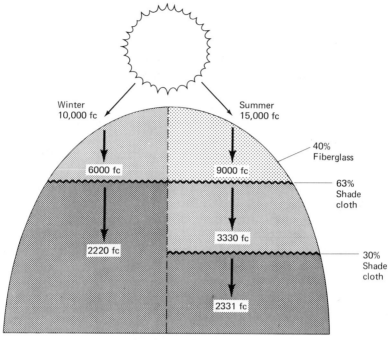

fc = foot candles

Figure 2-9.   When using shade cloth inside a greenhouse, be sure to calculate the percent reduction based on the level of light striking the cloth surface.

uncover chrysanthemums with black cloth, but most shading materials available are bulky. Savings in heat and increased growth rate can be obtained by using interior, movable shading systems.

Irrigation

Irrigation design should provide for overhead sprinklers as well as individual bench or pot watering systems. The basic plumbing should be located adjacent to post rows so that aboveground piping will not interfere with benches, mechanical equipment, or shade cloth. Overhead sprinklers in shade houses that are also used for frost protection should have an output equivalent to ¼ inch per hour or more to protect plants when temperatures drop to 25°F (−8°C) or lower [18]. Design of irrigation systems should be according to standard design procedures [1, 18, 21]. See Chapter 8.

Internal Greenhouse Design

Maximum utilization of internal space is essential in greenhouses and other structures owing to the high cost of energy (heating and cooling) and initial construction cost. Many U.S. greenhouses have been designed internally to utilize only 60 to 70 percent of the floor area, while European greenhouse operators often use 100 percent or more. Internal design depends on intended use (stock plants, pots, pot size) as well as labor and mechanization planned.

Space utilization will depend on many factors, including type of foliage crop to be grown, that is, stock plants, pots or baskets, pot size, and intended plant size. Structures designed for stock production can have narrow aisles, since there is little need to move large volumes of plant material, people, or equipment in and out.

Structures organized for potted plant production must allow carts, potting machines, plants, and people to move about freely. Benches should be no longer than about 50 feet, so people do not spend too much time walking to get to the other side. Generally, a wide central aisle is used with narrow side aisles. Greenhouses set up for potted plants are best designed with pyramid racks or regular benches with the aisle space above utilized.

Several possible designs for various purposes are shown in Table 2-4 to give an idea of potential usable space and yield. However, changes

TABLE 2-4   Influence of bench design and aisle width on yield in dollars[a]

Bench or space design[b]	Aisle width (inches)		
	18	24	30
Longitudinal benches with three center and two side benches per house. Each house with four 94 foot aisles of varying width with 3 foot end space at each end.	50,760	46,530	42,300
Longitudinal benches with three center and two side benches per house. Each house split crosswise with a 4 foot aisle, without end space at bench ends and varying width longitudinal aisles.	52,110	47,880	43,650
Perimeter benches with a 4-foot central aisle and cross aisles of varying width.	52,785	48,780	44,775

[a] Based on three 30- by 100-foot greenhouses and gross sales of $7.50 per square foot of bench space per year.

[b] Addition of 1000 square feet of hanging baskets to any of these designs would increase gross by $7500 per year.

made to increase effective square footage of bench space should not increase labor inputs or decrease plant quality.

Benches

Bench height should be such that workers of average height (approximately 5 feet 10 inches) can lean against the bench when they reach for plants near the center, which is usually 30 to 36 inches to the top of the side. Lower heights prevent people from leaning against the bench, and higher ones prevent short people from bending at the waist. Shorter bench heights are necessary when tall plants (3 to 6 feet) must be grown off the ground. Bottoms of benches must be 18 inches minimum above surfaces of treated soil to receive a sanitation certificate for shipment of plants grown on that bench into California and Texas. Top benches in a double-bench system should be 4 to 5 feet above the soil line to allow light entry.

Bench width for stock plant production can be 4 to 5 feet, while for potted plants up to 6 feet is often satisfactory. Cuttings from stock plants grown on benches wider than 5 feet are difficult to harvest near the bench centers. Side benches should be no wider than 2½ feet for stock production and 3 feet for potted plants. Use of wider benches and less aisle areas increases bench space within the growing unit but may reduce labor efficiency if not automated.

Bench orientation should be north to south according to most texts on commercial flower production so that sunlight strikes both sides of the benches evenly [23, 33]. This has been shown to be beneficial to tall, cut flower crops, but data do not indicate this is necessary for foliage plant production. Many foliage plants grown in benches are relatively short, and north to south or east to west orientation seems acceptable unless double or pyramid benches are used, in which cases orientation should be north to south. A major factor that determines bench orientation is location and placement of heating pipes. North to south orientation also allows headhouse structures to be attached to the north end for convenient movement of materials without shading effects.

Conventional flat benches are usually made of metal or wood frames set on concrete block or pipe supports (Figure 2-10). Metal frame benches are a better investment for stock production because wood framing usually rots rapidly. Treated wood framing is often satisfactory where wire bottom benches for pot production are to be used. Suggested bench materials are transite (corrugated asbestos) or flat asbestos where capillary mats are to be utilized, galvanized welded wire, rolled snow fence, and even styrofoam and other lightweight inert materials when properly supported. Transite is best where weight and long life are

Figure 2-10.   Conventional bench with transite (asbestos) bottom and sides.

Figure 2-11.   Double benching system with double benches alternated with a low single bench which allows light to penetrate to the lower section of the double bench.

factors, such as in stock beds, but welded wire on a metal frame covered with shade cloth to support the growing medium is also excellent and provides better aeration and heat transfer from under-bench heating pipes. Benches for potted plants can be made from most of these materials, including pressure-treated wood, but the most satisfactory seem to be metal or wood frame benches covered with 1- by 2-inch galvanized welded wire.

Double benches increase space utilization by using high benches (usually 3½ to 5 feet) planted on top and on ground level alternating with a low bench (usually 12 to 18 inches) (Figure 2-11). This system allows light to penetrate beneath high benches and permits the growth of low-light-requiring crops underneath. High benches should have a solid bottom to reduce drip on crops below and disease problems. This system can increase usable space by 25 to 40 percent.

Pyramid benches (A-frames) usually are used for plants that cascade or to increase usable space. Figure 2-12 shows a shelf type for pots, but rack types for hanging baskets are also popular. These are more expensive to build, but they increase space utilization up to 25 percent.

Movable benches have been developed, and their use in Europe is common. Figure 2-13 shows a type observed in use in the United States.

Figure 2-12. Pyramid benches are useful in increasing usable space as shown here with African violets.

Figure 2-13.   Movable benches are designed to increase percent usable space by eliminating most aisles.

Movable benches aid in increasing space utilization, and some can be mechanized so that they are filled and packed from the headhouse area.

Mechanical Equipment

Use of mechanical equipment should be considered in the internal design so that equipment such as automatic shade cloth or heating materials can be installed without obstacles such as bench, racks, vent equipment, and thermostats being in the way. Greenhouses should be designed to allow for automatic watering, fertilizing, spraying, and moving of people and plant materials. Any design that reduces the number of interior obstructions will be beneficial to mechanization.

Economics of Greenhouse Structures

Nursery owners should make thorough economic analysis during the planning process before deciding on the type of greenhouse to build. Factors to consider include initial land cost, capital expenditure per square foot for different designs and materials, life expectancy, internal improvements, operating and maintenance cost, insurance, interest, taxes, depreciation, and cash flow [42].

Initial land costs vary greatly within areas depending upon the real estate value and land use potential. For example, waterfront and land in heavily populated areas may cost several times more than inland or in rural areas. Open structures must be located on warm lands, but covered structures usually require heating and could be placed in colder and frequently less expensive locations.

Initial capital expenditure per square foot may vary as much as 100 percent or more depending upon the type of superstructure selected. Annual fixed costs for depreciation, repairs, maintenance, interest, taxes, and insurance vary among structures, with lower initial investment structures generally resulting in higher annual fixed costs than more substantial construction. Cost streams for initial investment and annual fixed costs are useful in evaluating different types of structures. Reported initial cost, annual upkeep, and life expectancy of several types of structures are compared in Table 2-5 using an investment analysis technique called discounted cash flow or net present value analysis. Investment and annual cost streams are discounted to give a single present-day value in dollars over the life of the investment. Polyethylene houses or steel frame and fiberglass covered houses would make best use of investment funds where a 10 percent minimum return on an investment is required. Availability of investment funds is usually a major problem, and initial construction cost must be given full consideration; therefore, wood, galvanized or steel-aluminum frames covered initially with UV-resistant polyethylene rank high for consideration. Polyethylene can later be converted to another longer-lasting cover with proper structural design. Maintenance costs for various structural designs in 1976 are listed in Table 2-5. The Quonset or vault structural design was not included in this study, and the advantages and disadvantages of this design should be evaluated also.

The internal improvement cost of benches, heating, cooling, walkways, and irrigation systems have been omitted in structural costs reported in Table 2-5, but must be considered in a total economic analysis. There are several individual internal improvements with wide structural cost variations, but costs of a specific type will not depend on the type of shell over it. Types of individual improvements within houses have different maintenance requirement costs, and these should be added in a total economic analysis.

Annual maintenance and cash flow are affected by factors such as relatively low initial investment for certain structures that have relatively large annual labor and maintenance cost versus greater initial costs and less annual maintenance cost. Before a greenhouse is built, a total economic analysis, including capital fixture cost, production, maintenance, depreciation, interest, and income expected by month, is highly recommended. The grower must have or be able to acquire adequate capital to

TABLE 2-5 Estimated cost per square foot, upkeep requirements, and life expectancy for several types of greenhouses in 1976[a] [17]

Type of construction	Cost/sq ft	Annual upkeep cost[b]	Life expectancy (years)	Remarks
Dutch-style glass	$2.13	$100	30	Glass may need resealing every 10 years
Steel post, extruded aluminum roof bars Long-life Tedlar	$1.41	$300	30 for structure 10 for fiberglass	Cost to replace fiberglass is $0.44/ft^2
Covered with regular fiberglass	$1.30	$300	30 for structure 5 for fiberglass	Cost to replace fiberglass is $0.31/ft^2
Covered with double-wall inflatable polyethylene	$0.99	$100	30 for structure	Plastic must be replaced every 2 yr at $0.12/ft^2
Treated wood structure, fiberglass Tedlar	$1.07	$300	20 for structure 10 for fiberglass	Will need razing every 6–8 yr
Treated wood structure with double poly cover	$0.80	$100	20 for structure	Poly replaced every 2 yr at $0.12/ft^2

[a] Based on the construction of one acre at 1976 prices.
[b] Based on structural costs—does not include costs associated with coverings (see Remarks).

make initial investments in land, structures, and facilities and cover cash operating expenses until the first plants are marketed.

Insurance coverage for liability, building contents and structural damage from fire, lightning, smoke, windstorm, hail, civil disorders, vehicle and aircraft damage, and explosives is available. Rates vary according to site location, area of the country, type of structure, and underwriter. Generally, complete coverage may be obtained on glasshouses, separate coverage on structures and covering for fiberglass houses, and structural only or no coverage on plastic houses. Growers should consult their insurance agent before initiating construction.

Depreciation rates vary with different types of structures and life expectancies. General depreciation rates allowed for tax purposes are given in Table 2-5.

The *straight line depreciation-method* probably more accurately allocates the investment cost of facilities over their useful life than *accelerated-methods*. Accelerated methods may provide tax advantages if net income is expected to decrease in the future and may be desirable because operators can retain current dollars in the business when cash flows are tight, although tax liability might increase later.

Taxes on land, structures, and improvements can be estimated by contacting local authorities [41].

Interest on construction and other loans is a cost of doing business. Greenhouse operations bought with equity capital should charge interest (opportunity cost) on this capital to reflect what could have been earned on this money had it been invested elsewhere.

REFERENCES

[1] Anonymous. 1976. *Florida irrigation society directory and handbook.* West Palm Beach, Fla., 64 pp.

[2] Augsburger, N. D., H. R. Bohanon, and J. L. Calhoun. 1973. *The greenhouse climate control handbook.* Acme Eng. Mfg. Corp. Form C7E-773. Muskogee, Okla.

[3] Baird, C. D., and D. R. Mears. 1976. Performance of a greenhouse solar heating system. In *Greenhouse solar heating, a progress report,* USDA publication.

[4] ———, W. E. Waters, and D. R. Mears. 1977. Greenhouse solar heating system utilizing underbench rock storage. Paper No. 77-4012, 1977 Annual Meeting of Am. Soc. Agr. Eng.

[5] Beattie, James H. 1952. Greenhouse construction and heating. *Farmers' Bull. 1318,* USDA publication, 38 pp.

[6] Buffington, D. E., and T. C. Skinner. 1974. Winter ventilation and heating requirements of greenhouses for condensation control in Florida. *Fla. State Hort. Soc. Proc.* 87:357–361.

[7] ———, and T. C. Skinner. 1977. Greenhouse ventilation. Agri. Eng. Fact Sheet AE-10, Fla. Coop. Ext. Serv.

[8] ———, and T. C. Skinner. 1977. Fans for greenhouses. Agri. Eng. Fact Sheet AE-12. Fla. Coop. Ext. Serv.

[9] ———, T. C. Skinner, and B. A. Barmby. 1977. Winter ventilation and heating requirements of fiberglass greenhouses for condensation control. Agr. Eng. Fact Sheet AE-13. Fla. Coop. Ext. Serv.

[10] Byrne, T. G., and R. P. Doss. 1976. Processed paper pads for greenhouse cooling. *Flower Nursery Rept.* Univ. of Calif. Jan–Feb., pp. 5–6.

[11] Carpenter, W. J., R. A. Mecklenburg, and W. H. Carlson. 1975. Greenhouse heating efficiency. *Flower Notes,* Mich. State Univ., vol. 17(4).

[12] Conover, C. A., and R. T. Poole. 1976. Calculations on shade and fertilization for foliage growers. Univ. of Fla. Agr. Res. Center-Apopka, Res. Rept. RH76-1. 4 pp.

[13] ———, and R. T. Poole. 1977. Influence of greenhouse design and cooling systems on temperature and energy requirements. Univ. of Fla. Agric. Res. Center-Apopka Res. Rept. RH 77-3. 8 pp.

[14] Duncan, G. A., and J. N. Walker. 1973. Preservative treatment of greenhouse wood. Univ. of Kentucky Dept. Agr. Eng. AEN-6 (4M-10-71; Rev. 5M-3-73). 5 pp.

[15] ———, and J. N. Walker. 1973. Greenhouse coverings. Univ. of Kentucky Dept. Agr. Eng. AEN-10 (8-73, 5M; 5M-8-75). 10 pp.

[16] ———, and J. N. Walker. 1973. Poly-tube heating-ventilation systems and equipment. Univ. of Kentucky Dept. Agr. Eng. AEN-7 (9-73, 5M). 9 pp.

[17] Halsey, L. A. 1975. Time is money—for greenhouse operators. *Fla. Flower Grower* 12 (1):7

[18] Harrison, D. S. 1965. Irrigation design for leatherleaf and plumosus fern in Florida. *Fla. Foliage Grower* 2(4):4–6.

[19] Hay, J., J. J. Hanan, and K. L. Goldsberry. 1976. Preliminary studies on cooling pad efficiency. *Colorado Flower Growers Assoc. Bull.* no. 314.

[20] Hodgman, C. D., R. C. Weast, and S. M. Selby, eds. 1958. *Handbook of chemistry and physics.* Cleveland, Ohio: Chemical Rubber Publ. Co.

[21] Karmeti, D., and J. Keller. 1975. Trickle irrigation design. Glendora, Calif.: Rainbird Sprinkler Mfg. Corp., 133 pp.

[22] Larsen, J. E. 1974. Evaluation of horizontal pad systems for evaporative cooling of glasshouse structures. *HortScience* 9:38.

[23] Laurie, A., D. C. Kiplinger, and K. S. Nelson. 1968. *Commercial flower forcing.* New York: McGraw-Hill, 514 pp.

[24] Lucas, R. F., and C. D. Baird. 1976. Application of solar heated water to greenhouses. AREC-Bradenton Res. Rept. GC1976-3.

[25] McConnell, D. B., and W. E. Waters. 1971. Central Florida well water analysis. *Fla. Foliage Grower* 8(2):1–5.

[26] Mastalerz, J. W. 1977. *The greenhouse environment: the effect of environmental factors on the growth and development of flower crops.* New York: Wiley.

[27] Mears, D. R., C. D. Baird, W. J. Roberts, J. C. Simpkins, and Paul Kendall. 1976. Greenhouse solar heating—a progress report. Biol. and Agri. Eng. Dept., Cook College, Rutgers Univ., Agr. Eng. Dept., IFAS, Univ. of Fla.

[28] ———, W. J. Roberts, and J. C. Simpkins. 1974. New concepts in greenhouse heating. Am. Soc. Agri. Eng. Paper No. NA74-112. 16 pp.

[29] Ministry of Agriculture, Fisheries, and Food. 1972. Glasshouse construction. Glazing, roof water collection and disposal. Short term leaflet 149. Great Britain Ministry of Agriculture, Fisheries, and Food. 10 pp.

[30] Monsanto Commercial Products Co. 1974. Monstanto '604' greenhouse film—Monsanto Report 12-817-0674-10. N. 8th St. and Monroe Ave., Kenilworth, N.J. 07033.

[31] Moore, E. L., and T. N. Jones. 1963. *Heating plastic greenhouses.* Mississippi State Univ. Agr. Expt. Sta. Bull. 666.

[32] Muller, Richard T. 1927. *American greenhouse construction, heating and equipment.* New York: A. T. De La Mare Co.

[33] Post, K. 1952. *Florist crop production and marketing.* New York: Orange Judd Publishing Co., 891 pp.

[34] Preston, F. G. (ed.). 1956. *The greenhouse.* London and Melbourne: Ward, Lock & Co.

[35] Roberts, W. J. 1970. Automatic black cloth shading for greenhouses. Rutgers University Coop. Ext. Serv., New Brunswick, N.J., Misc. Publ. 14 pp.

[36] Seeley, J. G. 1976. Some paints can cause plant injury. New York State Flower Industries, Inc., Bull. 72.

[37] Sheldrake, Ray, Jr. 1971. Air makes the difference. *Am. Veg. Grower,* Jan. 1971.

[38] Skinner, T. C. 1977. Some greenhouse considerations. Univ. of Fla. Coop. Ext. Serv. Circ. 429. 29 pp.

[39] ———, and D. E. Buffington. 1977. *Heating greenhouses.* Univ. of Fla. Coop. Ext. Serv. Agric. Eng. Fact Sheet AE-11.

[40] ———, and D. E. Buffington. 1977. Evaporative cooling of greenhouses in Florida. Univ. of Fla. Coop. Ext. Serv. Agri. Eng. Fact Sheet AE-14.

[41] U.S. Dept. of the Treasury, Internal Revenue Service. 1975. Farmer's tax guide, 1976 ed., Publ. 225, Oct. 1975.

[42] Van Horne, James C. 1974. *Financial management and policy,* 3rd ed. Englewood Cliffs, N.J.: Prentice-Hall.

[43] Vistron Corporation. 1975. Filon greenhouse panels. Filon Div., Vistron Corp., 12333 S. Van Ness Ave., Hawthorne, Calif. 90250 (7-75/10M #140).

[44] Walker, J. N., and G. A. Duncan. 1973. Rigid-frame greenhouse construction. Univ. of Kentucky Dept. of Agri. Eng. AEN-15 (6-73, 4M). 7 pp.

[45] _____, and G. A. Duncan. 1975. Estimating greenhouse heating requirements and fuel costs. Univ. of Kentucky Dept. Agri. Eng. AEN-8 (5M; Rev. 3-75, 5M). 5 pp.

[46] Waters, W. E., and C. A. Conover. 1969. Chrysanthemum production in Florida. Agri. Expt. Sta. Bull. 730. 64 pp.

[47] Watson, W. W., and J. A. Riley. 1960. Heater-hood improves circulation in plastic greenhouse studies in Mississippi Delta. Miss. State Univ. Agri. Expt. Sta. Bull. 607. 8 pp.

[48] Wright, W. J. 1947. *Greenhouses* (revised). New York: Orange Judd Publishing Co.

[49] Young, H. W., and C. E. Dean. 1961. Plastic greenhouse construction. NFES Mimeo Report 61-4. 6 pp.

three

Charles A. Conover
Glenn G. Blalock

mechanization

Labor constitutes the major expense in foliage plant production, and mechanization offers a method of limiting these costs. Other factors that favor mechanization include increased ability to meet production on time and improvement in plant quality. Practically, mechanization includes nursery design, organization of production, scheduling and materials flow, and the organization of labor and equipment to meet production plans. How these factors are combined into a well-organized and profitable foliage plant production unit is discussed in this chapter. Mechanization, however, is no cure for poor management.

Establishing a Need for Mechanization

Consideration should be given the need for mechanization [1] before new equipment is purchased, facilities built, or methods of handling jobs implemented. Such considerations include changes in labor productivity that may result; effects on energy usage (electricity, fuel) and on meeting peak demands for potting, watering, and packaging; influences on unit costs for growing products; and effects on possible cost increases in labor and/or supplies.

Labor Costs

Labor productivity or efficiency can have a tremendous effect on profitability. It has been shown [8, 9] that labor efficiency in terms of value of foliage plants sold per employee varied as much as 300 percent between the average of three high-profit and three low-profit foliage nurseries. Thus, the way labor is used and the efficiency of its use may well decide whether a mechanized foliage production unit is or will be profitable.

The objective of mechanization is to improve labor efficiency, not decrease it; therefore, time and motion studies must be a part in the determination of labor productivity. Just because a machine can accomplish a task in a shorter time interval than an individual does not economically justify its purchase [12]. Mechanization does not always contribute to whether the machine controls the worker or the worker controls the machine. In most instances, job satisfaction is highest when mechanization removes the drudgery of a job, but not the need and ability to make decisions about rate and/or quality of the finished product [14, 16].

Probably, the easiest method of establishing the need for mechanization is to examine individual existing segments of systems approach to production. The systems approach logically assumes that several jobs are grouped together in a specific sequence to reach the desired goal. An example of such sequence for potting plants could be soil mixing, transporting soil, pots, and plants to potting area, and potting and transporting plants to a greenhouse. Examination of each of these segments separately and combined in terms of the time required to accomplish each step mechanically and otherwise indicates whether savings are possible.

Someone conducting such analyses might consider the following segments in examining a soil-mixing operation. The time required to move pasteurized mix components by hand for 10 cubic yards of mix to a small shredder and shred is 6 hours. Switching to a front end loader that dumps directly into a batch loader might decrease this to 2 hours. However, labor savings would have to be compared with equipment costs and possibly the cost of more highly trained labor. Movement of prepared mix to the potting area by cart might entail hand loading or unloading, requiring 1 hour. This might be improved by utilizing carts that open to provide a potting area or a conveyer system to move mix. Before adding any equipment, a study should be made to assure that speeding up one operation will not result in a bottleneck somewhere else to negate the effect of mechanization [2].

Energy

Energy considerations are important presently and will become more so in the future as fossil fuels become scarcer and continue to escalate in price. Therefore, the energy costs of electrical equipment and gasoline engines used to mechanize should be considered against savings in labor or supplies, and the possibility of power outages should be considered [4]. One example of energy savings would be to pasteurize potting components in bulk prior to mixing (such as in an enclosed bin with pipe in the floor), rather than in a rotating cement mixer where the same amount of steam may be required, but the energy to rotate the drum for an hour or more is substantial. Additionally, in a large operation, a single mixer unit could produce more than double the output if steaming was accomplished outside the mixer, thus substantially reducing mix unit costs.

Energy costs should be calculated by estimating the number of hours specific equipment will be operating on a daily basis in terms of dollars per hour. This is accomplished by computing the kilowatt-hour rating on electrical equipment, fuel per hour on engines, and fuel per Btu on boilers.

Peak Needs

Satisfying peak needs is often an important goal in considering mechanization, but this may be unwise if peak needs occur infrequently, because the capital costs of designing and operating such equipment may be excessively high during other periods. With soil mixing equipment, it may be wiser to satisfy infrequent peak demands for potting media by providing a storage area for prepared mix and operating the mixing equipment for two shifts a day, rather than installing a second mixing unit. The problem may also be extended to the potting area, where an automated pot-filling machine might need double the normal weekly capacity of soil for a few weeks during the year. Several ways to alleviate problems of overdesigning would include operating in multiple shifts or filling pots early, and placing them in the growing unit and potting there. In any case, the final decision should be made only after labor costs associated with extra hours, capital, and operating costs of larger-sized equipment are compared.

Unit Costs

Unit costs of producing a particular foliage plant determine the selling price that will provide a satisfactory profit. Excessively high unit costs compared to the selling price of a particular foliage plant require one of several solutions: (1) delete the plant from the product line, (2) raise the wholesale price, (3) change the form of the plant (pot size, totem pole, hanging basket), (4) revise production and cultural systems to utilize less space, grow the same plant in less time, or otherwise improve quality to command a higher price, and (5) reduce costs of production through mechanization.

To consider the effects of mechanization on production systems, and thus unit costs, each segment of the system where mechanization will increase costs (capital investment) or decrease them (lower labor costs, growing more plants per unit area) must be analyzed.

Future Costs

Future cost escalations can be estimated to aid in justifying mechanization. For example, costs of labor probably will rise more

TABLE 3-1 Comparison of costs of mechanized potting with hand labor at selected points over 10 years (15,000 pots/day)

	Mechanized[a]	Nonmechanized
Year 1		
Equipment annual payment	$10,000	—
Equipment annual upkeep	2,500	—
Equipment energy requirement	200	—
Labor requirement[b]	49,000	$70,000
Interest	10,000	—
	$71,700	$70,000
Year 5		
Equipment annual payment	$10,000	—
Equipment annual upkeep	3,000	—
Equipment energy requirement	300	—
Labor requirement[b]	70,000	100,000
Interest	5,000	—
	$88,300	$100,000
Year 10		
Equipment annual payment	$10,000	—
Equipment annual upkeep	3,500	—
Equipment energy requirement	450	—
Labor requirement[b]	105,000	150,000
Interest	500	—
	$119,450	$150,000

[a] Mechanization equipment cost was $100,000 with an estimated life of 10 years and an interest rate of 10 percent.

[b] Seven people are required to operate the mechanized potting line and ten operate the nonmechanized line.

rapidly than other costs, except energy. Energy, however, is often a small part of mechanization, so other factors may become more important. An example of possible future cost escalations is shown in Table 3-1, where the mechanized column shows costs at 1, 5, and 10 years for operating a mechanized potting line, and column 2 shows the nonmechanized labor costs. These kinds of data can be generated for any mechanization proposal to examine short- and long-run effects.

Facility Design

The efficiency of any mechanization program will be determined by the design of the physical plant [7, 11]. Old production units with narrow aisles, steps between production units, and/or a supporting structure of posts limit the degree of mechanization possible without extensive renovation. The overall efficiency will be much greater if a new facility can be designed and built to accommodate mechanization. However, many improvements can be made in existing structures if careful thought is given to each segment of the production cycle [10].

Problems facing designers will vary depending on site selection, with level or slightly sloped sites having good drainage the best to work with and steeply sloped or poorly drained sites most difficult. Slope of the site also has a great effect on design, with square or nearly square sites easiest to design.

Design Considerations

Basic design considerations should consider future as well as immediate needs, such as size of soil mixing and potting facilities and storage. Many nurseries have been constructed with additional units being placed wherever space was available, rather than where it would best fit with the systems approach. This reduces efficiency to the point that profitability suffers. Figure 3-1 shows a basic systems approach pathway in a linear or straight line design for a medium-sized nursery. Major units are located so that additional capacity can be added without seriously disrupting daily operations or requiring changes in materials flow. Figure 3-2 shows the same nursery doubled in size, but with no major change in materials flow. Major components should be located where they are convenient and can be observed in Figures 3-1 and 3-2, with their functional use.

Major components of systems should be efficient in energy and labor use and require no more space than necessary. Prior to attempting location of equipment, components needed in a specific nursery should

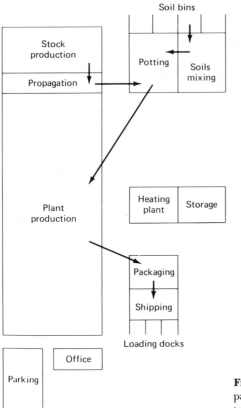

Soil bins

Stock production

Propagation

Potting

Soils mixing

Plant production

Heating plant

Storage

Packaging

Shipping

Loading docks

Office

Parking

Figure 3-1.   Foliage nursery with expansion potential designed for the systems approach to production.

be outlined. A nursery purchasing rooted cuttings, for example, need not plan for stock production, cutting preparation, or propagation areas, whereas a nursery growing its own stock must plan for these. The same situation would exist in a nursery that purchased premixed potting media, since mixing equipment would not be needed, but storage area would be necessary.

Location of Components

Locating basic equipment or components so they relate to each other and with materials flow is the first design step [2, 3]. Therefore, consideration should be given to every step necessary in moving a foliage plant from the stock area to shipping. Two types of basic equipment for this include (1) structures for housing supplies, equipment, and office and (2) plant growing structures. Movement of plants and supplies between structures should be limited to short distances where possible to

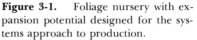

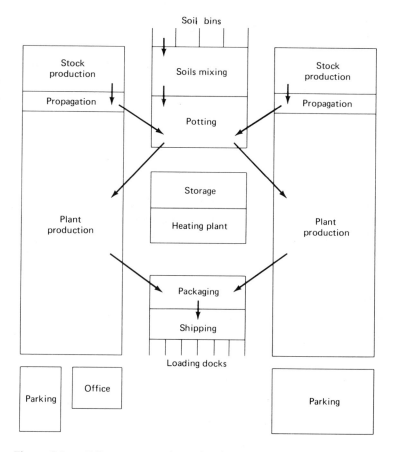

Figure 3-2. Foliage nursery shown in Figure 3-1 expanded to double its size, retaining the systems approach to production.

decrease movement time. Various components of the system should not be so close that people moving items such as plants, soil, and pots are in the way of each other. It takes approximately 1 minute to travel 100 feet at 1 mile per hour; thus at 5 miles per hour about 12 seconds will be expended. When determining time usage, be sure that time allowed to move plants is sufficient, since moving them at excessive speeds, especially over uneven surfaces, may cause physical damage or cause newly potted plants to shift in the pot. The following methods of estimating best speed and travel time may be useful when developing time estimates to aid in locating components:

1. A speed estimate can be obtained by walking beside a vehicle moving materials and counting the number of normal paces (approxi-

mately 3 feet per pace) taken in 20 seconds and dividing by 10 to give speed in miles per hour (mph).

$$\frac{\text{Normal paces in 20 seconds}}{10} = \text{mph}$$

2. Number of seconds required to cover a specific distance can be obtained as follows:

$$\frac{\text{Distance in feet} \times 0.68}{\text{mph}} = \text{seconds}$$

Several factors that should be considered in locating equipment include (1) the traffic caused by trucks delivering soil components, pots, and fuel, and picking up shipments from loading docks, (2) internal traffic of plants moving from potting to greenhouses and from greenhouses to packaging, and (3) internal services such as spraying. Driveways, turn-around areas, and service areas should be adequate for equipment that will operate within the complex. Typical areas in a foliage nursery that grows its own stock include stock production, cutting preparation, propagation, potting media and fertilizer storage and mixing, potting or transplanting, greenhouse production, maintenance support and vehicle storage, packaging and shipping, and offices. The size of each area is dependent on the production plan discussed previously.

Greenhouse Efficiency

Designing greenhouses for efficiency includes consideration of the structure and each component inside. Designs are usually handled by greenhouse manufacturing companies, but placement of doors, walks, benches, height of structure, and use of automated equipment is dependent on planned use and is largely up to the owner [21]. Chapter 2 contains information on greenhouse types and environmental equipment; the information provided in Table 3-2 relates to the influence of design factors on efficiency and mechanization.

Aisle width, floor area, bench height, and any other component used within greenhouses should be designed for maximum efficiency. Bench width, for example, should be designed for the size of pot, flat, or tray that will be used and the distance labor can comfortably reach to the center. The proper size for a greenhouse bench for growing 2¼-, 3-, or 4-inch pots, placed pot to pot, would be 36 inches or a multiple of 36 inches, because pots would completely fill that space without waste.

TABLE 3-2 Greenhouse design factors influencing mechanization efficiency

Design consideration	Advantages	Possible disadvantages
Greenhouse eave height of 9 to 10 feet	More room for equipment and also possible room for hanging baskets	Higher heating cost and somewhat higher construction cost
Wide main aisles	Ease of supplies and plant movement on carts or trailers	Reduction in usable bench space
Benches not more than 100 feet in length with major aisles on each end	Reduces walking time, increasing labor productivity	Slight reduction in usable bench space
Movable bench systems	Greater use of ground space through elimination of some aisles; bench sections can be loaded in the potting area and unloaded in the packaging area, thus saving labor	Increased investment in benching and equipment to move them; more difficult to detect and control pests; irrigation must be overhead or connected to each bench section
Multiple layers or tiers of plants	Increases number of units produced per greenhouse	May increase labor requirement and reduce plant quality owing to lower light levels and increased disease problems
Moving irrigation and/or spray booms	Reduces labor needs and provides uniform distribution, especially where movable benches are used	Efficiency of both spray and irrigation coverage is reduced as crops mature and foliage deflects water and spray materials

However, common sense should be used since bench size is partially controlled by greenhouse size, and adjustments of a few inches may be necessary. Close and detailed measurements for bench width are often negated by the need to change crops or pot sizes.

Supporting Facilities

Design of supporting facilities for efficiency can be as important to overall mechanization as greenhouse design. Important considerations include paving, size and location of storage and shipping, and other support structures.

Paving used throughout the nursery should be contiguous between work areas to allow easy movement in all weather, should not have rapid changes in elevation or bumps to damage or upset plants on carts, and should provide for both foot and vehicular traffic. Access to buildings should be easy, with wide access doors and sufficient head room so that equipment can move in and out. Placement of components within supporting facilities should provide for easy traffic flow without bottlenecks. Locations should allow potting materials such as soil, pots, and plants to reach the potting area without conflicting with plants moving off the potting line [19].

New Facilities

Designing new facilities may be the most important factor in the development of a new production unit. Obviously, it is easier to change a set of plans than to move buildings, walls, doors, heating pipes, or a multitude of other permanent items. Information provided in this section applies to design of new facilities. An additional point worth considering is the convertibility of the designed facility to other types and/or sizes of other crops. Changes occur in consumer demand over time; therefore, some consideration must be given during the design process to the possibility that different crops may have to be produced at a later date. One example is the use of fiberglass having 50 to 80 percent light exclusion. This percent of shade exclusion will increase in time, possibly becoming too great even for foliage plants; but it prevents its future use in the production of flowering pot plants, bedding plants, and other crops unless the fiberglass covering is changed.

Modifying Existing Facilities

Design and modification of existing facilities to adapt them to improved materials flow and plant handling systems and to mechanization of specific items such as soil mixing or potting requires as much planning as construction of new facilities. When building costs are high, it is often more economical to renovate existing facilities than to build new ones.

Improving materials flow is best accomplished by removing obstacles such as small doorways, replacing steps with ramps, paving unpaved areas, and providing additional storage space in key areas to aid in eliminating bottlenecks in the materials flow system.

Improving plant handling includes movement of cuttings to preparation areas and propagation benches or pots, getting rooted cuttings to potting and production areas, and, finally, packaging and shipping stations. Problems in existing facilities usually can be found in the way cuttings and/or plants are moved. Often the distance from bench to cart is too far or the number of plants moved each time is too few. Narrow aisles or the inability to move carts into a greenhouse also contributes to inefficiencies. When heating or structural posts are in the way, rebenching or designing an overhead trolley system may be desirable. Whatever system is selected, the cost of renovation must be balanced with proposed savings.

Improving shipping efficiency is often one of the easier improvements in mechanization, because most interior spaces can be modified to include efficient box storage and makeup, plant staging, boxing assembly, automated sealing, and rapid transit to shipping makeup areas.

Establishing a Production Plan

A production plan must be developed before mechanization of any production operation can occur. Such a plan should include determination of market needs and potential for a number of different products. Resources then must be analyzed that will support any decision to grow particular plant types. Market demand can be projected once product lines are developed by combining this with space and resources available to develop a production schedule.

Market Evaluation for Product Mix

Determining the product mix is the first step in being able to set up a production plan. This decision will depend on the quantity of what product in what sizes is necessary to reach a set goal.

Market evaluation is conducted daily by those involved in selling foliage plants. Thus, a primary source of useful information in determining product mix should come from in-house sales departments or, in the case of a new organization, from buying agents for retail, wholesale, and mass market outlets [18, 20]. Buying agents know from experience what markets want in terms of varieties, sizes, and forms and when they are desired in the greatest amount. Such information basically reflects consumer preference, which constantly changes, but not so rapidly that it cannot be followed.

Markets for particular varieties of foliage plants often reflect what interior designers are using and recommending in articles published in national magazines and by garden writers of newspapers. Sizes of plants desired often follow trends also, such as the terrarium fad of the early 1970s and the large plant boom of the late 1970s. Mostly, however, shifts are reflected in purchasing habits of buying agents.

Many factors influence peak market demands for foliage plants. The general trend for many years has been high demand for foliage plants from January through early June, with lowest demand from July to December. Even during periods of potentially high sales, other factors that influence the market include severe snowstorms or cold in major population centers, spring flooding, and changes in economic outlooks from such causes as talk about recession and strikes in major industries such as automobiles.

A producer must decide whether to specialize in particular product lines or provide full service to buying agents by growing or handling a wide product line. Small- and medium-sized producers often find that specialization in a few products and sizes maximizes profits, while large producers usually find they need many products to compete with other large growers. Regardless of the potential size of an operation, specializing in a few lines in the beginning is usually better so that a reputation for quality can be developed.

Resources

Available resources must be considered in selecting product lines from suggestions received from the sales department, outside marketing surveys, or buying agents. Several resources should be considered:

1. Is expertise available to grow specific product lines or to grow most lines? If a specialist grower is available to grow calathea, for example, and it has high market demand, this supports a decision to grow this crop. If no one in the organization knows anything about producing calathea, its selection would be poor even if good market demand existed.

2. Labor availability should strongly influence decisions to grow specific crops, since some crops are labor intensive; for example, two employees may be able to grow an acre of aglaonemas in 8-inch pots on a continuing basis, while ten may be necessary to grow 4-inch philodendron. Availability of trained and reliable labor is necessary to grow any crop, but it is especially true for labor-intensive ones.

TABLE 3-3   Analysis of yield per square foot of some foliage plants

Plant size and type	Yield in pots/ ft²/crop	Crop growing time (wk)	Yield in pots/ ft²/yr	Avg. selling price ($)	Gross/ yield/ ft²/yr
Philodendron (4 in.)	5.5	12	23.8	0.75	$17.85
Pilea (4 in.)	5.5	6	47.6	0.45	21.46
Dieffenbachia (6 in.)	1.5	10	7.8	2.50	19.50
Aglaonema (8 in.)	0.5	16	1.6	5.50	8.80
Philodendron[a] (6 in.)	1.5	20	3.9	2.50	9.75
Fern (3 in.)	11.0	6	95.3	0.30	28.60
Hoya (3 in.)	18.0	12	78.0	0.30	23.40
Norfolk Island pine (6 in.)	1.0	52	1.0	2.50	2.50

[a]Totem pole.

3. Space availability also affects decisions to grow specific crops, because crops are variably space intensive. For example, 7.8 pots of 6-inch dieffenbachia may be grown per square foot per year, whereas 23.8 pots of 4-inch philodendron can be grown in the same space. Figures in Table 3-3 indicate the trade between space and labor that can occur for a labor-intensive crop such as 4-inch pilea, and a space-intensive crop, such as 6-inch Norfolk Island pine. Where space is available and labor is limited, it is wise to select a space-intensive crop that has a satisfactory return on investment.

4. Capital for investment, especially for mechanization, may strongly influence crop selection. Use of available investment capital makes possible mechanization that will reduce labor needs on a crop so that it is no longer labor intensive [1].

Plant selection should be reduced to the most common denominator of the kinds of foliage plants in demand that a particular organization can produce in the pot sizes that maximize returns when analyzed against turnover time and space and labor required.

Developing a Production Plan

It is not difficult to develop a production plan once the product mix and pot sizes have been selected, but often in small- and medium-sized organizations no plan exists except in the mind of the owner or grower. A production plan should be documented and charted in a way that reflects the actual growing space available, the product to be grown in this space, and the turnover rate of the space and product (Table 3-4). The

TABLE 3-4   Typical production program for 4-inch philodendron showing steady input and shipping quantities and schedules

Bed no.	Jan.	Feb.	Mar.	Apr.	May.	Jun.	Jul.	Aug.	Sep.	Oct.
	(4-in. Plant	PHILO	SHIP 500)	(Plant	SHIP	500)	(Plant	SHIP	500)	
2	(		500)	(		500)	(		500)	
3	(		500)	(		500)	(		500)	
4	(			500)	(		500)	(		500)
5		(		500)	(		500)	(		500)
6		(		500)	(		500)	(		
7		(		500)	(		500)	(		
8		(			500)	(	500)	(		
9			(		500)	(	500)	(		
10			(		500)	(	500)	(		
11			(			500)	(	500)	(	
12				(		500)	(		500)	(

purpose of a production plan is to effectively utilize resources at hand to meet production objectives. When a production chart is established, it takes the guesswork out of production and provides information on profitability. This can be accomplished by using a weighted average profit analysis (the margin of profit of the production unit times the percent of space used).

Projecting Demand

Projecting demand is the most difficult part of developing the production plan. Based on demand information from purchasing agents and knowledge of market fluctuation throughout the year, however, some number of units can be planned for specific weeks or months. This can be adjusted with time and as experience dictates, but initial planning is necessary.

Using Space Efficiently

Space utilization throughout the year is necessary to obtain the highest efficiency in any operation. Few sales plans suggest equal sales units per week or even each month; therefore, it is not practical to plan a steady production cycle. All growing space should be utilized at all times; therefore, the plan must provide for low sales need periods. A producer, for example, may grow 4-inch philodendron on a regular schedule but have no market for them in July. During that period, a 6-inch totem pole philodendron, which takes about 1 month longer to mature, could be produced, giving full use with a high-priced item of the space not then needed for 4-inch philodendron (Table 3-5).

Scheduling Production

Tables 3-4 and 3-5 show a schedule for philodendron that may be excellent or not depending on the labor and space ratio of a particular organization. Similar schedules should be developed for all crops grown

TABLE 3-5 Typical production program for philodendron showing an irregular input schedule to utilize space and "span" a nonshipping month (July)

Bed no.	Jan.	Feb.	Mar.	Apr.	May.	Jun.	Jul.	Aug.	Sep.	Oct.
1	(Plant 4-in.	PHILO	SHIP 500)	(4-in.	PHILO	SHIP 500)	(4-in.	PHILO	SHIP 500)	
2	(		500)	(6-in.	PHILO	T.P.		100)		
3	(		500)	(				100)		
4		(		500)	(			100)		
5		(		500)	(				100)	
6		(		500)	(4-in.		PHILO	500)		
7		(		500)	(			500)		
8			(		500)	(		500)		
9			(		500)	(		500)		
10			(		500)	(	.		500)	
11			(		500)	(			500)	
12				(		500)	(		500)	

and all space available. Several controls must be set up to assure that production goals are met. Production schedules should outline objectives and results for the week, inventory, and per unit costs of production.

Development of a production plan and scheduling of production is the only way to determine the influences that mechanization may have on an organization.

Implementing Production Programs

Organizing each segment of a production plan into a cohesive unit is the key to mechanization. This requires that each step in production be analyzed to determine the most efficient method of accomplishing any task and incorporating it into a production model. If the method does not fit without disrupting the model, it must be revised (still maintaining the highest efficiency level possible) until it does fit.

Stock Sources

The decision to buy or produce cuttings or seedlings must be made. Logically, the method selected should depend on economics, quality, and reliability of delivery, but often the decision is made on price only.

Production of cuttings often improves the chances of having rooted cuttings when needed and ones of higher quality, because they do not spend several days in transit. The cost of producing cuttings must be determined since it may be advantageous to use space for finished plants rather than stock. Should cost economics be close to equal, the convenience of having cuttings at hand often swings the balance toward in-house propagation.

Purchase of cuttings should be considered when their price is lower than producing them. Local purchase might be better than foreign purchase because of transportation holdups and potential quarantine problems. However, certain types of cuttings such as cane can only be obtained from foreign sources. In selecting a cutting source, consider price, quality, and availability for production schedules.

Propagation

Seeds or cuttings can be propagated in beds or directly in pots. Each method can be incorporated into a mechanized production system, but plant quality often is the deciding factor between systems. Cuttings or seedlings propagated in beds can be hand graded when pulled, and when potted and grown properly often produce 95 percent or more salable plants. Plants grown from direct stick cuttings or seeds often have rejection rates as high as 10 percent. A labor analysis of the two methods will show the cost difference.

Bench propagation makes it difficult to mechanize if cuttings are carried to the propagation area and individually stuck. This requires considerable labor, and little can be done to improve efficiency unless a different system is devised. One possibility would be to stick cuttings into trays on a conveyer line, move them to the greenhouse, and place them on a bench.

Pot propagation is easy to mechanize, since pots can be filled automatically with a pot filler and cuttings stuck into them on a moving belt. Pots can be placed on a movable bench section, hauled to a greenhouse, or transported in trays and placed on a bench. This system works best with easy-to-root cuttings that have low cost ratios.

Potting

Potting of plants is the area of mechanization that has received the most attention, because it is perhaps the most labor-intensive part of foliage plant production [3, 10, 12]. Potting is accomplished in a permanent potting area in most large nurseries, while potting in the growing area is common in small nurseries.

Centralized potting is located where movement of supplies (soil, pots, and plants) to the potting area and potted plants to the greenhouse growing areas is most convenient. Equipment for centralized potting is often attached to the floor and the area climate controlled for employee comfort (Figure 3-3). Advantages of centralized potting include the use of large equipment and the ability to design permanent materials flow capability. The primary disadvantages are capital investments in equipment, the need to code plants to keep track of quality produced by various potters, and distances required to move plants to production areas [3].

High costs associated with development of a mechanized central-point potting operation require careful consideration of equipment. In some instances, it may be better to lease mechanization equipment rather than purchase it [2, 15]. Some factors to consider are the following:

1. Projections on equipment size to use for the job to be done.
2. Selection of equipment adaptable to the range of pot sizes likely to be grown.
3. Purchase of tough, well-designed equipment with standard indus-

Figure 3-3. Centralized potting systems capable of serving thirty potters with soil, plants, and pots.

trial components, such as motors, gears, bearings, and belts, so that local repair is possible. The entire potting operation can be stopped by an inoperative machine.

4. Selection of equipment with variable speed ranges, so the potting rate can be changed as personal experience levels change.

Figure 3-4 shows a materials flow plan for centralized potting, with soil moving from mixing area to storage to potting machine. Finished plants are then loaded on carts for delivery to production areas.

Potting in production areas can be advantageous where small- or medium-sized production units are involved. Movable potting benches on wheels or stationary benches located at strategic spots within a greenhouse range limit the distance plants must be moved. Other advantages to this system include lower investment costs and increased interest in doing a good potting job because of closer involvement with the entire growing operation. The main drawback to potting in production areas is transportation of soils, pots, and plants to be potted to potting benches or machines and housekeeping chores associated with soil, pots, and plants around the potting area.

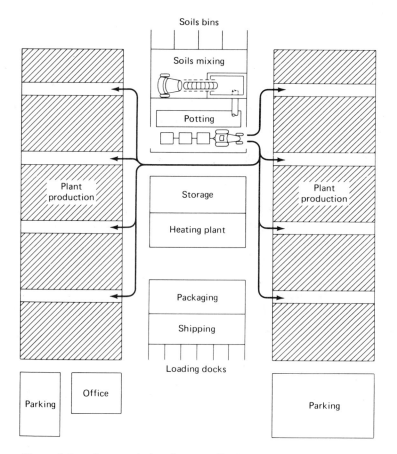

Figure 3-4. Systems design for centralized potting of foliage plants.

Several types of small pot-filling machines have been used in foliage nurseries for several years. These machines are mounted on wheels and can be moved between production units or placed in a centralized potting area. Figure 3-5 shows a materials flow plan for soils, plants, and pot delivery to potting areas within production units.

Transportation

Transportation within the nursery is of major importance to over-all materials flow. If the system of moving plants to the nursery is inefficient, much of the benefit of a well-designed or mechanized potting area will be lost.

Ground-operated transportation systems using electric carts or tractors hauling trailers are most commonly found inside production units.

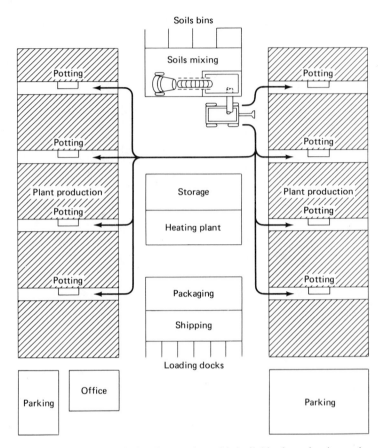

Figure 3-5. Systems design for potting with individual production units.

These systems require wide aisles, and trailers must be self-tracking so they will track behind pulling units (Figure 3-6). Use of electric carts or tractors is suggested because of pollutants generated inside production units by standard gas or diesel engines. Use of propane-fueled gas engines is the next best alternative to electric-powered units if such units cannot supply sufficient power. Pavement must be smooth for carts or plants may be injured from bouncing around.

Movable benches have become popular in recent years because they can be designed to eliminate aisle space. Such benches also are often used to move plants from potting to production areas and ultimately back to packaging and shipping. Such benches can be designed so that newly potted plants are placed on tracks at one end and finished plants removed at the other end on a weekly or monthly schedule.

Overhead transportation systems have been used by industry for years,

Figure 3-6. Ground operated transportation system using tractor and tracking carts carrying movable bench sections.

but only recently have they been incorporated into complete mechanized production units. These systems can be designed to operate over tops of benches to save space devoted to wide aisles, or they can be operated in wide aisles instead of using tractors and carts. Height is important when they are operated over top or plant damage can occur (Figure 3-7).

Fertilizing and Watering

Fertilization and watering systems can be mechanized to provide constant feeding as well as automatic watering as needed. These systems are discussed in more detail in Chapters 8 and 9 [13].

Plant Selection

Plant selection for shipping can be accomplished in the production area or in a portion of the central packaging area. The economics of each choice depends on whether plants and pots are to be cleaned and what is done with rejects.

Figure 3-7.   Overhead monorail system designed to carry movable bench sections which are rolled onto rails.

Selection of plants in the greenhouse production area is less efficient than if accomplished in the packaging area. Quality control is reduced because there is less supervision over labor and efficiency is less. This system is best adapted to small operations where only one or two people are required to select plants for shipping or when rush periods occur that cannot be handled in the shipping department. Several points to consider about selecting plants in greenhouses include the following:

1. There is a tendency for those doing the selection to place the best plants in one carton and the poor ones in another, resulting in considerable variation between cartons.
2. If plants are dirty, there are no provisions for cleaning.
3. Movement of trays and cartons into greenhouses and out to the shipping area is often inefficient.
4. Rejected plants can be left to grow, but often get in the way of the next crop. Therefore, rejects have to be moved to a different area or dumped. Time and motion studies in large operations have shown it to be more economical to dump rejects than to save them for finishing.

Selection of plants for the packaging operation is easily accomplished by moving all the finished product from the greenhouse to a work-center grading and staging area. The work-center concept encourages use of a specialized labor force concentrated in a specific work area under direct supervision. Such a work force can be briefed on acceptable quality of plants to be packaged, with rejects being dumped or returned to a special grow-out area. When this system is used, plants can be moved past those doing the grading and on to packers or can be graded or packed by the same personnel. Movement of plants from greenhouse production areas to a central selection area also allows provision for a cleaning operation, preferably prior to plants being graded. On an assembly-line basis, plants can be sprayed with water or other products that remove or mask residues on foliage. Some considerations concerning the use of a work-center grading and staging area include the following:

1. Increases in labor efficiency.
2. The potential for improving quality control before packaging.
3. Location of all activity involved with selection, packaging, and shipping in one centralized area, which improves overall supervision.

Packaging

Packaging includes all aspects of moving plants to the packaging area, making up shipping cartons, placing plants in cartons, and moving them to the staging area. The entire packaging operation is one that lends itself well to mechanization.

Moving plants from grading and selection to packaging can be accomplished on moving conveyer belts or carts. Mechanization of this part of the operation requires that packers be able to have products at their fingertips at all times, by automatic controls or by someone assigned to keep packers supplied with products.

Shipping carton makeup has historically required considerable floor space, because cartons had to be preassembled and stored, so they could be distributed to packers as required. Some improvement can occur through overhead storage on tracks, so boxes are automatically fed to packers as required. This saves considerable floor space and reduces labor requirements for carrying boxes to packers. Packers normally place cartons on a conveyer, where they move to someone who closes, seals, and labels the cartons.

More recently, mechanized equipment has been developed that allows cartons to be stored flat. The system unfolds the carton, and once

Figure 3-8. Mechanized packaging system designed to fold and seal cartons.

the product is inserted, it closes the top and bottom and seals it simultaneously. Use of automatic boxing equipment saves space and all the labor previously associated with preassembly and closing of shipping cartons. Once the box moves out of the packaging machine, it normally moves down a conveyer to someone who applies the label, and then to the shipping area (Figure 3-8). Movement of plants to the shipping area is usually on conveyers, but some operations utilize low carts or other wheeled equipment.

Shipping

Shipping of foliage plants is the culmination of the entire production and sales effort of an organization. Thus, it is important that plants reach their final destination on time, with the proper paperwork, and in good condition.

Order makeup requires necessary paper flow systems and controls established to follow the product flow from the selection process into packaging, shipping, and loading. Once labels are affixed to cartons, they must move to designated staging areas; thus, it is important to have supervisors present at all times who understand the exact size (number of cartons) and destination of each order.

Load makeup is most often accomplished at a shipping dock where the load can be preassembled on the dock. This allows cartons being received from packaging to be located within the load in the order that they will be delivered so that movement of one or more orders will not be necessary to get out a particular order at the delivery site. The entire order is loaded after it is assembled on the dock and checked and double-checked for completeness.

Loading is usually accomplished by hand, using roller conveyers to move cartons into trucks. This is labor intensive, but it allows fitting the load to the interior of the truck or trailer, and allows spacing so that heated or cooled air reaches all parts of the load. Shipment of large plants is often not in packages, but they are often sleeved and placed inside the truck one by one.

A few producers ship materials on pallets, but due to the wide variation in box sizes, it is difficult to assemble a complete stack that will hold together on a pallet, although heat-shrink materials are finding some application. Pallets also reduce packing space available in trucks.

Carts designed to be loaded in the packaging area, omitting cartons, that are then wheeled into trucks is a method used by some growers who own their trucks (Figure 3-9). This system works fine where delivery sites allow such carts to be unloaded inside in heated or cooled areas, but are not acceptable when unloading outdoors.

Figure 3-9.   Delivery system using carts with racks that are rolled onto trucks, canceling the need for cartons.

Organizing the Paperwork

Paperwork functions are the lifeline of any business, and proper organization of administrative services, such as personnel and accounting, is expected. For any foliage production unit to operate successfully, considerable paperwork relating to purchasing, sales, crop inventory control, scheduling crops, shipping labels, and other items must be handled. Computers have found application in the foliage industry [5, 6, 17] and are being used extensively to handle accounting jobs, but they are less used in maintaining plant inventories and keeping up-to-date sales analyses. The size of the operation and the paperwork required will determine the purchase or rental of a computer.

Production Paperwork

Production paperwork includes maintaining records of all factors involved in growing plants for sale, including purchasing materials and supplies, planting and harvest dates, schedules, plant inventory, and others. Some important records required include the following:

1. Inventory control: up-to-date information on plants available, space, and supplies.
2. Purchasing of plants and supplies, with controls on placement of purchase orders and receiving departments or individuals.
3. Scheduling of crops so that information is always available on what will be produced and when.
4. Growing records, including information on soils, temperatures, watering, pest-control requirements, and associated special needs of crops grown.
5. Analysis of shipping results to show the relationship of what was planted to what was sold.

Sales Paperwork

Sales paperwork includes a multitude of records necessary to keep track of sales and to be assured plants are shipped to reach destinations on time and in good condition. Some important records in this category include the following:

1. Maintenance of accurate sales records matched against inventory and future availability.
2. Scheduling order makeup, including plant pickup lists, packing lists with labels, invoices, and bills of lading.

3. Developing order assembly lists for scheduling delivery to packaging and transportation

4. Customer analyses relating to type, area of country, and quantities purchased.

Accounting Paperwork

Accounting paperwork involves all records necessary to meet city, county, state, and federal regulations relating to operation of the business. Of special importance are records relating to health and welfare of personnel and tax records. Accounting also maintains other records that are useful to the sales department, including the following:

1. Personnel records of employees, such as work history, insurance, and retirement.
2. Payroll records.
3. Accounts receivable, including costing analyses, sales analyses, and credit history of accounts.
4. Business insurance and tax records.

Computers

Computerization has the potential of relieving office staff of considerable drudgery, but although computer programmers have no trouble handling accounting problems, they have difficulty understanding the nature of programs needed in plant production. There are definite areas where computers have application within the foliage industry. The list that follows includes jobs already being accomplished in foliage nurseries:

1. Routine accounting jobs such as payroll, updating accounts receivable, general ledger accounting, accounts payable, and issuing invoices.
2. Plant inventory maintenance on weekly basis by plant variety and pot size.
3. Sales analyses of plants by variety, size, customer and customer group, with ability to total any group, plant, or pot size.
4. Cost analyses made on a continuing basis by comparing current dollars and percentages to previous years' expenditures and performance.
5. Scheduling of production based on previous years' sales, plus a weighted factor for sales projections to provide information on

when and how many cuttings are needed, when to pot, where to place in the production unit, and when to harvest.

REFERENCES

[1] Anonymous. 1966. Mechanization needs of the nursery industry. Survey conducted by Horticultural Research Institute, Washington, D.C. 12 pp.

[2] Anonymous. 1967. Mechanized systems for the handling of soil mixes. Kingston, Pa.: Royer Foundry and Machine Co., 20 pp.

[3] Anonymous. 1970. Mechanization at Alabama Nursery. *Nursery Business* 15(4):22-24, 56.

[4] Anonymous. 1978. Electric power outage and the floricultural industry. *Foliage Digest* 1(9):11, 12.

[5] Gammel, W. A., L. R. Poole, and R. T. Poole. 1978. Computers for the nursery industry. Part I. *Nursery Business* 23(8):54-57.

[6] ———. 1979. Minicomputers vs. computer services. Part II. *Nursery Business* 24(1):72-74, 80-81, 85.

[7] Gray, H. E. 1967. Using automation and improved layout to increase manpower output. *Roses Inc. Bull.,* Feb. 1967, pp. 16-19.

[8] Gunter, D. L. 1976. Business analyses of foliage nurseries in Florida—1975. Univ. of Fla. Food and Resource Economics Dept., Economic Information Report 60. 20 pp.

[9] ———. 1979. Business analyses of foliage nurseries in south Florida, 1977. Univ. of Fla. Food and Resource Economics Dept., Economic Information Report 104. 20 pp.

[10] Huffman, J. W., and R. A. Sciaroni. 1957. Mechanization and the U. C. system. *In* the U. C. system for producing healthy container-grown plants. *Univ. of Calif. Exp. Sta. Manual* 23:271-284.

[11] Lee, R. G. 1965. Efficiency in layout, operation and management can mean the difference between profit and loss. *Roses Inc. Bull.,* Dec. 1965, pp. 11-19.

[12] Levins, R. A., and R. Newton. 1975. Mechanizing your nursery, will it be profitable? Univ. of Fla. Food and Resource Economics Fact Sheet No. 1.

[13] Mastalerz, J. W. 1977. *The greenhouse environment.* New York: Wiley.

[14] Meadows, S. 1978. Worker productivity incentives. *Foliage Digest* 1(8):13-14.

[15] Moore, J. E. 1978. Owning versus leasing equipment. *Foliage Digest* 1(9):8-9.

[16] Moxley, C. C. 1977. Managing labor for higher profits. *Proc. 1977 National Tropical Foliage Short Course* 1:41-46.

[17] Rochford, T. E. 1979. Computer applications for the modern nursery. *Foliage Digest* 2(5):4-6.

[18] Scarborough, E. F. 1978. Marketing Florida ornamental crops—Fresh foliage plants. Federal-State Market News Service, Winter Park, Fla. 43 pp.

[19] Skimina, C. 1966. Mechanization of the nursery. *Florida Nurseryman* 1(1):1-5.

[20] Smith, C. N., and J. R. Strain. 1976. Market outlets and product mix for Florida foliage plants. *Proc. Fla. State Hort. Soc.* 89:274-278.

[21] Van Heyst, Jan J. S. 1977. Integrated production systems. *Proc. 1977 National Tropical Foliage Short Course* 1:179-184.

four

D. B. McConnell
M. R. Sheehan

plant classification and structure

Plant Classification

Correctly identifying plants and assigning them names is an activity humans have pursued for centuries. Initially, only a limited number of plants were known, and classification and identification were relatively simple. Theophrastus (ca. 300 B.C.), often considered the father of botany, described, classified, and differentiated approximately 480 kinds of plants in his book, *On the History of Plants.* Plants were classified by growth habit (tree, shrub, or herb), florial characteristics (superior or inferior ovary), and life cycle (annual, biennial, or perennial).

This type of classification is termed an artificial classification scheme because many plants have similar morphological features, but are not related. For example some *Aucuba* and *Codiaem* species have very similar leaves, but the plants are in different families. Most plant identification keys used are based on gross morphological features such as flower color, time of bloom, growth habit, and certain leaf and floral characteristics. Such keys are artificial, but they usually provide a system to quickly and reliably identify plants for which they are designed.

Use of artificial classification schemes reached its highest point when Linnaeus (ca. 1730) developed the sexual system of plant classification based on floral morphology, with emphasis on number of stamens and pistils. The system of Linnaeus worked well because reproductive structures remain relatively constant under different environments.

The publication of Charles Darwin's *On the Origin of Species* (1859) directed attention to evolutionary relationships among plants. Artificial plant classification systems were reevaluated and major emphasis placed on grouping closely related plants. The study of embryo development, chromosome number, conductive tissue structure, cell pigmentation, and other anatomical, biochemical, cytological, and morphological data have been used by taxonomists, in addition to floral morphology, to determine natural relationships among plants [2, 6].

The Plant Kingdom

When Linnaeus published *Species Plantarum* in 1753, he described about 6,000 species of the approximately 20,000 known plants. Today the plant kingdom is known to include over 350,000 plant species, ranging from blue-green algae to giant redwood trees. Taxonomists have not reached complete agreement on evolutionary relationships among plants because of the great diversity in the plant kingdom, absence of complete fossil records, and differences in interpretation of existing data. However, when naming plants they follow the International Code of Botanical Nomenclature [5] adopted by the International Botanical Congress. This states that "every individual plant belongs to a species, every species to a genus, every genus to a family, every family to an order, every order to a class, and every class to a division" [3]. As an example of this system of nomenclature, the foliage plant *Cordyline terminalis* is clasified as follows:

Kingdom:	Plant
Division:	Anthophyta
Class:	Angiospermae
Order:	Liliales
Family:	Agavaceae
Genus:	Cordyline
Species:	terminalis

Commercial plant growers are interested in classification of plants at the family, genus, and species level. A plant family is a grouping of one or more plant genera that have certain flower, fruit, and leaf characteristics in common. A plant genus is a grouping of one or more plant species that are closely related and have morphological characteristics in common. The species is the basic unit of taxonomic work and is the designation used most frequently by the horticulturists. Members of a species have more characteristics in common than members of a genus. The botanical name of a plant consists of the generic name and the species epithet, a system established by Linnaeus. Species epithets refer to plant characteristics, nativity or habitat, or to a person. Scientific names of plants are written in Latin or latinized forms of other languages. The use of two names to identify a plant is known as the binomial systems of nomenclature and is in accordance with the International Code of Botanical Nomenclature.

Some species are variable, and different forms occasionally occur, either in cultivation or naturally. A botanical variety is a naturally occurring subgroup within a species and is sufficiently different from the remaining members of the species to be easily distinguished. An example would be *Cordyline terminalis* var. *tricolor*. In addition to botanical varieties, commercial foliage growers and other horticulturists have selected, propagated, and named many variants with desirable characteristics. The International Code of Nomenclature of Cultivated Plants recognizes this as a special category, and it is designated as the *cultivar* (abbreviated cv.). The cultivar name is set off by single quotation marks or preceded by the abbreviation cv. and designates a variant that has originated or is maintained under cultivation. In writing the name of a cultivar, the cultivar name is written in common language rather than Latin and should not be italicized. For example, cultivars of ti plant are written as follows: *C. terminalis* 'Baby Doll' and *C. terminalis* 'Firebrand'. Cultivar names used before 1959 may be latinized as *C. terminalis* 'Amabilis'. Popular foliage plants are often bought and sold by cultivar name only, but it is important to use the binomial, since it specifies the exact plant in question and eliminates errors in identifying plants being bought and sold.

Structure

Commercial foliage plants vary from small herbaceous plants such as baby tears (*Soleirolia soleirolii*) to large tree forms such as schefflera (*Brassaia actinophylla*). Internally, these dissimilar plants are composed of comparable cell types arranged in similar patterns.

The plant body can be divided into the root, usually the underground portions of plants, and the shoot, usually the aboveground portions of plants. The shoot consists of stems, leaves, and reproductive structures as diagrammatically represented in Figure 4-1. Typical plant organs and variations of them occur in foliage plants, and commercial growers should be familiar with them to produce the best quality crop.

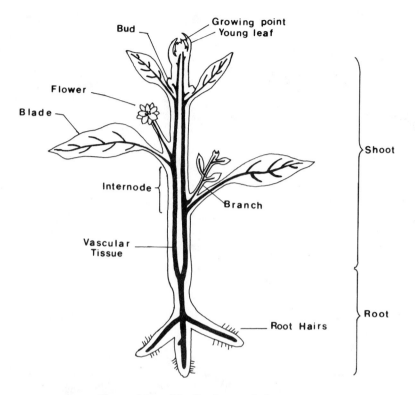

Figure 4-1. The fundamental plant parts.

Root Morphology

Plant roots are normally subterranean, which often causes their importance and extensiveness to be overlooked. Root systems grow by an irregular branching pattern, rather than a precise nodal pattern as with the stem. In some plants they account for more than half the dry weight of the plant. The extensive soil penetration facilitates absorption and translocation of water and nutrients from the soil to the stem, provides anchorage and support for the shoot, and may serve as the major storage organ for food reserves. Mature ti plants, for example, may have tuberous roots that weigh up to 300 pounds.

Two major types of root systems occur within foliage plant species, fibrous and taproot. Both systems begin with a primary root emerging from the embryo, and in a taproot system the primary root continues to develop vertically and enlarge with other roots branching from it. The primary root in a fibrous root system either dies or loses its dominance,

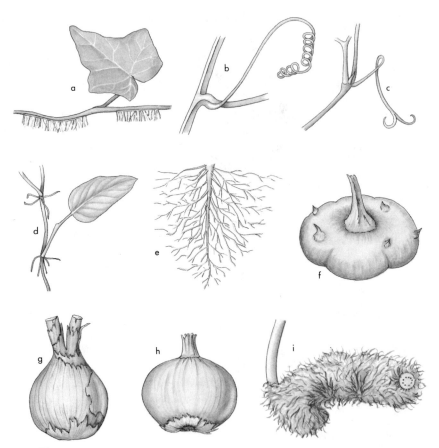

Figure 4-2.   Root and stem types: (a) Adventitious roots on stem of *Hedera helix;* (b) Stem tendril of *Passiflora* spp.; (c) Stem tendril of *Cissus* spp.; (d) Nodal adventitious roots of *Philodendron* ssp.; (e) Generalized taproot system; (f) Generalized corm with membraneous tunic; (g) Double-nosed bulb, an underground stem; (h) Generalized bulb, an underground stem; (i) Fern rhizome, an underground stem.

and an extensively branched root system develops, consisting of approx-imately equal-sized roots. Plants that form taproots when grown from seeds usually develop a fibrous system when grown from cuttings.

Many foliage plants have modified roots, adventitious roots, or roots with some leaf or stem functions. Adventitious roots are roots that develop from any portion of the plant other than another root. Members of the Araceae, Agavaceae, Araliaceae, Moraceae, and certain other plant families develop roots on stems or branches [1]. Adventitious roots often form along the entire stem of juvenile forms of *Hedera helix*

(Araliaceae) and originate from nodes in *Philodendron* spp. (Araceae) (Figure 4-2a,d). Adventitious roots may even possess chlorophyll and photosynthesize. Adventitious roots on branches of *Ficus* spp. develop into supplementary trunks in tropical climates.

Stem Morphology

Plant stems support leaves and flowers and provide the vital connection between the nutrient- and water-absorbing roots, photosynthesizing leaves, and other plant parts.

Continued stem growth in length and width results from cell divisions in meristematic regions. Cell divisions in apical and subapical meristems produce leaves, nodes, and internodes, resulting in stem elongation, while cell divisions in the vascular cambium result in increased stem girth. Branches develop from axillary meristems found where leaf bases and stems intersect, an area known as the leaf axil. Removing the apical meristem (growing point) of the main stem or branches promotes axillary bud growth.

Water, nutrients, vitamins, and products of photosynthesis are conducted through the stem via the vascular system. A cross section of the stem shows that the vascular system of the plant is composed of xylem, phloem, and cambial cells. The cambial cells separate the xylem and phloem and produce phloem cells toward the outside of the stem and xylem cells toward the inside of the stem. Most foliage plants are either dicotyledonous (dicots) or monocotyledonous (monocots) plants. The vascular system of a dicot is characterized by a complete or almost complete circle of xylem and phloem cells, whereas monocot stems are characterized by scattered vascular bundles. Consequently, monocots are seldom grafted owing to difficulties in joining the multiple separate cambial areas.

Stems have leaves attached at specific areas called nodes, with portions between nodes called internodes. Internode length under similar environmental conditions is relatively constant for each cultivar, but varies from species to species. As the distance betwen nodes becomes shorter and shorter, a point is reached where plants appear to have no internodes, a condition called acaulescent. Plants with distinct internodes or stems are called caulescent (Figure 4-3d,e).

Many foliage plants have erect single or multiple stems, but some lack sufficient rigidity to remain upright without supplemental support. Plants requiring some support for the stem can be divided into four groups [4]. Hook climbers, twining plants, plants with specialized climbing structures, such as tendrils, and root climbers (Figure 4-2). Hook

Figure 4-3. (a) Vining stem of *Philodendron scandens,* alternate leaves; (b) Stem of *Plectrantus australis,* opposite leaves; (c) *Nephrolesis exaltata,* an acaulescent plant; (d) *Spathiphyllum* spp., a short-stemmed plant; (e) *Cordyline* spp., a caulescent plant.

climbers or scramblers usually cling to a support by spines that curve backward. Twining plants climb by coiling their stems around a support, while plants like *Cissus* spp. climb by tendrils that wrap firmly around supports. Tendrils can be modified stems or leaves. Root climbers are plants that gain support via adventitious roots growing from the stem. Such roots elongate into crevices of the support to hold the stem erect. Root climbing plants make good subjects for "totems," and many members of the aroid family are commercially grown this way.

Leaves

A typical leaf is composed of the blade and petiole, but there are exceptions. The blade is usually a thin, broad, flat structure attached to the stem by a stalk called the petiole. A leaf with no petiole is called sessile, and those with petioles that wrap around the stem are called clasping. Leaves may be arranged on the stem alternately, or one leaf at each node; opposite, or two leaves emerging from the same node; and whorled, with three or more leaves at one node. Leaves that emerge one above another with no obvious internode between them have a rosette arrangement (Figure 4-4).

Figure 4-4. Leaf types: (a) Alternate leaf with petiole; (b) Alternate, sessile leaf; (c) Alternate, clasping leaf; (d) Opposite leaves; (e) Alternate leaves; (f) Whorled leaves; (g) Rosette leaves.

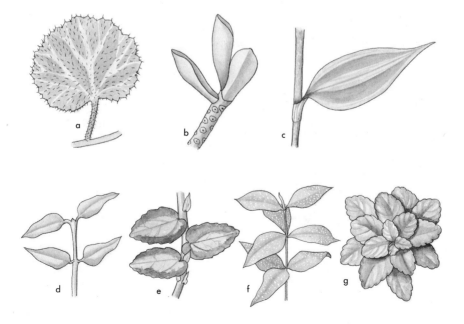

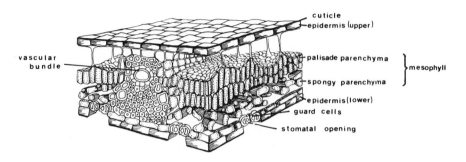

Figure 4-5.   Generalized structure of a plant leaf.

Internal Leaf Structure

Leaves differ greatly in external appearance, but in most their internal structure is similar in form and function. Leaves trap light energy and convert it to chemical energy in the form of organic compounds. A typical foliage leaf is shown in Figure 4-5. The cuticle forms a protective covering over the epidermal cells, and underneath there are one or more rows of elongated palisade cells. Usually, groups of loosely clustered spongy parenchyma cells are beneath the palisade cells, and like palisade cells they contain chloroplasts that photosynthesize. Each leaf has a variable number of openings called stomates through which gases diffuse, with the largest number of these on the lower leaf surface in most plants. Opening and closing of stomates is regulated by guard cells that surround them. A network of vascular bundles permeates the leaf blade. Xylem cells conduct water and mineral nutrients to the photosynthesizing cells; phloem cells carry photosynthetic products to other parts of the plant.

Variation in Leaf Forms

Several important variations in leaf forms are found in higher plants. Simple leaves have entire blades (Figure 4-6a,b,c,f,g), whereas a compound leaf consists of two or more blades attached to a single petiole. The blade may be attached to the petiole by a stalk called a petiolule or the blade may be sessile. Each individual blade and petiolule of a compound leaf is called a leaflet (Figure 4-6h,i,j). Pinnately compound leaves have leaflets attached to both sides of the leaf axis (rachis) and resemble a feather. Leaflets of palmately compound leaves all emerge from one point at the apex of the petiole (Figure 4-6h). The term decompound is used to describe leaves that have more than one leaflet per petiolule (Figure 4-6j). Some compound leaves are bipinnate

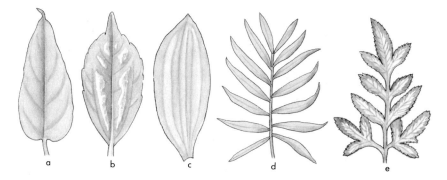

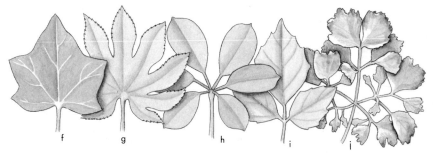

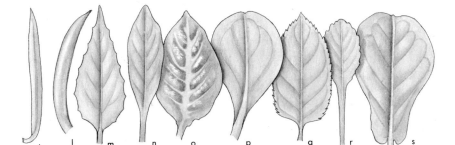

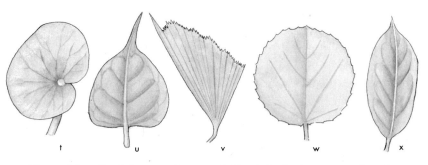

Figure 4-6. Leaf shapes and types: (a) Simple leaf, pinnate venation; (b) Simple leaf, pinnate venation; (c) Simple leaf, parallel venation; (d) Leaf compound, even pinnate; (e) Leaf compound, bipinnate; (f) Simple leaf, pedate margin; (g) Simple leaf, palmate venation; (h) Compound leaf, palmate; (i) Tricompound leaf; (j) Decompound leaf, bipinnate; (k) Linear; (l) Subulate; (m) Lanceolate; (n) Oblanceolate; (o) Ovate; (p) Obovate; (q) Oblong; (r) Spatulate; (s) Pandurate; (t) Reniform; (u) Deltoid; (v) Cuneate; (w) Orbicular; (x) Elliptic.

or tripinnate, with the primary divisions or leaflets divided once or twice again into leaflets (Figure 4-6j). A simple leaf is easily distinguished from a leaflet of a compound leaf by the presence of buds, which are found only in leaf axils.

Venation   Major vascular strands in leaf blades or leaflets are arranged in several different patterns depending on species. Leaves with pinnate venation have a central midrib (the main vascular strand), which extends from the petiole or base of the blade to the leaf apex, with secondary veins branching from the midrib and extending to the leaf margins (Figure 4-6a,b). Leaves with parallel venation have major vascular strands parallel to one another and to leaf margins (Figure 4-6c), and they may or may not have a midrib. Leaves with palmate venation have three or more major vascular strands originating at the leaf base and extending out to the leaf margins (Figure 4-6g).

Leaf forms   Simple leaves and leaflets of compound leaves vary considerably in form. Geometrical terms that approximate overall leaf shape are used so that leaf and other plant part descriptions will be consistent from author to author. Some of the more common terms and their definitions are as follows:

Linear   Elongated, narrow, with straight and approximately parallel sides (Figure 4-6k).

Subulate   Elongated, narrow, and awl shaped with sides that taper to form a sharp point on the end (Figure 4-6l).

Lanceolate   Shaped like the head of a lance, tapering toward the apex and broadest toward the base (Figure 4-6m).

Oblanceolate   Shaped like the head of a lance, but tapering toward the base of the leaf with the broadest part toward the apex (Figure 4-6n).

Ovate   Approximately egg shaped, with the widest part of the leaf just below the middle and narrowing toward the apex (Figure 4-6o).

Obovate   Approximately egg shaped, with the widest leaf part above the middle and narrowing toward the base (Figure 46p).

Oblong   Longer than broad, with almost parallel sides (Figure 4-6q).

Spatulate   Tending toward spoon shaped, with the lower half of the leaf very narrow (Figure 4-6r).

Pandurate   Approximately fiddle shaped, with the widest part of the leaf toward the apex (Figure 4-6s).

Reniform   Kidney shaped (Figure 46t).

Deltoid   Approximately shaped like an equilateral triangle (Figure 4-6u).

Cuneate   Wedge shaped with the widest point of the triangle toward the apex (Figure 4-6v).

Orbicular   Circular (Figure 4-6w).

Elliptic   Oblong, but broadest midway between apex and base (Figure 4-6x).

Leaf apexes   Leaf apexes are important diagnostic tools to aid in separating plants with similar leaf forms. Some common leaf apexes and their definitions are as follows:

Acuminate   Tapering to a sharp point, with the margins leading to the apex slightly concave (Figure 4-7a).

Acute   Tapering to a sharp point, with the margins leading to the apex meeting at an acute angle (Figure 4-7b).

Cuspidate   Abruptly and concavely constricted into a point (Figure 4-7c).

Obtuse   Blunt or rounded (Figure 4-7d).

Emarginate   Rounded, with a shallow broad notch at the apex (Figure 4-7e).

Obcordate   Deeply notched or two lobed, approximately heart shaped (Figure 4-7f).

Retuse   Rounded, but with a shallow narrow notch at the apex (Figure 4-7g).

Mucronate   Abruptly tipped with a short rigid point, which extends from the midrib. The midrib extension may or may not be accompanied by a small amount of leaf tissue (Figure 4-7h).

Caudate   Elongated into a somewhat tail-like extension at the apex (Figure 4-7i).

Leaf bases   Leaf bases are the closest points of leaf attachment to the plant. Some common bases and their definitions are as follows:

Attenuate   Drawn out, with lower sides constricting concavely, tapering toward the base (Figure 4-7j).

Oblique   One side larger than the other (Figure 4-7k).

Cuneate   Wedge shaped; may be broad or narrow (Figure 4-7l).

Acute   With straight margins that form less than a right angle (Figure 4-7m).

Truncate   Forming an almost straight line at a right angle to the midrib. (Figure 4-7n).

Hastate   Having a form similar to an arrowhead, but with a pair of basal lobes flaring outward (Figure 4-7o).

Figure 4-7. Leaf apexes (a)–(i), bases (j)–(u), and margins (v)–(hh): (a) Accuminate; (b) Acute; (c) Cuspidate; (d) Obtuse; (e) Emarginate; (f) Obcordate; (g) Retuse; (h) Mucronate; (i) Caudate; (j) Attenuate; (k) Oblique; (l) Cunate; (m) Acute; (n) Truncate; (o) Hastate; (p) Auriculate; (q) Obtuse; (r) Peltate; (s)–(t) Sagittate; (u) Cordate; (v) Entire; (w) Undulate; (x) Crenate; (y) Serrate; (z) Double-serrate; (aa) Serrulate; (bb) Fenestrate; (cc) Dentate; (dd) Lacerate; (ee) Palmatifid; (ff) Lobed; (gg) Pinnatifid; (hh) Crispate.

Auriculate   Characterized by two small earlike lobes on either side of petioles (Figure 4-7p).

Obtuse   Gently curved (Figure 4-7q).

Peltate   With a petiole attachment to the lower leaf surface inside the leaf margin (Figure 4-7r).

Sagittate   With lobes pointing downward or slightly inward (Figure 4-7s,t).

Cordate   With lobes forming a heart shape (Figure 4-7u).

Leaf margins and divisions   These provide additional assistance in identifying plants. The terms defined here are also used for petals, bracts, and other plant parts.

Entire   Smooth or uncut margins with no identation, but may be wavy or rolled (Figure 4-7u).

Undulate   Wavy margins that wind up and down rather than in and out (Figure 4-7w).

Crenate   Toothed margins, with each tooth blunt or rounded (Figure 4-7x).

Serrate   Toothed margins, with each tooth coarse, sharp, and directed forward (Figure 4-7y).

Double serrate   Margins with coarse teeth, each with small, fine teeth (Figure 4-7z).

Serrulate   Toothed margins with each tooth small, but sharp, pointed, and directed forward. Diminutive of serrate (Figure 4-7aa).

Fenestrate   With natural openings, often referred to as "windows" (Figure 4-7bb).

Dentate   Toothed margins, with each tooth sharp and coarse and directed outward at nearly right angles to the margin (Figure 4-7cc).

Lacerate   Indented margins cut irregularly from one half to two thirds the distance to the midrib. Margins of segments may be entire or toothed (Figure 4-7dd).

Palmatifid   Palmately cleft or parted margins (Figure 4-7ee).

Lobed   Coarsely divided margins with sinuses less than one half the distance from margin to midrib (Figure 4-7ff).

Pinnatifid   Indented margins pinnately cleft or parted almost but not quite to the midrib (Figure 4-7gg).

Crispate   Indented margins that are ruffled or curled in a vertical plane in small waves (Figure 4-7hh).

Inflorescence

Flowers and fruit represent sexual reproductive parts of plants, with fruit developing from flower parts. Flowers are borne in arrangements called inflorescences, which are constant within a species, making it possible to use this feature for identifying plant species. *Inflorescences* may consist of single flowers that arise from the base of a plant or from leaf axils, or groups of two or more flowers on a simple or branched stem. Many types of inflorescences exist, but the types most commonly occurring within foliage plants are the following:

Spike   An elongated, unbranched stalk of sessile flowers (Figure 4-8e, h).

Raceme   An elongated unbranched stalk of flowers, each having a pedicel holding it away from the main stem (Figure 4-8f).

Panicle   A branched inflorescence having flowers that open from the bottom of the inflorescence toward the tip (Figure 4-8g).

Cyme   Another branched, but determinate inflorescence in which terminal flowers open first (Figure 4-8c).

Corymb   A short, flat-topped inflorescence blooming from the outside toward the center.

Umbel   A flat-topped inflorescence with all flower pedicels arising at one point. It is indeterminate, since flowers open from the outer edge of the inflorescence toward the center.

Head   A group of sessile flowers gathered together tightly (Figure 4-8d).

Floral Morphology

Flowers are typically composed of sepals, petals, stamens, and pistils or carpels. When present, sepals are the outermost or basal whorl of floral parts. Sepals may be separate or fused, green and leaflike, or colored and petallike. Sepals may be reduced to hairs or entirely absent in some plants. Collectively, sepals are called the calyx (Figure 4-8i, j).

Petals are normally the most colorful portion of flowers and compose the second series of floral parts immediately above the calyx. They also may be separate or fused into a ring or an elongated tube with free tips (Figure 4-8i, j). Petals may be reduced to minute structures or may be entirely absent in some plants. Collectively, the petals are called the corolla.

The calyx plus corolla are called the perianth. They serve as protective envelopes for reproductive portions of flowers and as attractants

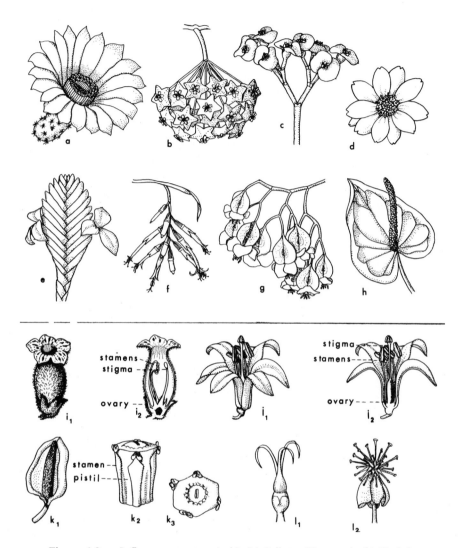

Figure 4-8.   Inflorescence types (a–h): (a) Solitary (*Cactaceae*); (b) Umbel (*Asclepiadaceae*); (c) Multiple inflorescence, cymelike (*Euphorbiaceae*); (d) Head (*Compositae*); (e) Spike (*Bromeliaceae*); (f) Raceme (*Bromeliaceae*); (g) Panicle (*Begoniaceae*); (h) Spike (*Araceae*); (i_1) Tubular zygomorphic flower; (i_2) Vertical section showing inferior ovary (*Gesneriaceae*); (j_1) Regular flower; (j_2) Vertical section showing superior ovary (*Liliaceae*); (k_1) Spathe and spike; (k_2) Bisexual flower from spike showing stamens and pistil, top view (*Araceae*); (l_1) Unisexual pistillate flower; (l_2) Unisexual staminate flower (*Euphorbiaceae*).

to pollinators, which carry pollen from stamens to stigma. Pollination occurs within the flowers of the same plant (self-pollinated) or between flowers on separate plants of the same or related species (cross pollinated).

Stamens compose the third set of flower parts and are male reproductive organs. Each stamen is composed of an anther and a filament (Figure 4-8i_2, j_2). Anthers produce pollen and are usually composed of two sections that open to disseminate pollen grains by lengthwise slits, flaps, or pores. Filaments are stalks that hold anthers, and their arrangement is specific to plant families and genera. Stamens may be free or attached to the perianth, grouped, or fused to each other to form a tube and vary from one to hundreds in flowers (Figure 4-8i_2, j_2, l_2). Collectively, stamens are referred to as the androecium.

The innermost whorl of floral parts is the female reproductive organs. The term carpel or pistil is used to designate the ovule-bearing organ. There may be from one to many carpels in a single flower, and these may stand separately or may be fused into a single structure. An individual, separate carpel or structure formed by the fusion of two or more carpels is also called a pistil. Collectively, carpels are referred to as the gynoecium (Figure 4-8i_2, j_2). A separate carpel or a pistil is made up of an ovary and a stigma, with the stigma often connected to the ovary by a slender or thick stalk called the style. Egg-containing organs or ovules within the ovary are arranged in a manner specific to the plant species. Two to many ovules may be arranged on side walls or on a central stalk, or there may be only a single ovule in the center of the ovary chamber attached to the bottom, side, or top.

Ovaries may be superior, inferior, or half-inferior. Superior ovaries are above the point of attachment of the perianth and stamens (Figure 4-8j_2). Inferior ovaries are below the point of attachment of perianth and stamens (Figure 4-8i_2), and half-inferior ovaries are in an intermediate position.

The ovary usually develops into the fruiting part of plants when eggs within ovules develop into seeds after being fertilized by pollen from stamens. The fruit, therefore, is a body containing seeds.

Flowers having sepals, petals, stamens, and pistils are called complete flowers. Not all flowers possess the four components, and if any are missing the flower is incomplete. An incomplete flower may lack one or both perianth parts, but if both the androecium and gynoecium are present, it is called a perfect flower. A flower that contains only one set of sex organs is unisexual; one having only stamens is a staminate flower (Figure 4-8l_2), and one having only pistils is a pistillate flower (Figure 4-8l_1). Some plants have pistillate and staminate flowers on different plants and are called dioecious. Plants with both types of unisexual flowers on a single plant are monoecious. Such flowers may be contained in the same inflorescence or on different inflorescences. Plants of both sexes are necessary for pollination.

Flower shape is important in identifying plants. Flower parts of a regular flower are formed so that the flower could be cut along any diameter, producing two equal halves (Figure 4-8a). If the flower parts are arranged so the flower can only be cut in one plane to produce two equal halves, it is bilaterally symmetrical or zygomorphic (Figure 4-8i).

Floral structures in major groups of foliage plants include many special types of flowers. For example the aroid family (Araceae) has an inflorescence composed of a special structure called a spadix subtended or enveloped by a spathe that is often large and colorful (Figure 4-8h). The spadix has bisexual or unisexual flowers. The pepper family (Piperaceae) has minute, often bisexual flowers without a perianth arranged on fleshy spikes. Inflorescences in the spurge family (Euphorbiaceae) vary, and some members, such as crown of thorns and poinsettia, have the inflorescence subtended by showy petallike bracts. Others have inconspicuous unisexual flowers.

Fruits

Fruits are seed-bearing structures of plants and are matured and ripened ovaries, often attached to or enveloped by associated floral parts. Fruit development depends on pollination, which occurs when ripened pollen is transmitted to stigmas at the proper stage of development. Secretions on the stigma start pollen tube growth down through the style and into the ovary, where it eventually reaches the ovule. Fertilization occurs when the male nuclei joins the female nuclei, after which repeated cell division and subsequent differentiation produce the seed or embryonic plant.

After pollination and fertilization occur, ovary growth begins. The ovary wall becomes the fruit wall. Ovules develop into seeds within the fruit.

Many types of fruit exist and are often used to identify plant genera and species. They may develop from a single pistil or from several pistils, be fleshy or dry, and may be dehiscent, meaning they open at maturity to disperse seeds, or indehiscent, retaining seeds within matured and fallen fruit.

1. Fleshy fruits include the following:
    (a) **Berry:** a succulent fruit with a soft pulpy interior and seeds embedded in the tissue or occasionally with a central seed (Figure 4-9a$_1$). Examples are aglaonemas, dates, dieffenbachias, and

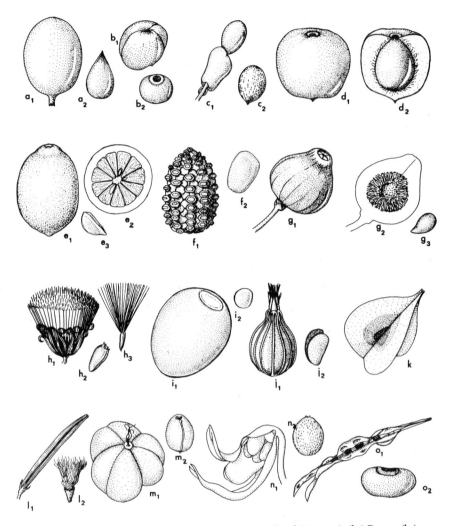

Figure 4-9.   Fruits and seeds; (a_1) Berry; (a_2) Seed (*Araceae*); (b_1) Berry; (b_2) Seed (*Liliaceae*); (c_1) Arilliate fruit; (c_2) Seed (*Podocarpaceae*); (d_1) Drupe; (d_2) Vertical section showing seed (*Palmae*); (e_1) Hesperidium; (e_2) Cross-section hesperidium; (e_3) Seed (*Rutaceae*); (f_1) Cone; (f_2) Seed (*Cycadaceae*); (g_1) Aggregate fruit; (g_2) Vertical section showing numerous achenes; (g_3) Single achene (*Moraceae*); (h_1) Seed head; (h_2) Achene; (h_3) Achene with pappus (*Compositae*); (i_1) Berry; (i_2) Seed (*Cactaceae*); (j_1) Capsule; (j_2) Seed (*Bromeliaceae*); (k_1) Capsule (*Begoniaceae*); (l_1) Follicle; (l_2) Seed (*Apocynaceae*); (m_1) Schizocarp; (m_2) Seed (*Euphorbiaceae*); (n_1) Fruiting structure showing nutlets; (n_2) Nutlet (*Labiatae*); (o_1) Legume; (o_2) Seed (*Leguminosae*).

tomatoes. Citrus is a special type of berry called a hesperidium (Figure 4-9e_1).

(b) **Drupe:** a fleshy one-seeded fruit with seed encased in a hard shell in the center. Examples are cycads, members of the Piperaceae, some palms, and peaches (Figure 4-9d_1).

(c) **Pome fruit:** central cores containing seeds, with the fleshy part being the flower receptacle. Examples include apples and quince.

2. Fruits that are dry include the following:

(a) One-seeded, indehiscent fruits:

(1) **Achenes:** small fruit with thin outside walls. Examples include *Senecio* spp. and *Pilea* spp. (Figure 4-9h_2).

(2) **Samaras:** winged achenes. Examples include the fruits of elm and maple.

(b) Dry fruits with two or more seeds that are released by splitting of pods:

(1) **Follicles:** seeds are released through a split along one side only (Figure 4-9l_1). Examples include *Stapelia* spp. and *Crassula* spp.

(2) **Legumes:** split along both edges of the pod. These include fruits of the legume family (Figure 4-9o_1).

(3) **Capsules:** a large group of fruits that open by various means such as by pores, lids, splitting along natural sutures, or splitting in the center of a wall. There may be two to several locules, each opening to disperse seeds (Figure 4-9k). Examples include some bromeliads, *Aphelandra* spp., and *Begonia* spp.

(c) Dry fruits that do not disperse the seeds, but rather split into achenelike segments when ripe, are schizocarpic fruits. Examples are fruits of the mint and carrot family (Figure 4-9n_1).

3. *Aggregate fruits* are composed of numerous fertilized ovaries that develop as a unit. Blackberries, roses, and strawberries are examples.

4. *Composite fruits* are formed from more than one flower and include breadfruits, pineapple, and figs. Individual flowers are fused together before being fertilized and continue to develop as a unit into a fleshy fruit (Figure 4-9g_1).

Seeds

A seed is a matured fertilized ovule consisting of an embryo and stored food, or endosperm, encased in a seed coat having an apical pore called the micropyle. The only exceptions to this are in the Orchidaceae and Podostemaceae, which have seeds devoid of endosperm.

Embryos are the portions of seed that produce new plants, since they are rudimentary seedling plants. The absence of a viable embryo renders the seed useless as a means of propagation.

The stored food, or endosperm, is the source of food for embryos and seedling plants and consists of starch, oil, protein, and/or sugar. Endosperm may be fleshy, oily, or boney in character and may be absorbed into the embryo as it matures, or it may be in the form of bulk food reserve surrounding the embryo. It is often the "meat" of a seed such as corn kernels, edible beans, coconut meat, or nuts, such as pecans.

Seed coats may be thick, thin, hard, soft, leathery, or fleshy. They may be textured with networks of veinlike sculpturing, bumps, pits, raised lines, or patterns of color and have raised protuberances, wings, or any of a variety of hairs, spines, or bristles in tufts over the entire surface, or they may be smooth. Most seeds have distinctive shape, color, and texture, which permit genus and often species identification.

Some seeds have an aril present, which is a thick and usually fleshy outgrowth on the seed. It may be at one end or as a cover over the entire seed (Figure 4-9c$_1$). Very hard or thick seed coats can be scarified in order to hasten germination.

Ferns

Ferns evolved before flowering plants; fossil records indicate that ferns were growing almost 400 million years ago [2]. Existing ferns never flower, fruit, or produce seed; they produce millions of microscopic one-celled structures called spores. Unlike most other spore-bearing plants, such as algae, fungi, and mosses, ferns have true leaves, stems, roots, and a complex vascular system to conduct food, minerals, and water; thus, ferns are classified as vascular plants.

Terms used to describe leaves and other parts of flowering plants apply to similar fern structures; however, special terms are used to describe life cycles of ferns and the ways spores are formed and distributed on fern leaves.

Ferns have two distinctly different photosynthesizing life forms during a complete life cycle. The form that has leaves and stems is called the sporophyte generation because it forms spores. After spores mature, they are released, and if a suitable environment is found, they germinate to produce a gametophyte generation with rootlike structures called rhizoids and small, green, usually flat, heart-shaped, leaflike structures called gametophytes or prothalli. The prothallus produces male and female sex organs on its lower surface after it matures. If kept moist, fertilization occurs and a sporophyte develops, which depends on the gametophyte for its initial nutritional needs. Soon leaf, root, and stem are produced, and the prothallus dies after the sporophyte develops secondary leaves. The primary root dies as the sporophyte continues to develop, and adventitious roots are produced from stems.

Stems of most horticulturally important ferns are rhizomes that grow horizontally on the soil or just beneath it. Fern rhizomes, as other stems, may have short or long internodes and be extensively or sparingly branched. Some ferns have erect unbranched stems, which may be extremely short, such as bird's-nest ferns (Figure 4-10f_1), or reach heights of up to sixty feet, as tree ferns (Figure 4-10e). Boston fern and a few others also produce long, slender, aboveground stems called stolons, which form new plants.

Fern leaves are called fronds and usually develop from a coil with the leaf tip in the coil center (Figure 4-10e). While still rolled up, they are called fiddleheads or crosiers, and this distinctive method of leaf development is known as circinate vernation. Some terms commonly used to describe parts of the fern leaf include stipe for petiole, pinna for primary leaflets, and rachis for portions of a compound leaf axis extending from lowest pinna to leaf apex (Figure 4-10a_1).

Fern fronds, whether simple or compound, can be divided into fertile, which produce spores, and sterile, which are sporeless. Sterile fronds and fertile fronds that differ significantly in size or shape are dimorphic. Dimorphic leaves may differ greatly, as in staghorn ferns, where sterile fronds are round and clasp supports, while fertile fronds are elongate and erect (Figure 4-10d_1).

Sori and sporangia are fruiting structures that develop on the lower surface of fronds and may appear as round dots or elongated oval shapes. Sori may be on leaf margins, scattered over leaves, or neatly arranged in rows, depending on genus and species. Marginal sori often have leaf edges rolled over them for protection as in *Adiantum* and *Pteris* (Figure 4-10a_2, b_3), while others have an umbrellalike cover called an indusium, which may be variously shaped as in *Rumohra* and *Polypodium* (Figure 4-10c_2, g_1). Other species have no covering and are termed naked, as in *Platycerium* (Figure 10f_2).

Each sorus is composed of sporangia, which are usually rounded bodies attached by stalks. They contain the spores. Many sporangia have an annulus, which is a row of thick-walled cells resembling half a zipper than runs from the bottom of sporangia just above the stalk over the top and partway down the opposite side (Figure 4-10g_2). When spores are mature, their case splits where the annulus is not present (Figure 10g_3). The annulus acts like a released spring, popping the sporangium open and scattering spores forcibly (Figure 4-10g_3).

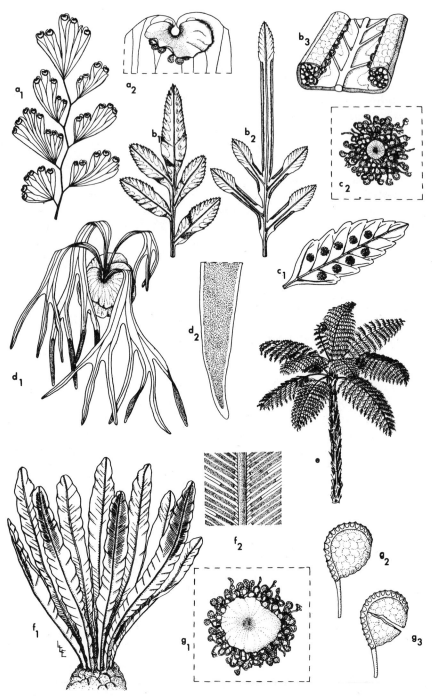

Figure 4-10. Ferns: (a₁) Compound fertile leaf; (a₂) Segment of fertile frond showing marginal soris (Adiantum); (b₁) Sterile frond; (b₂) Sterile frond; (b₃) Segment of fertile frond showing marginal sori (Pteris); (c₁) Fertile pinna; (c₂) Sorus (Runohra); (d₁) Dimorphic fern, fertile and sterile fronds; (d₂) Tip of fertile frond with sporangia (Platycerium); (e₁) Tree fern, circinate vernation (Cyathea); (f₁) Fern showing simple, fertile frond; (f₂) Detail of fertile frond showing sori (Asplenium); (g₁) Sorus with indusium; (g₂) Single sporangium (Polypodium).

REFERENCES

[1] Bailey, L. H., and E. Z. Bailey. 1976. *Hortus third.* New York: Macmillan.

[2] Foster, A. S., and E. M. Gilfford, Jr. 1959. *Comparative morphology of vascular plants.* San Francisco: W. H. Freeman.

[3] Gilmour, J. S. L., F. R. Horne, E. L. Little, Jr., F. A. Stafler, and R. H. Richens. 1969. *International code of nomenclature of cultivated plants.* Utrecht, Netherlands: International Bureau for Plant Taxonomy and Nomenclature.

[4] Jamieson, B. G. M., and J. F. Reynolds. 1967. *Tropical plant types.* New York: Pergamon.

[5] Lanjouin, J., ed. 1966. *International code of botanical nomenclature.* Utrecht, Netherlands: International Bureau for Plant Toxonomy and Nomenclature.

[6] Lawrence, G. H. 1951. *Taxonomy of vascular plants.* New York: Macmillan.

five

Gary J. Wilfret
T. J. Sheehan

development of new foliage plant cultivars

The development and introduction of new foliage plants into the commercial trade has depended basically upon natural mutations of commonly grown species, the introduction of new species, and observance and selection of mutations by growers. There would be little variability in foliage plants today if the foliage world had to depend on new cultivars from organized breeding programs. Fortunately, nature has provided the mechanism of natural or "spontaneous" mutation, with the result being many variations of species. Such mutants or sports have provided most of the variety and uniqueness available in an expanding industry.

The cultivar complex of *Dracaena deremensis* demonstrates the natural variation of a species and illustrates how small, naturally occurring differences have been successfully exploited. The cultivar 'Warneckei,' commonly grown as a house plant, has lanceolate leaves with a milky green center, bordered by a translucent white band on each side and thin bright green margins. 'Bausei' differs only in having a narrower center, with the white bands closer together. Leaves of 'Roehrs Gold' have a broad yellow center, bordered by white lines and edged with green, and 'Janet Craig' is a green sport of this species. Color is not the only variant existing, but other characteristics have been selected, such as the pendant corrugated leaves of 'Longii.'

The aroids (Araceae) are the dominant family in the foliage industry and have attracted hobbyists and a few commercial firms to produce improved genotypes through hybridization. One of the oldest "foliage" breeding programs began with *Caladium,* which has over 200 known cultivars with *C. bicolor* and *C. picturatum* as the main gene pool [8]. Inter- and intraspecific hybridization has produced many spectacular hybrids, from the white of 'Candidum' to the deep red of 'Freida Hemple.' This genus is easy to hybridize, since a single spadix has up to 200 ovaries, with each ovary producing about fourteen seeds. The fruits mature in 5 to 6 weeks, the seeds germinate in 8 to 10 days, and the colorful characteristics of the leaves are distinguishable within 3 to 4 months [6].

Two other aroids, *Aglaonema* and *Philodendron,* have received the attention of breeders, and interspecific hybridization has played an important role in these genera. *Aglaonema* Fransher. (*A. treublii* × *A. marantifolium tricolor*) has milky green leaves with white petioles, and *A.* Parrot Jungle (*A. curtisii* × *A. pictum tricolor*) has greenish silver leaves with green petioles in contrast with leaves of the common *A. commutatum,* which are deep green with silver-gray markings.

Philodendron, a genus comprised of some 200 species, was first hybridized in Italy in 1887 with the production of *P. corsinianum* (*P. lucidum* × *P. cariaceum*). The first U.S. hybrid, *P. mandaianum* (*P. hastatum* × *P. erubescens*) was developed by Manda in 1936 [16]. Since 1951, most of the outstanding philodendron breeding has been conducted by Bob McColley of Apopka,Florida, who has made twenty-five to thirty interspecific hybrids (including reciprocals), of which four or five have been accepted by the trade [16, 22]. Some of his more spectacular patented hybrids include 'Red Princess,' 'Emerald King,' 'Royal Queen,' 'Red Dutchess,' and 'Emerald Duke.' He classified philodendron into three groups based upon the sexual compatibility of the species [16]:

1. Aborescent or treelike plants (*P. selloum*).
2. Vines or "self-headers" (*P. wendlandii*).
3. Vines not crossable within or between sections (*P. scandens oxycardium*).

McColley hybridized species only within groups and not between them, with many species in the third group (such as *P. panduriforme*) being self-sterile. New cultivars from this program that have been recently developed include *Aglaonema* and *Dieffenbachia* hybrids to increase the variety and use of foliage plants.

Other aroid hybridization programs include work with *Zantedeschia* (calla lily) and *Anthurium,* although such programs can be called foliage breeding only technically since the objectives were to improve the modified leaf or spathe adjacent to or surrounding the spadix. The most complete work with calla lily is by Ryohitsu Shibuya of California [20], who studied the genetics of spathe color, leaf shape and size, corm size, pattern and distribution of leaf spots, and plant height and vigor, using three species (*Z. rehmannii, Z. albomaculata,* and *Z. elliottiana*) as parents. His most notable contribution was the finding that inheritance of anthocyanin and carotene pigmentation in the spathes was independent of each other, with both pigments controlled by multiple genes.

Anthurium species, many of which have very attractive leaves as well as colorful spathes, have been hybridized in Germany and Hawaii for at least 30 years. Many interspecific hybrids are reported, most of which have *A. andraeanum* (the commercial cut flower) as one parent. Research in Hawaii by Haryuki Kamemoto and his colleagues started in 1950 and has shown that a multiple allele system determines spathe color [9, 10]. R^r has been designated as the gene necessary for the production of the red pigment, R^o as the gene for orange, and rr as the white genotype. Genotypes of R^rR^r, R^rR^o, and R^rr are phenotypically red. R^oR^o is orange, rr is white, and R^or is coral pink. Modifying genes are involved in the expression of color intensity in the orange-coral pink series [10]. They also reviewed the inheritance of obake types, spadix color, double spathes, and sucker production [10, 11]. They have made interspecific hybrids among six species and are trying to improve leaf characteristics by crossing *A. andraeanum* with *A. crystallinum, A. warocqueanum,* and others of the velvety leaf group [10, 19]. This is also one of the few foliage programs where disease resistance is being considered [1, 11]. Breeding efforts on flowering foliage plants include hybridization with *Coleus* [18], *Begonia* [13], *Cordyline* [17], and *Dieffenbachia* [6].

Fern breeding has received less attention. A staghorn fern hybrid (*Platycerium* Cass hybrid) has been reported from Florida [5]. This was developed by Mr. Cass by combining spores of *P. grande, P. alcicorne, P. stemaria,* and *P. hillii,* resulting in a number of crosses [5]. Within the past five years, one intergeneric and several interspecific hybrids involving *Asplenium* have been reported [2, 3, 14, 15, 21]. These are *A. sollerense* (*A. majoricum* × *A. petrarchae*), *A. orelli* (*A. majoricum* × *A. trichomanes* subsp. *quadrivalens*), *A. litardierei* (*A. petrarchae* subsp. *petrarchae* × *A. trichomanes* subsp. *inexpectans*), *A. lessinense* (*A. fissum* × *A. viride*), and *Asplenoceterach barrancense* (*Asplenium majoricum* × *Ceterach officinarum*). This would indicate that species compatibility exists within many fern genera and ought to be pursued further by breeders to develop new genotypes.

Such a sparse list emphasizes the need for more hybridization of foliage plants. Growers should continue seeking sports in the large populations of plants raised, but this is a slow and often nonproductive undertaking. Breeders must utilize gene pools provided by nature to develop new plants for the industry.

Breeding Techniques

The majority of the plants grown as foliage plants are members of the Araceae family; thus, knowledge of breeding techniques used in this family is very important. Large numbers of foliage plants belong to other families, such as Agavaceae, Polypodiaceae, Lilaceae, Palmae, Bromeliaceae, Piperaceae, and Gesneriaceae. Techniques used in breeding these families differ from those used with the Araceae and will be discussed separately.

Flowers of Araceae are relatively small and may be bisexual or unisexual. Genera having bisexual flowers (e.g., *Anthurium*) have the entire spadix covered with flowers, whereas those having unisexual flowers (e.g., *Philodendron, Alocasia, Dieffenbachia*) have female flowers at the base of the spadix and male flowers at the apex. Usually, female flowers cover the lower one third of the spadix, and the males are positioned on the upper one third or two thirds of the spadix. The central portion of the spadix is sterile or covered with staminodes in plants where the male flowers cover only the upper one third of the spadix. Female flowers or the female portion of bisexual flowers are usually receptive one day before pollen is dehisced from male counterparts, which reduces the possibility of a flower being self-pollinated and ensures cross-pollination or sib-mating.

Techniques employed for breeding aroids depend on the type of inflorescence present. Two basic types are encountered. *Anthurium* will serve as an example of a plant with bisexual flowers on an exposed spadix (Figure 5-1), and *Philodendron* is a typical example of a genus with separate male and female flowers enclosed in a fleshy spathe (Figure 5-2).

Anthurium andraeanum, the anthurium of the florist's trade, has complete flowers on the exposed spadix, and although color and shape of the spathe and spadix may vary among species, the breeding technique is the same. The florescence will emerge from the leaf axil as new leaves mature, and at that time the spadix is enclosed in the leathery spathe. The spathe unfurls and exposes the spadix as the inflorescence matures and prior to the opening of the first flowers. Generally, the spadix will be yellow-orange overall as the spathe unfolds, but as the inflorescence develops and the basal flowers mature and start to open, the spadix begins to turn white at the base. The color change proceeds until the entire spadix is white as more and more flowers mature and open progressively toward the apex of the spadix. This transformation takes approximately two weeks, with new flowers maturing and opening each day. Stigmatic surfaces are receptive daily, and flowers that opened

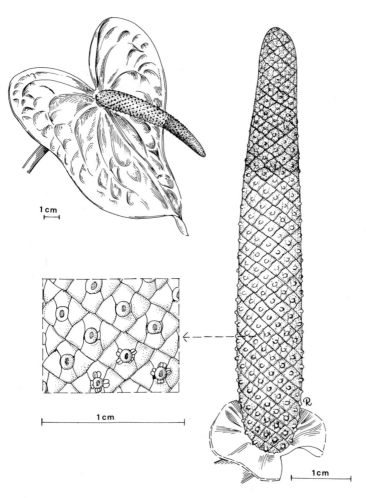

1 cm

1 cm

1 cm

Figure 5-1.   Vegetative and floral morphology of *Anthurium andraeanum*
(Araceae).

the day before will be shedding pollen. Pollination of *Anthurium* and
similar Araceae is relatively easy to perform at this time.

A decision as to whether to self-pollinate or cross-pollinate must be
made when considering pollination of this group. Self-pollination is a
simple task, since all that is needed is a small, fine camel's hair (or red
sable) paint brush. Each day the brush is gently brushed over the lower
area where the pollen is being dehisced and is drawn gently toward the
apex to bring fresh pollen in contact with the stigmatic surfaces of newly
opened flowers. Pollination will have to be repeated daily for 10 to 14
days to obtain a good seed set.

Some breeders pollinate *Anthurium* plants by gently stroking the spadix with thumb and forefinger from the base to the apex, but they must be extremely careful since too much pressure could damage the flowers or break the spadix. This technique also would have to be repeated daily for 10 to 14 days to assure a good seed set.

Crossing between different *Anthurium* species or genotypes is more difficult since anthers should be removed each day before they shed pollen. Afterward, the desired pollen can be applied to stigmatic sur-

Figure 5-2.   Vegetative and floral morphology of *Philodendron selloum* (Araceae).

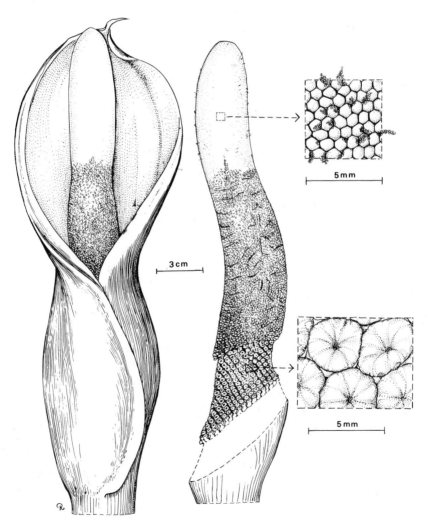

faces. If anthers are not emasculated, there is the possibility of pollen contamination and a selfed seedling would result.

Techniques used in breeding *Philodendron selloum,* which has its spadix enclosed in a fleshy spathe, are different from those employed in *Anthurium* breeding. The inflorescence arises from axils of leaves, and the spathe remains closed while flowers are maturing. The spathe opens for a short period of time when the female flowers are receptive and then closes, to open again, usually the following day, when male flowers are open and dehiscing pollen.

This short exposure period makes it imperative that breeders become familiar with the plant material to know when spathes will open. Many species have flowers that are receptive only at night, so those observing inflorescences only during the day may never see spathes open.

Spathes often shows signs of opening around 6:00 P.M. in nocturnal flowering species, which indicates inflorescences will be receptive later that night, with many receptive around 2:00 A.M.

A noticeable change in the temperature occurs within the spathe as female flowers approach receptability. The temperature change from 2° to 15°F (1° to 8°C) can be detected by placing the hand on unopened spathes. A spathe starting to unfurl during early evening which is warm to the touch a few hours later will have receptive female flowers that night.

The spathe should be removed when it unfurls to expose the spadix and especially the female flowers to make them readily accessible for pollination. Pollen from another inflorescence or from storage will have to be used for pollination since the male flowers will not be mature until the following evening. Pollen can be stored at 40°F (4°C) for 3 to 4 months in a sealed jar containing calcium chloride. The simplest method of pollinating flowers is to gently rub a fine camel's hair brush over stigmatic surfaces of female flowers. A small amount of stigmatic fluid will be transferred to the brush, making it slightly sticky and easier to pick up pollen. Dip the brush into the pollen and draw it again over the stigmatic surfaces of female flowers. Pollen should be applied to all flowers to ensure a good seed set.

The fruit will mature within 3 to 7 months after pollination, depending upon the species. All the fruit mature on a *Philodendron* spadix at approximately the same time, but *Anthurium* must be harvested over a 2- to 3-week period, relating to development of female flowers on the spadix at time of pollination.

Most Araceae seeds are enclosed in a fleshy, berry-type fruit. Seeds from a small number of fruit can be obtained by gently squeezing them out of the fruit just prior to planting. Large lots may be cleaned by putting fruit in a sieve or strainer and washing the pulp off by exposing them to a strong spray of water. The force of the water will break the skin of the fruit, wash the pulp through the sieve, and leave only the seeds.

Araceae seeds will germinate on a number of different media, but shredded tree fern, peat moss, and sphagnum moss are the most common ones used. The medium is placed either in a clay pot or standard greenhouse flat, depending on the number to be germinated. The medium should be 2 to 3 inches (5 to 7.5 centimeters) deep in the container. Seeds should be sprinkled on the surface of the medium and kept moist at all times to prevent drying. Moisture can be maintained by frequent misting or by covering containers with a sheet of glass. Once seedlings are large enough to handle, they should be transplanted into 2¼-inch (5.1-centimeter) pots for finishing. Plants generally will flower within 18 months of germination or up to a maximum of 3 years.

The Piperaceae family (*Peperomia*) has an inflorescence similar to that of *Anthurium,* except it is not subtended by a leafy bract. Morphologically, there are differences in the minute flowers, but the techniques used in breeding would be the same for both *Anthurium* and Piperaceae.

Most of the remaining plant families grown as foliage plants have relatively simple pollination systems, such as the Agavaceae (*Dracaena, Cordyline*), Bromeliaceae (*Aechmea, Cryptanthus*), and Acanthaceae (*Hemigraphis, Aphelandra*). The flowers are large enough in most cases so that various floral parts can be readily seen. Flowers to be selfed may be pollinated by taking an anther that is dehiscing pollen and gently rubbing it onto the stigmatic surface. Different techniques are used when different genotypes are to be crossed. First, select the flower to be used as the female parent and emasculate the anthers before pollen is dehisced; the flower is then ready for pollinating, assuming the stigmatic surface is receptive. Pollen from the desired male parent can be applied to the stigmatic surface of the female parent with a fine camel's hair brush. After pollination by either technique, flowers should be enclosed in a glassine or paper envelope or bag to prevent foreign pollen coming in contact with the stigmatic surface. If the style is long and strong, a small paper straw can be threaded over the stigma and style after pollination, and the distal end of the straw twisted to prevent foreign pollen from reaching the stigma. The envelope may be removed when fruit start to develop or may be left attached until fruit mature. The latter is often helpful, as the envelope will save any seed that dehisces from the pod if the breeder happens to overlook that fruit when it matures.

Palmae (*Chamaedorea, Rhapis*) plants have flowers that are relatively large and easy to handle as far as breeding is concerned, but a majority of the palms produce unisexual flowers, with few species having bisexual flowers. Species having unisexual flowers are generally monoecious, with only a few being dioecious. One must become familiar with the various types of inflorescences and arrangements of male and female flowers in order to breed palms. The sequence of floral opening must be observed to determine when pollen is shed and when stigmatic surfaces are receptive, but once these details are known, crosses can be made readily.

A technique for the cross hybridization of *Hoya* (Asclepiadaceae) has not been found. The authors have successfully selfed three clones, but have been unable to cross different genotypes.

The Polypodiaceae or fern family is the most difficult family to breed, and owing to their unique life cycles there are very few fern hybrids available today. Ferns have two life cycles, a gametophyte and a sporophyte generation. Plants sold as foliage plants or as seen in landscapes are members of the sporophyte generation and reproduce by spores. When mature spores are sown and germinate, they produce a prothallium, a very small, flat, green, mosslike structure, which is the gametophyte generation, and sexual reproduction takes place during this generation. Fertilization occurs, and the next sporophyte generation develops when the prothallium is still small. During the gametophyte stage, archegonium (eggs) and antheridium (pollen sacs) are formed on the prothallium. The antheridium produces mobile antherozoids, which swim to the archegonium and fertilize the eggs when the prothallium is covered with a film of water. Techniques must be developed to introduce desired antherozoids of one species or variety onto the prothallium of another species to produce hybrids. These must be introduced at the proper time to allow fertilization of egg cells before antherozoids of the female parent are released from the prothallium. This task is very exacting and difficult, so few people have been interested in breeding ferns.

Breeding Potential

The field of foliage plant breeding is still in its infancy. The few notable hybrids that have been produced are only the beginning: future possibilities are almost limitless. To attain these possibilities will require detailed studies of these plants, their sexual compatibility, and, eventually, of their genetics, but this can be done while new hybrids are being produced.

Those starting a breeding program with foliage plants cannot expect immediate success as results are slow. Several hundred crosses have been attempted with *Philodendron* alone, and over a million seeds were harvested and planted, but less than ten of these plants have become commercially acceptable [16]. Hybridization among species within a genus is not always successful, but the potential is there, since natural hybrids among species have been reported for almost all genera grown as foliage plants, including the ferns [5]. The authors have compiled a list of the chromosome counts of major spermatophytes grown as foliage plants and their allied species, which may be obtained by writing them individually. The chance of successful hybridization would probably be greatest by crossing species with a like chromosome number within a genus, but as the breeding program matures, crosses can be attempted among more diverse species.

Some areas in which breeding should be utilized include improving existing plants or developing hybrids adapted to very low light intensities. *Aglaonema* and *Aspidistra* are two genera that are in this category. If some of the basic characteristics of the *Aglaonema commutatum* complex could be combined with *A. modestum* (*A. simplex*), there could be interesting possibilities for colorful plants adapted to low light conditions. Developing dwarf or miniature forms of some of the more robust foliage plants is another area for breeding. For example, a diminutive form of *Monstera deliciosa* or *Philodendron selloum* for a table in a small room probably would be a very popular item. There are many other factors that could be considered, such as new leaf shapes (combining the heart-shaped leaf of *Hoya obovata* with the variegated leaves and short internodes of *Hoya carnosa*), intensified foliage color (red philodendrons that are adapted to low light areas), and more variegated plants (*Columnea*, *Ficus*).

Since many foliage plants are propagated vegetatively, another tool for rapid development of new plants is the use of irradiation (X ray, cobalt 60) or chemical mutagens to develop leaf chimeras, producing "sports" [4]. This is a method of accelerating chance natural mutation. Many of such mutants would be similar to variants already in existence, but the possibility exists for the development of a new variant. Irradiation of seed is the simplest method, but not necessarily the most productive for producing mutations. The authors have treated *Hoya darwinii*, *H. carnosa,* and *H. bandaensis* seed with X rays up to 16,000 roentgens (unpublished data), and many of the seeds at the highest rate produced albino plants or they failed to germinate. No obvious leaf chimera were observed at 4,000 roentgens, but a few were evident in the 8,000 roentgen treatments. If any irradiated plants produce fruit, some of the progeny may show mutant characteristics. Treatment of whole plants can achieve similar results, but generally this requires a large irradiation unit not often available to breeders. A small and easily handled amount of tissue can be irradiated with the advent of tissue culture [7, 12].

Excised stem tips or callus growing on standard nutrient medium in small test tubes could be treated in a small irradiator and the explants grown to maturity and evaluated for useful mutations.

All the aforementioned are possibilities, and with the guiding hands of competent plant breeders, they could soon become realities.

REFERENCES

[1] Aragaki, M., H. Kamemoto, and K. M. Maeda. 1968. Hawaii Agr. Exp. Sta. Tech. Prog. Rept. 169, 10 pp.

[2] Bennert, W., and D. W. Meyer. 1974. *Ber. Deut. Botan. Ges.* 87:21–28.

[3] ———. 1972. *Willdenowia* 6:461–470.

[4] Doorenbos, J., and J. J. Karper. 1975. *Euphytica* 24:13–19.

[5] Graf, A. B. 1970. *Exotica 3.* East Rutherford, N.J.: Roehrs Co., 1834 pp.

[6] Hartman, R. D., and F. W. Zettler. *Proc. Fla. State Hort. Soc.* 85:404–409.

[7] Hartman, R. D. *Phytopathology* 64(2):237–240.

[8] Hayward, W. 1950. *Plant Life* 6:131–142.

[9] Kamemoto, H., and H. Y. Nakasone. 1955. *Hawaii Farm Sci.* Jan. 1955: 4–5.

[10] ———, and M. Aragaki. *Proc. Am. Soc. Hort. Sci. Trop. Reg.* 12:267–273.

[11] ———, M. Aragaki, J. Kunisaki, and T. Higaki. 1975. *Proc. Am. Soc. Hort. Sci. Trop. Reg.* 19:269–274.

[12] Kunisaki, J. T. 1975. *HortScience* 10(6):601–602.

[13] Kusler, B. H. 1974. *Plants Gard.* 30(1):16–17.

[14] Lovis, J. D., and T. Reichstein. 1970. *Schweiz Botan. Ges. Ber.* 79:335–345.

[15] ———, A. Sleep, and T. Reichstein. 1970. *Schweiz Botan. Ges. Ber.* 79:369–376.

[16] McColley, R. H., and H. N. Miller. 1965. *Proc. Fla. State Hort. Soc.* 78:409–415.

[17] Moore, L. B. 1975. *New Zealand J. Bot.* 13:305–316.

[18] Reese, G. 1957. *Flora* 144:598–634.

[19] Sharma, B. R. 1961. *J. Ind. Botan. Soc.* 40:355–364.

[20] Shibata, K. 1962. *J. Agr. Sci. Tokyo Nogyo Daigaku* 8:49–62.

[21] Venkataswarlu, J., and N. R. Panugant. 1968. *Cytologia* 33:46–49.

[22] Watanabe, H. 1959. *Jap. J. Genet.* 34:162–167.

six

R. J. Henny
J. F. Knauss
A. Donnan, Jr.

foliage plant tissue culture

History

Plant tissue culture is the aseptic culture of plant tissue, such as protoplasts, cells, meristems, shoot tips, embryos, ovules, roots, or stem and leaf sections, in a vessel containing a microbe-free nutrient medium under environmental conditions suitable for plant development. The ability to study tissue and plant development under carefully controlled environmental conditions has led to the widespread employment of plant tissue culture as a commercial technique, and its use is increasing as more individuals become familiar with its potential benefits.

In 1902, G. Haberlandt was the first person to attempt to culture isolated plant cells [31, 82, 106]. He was unsuccessful in obtaining growth in his cultures, but stated that certain unidentified plant hormones were necessary for regulating cell division, growth, and differentiation. The first plant hormone to be identified was indoleacetic acid (IAA) in 1934 [54], and this opened the way to the discovery of many other hormone compounds important in the successful culture of plant tissue. The indefinite tissue culture of tomato roots was demonstrated in 1934 [116] and of tobacco callus in 1939 [117]. The addition of coconut milk to plant tissue culture media was found to stimulate the subsequent growth and development of the cultures [104, 113]. Investigations directed at discovering the active principle in coconut milk resulted in the discovery of the first cytokinin, kinetin, in 1956 [75].

Work on tobacco callus in 1957 [99] found that organogenesis was determined largely by concentrations of auxin and cytokinin in the tissue culture medium. High auxin levels induced root development and repressed shoot formation, while high cytokinin levels had the opposite effect. That the auxin to cytokinin balance has a major effect upon organogenesis has since been shown to be a general phenomenon.

The first extensive use of tissue culture for rapid propagation of ornamental plants was initiated by G. M. Morel with meristem culture to free cymbidium orchids of virus [78]. His interest as a pathologist was to eliminate virus by using the tissue culture method he devised, but astute readers of his report noted the multiplication potential of this technique. Thus, the orchid tissue culture industry was begun.

Today many individuals are involved in tissue culture studies of several ornamental crops, resulting in an increasing number of plants that can be cultured successfully. It is estimated that over 100 commercial tissue culture laboratories now operate in the United States.

Stages in Tissue Culture Development

Certain steps or stages must be completed in most commercial and research applications of plant tissue culture where eventual production of mature plants is the ultimate objective. The different steps are often referred to as stages I through IV [79]. This designation will be used in the following discussion.

Stage I, Initiation of the Tissue Cultures

The major objective of stage I is establishment of rapid developing, noncontaminated cultures that can be employed later in stage II. Stage I cultures are usually initiated with explants such as shoot tips, lateral buds, petiole or leaf sections, or other suitable plant parts, which must be determined by experimentation (Figure 6-1).

Contaminants in tissue cultures may adversely affect development, so they must be eliminated. Normally, this is accomplished through explant disinfestation by immersion in a chlorine-containing solution (usually with a surfactant added) or by dipping in a 70 to 95 percent alcohol solution. Further handling or cutting of explants from this point is done with sterile tools. Additional disinfestation may be required and is normally accomplished in more dilute chlorine solutions for shorter time periods to avoid injury to explants. Explants are normally rinsed several times in sterile deionized or distilled water after disinfestation.

Disinfestation usually eliminates the major source of contaminants

Figure 6-1. A single shoot tip of *Aglaonema* developing during Stage I of the tissue culture process.

that gain entrance into tissue cultures via the explant. Disinfestants have disadvantages since they can injure plant tissue and only eliminate surface contaminants. This presents problems if contaminants reside within internal tissues where disinfestants cannot penetrate. Where this occurs, placing the source plants in a cool, dry environment for several weeks before explant removal may assist in reducing contamination problems similar to those found for dieffenbachia [109]. Placing a glassine bag around tissue grown outdoors for a period prior to excision and disinfestation aids in reducing contaminant numbers. Any procedure that will keep plant tissue dry will probably reduce resident microbial populations.

A recent approach to establishing aseptic cultures is to develop plantlet lines in vitro that are indexed for microorganisms [109] and to maintain these in vitro as the explant source [19, 109]. Where this can be employed successfully, disadvantages of surface disinfestation can be eliminated. In this initial stage of development, light intensity and auxin-cytokinin levels are usually lower than in the next stage.

Stage II, Rapid Development of Tissue Cultures

Once tissues have developed sufficiently and are found contaminant free, they are transferred to this stage for rapid increase and development (Figure 6-2). Multiplication may involve formation of callus, from which adventitious organs or embryos develop, or stimulation of axillary shoot growth. The first method allows a faster increase in plantlet initials but can lead to production of genetically aberrant plants owing to reliance upon the callus stage of growth [79]. Plants developing from axillary buds are largely free from any genetic changes.

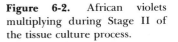

Figure 6-2. African violets multiplying during Stage II of the tissue culture process.

Stage III, Preparation of Plantlets for Greenhouse Development

Tissue cultured plantlets must be prepared for transfer to an in vivo environment after the rapid production of plantlets in stage II. Stage III is included in the process to achieve this objective. Stage II plantlets (usually unrooted) are transferred to stage III, where conditions have been adjusted to more closely simulate environments outside culture vessels. The shoot-promoting cytokinin is deleted or greatly reduced, and rooting is stimulated by inclusion of the proper auxin at a level to produce transplantable roots. Light intensity is increased two- to tenfold in preparation for greenhouse conditions. Plantlets persist in this stage from 2 to several weeks, often in large containers such as mason jars (Figure 6-3) or other similar vessels.

Stage III can consume relatively high levels of energy, which has stimulated several tissue culture laboratories to find ways of bypassing it. Some laboratories have placed stage III containers directly into the greenhouse environment for the period of adjustment. The time in culture before transplanting to soil is increased by several weeks when this is done. Some laboratories have eliminated stage III and successfully transferred stage II plantlets to the soil system where rooting and root development take place [26, 109].

Figure 6-3. Stage III culture of *Epipremnum aureum* (*Scindapsus aureus*).

Stage IV, Establishment in Soil

This stage in development has often caused the demise of otherwise successful tissue culture propagation programs. At this point in the tissue culture's development, plants are subject to drastic and somewhat hostile environmental changes compared to previous developmental history. The tissue cultures in stage IV are moved out of in vitro culture for the first time and planted in soil media under prevailing conditions in a growing structure such as a greenhouse. The greenhouse presents lower humidity and higher light intensity compared to conditions in the culture vessel. Tissue cultures may die or exhibit reduced subsequent development if compensation is not made for such drastic changes.

Newly planted tissue cultures must be covered with a facility to maintain various light and humidity levels and keep the temperature at an acceptable level for plant growth. Such cultures are particularly tender when first planted, and high humidity, reduced light, and moderate to warm temperatures must be maintained. The soil medium employed must be free of pathogens while providing sufficient soil aeration and moisture to stimulate rapid root development. The area employed may be as simple as a greenhouse bench covered with a plastic cover (Figure

Figure 6-4.   A protective structure for encasing plants after being transferred from Stage III tissue culture to soil.

6-4), as long as the preceding requirements are met and the area is free
of plant pathogens. A temperature sensor should be provided in the
adjustment area, and this should be connected to an alarm that will
arouse the proper personnel if temperatures approach levels that may
be injurious to the tissue culture plantlets.

One to several weeks after plantlets are in the adjustment area,
sufficient root development will have occurred to allow an increase in
light intensity and lowering of humidity. This should be done gradually
at first and continued until ambient conditions within the greenhouse
are reached. Use of pesticides during the adjustment period should be
discouraged. Should a special problem arise, however, use of the appropriate pesticide at one half the normally suggested concentration will
probably prove efficient and safe to plant tissues. Adjustment areas
should be cleaned and disinfested with appropriate compounds following each crop, after which they should be thoroughly rinsed prior to
placing plantlets in them to discourage buildup of potentially harmful
disinfestants.

No definite rules on the requirements and time of the adjustment
period are available, and tissue culturists should obtain help from others
or, in many cases, may have to work the details out for their own special
crops.

Laboratory and Culture Room Requirements

Tissue culture laboratories are of various designs and types of construction. A permanent facility with all activity areas under one roof is usually the most efficient; walls and roofs should be well insulated to reduce heating and cooling costs. Aerial contamination can be minimized by ensuring that the building is airtight and that all doors open outward. The laboratory should be conveniently located near water, gas, and electrical utility hookups. Objectives of a laboratory will dictate where the facility should be located. Laboratories that primarily do custom work and sell plants in stage III containers are more flexible in their location. Laboratories associated with nurseries are best located in close proximity to greenhouses where plants are to be transplanted into soil.

Most plant tissue culture facilities are divided into three major areas of activity: (1) glassware washing and media preparation area, (2) transfer room, and (3) culture or growth room. Easily accessible storage areas are also necessary. These activity areas should be located in separate rooms, yet blend together to allow efficient materials flow. The floor plan should allow entrance into the culture room without passing through the transfer room or the glassware washing and media preparation areas to reduce contamination. The activity areas should be on separate air-handling systems.

Equipment necessary for media preparation varies (Figure 6-5). Premixed formulations may be purchased from several commercial companies, or media can be made from basic ingredients and stock solutions. Analytical balances or less expensive units are employed to weigh media ingredients, and pH of the media is adjusted and measured using a pH meter that should be sensitive to 0.1 pH units. Tap water may be used in preparing media. In some instances, however, it may be necessary to have a source of deionized or distilled water if tap water has a high level of impurities. A source of heat is necessary to dissolve media ingredients, such as sucrose and agar, and a mechanical stirrer to agitate and prevent overheating is helpful when working with large quantities of media. Depending upon laboratory size, pressure cookers or commercial autoclaves can be used to sterilize media. Media may be dispensed in a variety of ways, such as pouring individual tubes or utilizing automatic dispensers.

Most laboratories use glass containers as culture vessels, which must be washed by hand or in a mechanical dishwasher. Commercial units or those designed for home use are satisfactory. A rinse in dilute acid followed by a rinse in distilled or deionized water may be advisable in addition to normal washing. Activities performed in these areas are

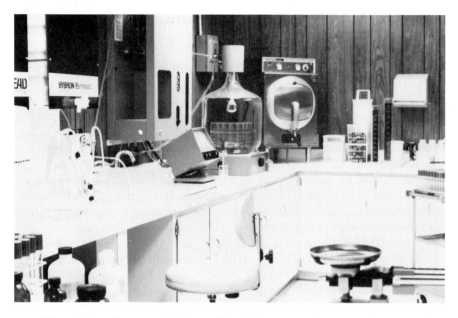

Figure 6-5.   A commercial tissue culture laboratory media preparation area and equipment.

Figure 6-6.   Laboratory worker dividing and transferring Stage II tissue culture plantlets.

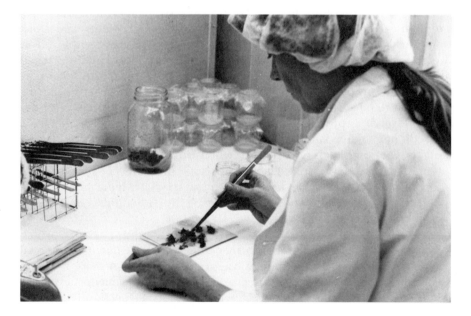

usually nonsterile and generate large amounts of heat, making it necessary to have a separate air-handling system.

The primary activity in the transfer room involves initiation of cultures or transferring cultures to fresh media (Figure 6-6). This work should be performed under laminar flow transfer hoods equipped with high efficiency particulate air (HEPA) filters to reduce rates of aerial contamination. A wide range of models is available from several suppliers. Under certain conditions, glove boxes or other commercially available transfer hoods may provide acceptable results.

The transfer room should have a separate air-handling system with provisions to exhaust fumes from disinfesting agents. The room should be provided with adequate electrical outlets and a supply of commercial gas, and have transfer hoods easily accessible to allow for efficient materials flow (Figure 6-7). Storage of media should be near hoods on permanent shelves or mobile carts.

The culture or growth room is in reality a large growth chamber. Construction should include ceilings, walls, and floors that are airtight, easy to clean, reflective to light, and well insulated. Adequate air circulation is necessary to eliminate dead spots where warmer temperatures occur and aerial contamination may be high. Several commercial laboratories have used horizontal air flow to correct this situation. Air exchange rates of once per 3 minutes may be necessary [70]. Filtration

Figure 6-7. Transfer room of a commercial tissue culture laboratory showing easy access to transfer hood, carts for media hauling, and separate culture room.

Figure 6-8.   Culture room of a commercial tissue culture laboratory.

may be provided by commercial furnace filters or air-cleaning units equipped with HEPA or similar filters. Individual air-quality standards will determine the amount of filtration necessary.

Humidity levels in growth rooms vary considerably. A variation between light and dark periods will occur, as well as the normal removal of moisture from air during cooling or heating cycles. Normal relative humidity will be approximately 30 to 50 percent at temperatures between 15° and 30°C unless moisture is added to the air [58]. Long-term cultures may suffer from dehydration and high salt levels in the medium unless water baths or humidifiers are used to increase relative humidity. Increased moisture levels may lead to greater amounts of contamination and will necessitate additional air conditioning to accommodate the latent heat of moisture.

Control of light intensity, duration, and quality is necessary. Light intensity may be varied by altering the distance between the shelves, the number of fixtures per unit area of shelf, or the type of fixture used. In some cases a rheostat may be used but is costly owing to special wiring and ballasts. Different plants have specific light requirements that vary from 1,000 to 10,000 lux for various stages of growth [79]. Most laboratories maintain a 16-hour photoperiod using cool white or Gro Lux fluorescent lights. Little information exists on effects of light quality on plant tissue cultures.

Normal culture room temperatures should range from 21° to 30°C, although lower temperatures may be necessary for certain plants [6], whereas a day-night fluctuation may be necessary for others [105]. Light ballasts should be placed outside the culture room to reduce heat loads. A thermostatically controlled system to shut off culture room lights and initiate an alarm when temperatures go above a present point is advisable. Safeguards against low temperatures should also be installed, although this problem is less likely to occur.

Shelf design and construction will vary with individual laboratories and even within a facility, with shelves normally 16 to 18 inches apart. Shelf areas should be designed for easy and constant observation of cultures (Figure 6-8), utilizing as much space as possible. Shelves may be of solid construction such as plywood or have perforations to allow air circulation.

Cost of Commercial Laboratory Operation

The objective of any tissue culture laboratory should be to produce uniform plants of a selected genotype at an economical cost. Selection of the proper plant, utilization of trained personnel, availability of capital, and the development of a successful marketing plan are essential before a commercial plant tissue culture laboratory can become a useful tool in a nursery operation. Initial capital investments vary depending upon a laboratory's size and purpose and can range from $20,000 to $250,000 [34].

The largest single cost factor of tissue culture produced plants is labor. In one case, wages and supervisory salaries amounted to 65.9 percent of the total cost of producing *Brassica oleracea* [2]. Other experience [26] has shown that wages, salaries, and associated costs amount to approximately 60% of the total operation cost of a commercial tissue culture facility. Other studies [11, 83] have shown a wide range in production costs on a per plant basis.

It has been demonstrated [34] that initial costs associated with the production of a specific plant are high owing to large labor costs involved with handling the initial explant and losses due to contamination in the establishment phase. As multiplication occurs and repeated subculturing is used, the cost curve moves downward and reaches a relatively stable level (Figure 6-9).

The overall production and marketing scheme of a laboratory will have a bearing on operating costs. Laboratories that utilize large numbers of personnel and have high operating costs require the production

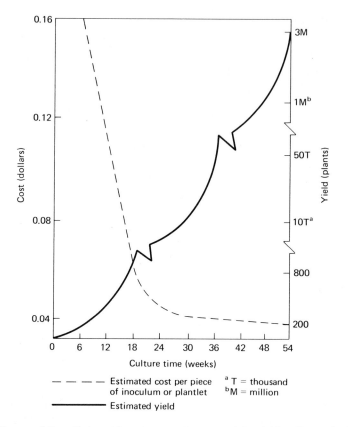

Figure 6-9. Estimated cost versus potential yield of producing *Spathiphyllum* using tissue culture [34].

of tremendous numbers of plants before the facility can operate at optimum cost efficiency.

Labor-saving methods such as mechanical homogenization, suspension culture, or the modification or elimination of labor-intensive procedures become necessary since labor is such a critical factor in commercial plant tissue culture. Eliminating the rooting of plants in vitro made it possible to reduce labor costs associated with *Ficus* and *Begonia* production by 56 and 37 percent, respectively [26]. Direct rooting in soil in the greenhouse may be applied to a large number of plants.

Accurate and diligent record keeping is necessary to make meaningful cost comparisons. A number of commercial plant tissue culture laboratories have indicated the advantages of specializing in a few product lines rather than producing many different types. A successful laboratory is one that has been able to integrate its product into the normal nursery production. Anticipating market demands requires the attention of all personnel involved in such a venture.

Media Components and Preparation

The choice of selecting a nutrient medium for a particular plant is difficult. A medium may be selected based on a literature search or on personal experience with crops similar to the one under study. Another method is to try several of the well-known media or a modification of them. The third approach is the most time consuming and requires a certain expertise since it incorporates a systematic way of determining the need for various ingredients in a nutrient medium. Probably the most extensive systematic method is the *broad spectrum experiment* [24].

Ingredients of plant tissue culture media can be categorized as (1) inorganic salts, (2) organic compounds, (3) complex natural preparation, and (4) inert supportive substances.

Several inorganic salt formulations or modifications thereof meet most requirements for plant growth [30, 52, 53, 60, 84, 86, 95, 118]. Specific elements for some commonly used salt formulations are shown in Table 6-1. A more complete summary of the composition of fifteen different inorganic salt formulations was published in 1976 [41].

The major categories of organic compounds are carbohydrates,

TABLE 6-1 Inorganic salt mixtures commonly used in plant tissue culture (milligrams per liter)

	Knudson [52]	Murashige and Skoog [84]	Schenk and Hildebrandt [95]	White [119]
NH_4NO_3	—	1,650	—	—
$NH_4H_2PO_4$	—	—	300	—
$(NH_4)_2SO_4$	500	—	—	—
H_3BO_3	—	6.2	5.0	1.5
$CaCl_2 \cdot 2H_2O$	—	440	200	—
$Ca(NO_3)_2 \cdot 4H_2O$	1,000	—	—	300
$CoCl_2 \cdot 6H_2O$	—	0.025	0.1	—
$CuSO_4 \cdot 5H_2O$		0.025	0.2	—
$Fe_2(SO_4)_2$	—	—	—	2.5
$FeSO_4 \cdot 7H_2O$	25	27.8	15	—
$MgSO_4 \cdot 7H_2O$	250	370	400	720
$MnSO_4 \cdot H_2O$	—	16.9	10.0	—
$MnSO_4 \cdot 4H_2O$	7.5	—	—	7.0
KCl	—	—	—	65
KI	—	0.83	1.0	0.75
KNO_3	—	1,900	2,500	80.0
KH_2PO_4	250	170	—	—
Na_2-EDTA	—	37.3	20	—
$Na_2MoO_4 \cdot 2H_2O$	—	0.25	0.1	—
$NaH_2PO_4 \cdot H_2O$	—	—	—	16.5
Na_2SO_4	—	—	—	200
$ZnSO_4 \cdot 7H_2O$	—	8.6	1.0	3.0

vitamins, and hormonal substances. Sucrose in concentrations of 2 to 3 percent is the most commonly employed carbohydrate, although glucose and fructose may be used in specific situations.

Many vitamins have been used in various nutrient media formulations (Table 6-2), but thiamine is the only one that has consistently been shown to be important. Other compounds elicit specific growth responses or, in the case of ascorbic and citric acid, may be included to retard oxidation of plant tissue.

Auxins and cytokinins are probably the most important organic components of a nutrient medium. These compounds (Table 6-3) will produce varied effects depending upon the type of compound and the· concentration. Normal auxin concentrations will range from 0.1 to 10 milligrams per liter and cytokinin concentrations from 0.03 to 30 milligrams per liter [79]. Auxins differ in activity, stability, and cost. IAA is the weakest but most commonly used auxin. In some cases two auxins or cytokinins may be used in the same media [14]. Of the cytokinins, 2iP is the most costly and most active. Gibberellins are often incorporated in media used to recover pathogen-free plant tissue.

Other organic compounds often included in plant tissue culture nutrient media are amino acids and amides, hexitols, and adenine or adenine sulfate. At least twenty-one amino acids and amides have been used in specific plant tissue culture formulations, with the L-isomer of these compounds being preferred. Inositol at a concentration of 100 milligrams per liter has been shown to be beneficial, but not necessary, for plant growth. Adenine or adenine sulfate has been shown to have varying effects on shoot formation [76].

Many substances that are chemically undefined are used in plant tissue culture media. These materials should be used only as a last resort since they are variable from batch to batch or when sources are changed. Commonly used materials include banana pulp, coconut extract, fish emulsion, and malt or yeast extract.

Inert supportive materials include things such as agar, charcoal, various gels, glass wool, and filter paper. Agar is most often used as a supportive agent for plant tissue culture media. Care should be taken to

TABLE 6-2 Vitamins for plant tissue culture nutrient media [41]

p-Aminobenzoic acid	Folic acid
Ascorbic acid	Nicotinic acid
Biotin	Pyridoxine hydrochloride
Calcium pantothenate	Riboflavin
Choline chloride	Thiamine hydrochloride
Cyanocobalamin	

TABLE 6-3   Auxins and cytokinins commonly included in plant tissue culture nutrient media

Auxin	Cytokinin
3-Indoleacetic acid (IAA)	N^6-Benzylaminopurine (BA)
3-Indolebutyric acid (IBA)	N^6-[Δ^2-Isopentenyl]-adenine (2iP)
1-Napthaleneacetic acid (NAA)	
(2,4-Dichlorophenoxy)acetic acid (2,4-D)	N^6-Furfurylaminopurine (kinetin)

determine the quality of different batches or sources of agar. Glass wool or filter paper bridges are used as platforms to support plant tissue when culture medium is a liquid. Charcoal at low concentrations will sometimes retard the inhibiting effects of certain substances in a medium and allow normal organogenesis to occur. Excessive concentrations can have adverse effects upon the activity of desired compounds [17].

Nutrient media may be bought premixed from commercial companies or made from individual ingredients. Commercial premixes are advantageous when large numbers of one plant type are being produced. Most premixes need only be dissolved in water, have their pH adjusted and agar added if desired, dispensed, and sterilized. Premixes may only include basic ingredients such as inorganic salts, vitamins, and sucrose. Hormones and other addenda may be added from stock solutions.

The second method of media preparation is from individual ingredients or stock solutions. Stocks of inorganic salts should be prepared by combining only those that do not coprecipitate. Organic compounds may be dissolved in water or, for those which are relatively insoluble, a solvent such as dimethyl sulfoxide (DMSO) may be required. Owing to possible phytotoxicity, a final concentration of 0.5 percent of DMSO should not be exceeded. Cytokinins may be dissolved in dilute hydrochloric acid (HCl) and auxins in dilute potassium hydroxide (KOH). The employment of 0.3 milliliters of the required solvent is usually sufficient to dissolve 10 milligrams of auxin or cytokinin.

The pH of the medium is adjusted with dilute HCl or KOH or sodium hydroxide (NaOH) before addition of agar. A pH in the range of 4.8 to 6.0 has been generally used, although agar may not gel properly at the lower values.

Agar is dissolved with heat and requires constant agitation to prevent burning. The media is normally sterilized by autoclaving 10 to 20 minutes at 121°C (250°F) at 15 pounds per square inch. Heat-labile compounds may be added to the nutrient medium with the use of a membrane filter when the temperature of the medium has cooled to 35° to 40°C.

Foliage Plants in Tissue Culture

A representative sample of foliage plants produced in tissue culture and the techniques involved are presented. Each plant or plants listed and the reference cited is followed by a summary of the procedures used for propagation. For some plants, more than one method is detailed. At the end of each discussion, additional pertinent references concerning the same or related genera, species, or cultivars are listed along with other plants cultured using the same techniques. All concentrations of media components are given in milligrams per liter unless stated otherwise, and explanations of the abbreviations are listed at the end of the discussion.

Adiantum Tenerum [50]

Fern spores are disinfested in sterile distilled water containing 2 percent Clorox and centrifuged to form a retrievable pellet. Spore pellets were suspended in sterile water and again centrifuged. This process was repeated two more times. Resuspended spores after last washing were streaked onto a cultured medium containing MS salts, sucrose (3 percent), T-HCl (0.4), agar (0.8), and at pH 5.7. Cultures were incubated for 16 hours daily under Gro Lux (1,000 lux) lights at 27°C. After 20 days, gametophytic growth was established, and tissue was divided, subcultured, and left to develop another 30 days. Sporophytic tissue that developed was discarded. One gram of gametophytic tissue was placed in 200 milliliters of MS salts (half-strength) and ground in a Waring blender for 5 seconds. Approximately 50 milliliters of solution was poured over the surface of sterile soil consisting of two parts Florida peat to one part coarse builder's sand amended with 7 pounds of dolomite limestone per cubic yard (4.2 kilograms per cubic meter) in new 4-inch (10.2-centimeter) plastic pots. Pots were sealed in plastic bags and watered by subirrigation. Plastic covers were removed after approximately 30 days and pots placed under intermittent mist for 3 weeks, and then fertilized with MS salts (half-strength) initially, and later with 20-20-20 at (0.25 pound per 100 gallon) (29.9 grams per 100 liters). The sporophytes reached salable size within another 30 to 60 days. More sporophytes than could be counted were formed in each pot using this method. This technique reduced the number of manual transfers compared to normal tissue culture procedures, as well as effectively eliminated known pathogens from propagative material.

Platycerium bifurcatum, Pteris ensiformis, leatherleaf, bear's claw, and bird's nest ferns appear to be adaptable to the same culture system.

Aechmea Fasciata [44]

Shoot tips were removed and placed in a solution of ascorbic acid (100.0) and citric acid (150) to prevent discoloration. Shoot tips were initiated in liquid medium of MS salts, sucrose (2 percent), NA (0.5), T-HCl (0.1), Gly (2.0), IBA (1.75), at pH 5.0, and rotated at 1 revolution per minute on a Brunswick roller drum apparatus. After 4 weeks enlarged shoot tips were transferred to stage II multiplication medium consisting of MS salts, sucrose (3 percent), NaP (85), AS (40), T-HCl (0.4), *i*-inositol (100), IAA (2.0), and Kin (2.0). After 6 weeks, clumps of new developing shoots were divided and moved to stage III medium of MS salts, sucrose (3 percent), T-HCl (0.4), *i*-inositol (100), and IAA (2.0). All cultures were held at 26° to 27°C with 16 hours of 1,000-lux light from Gro Lux lamps. Plants from stage III were rooted as small cuttings and moved into standard nursery practice.

This technique also proved successful with *Ananas comosus* 'Smooth Cayenne,' *Cryptanthus bivittatus* 'Cafe au lait,' *C.* 'Star,' *Cryptbergia meadii, Dyckia sulphurea,* and *Guzmania* 'Hummel's Supreme.'

Additional references   [64, 72, 120]

Anthurium Andraeanum [91]

Embryos were dissected and placed on half-strength MS salts, MS microelements, sucrose (3 percent), MS organic constituents (except edamin, IAA, and Kin), agar (0.7 percent), and at pH 5.8. Callus growth was slow initially and few embryos formed callus in dark at 25°C. PBA (1.0) induced callus growth. Some sprouts developed in dark, but were greatly stimulated after transfer of callus to constant fluorescent light (PL40W/57) at 25°C. (Note: PL40W/57 is a model number that means Philips Light 40 Watt/57 centimeters.) Subcultured sections of new sprouts yielded callus if PBA (0.5 to 1.0) was added and tissue incubated in dark. Callus further proliferated in 100 milliliters of liquid medium plus PBA (1.0) in 300-milliliter bottles rotated 120 revolutions per minute in dark. In addition to embryos, callus was obtained from leaf, spathe, petiole, and pedicel explants using the same basal medium plus PBA (1.0 to 5.0) and glucose (4 percent) instead of sucrose. Sprout development was again enhanced by transfer from dark to light at 25°C. Variations in callus production were observed between seedling and plant lines due to differing genetic makeup.

Additional references   [88, 89, 90]

Begonia Semperflorens [96]

Leaf and petiole segments were placed on modified WH medium with sucrose (2 percent) and agar (0.8 percent) at pH 5.8. Explants formed adventitious buds and embryolike structures when Kin (1.0) and CH (100) were added to basal medium. Cultures were incubated at 25°C and 55 percent relative humidity in diffuse daylight (intensity not stated). Response of both leaf and petiole sections was similar. Results of several other hormone combinations are also given. In general, auxin favored root formation and Kin induced adventitious buds.

Additional references   [4, 28, 74, 110, 115]

Caladium × Hortulanum [33]

Shoot tips were placed on a revised MS medium with edamin omitted and meso-inositol replacing myo-inositol. The agar was lowered to 0.8 percent and Kin (1.0) and IAA (15.0) were present. Material was incubated at 21° to 25°C with 12-hour light (7,500 lux) from a combination of incandescent and cool white fluorescent (CWF) bulbs. After 8 weeks of culture, excised shoot tips turned green and developed callus masses from which numerous shoot buds differentiated. After 18 weeks, plantlets with shoots and roots developed from shoot buds. This method was successful with *Colocasia esculenta* and *Xanthosoma sagittifolium*.

Additional reference   [1]

Coffea Arabica [38]

Leaf segments with portion of blade and lateral veins were placed on Staritsky medium [102] containing Kin (0.1) and 2,4-D (0.1) and were cultured in dark for 16 hours at 30°C and 8 hours at 25°C. Callus slowly formed, and after 60 days organoids formed on the edge of callus. Organoids were transferred to 16 hours (5,300 lux) of CWF light but did not develop into complete plantlets on Staritsky medium. The transfer of organoids to GD medium with NAA (0.1) resulted in root initiation after 60 days. After 4 months, light was increased to 10,000 lux, which increased plant growth rate. Plantlets were successfully transferred to sterile soil after 7 months total incubation.

Additional references   [101, 102, 111]

Cordyline Terminalis [73]

Shoot apices (3 millimeters) were placed on MS salts plus T-HCl (1.0), myo-inositol (100), sucrose (2 percent), 2,4-D (3.0), coconut water (10 percent by volume), and agar (0.9 percent) at pH 5.6. Cultures were incubated at 28° to 30°C at 1,000 lux continuous lighting (Gro Lux). Callus formed on cut surface of shoot apices in 2 to 4 weeks. The largest number of plants was produced if callus growth was maintained by transferring at monthly intervals two to three times on basal medium, and then allowed to differentiate on the same medium minus 2,4-D. No roots were induced by 2,4-D, whereas addition of NAA (5.0) improved root growth. Each shoot apex yielded 200 to 300 plants after 3 months callus growth and differentiation.

Additional references   [21, 22, 56, 62, 76].

Cryptanthus Bivittatus 'Minor' [20]

Buds were removed, placed in citric acid (150), sterilized, and placed in a liquid stage I medium containing MS salts, T-HCl (0.4), i-inositol (100), AS (80), NaP (170), citric acid (150), sucrose (3 percent), IAA (2.0), and Kin (2.0). Cultures were placed on a rotating wheel at 1 revolution per minute under 16-hour daily CWF light (750 lux) at 27°C for 4 to 6 weeks. For multiplication, buds were removed and placed in stationary culture in the same medium in larger containers. Incubation during the multiplication stage was at a higher CWF light level (3,000 lux) than initially. Every 4 weeks, cultures were subcultured by removing and transferring dominant shoots to stage III medium. Remaining callus and small shoots were returned to fresh stage II medium. Stage III cultures were grown in the same medium as stages I and II, except IAA was replaced by NAA (1.0) and agar (0.8 percent) was added. Light levels were at 9,000 lux 16 hours daily at 27°C. Forty stage III plantlets were grown per 946-milliliter mason jar for 5 to 6 weeks before being transferred to soil in a saran greenhouse. One mother plant with 25 buds yielded 10,000 plantlets in 10 months using these techniques.

Dracaena Deremensis 'Warneckii' [21]

Stem explants with dormant eye were cultivated on MS major elements (half-strength), NN minor elements, and sucrose (2 percent), agar (0.6 percent), at pH 5.8, and incubated with 17 hours of CWF fluorescent light daily (3,500 lux) at 22°C. Different levels of NOA, IBA, NAA, and 2,4-D were tested alone or in combination with Kin, 2iP, or BA. IBA (2.0) proved the best auxin for root induction. Callus formed from explants and differentiated into plantlets best with NOA or IBA (1.0) plus Kin or 2iP (1.0, 2.0, or 5.0). Plantlets developed also on callus pieces subcultured in media containing NOA (1.0) and Kin (5.0). Plantlets rooted best in medium with IBA (2.0) only. Approximately 90 percent of plantlets developed were of the parental type maintaining the normal chimeral structure, while 10 percent had a varied chimeral nature. Leaf tissue explants showed no response in culture.

Additional references   [22, 76]

Dieffenbachia maculata 'Perfection' [49]

This study details methods for developing single plantlets of dieffenbachia. Lateral buds and shoot tips (1 to 3 millimeters) developed into plants on medium of MS salts, sucrose (3 percent), agar (0.6 to 0.8 percent), T-HCl (0.4), i-inositol (100), NA (0.5), P-HCl (0.5), Gly (2.0), AS (80), NaP (170), IAA (0.1), plus either 2iP or Kin (0.1) at pH 5.7 to 5.8. Incubation was at 27°C with 16-hour light (1,000 lux) from Gro Lux fluorescent tubes. Plantlets developed on medium to sufficient size to be indexed.

Dieffenbachia maculata 'Perfection' [109]

Shoot tips (2 centimeters) taken from stock lines of known pathogen-free plantlets held in vitro were brought into active growth on a medium of MS salts, sucrose (3 percent), T-HCl (0.4), i-inositol (100), AS (80), NaP (170), agar (0.6 percent), IAA (2.0), 2iP (16.0) at pH 5.7. Cultures were maintained at 27°C with 16 hours of 1,000-lux Gro Lux light daily. After 30 to 40 days the dominant shoot was separated from its enlarged basal section, and both explants were put on fresh medium identical to the previous step. Within 30 to 45 days shoots developed from the basal section and were transferred to baby-food jars in a stationary liquid medium the same as above except Kin (2.0) replaced both IAA and 2iP and pH at 5.0. Shoots from this step and the previous step were placed back into the initial culture stage to serve as fresh explant source. After 30 to 60 days, more cuttings were removed from the expanding basal clump and rooted directly in sterilized soil or put back into step I of this procedure. A second flush of shoots formed on the remaining tissue within another 30 days of culture. Lateral buds (active or dormant) were not applicable to this procedure. Using these methods, it is theoretically possible to produce up to 70,000 cuttings or more per year.

Additional reference   [61]

Epipremnum Aureum (Scindapsus Aureus) [40]

Explants from the first and second nodes were cultured on MS major elements plus $MnSO_4 \cdot 4H_2O$ (25.8), KI (1.0), H_3BO_4 (10.0), $NaMoO_4 \cdot 2H_2O$ (0.25), $ZnSO_4 \cdot 4H_2O$ (10.0), $CuSO_4 \cdot 5H_2O$ (0.025), $CoCl_2 \cdot 6H_2O$ (0.025) as minor elements, plus Gly (2.0), myo-inositol (100), NA (5.0), P-HCl (0.5), T-HCl (0.5), biotin (0.05), folic acid (0.5), sucrose (2 percent), and agar (0.8 percent). Light was continuous from cool white fluorescent lamps (2,500 lux). Multiple shoot formation occurred when BA (10.0) was added to basal medium. Subcultured shoots elongated in medium with BA (1.0) and rooted when transferred to medium with NAA (1.0). This method was also successful with *Philodendron scandens oxycardium, Philodendron lacerum, Spathiphyllum* 'Clevelandii,' *Alocasia cucullata, Asparagus myriocladus* (failed to form roots, however), and *Zingiber officinale*.

Episcia Cupreata [42]

Explants (1 square centimeter) from mature leaves were cultured on MS salts and addenda plus several levels of Kin, IAA, and NAA under Gro Lux lamps (3,000 lux) with 16-hour photoperiod at 30°C. After 6 to 8 weeks of culture, callus and twenty to thirty shoots were formed on each leaf section on medium with Kin (0.2) and IAA (0.2). Reculturing callus in large containers produced several hundred more new shoots. Shoots 0.5 centimeter in length rooted in 1 to 2 weeks in MS medium with NAA (0.1 to 1.0). IAA did not induce root formation.

Additional reference   [9]

Ficus Benjamina [63]

Shoot tips (3 to 5 millimeters) were placed on MS salts with sucrose (3 percent), T-HCl (0.4), *i*-inositol (100), AS (80), NaP (170), IAA (0.3), and 2iP (30.0). Stages I and II were cultured at 1,000-lux Gro Lux light 16 hours daily at 27°C. New shoots were transferred to the same medium each 4 to 8 weeks. Rooting of shoots was also in the same medium minus IAA, 2iP, AS, and NaP. Adding activated charcoal (0.1 to 0.3 percent) appeared to be beneficial to rooting. Light at 7,000 to 10,000 lux was used for rooting and hardening before transplanting. These techniques also worked with *Ficus decora* 'Elastica' and *F. pandurata.*

Additional reference   [23]

Mammillaria Woodsii [68]

Plant tissue from 2-year-old plants was placed on solid MS medium containing IAA (2.0) and Kin (2.0) and incubated at 25°C in constant CWF light. Some cultures produced enough callus to be subcultured after 5 weeks. After 10 weeks of subculture on the same medium several shoots developed in some cultures. New shoots 1 centimeter long then rooted within 4 weeks in perlite. It was suggested that the addition of 2,4-D (no rate given) to culture media increased callus production.

Additional references   [43, 67]

Nephrolepsis exaltata bostoniensis [32]

Stage I cultures were initiated with shoot tip explants from rhizomes, runners, and crowns placed in MS salts with T-HCl (0.4), *i*-inositol (100), sucrose (3 percent), and agar (0.8 percent) at pH of 5.7 and incubated at 27°C with 16-hour daily light (1,000 lux) from Gro Lux lamps. In multiplication, explants from stage I cultures were placed on the same medium, except NaP (255), Kin (2.0), and NAA (0.1) were added. Light intensity was raised to 3,000 lux in stages II and III. Stage III cultures employed stage I medium. This method was also successful with *Microlepia strigosa, Adiantum cuneatum, Alsophila australis, Woodwardia fimbriata,* and several other ferns.

Additional references   [12, 13, 15]

Peperomia 'Red Ripple' [37]

Leaf discs were incubated on SH medium with sucrose (3 percent) and agar (0.6 percent) under 16-hour cool white fluorescent light (1,000 lux) per day at 27°C. Optimum shoot formation occurred with the addition of three concentrations of Kin (10.0, 5.0, or 2.5) in combination with NAA (0.05) or Kin (10.0) with NAA (0.5). Over fifty shoots were formed per leaf disc after 10 weeks. Roots were induced in 3 weeks using a mixture of Kin (0.01) and NAA (0.05) in the same basal liquid media shaken at 80 revolutions per minute in 50-milliliter flasks.

Additional references   [8, 35, 55]

Peperomia Scandens [55]

Leaf sections from fully developed leaves were placed on a medium of MS salts (minus edamin) at pH 6.0 with agar (concentration not given). Cultures were incubated at 22 to 24°C with continuous light (2,700 lux). No shoots developed on control medium without hormones after 16 weeks. In general, Kin (1.0 or 4.0) induced shoots and inhibited root formation, while IAA (2.0) produced roots only, and 2,4-D (1.0) induced a few shoots whose growth was inhibited. NAA (1.0 or 2.0) was the most effective auxin for regeneration of shoots and roots. Optimum regeneration of new shoots occurred in medium with Kin (4.0) and NAA (2.0).

Cultures initiated during the spring or summer yielded more shoots than those initiated from explants taken during winter. Leaf sections from basal leaf and petiole area produced more shoots than those from lateral parts of the leaf blade.

Additional references   [8, 35, 37]

Platycerium Stemaria [36]

Shoot tips were placed on MS salts plus T-HCl (0.4), P-HCl (1.0), NA (1.0), NaP (170), AS (80), sucrose (3 percent), agar (0.8 percent), and IAA (15.0). Cultures were incubated under 14-hour daily cool white fluorescent light (2,700 to 3,200 lux) at 25.5°C. After 35 days, frond development was obvious, and within 8 weeks two fronds and numerous shoot primordia were produced around the base. Initial explants were subcultured after 3 months, and subsequent transfers were made every 2 to 4 weeks thereafter. Cultures formed many shoots and relatively few roots. Roots would form, however, if the bases of the tubes were shielded from the light. This technique was also successful with *Platycerium wandae*, *P. veitchii*, and *P. wallichii*.

Saintpaulia Ionantha [16]

Leaf sections (10 square millimeters) were placed on MS salts plus sucrose (3 percent), NaP (170), inositol (100), T-HCl, P-HCl, and niacin each 0.4, with IAA (2.0), BA (0.8), and agar (0.9). Incubation was at 27°C with 1,000-lux Gro Lux light 16 hours daily. The same medium was used for stages I and II. Shoot production occurred within 30 days and multiple shoots after 60 days. Rooting occurred in the same medium minus IAA and BA at 10,000-lux cool white fluorescent light.

Additional references   [10, 27, 103]

Spathiphyllum Floribundum 'Clevelandii' [108]

Lateral buds and terminal shoots from the crown area were placed on two-thirds strength MS salts plus sucrose (3 percent), inositol (100), T-HCl (0.4), and agar (0.5 percent) (R. E. Strode, personal communication). Culture was at 1,000 lux for 16 hours daily at 27°C. Fifteen shoots developed per explant in 12 to 16 weeks, and from each subsequent subculture at 6-week intervals. Plants were rooted in the same medium except sucrose (4.5 percent) and IBA (15.0) were added and light was at 5,000 lux. Roots developed in 4 weeks.

Additional reference   [40]

Syngonium Podophyllum [76]

Shoot tips and lateral buds were cultured in liquid MS salts plus sucrose (3 percent), i-inositol (100), T-HCl (0.4), NaP (340), IAA (1.0), 2iP (3.0), and pH 5.0. The medium, rotated at 1 revolution per minute, yielded greater shoot elongation compared to stationary culture. During shoot multiplication, a stationary liquid medium identical to the preceding, except that IAA was omitted and 2iP increased to 20.0, was employed. Cultures were lighted 16 hours daily (1,000 lux) for stage I and at 3,000 lux during the multiplication stage. Pretransplant cultures were given 2 weeks of high-intensity light (10,000 lux). All cultures were incubated at 27°C. Once stage II was established, shoots were subdivided every 4 weeks. Employing this method, 5,000 syngonium could be produced from one initial explant in 1 year.

Three other foliage plants were tested in same study:

Cordyline terminalis: Shoot tips were initiated with stationary or rotating (1 revolution per minute on a roller drum) liquid culture. Medium was similar to the preceding with NaP (85 to 170), AS (80), IAA (3.0), and no 2iP. Multiplication medium contained agar (0.8 percent) with IAA (1.0) and Kin (3.0). A light intensity of 1,000 lux is suggested for shoot multiplication. On a 4-week subculturing schedule, 500,000 plants could be produced in one year from a single explant.

Additional references   [21, 22, 56, 62, 73]

Dracaena godseffiana: Propagation was as in the preceding study with the following changes. Stage I culture was best in liquid medium on filter paper bridge. The medium had AS (120), NaP (170), IAA (1.0), Kin (1.0), and pH 5.0. Liquid multiplication medium contained the same basic ingredients with IAA (1.0) and 2iP (3.0). Other aspects of culture were the same as with *Syngonium,* and 300,000 plants were estimated per year with a 7-week subculture schedule, assuming 8 new plants per interval. Environmental parameters remained unchanged.

Epipremnum aureum: Propagation was similar to the preceding, with cultures started using shoot tips or lateral buds on MS medium with agar (0.8 percent) or on filter paper bridges. The medium contained AS (160), NaP (170), IAA (10.0), and 2iP (3.0). Multiplication was on solid medium minus IAA and with 2iP increased to 10.0. It was estimated that 100,000 plants could be produced per year if subculture was performed every 4 weeks.

Additional reference   [40]

Tupidanthus Calyptratus [66]

Shoot tips (3 to 5 millimeters) were cultured on MS salts plus sucrose (3 percent), AS (40), T-HCl (0.4), *i*-inositol (100), NaP (85), agar (0.8 percent), IAA (0.3), and BA (3.0) during stages I and II. New shoots were transferred every 5 to 6 weeks. Cultures were at 5,000 to 10,000 lux for 16 hours daily at 27°C. Stage III medium was the same as stages I and II minus IAA and BA, and plus NAA (6.0).

Yucca sp [61]

Optimum proliferation was from lateral buds cultured on MS basal medium with BA (3.0) and NAA (1.0) at 28°C with 16-hour daily light (3,500 lux). Plantlets developed from the axillary buds at the base of each leaf. Maximum proliferation was a 3 times average biweekly increase over a 3-month period. Adventitious shoot formation also occurred from occasional callus masses. Plantlets were transferred to basal medium without hormones or to one with NAA (0.5 micromole) for rooting. Roots initiated in 3 weeks.

Abbreviations

Media

MS	Murashige and Skoog [84]
SH	Schenk and Hildebrandt [95]
NN	Nitsch and Nitsch [86]
WH	White [118]
GD	Gresshoff and Doy [30]

Components

IAA	indoleacetic acid
NAA	napthaleneacetic acid
IBA	indolebutyric acid
Kin	N^6-furfurylaminopurine
2iP	$N^6[\Delta^2$-isopentenyl]-adenine
2,4-D	(2,4-dichlorophenoxy)acetic acid
BA	N^6-benzylaminopurine
AS	adenine sulfate
CH	casein hydrolysate
NOA	napthoxyacetic acid
PBA	6-(benzylamino)-9-(2-tetrahydropyranyl)-9H-purine
AD	adenine
NA	nicotinic acid
P-HCl	pyridoxine-HCl
T-HCl	thiamine-HCl
Gly	glycine
NaP	$NaH_2PO_4 \cdot H_2O$

Problems Arising in Tissue Culture

The plant tissue culture technique is beset with many problems that can cause serious concern and make the difference between profitability or loss. The nature and control of these problems should be understood before the development of a plant tissue culture facility is considered.

Contamination

Contamination as used here denotes the presence of a foreign biological agent within an otherwise aseptic plant tissue culture environment. Contaminants most often encountered in plant tissue cultures are bacteria and fungi, although other agents may be troublesome at times. Contaminants may be plant pathogens, but most contaminants encountered in plant tissue culture are not; they are usually microorganisms that exist under normal plant culture in harmony with the plant. Such microorganisms may develop rapidly with available nutrients in the culture and can adversely affect the development of desired tissue.

Sources, dissemination, and reproduction   Tissue culture media usually provide an excellent environment for the growth of contaminants. Initial contamination results from the introduction of microorganisms into the culture system through (1) airborne, viable, reproductive units, (2) contact through operator, tools, or inadequately sterilized media, and/or (3) presence on or in initial explant.

The contaminating organism exists on dust particles or free within the air in the first instance. Contamination in this case is through an aerial route, and entrance into the culture vessel may occur whenever the vessel is opened or even when closed if the vessel is not adequately sealed. Air velocity and particle numbers within the culture room can determine contamination frequency under the latter conditions. Dust particles and fungal spores are easily moved around in the air because of their extremely light weight; thus, culture rooms that permit moderate to high air velocities will have increased movement of contaminants within the room. Culture contamination will increase with corresponding increases in air velocity, and rapid culture contamination will occur when air velocity and particle count increase concurrently. A low particle count and effective sanitation must be maintained if high air velocities occur within a culture room. In cases 2 and 3, contaminants are introduced into tissue culture systems primarily through direct contact of the culture medium with a contaminant. In these cases, the type (design) of culture vessel has little effect on contamination since the mode of dissemination is other than aerial.

Reproduction and recycling of contaminant units may occur unknowingly in commercial tissue culture units unless the source of the problem is located and eliminated. Major sources of contaminants may be related to tissue culture operators or to ineffective cleaning and disinfestation procedures, poorly designed air-filtration systems, inadequate sterilization equipment, and inadequate monitoring of essential equipment. Contaminant numbers may increase rapidly, if unchecked, to the point where their elimination from a culture room may constitute a major effort. Laboratories experiencing contamination problems should determine the sources as early as possible so that they can be eliminated before the problem goes beyond a point of simple solution.

Influence upon tissue cultures   Contaminants that develop within tissue culture media adversely affect tissue cultures through competition, antagonism, antibiosis, and, in some cases, pathogenesis. Tissue culture media contain nutritional substances adequate to sustain the growth and development of a wide range of contaminants. Contaminants may compete and rapidly utilize nutrients required by the tissue. Contaminant growth and development may be so rapid and extensive that it will completely cover the tissue cultures and cut off their supply of air and light. Microorganisms often have antagonistic and/or antibiotic effects upon the tissue cultures. Microorganisms develop and excrete biological substances during normal development that accumulate in high concentrations on or within the tissue culture media. These substances, common to the contaminant, are foreign to the tissue cultures and usually have an adverse effect upon their development.

Pathogenesis by a contaminant in a tissue culture system is rare but does occur. It has been isolated and demonstrated that a contaminant, which was visually difficult to detect in plant tissue cultures exhibiting decline in two commercial tissue culture laboratories, reproduced in healthy noncontaminated cultures identical symptoms of tissue decline [51]. The contaminant was identified to be *Erwinia carotovora,* an important plant pathogen of vegetable and ornamental crops. This organism apparently existed within these tissue cultures and to a degree restricted tissue growth, development, and multiplication, while further handling and stage II development of the tissue cultures provided a means for dissemination of the contaminating organism into an extremely high proportion of the cultures before its presence was detected.

More recently, experiments dealing with the rapid tissue culture multiplication [109] of lines of *Dieffenbachia maculata* 'Perfection,' indexed free of known pathogens and maintained in vitro, showed that dasheen mosaic virus as a contaminant within these indexed lines seriously affected growth and development of tissue cultures and their subsequent growth in stage IV. These studies showed that plants developed by tissue culture multiplication from a line free of all known pathogens except dasheen mosaic were, after several months of growth, three to four times smaller than comparative plants developed from lines free of all known pathogens including dasheen mosaic. Viral contaminants within plant tissue cultures, although incapable of growing outside plant tissues on the medium, may also seriously affect growth and development of tissue cultures and will probably go unnoticed by laboratory managers.

Detection of contamination   Commercial tissue culturists have relied almost completely upon visual observation for detection of contaminated cultures. Commercially, where rigorous visual detection is employed, contamination can be reduced but rarely eliminated. Visual scouting for contaminated cultures is especially important in detection and elimination of fungal contaminants. Fungi are relatively easy to see, and laboratory workers can be readily trained to recognize cultures contaminated with fungi.

Bacteria, on the other hand, may present special problems when detection is based primarily on visual observation. Bacteria may develop luxuriantly in most tissue culture media, but there are some whose growth is restricted [51], making visual observation difficult. Some bacterial contaminants of foliage plant tissue cultures do not develop well at pH 4.5 or below. The pH of culture medium can be rapidly reduced by the presence and activity of tissue cultures of the tropical foliage plant genera *Dracaena* and *Dieffenbachia*. Such reduction in pH probably occurs due to the production and release of acidic compounds into the media and can produce an environment that will not allow bacterial growth in the medium, while having no effect on bacterial contaminants within the plant tissue. Conditions such as this will restrict but not eliminate certain bacterial contaminants and foster widespread dissemination of contaminants within and among apparently noncontaminated cultures.

Recent studies were conducted (J. F. Knauss and M. E. Taylor, unpublished data) to determine the feasibility of employing variations of indexing methods [25] to detect fungal and bacterial contaminants prior to introduction of explants of *Philodendron selloum* and *Nephrolepsis exaltata* 'Bostoniensis' into multiplication state II. The explants were indexed after disinfestation and prior to placement into culture, and the resultant stage I cultures were indexed several weeks later. Most cultures proving positive for bacteria initially proved positive after indexing resultant stage I plants. There were, however, sufficient numbers of contaminated explants that were not detected in the initial indexing to prove this approach would not be completely effective in eliminating bacterial contaminants by indexing the initial explant.

Elimination, control, and antibiotics   Paramount in effective control of contamination is adherence to rules of aseptic culture. Sloppy, haphazard techniques will assist in the maintenance of a chronic contamination problem. Laboratory managers and technicians must develop and adhere to a philosophy of cleanliness that is based on a thorough understanding of aseptic culture. If training in this area is lacking, it should be sought out. Tissue culture programs to be successful must have direction from someone understanding aseptic culture and responsible for its implementation in management.

Culture rooms can be designed to provide various environmental capabilities. High air velocities employed necessitate adequate scrubbing and filtration of the air to remove contaminants and contaminant-infested dust particles. The greater the air velocity, the more likely airborne contaminants will find a route into the nutritious culture medium. Rooms with high air velocities of necessity require more rigid control over personal cleanliness of individuals entering the area. As much of the external body areas (especially hair and beard) as possible should be covered with clean coats, caps, and boots. This apparel can be of the disposable type, but if not, it should be cleaned and sterilized periodically. Individuals entering a clean area will contain higher contaminant numbers late in the day after visiting dust- and dirt-laden areas around the nursery or elsewhere. Work details requiring the culture room entrance to be open should be scheduled as briefly as possible and the number of entries kept to a minimum. The number of individuals working in the culture room should be few. Entrances into culture rooms should be built in such a manner that unfiltered air does not intrude when the room is entered.

Visitors to culture rooms should be forbidden, since visitors can carry a large number of contaminants into the transfer and culture rooms. Observation of the operation should be through a window.

Another important consideration is a thorough and periodic inspection of filtration and sterilization equipment. Coarse filters in laminar flow hoods should be changed regularly as determined by cleanliness of filtered air. HEPA filters should be inspected periodically for leaks and to determine whether air flow through them is adequate. If they contain holes that are irreparable or if air flow has been drastically reduced owing to long-term trapping of particles, they should be replaced.

Most laboratories employ autoclaves or pressure cookers to sterilize media and equipment. These units can malfunction, and periodic inspection and checks must be employed to assure proper functioning. Heat indicators available from medical supply houses will assay the effectiveness of sterilization equipment.

Additional information is available [5, 18, 69, 71] to assist in designing procedures and systems to control microbial contamination. Contamination of tissue cultures can occur even with the most effective aseptic technique and culture. This principally results from microorganisms that gain entrance into tissue culture systems in or on explants. Traditionally, plant tissue culturists have attempted to eliminate this problem by involved and elaborate disinfestation, washing, and excision procedures. Disinfestants containing chlorine in solutions of various strengths made from common laundry bleach or other sources are used. Such disinfestation of explant exteriors is effective where little or no internal contamination occurs, but will not effectively eliminate contaminants from within explant tissues. This is especially true of explants taken from many plants grown in warm, humid conditions. Explants taken from greenhouse-grown dieffenbachias proved to be highly contaminated no matter what disinfestation procedure was employed. In subsequent studies, placing dieffenbachias under cool, dry conditions for 3 or more weeks prior to explant removal reduced contamination to an acceptable level. With *Dieffenbachia maculata* 'Perfection' [49], this cultural change did more to reduce contamination in stage I than any disinfestation procedure attempted. This same result was noted in work with other dieffenbachias and foliage plant species (J. F. Knauss and M. E. Taylor, unpublished data).

Contamination control with antibiotics is a possible means of solving chronic problems that cannot be solved through previously mentioned methods of environmental adjustment and disinfestation. Antibiotics have largely been untested with plant tissue cultures. They have been employed in animal tissue culture, and readers can find detailed discussions and references on their value and shortcomings [5, 18]. Antibiotics should be employed in plant culture with caution and only where contamination cannot be solved by previously mentioned methods or where the method of maintaining indexed stock lines in vitro is not applicable.

The principal fault of antibiotics is that contaminants are usually inhibited but not killed by antibiotic activity. This allows inhibited and visibly undetectable contaminants to be perpetuated and readily disseminated among plant tissue in culture. When contaminants are not pathogens, no special problem exists, but when the opposite is true, pathogen spread can occur rapidly undetected.

Some precautions should be taken when using antibiotics. Test the compounds thoroughly for toxicity to tissue cultures before employing on a large scale. Use only on plant types that have never had a history of a systemic plant pathogen, especially bacterial agents such as *Erwinia chrysanthmi*. Be certain other methods of eliminating contamination have been tested and are inadequate before considering antibiotic use.

Production of Noncontaminated Cultures by Pathological Methods

Simple answers and methods to control contamination are not always the best. Plant pathologists have recognized the value of employing methods such as culture indexing [25], shoot tip [7, 33], shoot meristem [45, 65], and meristem [77, 78, 112] cultures as a means of freeing plant tissue of internal and external contaminants, especially pathogens. A combination of these methods and tissue culture multiplication with dieffenbachia [109] and carnations [19] has given in vitro methods of producing, maintaining, and increasing stock plant lines free of detectable contaminants including plant pathogens. The systems devised for dieffenbachia and carnations are concepts of plant handling that provide maximum control of plant contamination from all forms of agents, including pathogens, insects, nematodes, and other contaminants and fit into a progressive approach to ornamental tropical foliage plant production.

Genetic Modifications

Variation, mutation, and reversions may occur with plant tissue cultures, especially those repeatedly transferred for long periods in stage II without returning to stock plants to initiate new cultures. Laboratory managers should pay particular attention to any plant type until assured of its relative tendency not to change in the tissue culture system employed. Some plant mutations may be detected in stages II and III, but with plants like the variegated dieffenbachia, *D. amoena* 'Tropic Snow,' plantlets will all appear green in culture and not until they are grown out can any changes be observed. A percentage of cultures of this sport of *D. amoena* have been reported to revert back to the parent *D. amoena* type. Commercial tissue culture interests should be on guard continually for genetic changes within the plant tissue in culture. No hard and fast rule has as yet been formulated, but plant types that are sports (especially chimeras) and plant types that have a history of producing sports under normal growing conditions will require more rigid attention for possible change in culture.

Contaminating Pests

Insects and other pests may enter culture rooms on occasion where particular care has not been taken to eliminate portals of entry, possible attractants, and modes of dissemination. Certain saprophytic mites may be attracted to specific fungi and bacteria [29, 87, 100] and can be associated with these contaminating microorganisms. Mites and their eggs can often survive disinfestation procedures and conceivably could be transferred into tissue culture areas on infested plant tissues. Mite eggs might also be disseminated among cultural vessels on appendages of files [100]. Any movement of soil on shoes or mites on clothing presents a possible danger of mite entry into a culture area. Once established in culture areas where biological attractants (contaminants) exist, mites can disseminate contaminants by moving within and among culture vessels, especially those providing little or no physical barrier to their movement.

Flying insects can be particularly attracted into a culture room by light transmitted through cracks, holes, or crevices that have not been closed during construction.

Miscellaneous Problems

Two problems that can occur in stage IV and require attention are plant injury due to high soluble salts and/or disease development. Improper watering and/or fertilization techniques can produce foliar injury from soluble salts, which if left unchecked can cause serious losses to developing tissue culture plantlets. If such injury is sufficient and the environment proper for disease development, the ubiquitous, airborne fungus pathogen, *Botrytis cinerea,* will often develop on the injured tissue and ultimately cause a severe blight. Other disease problems can also arise if proper care is not taken to adequately free the soil medium, pots, benches, and tools of plant pathogens such as those belonging to the genera *Pythium, Phytophthora, Rhizoctonia, Sclerotinia,* and *Sclerotium.* Where pathogens are a problem during the development of newly transplanted tissue culture units, the appropriate fungicide used at one half the recommended concentration will probably provide control and avoid phytotoxicity. Use fungicides on young tissue culture plants only when other methods of control have proved ineffective.

Adverse Culture Room Environment

Fluorescent tubes should be tested periodically and their light intensity and quality recorded so that they may be replaced when efficiency drops below acceptable levels. Records on light and culture production should be kept for each crop so that one may correlate efficiency and determine the time interval at which tubes must be replaced for a particular plant type.

Another factor that may become a problem, especially in open culture vessels, is humidity. This is mentioned again briefly because rooms with low humidities can cause serious dessication of media, resulting in rapid increases in osmotic pressure and adverse effects upon tissue cultures.

When little or no fresh-air exchange exists within a culture room, tissue cultures may exhibit growth reduction and even death resulting from depletion of essential gases or from accumulation of gases that can be toxic. Tightly closed culture vessels without provision for air exchange can produce this condition.

Toxic Materials

Some ingredients or vessels employed in tissue culture media may contain materials toxic to the cultures. Reportedly, particular types of glassware can contain sufficient toxic materials that diffuse into culture media and affect tissue growth. Past experiences have shown that poor-grade agar and sucrose may contain inhibitory compounds. Under proper laboratory management, when media are prepared the source (manufacturer and lot number) of ingredients should be recorded. Once detected, knowing the manufacturer and lot number allows elimination of a toxic ingredient from the culture media and possible reimbursement from the supplier.

Communication

A tissue culture facility can be successful in production but fail to make a profit if communication with the nursery industry to determine industry needs is missing. Commercial laboratories should plan production wisely like any successful business. Managers of laboratories functioning in conjunction with nurseries should meet periodically with nursery executives in marketing, sales, and management to logically plan production for coming months. Tissue culture laboratory personnel rarely understand the business of profitable nursery production, and vice versa. An effective communication system must be planned before any serious steps are taken to add a tissue culture facility and support staff to an existing nursery.

Tissue culture facilities that plan contract or specialty work should keep lines of communication open to potential customers to determine needs and whether their product is handled properly. There have been cases where commercial laboratories have sold customers plant units that nursery personnel did not know how to grow on successfully. Systems of handling should be perfected so that customers will be confident and assured that tissue cultures bought will develop into healthy, quality plants.

Potentials of Plant Tissue Culture

The use of plant tissue culture as a propagative tool has been the subject of several review articles [39, 57, 79, 80, 81]. Tissue culture propagation of ferns [121] has already demonstrated the commercial applicability of in vitro propagation of foliage plants, and other commercial laboratories are reporting on their own successes [12, 20, 107]. Such potential is particularly important to growers or hobbyists with rare or unusual plants that are slow to propagate by normal sexual or asexual methods. Many of these individuals are not able to build and staff a laboratory of their own, thus making the availability of commercial laboratories that do contractual work of great importance to them. It is important, however, to realize that increasing costs of labor, energy, and materials may further limit the future use of tissue culture by larger commercial organizations as well as smaller firms. More research is needed to answer questions dealing with cost analysis [3] and alternative methods or shortcuts [50] in tissue culture methodology. Alternatives to the high-energy-requiring pretransplant stage (stage III) of culture should be investigated, along with problems encountered in the reestablishment of plants from test tubes to soil. Methods of economically handling the many thousands of plants that may be produced from a single explant in a year's time also need to be studied.

There is little doubt that tissue culture will continue to be an indispensable aid to researchers, particularly plant pathologists and plant breeders. Culture of ovules and ovaries [93] has been accomplished by plant breeders to overcome genetic incompatibilities [94]. Embryos are often cultured following interspecific crosses in which normal endosperm development does not occur or to replace a seed dormancy requirement [92]. These techniques all support standard breeding procedures. More revolutionary approaches to breeding involve another culture for production of haploid plants [85] and development of homozygous diploid plants or for uncovering mutations [97]. New types of genetic variability may occur naturally during the tissue culture process or be induced by use of mutagens and can lead to selection of new plant types [98]. Such practice is particularly useful for clonally propagated horticultural crops.

Most foliage crops are propagated vegetatively and are subjected to infection and dissemination of plant pathogens, in particular systemic fungi, bacteria, and viruses [46, 47, 48, 114], which detract from yield and salability of a plant. Production of pathogen-free plant material with the aid of tissue culture is economically important because of increased crop quality. Here it must be emphasized that plants which appear clean during culture are not necessarily pathogen free [59]. Indexing eighty-two dieffenbachia lines produced in tissue culture and which showed no visible signs of contamination revealed that thirty-two of these lines had bacterial and/or fungal contamination [49]. Detailed studies with dieffenbachia [49] and caladium [33] indicate that disease indexing of foliage crops is feasible and will become increasingly important in the future. Instructions on the proper methods of producing and handling indexed stock will have to accompany any release of such material, as only those producers who are able to maintain the stock's clean quality will benefit. Tissue culture can serve a dual role in this instance. Indexed lines would not only be initiated, but also maintained in culture to serve as constantly renewable sources of clean propagative material once a line was determined as pathogen free. This requires that plants in culture be grown out periodically to ensure the absence of any degradative mutations due to prolonged time in culture.

REFERENCES

[1] Abo El-Nil, M., and F. W. Zettler. 1976. Callus initiation and organ differentiation from shoot tip cultures of *Colocasia esculenta*. *Pl. Sci. Letters* 6:401–408.

[2] Anderson, W. C., and G. W. Meagher. 1978. Cost of propagating plants through tissue culture using lilies as an example. OSU Ornamental Short Course, Portland, Oregon.

[3] ———, G. W. Meagher, and A. G. Nelson. 1977. Cost of propagating broccoli plants through tissue culture. *HortScience* 12(6):543–544.

[4] Applegren, M. 1976. Regeneration of *Begonia hiemalis in vitro*. *Acta Hort.* 64:31–38.

[5] Armstrong, D. 1973. Contamination of tissue culture by bacteria and fungi. In *Contamination in tissue culture*, J. Fogh (ed.). New York: Academic Press, 288 pp.

[6] Bajaj, Y. P. S., and R. L. M. Pierik. 1974. Vegetative propagation of Freesia through callus cultures. *Neth. J. Agric. Sci.* 22:153–159.

[7] Baker, R., and D. J. Phillips. 1962. Obtaining pathogen-free stock by shoot tip culture. *Phytopathology* 52: 1242–1244.

[8] Berry, S. 1977. Regeneration of *Peperomia caperata* from callus. *In Vitro* 13(3):145 (Abstr.).

[9] Bilkey, P. D., and B. H. McCown. 1979. *In vitro* cultures and propagation of *Episcia* sp. (flame violets). *J. Am. Soc. Hort. Sci.* 194(1):109–114.

[10] ———, B. C. McCown, and A. C. Hildebrandt. 1978. Micropropagation of African violet from petiole cross-sections. *HortScience* 13:37–38.

[11] Boxus, P. 1978. La "Micropropagation", proceede industriel de multiplication rapide du fragarie. *Fruit Bllge.* No. 378.

[12] Burr, R. W. 1975. Mass production of Boston fern through tissue culture. *Comb. Proc. Int. Plant Prop. Soc.* 25:122–124.

[13] ———. 1976. Mass propagation of ferns through tissue culture. *In Vitro* 12(4):309–310 (Abstr.).

[14] Cheng, T. Y. 1975. Adventitious bud formation in culture of Douglas fir (*Pseudotsuga menziesii* Mirg. Franco). *Plant Sci. Lett.* 5:97–102.

[15] Cooke, R. C. 1977. The use of an agar substitute in the initial growth of Boston ferns *in vitro*. *HortScience* 12(4):339.

[16] ———. 1977. Tissue culture propagation of African violets. *HortScience* 12(6):549.

[17] Constantin, M. J., R. R. Henke, and M. A. Mansur. 1977. Effect of activated charcoal on callus growth and shoot organogenesis in tobacco. *In Vitro* 13(5):293–296.

[18] Corriell, L. L. 1973. Methods of prevention of bacterial, fungal, and other contaminants. In *Contamination in tissue culture*, J. Fogh (ed.). New York: Academic Press, 288 pp.

[19] Davis, M. J., R. Baker, and J. J. Hanan. 1977. Clonal multiplication of carnation by micropropagation. *J. Am. Soc. Hort. Sci.* 102:48–53.

[20] Davidson, S. E., and A. Donnan, Jr. 1977. *In vitro* propagation of *Cryptanthus* spp. *Proc. Fla. State Hort. Soc.* 90:303–304.

[21] Deberg, P. 1975. Intensified vegetative multiplication of *Dracaena deremensis*. *Acta Hort.* 54:83–92.

[22] ———. 1976. An *in vitro* technique for the vegetative multiplication of chimaeral plants of dracaena and cordyline. *Acta Hort.* 64:17–19.

[23] _____, and J. De Wael. 1977. Mass propagation of *Ficus lyrata. Acta Hort.* 78:361–364.

[24] de Fossard, R. A., A. Myint, and E. C. M. Lee. 1974. A broad spectrum tissue culture experiment with tobacco (*Nicotiana tabacum*) pith tissue culture. *Physiol. Plantarum* 31:125–130.

[25] Dimock, A. W. 1962. Obtaining pathogen-free stock by cultured cutting techniques. *Phytopathology* 52:1239–1241.

[26] Donnan, A., Jr., S. E. Davidson, and C. L. Williams. 1978. Establishment of tissue culture grown plants in the greenhouse environment. *Proc. Fla. State Hort. Soc.* 91:235-237.

[27] Flores, H. E., C. A. Fierro, and F. K. S. Koo. 1976. Tissue culture of African violet (*Saintpaulia ionantha* Wendl.) *Trop. Region Amer. Soc. Hort. Sci.* 24:449–453.

[28] Fonnesbech, M. 1974. The influence of NAA, BA and temperature on shoot and root development from *Begonia × cheimantha* petiole segments grown *in vitro. Physiol. Plantarum* 32:42–54.

[29] Forsberg, J. L. 1965. The relationship of *Pseudomonas marginata, Stromantinia gladioli,* bulb mites and chemical soil treatments to the occurrence and control of scab and Stromatinia rot of gladiolus. *Phytopathology* 55:1058 (Abstr.).

[30] Gresshoff, P. M., and C. H. Doy. 1972. Development differentiation of haploid *Lycopersicon esculentum* (tomato). *Planta (Berl.)* 107:161–170.

[31] Haberlandt, G. 1902. Cultuversuche mit isolienten pflanzenzellen. *Sitz-Ber. Mat.-Nat. Kl. Kais. Akad. Wiss. Wien.* 11:69–82.

[32] Harper, K., and T. Murashige. 1976. Clonal multiplication of ferns *in vitro*. M.S. thesis, University of California, Riverside, 168 pp.

[33] Hartman, R. D. 1974. Dasheen mosaic virus and other phytopathogens eliminated from caladium, taro and cocoyam by culture of shoot tips. *Phytopathology* 64:237–240.

[34] _____. 1979. Plant tissue culture from a propagator's viewpoint. *Foliage Digest* (in press).

[35] Harris, G. P., and E. M. H. Hart. 1964. Regeneration from leaf squares of *Peperomia sandersii* A. DC: A relationship between rooting and budding. *Ann. Bot.* 28:509–526.

[36] Hennen, G. R., and T. J. Sheehan. 1978. *In vitro* propagation of *Platycerium stemaria* (Beauvois) Desv. *HortScience* 13(3):245.

[37] Henny, R. J. 1978. *In vitro* propagation of *Peperomia* 'Red Ripple' from leaf discs. *HortScience* 13:150–151.

[38] Herman, E. B., and G. J. Haas. 1975. Clonal propagation of *Coffea arabica* L. from callus culture. *HortScience* 10(6):588–589.

[39] Holdgate, D. 1977. Propagation of ornamentals by tissue culture. In *Plant cell, tissue, and organ culture*, J. Reinert and Y. P. S. Bajaj, eds. New York: Springer-Verlag, pp. 18–43.

[40] Hosoki, T. 1975. Propagation of tropical plants by tissue culture. Ph.D. thesis. University of Hawaii. 112 pp.

[41] Huang, L. C., and T. Murashige. 1976. Plant tissue culture media: Major constituents, their preparation and some applications. *TCA Man.* 3(1):539–548.

[42] Johnson, B. B. 1978. *In vitro* propagation of *Episcia cupreata. Hort-Science* 13(5):596.

[43] Johnson, R. T., S. S. Koenigsberg, and R. W. Langhans. 1976. Tissue culture propagation of Christmas and Easter cactus. *HortScience* 11(3):70 (Abstr.).

[44] Jones, J. B., and T. Murashige. 1974. Tissue culture propagation of *Aechmea fasciata* Baker and other bromeliads. *Proc. Int. Plant Prop. Soc.* 24:117–126.

[45] Kartha, K. K., O. L. Gamborg, and F. Constabel. 1974. Regeneration of pea (*Pisum sativum* L.) plants from shoot apical meristems. *Z. Pflanzenphysiol.* 72:172–176.

[46] Knauss, J. F. 1975. Common diseases of tropical foliage plants. I. Foliar fungal diseases. *Florida Foliage Grower* 12(10):1–5.

[47] ———. 1975. Common diseases of tropical foliage plants. II. Bacterial diseases. *Florida Foliage Grower* 12(11):1–6.

[48] ———. 1976. Common diseases of tropical foliage plants. III. Soil-borne fungus diseases. *Florida Foliage Grower* 13(3):1–8.

[49] ———. 1976. A tissue culture method for producing *Dieffenbachia picta* cv. 'Perfection' free of fungi and bacteria. *Proc. Fla. State Hort. Soc.* 89:293–296.

[50] ———. 1976. A partial tissue culture method for pathogen-free propagation of selected ferns from spores. *Proc. Fla. State Hort. Soc.* 89:363–365.

[51] ———, and J. W. Miller. 1978. A contaminant, *Erwinia carotovora,* affecting commercial plant tissue cultures. *In Vitro* 14:754–756.

[52] Knudson, L. 1946. A new nutrient solution for the germination of orchid seeds. *Am. Orchid Soc. Bull.* 15:214–217.

[53] ———. 1951. Nutrient solution for orchids. *Bot. Gaz.* 112:528–532.

[54] Kogl. F., A. J. Haagen-Smit, and H. Erxleben. 1934. Uber ein neuses ausin ("Heteroaxin") aus harn. *Z. Physiol. Chem.* 228:90–103.

[55] Kukulczanka, K., K. Klimaszewska, and H. Pluta. 1977. Regeneration of entire plants of *Peperomia scandens* Ruiz. from different parts of leaves *in vitro. Acta Hort.* 78:365–371.

[56] Kunisaki, J. T. 1975. *In vitro* propagation of *Cordyline terminalis* (L.) Kunth. *HortScience* 10(6):601–602.

[57] ———. 1977. Tissue culture of tropical ornamental plants. *HortScience* 12(2):141–142.

[58] Langhans, R. W., ed. 1978. A growth chamber manual. Environmental control for plants. Ithaca, N.Y.: Comstock Publishing Association, Cornell University Press, 222 pp.

[59] ———, R. K. Horst, and E. D. Earle. 1977. Disease-free plants via tissue culture propagation. *HortScience* 12(2):149–150.

[60] Linsmaier, M., and F. Skoog. 1965. Organic growth factor requirements of tobacco tissue cultures. *Physiol. Plantarum* 18:100–127.

[61] Litz, R. E., and R. A. Conover. 1977. Tissue culture propagation of some foliage plants. *Proc. Fla. State Hort. Soc.* 90:301–303.

[62] Makino, R. K., and P. J. Makino. 1978. Propagation of *Syngonium podophyllum* cultivars through tissue culture. *In Vitro* 14(4):357.

[63] ———, P. J. Makino, and T. Murashige. 1977. Rapid cloning of *Ficus* cultivars through application of *in vitro* methodology. *In Vitro* 13(3):160 (Abstr.).

[64] Mapes, M. O. 1973. Tissue culture of bromeliads. *Comb. Proc. Int. Plant Prop. Soc.* 23:47–55.

[65] Marston, M. E. 1967. Clonal multiplication of orchids by shoot meristem culture. *Sci. Hort.* 19:80–86.

[66] Matsuyama, J., and T. Murashige. 1977. Propagation of *Tupidanthus calyptratus* through tissue cultures. *In Vitro* 13(3):169–170 (Abstr.)

[67] Mauseth, J. D. 1977. Cactus tissue culture: A potential method of propagation. *Cactus Succulent J.* 49:80–81.

[68] McCandless, D. W., N. C. Rosberg, and C. E. Cassidy. 1976. Vegetative propagation of the cactus *Mamillaria woodsii* Craig through tissue cultures. *Experientia* 32(5):668–669.

[69] McGarrity, G. J. 1975. Control of microbiological contamination. *Tissue Culture Assoc. Manual* 1:181–185.

[70] ———. 1977. Cell culture facilities. *Tissue Culture Assoc. Manual* 3:679–683.

[71] ———, and L. L. Coriell. 1971. Procedures to reduce contamination of cell cultures. *In Vitro* 6(4):257–265.

[72] Mekers, O. 1977. *In vitro* propagation of some Tillandsioideae (Bromeliaceae). *Acta Hort.* 78:311–320.

[73] Mee, G. W. P. 1978. Propagation of *Cordyline terminalis* from callus culture. *HortScience* 13(6):660.

[74] Mikkelsen, E. P., and K. C. Sink, Jr. 1978. *In vitro* propagation of reiger elatior begonias. *HortScience* 13(2):242–244.

[75] Miller, C. O., F. Skoog, F. S. Okumara, M. H. von Saltza, and F. M. Strong. 1956. Isolation, structure and synthesis of kinetin: a substance promoting cell division. *J. Amer. Chem. Soc.* 78:1375–1380.

[76] Miller, L. R. 1976. Tissue culture propagation of some tropical foliage plants. M.S. thesis. University of California, Berkeley. 119 pp.

[77] Miller, P. W., and R. O. Belkengren. 1963. Elimination of yellow edge, crinkle and veinbanding viruses and certain other virus complexes from strawberries by excision and culturing of apical meristems. *Plant Disease Reptr.* 47:303–310.

[78] Morel, G. M. 1960. Producing virus-free cymbidiums. *Am. Orchid Soc. Bull.* 29:495–497.

[79] Murashige, T. 1974. Plant propagation through tissue cultures. *Ann. Rev. Plant Physiol.* 25:135–166.

[80] _____. 1977. Current status of plant cell and organ culture. *HortScience* 12(2):127–130.

[81] _____. 1977. Clonal crops through tissue culture. In Barz, W., E. Reinhard, and M. H. Zenk., eds., *Plant tissue culture and its bio-technological application.* New York: Springer-Verlag, pp. 392–403.

[82] _____. 1978. Plant tissue culture: History, current status and prospects. *TCA Report* 12(2):41–47.

[83] _____. 1978. Tissue culture costs of producing plants. OSU Ornamental Short Course, Portland, Oregon.

[84] _____, and F. Skoog. 1962. A revised medium for rapid growth bioassays with tobacco tissue cultures. *Physiol. Plantarum* 15:473–497.

[85] Nitsch, J. P., and C. Nitsch. 1969. Haploid plants from pollen grains. *Science* 163:85–87.

[86] _____, and C. Nitsch. 1970. Obtention de plantes haploides a partir de pollen. *Bull. Soc. Bot. Fr.* 117:339–360.

[87] Noble, W. E., and S. L. Poe. 1972. Attractancy of several fungi and bacteria for bulb and soil mites frequenting diseased gladiolus corms. *Proc. Fla. State Hort. Soc.* 85:401–404.

[88] Pierik, R. L. M. 1976. *Anthurium andraeanum* plantlets produced from callus tissue cultivated *in vitro. Physiol. Plantarum* 37:80–82.

[89] _____, and H. H. M. Steegmans. 1975. Callus multiplication of *Anthurium andraeanum* Lind. in liquid media. *Neth. J. Agri. Sci.* 23:299–302.

[90] _____, and H. H. M. Steegmans. 1976. Vegetative propagation of *Anthurium scherzerianum* Schott through tissue culture. *Scientia Hort.* 4:291–292.

[91] _____, H. H. M. Steegmans, and J. J. Van Der Meys. 1974. Plantlet formation in callus tissues of *Anthurium andraeanum* Lind. *Scientia Hort.* 2:193–198.

[92] Raghavan, V. 1977. Applied aspects of embryo culture. In *Plant cell, tissue and organ culture,* J. Reinert and Y. P. S. Bajaj, eds. New York: Springer-Verlag, pp. 375–397.

[93] Rangaswamy, N. S. 1977. Application of *in vitro* pollination and *in vitro* fertilization. In *Plant cell, tissue, and organ culture,* J. Reinert and Y. P. S. Bajaj, eds. New York: Springer-Verlag, pp. 412–425.

[94] _____, and K. R. Shivanna. 1967. Induction of gametic compatibility and seed formation in axenic cultures of a diploid self-incompatible species of *Petunia. Nature* 16:937–939.

[95] Schenk, R. V., and A. C. Hildebrandt. 1972. Medium and techniques for induction and growth of monocotyledonous and dicotyledonous plant cell cultures. *Can. J. Bot.* 50:199–204.

[96] Sehgal, C. C. 1975. *In vitro* differentiation of foliar embryos and adventitious buds from the leaves of *Begonia semperflorens* Link and Otto. *Ind. J. Exp. Biology* 13:486–488.

[97] Sink, K. C., and V. Padmanabhan. 1977. Anther and pollen culture to produce haploids: progress and application for the plant breeder. *HortScience* 12(2):143–148.

[98] Skirvin, R. M. 1978. Natural and induced variation in tissue culture. *Euphytica* 27:241–266.

[99] Skoog, F., and C. O. Miller. 1957. Chemical regulation of growth and organ formation in plant tissues *in vitro. Symp. Soc. Exptl. Biol.* 11:118–131.

[100] Snyder, W. C., and H. N. Hansen. 1946. Control of culture mites by cigarette paper barriers. *Mycologia* 38:455–462.

[101] Sondahl, M. R., and W. R. Sharp. 1977. High frequency initiation of somatic embryos in cultured leaf explants of *Coffea arabica* L. *In Vitro* 13(3):146 (Abstr.).

[102] Staritsky, G. 1970. Embryoid formation in callus tissues of coffee. *Acta. Bot. Neerl.* 19:590–594.

[103] Start, N. D., and B. G. Cumming. 1976. *In vitro* propagation of *Saintpaulia ionantha* Wendl. *HortScience* 11(3):204–206.

[104] Steward, F. C., and S. M. Caplin. 1952. Investigations on growth and metabolism of plant cells. IV. Evidence on the role of the coconut milk factor in development. *Ann. Bot.* 16:491–504.

[105] Stimart, D. P., and P. D. Ascher. 1978. Foliar emergence and growth of *in vitro* generated bulblets from bulb scale explants of *Lilium longiflorum. HortScience* 13(3):36 (Abstr.).

[106] Street, H. E., and G. G. Henshaw. 1966. Introduction and methods employed in plant tissue culture. In *Cells and tissues in culture*, E. N. Willmer, ed. New York: Academic Press, pp. 459–532.

[107] Strode, R. E., and R. P. Oglesby. 1976. Commercial tissue culturing at Oglesby Nursery, Inc. *Proc. Fla. State Hort. Soc.* 89:367–368.

[108] ———, and R. P. Oglesby. 1978. Parameters in commercial propagation of *Spathiphyllum clevelandii* through tissue culture. *In Vitro* 14(4):356–357 (Abstr.).

[109] Taylor, M. E., and J. F. Knauss. 1978. Tissue culture multiplication and subsequent handling of known pathogen-free *Dieffenbachia maculata* 'Perfection.' *Proc. Fla. State Hort. Soc.* 91:233–235.

[110] Thakor, S. 1975. Differentiation of shoot buds and roots in petiole segments of *Begonia picta* Smith. *Ind. J. Exptl. Biology* 14:517–520.

[111] Townsley, P. M. 1974. Production of coffee from plant cell suspension cultures. *Can. Inst. Food Sci. Technol. J.* 7:79–81.

[112] Van Os, H. 1964. Production of virus-free carnation by means of meristem culture. *Neth. J. Plant Path.* 70:18–26.

[113] Van Overbeek, J., M. E. Conklin, and A. F. Blakeslee. 1941. Factors in

coconut milk essential for growth and development of very young *Datura* embryos. *Science* 94:350-351.

[114] Wehlburg, C., S. A. Alfieri, Jr., J. R. Langdon, and J. W. Kimbrough, 1975. Index of plant diseases in Florida. Fla. Dept. Agric. and Conserv. Serv., Div. Plant Ind., Bull. 11. 285p.

[115] Welander, T. 1977. *In vitro* organogenesis in explants from different cultivars of *Begonia* × hiemalis. *Physiol. Plantarum* 41:142-145.

[116] White, P. R. 1934. Potentially unlimited growth of excised tomato root tips in a liquid medium. *Plant Physiol.* 9:585-600.

[117] ———. 1939. Potentially unlimited growth of excised plant callus in an artificial nutrient. *Amer. J. Bot.* 26:59-64.

[118] ———. 1943. A handbook of plant tissue culture. Tempe, Ariz.: Jacques Cattel Press, Inc.

[119] ———. 1963. The cultivation of animal and plant cells, 2nd ed. New York: Ronald Press.

[120] Zimmer, K., and W. Pieper. 1976. Methods and problems of clonal propagation of bromeliads *in vitro*. *Acta Hort.* 64:25-27.

[121] Zumwalt, G. 1976. Plant propagation by tissue culture moves from academic theory into commercial production. *Florist* 10(1):72-81.

seven

R. T. Poole
C. A. Conover
J. N. Joiner

soils and potting mixtures

Soils may be defined as a naturally occurring mixture of weathered minerals and decaying organic materials that cover the earth in relatively thin layers. They are storehouses of water, air, and minerals needed by plants for growth and provide an anchor and support for roots. Soils in which plants grow are complex, living, dynamic systems with chemical and microbial actions that cause changes in physical, chemical, and biological characteristics.

The various foliage plants are found in many soil types in their natural habitats. There are large variations between plant genera listed as "foliage plants." Foliage plants grow on tree trunks or limbs, on rocks, and in heavy clay, sand, and organic soils. Certain foliage plants have specific soil or potting mixture requirements, but most grow in many soil types or in potting mixtures having widely varying physical and chemical properties.

Soil Characteristics

Little actual "soil" is used in foliage plant production except where stock plants are grown in the field or as a minor component of potting mixtures. The major factor in determining desirability of soils is physical structure, since fertility and pH can be adjusted.

179

Most native soils are composed primarily of mixtures of clay, silt, and sand. Particle size distribution determines the soils' usefulness because, among other properties, it determines aeration characteristics. Clay particles are 0.002 millimeters in diameter or smaller, silt from 0.002 to 0.02 millimeters, and sand from 0.2 to 2.0 millimeters in diameter [3]. Most native soils contain organic matter, which also varies in particle sizes and quantity.

Clay particles are negatively charged colloids with the number of charges depending on the type of clay. Too much clay present in container soils renders them almost useless for foliage production unless they are amended to provide aeration and drainage.

Silt particles have little nutrient-holding capacity, but good water-holding capacity. Size and percentage determine how beneficial they are in a particular soil.

Sand particles are large in comparison to other soil components and have low nutrient- and water-holding capacities, but most provide aeration and, when present in proper ratio with clay and silt, provide an excellent field soil. Sandy soils are usually amended with organic matter to increase water- and nutrient-holding capacities.

Field Soil Characteristics

Water infiltration rate can be determined by inserting a 15- to 20-centimeter-diameter, thin wall pipe (stove pipe) 30 centimeters into the soil without disturbing the structure. Thoroughly saturate this soil and allow to drain for 24 hours; apply 2.5 centimeters of water to the surface and determine the rate of infiltration. The soil is very well drained if the water infiltrates in 5 minutes or less, well drained if it takes 5 to 30 minutes, and poorly drained if it takes 30 minutes to 1 hour, although it can be acceptable for foliage stock production if amended. Soils that require more than 1 hour to drain are unacceptable for foliage plant production unless extensive modifications are made to change the structure.

Elevation of any soil relative to other land nearby determines surface and internal drainage potentials. Soils with poor internal drainage may be made acceptable for foliage stock production if surface drainage is rapid, but the same soil with slow or poor surface drainage would be unacceptable. Soils with a high water table or hardpan can prevent development of roots. Other important considerations include levels of salinity, herbicide residues, and nutrient- and water-holding capacities.

TABLE 7-1   Factors influencing selection of potting mixture components

Economic	Chemical	Physical
Cost	Cation exchange capacity	Aeration
Availability	Nutrient levels	Water-holding capacity
Reproducibility	pH	Particle size
Ease of mixing	Sterility	Density
Appearance	Soluble salts	Uniformity

Potting Mixture Characteristics

Ingredients used in containers or benches as potting mixtures have to be different than field soils because of physical limitations imposed by containers. Aeration is of major importance in container soils because they are shallow (have short column height) compared to field soils and do not drain well. The soil-filled container is an entity, with the container bottom acting as a perched water table preventing free water drainage and resulting in wetter potting mixtures in containers than would be true for the same mixture in the field after drainage [58, 59]. Another important factor is the reduced volume of soil available to plants from which needed water and nutrients must be obtained. Good potting mixtures must be retentive of sufficient water and fertilizer while allowing for excellent aeration [8, 29, 56, 57].

Small containers have short column height and, thus, might need frequent fertilization and irrigation at the risk of decreased aeration. Components for container potting mixtures should be chosen carefully, therefore, to provide good aeration and at the same time maximize water- and nutrient-holding capacities [62]. Some of the most important factors to be considered in selecting potting mixture components are listed in Table 7-1.

Selection of components will be affected by container size. Coarser materials should be used for smaller containers and finer-textured materials for larger containers. Larger pores in coarse potting soils permit better drainage in the small soil volumes, while the continuity of water in small pores permits good drainage in larger containers.

Physical Properties of Soils and Potting Mixtures

The importance of physical properties varies with intended use. A soil that is excellent in a field may be entirely unsatisfactory in a pot. Physical factors must be understood to properly manage any growing medium.

TABLE 7-2 Influence of soil amendments on weight of soil
(bulk density) with and without water [37]

Soil mix	Bulk density (kg/m³)	
	Dry	Wet
Pleasanton silt loam (100%)	1,520	1,776
Pleasanton + pine shavings (50% + 50%)	1,072	1,456
Pleasanton + redwood shavings (50% + 50%)	800	1,216
Pleasanton + white fir bark (50% + 50%)	912	1,296
Pleasanton + sphagnum peat (50% + 50%)	832	1,296
Pleasanton + pumice (50% + 50%)	1,100	1,472

Bulk Density

Bulk density expresses soil weight (grams per cubic centimeter) and takes into consideration solids and pore spaces between particles within a volume. High bulk densities generally indicate "tight" soils and low ones, "open" soils. Bulk densities in field soils often range from 1 to 1.75 grams per cubic centimeter, with 1.25 to 1.50 the desirable range [7]. This is equal to a dry weight of 1,250 to 1,500 kilograms per cubic meter. Weight is not an important factor in field soil, but is important in container soils, which are often transported considerable distances. A 30-centimeter container with field soil will weigh 28 to 33 kilograms dry, or nearly 40 kilograms wet. This is an excessive weight from labor and economic considerations. Bulk densities below 0.75 grams per cubic centimeter are best for container-grown crops, with values as low as 0.15 acceptable under some circumstances [29, 63].

Weight can be an advantage provided it is not excessive. Where wind is not a factor, a bulk density range between 0.15 and 0.50 is acceptable unless tall crops are grown in small pots. Foliage crops grown in shade houses or outdoors must be in heavier mixes or they will be toppled by wind or sprayer blasts. For such situations a bulk density range between 0.50 and 0.75 grams per cubic centimeter is desirable. Table 7-2 provides an indication of changes in bulk density when various amendments are added to one soil type.

Pore Space

Pore space (porosity or aeration) of a field soil or potting mixture is an important measure of its suitability for foliage plant production. Foliage plant growth is often reduced and sometimes plants are killed because of poor aeration caused by compaction, excessive rainfall, or overwatering of soils and potting mixtures with inadequate pore spaces [57, 60]. Roots cannot absorb water or nutrients except in the presence of oxygen. Roots emit carbon dioxide, which can become toxic unless sufficient air exchange exists between the media and atmosphere. Irrigation can aid air exchange, since it forces existing air from the medium, which is replaced as the water drains, provided the medium has sufficient pore space. Table 7-3 shows the change in rate of water movement through a soil after amending and the beneficial effects to be obtained.

There are several methods of measuring pore space. The most important is the percent of pore space remaining after water has drained owing to gravity. This is called noncapillary pore space and accounts for the macropores that provide aeration during periods of high water application. Plants have varying tolerances to inadequate aeration, but noncapillary pore space should be at least 3 to 5 percent in field soil and 5 to 10 percent or more in potting mixtures [29]. This is especially true with organic potting mixtures since they decompose with time, resulting in decreased noncapillary pore space. Container walls and bottoms also act to reduce noncapillary pore space by creating an interface of high surface tension to hold water [62].

Capillary pore spaces are smaller than noncapillary ones and account for many times the volume of the macropore spaces, but they are of little value to aeration because they are usually filled with water. Thus, a high percentage of capillary pore space may not guarantee proper aeration. The total voume of air-filled capillary and noncapillary pore space (after drainage) should be 5 to 30 percent. Excessive total pore space is not desirable, since it indicates a low water-holding capacity and causes more rapid drying of soil or potting mixtures.

Water-holding Capacity

Water-holding capacity is the ability of a soil or potting mixture to hold water against the pull of gravity and is measured as percent of dry weight or percent of volume of water held after gravitational drainage.

TABLE 7-3   Infiltration time of 1.3 centimeters of water in various soil mixtures [41]

Soil mixture	Time (min)
Fallbrook sandy loam	52
$\frac{2}{3}$ Fallbrook sandy loam, $\frac{1}{3}$ sphagnum peat moss	39
$\frac{2}{3}$ Fallbrook sandy loam, $\frac{1}{3}$ lignified redwood	2
$\frac{2}{3}$ Fallbrook sandy loam, $\frac{1}{3}$ calcified clay	6

TABLE 7-4   Water retention of various media [29]

Media	Maximum water retention	
	% Dry weight	% Volume
½ Peat, ½ sand	51	60
½ Pine bark, ½ sand	45	51
½ No. 3 vermiculite, ½ sand	34	43
½ No. 3 vermiculite, ½ pine bark	306	86
½ No. 3 vermiculite, ½ peat	411	94
⅔ Pine bark, ⅓ perlite	296	68

Percent of dry weight is adequate for field soils, whereas percent of volume is the best method to express water availability in a container because available water is restricted to the container. Table 7-4 shows the large difference in measuring water percent by volume versus weight of some potting mixtures.

Water-holding capacities of field soils in the range of 25 percent by weight are adequate since plant roots have an unrestricted growth potential, but the same range in container production is inadequate because root growth is artificially restricted. Drainage that occurs from containers depends on the surface area of the medium particles, absorptive properties of components, attractive forces acting between water and particles, and **medium** height. Small, shallow containers require a potting mixture with greater noncapillary pore volume than is needed in large containers. The capillary attraction of pot walls restricts drainage and partially counteracts effects of gravity, and the pot bottom produces the effect of a perched water table. Small pots containing mixtures with little noncapillary pore space and high water-holding capacity are often completely saturated for one or two days after watering because gravitational pull is not strong enough to remove water from the capillary pores. On the other hand, the same mix would be more satisfactory in a larger pot because better drainage would occur [32, 58, 62, 63]. Water-holding capacities should be in the range of 20 to 60 percent by volume, provided 5 to 30 percent total pore space is present after drainage.

Particle Size

Particle size of various constituents, such as clay, silt, and sand, determines the overall porosity of field soils and can be altered by tillage at the proper time of the year to promote granulation or by amending the soil with organic or inorganic materials. Ingredients of varying particle size placed in containers can result in less total volume of the mix than the volume of the separate ingredients used. If 1 cubic meter each of sand and coarse bark are mixed, the result is not 2 cubic meters of potting mix, but approximately 1¾ cubic meters. The sand fits between the bark particles, reducing volume and aeration. Another type of shrinkage is due to decomposition of organic components of the mixture. The area of the surface compared to the volume of particles is important. Finely ground organic components decompose more rapidly than coarse ones and can further reduce aeration. Thus, it is wise, especially when plants will remain in pots for 6 months or more, to select organic components resistant to decomposition that retain desirable characteristics.

Chemical Properties of Soils and Potting Mixtures

Chemical properties of soils and container potting mixtures have direct effects on production costs and quality in foliage plant production.

Carbon and Nitrogen

The carbon : nitrogen ratio (C : N ratio) indicates the amount of carbon present in a soil or amendment relative to total nitrogen. When the C : N ratio is high (high carbon, low nitrogen), most of the nitrogen will be required by soil microorganisms during decomposition of the organic components, and the higher the ratio, the more nitrogen required. Competition for available nitrogen between microorganisms and plants can cause nitrogen deficiency. For a high C : N ratio medium, 1000 : 1, extra nitrogen must be added to compensate for that required by microorganisms above that needed for plant growth [2, 6, 10, 30, 40]. Some amendments have such high C : N ratios that if used as a large part of a potting mixture they make it difficult to grow good plants even if excellent cultural procedures are used. Materials with high C : N ratios, such as sawdust and bagasse, should not be more than 20 percent by volume of the potting mixture.

Demand for nitrogen by microorganisms is strongly dependent on the C : N ratio, but other factors influencing this include temperature, pH, soil moisture, aeration, and medium particle size. Temperature, pH, soil moisture, and aeration levels most conducive to plant growth also are beneficial to soil microorganism activity. Particle size is important to microorganisms since it determines surface area and thus decomposition rate, which will be rapid if the surface area of a particle is nearly equal to its volume, and slow if its area is small compared to volume. For example, if sawdust is very fine, the effective C : N ratio will be approximately 1000 : 1, but if coarse (½ centimeter in diameter), the effective ratio will be a more acceptable 500 : 1. If sawdust or any other organic component with a high C : N ratio is to be used, it should be as coarse as possible. Material with a high C : N ratio can be composted 2 to 3 months with 8 kilograms of nitrogen per cubic meter of material to produce an acceptable medium component.

Cation Exchange Capacity

Cation exchange capacity (CEC) refers to the ability of soils or potting mixtures to retain fertilizer ions against the leaching effects of water and to release them for plant growth. Organic, silt, sand, and clay components of soils or potting mixtures have negative surface charges, and plant nutrients dissolve into negatively (anion) and positively (cation) charged ions in the soil solution. Cations, such as ammonia, potassium, calcium, magnesium, and sodium, are attracted to negatively charged soil particles and are resistant to leaching until displaced by another cation, usually hydrogen. Anions, such as nitrates, sulfates, and chlorides, are not held by the negatively charged soil particle and are leached more easily [7].

Organic materials are usually high in CEC and provide buffering action against rapid changes in nutrient availability and pH. Materials with high CEC have high nutrient reservoirs, whereas those with low CEC retain small amounts of nutrients and require more frequent applications of fertilizer. Rapid changes in soil acidity or alkalinity (pH) can be prevented by using a soil with high CEC, but if pH adjustment is necessary, more corrective material will be required.

Cation exchange capacity is usually measured by the number of units of nutrients held by a given quantity of soil, that is, milliequivalents (meq) per 100 grams (g) of dry soil. This measurement is satisfactory for field soils, but provides a poor estimate of the number of exchange sites available in potting mixtures containing large volumes of organic components and restricted in volume, as shown in Table 7-5 by the wide variation that exists when weight versus volume is used. A more acceptable measurement in container mixtures is milliequivalents per 100 cubic centimeters, which provides a basis for determining the number of exchange sites per container. A cation exchange capacity range between 2 and 5 milliequivalents per 100 grams is satisfactory for field soils, whereas a range of 10 to 100 milliequivalents per 100 cubic centimeters is satisfactory for container-grown plants.

Certain components, such as sphagnum peat, used in potting mix-

TABLE 7-5   Cation-exchange capacity of various media [29]

Media	Cation-exchange capacity		
	meq/100 g	meq/100 cm^3	meq/15-cm pot
½ Peat, ½ sand	4	4	41
½ Pine bark, ½ sand	3	3	33
½ No. 3 vermiculite, ½ sand	25	31	341
½ No. 3 vermiculite, ½ pine bark	125	35	385
½ No. 3 vermiculite, ½ peat	141	32	352
⅔ Pine bark, ⅓ perlite	24	5	55

tures have 200 to 700 milliequivalents per 100 cubic centimeters CEC levels, but are usually mixed with other components that lower the effective volume rate. Excessively high CEC levels may reduce nutrient loss to the point that soluble salts damage may result unless carefull attention is given to the fertilizer and water program. Leaching excess salts from potting mixtures with excessively high CEC is difficult [21].

Hydrogen Ion Concentration

pH is the negative logarithm of the hydrogen ion concentration of a particular medium in terms of normality and indicates the degree of acidity or alkalinity. A pH of 7 is neutral, below 7 is acid, and above 7 is alkaline. Each unit of measurement change decreases or increases the pH by a factor of 10. For example, a pH of 5 is 10 times more acid than pH 6 and 100 times more acid than pH 7; therefore, more lime is required to change the pH from 5 to 6 than to change it from 6 to 7. pH determines the solubility of the nutrients essential for plant growth, and although plants survive in a pH range from as low as 3.5 to above 7.5, extremes should be avoided. Most foliage plants should be grown in media having a pH range of 5.5 to 6.5.

Low pH can be increased by addition of liming materials such as dolomite, calcium carbonate, or calcium hydroxide, whereas high pH can be reduced by addition of finely powdered sulfur or other acidifying material. The amount of liming material or sulfur to change pH depends on the CEC and initial pH of the soil or potting mixture. Therefore, only small amounts of material are necessary to change the pH of a sandy soil, whereas large amounts are necessary to change the pH of peat (Table 7-6). The constant use of an acidic or basic fertilizer will also change the pH.

TABLE 7-6   Approximate amount of materials required to change the pH of soils and potting mixtures to 5.7 (kilograms per cubic meter)

Beginning pH	Sandy soil	Clay loam soil	50% Peat 50% Bark	Peat
		Add dolomitic lime or equivalent amount of calcium to raise pH to 5.7:		
5.0	0.6	0.8	1.5	2.1
4.5	1.2	2.1	3.3	4.4
4.0	2.1	3.0	4.7	6.8
3.5	3.0	4.4	6.2[a]	9.2
		Add sulfur or acidifying mixture to lower pH to 5.7:		
7.5	0.6	0.9[b]	1.2	2.0
7.0	0.3	0.6	0.9	1.5
6.5	0.2	0.2	0.6	1.2

[a] Additions of more than 6 kg of dolomite per cubic meter often cause micronutrient deficiencies.
[b] If plants are growing in a medium to be acidified, do not add more than ½ kg of sulfur per 10 m² per application.

Soluble Salts

Soluble salts levels of the potting medium higher than 1,000 ppm, based on a 1 : 2 soil or medium component to water by volume procedure prior to addition of fertilizer, are high. Field soils and potting mixtures can usually be leached provided good drainage exists. Potting mixture components should have less than 1,000 ppm soluble salts, with levels lower than 500 desirable. See Chapter 9 for information concerning soluble salts.

Amendments for Soils and Potting Mixture Components

Selection of one or several components depends on many factors in addition to the physical and chemical ones discussed previously. These include cost, uniformity, sterility, availability, reliability of supply, and ease of use. Each factor must be considered in relation to efficiency as potting mixture components represent approximately 2 percent of total production costs [25]. An alphabetical listing of common potting components and soil amendments follows:

Bagasse

Bagasse, or sugar cane pulp, is readily available in several southern states and tropical countries, but has a high C : N ratio and additional nitrogen is necessary to replace that used by microorganisms during rapid decomposition. Bagasse has high water-holding capacity, but in containers decomposes quickly, causing poor aeration and shrinkage; thus it is seldom recommended or used in potting mixtures. When used, less than 20 percent bagasse by volume should be added for foliage plants to be grown in containers more than 2 months. Research indicates that bagasse can be used for short-term crops and propagation [53, 54] if thoroughly composted. Bagasse is acceptable as a field soil amendment if it can be incorporated several months prior to foliage crops being planted and is especially useful with clay soils when incorporated, since decomposition leaves air spaces in the soil profile.

Bark

Bark is widely used as a soil amendment and component of potting mixtures. Bark is available in a number of sizes from finely ground, peatlike materials to particles 1 centimeter in diameter. Its intended use is important in size selection, as fine particles are better as field soil amendments, and coarse ones are better for use in potting mixtures. The most common size ranges in use as potting components are materials from 1.5 to 6 millimeters in diameter from cypress, fir, pine, redwood, and mixed hardwoods. Generally, barks have bulk densities that approximate peat moss, lower cation-exchange and water-holding capacities, and higher C : N ratios than peat, with hardwoods (oak, hickory, beech) having higher C : N ratios than softwoods (pine, fir).

Nitrogen requirements for microorganisms in decomposition of nine hardwoods were found to be 1.1 to 1.4 percent of the weight of the wood, and the values for nineteen softwoods were between 0.3 to 1.3 [2]. Bark of proper particle size provides good aeration when added to other potting mixture components and when used as a soil amendment.

Shredded and composted bark is a partial substitute for peat in potting mixes [44]. Preplant nitrogen to compensate for initial microbial activity proved valuable when applied at a rate of 150 kilograms of nitrogen per hectare or 100 grams per cubic meter [30]. Pine bark has a bulk density of 250 kilograms per cubic meter and a cation exchange capacity of 50 to 60 milliequivalents per 100 grams [6] with a pH of 4.0 to

5.5, so addition of lime is required in most cases. Nineteen plant species rooted as well or better in 100 percent pine bark with 65 percent of the bark between 0.4 and 2.4 millimeters in size, as in 1 : 1 by volume peat-sand or 1 : 1 peat-perlite [45]. A major disadvantage of fresh pine bark is the relatively high C : N ratio and initial decomposition rate, but this is not a problem with composted bark [31]. Redwood and eucalyptus bark may have toxic components, which should be leached or degraded by composting [37].

Hardwood bark can also be used as a partial substitute for peat [22, 23, 33, 34]. Bark-soil potting mixtures possess good physical properties and will keep these properties for a year [40]. Addition of nitrogen to hardwood bark, particularly ammonium nitrate, has proved helpful to prevent nitrogen deficiency problems [26], or hardwood and pine bark can be composted for 6 weeks or more prior to use with the same results.

Hardwood bark as a potting mixture component has been reported to suppress plant parasitic nematodes and soil-borne disease pathogens [39]. Softwood barks generally are uniform in size and quality, while hardwood barks are more variable due to the mixture of several species.

Approximately 5 centimeters of bark should be incorporated to a depth of 15 to 20 centimeters when used as a soil amendment. When used in potting mixtures for foliage plant production, a range of 25 to 75 percent by volume is acceptable. Foliage plants have been grown successfully in 100 percent bark, but watering and fertilizing practices are critical due to increased aeration.

Calcined Clay

Calcined clay is a granular fired clay of uniform size that resists compaction and has moderate water-holding and cation-exchange capacities. Calcined clay improves aeration in potting mixtures and is free of pathogens, insects, and weed seeds. Montmorillonite and attapulgite clays are heated to approximately 1,400°F, producing hard, sterile granules of calcined clay that contain many pore spaces, provide 500 kilograms per cubic meter of weight to pots, and are excellent in long-term potting mixtures because they do not decompose. It is generally used at rates of 10 to 20 percent by volume, although 100 percent can be used as a propagating medium [48, 49].

Cinders

Cinders from heating or manufacturing plants can be used in foliage potting mixtures, as can volcanic cinders commonly found in Hawaii. Cinders, which vary considerably in weight, provide excellent aeration and drainage and can be sized to complement other potting mixture components. Cinders provide little cation-exchange or water-holding capacity, but may contain excess salts of some nutrients, including sulfurous products, and should be leached prior to use. Cinders can be used as a soil amendment to provide aeration or in potting mixtures where 50 percent or less by volume will impart excellent aeration [16, 17].

Muck

Muck is more highly decomposed than peat, initially costs less, and has higher water-holding and cation-exchange capacities, but provides insufficient aeration for most foliage plants because particle sizes are small, eliminating pore spaces. It is sometimes high in contaminants, such as plant pathogens, nematodes, weed seeds, and herbicide residues. Growers often utilize muck just as it comes from the bog, and wide variation in physical and chemical properties between sources may exist. Fine sand mixed with muck often ranges from 5 to 25 percent, imparting radically different physical and chemical properties to potting mixtures. Low initial cost is usually offset by sterilization costs or increased plant losses and increased production costs; therefore, this material is not suggested as a medium component.

Garbage

Municipal garbage with solid materials such as cans, metals, glass, rags and some paper removed, often is pulverized, macerated, composted for various periods of time, and used as a medium component. Municipal compost has been evaluated as a component of potting mixtures [11, 24, 50], but its use by commercial growers is limited because of unavailability, particle-size variability, and toxic or high salts [11, 28]. Municipal compost may improve aeration and is high in cation-exchange and water-holding capacities. When present, high salts levels prevent use of more than 5 to 20 percent by volume in most potting mixtures.

Perlite

Perlite (sponge rock) is expanded siliceous volcanic rock produced by heating above 1500°F. Horticultural perlite is light (100 kilograms per cubic meter), provides excellent aeration, is sterile and uniform in quality, does not decompose, has low cation-exchange capacity, and a pH of 7.0 to 7.5. It is stable to chemical and steam fumigation, resists decay, is frequently used to propagate and produce foliage plants, and can be obtained in several sizes. Perlite contains sodium, aluminum, and small amounts of soluble fluorine, which can be injurious to some foliage plants, especially during propagation in a medium of low pH; however, they can be removed by leaching heavily two or three times prior to use [27]. Perlite is light, buoyant, and tends to float out of mixtures.

Peat Moss

Peat mosses are derived from decomposed remains of sphagnum moss (most Canadian and European peats), hypnum, sedges, and other aquatic plants (most U.S. and tropical peats) and are the most commonly used components of foliage plant potting mixtures.

Peat is high in cation-exchange and water-holding capacities and, unless finely ground, provides good aeration. It is resistant to rapid decomposition and is acid, with a pH usually less than 4.0 [38], but 4 to 7 kilograms of dolomite per cubic meter of peat will usually elevate pH to a satisfactory growing range. Peat has 1 to 2 percent nitrogen, but this should not be considered in a fertilizer program. Detrimental quantities of salts are sometimes found in peat, and when dry, peat is extremely difficult to wet. Table 7-7 provides data on a number of peat mosses and indicates that they all have high water-holding capacities, but vastly different noncapillary pore space. When noncapillary pore space is less than 7 percent, aeration will be poor. Some peats can be used at 100 percent by volume as potting mixtures but usually constitute 25 to 75 percent by volume of mixtures. Peat moss is an excellent soil amendment when 2.5 to 5 centimeters is incorporated to a 15- to 20-centimeter depth [9, 14].

TABLE 7-7 Noncapillary, capillary, and total pore space found in eleven peats from various sources in Germany, Canada, and Florida [14]

Product	Noncapillary pore space (%)	Capillary pore space (%)	Total pore space (%)
German sphagnum	21	58	79
German sphagnum	18	54	72
Florida peat moss	14	70	84
Canadian sphagnum	13	72	88
German sphagnum	12	66	78
Canadian sphagnum	11	81	91
Canadian sphagnum	9	70	79
Canadian sphagnum	8	63	71
Canadian peat moss	5	71	76
Canadian sphagnum	4	50	54
Canadian sphagnum	2	55	57

Rice Hulls

Rice hulls have been used in potting mixtures for several years by some foliage growers, and their use is increasing because of the high cost of several other commonly used components. Rice hulls provide a lightweight medium with good drainage and aeration and do not affect pH, soluble salts, or available nutrients [19, 20]. They resist decomposition, but if steamed may release toxic amounts of manganese. They are usually parboiled by producers to destroy pathogens, and nitrogen fertilization should be increased about 10 percent to compensate for the high C:N ratio. They should not comprise more than 25 percent of the potting mixture by volume, and when used as a soil amendment, 2 to 3 centimeters should be applied to the soil surface and incorporated 15 to 20 centimeters deep. Rice hulls are especially useful in improving aeration in heavy clay soils.

Sand

Sand is used in potting mixtures and may also be used to improve aeration of heavy clay field soils. Sand particle sizes should not be smaller than 0.1 nor larger than 1.0 millimeter, with an average between 0.25 and 0.50 [3], the range of most washed mason sands. Sand is the heaviest of the commonly used potting components, weighing as much as 1600 kilograms per cubic meter. It is useful for anchoring potted plants in windy production locations as well as for providing aeration. Sand has negligible water-holding and cation-exchange capacities, and usually not more than 25 percent by volume of sand is used because of its high bulk density, which increases handling and transportation costs. Sand originating from coral or volcanoes may have toxic elements and seashore sand might be high in salt content.

Sawdust

Sawdust has been used in potting mixtures for years, but can cause serious problems for those who do not understand its properties. Most sawdust (cypress and redwood excepted) has a high C:N ratio (about 1000:1) and requires heavy supplements of nitrogen before plant growth will occur. The finer the sawdust, the higher the nitrogen requirement [1, 10, 15]. Addition of at least 1 percent nitrogen to sawdust based on dry weight of the potting mixture has been suggested prior to planting [2]. This level is necessary to initiate plant growth, but an excess of salts may occur if fertilizer level is not reduced when microorganisms active in decomposition begin declining in number after several weeks.

Fine sawdust also has high water-holding capacities and decreases aeration when mixed with peat moss. Sawdust should not comprise more than 20 percent by volume of potting mixtures and not more than a 2-centimeter depth should be applied as a field soil amendment.

Shavings

Shavings are similar to sawdust in composition, are larger in size, provide excellent aeration, but have less water-holding and cation-exchange capacities. Shavings have a high C : N ratio, but their large volume compared with surface area reduces requirements for additional nitrogen. Potting mixtures containing as much as 50 percent shavings have grown good-quality plants [17]. Cypress shavings require no additional nitrogen, but pine and hardwood shavings need the equivalent of 50 kilograms of nitrogen per hectare as an initial application. Shavings can be used as a soil amendment at a rate of 2 to 3 centimeters incorporated 15 to 20 centimeters. Care should be taken that shavings and sawdust are not contaminated with pentachlorophenol.

Vermiculite

Vermiculite is hydrated magnesium silicate made by heating mica or clay materials 800°F to 1,100°F, which causes rapid water loss so the mineral flakes expand as much as twenty times original thickness. The resulting air spaces absorb and hold water readily. This material, available in several sizes, has a high cation-exchange capacity of 20 to 30 milliequivalents per 100 grams, but eventually compacts, with resultant loss of aeration and drainage. It is sterile, supplies a moderate amount of potassium, a small amount of calcium and magnesium, has a weight of 100 to 130 kilograms per cubit meter, and an alkaline pH varying from 7 to above 9 [43]. Vermiculite is not suggested for use in potting mixtures for long-term crops (more than 3 to 4 months) because of its compaction problems, nor as a soil amendment in the field, although it is an excellent material for germination of seeds [5].

Field Bed Design

Foliage plants are field grown in warm climates primarily for stock production, and maximum cutting yield can be obtained if well-drained, highly aerated soils are utilized. Selection of soils, as well as management, is important, since a farm establishment is a long-term situation. Proper soils should be selected, but if this is not possible, the following steps can be taken to increase and maintain aeration and drainage.

1. Design a drainage system that rapidly removes excess surface water from growing areas. This should include a large collector ditch at the low end of the farm to collect subsurface as well as surface water.
2. Design planting beds so that surface runoff leads directly to the collector ditch and subsurface drains have the least number of turns.
3. Slope aisles to the collector ditch with at least 0.5-meter drop per 100 meters of aisle.
4. Incorporate soil amendments into the top 15 to 20 centimeters of soil with a rototiller while adding liming materials. Select amendments that do not decompose rapidly, because crops may remain in beds for 2 to 10 years, depending on foliage species selected.
5. Install two or three mole drains under each 1-meter-wide stock bed to a depth of 0.4 to 0.6 meter. If tractors can be operated in the aisle, install drains after beds are made, but if not, install drains before amendments are incorporated.
6. Crown beds so water runs into aisles, and slope aisles into collector ditches to rapidly remove runoff water. Bed height of 15 to 25 centimeters above the aisles is suggested.
7. Do not allow organic debris to collect in aisles as this will reduce their efficiency in moving surface runoff.

Maintenance of soil amendments and soil structures will be improved if a mulch is maintained on bed surfaces. Materials that are good for this purpose include wood shavings, rice hulls, and bark.

Potting Mixtures and Selection

Foliage plants can be grown in sand or in 100 percent peat, but these media require precise cultural practices. There is no single best growing medium for foliage plants, and most potting mixtures are blends of two or more components formulated to combine physical and chemical properties to obtain better characteristics than one alone. For example, peat and sand, bark and sand, or peat and perlite combine cation-exchange and water-holding capacities of organic materials with drainage and aeration qualities of mineral components. Materials used should be readily available to growers, inexpensive, uniform, sterile, and free of plant toxins. Other factors to consider include weight, cation-exchange capacity, aeration or pore space, water-holding capacity, C : N ratio, pH, soluble salts level, rate of decomposition, and compaction. A good growing medium will produce quality plants in the shortest time with the lowest total production costs. Table 7-8 provides an indication of the

TABLE 7-8 Mean chemical and physical characteristics of twenty-seven soil media [62]

Media	Ratio	Mixing shrinkage (% volume)	Bulk density (g/cm³)	Moisture equivalent (% dry wt.)	Moisture equivalent (% volume)	Noncapillary air space (% in 2½-in. pots)
Builders sand (BS)		0	1.54	1.4	2.2	2.0
Shavings (Shv)		0	0.13	87.0	11.3	17.4
Perlite (Per)		0	0.12	103.3	12.4	30.1
German peat (GP)		0	0.10	184.2	18.4	5.7
Native peat (NP)		0	0.14	305.5	42.8	5.3
BS-GP	1:2	0	0.48	34.6	16.6	3.3
BS-NP	1:2	0	0.55	51.2	28.2	4.8
BS-GP-NP	1:1:1	7.5	0.67	32.9	22.0	4.1
BS-GP	2:1	0	0.92	9.9	9.1	2.5
BS-NP	2:1	0	1.11	15.7	17.4	2.9
Shv-GP	1:2	0	0.13	190.8	24.8	5.4
Shv-NP	1:2	0	0.16	215.6	34.5	3.4
Shv-GP-NP	1:1:1	0	0.15	187.3	28.1	3.8
Shv-GP	2:1	0	0.14	118.7	16.6	6.0
Shv-NP	2:1	0	0.15	162.5	24.4	4.1
Per-GP	1:2	0	0.12	207.7	24.9	4.0
Per-NP	1:2	7.5	0.15	225.0	33.8	3.2
Per-GP-NP	1:1:1	10.5	0.12	174.2	20.9	4.1
Per-GP	2:1	0	0.15	162.1	24.3	7.6
Per-NP	2:1	15.8	0.15	169.0	25.3	6.1
BS-GP-Shv	1:1:1	12.3	0.60	20.8	12.5	4.4
BS-NP-Shv	1:1:1	22.8	0.62	23.1	14.3	4.4
BS-GP-Per	1:1:1	17.5	0.65	21.4	13.9	4.4
BS-NP-Per	1:1:1	22.8	0.63	28.2	17.8	9.5
Shv-GP-Per	1:1:1	7.5	0.14	146.3	20.5	5.5
Shv-NP-Per	1:1:1	8.8	0.13	154.7	20.1	7.8
Shv-BS-Per	1:1:1	22.8	0.64	12.7	8.1	5.2

diversity that exists when five components are utilized in combinations of two or three components.

Considerable research has been conducted to determine the best soil mixtures for use in container growing of ornamental plants. Several universities have recommended specific component mixtures. The John Innes Soil Mix was one of the first developed; the University of California suggests several combinations of peat and sand, and Cornell University, Texas A&M University, and the University of Hawaii recommend specific plant mixes [3, 4, 5, 18, 61]. Auburn University conducted experiments with a variety of plants utilizing large numbers of combinations of potting materials, but did not find one medium superior to all others, and concluded that excellent plants could be grown in a large variety of media if they had proper physical and chemical properties [55]. Publications from the universities of Hawaii and California also indicated a satisfactory plant can be grown in a variety of mixes if proper aeration and water-holding capacities are provided [16, 17, 21, 36]. Foliage plants have been grown satisfactorily in many media [8, 12, 13, 35, 42, 50, 51, 52]. Optimum soil medium alone will not eliminate all production problems, but an understanding of the physical and chemical properties of soil mixes can reduce most soil-related problems. Because the physical and chemical properties of potting mixtures are the key to their value, a summary of these are listed in Table 7-9.

Some potting mixtures specifically suggested for ornamental plants include those from Cornell University, the University of Hawaii, Texas A&M University, and the University of Florida:

1. Cornell University foliage plant potting mixtures [42].
   (a) *Foliage plant mix* for plants that require a mixture with high water-holding capacity:
   2 parts sphagnum peat
   1 part horticultural vermiculite
   1 part horticultural perlite
   Each cubic yard of this mix also includes 8 pounds of ground limestone, 2 pounds of superphosphate, 1 pound of potassium nitrate, 2 ounces of fritted trace elements, 0.75 ounce of iron sulfate, and 2.5 pounds Osmocote (14-14-14).

TABLE 7-9 Summary of chemical and physical characteristics of commonly used components of potting mixtures (L = low, M = medium, H = high)

Amendment	Bulk density	Water-holding capacity	Porosity	Cation-exchange capacity	C:N ratio
Bagasse	L	H	L	M	H
Bark	L	M	M	M	M
Calcined clay	M	M	H	M	L
Cinders	M	L	H	L	L
Muck	L	M	L	H	M
Municipal garbage	L	H	M	H	M
Peat moss	L	H	H	H	M
Perlite	L	M	H	L	L
Rice hulls	L	L	H	M	M
Sand	H	L	M	L	L
Sawdust	L	H	M	H	H
Shavings	L	M	H	M	M
Vermiculite	L	H	M	H	L

	g/cc	% vol	% vol	meq/100 cm^3	
Low	0.25	20%	5%	10	1:200
Medium	0.25–0.75	20–60%	5–30%	10–100	1:200–1:500
High	0.75	60%	30%	100	1:500

(b) *Epiphytic mix* for foliage plants that require good drainage and can tolerate drying between irrigations:
1 part sphagnum peat
1 part horticultural perlite
1 part Douglas fir bark
Each cubic yard contains the same fertilizer amendments as in part (a), in the following amounts in pounds: 7, 4, 1, 2, 0.5, and 2.5, respectively.

2. University of Hawaii potting mixture for plants requiring good drainage:
1 part woodshavings
2 parts cinders

3. Texas A&M University growing mix for foliage plants [18]:
1 part sphagnum peat
1 part perlite

4. University of Florida foliage plant bench and potting mixtures [50]:

(a) *Raised bench* stock production [mixture (1) is for solid bottom benches and mixture (2) for wire bottom benches]:
(1) 3 parts peat
1 part sand
(2) 3 parts peat
1 part perlite

(b) *Propagation benches* [if fluorine is a problem in mixture (2) because sensitive cuttings are being propagated, substitute Styrofoam]:
(1) 100 percent peat
(2) 3 parts peat
1 part perlite

(c) *Potted foliage plants* [mixes (1) and (2) are excellent greenhouse mixtures]. Mix (1) has better aeration than mix (2). Mix (3) is best in larger containers and is heavy (good in shade house growing structures).
(1) 2 parts peat
1 part bark
1 part shavings
(2) 1 part peat
1 part bark
(3) 3 parts peat
1 part sand

Many other potting mixtures also will grow excellent foliage plants and may be used. Table 7-10 provides suggested standards for potting mixtures for foliage plants.

TABLE 7-10   Suggested standards for potting media used to grow foliage plants

Bulk density	0.30–0.75 g/cm^3 (dry), 0.60–1.2 g/cm^3 (wet)
Water-holding capacity	20–60% volume
Total pore space	5–30% volume after drainage
pH	5.5–6.5
Cation-exchange capacity	2–40 meq/100 g dry weight, 10–100 meq/100 cm^3
Soluble salts	400–1,000 ppm [soil/water ($\frac{1}{2}$) by volume]

Placing a fixed cost on potting mixes is difficult because there may be hidden costs associated with their acquisition, storage, mixing, potting, and use that are not evident at first. A recent survey in Florida indicated that the average cost of potting media equaled 2 percent of sales; however, this considered only observable costs such as the mixture components, labor, and equipment. Hidden costs that relate to production factors may include added costs of unsalable plants, reduction in quality, slow turnover, and increased labor costs due to drenching and weeding, which should properly be charged to the potting mix [46, 47]. Small growers might save by purchasing premixed potting mixtures rather than purchasing components and mixing them utilizing their own labor and equipment.

REFERENCES

[1] Adamson, R. M., and E. F. Maas. 1971. Sawdust and other soil substitutes and amendments in greenhouse tomato production. *HortScience* 6(4):397–399.

[2] Allison, F. E., R. M. Murphy, and C. J. Klein. 1963. N requirements for the decomposition of various kinds of finely ground woods in soil. *Soil Sci.* 96:187–190.

[3] Baker, K. F., ed. 1957. The U. C. system for producing healthy container-grown plants. Univ. Calif. Agr. Expt. Sta. Manual 23.

[4] Bewley, W. F. 1963. *Commercial glasshouse crops.* London: Country Life Limited.

[5] Boodley, J. W., and R. S. Sheldrake. 1977. Cornell peat-lite mixes for commercial plant growing. Cornell Plant Sciences Information Bulletin 43.

[6] Brown, E. F., and F. A. Pokorny. 1975. Physical and chemical properties of media composed of milled pine bark and sand. *J. Amer. Soc. Hort. Sci.* 100:(2):119–121.

[7] Buckman, H. O., and N. C. Brady. 1960. *The nature and properties of soils.* New York: Macmillan, 567 pp.

[8] Bunt, A. C. 1973. Some physical and chemical characteristics of loamless pot-plant substrates and their relation to plant growth. *Mededelingen Fakulteit Landbouw Wetenschappen Gent* 38(4):1954–1965.

[9] Christensen, O. V. 1971. The influence of some types of peat on the growth of *Hedera canariensis* Willd. 'Gloire de Marengo' and *Codiaeum variegatum* Bluem 'Gedulgig' and 'Hollufiana'. *Saertryk af tidsskrift for planteavl* 75:337–348.

[10] Conover, C. A., and J. N. Joiner. 1963. Effects of media, nitrogen and phosphorus on growth of container grown *Lantana* spp. 'Cream Carpet' and *Ligustrum japonicum*. *Proc. Fla. State Hort. Soc.* 76:445–449.

[11] _____, and J. N. Joiner. 1966. Garbage compost as a potential soil component in production of *Chrysanthemum morifolium* 'Yellow Delaware' and 'Oregon.' *Proc. Fla. State Hort. Soc.* 79:424–429.

[12] _____. 1967. Soil mixes for ornamental plants. *Florida Flower Grower* 4(4):1–4.

[13] _____, and R. T. Poole. 1974. Influence of media and fertilizer rates on *Aglaonema* 'Fransher.' *Proc. Fla. State Hort. Soc.* 87:431–435.

[14] _____. 1977. What do potting mixes cost. *Proc. 1977 National Tropical Foliage Short Course* 1:109–113.

[15] Cotter, D. J. 1974. Yields of successive cropping of tomato in sawdust and bark media. *HortScience* 9(4):387–388.

[16] Criley, R. A. 1973. Synthetic media for container grown plants. *Misc. Publ. Univ. of Hawaii. Coop. Ext. Ser.* 103:31–41.

[17] _____, and R. T. Watanabe. 1974. Response of chrysanthemum in four soilless media. *HortScience* 9(4):385–387.

[18] DeWerth, A. F., and R. E. Odon. 1960. A standard light weight growing medium for horticultural specialty crops. Texas Agricultural Experiment Station Misc. Pub. 420.

[19] Einert, A. E. 1972. Performance of rice hulls media for pot Easter lilies under three forcing systems. *HortScience* 7(1):60–61.

[20] _____, and E. C. Baker. 1973. Rice hulls as a growing medium component for cut tulips. *J. Am. Soc. Hort. Sci.* 98(6):556–558.

[21] Furuta, T. 1968. *Nursery management handbook. Section 6. Soil mixtures.* Univ. of Calif. Agr. Ext. Serv. AXT-284.

[22] Gartner, J. B., M. M. Meyers, and D. C. Saupe. 1970. Hardwood bark as a growing media for container-grown ornamentals. *Forest Products J.* 21(5):25–29.

[23] _____, S. M. Still, and J. E. Klett. 1973. The use of hardwood bark as a growth medium. *Proc. Int. Plant Prop. Soc.* 23:222–230.

[24] Gogue, G. J., and K.C. Sanderson. 1975. Municipal compost as a medium amendment for chrysanthemum culture. *J. Am. Soc. Hort. Sci.* 100(3):213–216.

[25] Gunter, Dan L. 1976. Business analysis of foliage nurseries in Florida, 1975. Univ. of Fla. Food and Resources Economic Department Economic Information Report 60. 20 pp.

[26] Harkin, J. M., and J. W. Rowe. 1969. Bark and its possible uses. U.S. Dept. Agr. Forest Serv. Res. Note. FPL-091. 42 pp.

[27] Henley, R. W., and R. T. Poole. 1976. We can live with perlite now. *Florida Foliage Grower* 13(11):4,5.

[28] Hortenstine, C. C., and D. F. Rothwell. 1969. Evaluation of composted municipal refuse as a plant nutrient source and soil amendment on leon fine sand. *Proc. Soil Crop Sci. Soc. of Fla.* 29:312-319.

[29] Joiner, J. N., and C. A. Conover. 1965. Characteristics affecting desirability of various media components for production of container-grown plants. *Pro. Soil Crop Sci. Soc. of Fla.* 25:320-328.

[30] _____, and C. A. Conover. 1967. Comparative properties of shredded pine bark and peat as soil amendments for container-grown pittosporum at different nutrient levels. *Proc. Am. Soc. Hort. Sci.* 90:447-453.

[31] _____, and C. A. Conover. 1969. Southern pine bark market in horticulture analyzed. *Forest Industries* 96(5):37.

[32] Juncker, P. H., and J. J. Madison. 1967. Soil moisture characteristics of sand-peat mixes. *Soil Sci. Soc. Am. Proc.* 31:5-8.

[33] Klett, J. E., J. B. Gartner, and T. D. Hughes. 1972. Utilization of hardwood bark in media for growing woody ornamental plants in containers. *J. Am. Soc. Hort. Sci.* 97(4):448-450.

[34] _____, and J. B. Gartner. 1975. Growth of chrysanthemums in hardwood bark as affected by nitrogen source. *J. Am. Soc. Hort. Sci.* 100(4):440-442.

[35] Laurie, A., D. C. Kiplinger, and K. S. Nelson. 1958. *Commercial flower forcing.* New York: McGraw-Hill.

[36] Lunt, O. R., and H. C. Kohl. 1957. Influence of soil physical properties on the production and quality of bench grown carnations. *Proc. Am. Soc. Hort. Sci.* 69:535-542.

[37] _____, and B. Clark. 1959. Horticultural applications for bark and wood fragments. *Forest Products J.* 9:39A-42A.

[38] McConnell, D. B., W. E. Waters, and R. T. Poole. 1972. The chemical properties of several peat sources. *Florida Foliage Grower* 9(7):1-4.

[39] Malek, R. B., and J. B. Gartner. 1975. Hardwood bark as a soil amendment for suppression of plant parasitic nematodes on container-grown plants. *HortScience* 10(1):33-35.

[40] Mazur, A. R., T. D. Hughes, and J. B. Gartner. 1975. Physical properties of hardwood bark growth media. *HortScience* 10(1):30-33.

[41] Morgan, W. C., J. Letey, S. J. Richards, and N. Valoras. 1966. Physical soil amendments, soil compaction, irrigation and wetting agents in turfgrass management. I. Effects on compactability, water infiltration rate, evapotranspiration and number of irrigations. *Agron. J.* 58:525-528.

[42] Mott, R. C. 1971. Cornell foliage plant mixes. *Florists' Rev.* 148(3839):22.

[43] Nelson, P. V. 1969. Assessment and correction of the alkalinity problems associated with Palabora vermiculite. *J. Am. Soc. Hort. Sci.* 94(6): 664-667.

[44] _____. 1972. Greenhouse media—The use of Cofuna, Floramull, pinebark, and Styromull. N.C. Agr. Exp. Sta. Tech. Bull. No. 206.

[45] Pokorny, F. A., and H. F. Perkins. 1967. Utilization of milled pine bark for propagating woody ornamental plants. *Forest Products J.* 17(8):43–48.

[46] Poole, H. A., and H. K. Tayama. 1976. Extension slants—soil costs—are you making the right decisions. Ohio Florists Assoc. Bull. No. 558, p. 4–6.

[47] _____, and H. K. Tayama. 1976. Extension slants—the hidden costs of poor soil : losses. Ohio Florists Assoc. Bull. No. 559, p. 6–7.

[48] Poole, R. T., B. A. Greaves, and J. A. Silva. 1968. Effect of soil media on container grown hibiscus and aralia. *Proc. Fla. State Hort. Soc.* 81:443–447.

[49] _____. 1969. Rooting response of four ornamental species propagated in various media. *Proc. Fla. State Hort. Soc.* 82:393–397.

[50] _____, and W. E. Waters. 1972. Evaluation of various potting media for growth of foliage plants. *Proc. Fla. State Hort. Soc.* 85:395–398.

[51] _____, and C. A. Conover. 1974. Media and watering effects of *Aechmea fasciata. Florida Foliage Grower* 11(12):1–2.

[52] _____, and C. A. Conover. 1975. Media, shade and fertilizer influence production of the Areca palm *Chrysalidocarpus lutescens* Wendl. *Fla. State Hort. Soc. Proc.* 88:603–605.

[53] Rodriguez, S. J., L. Rivera-Lopez, and A. Santiago. 1973. Performance of *Asparagus sprengeri* and *Dracaena sanderiana* in different potting and root-ing media. *J. Agr. Univ. Puerto Rico* 57(4):314–319.

[54] _____, and L. Rivera-Lopez. 1975. Performance of silverleaf fern, *Pteris ensiformis* 'Victoriae' and spider plant, *Chlorophytum comosum* 'Vittatum' in various growing media. *J. Agr. Univ. Puerto Rico* 59(2):125–128.

[55] Self, R. L., J. I. Ware, R. D. Rouse, and H. P. Orr. 1967. Potting mixtures and fertilization practices for container-grown ornamental plants. Au-burn Univ. Agr. Exp. Sta. Circ. 157.

[56] Spomer, L. A. 1975. Water and air in the soil. Illinois State Florists Assoc. Bull. No. 361.

[57] _____. 1976. Soil aeration and plant growth. Illinois State Florists Assoc. Bull. No. 363.

[58] _____. 1976. Container soils are different. Illinois State Florists Assoc. Bull. No. 365.

[59] _____. 1977. How much total water retention, and aeration porosity in my container mix. Illinois State Florists Assoc. Bull. No. 369.

[60] Swartz, Walter E., and Louis T. Kardos. 1963. Effects of compaction on physical properties of sand-soil-peat mixtures at various moisture con-tents. *J. Agronomy* 55:7–10.

[61] Voss, R. L., and D. P. Watson. 1968. U. H. potting mix. Univ. of Hawaii Coop. Ext. Serv. Circ. 424.

[62] Waters, W. E., W. Llewellyn, and J. NeSmith. 1970. The chemical, physical and salinity characteristics of twenty-seven soil media. *Proc. Fla. State Hort. Soc.* 83:482–488.

[63] White, J. W. 1974. Criteria for selection of growing media for greenhouse crops. *Florists' Rev.* Vol. 155, Issue No. 4009:28–30, 73–75 (Oct. 3, 1974).

eight

R. W. Henley
R. T. Poole

water
and foliage
plants

Foliage plants are composed of 80 percent or more of water. Water is essential as the matrix for cytoplasm, structural components of proteins and nucleic acids, a reagent of biological transformations, and as a climatic force of the environment. It acts as a carrier of essential nutrients and carbohydrates and permits reaction between molecules in solution and between enzymes and substrata.

The path of water through plants begins with absorption from the soil by roots and ends as a component of plant tissue or in the gaseous state emitted to the atmosphere by transpiration from leaves. Water maintains turgidity in plants, although some plants grown for indoor use, such as cacti, some dracaenas, maranta and peperomias, show little evidence of wilting even when moisture availability is extremely limited. Plants such as aphelandra, croton, and schefflera visibly collapse when water is lacking.

Most water in plants is found within cells, but it is also found in cell walls and between cells. It is found throughout plants from root tip to apical shoot, but the amount varies depending upon species, age, and environment. Distribution of water throughout plants forms the conductive system necessary for transport of essential materials. Water movement through plants occurs continuously, even though the environment may have a high relative humidity. Only a small proportion of water absorbed by plants remain in them, for they are inefficient users of water. They require a constant supply for optimum growth, but utilize only a small amount, which creates problems for commercial foliage growers in determining when, how much, and how to apply water to foliage plants.

Water Quality

An abundance of good water is not absolutely essential, but preferable, for production of foliage plants. Soft water or water low in calcium (Ca) and other minerals is desirable because less residue remains on the foliage from irrigation. Hard water can produce good growth, but plants grown with hard water must be washed to be aesthetically pleasing if overhead irrigation systems are used. Calcium and, to some extent, magnesium cause most of the hardness that results in water residue on foliage, except when less than 50 parts per million. Irrigation with hard water also increases the pH of media.

Water should be analyzed periodically because quality may vary. Pollutants are pumped directly into subsurface water in some areas, and there is the possibility of salt-water intrusion because of excessive pumpage of fresh water. Drought or heavy water use can also alter water quality.

Several parameters are used to determine water quality. The pH of water is important. Acids, acid-generating salts, and carbon dioxide lower pH, while carbonates, bicarbonates, and hydroxides increase it. A pH of 5.5 to 6.5 is most desirable for plant growth, but water with a pH of 6.5 to 7.5 is acceptable. Additions of lime to soil when pH is low and of sulfur when water pH is high may be necessary to keep it at the proper pH. Total salts or soluble salts are dissolved minerals from fertilizer addition and saline water. Soluble salts level of irrigation water should be less than 500 parts per million, but water with 1,500 parts per million has been used satisfactorily when plants are watered heavily and the proper medium is utilized. Increasing frequency of watering and the amount applied and reducing fertilizer applications and amounts will reduce the detrimental effects of water containing high soluble salts. Sodium (Na) is dissolved from many types of rocks and soils, and sodium concentrations create soils with poor structure, sticky when wet and hard when dry. Sodium is less a problem in most foliage media that contain high amounts of organic matter. Less than 20 parts per million of sodium is desirable, but 50 parts per million is not considered excessive. Problems of excessive sodium can be alleviated with additions of calcium. Chlorine (Cl) is found in most water and, in combination with sodium, is a common contributor to high soluble salts. Less than 50 parts per million of chlorine is desirable under proper cultural techniques.

Fluorine (F) is present in some water at levels as high as 7 parts per million. A zero level of fluorine is preferred; it can be neutralized with additions of calcium. Fluorine added to water for medicinal purposes is usually at a concentration of 1 part per million, which is not damaging to propagation and production of most foliage plants. Iron (Fe) is essential for plants, but an excess in the water will cause plants to be unsightly. Iron should be less than 0.1 part per million.

Several methods are available to improve water quality. Ion-exchange resins that exchange one ion for another are used to deionize or remove ions from water. Distillation removes impurities by evaporating the water and condensing pure steam. Reverse osmosis involves passage of water through a semipermeable membrane under pressure.

Water Usage by Plants

Use of water in a greenhouse can be as much as 400 kiloliters per hectare per week or more than 20,000 kiloliters per hectare during a year of continuous growing. Twenty liters of water per square meter of bench area at each irrigation is frequently used, which causes some leaching if the soil is 8 to 12 centimeters deep.

Most growers use more water than is necessary, wasting a large portion of the water and fertilizer, resulting in contamination of surface and groundwater. Plants can be grown with considerably less water than customarily used while maintaining good quality by reducing the amount applied and using saucers under pots. Excess irrigation results in poor aeration, waste of water and fertilizer, reduced plant growth, and eventual death. Roots of plants killed by overwatering deteriorate before tops, and damage is frequently irreparable before it is noted.

Excess water increases the incidence of root rot, causing growers to use fungicidal drenches when reduction in water would be all that is necessary for good growth. Plants die from lack of water when the soil is saturated because roots fail to function and because of rot due to poor aeration caused by overabundance of water. This causes wilted foliage from lack of oxygen, which prevents water absorption, similar to that found on plants growing in soil with insufficient moisture.

Water requirements of foliage plants vary considerably. Aphelandra and some ferns require three or four weekly irrigations, while epipremnum and dracaenas can thrive on weekly or biweekly irrigations. Irrigation frequency also varies with size of plants and containers, soil potting mixtures, soil and air temperatures, solar radiation, humidity, and air movement. A wilting problem frequently found in greenhouses during winter months is caused by large differences between the temperature of the atmosphere surrounding leaves and the temperature of the water around roots. Soil water may be less than 15°C on cold nights with thermostats turned down, whereas air temperature can be 10° to 15°C higher when hot air is forced from heaters. Under these circumstances, roots cannot absorb moisture fast enough to maintain turgidity in rapidly transpiring leaves, and wilting occurs. Water usage of most foliage plants increases as the cold, dark days of winter are replaced by the higher temperatures and light intensities of spring, and desiccation results if irrigation schedules are not altered. Changes in relative humidity and air movement also influence water usage of foliage plants.

Complete schedules cannot be given for irrigation of foliage plants. Each grower must use judgment in evaluating environmental conditions, appearance or feel of the soil medium, pot size, and the particular kind and size of plant in determining watering regimes. Misjudgment resulting in improper watering practices is one of the largest causes of reduced plant quality and yield in the industry. Mist is commonly used for propagation only during the day, but moisture should be supplied to cuttings when heaters are needed during cold nights [3].

Soil Moisture

Water necessary for foliage plant growth is stored in potting media; thus several factors should be considered in choosing media combinations (see Chapter 7). Porous material should be used to allow penetration of water, yet the medium should store sufficient water for plant use until the next irrigation. With each irrigation, sufficient water should be applied to thoroughly moisten the medium.

Water is stored in solid, liquid, and gas forms. Bound or hygroscopic water comprises the solid form, which is held so strongly by soil particles that it is unavailable to plants. The gaseous form is in the air within the pore spaces of the medium and can be absorbed by plants. The liquid phase comprises the largest portion, 90 to 99 percent of available moisture, which exists along capillary surfaces in the soil mass.

Some of the water applied to media is lost by leaching and some is held by the medium. Water adheres to soil particles and is held in soil pores by adhesive properties between water and soil and by the cohesive properties between water and water. Surface tension is created, which holds water against the pull of gravity, but which is not strong enough to prevent water uptake by plants. Soil properties and water quality determine the force of water retention or water suction. As water suction increases, plants are less able to absorb it; thus, soil suction determines soil moisture availability.

Availability is determined by the attraction of water to soil particles, matric suction, and effects of soil solutes on osmotic suction. Matric suction of soil particles determines movement and retention of water, whereas osmotic suction is influenced primarily by fertilizer application and resultant salt concentration. High osmotic suction or high salt concentration actually can withdraw water from plants. Soil pores hold most of the water available to plants, with many small pores retaining more water for plant use than a few large pores, but large pores supply oxygen.

Water Stress

Water stress or plant water deficit results when plants require more water than they are able to absorb from the soil, but this seldom occurs in commercial nurseries except from overwatering. A small variation in water content (10 percent) can significantly affect many plants, because processes required for growth function at reduced rates as water within the plant is reduced. This effect can occur without visible evidence. Wilting occurs as water deficiency becomes more acute, resulting in closing of stomata, preventing gas exchange, and growth is reduced or stopped entirely. Lack of gas exchange from too much water results in impaired photosynthesis, respiration, and protein synthesis. Reduction in the amount of water applied several weeks before sale of foliage plants may aid plants by improving their survival in the home. Frequent, heavy irrigations in commercial nurseries may produce luxuriant, attractive foliage, but small root systems, whereas reduction of water promotes enlarged root systems by allowing for better aeration.

Size of root systems relative to top, oxygen level in the potting medium, water-holding capacity of the medium, humidity, air movement, temperature, and light influence water absorption and success or failure of plants in indoor environments. During acclimatization, root system size can be improved by reducing nutrition and lengthening intervals between watering. This method reduces top growth while root growth continues, with an increase in the root-to-shoot ratio producing a plant less likely to wilt with infrequent watering. If soluble salts are high, however, reduction in water application may cause salt damage, so addition of fertilizer should be reduced or eliminated. Water deficit and high salts produce similar symptoms on foliage plants. Severe water deficit causes cells to become permanently injured, with marginal necrosis of leaves or general chlorosis resulting eventually in leaf abscission. Water stress and/or high light intensity causes leaves on some plants, such as aglaonema and calathea, to point upward, exposing a minimal amount of leaf surface to sunlight. Some plants such as Boston fern become gray or dull green when subjected to water stress.

Criteria for Selection of an Irrigation System

Often there are multiple objectives of an irrigation system, which may include irrigation by applying water to root systems, application of fertilizer to roots and/or foliage, application of pesticides, leaching of excess nutrients from root zones, maintenance of high or elevated humidity in crop areas, and/or cold protection. The type of irrigation system selected should be governed by the type of nursery and structures employed, which may vary from open fields with no structures to fabric shade houses and/or shaded greenhouses. The following criteria should be evaluated in selecting an irrigation system.

Size and topography of nursery   A large nursery often can justify the cost of sophisticated irrigation equipment that would be prohibitive in small nurseries consisting of only one or two small greenhouses or limited bed area. This is also true for related equipment connected to irrigation systems such as fertilizer injectors.

Organization of nursery   The nursery layout, including floor plan of beds or benches, is important when designing irrigation systems. When growing space is utilized efficiently by beds, benches, or plants, an automated irrigation system is feasible. Conversely, if beds or benches are broken into small, disorganized units, the feasibility of employing a modern automated system is reduced and hand watering may be the most economical.

Type of growing unit   The type of growing unit, such as raised benches or ground beds, can determine the type of irrigation system. Overhead irrigation can be used for most units, but raised or ground benches are required for subirrigation or capillary watering systems.

Most limiting factors   Factors other than irrigation may limit efficiency of crop production more than improvements upon an existing irrigation system. Improvements upon factors that most limit efficiency of crop production should be made before large expenditures are incurred in improving the irrigation system.

Flexibility to modify   New irrigation components and new crop culture technology are being developed constantly, so nursery owners should carefully plan a system for watering crops that can be modified with minimal expense as new technology becomes available or as the nursery is expanded.

Crop type   Crop species and plant size should be considered when planning an irrigation system. Overhead irrigation systems thoroughly wet plant canopies, causing them to be susceptible to disease attack and transmission due to free-standing water on foliage, splashing water, or high humidity around plants. Surface irrigation and subsurface irrigation systems are advised with disease-prone crops.

Container size and crop rotation   Nursery operations that use a standardized cropping system employing one container size in a regular rotation can use irrigation systems that deliver water directly to each container. However, nurseries that constantly change container sizes and spacing in given areas may not be able to do this.

Mobility   The degree of mobility for materials and labor can often be increased by carefully designing an irrigation system. Where flow patterns of labor, equipment, and materials must cross water pathways, irrigation lines should be placed overhead or underground. Buried irrigation lines or surface lines with risers could limit certain types of activity in beds or benches.

Quality of labor   The sophistication of an irrigation system adopted may be limited by the skills of nursery workers in operating equipment. Irrigation systems with elaborate controls cannot be understood or operated by many greenhouse workers.

Delivery rate   The amount of water required in a given time for a specific area is an important consideration. The capacity of wells, pumps, pipes and nozzle types, and spacing figure into delivery rates. Most nurseries are designed with several irrigation zones or areas that can be used sequentially to eliminate the need to water an entire crop section in a given time frame. Such a system of zoning reduces pump and well size requirements.

Uniformity of water application   Uniformity of water application to crops is dependent upon several factors, including the type of irrigation system employed. Usually, systems engineered to irrigate an area without wasting excessive amounts of water are most desirable. The surface irrigation systems and subirrigation technique, if properly operating, will do an excellent job, but overhead systems that will apply water uniformly and still result in a highly efficient system are difficult to design.

Air turbulence   Air turbulence within a production area influences the pattern of irrigation water applied overhead. The amount of wind or air turbulence should be carefully evaluated before irrigation design plans are finalized. Placement of irrigation heads and selection of head type can overcome many air turbulence problems associated with such systems. Surface or subirrigation techniques eliminate most water distribution irregularities created by air turbulence.

Water quality   Sources of irrigation water relatively high in soluble salts may influence the selection of an irrigation system. Water with a high mineral content usually has two inherent problems: (1) the accumulation of soluble salts or increase in salinity within a plant root zone, and (2) associated residue left on foliage and stems irrigated overhead (Table 8-1). Water containing suspended impurities also leaves prominent residues on plants. Should water with relatively high salinity values be used, the soil should be maintained in a moderately moist condition most of the time. As soil salinity increases, soil should be leached frequently enough to maintain salt values within acceptable limits. Leaching can be accomplished only through irrigation systems that apply water over the canopy of plants or at the soil surface. Subirrigation techniques using saline water usually result in rapid, high salt accumulations, especially at soil surfaces.

Moisture conservation   The importance of conserving high-quality water cannot be overemphasized owing to greater stresses

TABLE 8-1   Classification of water quality for growing foliage plants in high organic matter content soil mixes according to electrical conductivity and total dissolved salts

Class of water	Electrical conductivity (mho/cm × 10^{-5} at 25°C)	Total dissolved salts (ppm)
Excellent	Less than 15	Less than 105
Good	15–35	105–245
Acceptable	35–75	245–560
Poor	75–145	560–1,015
Unacceptable	More than 145	More than 1,015

being placed upon the environment. The type of irrigation system employed and its use in production are primary factors relating to conservation of moisture in nursery operations. Systems that apply water into containers or on only that portion of the nursery floor space used in crop production conserve considerable water compared to overhead sprinklers. To maximize efficient use of water, the portion of the system that regulates the amount of water applied to growing containers must be adjusted carefully. Conserving water for conservation's sake is enough, but occasionally a nursery is confronted with purchasing water from a municipal water system as a backup or as an only source of irrigation water. The cost of municipal water can often be high, making this a further incentive for utilizing irrigation systems that use water most efficiently.

Reliability and life expectancy   Reliability and life expectancy of an irrigation system or system component depend on the quality of components, usage, care, and weathering. Other factors, such as corrosive materials that contact the system and temperature extremes, should also be considered when applicable.

Cost of system   The degree of sophistication and quality of components and the ease of installation figure into the cost of irrigation systems. Ultimately, efficiency of the system becomes a part of the cost factor.

Economics of operation   Automated control systems for regulating irrigation save labor. Such systems prevent tying up labor that can be used for other jobs. One should not become too reliant on automated controls without adequate checking of controls and other components to see that they are functioning properly. Overall labor requirement is greatly reduced through use of sophisticated controls, but personnel necessary to manage and operate such controls must be well qualified.

Systems of Irrigation

Supersurface (Overhead) Irrigation

Several generalizations can be made regarding use of irrigation systems that apply water over the crop canopy. They are flexible within production areas for changing container sizes and/or plant spacing without adjusting the water distribution pattern, and this feature appeals to

TABLE 8-2 Influence of spacing, distance, distribution pattern, and container size on percentage of surface covered by containers and the number of containers per acre[a]

Distribution pattern of containers	Inches between containers	Percent of surface covered[b]			Containers per acre[c]		
		1 gal	2 gal	3 gal	1 gal	2 gal	5 gal
Square	0	79	79	79	174,240	128,118	77,786
0 0 0 0	1	58	60	64	128,118	99,000	63,130
0 0 0 0	2	44	48	53	99,000	77,786	51,857
0 0 0 0	4	28	32	38	63,130	51,857	37,230
	6	20	23	28	43,560	37,231	27,923
	12	9	11	14	19,360	17,355	14,235
Triangular	0	91	91	91	198,000	150,207	88,898
0 0 0 0	1	67	70	73	145,200	114,632	72,600
0 0 0 0	2	51	55	61	111,692	88,898	59,670
0 0 0 0	4	33	37	44	72,600	59,671	43,129
	6	23	26	33	50,069	43,129	32,267
	12	10	12	17	22,338	20,260	16,438

[a] Adapted from [9].

[b] Diameter of containers: 1 gallon = 6 inches, 2 gallons = 7 inches, and 5 gallons = 9 inches.

[c] Calculations are for a solid pattern without space for walks, drives, and so on.

many nursery owners. The relative low cost of some overhead systems appeals to others. Irrigation overhead raises relative humidity in growing areas temporarily, which may be good or bad and tends to reduce mite populations by the syringing action of airborne water particles. Water applied overhead reduces foliar-applied pesticide residues, but if the water is of poor quality, it may leave undesirable residue on plants.

A serious drawback to overhead irrigation is the tremendous waste of water, up to 90 percent, depending upon plant spacing and plant type. Container spacing, particularly close spacing, and placement patterns have a pronounced influence on water use efficiency when applied overhead. Efficiency of overhead systems is greatest when round containers are placed in a triangular pattern with tight spacing (Table 8-2).

Foliage canopies of many plants have a shielding influence or umbrella effect, deflecting most of the water from the foliage away from the container. Plant species and stage of development determine the efficiency of a canopy to repel water from overhead. A few plants, such as most bromeliads, produce a funnel effect that permits plants to capture more moisture than would enter a plant container exposed to overhead irrigation.

Hose and breaker   The tried and proved technique of manual application of water to crops with a flexible hose fitted with a breaker to fracture the coarse emerging stream of water into fine streams or blend it with sufficient air to decrease its impact on plants and soil surface is a satisfactory method for some situations (Figure 8-1). Water can be applied at the soil surface with large plants rather than overhead. Usually, garden-type hoses ranging from ⅝ to ¾ inch (1.6 to 1.9 centimeter) in inside diameter are used for this purpose with standard hose fittings or fast-connect fittings.

Manual watering with a hose has been replaced by more automated systems in many nurseries, but there are situations best served by a hand-held hose. These include initial irrigation of recently planted material, spot watering or spot liquid fertilizer applications to groups of plants with special requirements, or irrigation in holding areas for wholesaling or retailing.

The following points are critical if manual watering is to be effective: (1) selection of hose, breaker, and flow rate should be appropriate for the soil mix, plant type, and container being used, (2) individuals assigned to crop irrigation should recognize subtle signs of plant moisture stress from one plant to the next and monitor soil moisture levels, and (3) individuals should be methodical in their approach to watering plants and follow a definite pattern to minimize skips, water thoroughly when required, and use only the required amounts of water.

Stationary sprinklers   Spinning and impact sprinkler heads are used in many large areas to provide wide coverage from a single

Figure 8-1.   Water breakers and extension threaded for standard garden hose fittings.

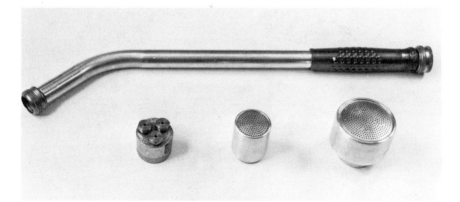

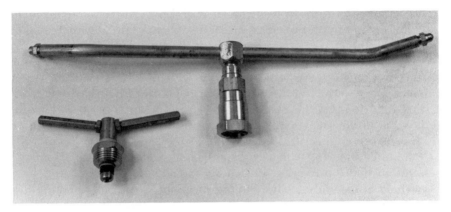

Figure 8-2.   Spinning-type sprinkler heads.

head, especially from impact types. Both types have capability for 360-degree patterns, and some impact types can be adjusted for narrower angles of distribution desirable at edges or corners of production areas (Figures 8-2 and 8-3). Sprinkler heads are available with a variety of features, including different delivery rate, range, angle of coverage, trajectory height, and droplet size. Additional flexibility is achieved by regulation of sprinkler height and pressure used. Most systems are installed with patterns that overlap to provide the most uniform distribution of water possible. A 50 to 70 percent overlap, depending upon sprinkler heads and air movement, should be used with all sprinkler

Figure 8-3.   Impact-type sprinkler heads.

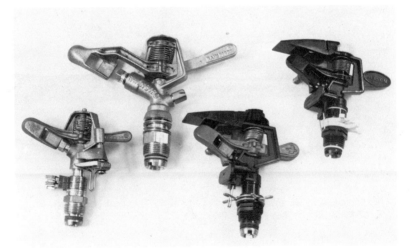

heads or coarse mist nozzles where uniform water distribution is required.

Under shadehouse or open-field conditions where wind influences distribution of water, lateral lines should be oriented 90 degrees to the direction of prevailing wind, with sprinklers spaced closer in the lines than the distance between lateral lines. Several technical publications on the design and selection of components for sprinkler irrigation systems are available [8, 16, 24]. A specialist is sometimes necessary to assist with layout and selection of equipment for specific applications unless a nursery employee is knowledgeable of irrigation systems.

Systems should be tested for uniformity of distribution after installation. An easy method is to place a series of calibrated cylindrical containers such as large cans in a grid pattern between overlapping sprinklers and irrigate. If much variation exists in amounts of water caught in test containers, adjustments in the system should be made. Engineers use a formula to determine the variation of water distribution within a test area. The formula for variance or coefficient of uniformity may be obtained from several sources [8, 9, 16].

Sprinkler irrigation is not a desirable method of cold protection for tropical foliage plants, but it is frequently used for protection of large stock plants and large potted trees grown under full sun in southern Florida and other areas with similar climate. An irrigation system installed to provide a dual function must have the capability of distributing 0.3 to 0.5 inch (8 to 13 millimeters) of water per hour over the entire crop area on a continuous basis. Nurseries equipped only for sequential irrigation of different zones cannot adequately protect plants.

Mobile sprinklers   Several sprinklers have been designed to limit investment in irrigation systems that use a single mobile unit equipped with one or more heads. These irrigate a large area each by moving through crop areas at speeds that distribute the desired amounts of water per unit area. A few systems involve a skid or ground trolley that supports the sprinkler head or heads on a riser at desired elevation; they are guided to opposite ends of the growing area by means of a track or line on the ground. These ground-level units perform the irrigation function and are relatively inexpensive but have never been popular, because they require close supervision to operate properly and provide an obstruction for mobility in growing areas since they normally operate in aisles.

Improved versions of moving sprinklers for greenhouse structures have been designed by several firms. They supply uniform applications of water to small plants in high-density plantings. These more sophisticated and costly systems consist of an overhead track suspended over the length of a greenhouse. Each track has an electrically propelled trolley equipped with solenoid valves, with an irrigation boom extending the width of the greenhouse. Numerous small nozzles with overlapping patterns provide uniform irrigation as the boom moves over the plants. Some systems designed for wide houses irrigate plants on one side as the trolley and boom travel to one end of track; then water is applied through the other half of the boom for irrigation of the remaining plants as the boom assembly returns to the starting position. Some overhead boom irrigation systems are also designed to apply pesticides. When pesticides are applied, the trolley moves faster to provide only a foliage spray rather than irrigation of root medium. Well-designed boom irrigation systems are usually more expensive than fixed sprinkler systems and partially obstruct traffic moving the length of houses, since they are normally suspended below head height.

Fixed spray heads   A variety of plastic and/or metal nozzles without moving parts has been developed for the nursery industry to apply irrigation water in circular or angular patterns. Some of these deflection-type nozzles produce larger droplets than nozzles designed specifically for mist propagation, but they are occasionally used for mist propagation and irrigation (Figures 8-4 and 8-5). Fixed spray nozzles usually have limited range (2- to 6-foot or 0.6- to 1.8-meter radius)

Figure 8-4.   Flat-pattern spray nozzles.

Figure 8-5. Overhead mist-spray system installed to provide water for both mist propagation and irrigation of rooted plants.

compared to spinning and impact types, which propel water much farther. Heads with distribution patterns of 4- to 8-foot (1.2- to 2.4-meter) diameter are usually selected in many greenhouses, shade-houses, and outdoors where irrigation or fertilization zones of a single bed width are desired.

Skinner lines   Skinner lines are mentioned here primarily for historical interest (although they were once used widely for irrigation of horticultural crops) [12, 20]. Skinner or nozzle lines [9] consist of a number of small, fixed, narrow-angle nozzles mounted with overlapping patterns on long rigid headers supported 5 to 8 feet (1.5 to 2.4 meters) above the ground on risers that permit headers to be rotated approximately 180 degrees. Drawbacks to skinner lines are the mechanical requirement to rotate the headers (manual or automated), the high trajectory of water when lines are turned to irrigate plants close to headers, and nonuniform pattern of water distribution.

Overhead mist systems   Mist systems are used primarily for propagation of cuttings. A detailed history of mist use for plant propagation was prepared by Snyder [23]. Leafy cuttings that lose water rapidly require frequent applications of water to prevent moisture stress in the propagule. The moisture requirements of plants vary tremendously depending upon plant species, temperature, relative humidity, and degree of rooting. Some material requires free moisture on the foliage at all times; other plants may only need mist applications a few times a day or less.

Most propagation mist systems employ small, deflection-type fixed nozzles that produce a flat, 360-degree pattern of fine droplets at line pressure of approximately 40 pounds per square inch (2.8 kilograms per square centimeter) and distribute 3 to 15 gallons (11 to 57 liters) per hour (Figure 8-6). Deflection nozzles have mostly replaced the modified oil-burner-type nozzles for mist propagation. Oil-burner-type nozzles modified for propagation will operate satisfactorily at line pressures of 30 to 40 pounds per square inch (2.1 to 2.8 kilograms per square centimeter), and some having nonclogging features, but they are more expensive than deflection types. Research has indicated that oil-burner-design nozzles that have a whirling action apply water more uniformly than deflection types [22].

Most mist propagation nozzles are designed to cover the general width of propagation beds (4 to 6 feet or 1.2 to 1.8 meters), permitting zone control of specific benches or bench sections. Nozzles should be installed with circular patterns overlapping approximately 50 percent to achieve maximum uniformity in water distribution. Many early propagation benches were designed with mist nozzles installed atop risers extending 18 to 24 inches (45 to 60 centimeters) above the bench. Most

Figure 8-6.   Mist nozzles used for intermittent mist propagation.

recent designs employ main lines suspended over the bench or bed with nozzles installed directly into the mains. Drip onto benches from nozzles on main lines suspended overhead can be minimized by installation of a low-pressure valve at the end of each main opposite the valve. These valves are maintained in open position when line water pressure is less than 3 to 5 pounds per square inch (0.2 to 0.3 kilograms per square centimeter). As pressure increases during the mist cycle, the low-pressure valve closes and then releases at the end of cycle, allowing excess water in the header to escape rapidly.

One or two filters in the line ahead of solenoid valves and mist nozzles are needed to prevent valves from sticking and clogging nozzles with suspended particulate material. Filters should be cleaned every 2 weeks or as frequently as required, depending upon purity of water and nozzle type. Fail-open-type solenoid valves can be used for mist systems to assure adequate moisture on plants being propagated in the event of electrical power failure [10].

Mist irrigation during propagation and early plant establishment of cuttings requires more sophisticated controls than those needed for established plants, because many cuttings in propagation beds need frequent applications of small amounts of water. As cuttings become rooted, the frequency and amount of mist used can be reduced. Staging the propagation mist to match plant requirements is easily accomplished with modern time clocks or irrigation programmers.

Fog systems   Fog systems have been in use to a limited extent by propagators for over 30 years. The concept of fog propagation is to provide a constant relative humidity of 100 percent around the plant parts without using excessive amounts of water. Fog systems are used most effectively on crops that have a low light requirement, permitting them to be grown in a heavily shaded greenhouse with minimum ventilation, and on crops that need exceptionally good aeration in the root zone [25]. Fog systems operating properly allow most of the fine moisture particles to evaporate before reaching crop level.

Fog generators are of two general types: centrifugal and high pressure. The centrifugal systems break water droplets into extremely fine particles as water is propelled from a specially designed disc spinning at high speed. Centrifugal units are most appropriately used for relatively small propagation areas where one or a few units can provide the fog required.

High-pressure mist has been used with varying degrees of success for over 30 years. Early use of high-pressure mist was primarily for evaporative cooling of greenhouses and to regulate humidity in production areas. Recent requirements in high-pressure systems have permit-

Figure 8-7. High pressure fog nozzles for propagation and evaporative cooling systems.

ted development of fog equipment that produces water particles with an average size of 10 microns that remain suspended in the air until they evaporate. Improved filter and nozzle design have created renewed interest in fog systems for numerous applications, including propagation (Figure 8-7). Heavy applications of fog will result in sufficient moisture in the air to provide a film of water on plants in propagation if desired. Since the pump, filter, regulator, gauges, and control are expensive, high-pressure fog systems should be considered primarily for large propagation areas.

Surface Irrigation

Systems that trickle or spray water onto soil surfaces under the plant canopy are referred to as surface irrigation systems. Surface irrigation water is normally restricted to the area where plants are growing and not wasted between containers or applied to foliage, where diseases and residues often develop.

Individual container tubes   The most popular type of surface irrigation used by the nursery industry for containers consists of a series of fine polyethylene tubes extending from a main line or from a series of lateral lines to each container within a block. Several authors

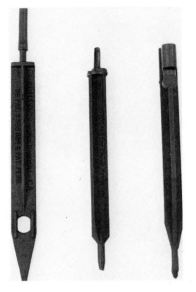

Figure 8-8.   Spray nozzle-stakes used in medium to large containers.

have discussed systems of tube watering for container plants [9, 13, 14, 15]. Tubes are equipped with anchor weights made of lead or plastic, which break the water stream into a series of drops that fall to the soil surface without disturbing it. Anchor weights on container tubes support tube openings slightly above the soil surface, minimizing chances of soil particles plugging the tubes after the water is turned off. Container tubes with anchor weights are most desirable in 5-inch (12.5-centimeter) diameter containers and larger where cropping is standardized in terms of container size and spacing. Occasionally, 4-inch (10-centimeter) diameter pots are equipped with container irrigation when plants are widely spaced and it is desirable to keep water off the foliage.

Some container tubes are equipped with special nozzles molded from plastic or made from metal and plastic with a stake on the lower end to anchor the nozzle in position on one side of the container (Figure 8-8). Spray from the nozzle is directed onto soil surfaces on the opposite side of the container from the input tube. Spray stake devices are usually designed for containers of 2-gallon (7.6-liter) capacity and larger. In large containers of 12-inch (30-centimeter) diameter and larger, some nursery owners use perforated tubular rings on the ends of tubes that are placed on the soil surface to provide numerous outlets for better water distribution. Technical data available from most manufacturers provides specifics on the number of tube units that should be installed per unit length of main line of a given size.

Container tube irrigation systems are especially useful for plants in

Figure 8-9. Irrigation tubes installed for hanging-basket plant production.

hanging baskets, which are often difficult to water by hand or other systems that do not confine water to containers. A highly functional system can be constructed by supporting plastic main lines with fasteners to metal or wood support members within a greenhouse at the desired height. These members also act as hanging supports for the baskets (Figure 8-9). A single valve at the end of each line can irrigate a long row of baskets. Plants in hanging containers constructed with snap-on basal saucers should be grown without saucers attached to facilitate drainage and minimize development of root rot.

Drip hoses or seep hoses   Several manufacturers of irrigation equipment and supplies have a line of perforated tubing that is made for irrigation of crops growing in soil benches or beds. The tubing is laid on the soil surface between rows of plants parallel to the bench length [13, 15]. Distance between irrigation hoses should be about 8 to 12 inches (20 to 30 centimeters). Foliage stock plants commonly grown in soil benches or beds usually lend themselves to drip hose irrigation.

Tubing design varies with the manufacturer and the use for which it is intended. Most of the tubing is made from 4- to 8-mil black poly-ethylene film, which is stitched or heat sealed together. Products with a sewn seam usually utilize the space around the threads for water to seep from the tube onto the soil surface. In other products the plastic hose is actually perforated to permit water to escape. Some of the least expensive hose is constructed with a single wall, but for long runs of over approximately 100 feet (30 meters), double-wall hoses are preferred because of more uniform pressure achieved throughout the line. The double-wall design has a smaller inner tube with widely spaced large ports that release water to the larger outer tube, which has closely spaced outlets to emit water. Operating water pressures recommended for most of the drip hose products are low, approximately 2 to 10 pounds (0.9 to 4.5 kilograms).

Drip hose irrigation applies moisture to crops in strips and relies on lateral movement of water in soil to wet the remaining volume of root medium. Downward movement of water occurs in close proximity to the hose on the surface, and essentially no leaching occurs between hoses. Periodic leaching with water applied overhead will make soluble salts levels more uniform in benches or beds that remain in production for long periods.

Surface-mounted nozzles   A few foliage plants, particu-larly stock plants in soil benches or beds, can be irrigated effectively with systems designed to spray water from small, flat, spray nozzles 1 to 3 inches (2.5 to 7.5 centimeters) above the soil surface at the perimeter or center of a bench or bed [13, 15, 20]. Systems of this type have been employed for many years in the production of cut flowers where basal leaves did not interfere with the flat lateral spray patterns or, in some instances, were removed to improve the distribution pattern. Systems with surface-mounted nozzles should be considered primarily for crops that have only stems exposed at the base. Plants with dense foliage near the soil prevent penetration of surface sprays.

An original design of this type, called the Ohio surface irrigation system [13], consists of a central main line of rigid pipe with 360-degree flat pattern nozzles tapped into the top of the pipe at approximately 3-foot intervals to provide for a 60 to 70 percent overlap of nozzle patterns. A shortcoming of these systems is that the outer edge of water distribution pattern extends into the aisle unless side boards are installed to contain it.

Another variation of the surface spray irrigation system employs a perimeter main line installed on the edges and ends of a bench or bed with 180-degree flat spray nozzles or 180-degree nozzles alternated with nozzles having greater range and narrower angle of distribution, usually 45 degrees. Narrow-angle nozzles are selected for corners to minimize water waste.

Subsurface Irrigation (Subirrigation)

Subsurface irrigation includes several techniques of introducing water to the bottom of the root medium, and, in the case of many containers, it is administered below containers. System designs vary greatly, including capillary benches, capillary mats, and individual containers with self-contained reservoirs. Techniques for subirrigation used by flower growers are discussed in other texts [13, 20]. Research has demonstrated that capillary irrigation of container-grown plants uses less than one half the water required with overhead systems [1].

Capillary benches   Watertight benches containing sand or other particulate materials are used by a few horticulturists for subirrigation of container-grown plants placed upon them. In some cases, water is maintained at a constant level below the bed surface; in other instances, the water level is raised and lowered or permitted to become depleted between irrigations. Weight of the particulate layer and water necessitates heavier construction and more elaborate preparation for watertight benches for this type of irrigation, which has decreased the popularity of capillary benches.

Capillary mats   Capillary mat irrigation involves the construction of benches that are flat and level or flat with a slight incline from side to side [15]. Benches are covered with a watertight film and a capillary mat material laid over the film. Most capillary mat products are fabricated from synthetic fibers $\frac{1}{8}$ to $\frac{3}{16}$ inch (3 to 5 millimeters) thick and are offered in rolls in one or more commonly used bench-top widths. Mat materials should be relatively durable, excellent for lateral movement of water applied, and provide good capillary contact with containers set on the surface. The benches should be as flat as possible to avoid pockets that trap excessive amounts of water and difficult-to-wet peaks. Level benches usually have water administered every 1 to 1.5 feet (30 to 45 centimeters), using either modified pot tube irrigation systems or seep hoses running the length of benches. The irrigation water should be introduced along the upper edge if the bench is designed with a slight incline of 1 inch (2.5 centimeters) in approximately 50 inches (1.2 meters) of bench width, and allowed to flow the width of the bench for sufficient time to irrigate containers placed upon mats (Figure 8-10).

Plastic pots with drainage holes in the bottom or at the extreme

Figure 8-10. Capillary mat irrigation system installed on an inclined bench. Water is introduced along the upper edge.

basal end of the container side wall function well with capillary mats [5], as do porous clay pots. Soil mixes selected for use with capillary mat irrigation should be well drained with plenty of large pore spaces.

Capillary benches and mats are especially well adapted to plants in small containers, up to 5 inches (12.5 centimeters), on close spacing; however, larger containers can be used. Pot size and spacing can be changed without modification of the irrigation system.

Many growers using capillary mats add fertilizer to irrigation water supplied to the mats. Considerable algae grow on moist mats after a period of several weeks, but the mats continue to function adequately with algae accumulation. Long-term crops grown on mats frequently develop high salinity in the root medium, especially near the soil surface. Soils of capillary irrigated crops should be tested periodically since water and fertilizers ascend from the bottom of the container, and the soluble salts tend to accumulate at the soil surface. If undesirable levels of salts accumulate, application of overhead water every 6 to 9 weeks to remove excessive fertilizer may be necessary.

Excessive algae growth can be removed by applying chlorine bleach or chlorine products used for swimming pools on the mat surface between crops. The chlorine material should remain on the moist mats long enough to permit all algae to be killed. After treatment, the mat should be flushed thoroughly with fresh water until the chlorine products are removed.

Figure 8-11. Self-subirrigated planter.

Self-subirrigating containers   Several firms recently have manufactured and/or marketed containers in the United States equipped with a water reservoir and capillary column that maintain a relatively constant moisture level in the root zone when reservoir water is maintained at an appropriate level (Figure 8-11). Many large, self-subirrigating, over 8-inch (20-centimeter) diameter containers require plants to be installed in finished sizes by installation specialists or consumers. Smaller containers, 4 to 8 inches (10 to 20 centimeters) in diameter, are frequently planted with small rooted plants and are finished in the self-subirrigating containers by commercial growers.

Container design and root medium vary with manufacturer and grower. The capillary column may consist of a number of materials depending upon container design. Some containers employ a wick that extends from the root zone portion of the container down into the water reservoir. A variation of the same principle is a container with a narrow, often tapered, column of root medium, inorganic and/or organic, which projects into the reservoir. Container systems that use coarse, open, porous, inorganic particles as the root medium usually use the lower zone of root medium column as the capillary column.

The selection of an inorganic material with the desired physical and chemical properties is extremely important to the success of the hydroponic system of culture. Most of the literature available on soilless systems provides formulas for nutrient solutions [2, 6, 7, 11, 20, 21]. Soilless systems for growing foliage plants are becoming more popular.

REFERENCES

Note: References [4], [17], [18], and [19] are not directly quoted in Chapter 8, but are listed to aid students and researchers.

[1] Auger, Edward, Charles Zafonte, and J. J. McGuire. 1977. Capillary irrigation of container plants. *Proc. Intern. Plant Prop. Soc.* 27:467–473.

[2] Biebel, Joseph P. 1958. Hydroponics—The science of growing crops without soil. Bulletin No. 180. State of Florida, Department of Agriculture, Tallahassee, Fla. 50 pp.

[3] Conover, C. A., and R. T. Poole. 1974. Foliage collapse of *Dieffenbachia picta* 'Perfection' during propagation. *Sou. Nurserymen's Assoc. Nursery Res. J.* 1(1):1–6.

[4] ———. 1977. Influence of fertilization and watering on acclimatization of *Aphelandra squarrosa* Nees. *Hort. Sci.* 12(6):569–570.

[5] ———. 1977. Influence of potting media and fertilizer source and level on growth of four foliage plants on capillary mats. *Proc. Fla. State Hort. Soc.* 90:316–318.

[6] Ellis, N. K., Merle Jensen, John Larsen, and Norman F. Oebker. 1974. Nutriculture systems—Growing plants without soil, State Bulletin No. 44. Purdue University Agricultural Experiment Station, West Lafayette, Ind. 20 pp.

[7] Epstein, Emanuel, and B. A. Krantz. 1965. Growing plants in solution culture, AXT-196. University of California, Agricultural Extension Service, Davis, Calif. 13 pp.

[8] Fry, A. W., Alfred S. Gray, et al. 1971. *Sprinkler irrigation handbook,* tenth ed. Glendora, Calif.: Rain Bird Sprinkler Manufacturing Corporation, 43 pp.

[9] Furuta, Tokuji. 1970. Nursery management handbook—Section VIII— Soil moisture, its application and control. AXT-323. California Agricultural Extension Service, University of California. 24 pp.

[10] Hartmann, Hudson T., and Dale E. Kester. 1968. *Plant propagation— principles and practices,* second ed. Englewood Cliffs, N.J.: Prentice-Hall, 702 pp.

[11] Kiplinger, D. C. 1956. Growing ornamental greenhouse crops in gravel culture, Special Circular 92. Ohio Agricultural Experiment Station, Wooster, Ohio. 37 pp.

[12] Laurie, Alex, D. C. Kiplinger, and Kennard S. Nelson. 1958. *Commercial flower forcing,* sixth ed. New York: McGraw-Hill, 509 pp.

[13] ———. 1968. *Commercial flower forcing,* seventh ed. New York: McGraw-Hill, 514 pp.

[14] Nelson, Kennard S. 1967. *Flower and plant production in the greenhouse.* Danville, Ill.: Interstate Printer –Publishers, Inc. 335 pp.

[15] Nelson, Paul V. 1978. *Greenhouse operation and management.* Reston, Va.: Reston. 518 pp.

[16] Pair, Claude H., Walter W. Hinz, Crawford Reid, Kenneth R. Frost, eds. 1975. *Sprinkler irrigation,* fourth ed. Silver Springs, Md.: Sprinkler Irrigation Association, 615 pp.

[17] Poole, R. T., and C. A. Conover. 1974. Media and watering effects on *Aechmea fasciata. Florida Foliage Grower* 11(12):1–2.

[18] ———. 1976. N, P and K fertilization of the bromeliad, *Aechmea fasciata* Baker. *HortScience* 11(6):585–586.

[19] ———, and W. E. Waters. 1974. Bud-break in canes of *Dracaena fragrans* Ker cv. Massangeana. *HortScience* 9(6):540–541.

[20] Post, Kenneth. 1959. *Florist crop production and marketing.* New York: Orange Judd Publishing Company, 891 pp.

[21] Sowell, Walter F. 1965. Hydroponics—growing plants without soil, Circular P-1. Auburn University, Cooperative Extension Service, Auburn, Ala., 11 pp.

[22] Stoltz, L. P., J. N. Walker, and G. A. Duncan. 1977. Mist nozzles. *Proc. Intern. Plant Prop. Soc.* 27:449–454.

[23] Snyder, William E. 1965. A history of mist propagation. *Proc. Intern. Plant Prop. Soc.* 15:63–67.

[24] Young, Virgil E. 1976. *Sprinkler irrigation systems,* third ed. Seattle, Wash.: Craftman Press, 132 pp.

[25] Warner, Zophar P. 1966. Fogging machines vs. intermittent mist. *Proc. Intern. Plant Prop. Soc.* 16:167–169.

nine

J. N. Joiner
C. A. Conover
R. T. Poole

nutrition
and fertilization

About 160 years ago scientists had determined that ten elements were required for plant growth. Three of these ten were supplied from air and water: carbon (C), hydrogen (H), and oxygen (O). The others, nitrogen (N), phosphorus (P), potassium (K), calcium (Ca), magnesium (Mg), sulfur (S), and iron (Fe), were obtained by plants from the soil or other growing medium. Six additional elements have been determined essential for plant growth, including manganese (Mn), zinc (Zn), copper (Cu), boron (B), molybdenum (Mo), and chlorine (Cl). These last six also are generally supplied through growing media.

The elements nitrogen, phosphorus, potassium, calcium, magnesium, and sulfur are called macro or major elements, and the remaining ones, iron, manganese, zinc, copper, boron, molybdenum, and chlorine, are micro, minor, or trace elements. They are so called because of the amounts of each required by plants for normal growth and production. Trace element deficiencies have become a recognizable problem in agriculture only in recent years owing to use of more refined, high analysis fertilizers. They were supplied years ago as impurities in unrefined fertilizer materials.

Nitrogen, potassium, magnesium, sulfur, and boron are soluble in the soil, and thus are leached by rainfall and irrigation. Nitrogen and potassium are the most easily leached and are used by plants in the highest concentrations; therefore, they must be regularly supplied by a fertilizer program. Magnesium is also easily leached, especially in sandy soils, but it is used in much smaller quantity by plants and, therefore, does not need to be supplied as frequently or in as high concentrations as nitrogen and potassium. Organic sources of nitrogen decompose to inorganic forms under conditions of high temperature and water relationships and are leached.

Sulfur is usually supplied as an impurity in several sources of fertilizers. Boron is required in very small concentrations and must be supplied with care. The other elements are insoluble in most soils and generally are not leached; therefore, they can be supplied less frequently (see section on Fertilizer Frequency, page 244).

Interactions Between Fertilization and Other Cultural Factors

Light Relationships

Adjusting fertilizer levels to light intensities is one of the major and most important problems faced by foliage plant growers. This relationship controls the type of growth, quality of product, propagational responses, and potential for acclimatization. Commercially, failure to properly balance fertilization with light intensity is one of the weakest links in production.

Results of the first quantitative research on light intensity/fertilizer relationships were published in 1918 by two German scientists [30], and later results through the years have confirmed their work. Under relatively low light and high fertilization rates, plants become leggy (long internodes) and have thin, weak stems and light green foliage. With a slight increase in light intensity and/or reduction of fertilizer, growers may produce plants that are vigorously vegetative and have dark green, large, thin leaves. These look excellent, but have little to no food reserves. By further increasing light intensity and/or reducing fertilizer application, plants will assume a more "normal" appearance, that is, green leaves, good, but not luxuriant vegetative growth, with ample food reserves to last through some periods of lower light intensity. Further increases in light intensity and/or reduction in fertilizer levels and plants become nitrogen deficient, being stunted with small, yellowish, thick leaves, and the plant becomes woody and brittle. The relationship between light intensity and fertilizer levels as described is relative and cannot be given quantitative terms, but it should indicate the importance of controlling fertilizer levels in terms of light intensities. Briefly, the greater the shade levels, the less fertilizer plants can use efficiently. Thus, growers should reduce fertilization during times of prolonged cloudy weather or if structures are erected that limit light admission.

Producing the most and highest quality plant material per acre is the object of foliage plant production; therefore, plants should be grown with the highest light intensity possible to utilize efficiently the largest amount of fertilization consistent with production of acclimatized plants [4, 5]. Many times, to obtain more vigorous growth with darker green color, growers add additional shade, whereas the proper answer would be to increase fertilization. By the same token, many grow under conditions of high shade levels without reducing fertilization, and thus obtain undesirable plant growth. Each plant has an optimum ratio of light and fertilization levels, and adjusting to this is a matter of trial and error using the recommendations given later in this chapter.

pH Relationships

pH is a measure of the alkalinity or acidity of soils, with pH 7 being neutral. Below this point is acid; above it is alkaline. pH is important only because it controls the availability of nutrients in the soil to plants. Nutrients are generally most available within a pH range of 5.5 to 6.2, and this is the range to which growing media should be adjusted for best growth response. At alkaline pH, most minor elements become unavailable and deficiencies appear. At very acid pH, these same elements become unavailable again, plus aluminum in the soil can become available to phytotoxic levels. Plants particularly susceptible to fluoride injury, such as many of the dracaenas, should not be grown in media having less than pH 6, for below this point fluorine can be sufficiently available to become toxic [17].

Temperature

Temperature largely controls the rate of plant growth and, thus, the fertilizer requirements of plants. The more growth by plants, the more fertilizer needed to sustain growth rate and quality. During times of high temperatures, more fertilizer can be applied per unit area than during periods when temperatures drop, especially below 65°F (18°C).

Temperature also affects preferential absorption of certain elements as well as total quantity. For example, iron is usually more difficult for plants to absorb in cold weather, and this should be given special attention [54].

Water

Many elements supplied through the soil are water soluble, and a high percentage absorbed by plants enters with inflow of water. As the amount of soil water increases, everything else being equal and ample aeration provided, the higher the quantity of elements in solution within the soil mass and immediately available for plant absorption.

Factors that affect water absorption by plants also affect nutrient absorption. Transpiration, which is the loss of water vapor from the leaves, usually results in higher absorption by roots and a higher inflow of nutrients. High light intensities and temperatures increase transpiration rate and, thus, nutrient absorption [47].

Media

The most important medium characteristics from a nutritional point of view should provide high cation-exchange and water-holding capacities and good aeration. Obtaining ideal levels of these three factors is not easy, and usually more than one constituent must be mixed together to obtain them.

Cation-exchange capacity (CEC) is the measure of the medium's ability to adsorb fertilizer materials to soil surfaces and retain them against leaching for slower, more gradual release to plant roots. The higher the CEC, the more fertilizer that can be added per application without burning plants and the less frequently fertilizers need be added. Water-holding capacity is also controlled by CEC, with higher CEC mixes holding the most water, thus necessitating less irrigation frequency [26].

Plant roots cannot absorb water or fertilizer elements except in the presence of air within the soil mass. Media must allow for constant and rapid air exchange (see Chapter 7).

Elements: Their Functions, Deficiency, and Toxicity Symptoms

Nitrogen (N)

Nitrogen is required by plants in higher concentrations than any of the other elements, except potassium in certain instances. Optimum levels of N in foliage plant leaves range from 1.5 to 4.5 percent on a dry weight basis, with most ranging from 2.5 to 4.0. Nitrogen is absorbed by plants in the nitrate (NO_3) or ammonium (NH_4) forms regardless of its source, changed in the plant to the amine form (NH_2), and then combined with soluble carbohydrates to form amino acids, which combine to form protein. Nitrogen is translocated primarily as amino acids and synthesized into proteins in the leaves. Proteins comprise a large percentage of the living component of plant cells. Nitrogen also is a part of nucleic acids, enzyme systems that activate metabolism (the life-giving processes in plants) and is a part of the chlorophyll pigment that is responsible for photosynthesis [54].

Nitrogen is very mobile within plants, and deficiency symptoms of this element first occur in older leaves. In cases of deficiency, proteins in older leaves degrade to amino acids, which are translocated to young tissue where they are resynthesized into proteins for new cell development. The first indication of N deficiency is development of a pale green color in older leaves, which then turns to green yellow, yellow green, yellow, and cream colored as the deficiency becomes more severe and young leaves become smaller. Chlorosis (yellowing) is general over the entire leaf area, and older leaves usually drop before death occurs [23].

Phosphorus (P)

Phosphorus is required by plants in amounts approximately one tenth that of nitrogen or potassium. Optimum leaf concentrations of this element in foliage plants range from 0.15 to 0.3 percent of dry weight. Although required in relatively small concentrations, it plays an extremely vital role in plant metabolism.

Phosphorus combines into a high-energy organic complex within plants and provides the energy required for chemical reactions necessary to maintain life and growth. These high-energy complexes are adenosine diphosphate (ADP) and adenosine triphosphate (ATP). Phosphorus is also a component part of certain fat globules found in living cells, nucleic acids, and in storage forms in seeds (primarily phytin).

Phosphorus is nonmobile and nonleachable in soils, but is extremely mobile within plants. Deficiency symptoms of this element, like nitrogen, are always found in the older tissue first. The beginning symptom is a loss of sheen or shine of the older leaves (some report this as a darker green color); leaves appear dull. Next red, yellow, and bluish pigments begin to show through the green, usually along the main veins on the under side of leaves, and this "fall" coloration spreads to other portions of leaves as the deficiency progresses. Young leaves during this time remain green, but become very small, often reduced to about one tenth of normal size. Old leaves usually drop before necrosis or death occurs, but if not, necrosis begins at leaf tips and progresses toward the base [23].

Potassium (K)

Healthy plant leaf tissue usually contains from 1.5 to 5 percent potassium on a dry weight basis. Like N, most foliage plants contain from 2.5 to 4.5 K, thus requiring K at about the same levels as N and at higher levels than other mineral elements. It is the only element that has never been found in organic combination within plant tissue and, thus, is exceedingly mobile, moving preferentially from old tissue to young, meristematic areas. Potassium is even leached directly from leaves during heavy rainfall and from cuttings in propagating beds under mist. Some other elements are also leached in these ways, but not to the same extent as K.

Deficiency symptoms of K are, like N and P, always found in old leaves first, although this is not a deficiency often found under commercial conditions. Usually, there is no chlorosis associated with K deficiency, but sections of leaves turn directly from green to brown. Necrosis begins at leaf tips or terminal margins of leaves and progresses toward the base, or occurs as irregular spots throughout the leaves, being more severe at leaf bases, or a combination of the two patterns. Occasionally, oily spots occur on the under side of basal leaves, which later develop into necrotic areas [23].

Magnesium (Mg)

Deficiency of magnesium is among the most prevalent nutritional problems in foliage plant production in Florida and other production areas. Few foliage operations have plants without symptoms of Mg deficiency. Reasons for the prevalence of this elemental deficiency is that it is leachable from the soil, as is K and N, and although not as leachable as N, is slightly more so than K. Magnesium is low in most Florida soils and in most organic materials used in growing media. This element needs to be constantly supplied through a fertilizer program, but unlike N and K it seldom is supplied in most commercial fertilizer mixes, and few growers think to add it as a separate or additional item. Magnesium becomes a special problem under alkaline soil conditions because of the competitive effects of calcium (Ca). Tissue levels of 0.35 to 0.5 percent dry weight should be maintained [27].

Magnesium deficiency symptomology is fairly specific in most pinnately (netted) veined leaves such as *Philodendron scandens* subsp. *oxycardium*. Chlorosis begins at upper margins progressing inward and downward in an arclike pattern. The chlorosis is actually a bronze yellow color, giving Mg deficiency the original name of bronzing disease. The chlorotic pattern progresses leaving a V-shaped tip of green on the leaf tip and an inverted V-shaped green area at the leaf base. As the deficiency becomes more severe, the tip loses its green color first, followed by the basal section, and by this time necrosis begins in the upper margins where chlorosis was first apparent. Necrotic areas spread in the same manner as the chlorosis and are usually rusty brown in appearance [23].

Magnesium is very mobile within plant tissue and, like the three previous elements, is preferentially translocated to terminal portions of stems and leaves; therefore, deficiencies occur in older leaves first.

Calcium (Ca)

Calcium is seldom a problem in plant production for it is usually provided in pH control. Calcium is found in healthy tissue in a range from 0.6 to 1.5 percent dry weight. When media are adjusted to the proper pH range (5.5 to 6.5) by any limiting material, sufficient Ca is provided for plant requirements. Liming materials are highly insoluble and, thus, not easily leached from media.

Calcium is immobile within plants, and deficiency symptoms generally occur at terminal points first. Usually, stem tips die when Ca is deficient, and further growth cannot occur. Terminal leaves become small, without a patterned chlorosis, and older leaves become thick and brittle.

Philodendron scandens subsp. *oxycardium* and *Epipremnum aureum* are two of the rare exceptions to the immobility of Ca in plants. In these two, and perhaps other vine types of foliage plants, the beginning symptoms of Ca deficiency appear as small yellow spots first on the vine's basal leaves, and symptoms move up the vine until, in severe cases, all or nearly all leaves show symptoms, with tip leaves the last to develop symptoms. Yellow chlorotic spots occur usually in the basal half of leaves, and expand to large, irregular, yellow areas that have numerous small oil-soaked-appearing spots scattered throughout larger chlorotic areas. In severe cases, leaf tissue breaks down into large necrotic spots, and leaves so affected frequently abscise [23].

Sulfur (S)

Commercially, S deficiency is seldom a problem in plant nutrition inasmuch as it is provided as a carrier for various sources of other elements, such as ammonium sulfate and potassium sulfate. Sulfur is immobile in plants, and deficiency symptoms appear first on younger leaves. Symptoms are identical to N deficiency (for example, a general yellowing of the entire leaf), but occur on younger rather than older leaves, which is opposite the case with N deficiency [23]. Sulfur deficiency has not been reported on any foliage plant as of this writing.

Iron (Fe)

Iron is probably the most common microelement deficiency in foliage plants and is particularly common where plants are grown at high pH. A satisfactory range in tissue is 50 to 100 parts per million.

Typical Fe deficiency begins as a mild interveinal chlorosis with veins and veinlets remaining green. The intervenous areas progressively turn from green yellow, to yellow green, to yellow, and finally to cream colored. By the time the deficiency is so severe that leaves have become cream colored, veins and veinlets have lost their persistent green color and the entire leaf is affected. Such leaves are small and frequently abscise. Deficiency symptoms always appear on younger tissue first, as is true with all microelements.

Manganese (Mn)

Deficiency symptoms appear on young tissue first and are very similar to Fe deficiency, except that the persistent band of green along veins and veinlets is broader, including tissue immediately adjacent to veins and veinlets. The interveinal chlorosis is not as severe as with Fe deficiency; it seldom progresses past the green yellow stage and there is little to no loss in leaf size. Severe cases of Mn deficiency symptoms have not been observed in foliage plants. Satisfactory tissue levels in healthy plants range from 50 to 100 parts per million.

Copper (Cu)

Copper deficiency first causes severe stunting of plants, with terminal leaves becoming exceedingly small (often only one fifth or less of normal size). Terminals die as the stunting advances, and multiple budding occurs immediately below the dead terminal. These buds will also die terminally, and often multiple buds will develop on each break, giving the plant a "witches broom" appearance. Normal tissue levels range from 5 to 15 parts per million.

Boron (B)

Boron deficiency is characterized first by internodes becoming noticeably shorter, with thickened stems that become tough and brittle and leaves that become small, stiff, and rigid. Black, sunken necrotic spots develop in stems just below nodes. In vine crops, nodal roots become thickened and stubby and slough off. Vines develop a characteristic curling at the nodes producing a "pigtail" appearance. Boron deficiency destroys geotropic responses in plants, causing them to grow laterally and in other abnormal ways. Terminal leaves of affected plants become very small, puckered, thickened, blunt, and have irregular streaks of chlorotic areas interveinally. Levels of boron in foliage plant tissue have not been determined.

Zinc (Zn)

Zinc deficiency has not been induced in foliage plants under experimental conditions and, therefore, the symptomology cannot be described. Satisfactory tissue levels range between 20 to 50 parts per million, but can be much higher.

Toxicity Symptoms

Toxicity symptoms for most elements have not been determined and defined. Excessive N and K cause salt burning effects that are the same as drought symptoms (e.g., marginal necrosis beginning at the tips of younger leaves). Severe leaching is the only way to overcome this problem. High Ca and P result in development of one or more microelement deficiency symptoms.

Among microelement toxicities, Fe toxicity usually is indicated by Mn deficiency symptoms, and Mn and Cu toxicities as Fe deficiency symptoms. Boron toxicity appears as whitish necrotic spots along leaf margins and in irregular spots within the leaf area.

The two most prevalent toxicity symptoms occurring in certain foliage plants are fluorine (Fl) and chlorine (Cl) injuries. Toxicity symptomologies for both of these elements are approximately the same: marginal and tip necrosis of leaves with older leaves showing symptoms first and most severely. Plants wilt prior to normal ones [9, 17]. Toxicity symptoms for other elements have not been delineated.

Fertilizer Sources

Plant nutrients can be obtained from many sources, and the methods used to obtain them vary from primitive to sophisticated. The slash and burn method, utilizing available nutrients in soils plus those obtained from wood ash, is common in many tropic areas. Manures from barnyards, stables, or feedlots are also sources of essential plant nutrients. Other sources of organic or natural fertilizers include bone, castor bean, cotton seed or fish meals, dried blood, sewage sludge, and garbage tankage. These sources contain varying amounts of N, P, and K and usually contain small amounts of microelements. Manures and natural fertilizers are used only to a small degree in growing foliage plants, since most foliage plants are fertilized with chemical or inorganic materials. Nutrients and the amounts required must be understood before selecting the source or sources of fertilizer to be used for foliage plant production, and commercial producers also must determine the method of applying them.

Nutrients can be applied liquid or dry, readily available or slow release, and in organic or inorganic forms or combinations. Liquid fertilizers are used often with frequency of application varied. Small amounts sometimes are used with every irrigation in an effort to maintain a constant level of nutrition in the soil mix, but equal or better quality plants can be grown with weekly, every other week, or even monthly applications in the case of stock plants [20]. Dry-form fertilizer usually is applied less frequently than liquid, with larger amounts applied each time. Excellent foliage plants have been grown with this method, even though nutritional levels in the soil mix probably fluctuate more with this system. Nutrients in liquid fertilizers are usually readily available for use by plants, but most dry fertilizers are available over a slightly longer period of time. Crops respond to available nutrients applied in solution just as they do to those applied as dry fertilizer. Nutrients in organic fertilizers are not readily available initially, while most inorganic compounds are completely available in a short time. Organic fertilizers are used sparingly by the foliage industry since their rate of availability is too variable for fast-growing crops, and the cost per unit of nutritional element is more expensive than for inorganic ones.

Slow-release fertilizers are widely used in the foliage industry since they supply adequate amounts of nutrition for extended periods of time (3 to 12 months) when supplied in proper amounts. A major advantage of slow-release fertilizers is the reduction in time required to apply the fertilizer program. The term "readily available" and "slow release" are misleading upon literal translation, and "completely available" and "incompletely available" or "controlled release" would be more exact. For example, when ammonium nitrate or potassium chloride is added to the soil, they dissolve into NH_4, NO_2, K, and Cl ions, and all are immediately available for plant absorption. All are not used immediately by plants, however, for some are lost by leaching and others are adsorbed to the soil complex; but initially all are available. Slow-release and/or organic fertilizers release nutrients slowly, but a portion is available immediately; therefore, good quality plants can be grown using liquid fertilizers or slow-release fertilizers exclusively if both are properly applied [32, 48].

Nitrogen for foliage plant fertilization is obtained from ammonium nitrate (NH_4NO_3), ammonium sulphate ($(NH_4)_2SO_4$), sodium nitrate ($NaNO_3$), potassium nitrate (KNO_3), calcium nitrate ($Ca(NO_3)_2$), or urea. Nitrate nitrogen (NO_3) dissolves readily, moves through the soil freely, and is very available to plants, but frequent irrigation or rainfall often removes much NO_3 from soils before plants can absorb it. Ammoniacal nitrogen, NH_4, also dissolves readily, but unlike NO_3, it resists leaching. Plants can utilize NH_4 directly, but bacteria convert much of this to NO_3. Low temperature, high moisture, and acidic soils retard bacterial activity, and sterilized soils probably will be lacking in them, which retards or stops this conversion. This is not a serious problem when NO_3 also is supplied to supplement NH_4 under such conditions, since plants grow best with a combination of NO_3 and NH_4 forms of N. Water-soluble organic N such as urea changes to the NH_4 form within a few days, but water-insoluble N is derived almost entirely from organic sources.

Soil microorganisms are required for conversion of water-insoluble N to readily available NO_3; thus, the water-insoluble form is more slowly available and remains in the soil mix for longer periods of time than soluble forms. Water-insoluble sources of N are often too slowly available for fast-growing foliage plants, particularly in cool weather.

The most common sources of P are single or treble superphosphates which are mixed into potting soils, but these might cause fluorine toxicity [17]. Ammonium and calcium phosphates are frequently used for liquid fertilizer applications. Phosphorus resists leaching unless soils are highly acidic and, even then, leaches slowly.

Potassium is supplied from potassium chloride, KCl, potassium sulfate, K_2SO_4, or potassium nitrate, KNO_3, and occasionally from potassium frit. Potassium frit used alone usually results in K deficiencies because it is too slowly available.

Foliage plants have fairly high requirements for Ca and Mg, which are usually incorporated into growing media. Dolomite is the best source of Ca and Mg and should be used where possible as an amendment in the media. Dolomite is slowly available and should be placed in the root zone. This material also increases media pH. Other sources of calcium include calcium nitrate $Ca(NO_3)_2$, calcium hydroxide, $Ca(OH)_2$, calcium carbonate, $CaCO_3$, and calcium sulfate, $CaSO_4$, and sources of magnesium include magnesium sulfate, $MgSO_4$. Overuse of liming materials can reduce availability of most microelements.

Potting media used for foliage plant production often have insufficient levels of micronutrients for long-term growth. For this reason, several blends of micronutrients are available in dry or liquid forms that can be incorporated into the mix prior to planting or on the surface after crop establishment.

There are many labels applied to fertilizer sources, such as organic, inorganic, liquid, solid, dry, slow release, readily available, acidic, and basic. Growers must determine a preferred method of application before selecting fertilizer sources. Any source mentioned will produce excellent quality foliage plants if the essential nature and properties of such sources are understood and proper procedures followed. See Table 9-1 for various properties of fertilizers commonly used in the foliage industry. Fertilizers should be selected for elemental analysis and rates of availability, solubility, and influence on pH.

TABLE 9-1 Common sources of required elements

		%				
	N	P_2O_5	K_2O	Availability	Solubility (lb/100 gals)	Influence on pH
Nitrogen (N)						
Ammonium nitrate, NH_4NO_3	33.5	0	0	Rapid	984	Acidic
Ammonium sulfate, $(NH_4)_2SO_4$	21	0	0	Rapid	568	Acidic
Calcium nitrate, $Ca(NO_3)_2$	15	0	0	Rapid	1,020	Basic
Sodium nitrate, $NaNO_3$	16	0	0	Rapid	757	Basic
Potassium nitrate, KNO_3	14	0	44	Rapid	110	Basic
Urea, $CO(NH_2)_2$	45	0	0	Rapid	High	Acidic
Potassium (K)						
Potassium nitrate, KNO_3	14	0	44	Rapid	110	Basic
Potassium chloride, KCl	0	0	60	Rapid	310	Neutral
Potassium sulfate, K_2SO_4	0	0	50	Rapid	98	Neutral
Phosphorus (P)						
Superphosphate, $Ca_2H(PO_4)_2$	0	20	0	Slow	Low	Neutral
Concentrated superphosphate $CaH_4(PO_4)_2$	0	45	0	Medium	Low	Neutral
Monoammonium phosphate	12	61	0	Rapid	120	Acidic
Diammonium phosphate	21	54	0	Rapid	120	Acidic
Phosphoric acid	0	52	0	Rapid	Highly soluble	Acidic
Calcium (Ca)						
Limestone	0	0	0	Slow	Low	Basic
Dolomite	0	0	0	Slow	Low	Basic
Calcium nitrate	15	0	0	Rapid	1,020	Basic
Superphosphate	0	20	0	Slow	Low	Neutral
Calcium hydroxide	0	0	0	Medium	1.5	Basic
Calcium sulfate	0	0	0	Medium	Low	Neutral
Magnesium (Mg)						
Dolomite	0	0	0	Slow	Low	Basic
Magnesium sulfate	0	0	0	Medium	Low	Basic

Methods of Fertilizer Application

Several methods of applying fertilizers to foliage plants exist, and each method can be suitable under various production regimes. The decision to use a specific method depends upon equipment available, type of plant grown, such as bedding and potted, growth cycle time, and size of operation. Methods used by growers include preplant incorporation and postplant surface and/or foliar application [2, 7, 8].

Preplant Application

Preplant incorporation of fertilizer is accomplished at the time of medium preparation. Types of fertilizer materials that can be used for this vary widely and include materials for pH adjustment as well as nutrients.

Materials used for pH control should be preplant incorporated at levels that will provide a pH range of 5.5 to 6.5. The amounts of liming materials to use will depend on soil type and components used in potting mixtures. Generally, if the pH must be raised more than 2 units, a combination of rapid- and slow-release components should be used such as limestone and finely ground dolomitic limestome. Dolomite (or dolomitic limestone) is available over many months and also supplies magnesium. The two limestone forms will provide pH control immediately and over long periods. Where pH changes are less than 2 units, dolomite, when incorporated, does an excellent job in raising pH within 2 to 4 weeks.

Superphosphate is often preplant incorporated to provide a slowly available, inexpensive source of P. Superphosphate contains approximately 1.5 percent soluble F, which is phytotoxic to a number of foliage plants at pH levels below 6.0 [9, 12, 17, 34, 35, 36, 37, 38, 39].

Micronutrients are often incorporated into soil and potting mixtures prior to planting. Chemical sources are rapidly available, while frits supply small amounts for a year or more. However, several frits contain levels of boron that can be phytotoxic to foliage plants at manufacturers' suggested rates.

Incorporation of small amounts of rapidly available fertilizer sources are sometimes made as a growth "starter," but the level must be low and no more than 1 to 2 ounces of nitrogen and 3 ounces of potash per cubic yard [1].

Incorporation of slow-release fertilizers containing N, P, and K has become popular in recent years, but use of these materials depends on an understanding of factors that influence their availability. These include microorganism population, moisture level, temperature, time, and several chemical reactions [51]. Materials should be selected that are compatible with individual crop growth period and rate. Incorporation of fertilizer sources in growing media can elevate soluble salts to toxic levels; thus, care must be exercised to be sure rates are calculated correctly and mixing is thorough, so variation does not occur within the soil mixture.

Postplant Application

Postplant application is a commonly used method to control fertility and maximize growth. Frequency of application depends on fertilizer materials used, whether production is in the field or under cover, container sizes, media, watering regime, and plant type. Methods of application include placement of dry or liquid fertilizers on the growing medium surface and liquid fertilizer on foliage (foliar feeding).

Dry application of dry chemical or slow-release fertilizers to media surfaces is the most conservative in fertilizer usage and cost, but may be expensive in labor used. The decision to use such a system should be based on total costs of the operation rather than just fertilizer cost, since cost of fertilizer material approximates only 2 percent of production costs.

The application of dry fertilizers to media surfaces can be time consuming unless mechanical equipment is used, because each application must be carefully measured for each pot or area of stock bench since incorrect rates often result in application of excessive levels of fertilizer and crop damage [6]. Care must be taken during application so that granules do not fall into the center of plants such as *Dracaena, Cordyline, Maranta,* or plants with whorls of leaves, or burning will result. Evenness of application is important, since placement in one spot will result in root damage from high salt concentrations even if the proper rate is used for the entire pot or bench area. Irrigation must be made to media surfaces when dry applications are used, to carry fertilizer into the growing medium. For these reasons, dry applications are best used in operations where equipment for liquid fertilization is not available, or in potted-plant production where containers are widely spaced and slow-release forms of fertilizer are used. In the latter instance, the cost of a slow-release fertilizer program on spaced container-grown foliage plants can be less than a liquid program. Surface application of dry fertilizers to minimize leaching has become more important recently, because of "no-discharge" laws relating to fertilizers in run-off irrigation water.

Liquid application is the most commonly used of postplant surface-applied systems and can be combined with media incorporation systems. Benefits include ease and uniformity of application, low labor requirements, and ability to automate the system [33]. Disadvantages include initial equipment costs, limitation on number of fertilizer materials that can be used, and potential excess runoff when applied overhead to widely spaced or canopied crops. Liquid fertilizer is usually applied directly to individual pots by hand or tube systems and to stock benches or beds by hand or soaker tubing or through sprinkler irrigation equipment. Overhead sprinkler irrigation is wasteful of fertilizer and inefficient in coverage owing to equipment and/or plant deflection. Under shade cloth, variations in water between pots are high owing to system design, and plants with a heavy foliage canopy may deflect as much as 75 percent of the fertilizer. Variation in watering and fertilizer rate between plants in the same block may be excessive; therefore, liquid applications should be made overhead by sprinklers only on stock beds or potted plants placed pot to pot. Fertilizers should be applied by individual pot watering systems where pots are spaced.

Interest in *foliar application* has recently increased for it can be combined with pest control procedures, since fertilizer is compatible with a number of pesticides. One objective of foliar application is to increase efficiency of fertilizer so that less need be supplied, but it serves best to correct problems that arise in the general fertilizer programs, such as inhibited absorption of soil applications owing to root damage or poor aeration or where a quick response is needed to correct deficiencies. Foliar fertilization is best adapted to nitrogen and microelements, since uptake of potassium and phosphorus from foliar sprays is limited. The system does not replace root fertilization, which is still necessary for most of the nutrients utilized [24, 28, 49].

Equipment

Equipment, which range from spoons to fully automated injection equipment, has been developed to reduce the labor requirements of fertilizer application. A summary of these and their potential uses follow.

Trap door hand applicators can be set to apply specific amounts of fertilizer or other pesticides. These are trigger operated by hand or a trip mechanism at the discharge point. Unfortunately, these applicators apply the material only at a single point unless a small spreader is attached at the outlet.

Cyclone spreaders in several sizes are available that can be calibrated for use to apply dry fertilizer to stock beds or containers placed side by side. This system serves a purpose where application is made to plants on which fertilizer cannot lodge in the leaf whorls and cause burning. However, uniformity of application may be poor, especially where foliage is thick and deflection of granules occurs.

Hose siphons are low cost and can be used to supply liquid fertilizers to small areas. These are as efficient and uniform as the human applicator because the rate applied depends on solution concentration, water pressure, friction loss, and area treated. The system is most applicable to small operations because of high labor requirements.

Numerous systems exist that utilize *pumps* or pumps and injectors. Each has its place, and decisions on which to use depend on investment costs and the area to be fertilized.

A simple method of applying liquid fertilizer is to mix the proper concentration in a tank and pump this directly to the area of use through any irrigation system. This method has a low equipment requirement if the pumping unit is shared with the irrigation system or if output desired is low, permits uniform applications to many containers, and may combine irrigation and fertilization.

Another slightly more complex method is to inject fertilizer contained in a mixing tank into the suction side of a centrifugal irrigation pump or pumping it directly into the discharge side of a deep well pump [25]. Injection is controlled by a valve or siphon, and specific amounts are applied to a known surface area. Care must be taken to ensure a rate of injection low enough to prevent plant damage. These methods may result in nonuniform applications because of variations in volume of water applied.

The best method of applying known levels of liquid nutrients to foliage plants is through use of an automatic metering device, which may be used with hose, sprinkler, seep tube, or individual pot watering systems. These devices (injectors) are designed to operate automatically whenever water is turned on and to maintain a uniform concentration over a range of water flow volumes. Injectors are automatically metered to deliver specific amounts of fertilizer solution into irrigation water being applied. Automatic recorders, cut outs, and alarms should be incorporated into the system to monitor operation and prevent the possibility of application of too low or too high fertilizer concentrations [25, 29].

Fertilizer Frequency

Researchers have demonstrated some benefits of applying fertilizers on a continuing basis through use of injection equipment in irrigation water, and others have tried to determine the longest interval between fertilizer applications that could be made without significant losses in quality [22].

Several factors influencing application frequency should be considered in developing fertilizer programs:

1. Plant growth rates. The faster the growth rate, the more frequently fertilizer should be applied.

2. Cation-exchange capacity of the media. The lower the cation-exchange capacity, the more frequently relatively low amounts of fertilizers must be applied.
3. Irrigation and/or rainfall. Heavy rainfall and/or irrigation leaches nutrients that must be replaced with frequent fertilization.
4. Soil volume in relation to plant size. Large plants grown in small containers require frequent fertilization.
5. Light intensity and temperature largely control growth rate; thus, the higher the light intensity and temperature, the more frequent applications should be made.

Stock plants growing in the ground require less frequent fertilization because of the large soil volume and depth of rooting. In most cases, monthly applications are adequate, but more frequent applications will not be injurious as long as rates of each application are reduced. Application frequency for stock grown on raised beds depends on the height of the sides and the rate of water application. Fertilizer applications every 2 weeks or monthly is adequate where side boards are 6 inches or more high and the medium is not subject to excessive rainfall. Beds with lower sides or those in outdoor locations subject to heavy rainfall may need to be fertilized weekly or every 2 weeks to prevent widely fluctuating nutritional levels, which can reduce stock yields. Constant-feed or slow-release fertilizers can be used in place of periodic fertilizer applications in any instance listed above.

Pot size also has a direct relationship to fertilization frequency. Small pots need to be fertilized more often because of limited media volume and the heavy leaching that occurs [6]. Foliage plants in small pots (1 to 4 inches) should be fertilized weekly or every other week or be on a constant fertilization program, liquid or slow release. Plants in larger containers should be fertilized weekly to monthly or placed on a constant program. Care should be taken when constant fertilization programs are utilized because the root-to-shoot ratio may be decreased, which could result in problems, particularly postproduction ones.

Fertilizer Ratios

Fertilizer ratios determined from research have shown that plant growth and quality are usually correlated with nutrient content in foliage, and leaf analyses for specific elements provide good information on amounts of each element needed relative to others (Table 9-2). Such information does not mean that ratios can be determined simply by dividing listed levels of elements into each other, because many other factors are involved. The data provided in Table 9-2 were primarily developed from research where 1-1-1 (N-P_2O_5-K_2O) ratio fertilizers were

TABLE 9-2 Tissue composition of high-quality foliage plants [44]

Botanical name	% Dry Weight				
	N	P	K	Ca	Mg
Adiantum raddianum	1.5–2.5	0.40–0.80	2.0–3.0	0.2–0.3	0.2–0.4
Aechmea fasciata	1.5–2.0	0.40–0.70	1.5–2.5	0.5–1.0	0.4–0.8
Aglaonema commutatum 'Franscher'	2.5–3.5	0.20–0.35	2.5–3.5	1.0–1.5	0.3–0.6
Aphelandra squarrosa	2.0–3.0	0.20–0.40	1.0–2.0	0.2–0.4	0.5–1.0
Asparagus myriocladus	1.5–2.5	0.30–0.50	2.0–3.0	0.1–0.3	0.1–0.3
Brassaia actinophylla	2.5–3.5	0.20–0.35	2.5–3.5	1.0–1.5	0.3–0.6
Chamaedorea elegans	2.5–3.0	0.20–0.30	1.0–2.0	0.4–1.0	0.3–0.4
Chlorophytum comosum	1.5–2.5	0.10–0.20	3.5–5.0	1.0–2.0	0.5–1.5
Chrysalidocarpus lutescens	1.5–2.5	0.10–0.20	1.0–2.0	1.0–1.5	0.3–0.6
Coffea arabica	2.5–3.5	0.15–0.25	2.0–3.0	0.5–1.0	0.3–0.5
Dieffenbachia exotica	2.5–3.5	0.20–0.35	3.0–4.5	1.0–1.5	0.3–0.8
Dizygotheca elegantissima	2.0–2.5	0.40–0.60	1.5–2.5	0.5–1.0	0.2–0.3
Dracaena deremensis 'Janet Craig'	2.0–3.0	0.20–0.30	3.0–4.0	1.5–2.0	0.3–0.6
Dracaena deremensis 'Warneckii'	2.5–3.5	0.15–0.30	3.0–4.5	1.0–2.0	0.5–1.0
Dracaena fragrans 'Massangeana'	2.0–3.0	0.15–0.25	1.0–2.0	1.0–2.0	0.5–1.0
Dracaena sanderana	2.5–3.5	0.20–0.30	2.0–3.0	1.5–2.5	0.3–0.6
Dracaena surculosa	1.5–2.5	0.20–0.30	1.0–2.0	1.0–1.5	0.3–0.5
Epipremnum aureum	2.5–3.5	0.20–0.35	3.0–4.5	1.0–1.5	0.3–0.6
Ficus benjamina	1.8–2.5	0.10–0.20	1.0–1.5	2.0–3.0	0.4–0.8
Ficus elastica	1.3–1.6	0.10–0.20	0.6–1.0	0.3–0.5	0.2–0.4
Maranta leuconeura kerchoveana	2.0–3.0	0.20–0.30	3.0–4.5	0.5–1.5	0.5–1.0
Monstera deliciosa	2.5–3.5	0.20–0.35	3.0–4.5	0.4–1.0	0.3–0.6
Philodendron scandens oxycardium	2.0–3.0	0.15–0.25	3.0–4.5	0.5–1.5	0.3–0.6
Sansevieria trifasciata 'Laruentii'	1.7–3.0	0.15–0.30	2.0–3.0	1.0–1.5	0.3–0.6
Stromanthe amabilis	2.5–3.0	0.20–0.50	3.0–4.0	0.1–0.2	0.3–0.5
Syngonium podophyllum	2.5–3.5	0.20–0.30	3.0–4.5	0.4–1.0	0.3–0.6

used [15, 19, 38, 45]. Several other factors influence the ratios at which nutrient elements should be applied, including (1) antagonisms of one ion to another owing to like electrical charges, such as calcium, potassium, and magnesium, (2) ingredients in potting mixtures that affect retention of certain elements against leaching, (3) differences in leaching rates of fertilizer elements as determined by the chemical replacement series, (4) fixative effects of certain soil types or potting mixtures or combinations that cause some elements such as P and certain microelements to become unavailable, and (5) differences among plant species in their requirements for and preferential absorption of certain elements.

Nitrogen is the most easily leached of the three primary plant nutrients normally supplied foliage plants, K is next, and P is leached practically not at all unless pH is low (below 5.5) and plants are in pots. Limited research indicates that $N-P_2O_5-K_2O$ ratios similar to 1-1-1 or 3-1-2 produce high-quality plants grown in pots with high organic mixes.

The 3-1-2 ratio appears best, since it reduces salt accumulation and cost [10, 14, 18, 41, 42]. Increasing P more than 15 percent of total N applied and K to more than 50 percent does not increase the quality of plants grown in pots containing high organic mixes.

In field soils where there is a good chance for P fixation, research on other crops indicates that a 1-1-1 ratio is probably best.

Fertilizer Analyses

Fertilizer analyses are represented by numbers on a fertilizer tag or bag. Generally, there are three numbers, and these represent N, P_2O_5, and K_2O; if these three are present, it is commonly called a complete fertilizer. This is misleading, however, as all the elements previously discussed are also needed. The first number on the fertilizer tag indicates the percentage of elemental N, the second is the percentage of P in the oxide form (P_2O_5), and the third is K as an oxide (K_2O). For example, a 20-20-20 analysis has 60 units of nutrients plus oxygen, while a 10-10-10 has 30. If a 20-20-20 is not more than twice the cost of a 10-10-10, it is a better buy, provided nutrients in both are 100 percent available. The higher the analyses are, the higher the percentage of fertilizer in the bag. There has been resistance to purchasing higher analyses fertilizers for years for fear they will burn roots, but they are as safe as lower analyses materials provided proper rates are used. High analyses fertilizers contain elements of high purity and usually are highly soluble, but they do not supply micronutrients that often might be present as impurities in low analysis fertilizer sources. To determine the ratio from the analyses, divide the smallest number into the other; that is, if there is no smaller number, as with a 20-20-20 analysis, the ratio is 1-1-1. With 18-6-12, the

TABLE 9-3 Present fertilizer analyses shown on fertilizer bags versus the elemental system (approximate)[a]

Present oxide system ($N-P_2O_5-K_2O$)	Proposed elemental system		
	N	P	K
18-9-9	18	4.0	7.5
18-6-12	18	2.6	10.0
20-20-20	20	8.8	16.6
20-5-30	20	2.2	24.9
25-10-10	25	4.4	8.3

[a]To convert P_2O_5 to P, multiply by 0.44. To convert K_2O to K, multiply by 0.83.

ratio is $18 \div 6 = 3, 6 \div 6 = 1$, and $12 \div 6 = 2$; the ratio would be 3-1-2 (N-P_2O_5-K_2O).

There is a possibility within a few years that fertilizer analyses will be reported in terms of actual elements rather than oxides of elements as N, P_2O_5, and K_2O, but there probably will be a dual system on bags for several years. Table 9-3 on ratios is based on the oxide system.

Fertilization Rates

The amount and the formula of fertilizers applied to foliage crops determine their quality. Quality may be assessed in several ways, including freedom from apparent nutritional deficiencies or good foliage color and longevity in areas of intended use (indoors). The rate of fertilization for quality depends on the following factors:

1. Plant species: Considerable variation exists in nutritional needs of tropical plants, and rates that may be excessive for one species may not be adequate to produce quality in another.
2. Light intensity: As light intensity increases, so should fertilizer rate; conversely, as light intensity decreases, so should fertilizer rate.
3. Rainfall: Fertilizer rates should be higher where plants are subject to excessive rainfall. Heavy rainfall leaches elements from media, and must be replaced.
4. Temperature: Fertilization rates should be higher in summer than in winter since this is the time of greatest growth. High light intensity and temperatures occur during summer to produce rapid growth rate.
5. Availability: Increases in temperature increase chemical reactions, including fertilizer availability, and temperature changes also affect pH, which in turn affects availability of nutrients. Low temperatures slow soil microorganism activities that convert certain fertilizers, particularly organic ones, from insoluble to soluble forms.
6. Fertilizer efficiency: Some fertilizer sources are less efficient than others. For example, only 60 to 70 percent of urea formaldehyde is available initially, while ammonium nitrate is 90 to 100 percent available. More urea formaldehyde (by weight) would have to be used to obtain the same initial plant growth responses, all other factors being equal.
7. Temperature controls the release rates of slow-release fertilizer sources; thus they become available more rapidly during summer than winter months.

TABLE 9-4 Suggested nutritional levels for production of some foliage stock plants

Botanical name	Light intensity (foot candles[c])	Fertilizer requirements (pounds/1000 ft²/yr[a,b]) N	P₂O₅	K₂O
Aglaonema spp.	1,500–2,500	28	9	19
Aphelandra squarrosa	500–1,000	34	11	23
Brassaia arboricola	7,500–10,000	48	16	32
Calathea spp.	1,500–2,000	28	9	19
Codiaeum variegatum	7,500–10,000	41	14	27
Cordyline terminalis	3,500–4,500	34	11	23
Dieffenbachia spp.	3,000–3,500	34	11	23
Dracaena deremensis (cultivars)	3,000–3,500	28	9	19
Dracaena fragrans (cultivars)	6,000–12,000	34	11	23
Dracaena marginata	6,000–12,000	41	14	27
Dracaena marginata 'Tricolor'	4,500–8,000	41	14	27
Dracaena sanderana	3,000–4,000	34	11	23
Dracaena surculosa	3,000–4,000	34	11	23
Epipremnum aureum	3,500–4,500	34	11	23
Ficus benjamina	8,000–10,000	56	19	37
Ficus elastica (cultivars)	8,000–10,000	41	14	27
Ficus lyrata	8,000–10,000	41	14	27
Maranta spp.	1,500–2,500	20	7	13
Monstera deliciosa	3,500–4,500	34	11	23
Nephrolepis exaltata (cultivars)	2,500–3,500	28	9	19
Peperomia spp.	2,500–3,500	20	7	13
Philodendron hastatum	3,500–4,500	34	11	23
Philodendron (hybrids)	3,000–3,500	34	11	23
Philodendron scandens oxycardium	3,000–4,000	34	11	23
Philodendron scandens scandens	3,500–4,500	34	11	23
Pilea spp.	2,500–3,000	20	7	13
Sansevieria spp.	6,000–12,000	20	7	13
Schlumbergera truncata	3,000–4,000	28	9	19
Syngonium podophyllum	3,000–4,000	34	11	23
Yucca elephantipes	10,000–12,000	41	14	27

[a] Based on a 3-1-2 ratio fertilizer source; if growing medium is known to fix phosphorus and potassium, they should be added at the same rate as nitrogen (i.e., use a 1-1-1 ratio fertilizer source).

[b] Pounds per square foot × 4.8 = kilograms per square meter.

[c] Footcandles × 10.7 = lux or × 0.01 = kilolux.

Average fertilizer rates for production of stock plants as well as acclimatized potted plants are listed in Tables 9-4 and 9-5. These rates are based on average production conditions, which include recommended light levels, soils or potting mixtures with high cation-exchange capacity, application of approximately 1 to 2 inches (2.5 to 5.0 centimeters) of water a week (irrigation and rainfall), and average night tempera-

TABLE 9-5 Suggested nutritional levels for production of some potted acclimatized foliage plants

Botanical name	Light intensity (footcandles[c])	N	P$_2$O$_5$	K$_2$O
		\multicolumn{3}{c}{Fertilizer requirements (pounds/1000 ft^2/yr[a,b]}		

Botanical name	Light intensity (footcandles[c])	N	P$_2$O$_5$	K$_2$O
Aglaonema spp.	1,500–2,500	28	9	19
Aphelandra squarrosa	1,000–1,500	34	11	23
Araucaria heterophylla	6,000–8,000	28	9	19
Asparagus spp.	3,500–4,500	20	7	13
Brassaia spp.	5,000–6,000	41	14	27
Calathea spp.	1,500–2,000	20	7	13
Chamaedorea elegans	2,500–3,500	28	9	19
Chamaedorea erumpens	4,500–6,000	34	11	23
Chrysalidocarpus lutescens	5,000–6,000	34	11	23
Codiaeum variegatum	7,000–8,000	34	11	23
Cordyline terminalis	3,500–4,500	28	9	19
Dizygotheca kerchoveana	5,000–6,000	28	9	19
Dieffenbachia spp.	2,500–3,500	28	9	19
Dracaena deremensis (cultivars)	3,000–3,500	28	9	19
Dracaena fragrans (cultivars)	3,000–3,500	28	11	19
Dracaena marginata	5,000–6,000	41	14	27
Dracaena (others)	3,000–3,500	28	9	19
Epipremnum aureum	3,000–4,000	34	11	23
Ficus benjamina	3,500–6,000	41	14	27
Ficus elastica (cultivars)	7,000–8,000	41	14	27
Ficus lyrata	5,000–6,000	41	14	27
Maranta spp.	1,500–2,500	20	7	13
Monstera deliciosa	3,500–4,500	34	11	23
Nephrolepis exaltata (cultivars)	2,500–3,000	28	9	19
Peperomia spp.	2,500–3,000	14	5	9
Philodendron selloum	5,000–6,000	41	14	27
Philodendron spp.	2,500–3,500	34	11	23
Pilea spp.	2,000–3,000	14	5	9
Sansevieria spp.	3,500–4,500	14	5	9
Schlumbergera truncata	3,000–4,000	28	9	19
Spathiphyllum spp.	1,500–2,500	28	9	19
Syngonium podophyllum	2,500–3,500	34	11	23
Yucca elephantipes	3,500–4,500	28	9	19

[a]Based on a 3-1-2 ratio fertilizer source; if growing medium is known to fix phosphorus and potassium, they should be added at the same rate as nitrogen (i.e., use a 1-1-1 ratio fertilizer source).

[b]Pounds per square foot × 4.8 = kilograms per square meter.

[c]Footcandles × 10.7 = lux or × 0.01 = kilolux.

tures of 60°F (15.6°C) or higher and day temperatures from 70° to 95°F (21° to 35°C).

Fertilizer Programs

Fertilizer programs must be adjusted to plants grown and the environmental and cultural conditions previously discussed. Many different programs will be necessary for varying conditions, and any program should be adjusted with time and production factors.

Fertilizer Elements to Incorporate During Potting Mixture or Soil Preparation

Incorporation of *dolomitic limestone* during soil or potting mixture preparation is usually necessary to adjust pH and provide Ca and Mg during the growing cycle of most potted crops. Field soils will also need to have dolomite added after several crops. Table 7-6 indicates the amount of dolomite to use for several situations, and it can be pasteurized without damage or loss of nutrients. Calcium and Mg must be supplied in the fertilizer program if not mixed into the growing medium preplant.

Superphosphate   Single superphosphate (approximately 20 percent P_2O_5) generally has been incorporated into potting mixtures at up to 5 pounds per cubic yard or 100 square feet to supply P, S, and Ca. Several genera of foliage plants, however, are sensitive to fluorides present in superphosphate as a contaminant [17, 36, 40]; thus, this material is not suggested as a soil amendment for all crops. Preferably, the concentrated or treble superphosphate form (approximately 45 percent P_2O_5) should be used at 1 pound per cubic yard (0.6 kilograms per cubic meter) or 2 pounds per 100 square feet (1.6 kilograms per square meter), since this reduces the amount of fluoride applied. Both single and treble superphosphate contain approx. 1.5 percent F, but only one half the amount of treble superphosphate need be applied because of its higher P_2O_5 content providing less fluoride. However, if superphosphate is pasteurized, it releases or volatizes fluorides. If superphosphate is incorporated into the medium, it is not necessary to supply P in the fertilizer program for 3 to 6 months.

Micronutrients   Micronutrients in most potting mixtures and many field soils are low, so they should be incorporated into the medium during preparation to achieve even distribution. This is especially true of insoluble forms, since it is the only way they can be properly handled. Do not pasteurize potting mixes or soils after additions of micronutrients since some can become so available to plants as to be phytotoxic.

Selecting a Program

Several types of fertilizer programs can be used singly or in combination to satisfactorily grow foliage plants, including periodic or continuous fertilization or a combination of both.

Periodic fertilization is based on application of a certain amount of fertilizer to the crop on a weekly, every 2 weeks, or monthly basis. Nutrient availability fluctuates somewhat with this system, but apparently this is not a serious problem with most foliage plants because little to no benefit has been observed from continuous applications. Any type of fertilizer can be used in such programs, including slow-release fertilizers, which are often applied periodically even though they provide continuous feeding for limited periods. Tables 9-6 and 9-7 provide information on recommended annual rates of fertilizers, which can be adjusted into portions for crops of short duration.

Constant fertilization indicates application of small amounts of fertilizer each time plants are watered. The fertilizer level with this system should never be higher than that of the applied solution as long as leaching occurs at each watering, and, since nutrients are replenished often, the nutritional status of potting mixtures remains fairly constant. As with any system, some problems may occur; the principal one is an accumulation of salts. Primary reasons for salt accumulations are improper leaching and high cation-exchange capacity, which traps fertilizer ions. To ensure proper leaching, a solution volume equal to 10 to 25 percent of pot volume should be leached through the potting mixture each time plants are fertilized. Another system is to apply fertilizer at every watering, except when pure water is used, on a periodic basis to leach excess salts. Quantity of water to apply will depend on the cation-exchange capacity of the medium, pot volume, and frequency of leaching.

Limited research has been accomplished on constant fertilization of foliage plants, except by use of timed release materials such as Osmocote. Recommendations for fertilization included in this chapter can be converted to constant programs by using information provided in the footnotes. Generally, 75 to 150 parts per million of N, 25 to 75 parts per million of P, and 75 to 150 parts per million of K should be used.

Fertilizers used for continuous fertilization through injectors must be 100 percent soluble or properly strained prior to placing in the injector. Impurities lodged in injector nozzles can render them inoperative or reduce the flow of fertilizer stock solution into irrigation water. Injectors take dissolved fertilizers in stock solutions and uniformly place them in a present ratio with irrigation water. For example, a 1 : 100 injector mixes 1 gallon of stock solution to each 100 gallons of water passing through it,

TABLE 9-6   Amount of several soluble fertilizers in pounds to be dissolved in 100 gallons of stock solution for use with 1:100 ratio injectors

Fertilizer analyses	50 ppm N[a]	100 ppm N	150 ppm N
9-3-6	44	88	132
18-6-12	22	44	66
20-20-20	21	42	63
20-5-30	21	42	63

[a]Based on the calculation parts per million of element = percentage of elemental analysis × ounces in 100 gallons × 75. Multiply by 1.28 for injectors with a ratio of 1:128 and by 2 for injectors having a ratio of 1:200.

while a 1 : 200 injector would mix 1 gallon of stock solution into 200 gallons of water. Accuracy of the injectors depends on stock solutions; therefore, care should be taken in mixing. If 50 pounds of a 20-20-20 fertilizer formula were dissolved in 50 gallons of water, it would provide 8 ounces of 20-20-20 per 200 gallons through a 1 : 200 injector, or 16 ounces per 100 gallons through a 1 : 100 injector. Rates for continuous fertilization are always expressed in parts per million (ppm). Table 9-6 provides basic information on determining the amounts of soluble fertilizer to utilize for stock solutions to make up various parts per million solutions.

Micronutrients

Micronutrients are required in limited amounts by foliage plants according to research, but growers have experienced many symptoms that appear to be micronutrient related and often are corrected by a "shotgun" application of essential micronutrients. Deficiency symptoms of iron, manganese, and boron have been reported on stock plants of *Dracaena surculosa* and *Dracaena sanderiana* in Puerto Rico, with iron reported to be the most common micronutrient deficiency noted [3, 46]. *Philodendron scandens oxycardium* and *Epipremnum aureum* were grown in sand culture for 6 months, and the only micronutrient deficiency noted was iron [23]. Cuttings of *Philodendron scandens oxycardium* and *Dieffenbachia picta* 'Exotica' and seedlings of *Syngonium podophyllum* grown for several months with and without a micronutrient blend were equal in quality and growth rate [34].

Copper deficiency has been noted on *Peperomia obtusifolia* and *Aglaonema commutatum* 'Fransher' when grown in pure peat moss or peat-bark combinations. Micronutrients seem needed most in stock areas or seedling crops and on plants grown for 6 months or longer in the same container.

Data on the nutritional status of good quality foliage plants and desired tissue levels of numerous foliage plants have been published [27, 44]. Generally, desired levels of micronutrients in leaves are copper, 5 to 15, iron, 50 to 100, manganese, 50 to 100, and zinc, 20 to 50 parts per million. Information on critical tissue levels of boron and molybdenum in foliage plants is unavailable.

Micronutrients can become available to plants in excess and may seriously reduce yield and quality [21]. Research has shown that inclusion of a micronutrient blend in propagation medium reduced rooting of three out of five foliage plants tested and did not improve it over controls [11]. No beneficial effect was noted when micronutrients were included in a potting mixture used in 4-inch pots for growing of aphelandra, brassaia, and philodendron, and higher rates of two mixtures injured aphelandra and brassaia. Such data would indicate the need for serious consideration of micronutrient levels, since reductions in growth may occur at relatively low levels of some of the elements [13, 43].

Acidity   Media pH strongly influences availability of microelements. At pH 5, Fe, Mn, Z, Cu, and B are readily available, but solubility (availability) decreases as the pH approaches 7 and deficiency symptoms, particularly of iron, may be noticed. Chelated iron is frequently used to supply this microelement to plants since the chelate prevents the metal from complexing with the soil, maintaining it in a soluble form available to plants. Molybdenum is more easily obtained by plants as pH increases.

TABLE 9-7   Suggested application rates of micronutrients

Element source	Spray application (lb/100 gal)	Soil drench (oz/1,000 ft^2)	Soil incorporation (oz/yd^3)
B: Borax	0.01	0.03	0.010
Cu: Copper sulfate	0.10	0.30	0.100
Fe: Iron sulfate	1.00	3.00	1.000
Mn: Manganese sulfate	0.50	1.50	0.500
Mo: Sodium molybdate	0.01	0.01	0.001
Zn: Zinc sulfate	0.30	1.00	0.300

Conversion factors

$B_2O_3 \times 0.31 = B$ $B \times 3.2 = B_2O_3$
$CuO \times 0.80 = Cu$ $Cu \times 1.2 = CuO$
$Fe_2O_3 \times 0.70 = Fe$ $Fe \times 1.4 = Fe_2O_3$
$MnO \times 0.77 = Mn$ $Mn \times 1.3 = MnO$
$MoO_3 \times 0.67 = Mo$ $Mo \times 1.5 = MoO_3$
$ZnO \times 0.80 = Zn$ $Zn \times 1.2 = ZnO$

Sources of microelements Microelements are found in some irrigation water, pesticides, growing media, and in various fertilizers supplying N, P, K, Ca, and Mg. When these sources do not supply adequate microelements, they must be added. Quantities (percentage) of microelements as listed on the fertilizer bag are misleading, as they are given as oxide forms, and the actual amount of the plant nutrient is less. Conversion factors that are needed to determine the actual amount of microelements purchased are listed in Table 9-7.

A survey of recommendations to prevent microelement deficiency in crops reveals a wide disparity in the amounts of these elements suggested. Foliage plants have been grown satisfactorily without supplemental applications of microelements, but there is no doubt that sufficient levels were present in the potting mixture or supplied by the fungicides used. If a deficiency is suspected and/or preventative measures desired, the rates in Table 9-7 are suggested.

Mixing Soluble Fertilizers

Some growers prefer to mix fertilizers rather than buy premixed ones because exact ratios and desired analyses can be developed. Mixing fertilizers and developing desired analyses are not difficult, but may be more trouble than it is worth, considering labor costs, storage space, and the need for careful mixing.

Determining analyses of fertilizer mixtures is accomplished by adding together the numbers in the analyses and dividing by the number of units. For example, mixing one part potassium nitrate with one part ammonium nitrate gives

$$
\begin{array}{lr}
\text{potassium nitrate} & 14\text{-}0\text{-}44 \\
\text{ammonium nitrate} & \underline{33\text{-}0\text{-}0} \\
& 47\text{-}0\text{-}44 \div 2 = 23\text{-}0\text{-}22
\end{array}
$$

This procedure works with any combination of components. Another example is a mixture of 3 parts ammonium nitrate, 1 part diammonium phosphate, and 2 parts potassium nitrate:

$$
\begin{array}{r}
33\text{-}0\text{-}0 \\
33\text{-}0\text{-}0 \\
33\text{-}0\text{-}0 \\
21\text{-}53\text{-}0 \\
13\text{-}0\text{-}44 \\
\underline{13\text{-}0\text{-}44} \\
146\text{-}53\text{-}88 \div 6 = \text{a } 24.3\text{-}8.8\text{-}14.6 \text{ formula}
\end{array}
$$

This is a good all-purpose fertilizer for greenhouse use as the ratio is near the desired 3-1-2 and the analysis is relatively high, reducing the need for the application of large amounts of fertilizer materials. The ratio of NH_4 to NO_3 is also near the desired 50 : 50 ratio; therefore, it is a usable material all year.

When mixing large quantities, place the proper proportions on a clean floor, mix with a shovel, and place back in bags, labeling correctly, or prepare in small plastic bags of a size appropriate for injectors. The mixture may not be completely uniform, but it is unlikely that the error will be greater than 10 percent, and inaccuracies will be canceled out as subsequent fertilizer applications are made.

Soluble Salts

Controlling and accurately measuring soluble salts levels in soil or potting mixture solutions is a continuous problem for most foliage growers. Salts accumulate in growing media primarily from applied fertilizer and salty irrigation water, but small amounts are contributed by decaying organic matter. Soluble salts are composed predominantly of ammonium, calcium, magnesium, potassium, sodium, bicarbonate, chloride, nitrate, and sulfate ions.

Soluble salts levels when too high damage plant roots (burn) and reduce their ability to absorb water and nutrients. Salt concentrations of soils or potting mixtures that exceed concentrations inside plant roots cause water to move out of roots into the soil, resulting in partial or complete dehydration and death. Other symptoms of high soluble salts include stunting, excessive wilting, marginal leaf burn, yellowing of new growth and small flowers, and, in mild cases, reduction in growth may occur without other visible symptoms.

Soil or potting mixture samples normally are analyzed for soluble salts by one of three different procedures; therefore, growers must understand these different testing procedures and how to interpret them. Extreme variations occur in parts per million of soluble salts obtained on the same sample by the three procedures. These three salts testing procedures are (1) 1 : 2 soil to water dry weight, (2) 1 : 2 soil to water volume, and (3) the saturated paste. The information presented should provide rough guidelines on the interpretation of salts analyses from the different procedures.

Interpretation of Soluble Salts for 1 : 2 Dry Weight Procedure

In the 1 : 2 dry weight procedure, results are reported as parts per million of salts by weight of air dry soil. This makes the bulk density of media an important factor in interpretation, since with lightweight media larger volumes are required to equal a given weight than with heavier ones, yet both are mixed in the same volume of water. Therefore, in establishing high and low salinity values as shown in Table 9-8 for lightweight media by the dry weight method, values other than those recommended for sandy soils must be used. Lightweight media frequently contain moderate quantities of moisture after air drying, which also affect the results of this procedure.

A mixture of one part soil by weight and two parts water is read on a Solu-Bridge at 25°C. The Solu-Bridge is calibrated to read specific electrical conductance (EC) of the solution from 10 to 1,000 siemens $\times$ 10^{-5} or 0.1 siemens $\times$ 10^{-3} for newer models.

The parts per million of salts for the dry weight procedure are calculated by multiplying the EC $\times$ 700 $\times$ 2, where EC equals electrical conductivity in siemens per cubic centimeter or "Solu-Bridge reading" in siemens $\times$ 10^{-3}, 700 represents the average factor for converting conductivity readings to parts per million of salts, and 2 is the water weight dilution factor. For example, if the Solu-Bridge reading was 0.48,

$$0.48 \times 700 \times 2 = 672 \text{ ppm of salts}$$

For Solu-Bridge designed to read in siemens $\times$ 10^{-5}, use a factor of 7 instead of 700. For lightweight mixes with high water-holding capcity, it

TABLE 9-8   Interpretation of soluble salts readings (ppm) of 1:2 mixture of dry soil to water by weight for foliage plants

	(ppm) Salts for three media, rough guidelines[a]		
	Sandy soil	Sand:Peat (1:1 ratio)	Peat or lightweight mixes
Low	400	1,000	2,000
Medium	800	3,000	5,000
High	1,200	5,000	8,000
Very high	1,600	6,500	10,000
Excessive	1,600+	6,500+	10,000+

[a]These readings are based on medium salts-tolerant plants such as dieffenbachia and philodendron. For salts-sensitive plants such as calathea and maranta, these levels should be decreased by approximately 25 percent.

may be necessary to use a $1:4$ mixture of soil to water by weight, in which case a water dilution factor of 4 should be used instead of 2.

Interpretation of Soluble Salts for $1:2$ Volume Procedure

Soluble salts in this procedure are easily estimated by mixing 1 part by volume air dry soil to 2 parts water and reading on the Solu-Bridge at 25°C. Results are reported as parts per million of salts in a volume of water equivalent to the volume of soil sample. In the $1:2$ volume procedure, the same formula as for the dry weight method (EC $\times$ 700 $\times$ 2) is used for calculations where EC and 700 are the same as for the dry weight procedure, and 2 represents the water volume dilution factor. Again it might be necessary to use 4 volumes of water for peat and lightweight soil mixes, and a water dilution factor of 4 must be used in the calculation (Table 9-9).

The $1:2$ soil to water volume method is the procedure most commonly used by growers with their own Solu-Bridge. Variations (with this method) in salinity readings of media with different bulk densities at a given fertilization rate are much less than with the $1:2$ dry weight pro-

TABLE 9-9 Interpretation of soluble salts readings (ppm) for 1:2 air dry soil to water mixture by volume [53]

Media	Solu-Bridge reading (siemens g 10^{-5} on 1:2 volume)[a]	(ppm) salts[b]	Salts rating	Remarks
Sandy soils	Below 25	0–325		
1:1, peat:sand	Below 33	0–460	Low	Needs fertilizer
Peat or lightweight mixes	Below 50	0–700		
Sandy soils	25 to 50	350–700		Satisfactory
1:1, peat:sand	33 to 66	460–925	Low to medium	for growth in
Peat or lightweight mixes	50 to 100	700–1,400		upper range
Sandy soils	50 to 100	700–1,400		Desirable salt range,
1:1, peat:sand	66 to 130	925–1,820	Medium to high	no fertilizer needed;
Peat or lightweight mixes	100 to 175	1,400–2,450		but light applications can be made
Sandy soils	100 to 150	1,400–2,100		Do not fertilize or
1:1, peat:sand	130 to 200	1,820–2,800	High to very high	allow soil to become
Peat or lightweight mixes	175 to 275	2,450–3,850		dry; leach media if readings are near top of these ranges

[a] These readings are based on medium salts-tolerant plants such as Dieffenbachia and Philodendron. For salts-sensitive plants such as Calathea and Maranta these levels should be decreased by approximately 25 percent.

[b] EC (Solu-Bridge reading in siemens $\times$ 10^{-5}) $\times$ 7 $\times$ 2 = ppm salts.

cedure since volume measure offers partial compensation for variations in bulk density. As with the dry weight method, however, excessive soil moisture in the sample at the time of analysis, especially with lightweight media, will reduce salinity readings; therefore, *the initial soil sample should be air dried.*

Interpretation of the Saturated Paste Procedure for Soluble Salts and Specific Nutrients

The saturated paste extraction procedure of testing salinity was initially developed by the U.S. Salinity Laboratory in Riverside, California, for saline and alkali soils and later was expanded at the Agricultural Research and Education Center, Bradenton, Florida, to evaluate intensity (total salts) and balance of various ions in the salts extract, hence, the intensity and balance or I & B concept of soil testing presently in use in Florida [53].

Sufficient water is added in the procedure to the soil media to bring the sample to a glistening, saturated paste for 1 to 2 hours, and the moisture is then extracted from the soil under slight vacuum. Results are reported as parts per million of salts in the soil solution at maximum soil moisture-holding capacity after gravitational drainage. Readings are calculated as follows: EC_e represents electrical conductivity in siemens per cubic centimeter (Solu-Bridge reading) of the saturation extract, 700 represents a standard conversion factor, and moisture factor (MF) represents the ratio of moisture percentage at saturation (by dry weight) to moisture-holding capacity percentage (by dry weight). The MF changes with soil or media composition, as well as with the pot size for container-grown ornamentals. The MF for any soil or media can be computed by

$$MF = \frac{\text{percent of soil moisture on weight basis at saturation}}{\text{percent of soil moisture on weight basis at field moisture capacity}}$$

For field soils and ground beds the moisture factors normally used are 2.0 for sandy soils, 1.2 for organic soils, and 1.5 for 1 : 1 sand and peat mixtures. For example, if the Solu-Bridge reading was 120, $120 \times 7 \times 1.37 = 1109$ ppm of salts in a peat mix in a round pot (Table 9-10).

Moisture-holding capacities of soils in containers are affected by soil mixture and container size and height. Moisture-retention properties of media in containers are affected by a media-container interface phenomenon that acts as a barrier to free drainage, and media water retention is also a function of container depth.

TABLE 9-10 Factors to convert electrical conductivity of saturated paste extract (EC_e) to parts per million of soluble salts at field moisture capacity for several soil media mixtures

Media mixtures	Factors for various-sized plastic pots					
	2¼-inch square pot		5-inch round pot		7-inch round pot	
	Moisture factor (MF)	MF × 7	Moisture factor	MF × 7	Moisture factor	MF × 7
Muck	1.1	7.7	1.3	9.1	1.8	12.6
European or native peat	1.14	8.0	1.37	9.6	1.8	12.6
Wood shavings	1.39	9.7	1.43	10.0	2.1	14.7
Shavings and peat combined	1.2	8.4	1.43	10.0	1.7	11.9
Perlite and peat (not over 66% of either)	1.3	9.1	1.43	10.0	1.8	12.6
Shavings, peat, and perlite mixture at 1:1:1	1.3	9.1	1.43	10.0	1.9	13.3
Sand[a] and peat, 1:1 volume	1.3	9.1	1.43	10.0	1.8	12.6
Sand:peat:perlite at 1:1:1 volume	1.2	8.4	1.43	10.0	1.7	11.9
Sand:peat:shavings at 1:1:1 volume	1.3	9.1	1.43	10.0	1.7	11.9
Perlite and shavings at 1:1 volume	1.5	10.5	1.65	11.5	2.4	16.8
Builders sand alone	1.6	11.2	1.8	12.6	2.2	15.4
Sand:shavings: perlite at 1:1:1 volume	1.5	10.5	2.2	15.4	2.4	16.8

[a] Builders sand.

Moisture factors have been determined for several soil media in different containers (Table 9-10) for use in determining soluble salts by the saturated paste technique for container-grown crops.

The media sample is brought to a saturated paste prior to salts determination; therefore, initial soil moisture, sample volume, bulk density, water-holding capacity, or media composition are not critical factors in the accuracy of determinations. The saturated paste technique is superior in dealing with media with wide ranges of bulk density and water-holding capacity and, in cases where it is not practical to use this procedure, the air dry volume based technique is more convenient than the dry weight method. The 1:2 dry weight method has advantages for sandy soils over the volume technique, but both are inferior to the saturated paste method.

Approximate low, medium, and high levels of soluble salts (parts per million) as determined by the saturated paste technique for ornamentals are given in Table 9-12 with emphasis that these are approximations.

Interpretation of Soluble Salts in Irrigation Systems

Quality of irrigation water is important in plant production because of the undesirable effects of total soluble salts and certain specific toxic chemicals found in some waters. A complete water analysis should be made before using water from a new well.

Concentrations of soluble salts in Florida well waters range from less than 50 parts per million to several thousand. Generally, wells can be classified as low, medium, and high according to salts content, with wells containing less than 700 parts per million of total soluble salts the low category, which usually does not cause trouble (Table 9-11). Wells containing from 700 to 1,500 parts per million of salts are in the medium salts range and may cause problems, especially during dry seasons or where frequent but light overhead irrigation is practiced. Wells containing over 2,000 parts per million of salts should be avoided as much as possible for foliage plant production (Table 9-12).

To convert Solu-Bridge Model RD-15 readings on well water or other irrigation water, multiply the reading of the water in siemens $\times$ 10^{-5} by 7. This will approximate the ppm total soluble salts in the water. For example, if the Solu-Bridge reading was 48,

$$48 \times 7 = 336 \text{ ppm of total soluble salts in the water}$$

If the Solu-Bridge reads in siemens $\times$ 10^{-3}, then multiply the 0.48 by 700 instead of 7.

TABLE 9-11   Classes of irrigation water and permissible limits of constituents [50]

Class of water	Electrical conductance (EC $\times$ 10^{-5}) at 25°C	Total dissolved solids (salts, ppm)	Sodium percent of total solids	Boron (ppm)
1. Excellent	Less than 25	175	20	0.33
2. Good	25–75	175–525	20–40	0.33–0.67
3. Permissible	75–200	525–1,400	40–60	0.67–1.00
4. Doubtful	200–300	1,400–2,100	60–80	1.00–1.25
5. Unsuitable	More than 300	2,100	80	1.25

TABLE 9-12 Interpretation of low, medium, and high soluble salts levels (ppm) for foliage plants as determined by saturated paste technique[a]

Crop response	Low	Optimum	High
Salts sensitive	900	1,800	2,700
Range	Up to 1,400	1,400–2,300	2,300–3,000
Medium salts tolerant	1,500	3,000	4,500
Range	Up to 2,200	2,200–3,800	3,900–5,200
High salts tolerant	3,500	4,500	5,500
Range	Up to 4,000	4,000–5,000	5,000–6,000

[a] These readings are based on medium salts-tolerant plants such as dieffenbachia and philodendron. For salts-sensitive plants, these levels should be decreased by approximately 25 percent.

Avoiding High Salts Problems

Salts from irrigation water may reduce water absorption, produce nutritional imbalances and toxicities, and adversely affect physical conditions of soils. Sodium tends to make clay and organic soils "run together," to be wet, nonaggregating, and subject to poor drainage and aeration [52]. Sodium also interferes with absorption of other positively charged ions that are nutritionally important, such as potassium, magnesium, and calcium. Excess sodium may induce calcium deficiency or poor quality of plant products owing to low calcium availability. Potentially toxic elements in irrigation water include boron, fluoride, lithium, and bicarbonate. Proper fertilization must be adjusted according to amounts of boron and other ions present in the irrigation water. Analyses of water and leaf samples will aid in clarifying this situation.

Large amounts of negatively charged ions, such as bicarbonate, are undesirable. Bicarbonate present in excess of chloride plus sulfate content often results in precipitation of calcium and magnesium, and results in sodium-saturated soils that have poor physical condition. Bicarbonate ions also increase the incidence of iron deficiency.

To reduce or eliminate the effects of high soluble salts, the following procedures are helpful:

1. Avoid excess use of chloride, sodium, and sulfate in fertilizer to reduce the salts input of unnecessary elements.
2. Test irrigation water and soils regularly.
3. Select sources of water of the best quality available.
4. Provide good drainage to remove salts.
5. Be careful to avoid letting very light soils dry out, since a 50 percent loss of available soil moisture approximately doubles the salts concentration.

6. Leach salts out of soil when possible, even with slightly salty water. Overhead irrigation is the only way to remove salts by leaching, and the saltier the water, the more leaching is required.

7. Salts accumulate in hardpan subsoil pockets of field soils or depressions in the hardpan profile. These small areas will damage a planting and should be corrected by breaking the hardpan at the center of affected areas and leaching the salts. Surprisingly, these areas will persist with heavy rains or heavy irrigation unless the hardpan is broken. Once located, these areas should be watched since the hardpan may reseal itself where broken.

A physiological character of root growth is their failure to grow into a zone of high soluble salts because of water limitations to the root. If fertilizer is placed too close to roots, they will probably be burned, since salts levels outside roots will cause water to move from them into the soil. If soluble salts build up too high in soils, plants will make little growth and leaves may be burned.

Soil and Tissue Analyses

Determining the amounts of nutrients in soils and plant tissue aids in regulating fertilizer application. However, such knowledge must be translated into specific recommendations, which depend upon accurate sampling and analyses evaluations using research data. Soil and plant analyses supplement each other, each having advantages and disadvantages. Soil analyses have the advantage of determining nutrient content, salinity, and pH of the soil prior to planting and can be used periodically during crop growth. Such information can be used to adjust soil pH, nutrient content, and salinity prior to planting and to help maintain desired levels during crop growth. Tissue analyses are more reliable in providing exact information on the content of specific elements, and when combined with soil analyses, they can aid in adjusting fertilizer programs to provide proper amounts of nutrients for maximum yield and quality.

A simple method of estimating fertilizer level is the use of a Solu-Bridge to determine soluble salts. A low salts reading indicates that insufficient fertilizer is available, and a high reading indicates excessive and possible toxic amounts of fertilizer. The problem with this method is that amounts of individual elements are not indicated, nor is there any differentiation between salts of usable and salts of unusable elements. There are many methods of determining individual amounts of elements, some simple and relatively inexpensive, others sophisticated and more costly, and a good procedure to follow employs the use of both methods. Soil test kits are available that allow growers to make determinations on a regular, frequent schedule; if correlated with growth responses of various crops, they can become a valuable cultural tool. Less frequently, samples can be sent away for more precise and accurate determinations and both systems compared with each other, relying on the precise system as the check. In this way, relative reliability of the quick test system can be estimated to provide quick inputs on the nutritional status of a crop.

Samples should be taken at intermediate intervals between fertilizer applications, as soil samples taken immediately before fertilization will indicate soil fertility at its lowest level, while samples taken immediately after fertilization will indicate fertility at its highest level. Several composite samples from the same area or potting mixture should be analyzed. If sampling prior to potting, the potting mixture should be thoroughly blended and samples taken only after all ingredients are mixed. Samples from ground beds or raised benches that are to be analyzed should be removed from several widely spaced locations, and the entire profile containing plant roots should be included. Slow-release fertilizers added to media can result in misleading information from soil analyses depending upon analytical procedures used, since crushing or otherwise breaking of such materials can release the fertilizer materials contained in them. As analytical techniques vary between laboratories, results also vary, and it is best to stick with one laboratory or technique and check results against crop responses [31]. Growers should follow suggestions of the laboratory when determining whether a particular element in the soil or tissue is low, optimum, or high, and use these results to establish optimum standards for a particular situation and crop.

Plant tissue analyses determine the present nutritional status of plants and are useful in diagnosing existing problems. Plant analyses are not as useful for short-term crops as for long-term ones. For many fast-turnover foliage plant crops, the results of tissue samples are often not available in time to correct deficiencies or other problems, but they are useful in preventing similar mistakes on subsequent crops.

Analyses of plant tissue also are useful in evaluating fertilization programs. Tissue composition of good quality foliage plants can be found in Table 9-2. There is much less variation in tissue analyses than in those for soils; however, the area of the plant from which tissue samples are obtained is important. Generally, the most recently matured leaves of plants are utilized. Old leaves and young immature leaves should be avoided. Leaves taken for tissue analyses should be clean, and if pesticides containing iron, zinc, copper, manganese, or other heavy metals have been applied to the leaves, results will be misleading for each particular element.

The prime disadvantage of soil and plant tissue analyses for most commercial foliage growers is the time lag between sampling and receiving results. Many universities analyze samples, but a month often passes before results are known. Commercial laboratories are usually faster, but even there, 1 to 2 weeks may lapse before sample results are received. Growers who own a pH meter and a Solu-Bridge at least can have immediate knowledge of pH and soluble salts levels and can alter programs accordingly. An occasional comparison of these results with those of a university or commercial laboratory is useful and will provide a basic check of methods and results.

REFERENCES

[1] Baker, K. S. 1957. The U. C. system for producing healthy container grown plants. Univ. of Calif. Agr. Exp. Sta. Manual 23. p. 332.

[2] Boodley, J. W. 1965. Steaming and fertilizers. *N.Y. State Flower Growers Bull.* 241:2–4.

[3] Cibes, H., and G. Samuels. 1960. Mineral deficiency symptoms displayed by *Dracaena godseffiana* and *Dracaena sanderiana* grown under controlled conditions. Univ. of Puerto Rico Agr. Exp. Sta. Tech. Paper 29.

[4] Collard, R. C., J. N. Joiner, C. A. Conover, and D. B. McConnell. 1977. Influences of shade and fertilizer on light compensation point of *Ficus benjamina* L. *J. Am. Soc. Hort. Sci.* 102(4):447–449.

[5] Conover, C. A. 1972. Influence of nutrition on foliage quality and longevity. *Florida Foliage Grower* 9(3):1–4.

[6] ———. 1972. Greenhouse production of potted foliage in the southern United States. *Florida Foliage Grower* 9(11):1–7.

[7] ———. 1978. Fertilizer facts for foliage growers. Agr. Res. Center Apopka, Res. Rept. RH-78-2.

[8] ———. 1978. Fertilizer facts for foliage growers. Univ. of Fla. Agr. Res. Center Apopka, Res. Rept. RH-78-2, p. 7.

[9] ———, and R. T. Poole. 1971. Influence of fluoride on foliar necrosis of *Cordyline terminalis* cv. Baby Doll during propagation. *Fla. State Hort. Soc. Proc.* 84:380–383.

[10] ———. 1972. Influence of shade and nutritional levels on growth and yield of *Scindapsus aureus, Cordyline terminalis* 'Baby Doll' and *Dieffenbachia exotica. Proc. Am. Soc. Hort. Sci. Trop. Reg.* 16:277–281.

[11] ———. 1972. Influence of propagation bed nutritional amendments on selected foliage plants. *Fla. State Hort. Soc. Proc.* 85:392–394.

[12] ———. 1973. Factors influencing notching and necrosis of *Dracaena deremensis* 'Warneckii' foliage. *Proc. Am. Soc. Hort. Sci. Trop. Reg.* 17:378–384.

[13] Conover, C. A., and R. T. Poole. 1973. Factors influencing micronutrient

use in tropical foliage production. Apopka ARC Research Report RH-73-1. 5 pp.

[14] _____. 1974. Influence of shade, nutrition and season on growth of *Aglaonema, Maranta* and *Peperomia* stock plants. *Proc. Am. Soc. Hort. Sci. Trop. Reg.* 18:283–287.

[15] _____. 1974. Influence of media and fertilization on *Aglaonema* 'Fransher.' *Proc. Fla. State Hort. Soc.* 87:431–435.

[16] _____. 1974. Influence of shade and fertilizer source and level on growth, quality and foliar content of *Philodendron oxycardium* Schott. *J. Am. Soc. Hort. Sci.* 99:150–152.

[17] _____. 1974. Fluoride toxicity of tropical foliage plants. *Florists' Review* 157:23, 59.

[18] _____. 1975. Influence of shade and fertilization on growth of container grown *Araucaria, Dieffenbachia, Dizygotheca* and *Dracaena. Proc. Amer. Soc. Hort. Sci. Trop. Reg.* 19:247–252.

[19] _____. 1975. Influence of shade and fertilizer levels on production and acclimatization of *Dracaena marginata. Proc. Fla. State Hort. Soc.* 88:606–608.

[20] _____. 1976. Light and fertilizer recommendations on production of foliage stock plants and acclimatized potted plants. ARC-A Res. Rept. RH-76-6. 5pp.

[21] _____, D. W. Simpson, and J. N. Joiner. 1975. Influence of micronutrient sources and levels on response and tissue content of *Aphelandra, Brassaia* and *Philodendron. Proc. Fla. State Hort. Soc.* 88:599–602.

[22] Dickey, R. D., R. T. Poole, and J. N. Joiner. 1961. Effects of nitrogen and potassium levels and two application intervals on growth and chemical comparison of Rhododendron ineicum in vivernum suspension. *Proc. Fla. State Hort. Soc.* 74:436–440.

[23] _____, and J. N. Joiner. 1966. Identifying deficiencies in foliage plants. *Southern Florist Nurseryman* LXXIX(20):38, 42–43.

[24] Furuta, T. 1964. Foliar feeding can produce quality woody ornamentals grown in containers. *Southern Florist Nurseryman* 76(45): 42, 43, 46, 48–50.

[25] Harrison, D. S. 1968. Injection of liquid fertilizer materials into irrigation systems. *Univ. of Fla. Agr. Ext. Serv. Circ.* 276A. 11 pp.

[26] Joiner, J. N., and C. A. Conover. 1965. Characteristics affecting desirability of various media components for production of container grown plants. *Soil Crop Sci. Soc. of Fla.* 25:320–328.

[27] _____, and W. E. Waters. 1970. The influence of cultural conditions on the chemical composition of six tropical foliage plants. *Proc. Am. Soc. Hort. Sci. Trop. Reg.* 14:254–267.

[28] Jones, W. W., and T. W. Embleton. 1965. Urea foliage sprays. *California Citrograph* 50(9):334, 355–359.

[29] Koths, J. S., R. W. Judd, J. J. Maisano, G. F. Griffin, J. W. Bartok, and R. A. Ashley. 1976. Nutrition of greenhouse crops. Univ. of Conn. Misc. Pub. 76-14. 17 pp.

[30] Kraus, E. J., and H. R. Kraybill. 1918. Vegetation and reproduction with special reference to the tomato. Oregon Agr. Expt. Sta. Bull. 149.

[31] Labanouskas, C. K., and M. F. Handy. 1975. Comparative wet-digestion and dry-ashing of orange and schefflera leaves for nutrient determinations. *HortScience* 10(6):596–597.

[32] Langhans, R. W., R. C. Mott, J. H. Kumpf, and P. A. Hammer. 1972. Osmocote used successfully with foliage plants. *Florists Rev.* October 19, 1972, pp. 35, 49.

[33] Peters, R. B. 1978. A system of greenhouse soil fertility control. Allentown, Pa.: Robert B. Peters Co., Inc., 20 pp.

[34] Poole, R. T., and C. A. Conover. 1974. Nutritional studies of three foliage plants. *Southern Nursery Assoc. Nursery Res. J.* 1(2):17–26.

[35] _____. 1974. Foliar chlorosis of *Dracaena deremensis* Engler cv. Warneckii cuttings induced by fluoride. *HortScience* 9:378–379.

[36] _____. 1975. Influence of culture on tipburn of spider plant, *Chlorophytum comosum*. *Proc. Fla. State Hort. Soc.* 88:441–443.

[37] _____. 1975. Fluoride induced necrosis of *Dracaena deremensis* Engler cv. Janet Craig. *HortScience* 10:376–377.

[38] _____. 1975. Influence of media, shade and fertilizer levels on production of *Chrysalidocarpus lutescens*. *Proc. Fla. State Hort. Soc.* 88:603–605.

[39] _____. 1975. Influence of propagation media and amendments on fluoride toxicity of *Cordyline terminalis* 'Baby Doll'. *Fluoride* 8:85–92.

[40] _____. 1976. Influence of liming materials on soil pH, leaf chlorosis and necrosis and elemental composition of *Dracaena deremensis* 'Warneckii'. *Southern Nursery Assoc. J.* 3(2):21–25.

[41] _____. 1976. Nitrogen, phosphorus and potassium fertilization of the bromeliad, *Aechmea fasciata* Baker. *HortScience* 11(6):585–586.

[42] _____. 1977. Nitrogen and potassium fertilization of the *Aglaonema commutatum* Schott cvs. Fransher and Pseudobracteatum. *HortScience* 12(6): 570–571.

[43] _____. 1978. The importance of micronutrients in tropical foliage production. *Proc. 1978 National Trop. Foliage Short Course*, pp. 121–125.

[44] Poole, R. T., C. A. Conover, and J. N. Joiner.1976. Chemical composition of good quality tropical foliage plants. *Proc. Fla. State Hort. Soc.* 89:307–308.

[45] _____, and D. B. McConnell. 1974. Fertilization of *Philodendron selloum*. *Southern Nursery Assoc. Res. J.* 1(1):7–12.

[46] Samuels, G., and H. R. Cibes. 1953. Iron chlorosis on *Dracaena sanderana*. *J. Agr. Univ. of Puerto Rico* 37(4):265–272.

[47] Sutcliffe, J. F. 1962. Mineral salts absorption in plants. New York: Pergamon Press.

[48] Trapp, J. A. 1973. Growing *Philodendron oxycardium* in soilless media with slow-release fertilizers. Pennsylvania Flower Growers Bulletin No. 261.

[49] Tukey, H. B. 1965. Foliar feeding. *American Fruit Grower* 85:14, 15, 40.

[50] Waters, W. E., and C. A. Conover. 1969. Chrysanthemum production in Florida. Univ. Fla. Exp. Station Bull. 730:21.

[51] ———, and W. Llewellyn. 1968. Effects of coated-slow-release fertilizer on growth responses, chemical composition and soil salinity levels for foliage plants. *Proc. Fla. State Hort. Soc.* 81:380–388.

[52] Wallihan, E. 1961. Effect of sodium bicarbonate on iron absorption in orange seedlings. *Plant Physio.* 36:52–53.

[53] Waters, W. E., J. Nesmith, C. M. Geraldson, and S. S. Waltz. 1972. Interpretation of soluble salt tests and soil analysis by different procedures. Univ. of Fl. Agr. Res. and Ed. Center. Bradenton Mimeo Report. G. C. 1972 –4. 9 pp.

[54] Webster, G. C. 1959. Nitrogen metabolism in plants. Evanston, Ill.: Row-Peterson Biological Monographs.

ten

C. A. Conover
R. T. Poole

environmental factors

Growth and quality of foliage plants depend on interactions between environmental factors and the genetic constitution (gene pool) of a particular plant. Each plant has inherent characteristics such as color, leaf shape, size, and growth rate that determine its potential for consumer satisfaction, but its ultimate potential is controlled by environments under which plants are grown. Environmental factors, thus, determine profitability of foliage plants, because they influence quality, size, and turnover time, which determines unit cost of production. Maximum yields are not achieved in many commercial foliage plant production units because of improper light intensities, temperature, and/or other factors, but economic considerations are necessary before making environmental changes, since the cost of changes may be greater than potential increases in yield.

Light

Light in the presence of water and carbon dioxide in the chlorophyll of living plants triggers internal mechanisms that synthesize sugars. Light energy that is received by a leaf activates chloroplasts to convert radiant energy to chemical energy, which is used to join carbon dioxide with water to form carbohydrates, with oxygen evolved in this photosynthetic process. Plants are unique in their ability to produce their own food supply. Soluble carbohydrates formed in photosynthesis can be further synthesized into starch, hemicellulose, and cellulose, which constitute the major structural portions of plants and are necessary for respiration, which provides energy for growth and development. Carbohydrates are also building blocks for fats and proteins, which are major components of living cells [27]. The amount of light plants receive within a broad range determines amounts of carbohydrates synthesized and resultant growth and quality potential. The photosynthetic rate can be reduced when excessive light energy is received by plants because of limited CO_2 or photooxidation. Under conditions of excessive light and high temperature, photooxidation or sun scald of foliage results from a reversal of the photosynthetic process in that oxygen is absorbed and cells are consumed.

As light is decreased below the optimum point, carbohydrate production per unit of time also decreases until the light compensation point is reached. This is the intensity at which carbohydrate production is just sufficient to equal that utilized by respiration, with none left over for other plant functions. Plants cannot long survive light intensities as low as the compensation point or less.

Effectiveness of light in the production of carbohydrates is closely correlated with nutrition. The higher the light intensity, other factors being favorable, the larger the amount of fertilizer foliage plants can use efficiently and effectively until light levels become excessive or the light saturation point (LSP) is reached.

Growth of foliage plants under specific light intensities is an important aspect of production, since many plant genera included in the foliage plant group evolved under widely divergent environmental conditions of light intensity, temperature, humidity, and soil type. These conditions range from tropical forest understories, where light intensities may be no more than 200 footcandles (2 kilolux) to open savannas where 10,000 footcandles (110 kilolux) are reached. Research has shown that foliage plants can tolerate higher light levels when there is sufficient air movement to prevent reaching lethal temperatures at the leaf surface [3]. However, air movement is not normally considered when selecting shade levels in commercial nurseries.

The ability of plants to acclimate to varying light intensities has been known for years [1, 32, 41]. This process can result in foliage plants of the same species having different anatomical and physiological features depending on the light intensity received during production. Sun leaves of *Ficus benjamina,* for example, are smaller, thicker, and lighter green in color than shade leaves and are often folded at the midrib. Chloroplasts in sun leaves often have vertical orientation and contain rudimentary grana with the same orientation, whereas chloroplasts in

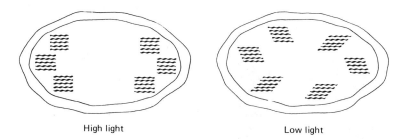

High light   Low light

Figure 10-1.   Stylized example of nondispersed chloroplasts and vertically oriented grana in a cell of a sun-grown plant (left). At right, dispersed chloroplasts and grana of a cell from a shade-grown plant.

shade leaves have well-defined grana which are better dispersed within cells with predominately horizontal orientation (Figure 10-1). Determination of proper light intensities for production of foliage plants depends on production techniques, especially nutrition, as well as final use factors [12].

Light Effects on Stock Plant Production

Yield of cuttings should be maximized in stock plant production and quality maintained. Yield, foliage color, foliage size and/or shape, density of foliage, amount of stored carbohydrates, and susceptibility to diseases or insects influence determinations of proper light intensities.

Color   Foliage color of green foliage plants becomes deeper or more intense to a point as shade level increases at constant fertilizer level [9, 37, 40]. Color intensity of colorful plants such as *Cordyline terminalis* and *Codiaeum variegatum* are severely reduced as light intensity is decreased below 3,000 footcandles (32 kilolux) [5]. Foliage plants with variegated leaves, such as *Epipremnum aureum*, have less yellow variegation when light levels are less than 4,000 footcandles (43 kilolux) [5], while *Dracaena sanderana* or *D. deremensis* 'Warneckii' produce wider white stripes at less than 2,000 footcandles (22 kilolux) than at higher levels (Figure 10-2).

Foliage size and shape   Foliage size and shape vary considerably as light intensity changes. *Philodendron scandens oxycardium* [9] produces larger leaves and greater stem caliper under 40 percent shade than under 80 percent. Since growers desire medium-sized foliage, they usually select an intermediate light intensity to produce the wanted size and quality. Plants with lance-shaped leaves, such as *Dracaena marginata*,

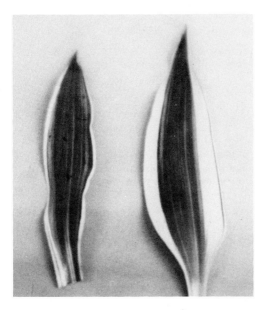

Figure 10-2. Leaves of *Dracaena sanderana* grown at approximately 1,500 ft-c (16 Klux) (right) and 3,000 ft-c (32 Klux) (left); note increase in width of the white found under lower light intensity.

produce longer and narrower leaves under high shade than under low shade levels [15], while the petiole length of plants such as *Brassaia actinophylla* may be so lengthened under heavy shade that plants become unsalable.

Related problems   Disease, pest, and physiological problems are not necessarily related to light intensity directly, but growth of stock plants under polypropylene shade cloth rather than in full sun frequently increases disease problems because of higher humidity, which means foliage and potting medium remain wet for longer durations. An example of this is increased problems with *Fusarium* on *Dracaena marginata* when grown under shade rather than in full sun. Incidence of fluoride toxicity increases as light intensity increases [7], due to increased transpiration increasing the movement of free fluoride in soil solutions. Increased levels of mite infestations on susceptible plants occur more frequently on stock plants grown under fiberglass or glass due to lack of rainfall or overhead application of water.

Cutting yield   Cutting yield is directly related to light intensity, with too much or too little light reducing yield. Ultimate use of plants must be considered when making decisions on light levels for stock plants, since cuttings grown under high light intensity produce plants having reduced quality under interior conditions if their production time is short, owing to lack of proper acclimatization prior to placement under low interior light levels [8, 39]. Table 9-4 provides suggested light levels for the production of stock plants of major foliage genera as determined by research [5, 7, 9, 11, 14, 15, 16, 37] and observations in the United States and the tropics. Yield of *Epipremnum aureum* increased nearly 100 percent when grown under 40 percent shade rather than 80 percent [5], and *Peperomia obtusifolia* was increased 77 percent when the shade level was decreased from 80 to 60 percent [11]. Placement under higher than recommended light intensities resulted in lower quality of most foliage plants, as evidenced by poor color and/or reduced leaf size [5, 7, 11].

Light Effects on Potted Plant Production

Plants grown for indoor use should be acclimatized during production for the low light conditions found in most building interiors. Acclimatization techniques determine plant quality for consumers, since leaves developed under high light and nutritional levels have higher light compensation points than those grown under lower levels [4, 10] and, thus, cannot survive low light stress as well as plants produced under lower light intensities. The light compensation point is that point at which energy (food) required by the plant during respiration is equal to the amount produced by photosynthesis. Proper production light intensity is important, as is placement of plants under gradually reduced light levels to lower the compensation point before placement indoors [13, 21]. The importance of compensation points is demonstrated by the fact that 100 footcandles (1 kilolux) of light 10 to 12 hours daily may be sufficient for shade-grown plants, while 200 footcandles (2 kilolux) may not be sufficient for sun-grown plants [18].

Light intensities suggested for stock production are frequently too high for pot plant production, since they can cause foliage to be an unacceptably light green or yellowish in color. This off green color is associated with reduced chlorophyll levels under high light [15, 18, 38] and can be corrected in most cases with increased fertilizer levels or a reduction in light intensity. Increased levels of fertilizer often cause soluble salts problems and increased light compensation points; thus, the suggested method of correcting the problem with potted plants is reduction of light levels.

Several foliage plant groups exhibit other problems in addition to color differences when receiving incorrect light levels. *Aglaonema* and *Dieffenbachia* leaves assume a nearly vertical position when grown under excessive light, which reduces plant quality, since surfaces of leaves cannot be viewed from the side. *Aphelandra* develops sunken and uneven leaf surfaces, which detract from its appearance. Growth of pot plants, including plant size and shape, is as fast and sometimes faster under proper light intensities than higher or lower levels [15]. Table 9-4 provides suggested levels in footcandles for some of the most important foliage plant genera.

Minimum light intensities are necessary for adequate flower production in many potted plants sold as flowering foliage plants [26, 34]. *Aphelandra, Pachystachys, Saintpaulia,* and others grown for flower production must accumulate carbohydrates before flower initiations can occur; therefore, relatively high light intensities are necessary for flowering, but may not be best for production of acclimatized plants.

Some flowering foliage plants are photoperiodically responsive [33] and can be induced to flower through short-day or long-day treatment. Flowering on demand might be induced in many other species through day-length control once research is conducted to determine which are photoperiodically responsive.

Temperature

Temperatures affect growth rate of foliage plants as much as any other factor by influencing rates of photosynthesis and respiration [23, 24, 42]. Temperature needs of each foliage plant species should be determined, since some are tropical, others subtropical, and others temperate in their requirements. Growers must provide proper temperature regimes to maximize carbohydrate production during the day and control its consumption at night through respiration so as to obtain the greatest plant growth. A differential between day and night temperatures is necessary for best quality growth.

Research information is available on day/night temperature differentials for roses, chrysanthemums, and other horticultural crops, but is very limited on foliage plants. Indications are that some benefits can be obtained with differentials in day and night temperatures of 5° or 10°F (2.7° to 5.5°C). Night temperatures below 65°F (18.3°C) can seriously reduce growth of many tropical and subtropical foliage plants, especially *Aglaonema, Dieffenbachia,* and *Epipremnum,* but *Hedera, Ardisia, Podocarpus, Pittosporum,* and other temperate foliage plant genera can tolerate lower temperatures without serious loss in growth or quality.

Maximum day temperatures maintained by commercial foliage growers vary extensively. Recent data accumulated by monitoring six greenhouse ranges used in foliage production showed variations from 80° to 105°F (26.7° to 40°C) [19]. Even with such variable and often high daily temperatures, no serious loss in quality was observed. Observations have indicated that quality loss occurs on *Aglaonema, Calathea, Maranta,* and other genera when day temperatures are above 90°F (32°C). Maximum daily temperatures often exceed 95°F (35°C) during dry seasons in tropical areas of Central America where considerable stock is produced. The best plant growth is observed on *Philodendron, Ficus,* and *Epipremnum* under these conditions. The best general day/night temperatures for foliage plant production appear to be approximately 70°F (21°C) night and 90°F (32°C) day, but when heating and cooling energy costs are taken into consideration, some adjustment might be desirable. During winter when heating is necessary, night temperatures of 68°F (20°C) are acceptable, and heating to 75°F (24°C) during the day is adequate, except where sun heating is available; then day temperatures of 85° to 90°F (29° to 32°C) should be maintained. Night temperatures of 70° to 75°F (21° to 24°C) are acceptable during summer, as is 90° to 95°F (32° to 35°C) during the day, provided this does not severely influence labor productivity.

Soil temperatures do not fluctuate as much as air temperatures because of the insulating effects of soil; thus, daily soil temperatures stay near or slightly above night temperatures, which are often too low for good foliage plant growth during winter months. This problem is further complicated by the use of forced air heaters with thermostats located several feet above benches, which result in soil temperatures several degrees below the lowest controlled night temperatures. Desiccation of leaves often occurs under these conditions when warm air is forced across plants having roots in cold soils.

Research on propagation benches used for rooting of foliage plants [35] has shown that rooting can be advanced by several weeks when medium temperature is maintained at 80°F (27°C), rather than at 65° to 70°F (18° to 21°C) (Figure 10-3). The same response has been shown in caladium production [6] in that root growth was greatly increased at 80°F (27°C) over check plants at 65° and 70°F (18° and 21°C), and germination time for palm seed decreased and growth rate increased at these temperatures [36]. Commercial foliage stock plant producers often recognize benefits of increasing soil temperatures through the use of bottom heat, and practice this technique by using steam or hot water pipes beneath benches and skirting the benches to retain heat, by using forced hot air through convection tubes, or by placing heating cables in benches.

Use of cold irrigation water lowers soil temperatures during winter months and can injure foliage of several species by foliage contact. Water of 45°F (7°C) can injure *Aglaonema, Dieffenbachia, Philodendron, Saintpaulia,* and *Sansevieria* foliage when air temperature is 60°F (16°C) or higher [17, 20] (Figure 10-4). Water pumped directly from the ground in southern parts of the United States is usually 60°F (16°C) or

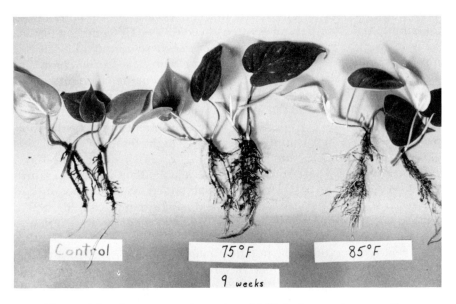

Figure 10-3. Improvement in rooting of *Philodendron scandens oxycardium* when the propagation medium is maintained at 75°F (24°C) or 85°F (29°C) versus a 65° to 70°F (18° to 21°C) control.

Figure 10-4. Spotting of *Philodendron scandens oxycardium* caused by cold water of 35° to 45°F (4.5° to 7°C) falling on warm foliage.

higher, but sometimes it is stored outdoors or in buildings where it cools overnight or between use. Water should be heated to 50°F (10°C) or more in colder climates prior to use to prevent foliar damage.

Relative Humidity

Relative humidity is the percentage of moisture in the air relative to the amount of moisture the air could hold if saturated at any given temperature. A relative humidity of 100 percent means the air is saturated with water at that temperature, while one of 50 percent means the air contains only half the amount of water it could hold at that temperature. An increase in temperature without a corresponding increase in water vapor decreases the relative humidity; conversely, a drop in temperature without a decrease in water vapor increases the relative humidity. Relative humidity is important because of its effects on plant-water relations, greenhouse condensation, and disease incidence [22].

Relative humidity affects transpiration rate and hence water usage. The lower the relative humidity, the more often watering will be required to keep water available to plant roots and prevent water deficits. Even though relative humidity in a greenhouse may be 50 percent, transpiration from a leaf may be based on a lower relative humidity level because, even though the greenhouse air temperature may be 68°F (20°C), leaf temperatures may be 77°F (25°C); hence they will lose water vapor faster because the loss is based on a lower effective relative humidity. This water loss problem can be serious when soil temperatures are low, because roots will absorb water slowly, and sufficient water may not be available to foliage to prevent desiccation. Commercial growers generally maintain relative humidity levels of 50 percent or more in greenhouses, although there is a lack of information to substantiate this level as a requirement for foliage plant growth. Maintenance of extremely high relative humidities (80 to 100 percent) at all times can severely reduce root-shoot ratios and cause potential problems when plants are subjected to moisture stress in nurseries or after placement indoors.

Greenhouse condensation is most severe in cold climates, but it can be a problem everywhere, as is water condensation on plant foliage. Major problems caused by condensation include increased foliar disease incidence, cold water spotting on foliage, and reduced light intensities.

Condensation is most likely to form inside greenhouses and on foliage when humidity is high and greenhouse temperatures are as warm as or only a few degrees warmer than the outside temperature reading. This occurs most commonly when moisture in the warmer air condenses on cooler leaf and greenhouse surfaces. The best method of preventing condensation is to raise the greenhouse temperature a few degrees above that outside and ventilate the warm air containing high levels of water vapor [2]. Many growers will not do this because of fuel costs to heat the air, and thus condensation continues a problem. Another practice that causes severe condensation inside greenhouses is closing ventilators at night to conserve heat and not providing heat inside to keep the greenhouse at desired temperature levels. Cold air inside greenhouses cannot hold as much water as heated air, and condensation results.

Commercial producers often increase humidity by shading or misting to reduce transpiration rate during periods of low humidity. Application of water to walks or under benches is an inefficient method of increasing relative humidity, because the effect only lasts for 15 to 30 minutes.

Rainfall

Foliage plants produced under shade cloth or in open fields are subjected to rainfall, which in some areas of the tropics may be more than 200 inches a year and in other areas not more than 20. Allowing rain to reach leaves of foliage crops often results in fertilizer leaching, saturated soils, and increased disease problems.

Foliage plants produced outdoors may be subjected to saturated soils during periods of heavy rains when an inch or more may occur every day for several weeks. Under these climatic conditions, severe root loss may occur on plants in containers or in ground beds unless open, well-drained soil media are utilized. Oxygen concentrations may decrease to the point that root damage occurs owing to insufficient non-capillary air space.

Excessive rainfall or overhead irrigation increases leaching of nutrients from foliage and soils and requires high levels of fertilizer. During excessive rainfall periods, several inches of water may fall in one day, and in some areas 4 to 6 inches (10 to 15 centimeters) is common. Such conditions can remove 50 percent or more of the fertilizer available to plants; when this occurs, plants should be refertilized based on the date of the last application as well as the planned interval between applications. For example, if plants are fertilized daily or several times per week on a constant fertilization program, they should be refertilized immediately, but if plants are fertilized every 2 weeks or monthly, a partial application should be made depending on the percentage of time remaining prior to the next fertilization.

Many disease problems become more severe when plants are grown in the open or under shade cloth because of increased periods of wet foliage (see Chapter 14). This is often a more severe problem under shade cloth than in the open.

Hail may occur in conjunction with thunderstorms in many tropical and subtropical areas where plants can be grown outdoors or in temperate areas during summer months. Hail damage to foliage plants can render them totally unsalable; therefore, the possibility of hail must be considered when selecting an area for open field stock or plant production. Foliage plants grown under lath or slat shade are also vulnerable, since hail can enter between slats. Production under polypropylene shade cloth is advised where hail is a relatively common occurrence since it protects plants from physical damage, provided the structure is strong enough to support the accumulation of hail. Foliage plant genera particularly susceptible to hail damage include *Dieffenbachia, Philodendron, Aglaonema,* and soft plants such as *Pilea* and *Pellionia.*

Wind

Production of foliage plants in locations where high winds may occur should be considered in view of the risks involved, because even slight physical damage can seriously reduce quality. Many foliage plants can tolerate temperatures as low as 35° to 45°F (2° to 7°C) if they are protected from wind, but these temperatures can cause severe damage in a 10 to 20 mile per hour (16 to 32 kilometer per hour) wind because of dehydration and cooling effects (wind chill factor). The best solution to this problem is installation of windbreaks around production units to prevent entry of wind or reduce it below levels that will cause damage. Wind speeds of 5 miles per hour (8 kilometers per hour) or below will not damage plants capable of withstanding low temperatures in most cases. Use of shade cloth on sides of structures will produce a desired windbreak effect but may need to be moved in hot summer months because of reduction of air movement.

Leaf tipburn also may occur on plants grown under high light regimes when low humidities (less than 40 percent) occur in conjunction with winds of 10 to 20 miles per hour (16 to 32 kilometers per hour) or more. This condition often occurs in the tropics during dry seasons and can be prevented by use of sprinkler irrigation and windbreaks.

Proper selection of containers and soil mixture components will prevent plants from blowing over in areas subject to wind. Containers should have relatively straight sides, and their height should not be greater than one and a half times the bottom diameter. Potting media should contain some heavy component so it will not be too lightweight, especially when dry. Peat or peat-bark combinations are too light, but if they contain sand, tip over is less likely to occur. Potting mixtures containing sand are sometimes too heavy for shipping; thus other methods to prevent toppling include running a steel stake through the bottom of the pot into the ground, placing plants in racks or wire mesh, tying tall trees to wire run between posts, and use of wind screens.

Carbon Dioxide Level

Research has shown that carbon dioxide (CO_2) levels inside greenhouses often become deficient [29, 31], especially during winter months when greenhouses are closed, air circulation is reduced, and sunlight is less available. Carbon dioxide deficiencies are more likely to occur in plastic greenhouses, as they are tighter than glass houses and less exchange of air with the outside atmosphere occurs.

Specific research on effects of injected CO_2 in structures containing foliage crops is not available, but there is information on other crops [28, 30] and reports of some trials by foliage plant growers [25].

Green plants combine carbon dioxide and water in the presence of light (photosynthesis) to produce carbohydrates or sugars and oxygen; these are consumed in respiration to produce the energy necessary for growth and yield CO_2 as a by-product. The three principal environmental factors controlling photosynthetic rate are light intensity, temperature, and CO_2 level. A deficiency of any one of these factors limits photosynthetic rate. In closed greenhouses, CO_2 is often a limiting factor, if a satisfactory temperature is maintained and light levels are adequate.

Under low light intensities but adequate temperature and CO_2 levels, photosynthesis can occur only as fast as light levels will permit until light becomes the limiting factor. This would normally occur on overcast days, and the addition of CO_2 would have little effect on photosynthesis under this condition.

Low temperatures also limit photosynthesis, even though light and CO_2 levels are adequate for higher rates of food manufacture. High temperatures, on the other hand, may cause wilting of foliage and closing of leaf stomates, which would prevent proper exchange of CO_2 and oxygen through leaves, thereby reducing photosynthetic rate. High temperatures also increase respiration rate, which may be increased to the point where sugars consumed exceed that manufactured by photosynthesis.

The normal atmosphere contains 78 percent nitrogen, 21 percent oxygen, 0.03 percent carbon dioxide, and 0.97 percent other gases. The level of CO_2 usually averages 0.03 percent or 300 parts per million, but varies slightly with barometric pressure. In a closed greenhouse, however, CO_2 levels can drop rapidly to 100 to 150 parts per million soon after sunrise when photosynthesis begins, and within a few hours it can become the limiting factor in photosynthesis. Use of CO_2 generators appears desirable in temperate regions, but would be of less value in tropical and subtropical areas where ventilators are open most of the time.

REFERENCES

[1] Anderson, J. M., D. J. Goodchild, and N. K. Boardman. 1973. Composition of the photosystems and chloroplast structure in extreme shade plants. *Biochem. Biophys. Acta* 325:573–585.

[2] Augsburger, N. D., H. R. Bohanon, and J. L. Calhoun. 1969. The greenhouse climate control handbook. Muskogee, Okla.: Acme Engineering and Manufacturing Corporation. 32 pp.

[3] Carpenter, W. J., and J. P. Nautiyal. 1969. Light intensity and air movement effects on leaf temperatures and growth of shade requiring greenhouse crops. *J. Am. Soc. Hort. Sci.* 94:212–214.

[4] Collard, R. C., J. N. Joiner, C. A. Conover, and D. B. McConnell. 1977. Influence of shade and fertilizer on light compensation point of *Ficus benjamina* L. *J. Am. Soc. Hort. Sci.* 102(4):447–449.

[5] Conover, C. A., and R. T. Poole. 1972. Influence of shade and nutritional levels on growth and yield of *Scindapsus aureus, Cordyline terminalis* 'Baby Doll' and *Dieffenbachia exotica. Proc. Am. Soc. Hort. Sci. Tropical Region* 16:227–281.

[6] ———, and R. T. Poole. 1973. Influence of shade level and soil temperature on forcing of *Caladium bicolor. Fla. State Hort. Soc. Proc.* 86:369–372.

[7] ———, and R. T. Poole. 1973. Factors influencing notching and necrosis of *Dracaena deremensis* 'Warneckii' foliage. *Proc. Am. Soc. Hort. Sci. Tropical Region* 17:378–384.

[8] ———, and R. T. Poole. 1973. *Ficus benjamina* leaf drop. *Florists' Rev.* 151(3925):29, 67, 68.

[9] ———, and R. T. Poole. 1974. Influence of shade and fertilizer source and level on growth, quality and foliar content of *Philodendron oxycardium* Schott. *J. Am. Soc. Hort. Sci.* 99:150–152.

[10] ———, and R. T. Poole. 1974. Influence of light conditioning and interior light levels on keeping quality of Ficus and Schefflera under interior environments. *Proc. SNA Research Conf.,* pp. 126–129.

[11] ———, and R. T. Poole. 1974. Influence of shade, nutrition and season

on growth of Aglaonema, Maranta and Peperomia stock plants. *Proc. Am. Soc. Hort. Sci. Tropical Region* 18:283–287.

[12] ———. 1975. Acclimatization of tropical foliage plants. *Am. Nurseryman* 142(5):64, 65, 68–71.

[13] ———, and R. T. Poole. 1975. Acclimatization of tropical trees for interior use. *HortScience* 10(6):600–601.

[14] ———, and R. T. Poole. 1975. Influence of shade and fertilization on growth of container grown *Araucaria, Dieffenbachia, Dizygotheca* and *Dracaena. Proc. Am. Soc. Hort. Sci., Tropical Region* 19:247–252.

[15] ———, and R. T. Poole. 1975. Influence of shade and fertilizer levels on production and acclimatization of *Dracaena marginata. Fla. State Hort. Soc. Proc.* 88:606–608.

[16] ———, and R. T. Poole. 1976. Light and fertilizer recommendations on production of foliage stock plants and acclimatized potted plants. ARC-Apopka Research Report RH-76-6. 5 pp.

[17] ———, and R. T. Poole. 1976. Influence of nutrition on yield and chilling injury of *Sansevieria. Fla. State Hort. Soc. Proc.* 89:305–307.

[18] ———, and R. T. Poole. 1977. Effects of cultural practices on acclimatization of *Ficus benjamina* L. *J. Am. Soc. Hort. Sci.* 102(5):529–531.

[19] ———, and R. T. Poole. 1977. Influence of greenhouse design and cooling systems on temperature and energy requirements. ARC-Apopka Research Report RH-77-3. 8 pp.

[20] Culbert, J. R., and D. Hickman. 1966. African violets. Univ. of Ill. Coop. Ext. Circ. 695. 32 pp.

[21] Fonteno, W. C., and E. L. McWilliams. 1977. Light compensation points and acclimatization of *Philodendron scandens oxycardium, Epipremnum aureum, Brassaia actinophylla* and *Dracaena Sanderana. J. Am. Soc. Hort. Sci.* 103:52–56.

[22] Freeman, R. N., and M. T. Cinque. 1976. Relative humidity—a review. Focus on floriculture. N.Y. State Coop. Ext. Serv. January, 1975, 2 pp.

[23] Gates, D. M. 1968. Transpiration and leaf temperature. *Ann. Rev. Plant Physiol.* 19:211–238.

[24] Hadfield, W. 1968. Leaf temperature, leaf pose and productivity of the tea bush. *Nature* 219:282–284.

[25] Humphrey, W. A., and P. E. Parvin. 1967. Foliage plants response to increased CO_2. *Florida Foliage Grower* 4(3):5.

[26] Joiner, J. N., E. R. Gruenbeck, and C. A. Conover. 1973. Effects of shade and dwarfing compounds on growth and quality of *Pachystachys lutea. Fla. State Hort. Soc. Proc.* 86:382–384.

[27] Leopold, A. C. 1964. Plant growth and development. New York: McGraw-Hill.

[28] Lindstrom, R. S. 1964. The effect of increasing the carbon dioxide concentration of floricultural plants. *Michigan Florist* 398:12–13, 19, 22.

[29] Miller, E. S., and E. O. Burr. 1935. Carbon dioxide balance at high light intensities. *Plant Physiol.* 10:93–114.

[30] Nelson, P. V., and R. A. Larson. 1969. The effects of increased CO_2 concentrations on chrysanthemum (*C. morifolium*) and snapdragon (*Antirrhinum majus*). N.C. Agri. Exp. Sta. Tech. Bull. No. 194.

[31] Owen, O., T. Small, and P. N. Williams. 1926. Carbon dioxide in relation to glasshouse crops. *Ann. Appl. Biol.* 13:550–576.

[32] Park, R. B. 1965. The chloroplast. Plant biochemistry. J. Bonner and J. E. Varner, eds. New York: Academic Press, pp. 124–149.

[33] Poole, R. T. 1971. Flowering of Christmas cactus as influenced by nyctoperiod regimes. *Fla. State Hort. Soc. Proc.* 84:410–413. Also in *Proc. SNA Research Conf. 1972.* 17:22.

[34] ———, and D. B. McConnell. 1971. Effects of shade levels and fertilization on flowering of *Anthurium andraeanum* 'Nitta' and 'Kaumana.' *Proc. Amer. Soc. Hort. Sci. Tropical Region* 15:189–195.

[35] ———, and W. E. Waters. 1971. Soil temperature and development of cuttings and seedlings of tropical foliage plants. *HortScience* 6:463–464.

[36] ———, and C. A. Conover. 1974. Germination of 'Neanthe Bella' palm seeds. *Fla. State Hort. Soc. Proc.* 87:429–430.

[37] ———, and C. A. Conover. 1975. Influence of media, shade and fertilizer levels on production of *Chrysalidocarpus lutescens. Fla. State Hort. Soc. Proc.* 88:603–605.

[38] ———, and C. A. Conover. 1975. How to improve caladium leaf color. *Grower Talks* 39(8):24–26.

[39] ———, and C. A. Conover. 1975. Light requirements for foliage plants. *Florists' Rev.* 155(4024):44, 45, 94–96. Also in *Florida Nurseryman* 20(3):9, 10, 25, 26, 66.

[40] ———, and C. A. Conover. 1975. The importance of maintaining vigorous stock plants. *Florida Foliage Grower* 12(5):4, 5.

[41] Ulvin, G. B. 1934. Chlorophyll production under various environmental conditions. *Plant Physiol.* 9:59–81.

[42] Went, F. W. 1953. The effect of temperature on plant growth. *Ann. Rev. Plant Physiol.* 4:347–362.

eleven

J. N. Joiner
R. T. Poole
C. A. Conover

propagation

Propagation of selected plants or groups of plants that have specific value to foliage producers is an important aspect of production. Seedlings or recently rooted plants account for a significant portion of sales. Such plants spend a large portion of time in propagating areas and little time in production areas.

Foliage plants are propagated by cuttings, seed, air layers, division, and spores, but propagation by cuttings is most common [3]. Plants propagated from cuttings and seed are often rooted or germinated in flats or benches, but direct potting is common. *Philodendron scandens oxycardium* and *Peperomia floridana aurea* cuttings produced more growth when placed directly in pots than cuttings placed in propagating benches and transplanted to pots after root initiation [11]. Seed propagation is becoming more important in foliage production and is the best way to produce many foliage types. Major problems of foliage plant propagation include sanitation, propagation media, environmental conditions, and fertilization [4, 13, 16, 21].

Methods of Propagation

Seed

A number of foliage plants, including coffee, false aralia, ardisia, Norfolk Island pine, *Philodendron selloum,* palms, schefflera, and nephthytis, are grown from seed. Seed propagation reduces transmission of a number of disease organisms that are transmitted with vegetative plant parts.

The pulp of fleshy seeds should be separated immediately after harvest to prevent spoilage by fermentation and other causes. The pulp should be mascerated or shredded without damage to the seed. Pulp and seed then can be separated by flotation, which involves placing seeds in water where the heavy, viable ones sink and the light pulp, poor seed, and other extraneous materials float. Longevity of seed extracted from pulpy fruit is often short, sometimes only 3 to 10 days. Pods and capsules containing seed should be air dried to increase ease of seed removal, which can then be accomplished by use of a rubber prong hammermill or by rubbing through screens.

Seed propagation requires careful manipulation of germination conditions, plus knowledge of individual seed requirements; however, little is known about the exact requirements of tropical seed storage and germination. Table 11-1 lists percentage and germination time of some foliage plant seeds.

Seed of tropical foliage plants should be planted as soon as they are ripe or percentage of germination may be reduced. For example, a 2-month delay in planting time of 'Neanthe Bella' palm seed reduced germination considerably, and germination percentage was higher from seed stored in an atmosphere of 25°C with 90 to 100 percent relative humidity (Table 11-2) [24]. *Chamaedorea elegans* and *C. erumpens* planted

TABLE 11-1   Germination of seed of foliage plants [19]

Species	Percent germination	Days to germination
Agave filifera	20	13
Aglaonema commutatum	56	65
Araucaria excelsa	56	33
Ardisia crenulata	65	57
Asparagus setaceus	31	26
Asparagus sprengeri	69	25
Asparagus myersii	57	27
Beaucarnea recurvata	49	25
Brassaia actinophylla	76	24
Carica papaya	80	20
Coffea humilis 'Dwarf'	50	55
Coffea arabica	60	50
Cyperus alternifolius	70	17
Dracaena draco	75	32
Ficus elastica 'Decora'	70	11
Ficus elastica	34	29
Ficus microphylla	11	27
Hypoestes sanguinolenta	95	5
Nephthytis sp.	37	28
Philodendron selloum	76	15
Podocarpus macrophyllus	35	39
Sempervivum tectorum	48	14

TABLE 11-2 Effect of planting date and storage temperature on germination of 'Neanthe Bella' palm [24]

	Percent germination, 1974		
	March 8	May 17	July 26
Storage temperature			
25°C	2	16	34
5°C	2	8	19
Planting date			
October 19	11	34	61
November 16	0	21	32
December 14	0	3	7

in May required 127 to 300 and 124 to 255 days to germinate with 81 and 45 percent germination, respectively [15].

Poor seed germination often results from improper planting depth. Seeds planted deeper than one or two times their diameter often germinate poorly. Palm seeds germinate readily when planted 2 centimeters deep and *Aglaonema, Podocarpus,* false aralia, and *Philodendron selloum* at 0.5 centimeters. Coffee and schefflera germinate readily when lightly covered. Norfolk Island pine seed germinate best when placed on top of the propagating medium, but high relative humidity must be maintained.

Cuttings

Cuttings most frequently used to propagate foliage plants include tip, single- or double-eye, leaf, and cane (Figures 11-1 to 11-3). Foliage plants grown from cuttings reflect growing conditions of stock plants and, therefore, should be obtained from healthy, turgid, disease- and insect-free stock plants with no nutritional deficiencies [2]. Such cuttings will root faster, be of higher quality, produce more roots, reach maturity in a shorter time, and require less maintenance than poor cutting material [10, 16, 25]. Cuttings taken from stock plants 2.5 months after treatment with a variety of herbicides or 2 months after treatment with growth retardants rooted as well as untreated plants [23, 31].

Ninety-seven percent of single-eye cuttings taken from *Ficus* 'Decora' grown in full sun in 30-centimeter pots fertilized with 21 grams of 18-6-12 each 4 months rooted, but only 70 percent rooting was obtained from cuttings taken from plants grown in 30 percent shade and fertilized with 7 grams of the same material [26]. Maximum leaf surface should be left on cuttings for fastest and best rooting response since any reduction of leaf surface to reduce water loss is detrimental to the root-

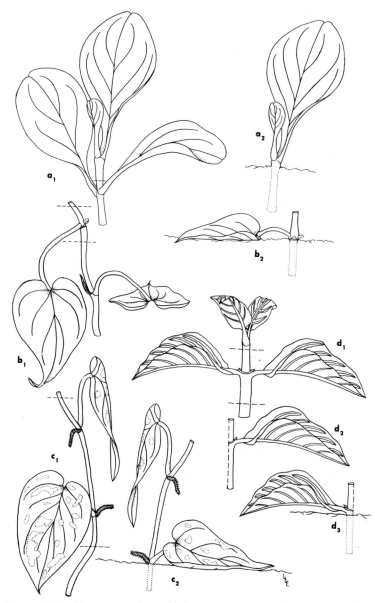

Figure 11-1. Types of cuttings and placement in root medium. (a_1) and (a_2): tip; (b_1) and (b_2): single-eye leaf bud; (c_1) and (c_2): double-eye leaf bud; (d_1), (d_2), and (d_3): split single-eye leaf bud.

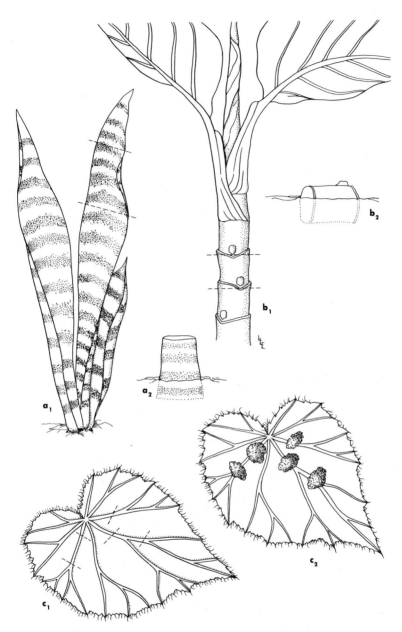

Figure 11-2. Types of cuttings and placement in/on rooting medium. (a_1) and (a_2): leaf section; (b_1) and (b_2): cane; (c_1) and (c_2): leaf vein.

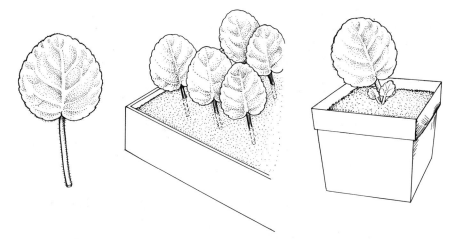

Figure 11-3. Leaf cuttings are commonly used to propagate *Saintpaulia*.

ing process. Leaves provide carbohydrates and hormones essential for root development; therefore, misting should be used to reduce transpiration or water loss from cuttings rather than reducing leaf area.

Tip cuttings Tip cuttings are a popular way of producing *Dracaena, Aglaonema, Peperomia, Dieffenbachia,* and many others (Figure 11-1). They usually produce desirable plants in a short period of time [10], but tip cuttings have a longer production time than other cuttings; therefore, they are more expensive. However, mature stem cuttings of dwarf brassaia root better than terminal cuttings [33]. Tip cuttings should usually be 10 to 15 centimeters long, although larger material can be rooted (Table 11-3). Small cuttings usually root faster and require less space. Only enough lower foliage should be removed to allow sticking,

TABLE 11-3 Effect of cutting size on subsequent vine length of *Philodendron scandens oxycardium* [25]

Size of cuttings: July 2		Vine length (cm), September 29
Weight (g)	Leaf length (cm)	
4.4	13	20
2.9	11	15
2.4	11	14
1.8	9	10

since increased photosynthetic area of remaining leaves decreases rooting time and improves root quality. Depth of sticking cuttings is important since root initiation and growth require large amounts of oxygen. Cuttings should be stuck just deep enough for support and preferably no deeper than 3 to 5 centimeters. Shallow sticking places the rooting zones of cuttings near medium surfaces where maximum exchange of air and, thus, oxygen occurs and harmful excesses of CO_2 are removed. *Dracaena marginata* cuttings hardened or allowed to suberize in an open greenhouse in Hawaii for 4 days had a 100 percent survival rate without infection compared to only 30 percent of those cuttings that were not hardened or suberized [28].

Leaf bud cuttings Single- and double-eye leaf bud cuttings are used to produce many vine-type foliage plants such as *Philodendron scandens oxycardium* and *Epipremnum aureum* (Figure 11-1). Single-eye cuttings consists of a short stem section with an attached leaf. Stem sections, 2 to 4 centimeters long, are usually selected, and those from the extreme tip or base of vines may be slower to root owing to age of such cuttings [17, 33]. Recently matured stems are better for propagating purposes than older material or young cutting material, which frequently wilts. Single-eye cuttings should be stuck into the rooting medium until the eye is slightly below or at the surface, since new roots arise from that point (Figure 11-1). New vine growth arises from axillary buds, which are provided food by the attached leaf [25]. Leaf bud cuttings do not produce a salable plant as fast as terminal cuttings, but their initial cost is much less. Double-eye leaf bud cuttings are sometimes used for totem poles because they grow more rapidly than single-eye cuttings. Single-eye cuttings of *Ficus* 'Decora' produced stems 30 centimeters long in 6 months [26]. Ninety percent of the cuttings rooted.

Leaf cuttings Leaf cuttings are utilized to propagate plants such as rex begonias, violets, peperomia, and species of sansevieria that do not have chimeras (Figures 11-2 and 11-3). This method of propagation supplies the largest number of plants from the least propagative stock material. Sanitation is important when using leaf cuttings or segments, for detached parts are easily attacked by disease organisms.

Cane cuttings Cane cuttings provide economical propagating material for *Dieffenbachia, Dracaena,* and similar genera, although rooting and growth of such cuttings take longer than for tip cuttings [13] (Figure 11-2). Cane is usually cut with one eye per section or internode, but stem sections of 30 to 120 centimeters are used for *Dracaena* 'Massangeana.' *Dieffenbachia* cuttings of large diameter taken from the upper part of stems and allowed to suberize before planting produce the largest plants. Cuttings should be pressed into the potting medium until the cane is barely visible, with the eye facing up and out of the media [17]. Optimum conditions for periderm formation of *Dieffenbachia* are 28° to 34°C and 91 to 100 percent relative humidity [18]. High humidity should be maintained for all cane cuttings, and soaking canes of *D*. 'Massangeana' before sticking improves their propagation percentage. If such canes are waxed, a small portion of the waxed end should be removed prior to soaking [29].

Layering

Layering is the development of roots on the base of a large cutting while it is still attached to the parent plant (Figure 11-4). This method utilizes the parent plant as a source of water and nutrients during rooting processes and is widely used with *Ficus* species, large-sized crotons, *Monstera*, and *Philodendron*. Major benefits of air layers include the large plant-size cuttings, which can be rooted with a minimum of reduction in leaf area.

Important factors in the layering process include type of cut and amount of sphagnum moss used around the cut. Two types of cuts are used in air layering; a slanting cut upward at a 45-degree angle about one half through the stem is the most common and least expensive. A wedge is placed in the cut or the knife is twisted to spread the cut and prevent cambia from uniting before root formation. Another method consists of removal of a ring of bark about 2 centimeters long, which is more time consuming. The amount of moist sphagnum moss used to wrap the cut helps determine the size of the root system that develops; therefore, a large handfull should be used for each layer. A covering of aluminum foil around the moss is better than plastic and should be applied with a collar around the top to catch moisture from rain or irrigation.

Air layering is a high labor requirement plus the problem of desiccation of the material covering the wound during dry periods and excessive moisture during wet periods.

Division

Division is used for some *Sansevieria* species that are chimera, since they will not reproduce true to type from leaf cuttings (Figure 11-5). Propagation of ferns, *Calathea,* and other genera are also obtained by division from parent plants. Zamias can be propagated by tubers by removing the lower third of the tuber and planting it with the apex just below the soil line in a mixture of peat, bark, and shavings [8].

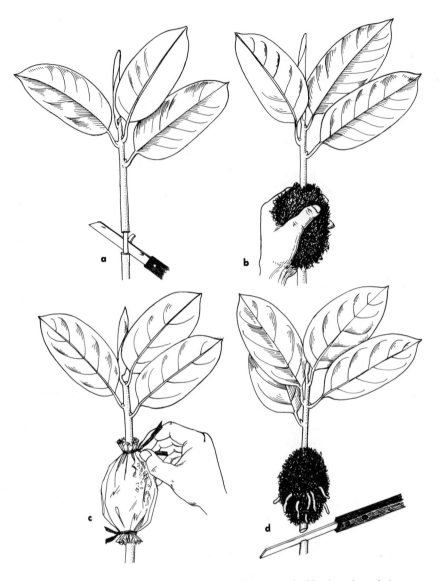

Figure 11-4. Steps in air layering *Ficus:* (a) removal of bark and cambrium layer; (b) wrapping prepared area with sphagnum moss; (c) enclosing sphagnum moss with plastic or aluminum foil; and (d) removal of rooted air layer from parent plant.

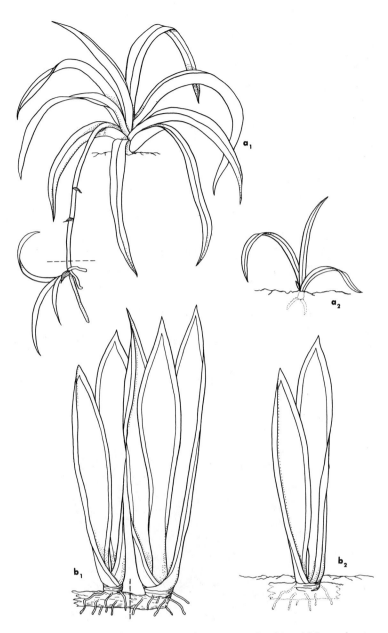

Figure 11-5. *Chlorophytum somosum:* (a₁) produce plantlets which can be removed and planted (a₂); *Sansevieria* (b₁) and (b₂) propagated by rhizome division to maintain chimera.

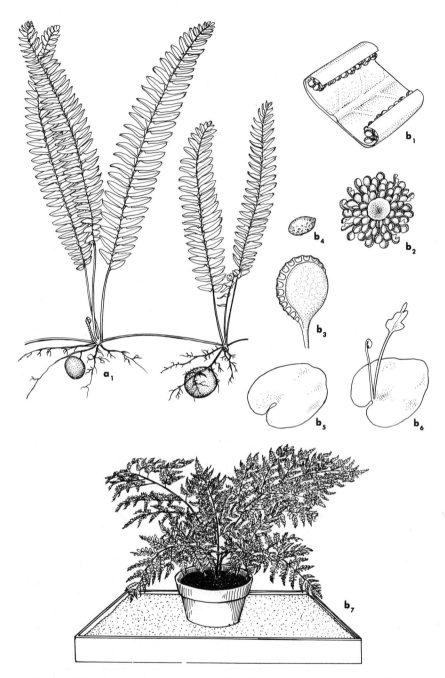

Figure 11-6. Ferns can be propagated by division (a₁) or spores (b₁–b₇). Growth of a fern from spores: (b₁) leaf section containing sori; (b₂) sorus; (b₃) sporangium; (b₄) spore; (b₅) prothallium; (b₆) prothallium with young sporophyte; and (b₇) mature fern over a medium for spore collection and germination.

Clean, healthy stock is especially important when division is used as a method of propagation since nematodes and other soil-related problems are transferred with the plant division. Detrimental pathogens and nutrient deficiencies also remain with divided portions of plants.

Spores

Spores are used to propagate many fern cultivars (Figure 11-6). Spores from mature ferns are placed on a rooting medium, usually peat, and misted or maintained under moisture-tight cover until plants are large enough to pot. Spores can be gathered from mature fronds by taping intact or excised fronds over a sheet of paper or an open envelope, or mature fronds can be grown in or above the propagation bed. A dry atmosphere will promote release of spores. Research has shown that increasing the pH of peat to 5.0 and adding a weak fertilizer solution (5 cubic centimeters per 4 liters of 20-9-17, N-P-K) prior to placement of spores improve spore germination [12]. Light should be 5 to 10 kilolux [14]. Phosphorus prevented germination of spores and retarded growth of tree fern [27].

Common methods of propagating various foliage plants are compared in Table 11-4.

Environmental Considerations

Propagation Media

The propagation medium selected should be easily obtained, uniform, and available in quantity so that plant propagators can use the same material repeatedly [22]. It must be firm enough to support cuttings without deep sticking of cuttings and of a consistency to allow cuttings to be easily removed after development of root systems. Plants should be removed before roots are too long, or damage may occur when they are removed from the medium.

A pH of 5.5 to 6.5 will result in satisfactory rooting of most foliage plants. Since most imported and native peats have a pH of 3.5 to 5.0, 3 to 6 kilograms of dolomite per cubic meter should be added to raise the pH to a satisfactory range. Leaf bud cuttings of *Ficus robusta* rooted best when pH was 4.5 to 5.5 [20]. Dolomite at 4 kilograms per cubic meter of peat increased the pH of peat from 4.5 to 5.5, and improved root grades of *Aglaonema* 'Franscher' and *Aphelandra* 'Dania,' but not *Dieffenbachia* 'Perfection,' *Maranta* 'Red Nerve,' *Philodendron scandens oxycardium,* and golden pothos [6].

TABLE 11-4 Methods of propagating foliage plants

Botanical name	Common-name	Air layers	Cane cuttings	Divisions offsets	Leaf cuttings	Seed	Eye cuttings	Spores	Tip cuttings
Aechmea spp.	Bromeliad			2		1			
Adiantum spp.	Maidenhair fern			2				1	
Aglaonema spp.	Aglaonema		2						1
Aphelandra squarrosa	Zebra plant						2		1
Araucaria excelsa	Australian pine	2				1			2
Ardisia crenata	Coral ardisia					1			
Asparagus spp.	Asparagus					1			
Aspidistra elatior	Cast-iron plant			1					
Begonia spp.	Rex begonia				1	1			
Brassaia actinophylla	Schefflera								2
Calathea spp.	Calathea			1					
Chamaedorea elegans	Parlor palm					1			
Chlorophytum comosum	Spider plant			1					
Cissus antarctica	Kangaroo vine						1		1
Cissus rhombifolia	Grape ivy						1		1
Codiaeum variegatum	Croton	2							1
Coffea arabica	Coffee					1			
Cordyline terminalis	Ti		2			3			1
Crassula spp.	Jade plant				2				1
Dieffenbachia spp.	Dieffenbachia		2						1
Dizygotheca elegantissima	False aralia					1			2
Dracaena fragrans	Massangeana		1						1
Dracaena godseffiana	Dracaena		2						1
Dracaena marginata	Marginata								1
Dracaena sanderiana	Sanderiana								1
Episcia spp.	Episcia			3	2	4			1
Epipremnum spp.	Pothos						1		2

Scientific name	Common name						
Ficus elastica	Rubber plant	1				2	3
Ficus lyrata	Fiddle-leaf fig	1				2	2
Hoya carnosa	Wax plant					1	1
Kalanchoe spp.	Kalanchoe				2	1	1
Maranta spp.	Maranta	1					1
Monstera deliciosa	Monstera	1			2	2	1
Nephrolepis exaltata	Boston fern	1			2		
Palm spp.	Palms			2	1	2	
Peperomia spp.	Peperomia			2	2	2	1
Philodendron florida	Florida philodendron	3				2	1
Philodendron hastatum	Hastatum	3				2	1
Philodendron micans	Micans				1	1	
Philodendron scandens oxycardium	Heart-leaf philodendron				1	1	
Philodron panduriforme	Panduriforme					2	1
Philodendron selloum	Selloum				1	2	
Pilea cadierei	Aluminum plant				1		1
Platycerium spp.	Staghorn fern			2		1	
Podocarpus macrophylla	Podocarpus			2	1		2
Polyscias spp.	Aralia		2				1
Pteris spp.	Pteris fern			2			1
Saintpaulia spp.	African violet				1		
Sansevieria hahnii	Hahnii sansevieria			2	1		
Sansevieria trifasciata	Sansevieria			2	1		
Sansevieria trifasciata 'Laurentii'	Sansevieria			1			
Spathiphyllum spp.	Spathiphyllum			2	1		
Syngonium spp.	Nephthytis (var.)				1	1	
Syngonium spp.	Nephthytis (green)				1	2	
Zygocactus spp.	Christmas cactus						1

Numbers indicate preference: 1, first choice; 2, second choice; etc.

Propagation media should have a water-holding capacity of 50 to 75 percent by volume so that frequent irrigations will not be necessary when a mist system is not used. Water conductivity should be at least 10 centimeters per hour when cuttings are under mist or are watered heavily so it will not become saturated. Aeration also is important with the medium having 15 to 25 percent noncapillary pore space to allow water flow and ensure gas exchange for an ample oxygen supply around rooting surfaces.

Cation-exchange capacity (CEC) is not as important in a propagation medium as in a potting medium; however, a moderately high CEC is desirable so that fertilizer applied after rooting can be held after cuttings have initiated roots and the amount of water applied is reduced. Soluble salts levels of media should be low to prevent burning of developing roots. Shrinkage and rate of decomposition of propagation media are important if the medium is to be used for a long time. Aeration will decrease with time owing to decomposition, and additional medium should be added to maintain original volume. Weight of propagating media is relatively unimportant as long as they perform as required and do not require physical handling.

Peat is a satisfactory medium for propagation of most foliage plants. Imported and domestic peats may be used, and both should be sterilized to control weeds, plant pathogens, and nematodes. Aerated steam sterilization is the best method of preparing contaminated media for plant propagation, but conventional steam sterilization, heat, or chemicals are satisfactory. Highly decomposed fine-textured peats should be avoided, as should peats with soluble salts levels over 1,000 parts per million extracted as 2/1 (v : v) water/soil. Calcined clay, bark, wood shavings, rice hulls, perlite, vermiculite, and sand can be mixed with peat, each other, or used singly for propagation. *Philodendron scandens oxycardium* and golden pothos growing in German peat produced longer vines than cuttings placed in calcined clay (Table 11-5).

Products made of compressed peat, treated wood fiber, or a synthetic product such as styrofoam also are available. All media should be completely moist before sticking of cuttings. Many media may be used for propagation of foliage crops and left in benches for 1 to 2 years, but they should be leached with water to remove excess salts and sterilized each time before new cuttings are stuck.

Light

Light intensity is important in determining the speed and success of rooting. The use of low light intensities was common in the past to reduce transpiration; however, automatic mist systems maintain high

TABLE 11-5   Effects of medium on vine length in centimeters during 8 weeks of propagation [22]

			Time of sticking		8 weeks	
Medium	*P.s.* *oxycardium*	Golden pothos	pH	siemens $\times 10^5$	pH	siemens $\times 10^5$
Calcined clay	6.5	9.9	6.8	1	7.4	1
German peat	8.0	11.6	3.8	21	6.9	10

water relationships on cuttings, and higher light intensities can and should be used. The highest intensity of light the plant material will tolerate without loss of quality under conditions of propagation should be utilized. Light is required for production of carbohydrates (sugars) and auxins; thus the higher the light intensity a plant can tolerate during the rooting process, the larger the amount of carbohydrates and auxins that will be produced to stimulate root and bud initiation and growth.

Chlorophytum, spider plant, is propagated from plantlets at the end of runners. Eight-hour days stimulate runner production and plantlet formation, but day lengths of 14 and 18 hours inhibit plantlet production [12].

Cuttings rooted with insufficient light take longer to root and are lower in quality than those rooted under optimum light levels. Optimum light requirements vary among foliage plant genera; therefore, a level must be selected for the propagating house that will allow maximum carbohydrate production without injury to cuttings. Light levels of 10 to 25 kilolux provide the best average light intensity for foliage propagation benches, with the higher light intensity being especially valuable in aiding bud break and decreasing time in propagation benches. Light intensity should be lowered to 5 to 10 kilolux when mist systems are not utilized in propagation. Light intensities of 20 to 30 kilolux are satisfactory for propagation from seed as long as the surface layer of the media is not allowed to dry.

Water

Mist systems provide the best method of maintaining high water relationships within cuttings during rooting and have been instrumental in increasing propagation success. Mist systems are successful with cuttings that require short or long periods for rooting and make rooting possible under conditions of high light intensities. Misting also aids in producing high rooting percentages in less time, better rooting quality, and fewer problems from insects and disease pathogens. Mist can lower medium temperatures and may slow rooting, especially during winter months, unless bottom heat is supplied. The primary function of mist is to provide a continuous film of water over the entire cutting surface; therefore, the finer the droplet size of the water, the better the coverage. Mist systems should operate the minimum time necessary to maintain this water film. Mist systems normally should be turned on at sunrise and off at sunset by time clocks, except where forced air heaters are used during winter months, which might require night misting for some plant materials [7]. Interval timers should be used to provide minimum cycles of mist while the system is on to reduce water usage and leaching of nutrients from foliage. A common mist cycle used in the foliage industry is 15 seconds of mist every 30 minutes, although 12 seconds every 6 minutes has been shown best for *Dracaena* spp. [32] and 24 to 48 seconds every 6 minutes for *Brassaia arboricola* [33]. Systems should be adjusted for air movement, temperature, humidity, and light intensity to prevent desiccation of foliage.

Uneven mist application can be a problem in foliage plant propagation owing to improperly spaced or partially clogged nozzles or air movement in greenhouses. Uneven mist application results in uneven speed of rooting, different rates and quality of growth, or death. Failure of a mist system can result in heavy to complete losses; therefore, it is wise to utilize an alarm system.

Cuttings such as *Philodendron, Sansevieria,* and *Syngonium* can be propagated without the use of mist systems, but they should be syringed two or more times daily to maintain high humidity and rooted under a light intensity of 10 to 15 kilolux.

Moisture in media is important for optimum seed germination and must be adequately maintained after seeds are sown. Subirrigation is preferred since it prevents disturbing seeds and possibly breaking germinating roots. The medium and air surrounding germinating seed must remain moist at all times during and after germination, since moisture is critical at these times. Seed requires high amounts of oxygen to germinate; therefore, too much moisture as well as too little results in death of plants.

Temperature

Day air temperatures of 25° to 35°C and night temperatures of 22°C are within the best range for propagation of most foliage plants. The growing medium temperature at these air temperatures usually ranges 4° to 8°C lower, except during summer months. Propagating medium temperatures in winter may fall as low as 15°C during the night and early morning or after misting or watering, and rise no higher than

TABLE 11-6 Root grade (1, no roots; 3, heavy rooting) of plants propagated at various soil temperatures [30]

Plant	15-25°C	25°C	30°C
Dieffenbachia picta (nodes)	1.7	2.2	2.1
Cordyline 'Baby Doll'	2.1	2.4	1.8
Rhaphidophora 'Pothos'	1.4	2.2	2.5
Philodendron scandens oxycardium	1.8	2.2	2.4
Peperomia obtusifolia	2.3	3.0	2.1

20°C during the day. Use of bottom heat can reduce propagation time of many foliage plants by 50 percent during cool months if the medium is maintained at 25°C. Table 11-6 indicates the effects of temperature on root grade.

Higher media temperatures encourage root initiation but retard root development. An economical way of heating propagating beds is to support them with steam lines and trap heat with plastic dropcloths on the sides. Air temperature can be reduced 5° to 10°C if the propagating medium is maintained at the desired temperature.

Seed germinates faster at warm temperatures, and the optimum germinating temperature range for most foliage seedlings is 25° to 30°C. Temperatures should be maintained within this range if possible, but temperatures varying 5°C between night and day stimulate germination compared with constant daily temperatures. If propagating medium temperatures above 28°C are utilized for seed germination, temperatures should be reduced to 28°C or below when roots emerge. In most cases a range of 24° to 28°C provides excellent seed germination and seedling growth.

Carbon Dioxide

Carbon dioxide concentration up to 1,500 parts per million will increase plant growth and decrease the time required to propagate foliage plants. Atmospheric content of CO_2 is normally 300 parts per million, but in closed greenhouses the level may drop to 100 parts per million or less during daylight hours. Carbon dioxide addition is helpful only during daylight hours when vents are closed.

Some growers vent exhaust air from heaters into their greenhouses to increase CO_2, but this is not recommended because of the possibility of emission of *harmful gases,* primarily ethylene. An inefficient burner can cause the *loss* of an *entire crop.* There are several liquid gas CO_2 generators available that will safely increase CO_2 in greenhouses, and detectors to measure CO_2 and ethylene are on the market.

Spacing

Spacing of cuttings varies with the size and type of plant material and size of the root system produced. Single-eye cuttings with leaves such as those taken for *Philodendron* should be spaced at approximately 5 × 5 centimeters, and small tip cuttings should also be stuck at 5 × 5 centimeter spacing. Larger tip cuttings, such as some *Dieffenbachia* species, should be spaced 7 × 7 centimeters or more. Sufficient space should be maintained between plants so that light will be available to leaves and to permit adequate air movement between plants.

Fertilizer

Foliage plants in propagating benches should receive fertilizer as soon as they produce roots. This practice rapidly replaces nutrients in tissue lost through leaching due to misting and aids in stimulating bud break and new growth. Two methods of fertilization can be used separately or together, chemical liquid fertilizers applied overhead or slow-release fertilizer mixed in the medium [4, 5].

The type of liquid fertilizer program to follow depends on how the propagating medium was amended at the time of mixing. Where only calcium and magnesium were premixed into the medium, use a 20-9-17 or similar soluble formula. Slow-release fertilizers should be premixed into the propagating media at the time initial applications of calcium and magnesium are incorporated. One-half kilogram of nitrogen per cubic meter or 10 square meters will supply sufficient nutrition with only one application of slow-release fertilizer applied per crop (Table 11-7).

Rooting Hormones

Use of rooting hormones on foliage plants has not been investigated thoroughly, but such materials are used in the industry. Some producers claim hormones greatly aid propagation, while others say they have no effect. Hormones, or auxins, should not be used indiscriminately as they may have no effect at one concentration, stimulate rooting at a higher concentration, and inhibit and injure cuttings at still higher

TABLE 11-7   Fertilizer programs for foliage plant propagation [5]

1. Three to six kilograms of incorporated dolomite per cubic meter and bi-weekly applications of 20-20-20, one kilogram per 40 square meters.
2. Three to six kilograms of dolomite per square meter, ½ kilogram of Perk, and 4 kilograms per cubic meter of slow-release 14-6-11.

TABLE 11-8 Influence of hormones on rooting of foliage plants (1, no roots; 3, heavy rooting) [28]

Plant	Control	Hormodin 2 [a]	Patio [b]
Aglaonema 'Silver Queen'	2.7	2.5	2.6
Aphelandra 'Dania'	1.8	2.9	2.8
Dieffenbachia 'Exotica'	2.3	2.7	2.3
Dracaena sanderiana	2.8	2.7	2.9
Ficus benjamina	1.7	2.4	2.1
Maranta leuconeura	2.7	2.9	2.7
Peperomia 'Marble'	2.5	2.5	2.7
Peperomia 'Variegate'	2.0	2.0	2.0
Polyscias balfouriana	1.6	2.7	2.9
Syngonium podophyllum	1.5	2.3	1.7

[a] Hormodin 2: 0.3% IBA.
[b] Patio: 0.07% IBA, 0.05% NAACT (naphthaleneacetimide), 0.05% NAA, 2.0% captan, and 2.0% thiram.

amounts. The range between beneficial and toxic levels is often narrow, since such materials applied by a propagator enhance or counteract naturally produced hormones in plants [1]. Natural levels of hormones in plants vary seasonally owing to temperature changes, fertilizer levels, water practices, and stage of growth of plants, so the same amount of auxin that may stimulate rooting at one time may prevent rooting at another. Most foliage plants root easily, and for such plants, additions of auxins generally retard rooting. Hormones should not be used before careful testing, using varying concentrations at different seasons.

Convenient auxin application methods are dipping, spraying, or dusting basal ends of cuttings with powdered talc containing auxin. Several commercial preparations are available that contain various concentrations of different materials. The auxins most commonly used and that have proved most successful are indoleacetic acid (IAA), indolebutyric acid (IBA), and naphthaleneacetic acid (NAA). Combinations of IBA and NAA are effective with many plant materials. The more difficult to root material should be treated with higher concentrations of the compounds than less difficult to root species. Three thousand parts per million of IBA improved root index of *Dracaena marginata* [34]. Rooting hormones have been shown to improve root grade of some foliage plants (Table 11-8).

Subterminal and cane cuttings usually respond to auxin treatments more than tip cuttings because older wood is involved. Auxins are produced primarily in apical portions of the stem; therefore, young plant materials normally have more natural auxin than old tissue. Unfortunately, some propagators believe auxins are a substitute for proper

TABLE 11-9 Influence of days from harvest to sticking on leaf drop and root grade
(1, no roots; 3 heavy rooting) of crotons [9]

Days from harvest to sticking	No. leaves lost/cutting		Root grade	
	'Bravo'	'Oakleaf'	'Bravo'	'Oakleaf'
3	0.5	4.2	1.8	1.6
5	1.0	5.0	1.6	1.3

propagating techniques, which is not true. All factors for successful plant propagation such as temperature, light, and moisture conditions of the cuttings should be maintained optimally.

Shipping

Many cuttings are produced in one area and shipped to another location. Temperature should be maintained near 21°C with humidity kept high. Cuttings should be shipped as rapidly as possible and placed in propagation areas immediately after receipt [2]. An increase in shipping time increased leaf drop and reduced root grade of crotons (Table 11-9).

REFERENCES

[1] Chadwick, L. G., and D. C. Kiplinger. 1938. The effect of synthetic growth substances on the rooting and subsequent growth of ornamental plants. *Proc. Am. Soc. Hort. Sci.* 36:809–816.

[2] Conover, C. A. 1976. Postharvest handling of rooted and unrooted cuttings of tropical ornamentals. *HortScience* 11(2):127–128.

[3] _____, and R. T. Poole. 1970. Foliage plant propagation. *Florida Foliage Grower* 7(4):1–8.

[4] _____, and R. T. Poole. 1970. Methods of propagating foliage plants. *Florida Foliage Grower* 7(5):1–4.

[5] _____, and R. T. Poole. 1972. Fertilization practices for foliage plant propagation. *Florida Foliage Grower* 9(3):4–5.

[6] _____, and R. T. Poole. 1972. Influence of propagation bed nutritional amendments on selected foliage plants. *Proc. Fla. State Hort. Soc.* 85:392–394.

[7] _____, and R. T. Poole. 1974. Foliage collapse of *Dieffenbachia picta* 'Perfection' during propagation. *Sou. Nurseryman's Assoc. Nursery Res. J.* 1(1):1–6.

[8] _____, R. T. Poole and D. B. McConnell. 1978. Propagation of Zamia tubers. *Proc. Trop. Reg. Amer. Soc. Hort. Sci.* 22:(in press).

[9] _____, and R. T. Poole. 1978. Leaf retention of crotons during propagation. *Foliage Digest* 1(4):6.

[10] Fukuda, S., and F. D. Rauch. 1975. Panax propagation. *Univ. Hawaii Hort. Digest* 26:2.

[11] Gruis, J. T., and J. N. Joiner. 1959. Effect of various pots and rooting methods on the growth of *Philodendron oxycardium* and *Peperomia floridiana aurea. Proc. Fla. State Hort. Soc.* 72:369–373.

[12] Hammer, P. A., and G. Holton. 1975. Asexual reproduction of spider plant, *Chlorophytum elatum,* by day length control. *Florists' Rev.* 157(4057):35, 76.

[13] Hartman, H. T., and D. E. Kester. 1968. *Plant Propagation.* Englewood Cliffs, N.J.: Prentice-Hall.

[14] Henley, R. W., and R. T. Poole. 1975. Propagation of *Pteris ensiformis* Burm. 'Victoriae' by spores. *Proc. Fla. State Hort. Soc.* 88:407–410.

[15] Ishihata, I. 1973. Studies on the morphology and cultivation of palms: On the germination of seed in ornamental palms. *Bull. Faculty Agr., Kagoshima Univ.* 24:11–23.

[16] Laurie, A., D. C. Kiplinger, and K. S. Nelson. 1958. *Commercial Flower Forcing.* New York: McGraw-Hill.

[17] Marlatt, R. B. 1969. Propagation of *Dieffenbachia. Economic Botany* 23(4):385–388.

[18] _____. 1970. Suberin and periderm formation in *Dieffenbachia. HortScience* 95(1):32–33.

[19] Mikorski, D. J., and J. W. White. 1977. Foliage plants—seed propagation and transplant research. *Florists' Rev.* 160(4153):55, 99–101.

[20] Morgan, J. V., and H. W. Lawlor. 1976. Influence of external factors on the rooting of leaf and bud cuttings of *Ficus. Acta Hort.* 64:39–46.

[21] Nehrling, A., and I. Nehrling. 1962. *Propagating House Plants.* New York: Hearthside Press.

[22] Poole, R. T. 1969. Rooting response of four ornamental species propagated in various media. *Proc. Fla. State Hort. Soc.* 82:393–397.

[23] _____. 1970. Influence of growth regulators on stem elongation and rooting response of foliage plants. *Proc. Fla. State Hort. Soc.* 83:497–502.

[24] _____, and C. A. Conover. 1974. Germination of 'Neanthe Bella' palm seeds. *Proc. Fla. State Hort. Soc.* 87:429–430.

[25] _____, and C. A. Conover. 1975. The importance of maintaining vigorous stock plants. *Florida Foliage Grower* 12(5):4–5.

[26] _____, and C. A. Conover. 1976. Propagation and growth characteristics of *Ficus elastica* 'Decora' in central Florida. *Proc. Trop. Reg. Am. Soc. Hort. Sci.* 20:438–448.

[27] _____, C. A. Conover, and D. B. McConnel. 1978. Spore propagation

and production of the Hawaiian tree fern, *Cibotium glaucum* (Sm.) Hook & Arn. *Proc. Trop. Reg. Am. Soc. Hort. Sci.* 22:(in press).

[28] _____, C. A. Conover, and C. A. Robinson. 1980. Rooting hormones and foliage plants. *Foliage Digest* 3(8):4.

[29] _____, C. A. Conover, and W. E. Waters. 1974. Bud-break in canes of *Dracaena fragrans* Ker. cv. Massangeana. *HortScience* 9(6):540–541.

[30] _____, and W. E. Waters. 1971. Soil temperature and development of cuttings and seedlings of tropical foliage plants. *HortScience* 6(5):463–464.

[31] _____, W. E. Waters, and A. J. Pate. 1972. Herbicides and the foliage industry. *Florida Foliage Grower* 9(2):1–6.

[32] Rauch, F. D. 1976. Rooting response of *Dracaena* spp. *Univ. Hawaii Hort. Digest* 30:3.

[33] _____. 1976. Factors influencing rooting of dwarf *Brassaia* cuttings. *Misc. Publ. Univ. Hawaii Coop. Ext. Serv.* 134:37–41.

[34] Stevens, G. A. 1976. Propagation of *Dracaena marginata* Lam. Proc. 3rd Annual Nurserymen's Short Course. Univ. of Hawaii Misc. Publ. 134.

twelve

D. B. McConnell
R. T. Poole

growth regulators

Growth regulators are chemical compounds that control or alter plant growth. Endogenous growth regulators are produced by plants and exogenous ones are synthetic materials applied externally. Those produced internally or absorbed through the foliage or roots promote, inhibit, or otherwise alter plant physiological processes.

Growth regulators include auxins, gibberellins, cytokinins, ethylene, growth inhibitors, and growth retardants, and are used commercially to modify plant growth.

Auxins

Auxins are defined as chemicals that produce cell elongation in oat coleoptiles in a manner similar to indoleacetic acid (IAA), a naturally occurring hormone. The discovery of auxins started with experiments [24] to explain phototropism in plants, and later investigations showed that cell elongation was caused by a diffusable chemical (auxin) produced in the apical portion and translocated toward the base of plants [99]. Naturally occurring auxins are indole compounds, and synthetic auxins include naphthaleneacetic acid (NAA), indolebutyric acid (IBA), (2,4-dichlorophenoxy)acetic acid (2,4-D), and (2,4,5-trichlorophenoxy)-acetic acid (2,4,5-T) (Figure 12-1).

Investigators agree that IAA is the only naturally occurring auxin,

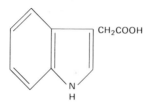

Indoleacetic acid (IAA)

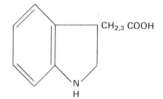

Indolebutyric acid (IBA)

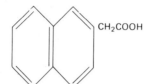

α-Naphthaleneacetic acid (NAA)

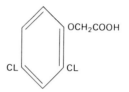

2,4-Dichlorophenoxyacetic acid (2,4-D)

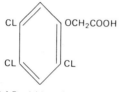

2,4,5-trichlorophenoxyacetic
acid (2,4,5-T)

Figure 12-1. Structure of commonly used auxins.

but it is not used commercially because it is unstable in solution or when applied to plants. Most synthetic auxins have greater stability and, thus, have found widespread agricultural use. The most common synthetic auxins include 2,4-dichlorophenoxyacetic acid (2,4-D), and 2,4,5-tri-chloro-phenoxyacetic acid (2,4,5-T) (Figure 12-1).

Research since the 1920s has shown auxins to be involved with a multitude of plant responses. Auxins used as root-promoting compounds are discussed in Chapter 11. Application of auxins to plants has induced flowering in bromeliads and other plants (17), shifted sex expression in flowers [42], and insured fruit set [42, 54].

Gibberellins

Gibberellins are naturally occurring growth regulators that were discovered by a Japanese plant pathologist in 1926 [50] in an extract from the fungus *Gibberella fujikuroi,* but were not isolated until 1935 [104]. Intensive investigation of gibberellin growth-regulating properties did not begin until 1950 when procedures for large-scale gibberellin production were established.

Gibberellins are compounds that have a gibbane structure (Figure 12-2) and stimulate cell division and/or cell elongation. More than fifty-two gibberellins have been extracted from fungal cultures or plant materials, usually immature seeds. They are complex chemical structures that are difficult to synthesize and are produced commercially from fungal cultures similar to antibiotics. The best known and most widely used gibberellin is GA_3.

Various bioassay techniques have been developed to detect the presence of gibberellins, including dramatic response of shoot elongation in certain plants [98]. Single-gene dwarf mutants of corn (*Zea mays*) and pea (*Pisum sativum*) respond to a number of gibberellins [5, 74] and are used in bioassays.

Since the 1950s, gibberellins have been shown to be involved in a multiplicity of plant responses, including reduction in time for seed germination [46], stimulation of enzyme hydrolysis of starch reserves [72], and orientation of seedling leaves to light [59]. Gibberellin sprays induce flowering in many plants that normally require vernalization or long days to develop flowers [51].

Floral sex expression may be modified by GA treatment with staminate or male flowers normally induced [33, 66], but some plants produce an increased number of pistillate or female flowers [39, 86, 105]. Gibberellins also have changed floral morphology, inducing style elongation in tomatoes [6] and anther and pollen development in stamenless tomato mutants [73]. Parthenocarpic fruit set is stimulated by gibberellin application in a variety of species, often in plants that fail to respond to auxin treatment [18], and floral maturation and anthesis are accelerated in other plants [57]. Gibberellins are not of great commercial importance in foliage plant production. They could, however, be used to

Figure 12-2. Structural formula of the gibbane skeleton and GA_3.

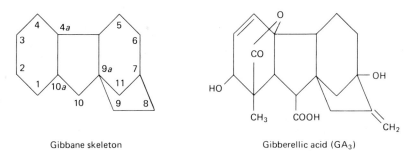

Gibbane skeleton   Gibberellic acid (GA_3)

increase seed germination, to stimulate elongation of axillary buds, and to influence flowering.

Cytokinins

Cytokinins are plant growth regulators that promote cell division in excised plant tissues when auxin is present. Plant physiologists long suspected plant growth substances other than auxins stimulated cell division, but it was not until 1955 that kinetin, a substance that stimulated cell division in cells that normally did not divide, was identified [64]. This compound, 6-furfurylaminopurine, was not endogenous, but several purine cytokinins have been isolated from plants, with *zeatin* being first [56]. Several bioassays have been developed to determine the activity of

Figure 12-3. Structure of selected synthetic and naturally occurring cytokinins.

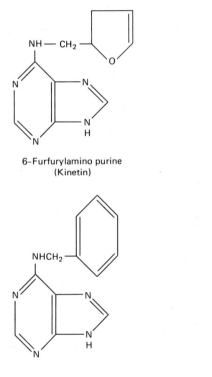
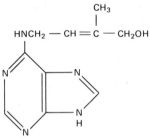

6-Furfurylamino purine
(Kinetin)

Zeatin

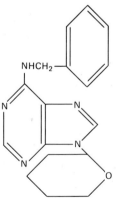

6-Benzylamino purine (BA)

6-(Benzylamino)-9-(s-tetrahydropyranyl)
9H-purine (PBA)

synthetic and naturally occurring cytokinins [98]. The structure of several synthetic and naturally occurring cytokinins is shown in Figure 12-3.

Cytokinins influence a variety of plant physiological responses, including regulation of cell division and differentiation, cell enlargement, flower bud dormancy, vegetative bud break, seed germination, fruit set, and delay of senescence. Plant responses to cytokinins depend on amount and kind of cytokinin present and the active level of other growth regulators, particularly auxins. Successful tissue culture of foliage plants depends on the cytokinin-auxin balance in inducing cell division and regulating differentiation in excised tissues. Successful tobacco pith tissue culture required cytokinins and auxins in correct balance [88]. Low cytokinin, high auxin levels induced root development, while high cytokinin, low auxin levels induced shoot development. Low auxin, relatively high cytokinin levels induced bud initiation in *Plumbago indica* [71]. Spray application of PBA 6-(benzylamino- 9(2-tetrahydropyranyl)-9H-purine suppressed apical dominance and increased lateral branching on a variety of horticultural crops [8, 9, 10, 22, 23, 100]. This response could be useful on foliage plants with a strong apical dominance to increase branching and aesthetic appeal. Golden pothos (*Epipremnum aureus*) sprayed with PBA produced more enlarged axillary buds, but had less new growth compared to untreated plants [60].

Cytokinin treatment, substituted for light requirement in germination of lettuce seed, increased germination at supraoptimal soil temperatures [3], and delayed chlorophyll breakdown in detached [80] and attached leaves [55]. Plant leaves or portions of plant leaves treated with cytokinins mobilized nutrients, amino acids, and other assimilates from untreated portions of the plant to the treated portion [68]. This cytokinin property might delay leaf senescence during transport and initial acclimatization of foliage plants.

Ethylene

Ethylene (C_2H_4) is a simple chemical compound (Figure 12-4) compared to the other compounds mentioned in this chapter and is a gas, but it is classified as a growth regulator. Ethylene has a broad spectrum of physiological activities, inducing vegetative and reproductive plant responses such as abscission, tropistic responses, elongation, dormancy, fruit ripening, flower maturation, and bud development.

Plants produce ethylene in small amounts [53], with flowers and fruits emitting larger amounts than vegetative plant parts. Ethylene is

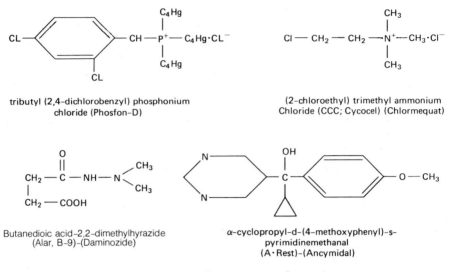

tributyl (2,4–dichlorobenzyl) phosphonium chloride (Phosfon-D)

(2-chloroethyl) trimethyl ammonium Chloride (CCC; Cycocel) (Chlormequat)

Butanedioic acid–2,2–dimethylhyrazide (Alar, B–9)–(Daminozide)

α–cyclopropyl-d-(4-methoxyphenyl)-s-pyrimidinemethanal (A·Rest)-(Ancymidal)

Figure 12-4.   Structure of common growth retardants.

produced by combustion of organic materials, frequently in damaging quantities, and various chemical compounds also release ethylene.

Ethylene is active alone or in interactions with other plant hormones, notably auxins. Ethylene reduces auxin level and lessens auxin transport and synthesis [28]. Reduced synthesis and enhanced destruction of auxin may result from inhibited tryptophan conversion to auxin, as well as increased IAA oxidase activity.

Symptoms of ethylene injury include thickening of stems, shortening of internodes, leaf distortion, and abscission [38, 82, 91]. Ethylene has been used to induce flowering in bromeliads [76], retard growth of poinsettias [84], chemically pinch azaleas [4], and defoliate deciduous trees and shrubs [52].

Growth Inhibitors

Growth inhibitors are compounds that suppress apical dominance by inhibiting cell division in the apical meristem [11]. Morphactins and maleic hydrazide suppress or inhibit plant growth by disrupting the function of apical meristem [20, 48, 92], preventing normal leaf and flower initiation. Distorted growth produced by most growth inhibitors has discouraged their use by foliage plant growers.

Morphactins produce morphological changes in many plants, with plants appearing stunted and dark green. The compounds are absorbed by leaves and roots and are readily translocated to the growing tip [93]. Morphactins have a structure similar to gibberellic acid, and the two most common ones used are flurenol and chloflurenol.

Maleic hydrazide also has striking effects on plant growth, development, and flowering [20, 30, 69], including growth inhibition, loss of apical dominance, increase or decrease in leaf size, development of dark green leaves with chlorotic areas, and dieback of suckers and terminal portions of the plants.

Growth Retardants

A number of organic chemical compounds have been synthesized since 1949 [65] that function as plant growth retardants. Retardants have been defined as substances that slow cell division and elongation in the subapical meristem, but do not completely inhibit these processes [11]. The result on responsive plant species is a compact plant with shorter internodes, but approximately the same number of nodes as an untreated plant. Other effects may include darker green leaves, accelerated or delayed flowering, increased drought tolerance, increased resistance to air pollutants, and diseases, and delayed senescence.

Growth retardants have become widely used in the ornamental industry since treated plants usually do not show growth malformations or reduced vigor, and plants respond over a wide range of concentrations. Shortened internodes usually result in more aesthetically pleasing plants, especially potted ones, and provide better support for leaves and flowers. Their use often permits commercial plant growers to better program production and assure crop uniformity.

The most commonly used growth retardants are ancymidol (A-Rest), chlormequat (cycocel), phosphon, and Daminozide (Alar, B-9) (Figure 12-4). These compounds are available commercially, are widely used in the floricultural industry, but have only recently been evaluated for use in the foliage industry [12, 21, 29, 31, 41, 61, 75, 77]. A list of growth retardants and responsive plants is shown in Table 12-1.

ACPC, formerly known as AMO-1618, is a quaternary ammonium compound whose growth-retarding properties were first reported in 1950 [101]. Only a limited number of plant species respond to treatment with ACPC [12, 13], but plants that do have shorter internodes, darker green leaves, and compact growth habits. Horticulturally important crops are among the limited responsive species, although no commercial use of ACPC has developed because it is too expensive. Limited investigations continue to be conducted because it persists in the soil for 10 years [13], and no undesirable side effects have been reported.

TABLE 12-1   Response of selected foliage plants to growth retardants

Plant	Phosfon	Chlormequat (Cycocel)	Daminozide (Alar, B-9)	Ancymidol (A-Rest)	Reference
Abutilon sp.	+[a]	+	−[b]	NA[c]	[21]
Aglaonema modestum	−	−	−	−	[21]
	−	−	−	−	[12]
Alternanthera amoena	NA	NA	+	+	[29]
Aphelandra squarrosa	NA	NA	NA	+	[21]
	−	−	−	+	[12]
Ardisia crispa	NA	NA	NA	+	[21]
	NA	−	−	−	[41]
Araucaria heterophylla	−	NA	−	−	
Aucuba japonica	−	−	−	+	[12]
Brassaia actinophylla	NA	−	−	+	[41]
	NA	NA	+	+	[29]
	−	−	NA	−	[21]
	+	+	NA	NA	[13]
Caladium bicolor	NA	NA	NA	+	[21]
Cissus rhombifolia	−	−	−	+	[12]
Chlorophytum cosmosum	−	−	NA	−	[21]
Codiaeum variegatum	NA	−	NA	+	[21]
Coffea arabica	NA	NA	NA	+	[77]
Coleus blumei	+	+	NA	NA	[13]
	−	−	−	+	[21]
	−	−	−	+	[12]
Cissus discolor	+	+	NA	+	[21]
Cordyline terminalis	NA	NA	−	+	[29]
Crassula arboressens	NA	NA	NA	+	[21]
Cyanotis kewensis	NA	+	+	+	[41]
Dieffenbachia picta	−	−	−	−	[21]
	−	−	−	−	[12]
Dieffenbachia sp.	−	−	NA	NA	[13]
Ficus elastica	−	−	NA	−	[21]
Fatshedera lizei	−	+	+	+	[21]
	−	+	NA	NA	[13]
Ficus nitida	NA	NA	+	NA	[21]
Ficus retusa	NA	NA	NA	+	[21]
	−	−	−	+	[12]
Graptophyllum pictum	NA	−	−	+	[21]
Gynura sarmentosa	−	+	+	+	[12]
	NA	NA	−	+	[29]
	NA	−	−	+	[41]
Hedera helix	−	+	+	+	[21]
	−	−	+	+	[12]
Hemigraphis 'Exotica'	+	+	+	+	[12]
Hemigraphis metallica	+	+	+	+	[21]
Hypoestes sanguinolenta	NA	NA	NA	+	[21]
Impatiens holstii	−	−	+	+	[12]

TABLE 12-1   Response of selected foliage plants to growth retardants (Continued)

Plant	Phosfon	Chlormequat (Cycocel)	Daminozide (Alar, B-9)	Ancymidol (A-Rest)	Reference
Impatiens sultanii	+	+	NA	NA	[13]
Iresine herbstii	−	−	+	NA	[70]
Kalanchoe blossfeldiana	−	+	+	+	[12]
Kalanchoe diagremontiana	−	+	NA	NA	[13]
Monstera deliciosa	NA	NA	NA	+	[21]
	−	−	−	+	[13]
Nephthytis sp.	NA	−	−	+	[21]
Nephthytis gravenreuthii	−	−	−	+	[12]
Pellionia pulchra	NA	+	NA	NA	[21]
	NA	+	−	−	[41]
Peperomia caparata	NA	−	NA	+	[21]
	NA	NA	NA	+	[97]
Peperomia crassifolia	NA	−	NA	+	[21]
	−	−	NA	+	[97]
Peperomia griseo-argentea	NA	−	NA	+	[21]
	−	−	NA	+	[97]
Peperomia metallica	NA	−	NA	+	[21]
	−	+	NA	+	[97]
Peperomia obtusifolia	+	−	NA	+	[21]
	−	−	−	+	[12]
Peperomia rotundifolia	−	−	NA	NA	[13]
Philodendron oxycardium	NA	−	−	−	[41]
	−	−	+	NA	[75]
	−	−	NA	NA	[13]
	NA	NA	−	+	[29]
Philodendron micans	+	NA	NA	NA	[21]
Philodendron panduraiforme	−	−	NA	NA	[13]
Philodendron scandens	−	−	−	+	[12]
Pilea cadierei	+	+	+	+	[21]
	NA	+	+	+	[41]
	NA	NA	−	+	[29]
	+	+	NA	+	[97]
Pilea depressa	NA	NA	NA	+	[21]
	+	+	NA	+	[97]
Pilea involucrate	NA	−	−	+	[41]
	+	+	−	+	[21]
Pilea microphylla	NA	+	−	−	[41]
	NA	NA	NA	+	[21]
Pilea 'Norfolk'	+	+	NA	+	[21]
Pilea nummularifolia	+	+	NA	+	[21]
Pilea serpillacea	+	+	NA	+	[97]
	−	−	−	−	[21]
Pilea 'Silver Tree'	+	+	−	+	[21]
Plectranthus coleordes	−	+	−	+	[21]
Podocarpus macrophylla	NA	−	−	−	[41]

(*continued*)

TABLE 12-1   Response of selected foliage plants to growth retardants (Continued)

Plant	Phosfon	Chlormequat (cycocel)	Daminozide (Alar, B-9)	Ancymidol (A-Rest)	Reference
	NA	−	−	−	[21]
Pseudoeranthemum sp.	NA	−	NA	+	[21]
Sanchezia nobilis	NA	+	NA	NA	[21]
Saxifraga sarmentosa	NA	NA	NA	+	[97]
	+	−	NA	−	[21]
Scindapsus aureus	−	−	+	+	[21]
	−	−	+	NA	[75]
	NA	NA	NA	+	[61]
	−	−	−	+	[12]
	NA	NA	−	+	[29]
Sedum anglicum	NA	+	NA	+	[21]
	+	+	NA	+	[97]
Strobilanthes dyerianus	NA	NA	−	+	[29]
	+	+	−	+	
Strobilanthes exotica	+	+	−	+	[21]
Syngonium podophyllum	NA	−	−	−	[41]
	−	−	−	−	[21]
	−	−	+	NA	[75]
Syngonium podophyllum anthophilum	NA	NA	−	+	[29]
Zebrina pendula	NA	NA	+	+	[29]

a +, active.
b −, inactive.
c NA, not applied.

Phosphon D is a quaternary ammonium compound that contains a phosphonium cation whose properties were first reported in 1955 [1]. Soil drenches of phosphon retard vegetative growth of a variety of plants [11, 13, 62, 63], promote flowering of azalea [89], camellia [34], and holly [63], and increase fruit set on grape [19].

Phosphon retards growth of some foliage plants, but fewer plants respond to it than to chlormequat, daminozide, or ancymidol (Table 12-1). Phosphon retains biological activity in the soil for over a year and provides long-term growth control for responsive plants.

Phosphon was incorporated at 0.16, 0.8, and 4 grams per cubic foot of soil mix and the activity determined on a variety of horticultural plants [13]. Only schefflera (*Brassaia actinophylla*) had less growth than untreated plants of the seven foliage plants included in the experiment.

Phosphon at 0.28, 0.55, and 1.11 grams per 6-inch pot was soil incorporated to determine its effectiveness on six foliage plant species (*Peperomia crassifolia, P. metallica, Pilea cadierei, P. depressa, P. serpillacea, Sedum anglicum*) used in terrariums [97]. Moderate growth retardation was reported on *Pilea cadierei, P. depressa, P. serpillacea,* and *Sedum anglicum;* also, *S. anglicum* exhibited chlorosis at the 0.55-g rate, and leaf tips were necrotic at the 1.1-g rate. Phosphon-induced chlorosis and marginal leaf burn were reported at high rates in other studies [13].

Chlormequat [(2-chloroethyl) trimethylammonium chloride)] or Cycocel was the most active of a new group of quarternary ammonium compounds first reported by Tolbert [94]. The number of plant species responsive to chlormequat is greater than phosphon [12, 13] and includes several important commercial floricultural crops. The possibility of using chlormequat commercially on poinsettia, *Eupharbia pulcherrima*, to produce compact plants was reported by several investigators who recommended methods and levels of application [14, 45, 49]. Other plant responses illicited by chlormequat include increased number of flowers [24, 44, 89] and earlier flowering of woody and herbaceous plants [85, 94, 103].

More ornamental plants respond to chlormequat treatment than to ACPC or phosphon, but few foliage plants are responsive; these have been limited to the following genera: *Gynura* spp., *Kalanchoe* spp., *Pilea* spp., and *Sedum* spp.

Chlormequat was reported phytotoxic to two of the six species it retarded [97], and *Pilea cadierei* was killed at concentrations of 1.1 grams per 6-inch pot, while other *Pilea* spp. showed leaf tip chlorosis at 0.55 grams per 7-inch pot or higher. Chlormequat was found toxic to some foliage plants in another study [41], but at low concentrations growth stimulation was reported [79].

Daminozide (butanedioic acid 2,2-dimethylhydrazide) has growth-retarding effects that were first reported in 1962 [81]. A large number of herbaceous and woody dicotyledonous plants were found to respond to treatment and, later, a wide range of ornamental plants [12, 15, 21, 28, 35, 40]. Internodes were shorter, terminal growth was suppressed, and foliage was darker green in responsive plants. Daminozide usually does not cause toxic effects, but certain formulations have phytotoxic effects in high concentrations.

Daminozide is recommended as a foliar spray to minimize internode elongation and produce a more marketable plant for azaleas, bedding plants, chrysanthemums, gloxinias, hydrangeas, and kalanchoes [40]. It also has been used successfully to control growth on a variety of nursery and landscape shrubs and trees [83, 90].

Rapid foliage plant growth is desirable during early production phases, but continued rapid growth may reduce plants' aesthetic and commercial value. Daminozide inhibited internode elongation of cordatum (*Philodendron scandens oxycardium*), pothos, (*Epipremnum aureum*) and nephthytis (*Syngonium podophyllum*) without phytotoxic effects [75]. Plants treated twice with Daminozide had less new growth than plants treated once. Later work [41] indicated that Daminozide was not effective in reducing internode elongation, but the variable results may have resulted from different environmental factors during application periods. Growth retardation with daminozide applications may depend on temperature and humidity [83]. Daminozide-responsive plants grown under low humidity and high temperatures showed little or no treatment effects. Daminozide produces variable results when used on foliage plants [12, 28, 40, 75]. Foliage plants responsive to daminozide treatment are listed in Table 12-1.

Daminozide treatments often modify or alter flower and fruit development in addition to its growth-retarding properties. However, investigators have shown that daminozide's effects on flowering depend on time of application and concentrations used. Daminozide sprays have increased the size and number of flowers in azaleas [89], promoted floral induction in young lemon trees [67], and increased total number of flowers in apples, peaches, pears, blueberries, and bougainvillea [2, 25, 36, 87]. However, flowering delay of 3 to 7 days occurred in garden annuals treated at the time stem elongation was most rapid [15], and flowering also was delayed but number of flowers per cluster increased in treated tomatoes [78]. Sex expression of some cucurbits has been altered with daminozide, with an increase in the number of female flowers produced in muskmelon [37] and an increase in male flowers in squash [43].

Daminozide increased fruit set in some grape varieties [96] and pears [35], reduced respiration rate and improved storage and shelf life of treated apples [58], and hastened maturity of peaches [7] and cherries [16]. These properties of daminozide could have limited usage in foliage plant breeding and seed production.

Ancymidol's [a-cyclopropyl-a-(p-methoxyphenyl)-5-pyrimidine-methanol] activities in growth retardation were first reported in 1970 [95]. Investigators showed ancymidol effectively reduced internode elongation on a variety of ornamentals [26, 27, 31, 32]. Ancymidol was effective as a soil drench or a foliar spray although soil applications were variable [32], depending on media, moisture, and stage of root growth [12]. Pine bark in the media has been reported to inactivate ancymidol when ancymidol is used as a soil drench [102].

Ancymidol retards the growth of more foliage plants than any other growth retardant (Table 12-1) when used as a soil drench or foliar spray. Foliar sprays of 50 to 150 parts per million retarded growth of nephthytis (*Syngonium* spp.), schefflera (*Brassaia actinophylla*), aluminum plant (*Pilea cadierei*), aphelandra (*Aphelandra squarrosa*), and grape leaf ivy (*Cissus rhombifolia*) [31]. Foliar sprays of 100, 200, 300, and 400 parts per million and soil drenches of 0.5, 1.0, 1.5, and 2.0 milligrams per 4-inch pot retarded growth of coffee (*Coffea arabica*), cordatum (*Philodendron scandens oxycardium*), nephthytis (*Syngonium podophyllum*), and pothos (*Epipremnum aureum*) [77].

When 0.125, 0.25, 0.50, 1.0, and 2.0 milligrams of ancymidol per 6-inch pot of soil were incorporated, noticeable growth retardation of *Peperomia crassifolia, P. caperata, P. griseo-argentea, Pilea cadierei, P. serpyllacea,* and *Saxifraga stolonifera,* which are often grown as terrarium plants, occurred; with 0.5 and 1.0 milligrams of ancymidol producing plants with the greatest aesthetic appeal. At 2 milligrams per 6-inch pot, leaf distortion of *Peperomia griseo-argentea* and *P. caperata* was observed [97]. A foliar spray of 50 parts per million of ancymidol retarded shoot elongation of schefflera (*Brassaia actinophylla*), teddy bear vine (*Cyanotis kewensis*), purple passion (*Gynura sarmentosa*), aluminum plant (*Pilea cadierei*), and friendship plant (*Pilea involuerata*) [41].

Foliar sprays of 100, 200, and 300 parts per million of ancymidol applied weekly for three weeks to golden pothos (*Epipremnum aureum*) produced plants with short internodes, and there were no differences between concentrations [60]. In subsequent research, golden pothos was sprayed weekly for 8 weeks with concentrations of 1.0, 2.5, 5.0, 7.5, 10.0, 15.0, and 20.0 parts per million of ancymidol. Treated plants were shorter than controls, and concentrations of 1 part per million produced 50 percent new growth compared to controls. Internode, petiole and leaf blade length, vine fresh weight, and number of new nodes were not affected by concentrations used [61].

Eleven species of foliage plants were treated once with foliar sprays applied at rates of 0.625, 1.25, 2.5, and 5 milligrams per square foot [29]. Ancymidol treatment produced premium plants at the 0.625 rate for babydoll ti plant (*Cordyline terminalis*), schefflera (*Brassaia actinophylla*), and pothos (*Epipremnum aureum*). It took 1.25 milligrams per square foot to provide premium plants for alternanthera (*Alternanthera ficoidea*), cordatum (*Philodendron scandens oxycardium*), and wandering jew (*Zebrina pendula*), while the 2.5 rate was required for nephthytis (*Syngonium podophyllum*), bluebell (*Strobilanthes dyerianus*), and purple passion (*Gynura sarmentosa*).

The broad range of activity makes ancymidol the most effective growth retardant for most foliage plants. However, supraoptimal concentrations of ancymidol may stop node formation and leaf expansion, and leaves may develop crinkled indentations between veins.

Growth regulators are used as aids in foliage plant production, and their future use will undoubtedly increase. Caution must be exercised when using growth regulators, as excess application can damage foliage plants. Application of growth regulators may be beneficial, but their use may be illegal because of lack of registration; therefore, producers should exercise caution when trying a growth regulator on crops for the first time. The growth regulator must be nontoxic to the crop and registered for the particular use.

REFERENCES

[1] Anonymous. 1955. Natl. Acad. Sci. Natl. Res. Counc. Publ. 384. Chemical Biological Coordination Center Positive Data Series No. 2. 45 pp.

[2] Batjer, L. P., M. W. Williams, and G. C. Martin. 1964. Effects of N-dimethyl amino succinamic acid (B-nine) on vegetative and fruit characteristics of apples, pears, and sweet cherries. *Proc. Am. Soc. Hort. Sci.* 85:11–16.

[3] Braun, J. W., V. S. Rao, and A. A. Kahn. 1976. Release of lettuce seed thermodormancy by plant growth regulators applied in organic solvent. *HortScience* 11:29–30.

[4] Breece, J., L. Pyeatt, and T. Furuta. 1970. Increased effectiveness of chemical pinching agents in azaleas. *Flower Nursery Rpt.* July, pp. 1–3.

[5] Brian, P. W., and H. G. Hemming. 1955. The effect of gibberellic acid on shoot growth of pea seedlings. *Physiol. Plantarum* 8:669–681.

[6] Bukovac, M. J., and S. Honma. 1967. Gibberellin-induced heterostyly in the tomato and its implication for hybrid seed production. *Proc. Am. Soc. Hort. Sci.* 91:514–520.

[7] Byers, R. E., and F. H. Emerson. 1969. Effects of succinamic acids 2,2-dimethyl-hydrazide (Alar) on peach fruit maturation and tree growth. *J. Am. Soc. Hort. Sci.* 95:641–645.

[8] Carpenter, W. J., and W. H. Carlson. 1972. Improved geranium branching with growth regulator sprays. *HortScience* 7:291–292.

[9] ———. 1972. The effect of growth regulators on chrysanthemums. *J. Am. Soc. Hort. Sci.* 97:349–351.

[10] ———. 1975. Foam sprays of plant growth regulating chemicals on rose shoot development at cut back. *HortScience* 10:605–606.

[11] Cathey, H. M. 1964. Physiology of growth retarding chemicals. *Ann. Rev. Plant Physiol.* 15:271–302.

[12] ———. 1975. Comparative plant growth-retarding activities of ancymidol with ACPC, Phosfon, Chlormequat, and SADH on ornamental plant species. *HortScience* 10:204–216.

[13] ———, and N. W. Stuart. 1961. Comparative plant growth retarding activity of Amo-1618., Phosfon and CCC. *Botan. Gaz.* 123:51–57.

[14] ———, and R. L. Taylor. 1963. Growth control of poinsettias *Euphorbia pulcherrima* by use of cyclic lighting and (2-chlorophyl) trimethyl ammonium chloride. *Proc. Am. Soc. Hort. Sci.* 82:532–540.

[15] ———, J. Halperin, and A. A. Piringer. 1965. Relation of N-dimethyl aminosuccinamic acid to photoperiod, supplementary light, and night temperatures, in its effect on the growth and flowering of garden annuals. *Hort. Res.* 5:1–12.

[16] Chaplin, M. H., and A. L. Kenworthy. 1970. The influence of succinamic

acid, 2,2-dimethylhydrazide on fruit ripening of the 'Windsor' sweet cherry. *J. Am. Soc. Hort. Sci.* 95:532–536.

[17] Clark, H. E., and K. R. Kerns. 1942. Control of flowering with phytohormones. *Science* 95:536–537.

[18] Coggins, C. W., Jr., H. Z. Hield, R. M. Burns, I. L. Eaks, and L. N. Lewis. 1966. Gibberellin research with citrus. *Calif. Agr.* 20:12–13.

[19] Coombe, B. G. 1965. Increase in fruit set of *Vitis vinifera* by treatment with growth retardants. *Nature* 205:305–306.

[20] Crane, J. C., and H. M. Nelson. 1970. Apricot fruit growth and abscission as affected by maleic hydrazide-induced seed abortion. *J. Am. Soc. Hort. Sci.* 95(3):302–306.

[21] Criley, R. A. 1976. Vaeksthaemmende midler til bladplanter. *Gartner Tidende* 92(26):385–386.

[22] ———, and S. Oka. 1976. Stimulating bud break on dieffenbachia cane pieces. *Hort. Digest. Univ. Hawaii* 29:1.

[23] ———, and G. A. Stevens. 1976. Cytokinins stimulate bud initiation on *Cordyline* cuttings. *Hort. Digest* 31:1.

[24] Darwin, C. R. 1897. The power of movement in plants. New York: D. Appleton & Company, Inc.

[25] Edgerton, L. J. 1966. Some effects of gibberellin and growth retardants on bud development and cold hardiness of peach. *Proc. Am. Soc. Hort. Sci.* 88:197–203.

[26] Einert, A. E. 1971. Response of pot chrysanthemums to growth retardant El 531. *Ark. Farm Res. Mar.* Apr., p. 7.

[27] ———. 1971. Reduction in last internode elongation of cut tulips by growth retardants. *HortScience* 6:459–460.

[28] Ernest, L. L., and J. G. Valdoirnas. 1970. Regulation of auxin levels in *Coleus blumei* by ethylene. *Plant Physiol.* 48:402–406.

[29] Frank, D. G., and A. Donnan, Jr. 1975. Influence of A-Rest on tropical foliage plants. *Fla. State Hort. Soc. Proc.* 88:531–534.

[30] Foote, L. E., and B. F. Himmelman. 1971. MH is a roadside grass retardant. *Weed Science* 19(1):86–90.

[31] Furuta, T., W. C. Jones, W. Humphrey, and J. Breece. 1972. Ancymidol retards growth of many plants. *Florists' Rev.* 150:23, 45.

[32] ———, W. C. Jones, T. Mock, W. Humphrey, R. Maire, and J. Breece. 1972. Ancymidol applications retard plant growth of woody ornamentals. *Calif. Agr.* 26:10–12.

[33] Galun, E. 1959. Effects of gibberellic acid and naphthaleneacetic acid on sex expression and some morphological characters in the cucumber plant. *Phyton* 13:1–8.

[34] Gill, D. L., and N. W. Stuart. 1961. Stimulation of camellia flowerbud initiation by application of two growth retardants—a preliminary report. *Amer. Camellia Yearbook,* pp. 129–135.

[35] Griggs, W. H., and B. T. Iwakiri. 1968. Effects of succinic acid, 2,2-dimethylhydrazide (Alar) sprays used to control growth in 'Bartlett' pear trees planted in hedgerow. *Proc. Am. Soc. Hort. Sci.* 92:155–166.

[36] Hackett, W. P., and R. M. Sachs. 1967. Chemical control of flowering in bougainvillea 'San Diego Red'. *Proc. Am. Soc. Hort. Sci.* 90:361–364.

[37] Halevy, A. H., and Y. Rudich. 1967. Modification of sex expression in muskmelon by treatment with the growth retardant B-995. *Physiol. Plantarum* 20:1052–1058.

[38] Heek, W. W., and E. G. Pires. 1962. Effect of ethylene on horticultural and agronomic plants. Texas Agr. Exp. Sta. MP-613.

[39] Heide, O. M. 1969. Environmental control of sex expression in *Begonia. Zeit. Pflanzenphysiol.* 61:279–285.

[40] Heins, R. D., R. E. Widmer, and H. F. Wilkins. 1976. Growth regulator recommendations for floricultural crops. Minn. State Florist Bulletin.

[41] Henley, R. W., and R. T. Poole. 1974. Influence of growth regulators on tropical foliage plants. *Proc. Fla. State Hort. Soc.* 87:436–438.

[42] Heslop-Harrison, J. 1959. Growth substances and flower morphogenesis. *Jour. Linnean Soc. London Botan.* 56:269–281.

[43] Hopp, R. J., and H. Rochester, Jr. 1967. Responses of butternut squash to *N*-dimethyl amino succinamic acid. *HortScience* 2:160–161.

[44] Joiner, J. N., and R. T. Poole. 1962. Variable photoperiod and CCC. Effects on growth and flowering of *Gardenia jasminoides* 'Veitchii.' *Proc. Fla. State Hort. Soc.* 75:449–451.

[45] ———, and T. J. Sheehan. 1962. Effects of photoperiod, propagation date and dwarfing compounds on growth and flowering of poinsettias. *Proc. Fla. State Hort. Soc.* 75:451–456.

[46] Kahn, A. J., A. Goss, and D. F. Smith. 1957. Effect of gibberellin on germination of lettuce seed. *Science* 125:645–646.

[47] Kender, W. J. 1974. Ethephon induced flowering in apple seedlings. *HortScience* 9:444.

[48] Khan, A. A. 1967. Physiology of morphactins: effect on gravi- and photo-response. *Physiol. Plantarum* 20:306–313.

[49] Kofranek, A. M., R. H. Sciaroni, and T. G. Byrne. 1962. Shortening poinsettias with CCC for better proportioned plants. *Calif. Agr.* 16(12):4–5.

[50] Kuroswa, E. 1926. Experimental studies on the secretion of *Fusarium heterosporum* on rice plants. *Trans. Nat. Hist. Soc. Formosa* 16:213–227.

[51] Lang, A., J. A. Sandoval, and A. Bedri. 1957. Introduction of bolting and flowering on *Hyoscyanum* and *Samolus* by a gibberellin-like material from a seed plant. *Proc. Natl. Acad. Sci.* 43:960–964.

[52] Larsen, F. E. 1970. Promotion of leaf abscission of deciduous nursery stock with 2-chloroethyl phosphonic acid. *J. Am. Soc. Hort. Sci.* 95:662–63.

[53] LaRue, T. A. G., and O. L. Gamborg. 1971. Ethylene production by plant cell cultures. *Plant Physiol.* 48:394–398.

[54] Leopold, A. C. 1958. Auxin uses in the control of flowering and fruiting. *Ann. Rev. Plant Physiol.* 9:281–310.

[55] ———. 1964. Kinins and the regulation of leaf senescence. In Nitsch, ed. *Regulateurs naturels de la croissance vegetale*, pp. 705–718. Paris: Centre National de la Recherche Scientifique.

[56] Letham, D. S., J. S. Shannon, and I. R. McDonald. 1964. The structure of zeatin, a factor inducing cell division. *Proc. Chem. Soc. (London.)*:230.

[57] Lindstrom, R. S., S. H. Wittwer, and M. J. Bukovac. 1957. Gibberellin and higher plants, IV. Flowering responses of some flower crops. *Quart. Bull. Agr. Exptl. Sta.* 39:673–681.

[58] Looney, N. E. 1967. Effect of N-dimethyl amino succinamic acid on ripening and respiration of apple fruits. *Can. J. Plant Sci.* 47:549–553.

[59] Loveys, B. R. 1970. The phytochrome and hormonal control of unrolling in etiolated wheat. Ph.D. thesis. Univ. of Wales, Aberystwyth. 240 pp.

[60] McConnell, D. B., and R. T. Poole. 1972. Vegetative growth modification of *Scindapsus aureus* by ancymidol and PBA. *Proc. Fla. State Hort. Soc.* 85:387–389.

[61] ———. 1973. Influence of ancymidol on *Scindapsus aureus*. *Southern Nurseryman's Res. J.* 1:13–18.

[62] Mahmoud, T. A., and P. L. Stephonkus. 1970. A differential response of two cultivars of chrysanthemum morifolium to phosfon applications. *J. Am. Soc. Hort. Sci.* 95:292–295.

[63] Marth, P. C. 1963. Effect of growth retardants on flowering, fruiting and vegetative growth of Holly (Ilex). *Proc. Am. Soc. Hort. Sci.* 83:777–781.

[64] Miller, C. O., F. Skoog, F. S. Okumura, M. H. Von Saltza, and F. M. Strong. 1955. Structure and synthesis of a kinin. *J. Am. Chem. Soc.* 77:2662–2663.

[65] Mitchell, J. W., J. W. Wirville, and I. L. Weil. 1949. Plant growth-regulating properties of some nicotinium compounds. *Science* 110:252–254.

[66] Mitchell, W. D., and S. H. Wittwer. 1962. Chemical regulation of flower sex expression and vegetative growth in *Cucumis sativa*. *Science* 136:880–881.

[67] Monselise, S. P., and A. H. Halvey. 1964. Chemical inhibition and promotion of citrus flower bud induction. *Proc. Am. Soc. Hort. Sci.* 84:141–146.

[68] Mothes, K. 1960. Uber das altern der Blatter und die Moglichkeit ihrer Wiederverjungung. *Naturwiss* 47:337–350.

[69] Naylor, A. W., and E. A. Davis. 1950. Maleic hydrazide as a plant growth inhibitor. *Botan. Gaz.* 112:112–126.

[70] Nightingale, A. E. 1974. The influence of growth retardants on *Iresine*. *HortScience* 9:379–381.

[71] Nitsch, C., and J. P. Nitsch. 1967. The induction of flowering *in vitro* in stem segments of *Plumbago indica* L.I. The production of vegetative buds. *Planta (Berl.)* 72:355–370.

[72] Paleg, L. G. 1960. Physiological effects of gibberellic acid, II. *Plant Physiol.* 35:902–906.

[73] Phatak, S. C., S. H. Wittwer, S. Homna, and M. J. Bukovac. 1966. Gibberellin-induced anther and pollen development in a stamenless tomato mutant. *Nature* 209:635–636.

[74] Phinney, B. O. 1956. Growth response of single-gene dwarf mutants in maize to gibberellic acid. *Proc. Natl. Acad. Sci. U.S.* 42:185–189.

[75] Poole, R. T. 1970. Influence of growth regulators on stem elongation and rooting response of foliage plants. *Fla. State Hort. Soc. Proc.* 83:497–502.

[76] ———, and C. A. Conover. 1975. Flowering of bromeliads. *Fla. Foliage Grower* 12(6):1–2.

[77] ———, and D. B. McConnell. 1972. The effect of ancymidol on various foliage plants. *HortScience* 7:332.

[78] Read, P. E. and D. J. Fieldhouse. 1970. Use of growth retardants for increasing tomato yields and adaptation for mechanical harvest. *J. Am. Soc. Hort. Sci.* 95:73–78.

[79] ———, V. L. Herman, and D. A. Heng. 1974. Slow-release chlormequat: a new concept in plant growth regulators. *HortScience* 9:55–57.

[80] Richmond, A. E., and A. Lang. 1957. Effect of kinetin on protein content and survival of detached *Xanthium* leaves. *Science* 125:650–651.

[81] Riddell, J. A., H. A. Hageman, C. M. J'Anthony, and W. L. Hubbard. 1962. Retardation of plant growth by a new group of chemicals. *Science* 136:391.

[82] Rubinstein, B., and F. B. Abeles. 1965. Relationships between ethylene evolution and leaf abscission. *Botan. Gaz.* 126:255–259.

[83] Sachs, R. M., and R. G. Maire. 1967. Chemical control of growth and flowering of woody ornamental plants in the landscape and nursery: tests with maleic hydrazide and Alar. *Proc. Am. Soc. Hort. Sci.* 91:728–734.

[84] Shanks, J. B. 1970. Chemical growth regulation for floricultural crops. *Florists' Rev.* 147(3209):34–35, 50–58.

[85] ———. 1972. Chemical control of growth and flowering in *Hibiscus.* *HortScience* 7:574.

[86] Shifriss, O. 1961. Gibberellin as a sex regulator in *Ricinus communis. Science* 133:2061–2062.

[87] Shutak, V. G. 1968. Effect of succinic acid, 2,2-dimethylhydrazide on flower bud formation of the "Coville" highbush blueberry. *HortScience* 3:225.

[88] Skoog, F., and C. O. Miller. 1957. Chemical regulation of growth and organ formation in plant tissue culture *in vitro. Symp. Exptl. Biol.* 11:118–131.

[89] Stahly, E. A., and M. W. Williams. 1967. Size control of nursery stock with N-dimethylaminosuccinamic acid. *Proc. Am. Soc. Hort. Sci.* 91:792–794.

[90] Stuart, N. W. 1965. Controlling the flowering of greenhouse azaleas. *Florist Nusery Exchange* 144:22–23.

[91] Tjia, B., M. N. Rogers, and D. E. Hartley. 1969. Effects of ethylene on morphology and flowering of *chrysanthemum morifolium* Ramat. *J. Am. Soc. Hort. Sci.* 94(1):35–39.

[92] ———, D. C. Kiplinger, and P. C. Kozel. 1973. Studies of morphactin on the growth and auxin distribution of *chrysanthemum morifolium* Ramat. *J. Am. Soc. Hort. Sci.* 98(2):186–193.

[93] Tognani, F., A. A. De Hertagh, and S. H. Wittwer. 1967. The independent action of morphactins and gibberellic acid on higher plants. *Plant Cell Physiol.* 8:231–239.

[94] Tolbert, N. E. 1960. (2-chlorethyl) trimethylammonium chloride and related compounds as plant growth substances. *J. Bio. Chem.* 253:475–479.

[95] Tschabold, E. E., H. M. Taylor, J. D. Daveport, R. E. Hackler, E. V. Krunkalns, and W. C. Meredith. 1970. A new plant growth regulator. *Plant Physiol.* 46:519.

[96] Tukey, L. D., and H. K. Fleming. 1968. Fruiting and vegetative effects of N-dimethylaminosuccinamic acid on 'Concord' grapes. *Vitis labrusca* L. *Proc. Am. Soc. Hort. Sci.* 93:300–310.

[97] Vienrevee, K., and M. N. Rogers. 1974. Growth control of terrarium plants with ancymidol. *Florists' Rev.* 155(4008):24–25, 67–71.

[98] Weaver, R. J. 1972. *Plant Growth Substances in Agriculture,* pp. 52–61 (gibberellins), pp. 62–66 (cytokins). San Francisco: W. H. Freeman.

[99] Went, F. W. 1928. Wuchsstoff und Uachstum. *Rec. Trav. Bot. Neerl.* 25:1–116.

[100] Williams, M. W., and E. A. Stahly. 1968. Effect of cytokinins on apple shoot development from axillary buds. *HortScience* 3:68–69.

[101] Wirville, J. W., and J. W. Mitchell. 1950. Six new plant growth inhibiting compounds. *Botan. Gaz.* III:491–494.

[102] Witte, W. T. 1973. A-Rest effectiveness reduced by pine bark. *Fla. Flower Grower* 10:4.

[103] Witter, S. H., and N. E. Tolbert. 1960. (2-chlorethyl) trimethylammonium chloride and related compounds as plant growth substances III. Effect of growth and flowering of the tomato. *Am. J. Botany* 47:560–565.

[104] Yabuta, T. 1935. Biochemistry of the 'bakanae' fungus of rice. *Agr. Hort. (Tokyo)* 10:17–22.

[105] Zimmerman, C. E., S. N. Brooks, and S. T. Likins. 1964. Gibberellin A_3-induced growth responses of Fuggle hops (*Humulus lupulus* L.) *Crop. Sci.* 4:310–313.

thirteen

R. W. Henley

diagnosing plant disorders

Diagnosis of plant problems is a challenging task that requires knowledge of plant growth processes and an understanding of the influences of environmental factors (light, temperature, moisture, nutrition, gases, plant pathogens, pests, pollutants, and other agents) on plant growth and quality. Specific crop history information preceding development of a problem and access to services of experts in the fields of plant physiology, plant pathology, entomology, nematology, soil science, and fertilizer chemistry are helpful when symptoms alone are insufficient to provide an answer to a plant problem. Plant problem diagnosis relates closely to many chapters of this book pertaining to foliage plant culture and pests; therefore, the reader will be referred to appropriate chapters for additional background information on some aspects of problem diagnosis.

Several textbooks on floriculture, nursery plant science, and plant propagation have specific chapters that pertain to diagnosing plant problems [15, 16, 19, 24] or discuss disorders in relation to specific environmental factors in separate chapters [2, 5, 7]. A few technical publications address the issue of diagnosing plant problems, including some foliage plants [3, 4, 6, 10, 11, 12, 13, 14, 23]. Pirone [22] provided a discussion of a broad range of plant problems including symptoms, causes, and hosts, but its coverage of foliage plant problems is limited. The two volumes by Westcott [25, 26] also provide good introductory chapters on diseases and insects of garden plants, respectively, but include only a few foliage plants as hosts. A few publications written primarily for amateur horticulturists on subjects of house plant problem diagnoses are insufficiently technical to be of much value to commercial foliage plant producers [1, 20, 21].

Much diagnostic work and preventative maintenance monitoring can be done by nursery personnel, preferably several employees who work with plants on a day to day basis in the production areas or in retail displays. Seldom can one person be trained to detect and report all plant problems.

The person or persons charged with production quality control must observe and survey plants on a regular schedule, daily if possible. Details such as needs for watering may require more frequent inspection. Unnecessary losses are encountered too often due to infrequent checks for infestations of insects or mites, pathogens, or other factors. Heavy losses can usually be avoided if problems are detected early and corrective measures initiated quickly.

Many firms have some or all of the diagnostic work done by outside specialized laboratories. Soil, water, and plant tissue samples and plant samples that are suspected of having pests or pathogens can be sent to laboratories that specialize in one or more diagnostic services. In some states the Cooperative Extension Service is well equipped to handle many of these problems, but in others the use of private laboratories and consultants is advisable.

Major Problem Areas and Tools for Diagnosis

Plant growth rate is influenced by the intensity of several essential environmental factors, such as light, nutrients, temperature, and water. A hypothetical model of plant response to intensity of these factors is displayed in Figure 13-1. The two regions, hidden deficiency and hidden excess, on the plant growth curve designate restrictions that may be economically significant but usually go undetected unless certain environmental factors are monitored carefully and accurate crop productivity records are maintained. Measurement of factors such as light intensity, soil pH, soil salinity, concentration of specific elements in soil and plant tissue, air and soil temperature, and soil moisture should be recorded as frequently as feasible. Such procedures should be part of a preventative maintenance program rather than used only as emergency measures to aid in diagnosing serious, large-scale problems.

Other agents in the plant environment operate primarily in a negative sense to retard growth or injure plants. Plant pathogens, certain insects and mites, parasitic nematodes, some pesticides, and injurious

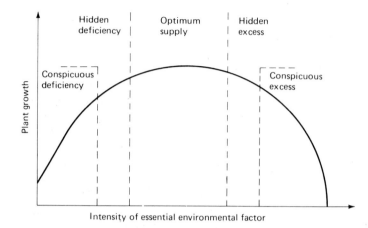

Figure 13-1. Plant growth as influenced by the intensity of an essential environmental factor.

pollutants of the atmosphere, water, and soil are examples of such factors, and the intensity of these is inversely proportional to plant growth. A hypothetical model of the influence of agents primarily detrimental to plants is presented in Figure 13-2.

Numerous factors that influence plant growth may exist singularly or in combination, and the intensity and exposure duration of each

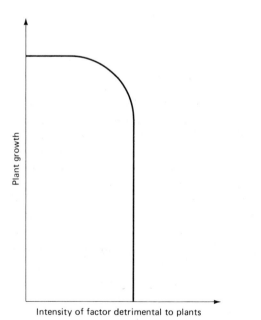

Figure 13-2. Influence of intensity of a detrimental factor on plant growth.

alters the condition of a given plant. A significantly detrimental change in plant condition results in visual symptoms of the malfunction. Table 13-1 provides a list of plant disorder symptoms and some factors that cause them. Many symptom and cause categories are broad since some foliage plant species respond differently to the same stimulus. The matter of factor intensity and interaction of factors should always be kept in mind. No attempt is made in Table 13-1 to categorize injury symptoms resulting from a combination of two or more factors.

Plant Examination and Optical Aids

Injury from a specific pest, presence of a pest, expression of disease, phytotoxicity symptoms, or evidence of mechanical injury often is so obvious on aerial plant parts that no further inspection is necessary to properly identify the problem. Where symptoms on aerial plant parts alone do not provide sufficient clues to the cause of disorder, the basal portion of the stem and the root system should be examined. Plants with an underdeveloped or partially destroyed root system rarely have vigorous top growth, and, conversely, plants may have excellent root systems but due to some injury, nutritional imbalance, or other limiting environmental factor, may be stunted or fail to develop normal foliage or stems. A hand lens, approximately 10 to 20 power, is useful to the diagnostician since many pests and symptoms of injury are not easily seen with the unaided eye. A binocular microscope with magnification capabilities between 20 to 80 power also is an ideal optical instrument for dissection of plant material and general diagnostic work.

Isolation of some microorganisms associated with affected plant tissue for identification purposes may be desirable. These procedures should be done or supervised by a person with a background in plant pathology and nematology in a laboratory equipped adequately for culturing and observation of isolated pathogens and pests. A compound light microscope with a magnification range of 100 to 1,000 power is needed when working with fungi and bacteria. Large nurseries should consider trying to handle isolation and culture of pathogens in house because of the costs involved.

Light Intensity and Light Meters

Major fluctuations in weather or changes in climate due to changing seasons or other climatological reasons should be considered when diagnosing foliage plant problems. Shade density of a structure cover must be changed for some crops from winter to summer, and vice versa, to maximize growth and retain plant quality. As light levels increase

TABLE 13-1   Foliage plant malady symptoms and possible causal agents

Plant part affected and symptoms	Possible cause
Foliage	
Chlorosis (general)	Low soil fertility Excessively high light intensity Excessively high temperatures
Chlorosis (younger leaves)	Inadequate supply of iron or manganese and possibly copper or zinc Plants excluded from light for extended period Phytotoxicity from pesticides
Chlorosis (older leaves)	Low nitrogen or potassium supply High soil salinity Overwatering Poorly aerated soil mix
Marginal chlorosis	Low magnesium and potassium supply (primarily lower leaves) High soil salinity Cold drafts (primarily lower leaves) Spider mite feeding injury (primarily lower leaves) Phytotoxicity from pesticides
Interveinal chlorosis	Deficiency of iron or manganese (upper leaves affected first) Spider mite feeding injury Sulfur dioxide air pollution injury Phytotoxicity from pesticides
Veinal chlorosis	Injury from certain herbicides
Round chlorotic spots	Fungal or bacterial leaf spots Phytotoxicity from pesticide, fertilizer, or pollutant
Irregular, chlorotic spots	Cold-water injury Fungal or bacterial leaf spots Virus or viruslike infection Phytotoxicity from pesticides, fertilizers, or pollutants
Stippled, chlorotic pattern not associated specifically with veins or interveinal areas	Feeding injury from spider mites, plant hoppers, leafhoppers, or thrips
Mosaic, chlorotic pattern	Cold-water injury of some plants Virus or viruslike infection Phytotoxicity from pesticides
Spots or sectors of leaves that appear water soaked or have a greasy color	Early stages of high-temperature injury often associated with high light intensity or high temperatures which plants are subjected to when improperly handled during shipment

TABLE 13-1   Foliage plant malady symptoms and possible causal agents (Continued)

Plant part affected and symptoms	Possible cause
	Early stages of cold injury from either low air temperatures or very cold water dropping onto foliage Certain foliar diseases caused by bacterial or fungal pathogens Foliar nematodes in fleshy tissue Early stages of phytotoxicity from improper use of pesticides or fertilizers
Necrosis of leaf margin or tip	Nutrient deficiency: potassium (lower leaves first) Boron excess High soil salinity Fluoride phytotoxicity of susceptible plants High-temperature injury Low-temperature injury Desiccation injury Low relative humidity, particularly indoors Spider mite feeding injury Foliar bacterial diseases Phytotoxicity from pesticides or fertilizers
Necrotic spots or sectors within the lamina	Cold-water injury Leaf miner feeding injury Leaf spot diseases: fungal and bacterial Foliar nematode feeding injury Phytotoxicity from pesticides or fertilizers
Combination of marginal and internal necrotic areas	Sun scorch Cold injury from low air temperatures or very cold water Foliar diseases and injury from several foliar feeding pests Air pollution injury Phytotoxicity from pesticides or fertilizers
Leaves abnormally large	Plants received a high level of nutrition Plants grown under moderate to low light intensity Stock plants not harvested frequently enough Old specimens with large root system
Leaves abnormally small	Plants grown under low nutritional program Lack of copper, which occurs first in new leaves and may be associated with some chlorosis High soil salinity Plants grown under excessively high light intensity Low light and low humidity

(continued)

TABLE 13-1   Foliage plant malady symptoms and possible causal agents (Continued)

Plant part affected and symptoms	Possible cause
	Container-grown plants that become root-bound Root mealybugs or nematodes Root diseases Phytotoxicity from certain pesticides Tarsonemid mite injury
Petiole (leaf stem) too long	Low light intensity
Petiole very short	High light intensity
Lamina (leaf blade) long and narrow	Low light intensity
Lamina short	High light intensity
Lamina very thin	High nitrogen nutrition Low light intensity
Lamina extremely thick	Virus or viruslike disease Phytotoxicity from pesticides High light intensity Tarsonemid mites
Splitting of lamina along margins	Mechanical injury to developing or fully expanded leaves Fluctuating moisture supply Phytotoxicity from pesticides
Cupped lamina	Nutritional disorder Aphid injury Injury from certain mites: broad mite and cyclamen mite Virus or viruslike disease Air pollution Phytotoxicity from pesticides
Abnormally tight rosette pattern of new foliage	Injury from broad mites, cyclamen mites, etc.
Loss of sinuses or holes in new foliage of split-leaf plants	Reduced light intensity, especially once the plants are placed indoors
Leaf margins notched	Mechanical injury Injury from chewing insects Phytotoxicity from pesticide sprays
Translucent-tunnel pattern in foliage	Leaf miner feeding injury
Holes in foliage	Mechanical injury

TABLE 13-1   Foliage plant malady symptoms and possible causal agents (Continued)

Plant part affected and symptoms	Possible cause
	Feeding injury from caterpillars, snails, or slugs Dead areas that drop from leaf after tissue is killed by foliar pathogens Phytotoxicity from pesticides
Windowpane effect (only a thin layer of cells left in damaged area of foliage)	Larvae feeding injury, usually from very small larva
Abnormally glossy leaf surface	Excessive amount of plant polish or plant shine product applied to leaf surface
Solution dripping from edges of foliage that is otherwise dry	Guttation: the loss of water from tiny holes that are present along the leaf margin of some species; most guttation occurs at night and early morning and is a noninjurious physiological process
Defoliation of plant	High soil salinity Plants moved from high to low light intensity Prolonged period in shipping container without light or gas exchange Chilling injury Excessive desiccation between irrigation periods or between propagation mist intervals Reduced humidity Poor soil aeration Injurious soil insects Foliage injury from mite feeding Parasitic nematodes Root rot pathogens Air pollution, especially elevated levels of ethylene Phytotoxicity from pesticides
Stems	
Stem tips stunted	Lack of nutrients such as boron, calcium, or copper Injury from certain mites, including broad mite and cyclamen mite Phytotoxicity from pesticides
Few lateral branches on plants that naturally branch freely	Insufficient light in growing area Close plant spacing
Holes or tunnel in stems	Borers or other larva, such as fungus gnats, feeding on stem
Fasciated stems	Genetic variation Virus or viruslike disorders Herbicide injury

(continued)

TABLE 13-1 Foliage plant malady symptoms and possible causal agents (Continued)

Plant part affected and symptoms	Possible cause
Stem severed at or near soil surface	Cutworm Rodent damage
Basal stem rot or breakdown	High soil salinity Slow-release fertilizer placed against stems Excessive irrigation Poorly drained soils Fungus gnat infestation Fungal pathogen infection Bacterial pathogen infection Phytotoxicity from pesticides
Lesions or cankers on stem	Sun scald Mechanical injury Pest feeding injury Fungal infection Bacterial infection
Foliage and/or Stems Wilted foliage and/or stems	High soil salinity High leaf temperature and cool soil Excessively high temperature Insufficient water supply in soil Low humidity Cuttings or plants not rooted adequately Roots that developed outside of container were severed Root mealybugs or parasitic nematodes Reduced root size from fungal root pathogens
Cracked leaf and/or surface	Mechanical injury
Etched or pitted leaf and/or surface	Excessively high temperature Phytotoxicity from pesticides
Thin cork layer (tan or brown), which develops on leaves and stems as spots or streaks	Thrips or false spider mite feeding injury Certain plant pathogens Phytotoxicity from pesticides
Tip dieback or blight	Deficiency of calcium, copper, or boron Desiccation injury Mites such as broad mite and cyclamen mite Fungal infection Phytotoxicity from pesticides
Epinasty of young shoots and leaves	Aphid feeding injury Virus or viruslike diseases Phytotoxicity from pesticides, particularly some herbicides

TABLE 13-1   Foliage plant malady symptoms and possible causal agents (Continued)

Plant part affected and symptoms	Possible cause
Stems and leaves bent or oriented to one side	A phototropic response to side lighting
Bud and flower drop on some foliage plants with flowers	Temperature extremes Plant moisture stress Low humidity Reduced root system from numerous causes Mechanical injury Ethylene injury Phytotoxicity from pesticides
Stems exceedingly thin and weak, wide spacing between leaves	Excessive fertilizer Inadequate light Tight spacing of plants Temperature too high
Stem thicker than normal and leaf spacing usually very close	High light intensity Wide plant spacing Air turbulence
Unusual amount of red pigment	Phosphorus deficiency Cool temperatures Root rot pathogens Nematodes or root mealybugs
Development of a new color pattern	Segregation of vegetative tissues in a chimeral plant Mutation in meristematic region resulting in a chimera
Loss of variegation	Excess fertilizer Low light intensty in production or holding areas Excess photoperiod indoors Leaf aging in some plants Segregation of vegetative tissues in a chimeral plant
Small, translucent artifacts from living creatures	Molted skins or empty pupa cases from certain insects or mites
Whitish to darker-colored residue on surface of plant	Calcium, magnesium, and sodium compounds found in some water supplies, which leave an objectional deposit on foliage Some fertilizer materials that contribute to deposits on the foliage Residue from certain pesticides, particularly wetable powder formulations of a given compound are preferred for appearance when safe Airborne particulate material adhering to plant
Small inanimate bodies on	Fecal deposits from pests

(continued)

TABLE 13-1   Foliage plant malady symptoms and possibly causal agents (Continued)

Plant part affected and symptoms	Possible cause
surface of foliage or stems or on soil surface	Dead insects Saprophytic fungal spore masses Soil particles Weed seeds Encapsulated or granular fertilizers Pesticide or fertilizer granules
Small, round, or cylindrical-shaped objects fastened to the leaf or stem directly or on a stalk, solitary or clustered	Insect eggs
Green deposit on plant surface	Algae
Sticky substance on plant surface	Honeydew exudate from bodies of aphids, mealybugs, scales, or whiteflies
Black powdery growth on plant surface	Sooty mold fungus growing on the honeydew from aphids, mealybugs, scales, or whiteflies
Loose, powdery material on plant surface	Wind-blown, particulate matter: dusts and soots of various types Pesticide dusts, normally not used
Small, vinelike plant growing on ornamental host with stems attached into the host by means of rootlike structures (haustoria)	Dodder
Brown to rusty red film on foliage	High iron content in water used for overhead irrigation Heavy false spider mite infestation
Fine webbing on leaf or between leaflets	Spider mites and a few other mite species
Glossy or glazed streaks across the surface of foliage, stems, or container	Snails or slugs
Roots Roots very shallow; fail to penetrate deep into the soil	Excessive bottom heat Soil kept too wet Soil-mix texture very fine with few large pore spaces Soil-mix compacted excessively Soil infested with root-rotting fungi, parasitic nematodes, or other root-infesting pests

TABLE 13-1   Foliage plant malady symptoms and possible causal agents (Continued)

Plant part affected and symptoms	Possible cause
Roots exposed at top of container	Inadequate quantity of soil added to container at time of potting Soil washed out by splashing water Excessive soil-mix shrinkage in certain mixes Poor soil aeration Development of extensive root systems in some species, which push the plants upward in the container
Root system slow to develop	Factors listed as causing the previous problem plus: High soil salinity Soil temperature extremes Plant potted too deep Toxic components in soil mixture (e.g., certain types of bark) Phytotoxicity from pesticide drenches
Portions of exposed roots eaten	Snail or slug feeding damage
Root rots	High soil salinity Soil kept too wet Soil-mix texture very fine with few large pore spaces Soil mix compacted excessively Parasitic nematodes Root-rot pathogens, usually fungi
Roots develop extensively through bottom of container	Plant container placed on moist medium that supports root growth Plant left in production area or retail display too long
Knots or swollen areas on roots	Root-knot nematode injury Tuberous roots that develop naturally on some plants
Excessive root system tightly bound in containers	Plants not sold on schedule or not stepped up to a larger container
White or gray fuzzy masses on roots	Root mealybugs present Noninjurious saprophytic fungi
Whole Plant	
Tissue torn or mashed	Mechanical injury during growing, handling, packing, or shipping
Galls on foliage, stems, or roots	Insect oviposition injury and injury from developing immature insects

(*continued*)

TABLE 13-1 Foliage plant malady symptoms and possible causal agents (Continued)

Plant part affected and symptoms	Possible cause
	Bacterial crown gall
Shrinkage of leaf, stem, or root tissues	High soil salinity
	Injurious soil insects
	Parasitic nematodes
	Fungal root rots
	Phytotoxicity from pesticides
Reduced rate of growth without drastic changes in typical plant characteristics	One or more essential elements in limited supply
	Excessive soil salinity
	Soil pH extremes
	Extremely low light levels, usually indoors
	Temperature extremes
	Excessive soil moisture
	Poor soil aeration
	Poorly drained container
	Low humidity
	Seedling variation in some plants
	Pot-bound root system
	Presence of plant pathogens or other pests that affect the root system or vascular system
	Phytotoxicity from pesticides
Small, usually mobile creatures on surface of leaves, stems, or roots	Insects, mites, slugs, or snails
Seeds	
Seeds fail to germinate	Nonviable seeds
	Seeds harvested prematurely
	Seeds stored for excessive periods
	Seeds stored at improper temperature or humidity
	High salinity of germination medium
	Germination medium dried during germination
	Destruction of seeds prior to emergence by rodents, insects, or plant pathogens
Seeds fail to germinate in expected time	Insufficient time for germination
	Impermeable seed coat
	Chemical inhibitors in seed
	Germination medium temperature too low
	Poor soil aeration
Seedlings	
Damping-off	High salinity of germination medium
	Fungal stem and root rot pathogens
Some seedlings are white	Genetic, albino seedlings common to certain species

TABLE 13-1   Foliage plant malady symptoms and possible causal agents (Continued)

Plant part affected and symptoms	Possible cause
Soil	
Organisms on soil surface	Algae
	Mosses or liverworts
	Slime molds, bird's-nest fungi, or other saprophytic fungi
	Some plant pathogens
Weeds	Soil mix improperly pasteurized or fumigated
	Seeds dispersed by weeds established in production area
	Airborne seeds entered production area
	Weed seeds introduced through irrigation water
Small, translucent, capsulelike structures on soil surface or in soil	Capsules from encapsulated, slow-release fertilizer products
White to tan to brown, mustard-seed-like structures massed on soil surface	Resting stage of the pathogen *Sclerotium rolfsii*
White to light-brown, crusty layer on soil surface and pot rim	Accumulated soluble salts
Brownish slippery bodies or dried, somewhat powdery masses on leaf or stems or on soil surface	Slime mold, actively growing and sporulating stages, respectively

during spring months, many growers find a number of plants injured from excessively bright light under structures when shade was not increased to compensate for increased external light levels. Others experience poorer growth during winter months because summer shading levels were maintained during lower light levels of winter. Suggested light intensity ranges for production of selected plants and a detailed discussion of problems arising from too much or too little light are presented in Chapters 9 and 10.

Foliage plant producers, retailers, and interiorscape contractors should be concerned with the light intensity under which plants are grown and displayed. A light meter that measures incident light and reads directly in footcandles or lux units should be part of a professional's equipment. An incident light meter with a range up to 10,000 footcandles is adequate for use in production structures and interiors. An expanded range would permit the meter to be used under full sun in areas where light intensity exceeds 10,000 footcandles.

Temperature Measurement and Regulation

Temperature regulation is critical for maintenance of reasonably vigorous tropical foliage plants. Severe chilling injury or localized injury from cold water dripping onto foliage or where plant parts contact cold greenhouse coverings is frequently striking, resulting in chlorotic and necrotic tissues. Slight chilling of plants, which stunts growth, is a more common problem and is often difficult to diagnose. Retardation of plant growth from chilling makes it difficult, if not impossible, to project production schedules. Temperatures less than 70°F (21°C) will result in significantly less growth with many species than when temperatures are maintained at 70°F (21°C) or above. Cold injury occurs when structures are improperly engineered to provide sufficient heat during cold weather, when heating or air circulation systems fail, when cold-water condensate drips onto plants from greenhouse roofs, when cold water is used for irrigation, or when plants are not properly protected from low temperatures during shipment or relocation within a nursery [18].

Injury may also be caused by excessively high temperatures from ventilation and/or cooling system failure or when plants are elevated in a greenhouse where temperatures are higher than levels where most plants are grown. Plants subjected to above-optimal temperatures are often stunted and, when combined with excessively high light levels, may become chlorotic. Leaves of sensitive plants may partially collapse and/or develop leaf scorch from combined influences of high temperature and excessive light.

Producers should measure temperatures within structures at crop level and keep thermometers and thermostats accurately calibrated. For more specific information on the influences of temperature on foliage plants, techniques of temperature regulation, and specific temperature requirements, refer to Chapter 10.

Soil Mixtures and Water Use

A major problem of growing foliage plants is the lack of free pore space in soil mixes owing to a variety of interrelated factors, including small particle size, biological breakdown of certain particles in a mix, and excessive compaction of soil during potting of plants or plant parts, as discussed in Chapter 7. Root systems decline from lack of oxygen without adequate aeration, and this problem is often compounded by development of fungal root rot organisms that thrive in poorly drained soils. Growers are advised to use the best soil mix components available and to irrigate soils only when required. Use of excessive amounts of water serves to restrict soil aeration, necessitates use of extra fertilizer, and stimulates growth of algae on surfaces of media, a problem that further restricts air movement through soils. Overuse of water is observed more frequently in the foliage plant industry than insufficient irrigation.

Several commercial laboratories are equipped to evaluate the physical and chemical properties of soils and advise growers of appropriate combinations of media to formulate desirable mixtures. Soil tests of this type are an excellent investment for those attempting to improve their present soil mixture, although they are infrequently used.

Soil Salinity, pH, and Testing of Soil and Water

Obvious factors contributing to changes in soil salinity (soluble salts concentration) and pH are the amount and type of fertilizer applied, amount and quality of water used, and quality of soil mix components employed. These and other factors that influence soil fertility and pH are discussed at length in Chapters 7, 8, and 9, respectively.

Many nurseries attempt to handle routine monitoring of soil fertility and water quality on an in-house basis because soil and water can be tested easily for salinity and pH. A good quality Solu-bridge and pH meter plus a few supply items can be purchased to accomplish these tasks. The grower or person assigned to operate a nursery laboratory can quickly determine if total soluble salts or pH of irrigation water or soil solution are within acceptable limits with a few basic instruments.

Suggested ranges for both pH and Solu-bridge readings for water and foliage plant soil mixes are presented in Chapters 7 and 8, respectively.

Testing Soil, Water, and Plant Tissue Samples for Specific Elements or Ions

Soil and water tests for specific elements or ions and plant tissue tests for total nutrient composition are usually handled by specialized laboratories associated with state universities or private diagnostic firms that specialize in ornamental plant problems. The latter point is especially important since interpretation of test results from laboratories dealing primarily with crops other than ornamentals is often inadequate. Soils used for container-grown foliage plants and nutritional programs for ornamentals are unique, so they require sample processing and interpretation of test results by someone familiar with these crops if recommendations are to be meaningful. Test results from different laboratories can be made only if the analytical procedures used by the laboratories are the same. Differences in analytical procedures usually account for variations in test results, especially in soil testing, where the extraction technique has tremendous influence on results. Services of a single laboratory should be used to assure accurate comparisons over a long term, assuming service and charges by the firm are satisfactory.

Certain measurements in soil test reports, particularly the soluble salts values, can shift quickly, depending upon amount of fertilizer or amount of water applied. Even where soluble salts levels in soil test reports are within acceptable limits, injury from high salinity might have occurred earlier.

Records of soil and water tests and plant tissue analyses should be retained so they can be plotted for each crop tested. Records of this type permit growers to understand the influences of changes in crop culture on soil and plant analyses report data. Maintenance of records on pests and other disorders found on specific plants as they are determined is also desirable. A compilation of diagnostic information over a period of time will provide the producer with an invaluable data base for solving future problems. The optimum ranges of essential elements in leaf tissue of selected foliage plants are listed in Chapter 9.

Phytotoxicity from Pesticides Applied to Plants

Reduction in plant growth and blemishes that lessen product quality are always possibilities when agricultural chemicals are applied to crops. Phytotoxicity from fertilizers and pesticides is discussed in considerable detail in Chapters 9, 14, and 15.

Only products that are labeled for foliage plants or ornamental crops and tested on an experimental basis under the production environment should be used. Accurate records of materials used, their concentrations, and other factors will assist in linking a specific injury symptom to the use of a particular fertilizer, pesticide, or other chemical.

Air Pollution

Occasionally, greenhouse operators encounter air pollution problems caused by improper combustion of fuel in heating units. Ethylene is usually the primary gas responsible for pollution injury. Relatively inexpensive kits are available that measure propylene and acetylene concentrations in parts per million. Kits of this type are often used in deep mines where dangerous gases accumulate and are sold through many safety supply firms. Sampling of greenhouse air for toxic components should be done on cool nights when structures are closed and heaters are operating.

Ornamental plants are severely damaged from exposure to airborne pollutants that originate outside greenhouses or production areas in many parts of the country. Such air pollutants fall into several categories, including products of photochemical reactions with airborne hydrocarbons and nitrogen oxides, pollutants such as sulfur dioxide and fluorides released to the air by certain industries, combustion products, particularly ethylene, accidental spillage of materials like ammonia and chlorine, and pesticide drift, particularly of herbicides, applied outside production areas [8, 9].

Crop injury from pollutants originating outside growing areas may be difficult to prove. Assistance from local Cooperative Extension Agents, pollution control agencies at state and national levels, local meteorologists, and independent consultants may be necessary to associate and document the cause with the injury. Metering instruments can be used in a few instances when air pollutants are sustained at an injurious concentration for an appreciable period beyond the point where crop injury is observed. The kit mentioned previously for testing greenhouse air may be useful if certain gases such as sulfur dioxide are suspected. Unfortunately, some crop injury is caused by relatively short exposure to an aerial pollutant, which makes detection of that pollutant difficult or impossible with conventional monitoring equipment.

Water and Soil Pollution

Introduction of pollutants into surface or subsurface water supplies and/or soil components used for foliage plants has increased with widespread use of herbicides and accidental spillage of other types of industrial and agricultural chemicals. The same agencies indicated for air pollution should be contacted when pollution of soil or water is suspected. The manufacturer of a suspected chemical pollutant can often provide laboratory assistance to determine if an injurious level of their product is present in water or soil.

Mechanical Injury to Plants

Cracked, torn, or crushed foliage, bruised or broken stems or roots, and scraped or torn bark are a few examples of mechanical injury, which usually result from improper plant handling [17]. Mechanical injury can occur at any stage of plant culture from seed or stock plant through finished product, but it happens most frequently during packaging and shipping. The quality of ornamental plants is dependent upon perfection; therefore, mechanical injury should be avoided at any time during production, packaging, and shipping.

Most mechanical injury is obvious immediately after it is inflicted, and diagnosis of the cause is usually easy; but sometimes several steps in the culture and/or plant handling processes must be studied to determine the specific cause of injury.

Collection of Crop History Information

Foliage plant problem diagnosis should be a thorough, systematic process with no substitutes for examination of fresh plant material. The appearance of healthy foliage plants must be known before deviations in appearance of color, leaf shape, vigor, and the like, can be recognized.

Some plant abnormalities caused by different agents are similar in appearance, which makes it important to obtain detailed crop records before attempting to determine their cause. Occasionally, several factors injure or induce abnormal growth not attributable to a single cause. The foliage plant diagnostic form (Figure 13-3) can serve as an outline for collection and tabulation of basic information on crop environment and cultural procedures needed to determine many plant disorders. A benefit of using a diagnostic form partially completed by the producer is that the data requested require the producer to recall environmental elements, cultural procedures, chemical treatments, and other factors used in the production cycle. Frequently, a grower will suspect a particular factor when he or she has completed the form simply from having been forced to review and outline the crop production program. For such a form to be a useful tool, it must be completed as accurately and thoroughly as possible.

The plant diagnostic process should continue with examination of the aerial plant parts to note changes from desired or normal growth or presence of pests. Restricted growth or slight changes in morphology may be difficult to detect in rare or unusual plants unless some healthy plants are available for comparative purposes. Determine whether abnormal plants received the same treatment as healthy ones of the same type that are located nearby and if additional plant species in the area have the same or similar symptoms. Most disease-causing organisms and some other pests are highly specific to individual plant species or closely related plants. A general problem on all plant types in a production area is not indicative of those caused by pathogens or other pests.

Information provided by producers and reports from analysis of soil, water, and plant tissue may not provide sufficient information to establish the problem source, and specialists may need to visit the production location to review all aspects of the crop environment inside and

COMMERCIAL FOLIAGE PLANT DIAGNOSTIC FORM

(One form should be completed for each plant problem) _____

Date Submitted

Part A. PRODUCER INFORMATION AND CROP HISTORY (Producer should complete Part A):

Nursery	Mailing address	
City	County	State	Zip code

Contact person _____ Telephone number _____

Crop _____ Crop age _____

Symptoms of injury or crop problem: _____

_____

Distribution of problem: _____ General _____ Localized _____ Scattered
Severity of problem: _____ Slight _____ Moderate _____ Severe

Date problem was first observed: _____

Crop environment: Plants in:

____ Under glass, fiberglass, or plastic film   ____ Containers on raised benches
____ Under fabric shade or lath shade   ____ Containers on ground
____ Open field   ____ Planted in raised benches
   ____ Planted in ground beds

Light intensity (footcandles or lux units) or percent shade (estimated): _____

Soil mixture (indicate amendments—peat, sand, bark, etc.—and percent by volume): _____

_____

Other soil amendments—(Dolomite, microelements, etc. Indicate type and amount.): _____

_____

Soil treatment: Irrigation system:

____ Steam pasteurization   ____ Pot watering tubes
____ Chemical fumigation (indicate chemical)   ____ Drip irrigation hoses on benches or
     beds
____ None   ____ Overhead sprinklers
   ____ Hand water with hose
Fertilizer program: ____ Capillary mat ( ) or bench ( )

Analysis _____
Rate applied _____   Irrigation frequency:
Frequency applied _____   Once every __ days
     (Indicate number of days)

Fertilizer application technique

____ Incorporated into soil mixture
____ Liquid on soil surface
____ Dry on soil surface

Temperatures in production area: Days: ____ to ____ °F   Nights: ____ to ____ °F

Pesticides—(Insecticides, miticides, fungicides, herbicides, or other chemicals applied):

Material and formulation used	Concentration applied	Date of application
_____	_____	_____
_____	_____	_____
_____	_____	_____

(*continued*)

Figure 13-3.   Foliage plant diagnostic form.

Part B. TEST REPORTS: (Producer should complete those portions which are applicable):

Soluble salts of soil extract: (ppm) _____ pH: _____

Other test results from plant tissue, soil, or irrigation water samples, if available: _____

_____
_____
_____
_____

Part C. REFERRALS: (Producer should complete those portions which are applicable): _____

_____ Sample & copy of diagnostic form referred to: _____

Name

Firm or Institution

Mailing address

| City | State | Zip code |

Part D. DIAGNOSIS AND RECOMMENDATIONS: (To be completed by diagnostic institution or firm):

Diagnosis: _____
_____
_____
_____

Recommendations: _____
_____
_____
_____

Person making recommendation: _____

Date: _____

outside production structures. Often plant problems develop in specific patterns recognizable by specialists, which provide valuable clues as to the cause.

Symptoms of Plant Injury

Descriptions of plant problem symptoms should be prepared carefully using terms familiar to trained horticulturists. A partial list of terms used to describe plant disorder symptoms follows:

Atypical leaf shape: Leaves that are distorted or misshapen owing to phytotoxicity, disease-causing organisms, feeding by insects, mites, or nematodes, nutritional disorders, or environmental factors.

Blight: Diseases caused by pathogens that kill primarily new expanding tissues of shoots and young leaves. Most blights are attributed to fungal and bacterial pathogens.

Blotch: Irregular spot diseases that vary in shape and lack a clean line of demarcation between infected and noninfected tissue.

Burn: A nontechnical term applied to a variety of injury symptoms induced by pesticide sprays, excessive light, excessive fertilizer, excessively high temperatures, and pollutants.

Canker: Commonly localized, sunken lesions on stems that may crack open as they develop. Most cankers are caused by fungi or bacteria.

Chlorosis: The lack of chlorophyll in plant tissue, usually the foliage, giving it an abnormal light green to yellow coloration. Chlorosis can be caused by nutrient deficiencies, nutrient excesses, nutrient imbalances, root rots, insect or mite feeding, excessive light, chilling injury, or phytotoxicity from pesticides or pollutants.

Damping-off: The decay of seeds or roots and/or stems of seedlings near the soil line. It is usually caused by soil-borne fungi.

Decay: A broad term that describes breakdown of tissues caused primarily by fungi and bacteria.

Defoliation: Loss of leaves caused by a number of factors, including root rots, insufficient or excessive water in the root zone, low nutrition, pesticides, wounding, high atmospheric ethylene or other toxic gases, and chilling.

Dieback: A condition where shoots are killed back by varying degrees depending upon severity of injury or disease infestation. Most dieback of pathogenic origin is caused by fungi or bacteria.

Dwarfing: A nontechnical term that refers to restriction of plant growth, usually through manipulation of cultural procedures. Pruning, restriction of root zone, and withholding nutrients and water will dwarf most plants when done individually or collectively. Chemical growth retardants or phytotoxic effects of pesticides may also dwarf plants.

Epinasty: Curled and contorted leaves and stems developed from plants that have been exposed to growth regulators such as 2,4-D, and similar phenoxy compounds, on ethylene gas or plants that have been fed upon by certain insects that induce abnormal growth. Other factors, including pollutants, may also induce epinasty.

Fasciation: Plant organs or axes that abnormally grow together or become flattened, resulting in an abnormally irregular, thickened configuration of such organs, such as stems, leaves, flowers, and fruits. The cause of most fasciations is not well understood.

Gall: Swollen abnormal growths that assume a variety of shapes and sizes and can occur on practically any plant organ. Some galls are hollow; others are nearly solid tissue. They may be induced by insects, mites, nematodes, bacteria, and fungi.

Gumosis: A condition within vascular systems of stems, usually caused by systemic bacterial or fungal pathogens, which causes a gumlike exudate to be emitted from stem surfaces.

Lesion: Wounds on plant surfaces, which are usually induced by disease-causing organisms, mechanical means, pests, or through contact with phytotoxic chemicals.

Mold: The development of fungal mycelia (hairlike branches) and spores over the surface of infected tissues on decaying organic material.

Mosaic: An abnormal pattern of coloration usually expressed in the foliage, but may also be found in flowers and other plant organs. Mosaics may range from slight chlorotic patterns to stunning variegated patterns in some plants. Most mosaics are caused by viruses or mycoplasmalike organisms and often result in reduced plant vigor.

Mottling: A stippled pattern of chlorosis, which often develops when leaves have hosted spider mites, leafhoppers, or thrips. Mottled patterns can be induced from the application of pesticides, deficiency of essential elements, and exposure to pollutants.

Necrosis: Dead plant tissue, which has been caused by a variety of factors, including disease-causing organisms, pesticide phytotoxicity, pollutants, certain pests, temperature extremes, and others. Such tissue is usually tan, brown, or black in color.

Oedema: A physiological disorder that results when plants absorb water faster than it is lost through evapotranspiration, causing cells to swell and rupture certain soft tissues, often on the underside of foliage. Such wounds usually heal as cork-covered bumps.

Residue: Foreign material on plants, which often is sufficiently conspicuous to detract from plant quality. Residues originate from various sources, including pesticide sprays, especially wetable powder formulations, mineral deposits from irrigation water, aerial particulate matter, and others.

Rot: Deterioration of plant tissue caused by a plant pathogen, usually a fungus or bacterium. Some rots have foul odors; others are relatively odorless, depending upon the pathogen or secondary organisms involved.

Scorch: A collective term that includes necrotic areas usually caused by excessive light levels, often coupled with high temperatures, which destroys foliage and/or stem tissue.

Spindly vegetative growth: Describes plants grown under dark conditions that have stems that elongate excessively and become thin and weak. This is a nontechnical term.

Spots: Caused by disease-causing organisms, primarily fungi and bacteria, chemical injury, and certain environmental factors. Spots vary in size, shape, and color and occur primarily on foliage and stems.

Stunts: Diseases caused by specific systemic organisms such as fungi, bacteria, and viroid particles that reduce the rate of water and food movement within infected plants and drastically slow growth.

Wilt: Plants that cannot absorb water to replace that which is lost through evapotranspiration owing to blockage of vascular tissues from systemic plant pathogens have a category of diseases known as wilt. Plants also wilt from moisture stress caused by numerous other factors.

Witches'-broom: A condition that results in proliferation of shoots from specific regions of a stem. It can be caused by pathogens on some hosts, by insects and mites on others, and by boron or copper deficiencies.

REFERENCES

[1] Abraham, Doc, and Katy Abraham. 1976. *Houseplant Rx.* Barrington, Ill.: Countryside Books. 119 pp.

[2] Baker, Kenneth F. 1972. *The U.C. system for producing healthy container-grown plants.* Manual 23. Division of Agricultural Sciences, University of California. 331 pp.

[3] Dickey, R. D. 1977. Nutritional deficiencies of woody ornamental plants used in Florida landscapes. Bulletin 791. Agricultural Experiment Stations, Institute of Food and Agricultural Sciences, University of Florida, Gainesville, Fla. 63 pp.

[4] _____, and J. N. Joiner. 1966. Identifying elemental deficiencies in foliage plants. *Southern Florist Nurseryman* 79(20):38, 42, 43.

[5] Furuta, Tokuji. 1974. *Environmental Plant Production and Marketing.* Arcadia, Calif.: Cox Publishing Company. 232 pp.

[6] Hamlen, R. A., D. E. Short, and R. W. Henley. 1978. Detection and identification of insects and related pests of the commercial foliage industry. Circular 432. Florida Cooperative Extension Service, Institute of Food and Agricultural Sciences, University of Florida, Gainesville, Fla. 23 pp.

[7] Hartman, Hudston T., and Dale E. Kester. 1975. *Plant Propagation—*

Principles and Practices, third ed. Englewood Cliffs, N.J.: Prentice-Hall. 662 pp.

[8] Hindawi, Ibraham J. 1970. Air pollution injury to vegetation. National Air Pollution Control Administration Publication No. AP-71. Washington, D.C.: U.S. Government Printing Office. 44 pp.

[9] Jacobson, Jay S., and A. Clyde Hill. 1970. *Recognition of air pollution injury to vegetation—A pictorial atlas.* Pittsburgh, Pa.: Air Pollution Control Assoc. 128 pp.

[10] Kiplinger, D. C. 1975. Pointers on diagnosing problems with foliage plants. *Ohio Florists Assoc. Bull.* 554:5–8.

[11] Knauss, J. F. 1973. Common diseases of tropical foliage plants. I—Foliar fungal diseases. *Florists' Rev.* 152:26, 27, 55–58.

[12] _____. 1973. Common diseases of tropical foliage plants. II—Bacterial diseases. *Florists' Rev.* 153:27, 28, 73–80.

[13] _____. 1974. Common diseases of tropical foliage plants. III—Soil-borne fungus diseases. *Florists' Rev.* 154:66, 67, 114–121.

[14] _____. 1977. Diagnosis of foliage plant problems indoors. *Proceedings of 1977 National Tropical Foliage Short Course,* pp. 123–129.

[15] Laurie, Alex, D. C. Kiplinger, and Kennard S. Nelson. 1968. *Commercial flower forcing,* seventh ed. New York: McGraw-Hill. 514 pp.

[16] _____, and Victor H. Ries. 1950. *Floriculture—fundamentals and practices,* second ed. New York: McGraw-Hill. 525 pp.

[17] Marousky, F. J., and B. K. Harbaugh. 1978. Deterioration of foliage plants during transit. *Proceedings of 1978 National Tropical Foliage Short Course,* pp. 33–39.

[18] Mastalerz, John W. 1977. *The greenhouse environment.* New York: Wiley. 629 pp.

[19] Nelson, Kennard S. 1967. *Flower and plant production in the greenhouse show.* Danville, Ill.: Interstate Printers and Publishers. 335 pp.

[20] Nicholls, Richard. 1975. *The plant doctor.* Philadelphia: Running Press. 108 pp.

[21] Pechnold, Paul C., Walter R. Stevenson, and Donald H. Scott. 1976. Plant disease control—house problems. BP-1-12. Cooperative Extension Service of Purdue University, West Lafayette, Ind. 4 pp.

[22] Pirone, Pascal P. 1978. *Diseases and pests of ornamental plants,* fifth ed. New York: Wiley. 556 pp.

[23] Poole, R. T., and C. A. Conover. 1976. Use of microelements in foliage plant production. *Florida Foliage Grower* 13(9):3–6.

[24] Post, Kenneth. 1949. *Florist crop production and marketing.* New York: Orange Judd Publishing Co. 891 pp.

[25] Westcott, Cynthia. 1960. *Plant disease handbook,* second ed. New York: Van Nostrand Reinhold. 825 pp.

[26] _____. 1964. *The gardner's bug book,* third ed. Garden City, N.Y.: Doubleday. 625 pp.

fourteen

J. F. Knauss
S. A. Alfieri, Jr.
R. B. Marlatt
F. W. Zettler

foliage plant disease

Disease Conditions

Diseases in plants are often misunderstood and occasionally mistaken for other factors that cause plant damage. In simplest terms, plant disease results from the interactions of the three basic factors shown in the following diagram:

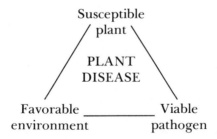

Susceptible plant

PLANT DISEASE

Favorable environment _____ Viable pathogen

Disease only occurs when the three factors of the disease triangle are present simultaneously. The absence of any one or more of these factors will result in no disease.

The Susceptible Plant

The susceptible plant is the entity that becomes diseased; it is often referred to as the "suscept" or "host" to denote its generic inability to inhibit invasion of disease-causing plant pathogens when environmental conditions favorable for disease development are present. Plants differ in their susceptibility depending on the type of tissue attacked, with one part possibly susceptible and other parts of the same plant seemingly resistant. This is evident in many pathogens that cause only leaf spots or root rots. Susceptibility or resistance to pathogen attack is related to the physiological status of tissue, presence or absence of mechanical or biochemical barriers, and influence of prevailing chemical, physical, and biological environments.

The Pathogen

Pathogen is the term given the agent (fungus, bacterium, virus, or mycoplasm) that invades and usually develops within a susceptible plant causing disease symptoms, the plant's response to the pathogen's presence. The pathogen's ability to develop and cause disease is determined by its genetic complement, which is, in turn, influenced by certain chemical and physical environmental factors.

The Environment

The environment probably plays the most important and moderating role and is generally the most difficult to control of the three major factors affecting disease development. The environmental factors that are most influential are moisture and temperature.

Moisture is present within the environment in the soil, in and on the plant, and in the air. Moisture normally affects plant disease development in varying degrees. Free moisture on foliage (except for powdery mildews) is necessary for fungal spore germination and bacterial invasion. Moisture at various levels in the soil is necessary for pathogen development and survival, while high levels of humidity in the atmosphere and subsequent condensation favor attacks by foliar and basal stem pathogens.

Temperature affects plant disease in a variety of ways. Many disease problems only occur at certain times of the year, usually because of the direct effect temperature has upon growth and increase in pathogens. As might be expected, warm and hot weather pathogens when tested for growth under laboratory conditions have been found to grow at optimum rates at or near the temperatures under which the disease they cause is most severe. When temperatures are reduced, plants tend to grow slower and become more hardened, frequently resulting in some degree of resistance to pathogen invasion. A possible exception would be prolongation of the susceptible seedling stage by temperatures less than optimum for best growth.

When sufficient temperature changes occur between day and night, the relative humidity within growing structures may reach 100 percent and condensation will occur. Wetting of foliage from condensation is no different from that caused by overhead irrigation and, if of sufficient duration, can promote pathogen activity and subsequent foliar disease.

Disease Development and Foliage Plant Culture

Production Under Full Sun and Shade

Foliage plants, especially larger types, are often grown in open sun or under slat or plastic screen shade houses. Such plants are exposed to natural elements and require different disease considerations than those grown under more manageable conditions of glass- or fiberglass-covered structures.

Wood treated with preservatives to slow rotting is often employed in the construction of shade houses used for outside production. Creosote and pentachlorophenol preservatives should be avoided as their vapors are toxic to plants, and this toxicity can be mistaken for disease. A more satisfactory material for wood preservation is copper naphthenate.

Foliage plants grown outside should be in slightly raised ground beds since soil in these beds may be infested with many plant pathogens and should be treated to eliminate such pathogens prior to planting. Methyl bromide alone or in combination with chloropicrin is the fumigant most widely employed to kill pathogens, nematodes, insects, and weed seeds. This material is applied to prepared soil in an area covered with a plastic sheet that has the edges sealed with soil or boards to prevent gas escape. Pots or flats should be placed on the soil before laying the plastic to elevate the plastic sheet off the soil surface and provide space to contain the methyl bromide gas during a suggested treatment period of at least 24 hours. A 48-hour aeration period or more is needed for the fumigant to dissipate from the soil after removing the plastic and prior to planting. Chloropicrin, a more thorough but more expensive soil fumigant, is normally applied in furrows 12 inches apart that are immediately closed by tractor-drawn equipment. Wetting the soil surface seals in the fumigant and a plastic sheet is not needed. Chloropicrin is applied at 480 pounds per acre with at least a 2-week aeration period required after treatment. Methyl bromide and chloropicrin are very poisonous if inhaled, and chloropicrin can cause eye damage. Careful handling is required when using these compounds, especially when their use is confined to areas such as a shade house. The use of respirators and airtight goggles by operators is necessary.

Media employed in growing potted plants outside should be treated by fumigation, free-flowing steam pasteurization, or aerated steam treatment to eliminate plant pathogens. Aerated steam treatment is preferred where possible because it is less costly than free-flowing steam, does not eliminate all soil antagonists or competitors of pathogens, has a quicker cool down time, and is safer for workers.

Plants grown in direct sunlight or shade houses are exposed to prevailing weather conditions. Cold temperatures injure or kill foliage plants; thus their production outside is limited to subtropical and tropical areas. Air temperatures below 50°F (10°C) are known to injure certain foliage plants, and low soil temperatures also can prove unsuitable for their growth. The subtropical and tropical areas are preferred areas of production, and in these locations soil temperatures may reach levels high enough to be injurious to roots next to pot walls. Dark-colored containers absorb more of the sun's infrared or heat waves, and soil temperatures on sunny sides of dark metal or plastic pots may reach lethal temperatures of 130° to 140°F (54° to 60°C). The injured plants may have healthy roots on only one side, a symptom of decay that can easily be mistaken for a fungal root rot. Employment of light-colored containers should be considered where hot soils might be a problem.

Another consideration in open or shaded areas is the use of potting mixes suitable to prevailing weather conditions. Subtropical and tropical areas often have rainy and dry seasons, and potting media used during rainy seasons must allow excellent drainage to discourage activities of water-loving pythiaceous pathogens belonging to the genera *Pythium* and *Phytophthora*.

Rain and overhead irrigation, common in outdoor culture, provide an effective mechanism for dissemination of fungal and bacterial pathogens. Little can be done about rain, but overhead irrigation applied less frequently and when good drying conditions exist will enable foliage to dry quickly, thus assisting in foliar disease control. Foliar sprays of disease control compounds are required every 3 to 7 days during wet seasons and every 10 to 21 days at other times of the year to grow quality plants outside.

Rain and overhead irrigation cause splashing, which assists in moving soil-borne pathogens from infested soil into and among pots, containers, and ground beds; thus containers less than 1 foot tall should rest on high pallets or on benches raised above splash height. Containers are often placed on plastic sheets to discourage splashing of soil and to assist in weed control. Drainage of irrigation water or rain can be a problem with this cultural method. Indentations in plastic sheets caused by pot weight can hold water sufficiently deep to prevent drainage from side holes, causing roots in the continually water-saturated bottom of such containers to suffer from lack of air. Water-saturated media are ideal for development of root diseases caused by species of *Pythium* and *Phytophthora*. Pots containing soil mixes that drain poorly and stay saturated for long periods are prime targets for root diseases when grown outdoors, especially where poor drainage of surface water is common.

Production under Permanent Cover

Production of ornamental tropical foliage plants under structures with permanent cover (glass, fiberglass, plastic, and so on) is increasing. Permanent cover assists in control over environmental variabilities, which is fundamental to provide freedom from disease and production of quality foliage plants. Permanent structures for plant growth are practical and realistic in control and manipulation of environmental variables such as temperature, light, humidity, water, and nutritional requirements that enhance plant growth in the absence of disease-causing organisms.

Permanent structures for growing plants To assure growth of healthy plants, structures should (1) be free from leaks or cracks that could provide entry of rain or soil that may aid in pathogen dissemination, (2) be equipped with adequate temperature, humidity, and aeration controls, (3) be furnished with watering systems that minimize excess foliar wetting, (4) provide sufficient light for healthy plant growth, (5) be equipped with raised benches for growing plants and cement walkways to minimize hazards of contamination from ground areas, and (6) have a pathogen-free source of water, since recycled irrigation water can lead to many plant disease problems [210].

Healthy stock plants Starting production with stock plants free of pathogens is of primary importance to quality plant production. Other precautions in the control of plant diseases are essentially negated if stock plants are diseased and introduce pathogens into propagative areas with eventual carry over to finishing and sales areas. Whenever possible, stock should be obtained from nursery owners or specialist propagators that have pathogen-free stock. Growers can often improve existing stock by taking tip cuttings, growing plants on frames [130], controlling certain environmental factors, employing certain culturing methods (tissue culture indexing), heat treatment of propagative plant materials, chemical treatment for pathogens carried externally, and roguing. Detailed information is available on methods to obtain and maintain clean propagative stock [19].

Stock plant area   Growing stock plants on raised benches or beds ensures a greater degree of control over plant diseases compared to ground beds. In raised beds, the type of growing medium (soil) can be manipulated and heat treated by pasteurization or aerated steam to free it of pathogens while reducing the risk of recontamination. Advantages of pasteurization and aerated steam treatment have been verified and supported by others [25, 26, 44, 45, 53, 57, 75]. The use of aerated steam and controlled temperature treatment of soils has been fully discussed [20, 160, 196]. Soil for plant growth in greenhouses also can be treated chemically, usually with a material having fumigant action capable of eliminating most plant pathogens. Some common treatments are methyl bromide, ethylene dibromide, chloropicrin, Vapam, and formalin. These compounds are utilized for soil preplant treatment, since they are phytotoxic. They also are hazardous to personnel and require cautionary measures relative to proper equipment in safe handling. Their effectiveness is dependent on a number of factors, such as the temperature, moisture content, and tilth of the soil at the time of treatment [19, 53, 175, 206].

Plant propagation area   Foliage plant propagation should be carried out on raised benches containing media free of plant pathogens. Peat is an important component of soil media employed for growing foliage plants and should be from pathogen-free sources, especially if used in media that will not be treated with heat or by fumigation. Peat from shallow bogs previously cropped to vegetables or ornamental plants should be fumigated or steam pasteurized prior to use, because it usually contains plant pathogens [96]. Following suitable growth and plant removal from propagation benches, extraneous plant tissue should be removed and new peat added to replace that utilized in the propagation of the preceding crop, and the bench steam pasteurized and leached prior to reuse. If steam pasteurization is impossible, the medium should be fumigated or a preventive soil fungicide program utilized to achieve as low a population of pathogens as possible. Materials employed in preventive soil fungicide programs will be noted later and are normally applied as a preplant dip for cuttings or cane pieces and/or as a drench to propagative media. Drench treatments should be made prior to planting leafy cuttings and immediately after sticking nonleafy cuttings, cane sections, or seed [96]. Drenches applied should be at recommended concentrations and rates since poor results can occur if used otherwise. Foliage plant species should be rotated where unsterilized media must be used. Some foliage species especially prone to greater disease losses when cropped repeatedly in the same medium without sterilization are species of the genera *Syngonium, Epipremnum* (pothos), *Aglaonema, Dief-*

fenbachia, Brassaia (schefflera), *Chamaedorea* (neanthe bella palm), and *Peperomia.*

Plant finishing area   Rooted plants should be transplanted into clean or new pots containing noninfested potting media. Tools, equipment, benches, and work areas should be clean or disinfested and free of old plant debris to eliminate risks of dissemination of plant pathogens to noninfested plants, soil, or growing areas. Without attention to these factors, apparently healthy foliage plants occasionally will progressively deteriorate in finishing or holding areas because they were infected at the time of potting or contaminated during potting with infested media. An unclean, pathogen-infested potting work area and careless transportation and hauling of healthy plants can contribute to infection and later disease development. A broad-spectrum soil fungicide drench soon after potting is often a good practice. Normally, a single treatment suffices for most plants, but treatment should be made once every 3 months for plants held in the nursery over extended periods of time [96]. Additional measures that aid in reducing disease development due to soil-borne pathogens include (1) the use of well-aerated, well-drained soil mixes, (2) careful irrigation, and (3) placement of potted plants on surfaces that allow unrestricted drainage, such as an adequately firm wire mesh screen or similar material.

Foliar Fungus Diseases of Foliage Plants

Foliage plant production employs intensive methods of culture and long-term maintenance of stock sources that enhance the probability of disease caused by foliar-attacking fungi. The demand for blemish-free plants by consumers requires as complete control of foliar pathogens as possible. This at times has resulted in excessive fungicide use that could have been avoided had growers a better understanding of how and why foliar fungal diseases developed.

Pathogenic fungi may be spread by irrigation and/or rain or may be airborne and therefore do not require moisture for dissemination. Foliar infections are initiated when fungal infective units (usually spores) have been in contact with susceptible plant tissue for a sufficient length of time under proper environmental conditions for spore germination and tissue invasion. For each pathogen-plant combination, the optimum time of foliar wetting and temperature requirements for spore germination, invasion, and disease development usually will differ somewhat, causing certain diseases to appear during particular times of the year. Knowledge of environmental conditions necessary for the preceding spore germination aids growers in determining and forecasting when certain diseases will develop.

Fungi that cause foliar spotting exist and persist primarily on living, infected plants or in debris that has accumulated from previously diseased plants. Spore survival in some cases may occur in soil media, thereby making soil sterilization or fumigation essential in total disease-control programs. Pathogen genera such as *Botrytis* and *Cercospora* are ubiquitous and are easily disseminated to susceptible plant tissue. Pathogens of this type can be controlled culturally only by eliminating foliar wetting and long periods of condensation.

In foliar attacks, a variety of symptoms may result, depending upon the specific pathogen-plant combination, their physiological state at the time the attack occurs, and the duration of environmental conditions optimum or conducive to disease development. Spots and blights commonly occur after fungal invasion of foliage. Spots may be varied in color, necrotic, may have chlorotic margins, and in many cases a definite transition zone will be evident between diseased and apparent healthy tissue. In some cases (many *Cercospora* infections) (Figure 14-1) raised leaf swellings that are called edemas may appear. Leaf blights refer to infections that seemingly encompass all healthy tissue, causing rapid death and decay. With this type of infection, dark-colored necrotic tissues usually are most evident, with noticeable evidence of the pathogen present in the form of mycelium or reproductive structures. Multiplicity of diseaselike symptoms occur on tropical foliage plants (in addition to

Figure 14-1.   Typical symptoms of *Cercospora* on *Peperomia obtusifolia*.

true foliar fungal diseases) that are caused by physiological (noninfectious) factors such as excessive or deficient nutrition, injuries from environmental factors (light, temperature, water, gases, particulate matter in the atmosphere), insects, and handling by personnel. Such problems are difficult to diagnose and often require the opinions of specialists.

Foliar fungal pathogens of foliage plants are numerous and varied [3, 5, 6, 8, 11, 13, 37, 53, 64, 82, 83, 91, 100, 105, 123, 128, 130, 143, 153, 154, 165, 174, 175, 183, 189, 194, 200, 203, 221, 226, 228, 233, 236]. Some common and economically significant genera of fungus pathogens occurring on tropical foliage plants follow.

Alternaria

This genus [29, 168] occurs universally and may be found on dying and necrotic debris or in soil; it is disseminated by wind, splashing rains, and irrigation water. It is the most serious foliar pathogen of *Brassaia actinophylla* [100, 149, 152, 228] and causes disease on *Coleus, Fatsia, Gynura, Polyscias* [228], and *Passiflora* [175]. This fungus is a particular problem during warm months when excessive wetting of foliage occurs for long durations, especially where plants are watered overhead and crowded together. Leaf spots on schefflera may range from small circular to large irregular tan to dark, brownish black lesions. A chlorotic halo may develop around lesions, with the entire leaf eventually turning yellow and abscissing from the plant. Dark brown to black petiole and stem cankerous lesions may occur, but are less common.

Ascochyta

This genus is not generally a serious leaf pathogen of foliage plants, but it occurs on *Aspidistra* [13], *Coffea* [190], *Rumohra* (leatherleaf fern) [80, 82], and *Clusia* (autograph tree) [228]. This pathogen is the worst under cool, wet environmental conditions.

Botrytis

This genus exists as a saprophyte or pathogen and has a broad host range. It can be serious and destructive to tropical foliage plants when proper conditions exist and is referred to as "gray mold," because infected tissue is usually covered with a thick mat of fuzzy, moldy growth of spores and mycelium of the pathogen. It can cause serious problems on *Aphelandra* [228], *Begonia* [13, 228], *Coleus* [13], *Dracaena* [228], *Ficus* [3, 175, 228] (Figure 14-2), *Nephrolepis* [13], *Pilea* [228], and *Saintpaulia* [13, 53, 175, 228, 233] and has been noted on other foliage plant types. The

Figure 14-2.   *Botrytis* infection on *Ficus elastica* 'Decora'.

fungus usually attacks dead or senescent plant tissue, using this as a good base for the development and production of toxic metabolites that kill healthy plant tissues in advance of its movement. Thus, during times of the year when environmental conditions (warm days and cool nights) promote condensation necessary for *Botrytis* development, growers should be especially careful to control plant injury. Proper spacing of plants to allow adequate aeration and drying, removal and destruction of infected leaves and debris, application of proper protective fungicides, careful watering to avoid foliar wetting, and environmental management to discourage condensation will aid in controlling this pathogen.

Cephalosporium

This fungal genus has been noted only on a few foliage plants, but caused considerable losses before industry changed to modern cultural practices and management. Lesions appear usually as small, circular or irregular bright reddish-brown leaf spots with pale yellow margins. Infection takes place on nonmature leaf tissue, with hundreds of spots on a single leaf not uncommon. Hosts are *Syngonium* [12, 114] (Figure 14-3), *Dieffenbachia* [13, 53, 115], *Ficus* [13], and *Aglaonema* [228].

Figure 14-3.   Leafspots on *Syngonium* produced by *Cephalosporium*.

Cercospora

This versatile, universally present fungus attacks an extremely wide range of plants; it has a host list in excess of 2,500 named plant species. *Cercospora* attacks foliage, producing definite spots (often having chlorotic margins) or small edemalike swellings on plants such as *Peperomia* [3], *Pilea*, and *Brassaia*. Soft rots are never produced. Spores (conidia) are usually produced in abundance on dying and necrotic host tissues and are spread by wind, splashing rain, overhead irrigation, insects, and people [145]. Disease development is most severe during warm periods coupled with high humidity. Important hosts are *Asparagus* (asparagus fern) [13, 228], *Asplenium, Begonia* [37, 228], *Ficus* [123, 228], *Coffea* [13, 37, 221, 228], *Cordyline, Hedera, Nephrolepsis, Pilea, Platycerium, Epipremnum* (pothos), *Araucaria* [228], and *Codiaeum* [37, 228].

Figure 14-4.   Leaf infection on *Hedera helix* caused by *Collectotrichum*.

Colletotrichum

Worldwide in distribution, this pathogen genus causes many serious diseases of economic crops. Symptoms caused by *Colletotrichum* are generally referred to as anthracnose because of the nature of the lesions produced. Within the lesions normally appear fruiting structures that contain dark black, sterile, hairlike projections called setae, which can be viewed easily with a 10× to 20× hand lens, making field diagnosis easy. Dissemination occurs mainly by splashing water (rain or irrigation). *Colletotrichum* has been reported on *Coffea* [13, 228], *Araucaria* [179], *Dracaena, Pilea* [72], *Codiaeum, Dieffenbachia, Ficus, Hedera* [181, 228] (Figure 14-4), *Aspidistra* [13], *Dionaea* (venus fly trap) [85], and *Philodendron* [228]. Elimination of foliar wetting and proper sanitation are important in eliminating *Colletotrichum* from growing areas.

Corynespora

This genus occurs frequently on foliage plants and its role is not clearly understood. On *Aphelandra* [143] it causes black necrotic spots on injured leaf tissue. It has also been reported on *Brassaia, Hedera, Hoya,* and *Peperomia* [228].

Coniothyrium

Though uncommon on foliage plants, this genus causes a severe disease of *Yucca* [224] that can be particularly devastating outdoors or under covered structures where foliage remains wet for long periods. The spots are small, numerous, oval, slightly sunken, and initially appear light brown with a dark center. Mature spots turn dark brown to black and may show concentric rings of light and dark leaf tissue. Spots coalesce to produce larger necrotic areas of varying shapes and sizes.

Curvularia

This genus apparently does not have a wide host range on foliage plants, but causes necrotic leaf spots and distortion on *Rhoeo* [153, 228].

Cylindrocladium

This genus can be a leaf-spotting and root-rotting pathogen. It generally attacks plants during warm, wet months. The primary hosts among tropical foliage plants are *Rumohra* (leather leaf), *Nephrolepsis*, *Asparagus* (asparagus fern), and the palms, *Chamaedorea* and *Howea* [200].

Cytosporina

Though rare as a pathogen of foliage plants, this genus causes a disease of *Yucca* called gray leaf spot and tip necrosis [224]. Lesions are large and gray with a brown margin, often with concentric zones of dark to light color. The gray part of the lesions contains visible, small black spots, which are the fruiting bodies of the fungus.

Dactylaria

This genus is a common pathogen of *Philodendron scandens oxycardium* [105] grown under warm to hot, wet and humid conditions where foliage remains wet for extended periods and splashing occurs. It is particularly prevalent where plants are grown in ground beds under slat or saran cover. Only immature, developing leaves are susceptible. Infection is prominent on the leaf undersurface and appears as numerous, yellowish green to tan circular lesions that collapse in the center and give the appearance of insect feeding. When viewed from the upper surface, lesions are circular and prominent yellow.

Erysiphe

This genus is representative of the group of fungi called powdery mildews. These are obligate parasites attacking leaves and tissues such as young shoots, buds, and fruits and producing a characteristic thatch of white or near white powdery growth, from which they derive their name. The spores (conidia) are extremely light and powdery and easily distributed by the wind. Powdery mildews do not require free moisture on the foliage for germination and infection and are in fact inhibited if foliage stays wet for long periods. They are rarely seen in subtropical or tropical areas but may be important in cooler climates. Nevertheless, they can be destructive pathogens, rendering plants unsightly and unsalable. *Erysiphe* occurs on *Begonia* [163, 175, 223], *Hedera* [13, 175, 233], and *Gardenia* [175, 233].

Exosporium

This genus causes a common leaf spot of palms [129] and appears initially as minute, circular, tan spots that are transparent when held to light. The lesions develop to become circular to elongate, depressed and light brown in color, with a dark brown to black center, entirely surrounded by a diffuse yellow halo. Lesions may eventually coalesce to form irregularly shaped spots.

Fusarium

This genus is an important leaf-spotting pathogen affecting tropical foliage plants. It generally produces light chlorotic spots that mature to become reddish brown in color. Leaf distortion is common, since only young developing leaf tissue is subject to attack. *Fusarium moniliforme* is a species that can cause serious leaf spotting on *Cordyline* [228], *Dracaena* and *Pleomele* [226, 228] (Figure 14-5), and *Sansevieria* [13, 53, 228].

Gloeosporium

In addition to its perfect state *Glomerella,* this genus is not generally considered a serious anthracnose pathogen but can cause damage to plants that have been injured or are under stress. Spores are disseminated by splashing rains or water, insects, and birds [216]. *Gloeosporium* occurs on *Hedera* [64], *Ficus* [221], *Dracaena* [13, 233], *Sansevieria* [13, 228], *Caladium* [233], *Begonia* [13, 175, 233], *Codiaeum* [13], *Crassula* [175, 233], *Dieffenbachia* [228, 233], *Fatshedera,* and *Hoya* [228]. Chemical control is generally not necessary if ornamental foliage plants are maintained free of injuries.

Figure 14-5.   Typical leaf spots on *Dracaena marginata* produced by *Fusarium moniliforme*.

Gliocladium

This genus is capable of causing considerable damage on several ornamental palms [142, 178]. The first symptoms of infection appear as dark brown necrotic areas on stems at the soil line or as much as 2 to 3 feet up the stem on large specimens. Oozing gum is often found associated with the necrotic areas. Frond death is preceded by necrotic streaks from the base of the rachis outward, with pinnae often turning yellowish brown on one side of the rachis. Masses of pink spores of the fungus are evident on infected leaf sheaths and stem tissue. The disease appears to be favored by cool weather and extended periods of foliar wetting from rain and/or overhead irrigation.

Helminthosporium

This genus is not particularly common to foliage plants but causes leaf spots that can pose a serious production problem on *Caladium* [13],

Aechmea [128], asparagus fern [13, 228], the palms *Chamaedorea, Chrysalidocarpus, Howea,* and *Rhapis* [228], and *Cactus* [180].

Leptosphaeria

This genus causes a leaf spot of *Dieffenbachia* [120] and *Monstera* [228] and has been found to produce stem cankers on *Codiaeum* [228]. Older leaves of *Dieffenbachia* are more susceptible and may exhibit numerous brown lesions, ranging from several millimeters to several centimeters in size. Severely infected leaves turn yellow, collapse, and die. The disease is most prevalent during late winter and early to mid-spring months, especially if plants are not under permanent cover and in ground beds where extended wetting from rain and/or overhead irrigation occurs. Proper culture can effectively control this disease.

Myrothecium

This genus is rarely reported as a serious pathogen of foliage plants but has been found on necrotic leaf tissues of *Aeschynanthus, Aglaonema, Ajuga* [228], *Dieffenbachia, Gardenia* [233], and *Peperomia*. It has never been proved conclusively as a pathogen on these plants, but the high degree of association of the pathogen with young developing lesions suggests the possibility of pathogenicity. It most commonly occurs under warm to hot, wet and humid conditions. Sanitation, environmental management, and careful attention to provide control of the pathogen in stock areas will greatly aid in eliminating this problem.

Phomopsis

Generally, this genus is a stem-inhabiting wound pathogen, but occasionally it occurs on leaves. It causes stem cankers on *Gardenia,* which results in stunted, weakened, and dull green plants [4, 53, 141, 175, 233] and produces leaf spots on the palms *Chrysalidocarpus, Caryota,* and *Phoenix* [228], on *Codiaeum* [228], and on *Crassula* [233]. Employment of disease-free propagating stock, "clean" soil, and pruning equipment, minimizing plant injury, avoiding splashing water, and dipping of cuttings in ferbam [4, 43] aid greatly in pathogen control.

Phyllosticta

This genus occurs on a wide range of host plants. Leaf spots are usually discrete, with a definite border of contrasting color that may have a chlorotic margin. Among its hosts are *Epipremnum* [13, 175],

Figure 14-6. Leaf spots on *Philodendron scandens oxycardium* produced by *Phytophthora.*

Cissus [233], *Clusia* [13], *Codiaeum* [13, 175], *Coffea* [221], *Fatshedera* [228], *Hedera* [13, 53, 175, 228, 233], *Cordyline* [13, 195, 228], *Dracaena* and *Ficus* [195, 228], *Pteris* [233], *Aechmea* [228], *Beaucarnea* [228], *Begonia* [13], *Calathea* [13, 228, 233], *Chamaedorea* [228], *Coleus* [13], *Dieffenbachia, Fatsia* and *Monstera* [228], *Nephrolepsis* [13, 228], and *Philodendron* [228].

Phytophthora

The genus name means "plant destroyer," a fitting description for this serious foliar pathogen of some foliage plants. It causes spots or blights of *Cordyline* [214], *Philodendron* [183, 184] (Figure 14-6), *Dieffenbachia* [91, 100], *Brassaia* [234], and *Monstera* [228], which if unchecked under favorable environmental conditions can severely affect plant foliage. Infection by this pathogen occurs primarily where plants are close to soil and where splashing and extended periods of wetting are produced from rain and/or overhead irrigation. Where plants cannot be grown on raised beds, providing a suitable barrier between the plant and soil to prevent splashing of soil will help to eliminate this aid to infection. Growing under permanent cover in raised beds employing nonwetting watering techniques will control foliar attack.

Puccinia

This genus is a rust fungus that may be important and serious on rare occasions on foliage plants. Rusts get their name from their characteristic lesions, which produce numerous reddish brown spores giving affected tissue a rusted appearance. It has been reported on asparagus fern [228], *Calathea* [13], *Codiaeum* [228], *Saxifraga*, and *Ruellia* [233]. Providing for good aeration among plants, reducing relative humidity, and avoiding overhead irrigation are effective aids in the control of this pathogenic group.

Rhizoctonia

This genus occurs as a serious pathogen on a wide array of plants and is capable of attacking any plant part. It is common in most natural soils and most serious in attacking underground plant parts. Affected leaf or stem tissue rot become a wet, brownish black, which normally turns tan to brown upon drying. Diagnosis of this problem is usually easy because fungal strands of this pathogen are normally evident on and between infected foliage, matting them together and making them difficult to pull apart. Foliage plants affected in this manner are *Brassaia*, *Philodendron, Epipremnum, Pilea, Syngonium* [91, 100], *Gardenia* [175], and undoubtedly many others. Noninfested soil, noncrowding of plants, maintenance of dry foliage, and proper fungicide application are important in control of this pathogenic group.

Sphaceloma

This genus is not common on many foliage plants. It causes malformation of leaves and produces raised, roughened growths on stems, fruits, and leaves. Foliage plants affected by this pathogen include *Codiaeum, Dizygotheca* [228], and *Hedera* [13, 175, 233]. Selection of healthy propagative material and planting stock, elimination of foliar wetting, and applications of effective fungicides will control this pathogen group.

Stemphylium

This genus is rare as a pathogen of foliage plants, but it can cause a serious disease of *Kalanchoe* [199]. Symptoms resulting from infection on this host have been attributed to a physiological condition called edema but are truly the result of the activity of *Stemphylium*. Infection occurs on both leaf surfaces and appears normally as circular 2- to 15-millimeter, brown to black, raised, often corky lesions. This pathogen is normally disseminated in splashing water and can be effectively controlled by keeping foliage dry.

Cephaleuros virescens

This parasitic alga is mentioned in this section because it is often mistaken for a fungus and may be common on tropical and subtropical plants that tend to have leaves of smooth, somewhat stiff, leathery texture. Normally restricted to upper leaf surfaces, it is commonly called "green scurf" because of its grayish green color and rough texture [7]. It occurs on a wide range of plants, such as *Ardisia, Brassaia, Clusia* [13], *Citrus* [51, 161], *Coffea* [13, 221], *Fatshedera, Ficus* [228], *Gardenia* [175, 233], *Hedera* [228], *Platycerium* [228], and *Sansevieria* [228].

Bacterial Diseases of Foliage Plants

Published reports of tropical foliage plant diseases caused by bacteria are less numerous than those caused by fungi, but these diseases are nevertheless among the most insidious and difficult to control. Bacteria affecting foliage plants are prevalent and rapidly disseminated in the warm to hot subtropical and tropical environments where sufficient moisture provided by rain or overhead irrigation is usually present.

Plant pathogenic bacteria are small, one-celled microorganisms that do not form resting spores or resting structures comparable to those of fungi and nematodes. Bacteria remain dormant, yet viable, in association with seeds, perennial plant hosts, insects, plant residues, soils, and other nonhost materials [41].

Cells of many bacterial pathogens have one or more whiplike appendages called flagella to assist in their micromovement, but these appendages have little to do with their spread and dissemination. Bacterial pathogens are probably moved from place to place or plant to plant in and/or on (1) splashing water produced by rain or overhead irrigation, (2) hands, tools, cutting knives, or shears that become infested in handling diseased materials, (3) infested or infected plant materials moved into clean areas, (4) infested or infected seed, and (5) possibly windblown soil [32, 38] or vectors such as nematodes [176] or insects [41, 52, 170, 191].

Bacteria normally invade plant tissues through wounds or natural openings such as stomata, hydathodes, nectaries, or lenticels, with free moisture on the plant surface greatly facilitating invasion. The major reservoir of foliage plant bacterial pathogens is stock plants used for

propagation. These plants often contain bacterial pathogens that go undetected, thereby allowing bacterial pathogens easy access to noninfested
propagation, potting, and finishing areas in cuttings taken from them.
Bacteria also persist under dry situations, which promote extended survival in plant residues. Plant pathogenic species of *Xanthomonas*, for
example, have remained viable and pathogenic in dry, infected plant
tissue for years [169, 193]. Plant residues on or near soil surfaces in
nurseries provide situations more favorable to bacterial survival than
plant residues that have been incorporated into the soil. Bacteria may
also exist as natural residents in or on apparently healthy plant parts
such as shoots, stems, leaves, and buds [76, 193], and those persisting in
this manner can serve as a primary inoculum for subsequent disease
initiation [65]. Latent bacterial infections can go unnoticed [69] until an
external physical force causes injury to the infected, symptomless plants
[215], thereby providing the stimulus for symptom development.

Figure 14-7. Typical leaf spots on *Syngonium* caused by *Erwinia chrysanthemi.*

Figure 14-8.   Foliar infection of *Dieffenbachia amoena* by *Erwinia chrysanthemi*.

Diseases Caused by Erwinia chrysanthemi

This is the single most destructive bacterium affecting foliage plants. Initially discovered on *Chrysanthemum,* from which it derives its species name [36], it probably attacked this host plant from the Florida plant ecosystem when the chrysanthemum industry began out-of-doors in Florida in 1949 [217]. Shortly after this there was evidence of the pathogen on *Philodendron* [151], *Syngonium* [109] (Figure 14-7), *Aglaonema* [140], *Dieffenbachia* [23, 136, 164] (Figure 14-8), and other foliage plants.

Erwinia chrysanthemi is not restricted to foliage plants and chrysanthemums. Scientists working with floricultural and bedding plants have found it to be the causal agent in diseases of *Saintpaulia* [107], *Begonia* [187], *Dianthus* [112, 205], *Dahlia* [188], orchids [30], *Euphorbia* (poinsettia) [73], *Sedum* [30], and shasta daisy [30, 36]. Edible crops such as carrot [213], corn [78, 131], sweet potato [109], and pineapple [113] have been found naturally infected with this disease organism. Plants found susceptible when experimentally inoculated include cabbage, cauliflower, celery, eggplant, lettuce, morning glory, onion, pepper, petunia, potato, radish, tobacco, tomato, and turnip [23, 30, 187]. The potential host range of this pathogen is wide, and undoubtedly many other foliage plants will be found to be susceptible.

Symptoms induced by *E. chrysanthemi* may result from systemic (internal) invasion, usually seen as a yellowing, collapse, and wilting of foliage. Often also present is a rapid, mushy decay of stems, especially at and near the soil line.

The environment plays a major role in symptom expression with *E. chrysanthemi* infected plants. Infected stock or production plants grown under cool and/or dry conditions may not exhibit noticeable symptoms, and can go undetected, but plants grown from cuttings taken from these stock sources may rapidly exhibit symptoms of collapse, wilt, and necrosis when warm to hot, wet conditions prevail. Culture-indexed material should be used where possible, but if unavailable, plants or cuttings destined to be stock plants should be selected when environmental conditions conducive to optimum disease development exist to lessen the likelihood of selecting infected stock.

A mushy collapse of stem tissues often accompanied by a foul odor develops rapidly when infected cuttings are exposed to optimum conditions. Cuttings of some species of *Aglaonema, Dieffenbachia, Dracaena,* and *Philodendron* often exhibit this form of decay. If environmental conditions necessary for rapid disease development exist in the stock areas, infected stock plants exhibit an identical rapid collapse at the cut stub remaining after removal of cuttings. Rapid decay of propagative cane pieces of *Dieffenbachia, Aglaonema, Syngonium,* and others also can occur when propagation units are infected with this pathogen.

The pathogen can cause foliar infection if disseminated aerially. Evidence of such infection is seen initially as a discrete water-soaked, usually greasy appearing spot, which may enlarge rapidly and coalesce with other spots to result in a mushy foliar collapse typical in *Aglaonema* [140] and various philodendrons [151], particularly *Philodendron selloum, P. bipennifolium, (panduraeforme),* and the hybrid *P.* 'Florida' (Figure 14-9). Discrete spots having a peppered appearance upon drying are more common on the undersurface of infected leaves of *Syngonium* [109].

Invasion by *E. chrysanthemi* of some foliage plants, such as *P. selloum,* may produce all the preceding symptoms plus several more. When optimum conditions for disease development are present, attacks on *P. selloum* can result in total destruction of all plant tissue within a relatively short time [108, 151]. Even root tissue is susceptible to attack in infections to chrysanthemums [36] and poinsettias [73]. Root attack by this pathogen on foliage plants is probably more common than is recognized. Diagnosticians of plant diseases should be aware that root decay symptoms resulting from invasion by *E. chrysanthemi* may be identical to

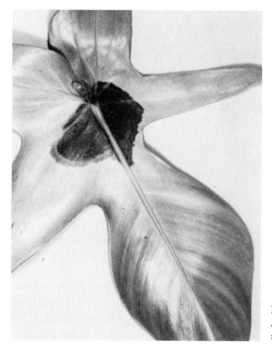

Figure 14-9. Foliar infection of *Philodendron* 'Florida' caused by *Erwinia chrysanthemi*.

those resulting from invasion by pythiaceous fungi [36, 108] and should therefore determine the identity of the causal agent by appropriate means and not on visual symptoms alone.

Diseases Caused by Erwinia carotovora

This bacterium is commonly associated with decay of vegetables, particularly storage organs [216], although there are a few reports of this pathogen on foliage plants [33, 106]. Recently [220], it has been indicated as the probable cause of disease on *Aglaonema, Anthurium, Aphelandra, Cactus, Caladium, Chlorophytum, Crassula, Dieffenbachia, Dracaena, Epipremnum, Ficus, Maranta, Monstera, Philodendron, Sansevieria, Syngonium,* and others. It is widespread within the foliage plant industry and is responsible, alone or in combination with other pathogens, for many diseases affecting overall production.

Infection by *E. carotovora* occurs on all types of plant tissues and closely resembles in symptomatology disease caused by *E. chrysanthemi.* In *Sansevieria,* for example [33], it causes chlorosis and water-soaked spotting of the foliage. The leaves collapse and fall over, and a basal rot and straw-colored discoloration of the rootstock occurs. In advanced stages the roots shrivel and desiccate.

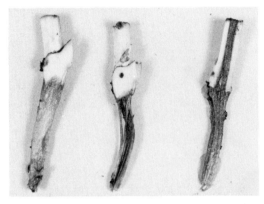

Figure 14-10. Rapid cutting decay of *Epipremnum* caused by *Erwinia carotovora*.

Rapid decay of *Epipremnum aureum* [106] due to *E. carotovora* was noted in 1961 [135]. It can act alone on this host, but may attack in conjunction with the fungus *Pythium splendens* [88], thereby causing major difficulty in controlling *E. aureum* decay.

Erwinia carotovora invades leaves and petioles of potted *E. aureum* and the stems, leaves, and petioles of unrooted and rooted cuttings. Infections can occur through intact plant tissue but are enhanced by wounds in the plant epidermis. Initially, infected tissues have discrete water-soaked, grayish green areas that enlarge rapidly, become mushy, and turn brown to black, eventually resulting in the complete collapse of the affected plant units. If the environment becomes dry during disease development, lesions turn a dry, brownish black, often with yellow margins. Cuttings taken near vine apexes and those taken from rapidly growing vines are most susceptible to the pathogen. Infection of unrooted cuttings usually occurs through cut ends or locations where aerial roots have been removed (Figure 14-10); the resultant decay eventually progresses into the petiole and lamina of parent leaves. Complete collapse of cuttings can occur within 2 to 4 days. Parent leaves of cuttings attacked by *E. carotovora* usually turn a bright yellow as the result of stem infection.

Diseases caused by *E. carotovora* often appear as rapid, mushy decays of leaves, petioles, cuttings, or propagative cane sections. As with vegetables, a foul odor may accompany invasion and is usually detected during the rotting process. Rots caused by this pathogen are favored by extended periods of warm to hot, wet weather, and physical injury to the susceptible plant generally intensifies disease development.

Diseases Caused by *Xanthomonas* spp.

Relatively few diseases caused by members of the bacterial genus *Xanthomonas* have been recorded on tropical foliage plants, the earliest being a report of a disease of *Hedera helix* caused by *Xanthomonas hederae*

Figure 14-11. Typical leaf spots of *Hedera helix* caused by *Xanthomonas hederae.*

[35, 49] (Figure 14-11). Only the foliage is attacked, with initial symptoms appearing as small, circular, water-soaked spots, which are more visible when viewed from the under surface of leaves. The spots enlarge into circular to angular areas with greenish brown, water-soaked margins and reddish brown to black centers as the disease develops. Frequently, a chlorotic yellow halo surrounds older lesions. On older leaves where lesions develop and infected plant tissues have gone through subsequent wetting and drying, the water-soaked margins tend to disappear, and necrotic tissue in the lesions usually cracks upon drying. This disease can be particularly severe on this host when warm to hot temperatures exist and long periods of foliar wetting are prevalent.

Probably the most important pathogen of foliage plants within *Xanthomonas* was first observed and described in 1939 on *Dieffenbachia picta* [134] and subsequently named *X. dieffenbachiae*. On this host, only leaf tissue, excluding midrib and petiole, is susceptible. Initially, infection appears as tiny, translucent specks that enlarge from several millimeters to 1 centimeter in diameter. Individual spots are circular to elongate and yellow to orange yellow in color. Close examination reveals central areas of dull, watery, green tissue surrounded by a border of orange brown with an irregular outer margin. Lesions appear translucent with a pale greenish yellow center and a bright yellowish orange color when viewed with transmitted light. Lesions located near leaf veins fail to expand beyond them. Usually, many reddish brown specks are noted in a ring between the lesion center and its outer margin. During unfavorable conditions for disease development, young lesions do not enlarge and remain as small, dry, red-brown specks. Infection sites coalesce to form large lesions that wilt, become yellow, and dry when infections are numerous and conditions are favorable for disease development, and leaf tissue adjacent to such areas becomes yellow and dies. A few lesions, strategically located, can result in the death of large areas of a leaf. Dead leaves appear dull tan or light brown, are thin and tough (not brittle), and the lesions appear dark brown by reflected light and pale green and translucent when viewed by transmitted light. Considerable exudation, consisting mostly of bacteria, is prominent on lesions on the lower surface of infected leaves. The exudate is soft when moist, but upon drying, becomes waxy, with a thin silvery white layer covering, which occasionally flakes off from the lesion. Only during advanced cases of the disease does this exudate appear on the upper leaf surface.

Although first observed on dieffenbachia, *X. dieffenbachiae* was first noted in 1963 [138] and described [139, 222] on its most important host plant *Philodendron scandens oxycardium*. In the period 1963 to 1971, *X. dieffenbachiae* was disseminated to this host throughout most of the foliage plant industry, resulting in the industry's most pressing disease problem.

It remains today a common and important disease problem. Few stock areas of *P. scandens oxycardium* are completely free of this pathogen, because the pathogen moves rapidly within the industry and is facilitated by the sale of infected plants from grower to grower. Disease symptoms appear 7 to 10 days after infection and are small water-soaked leaf spots that soon become yellow, with centers turning brown with increased age. The most common symptom is a yellowing along leaf margins, initiating at the pointed leaf tip. During hot, wet weather, infected leaf margins become necrotic and turn reddish brown, a symptom leading to the common name "red edge" given it by growers. The affected leaf turns yellow, drops from the stem, and that node is practically useless as a propagative unit. Extensive leaf drop within stock areas severely limits the number of cuttings available. Infected leaves appearing free or nearly free of the pathogen when planted into propagative beds often turn yellow and die soon after planting. The disease is most active during the warm, wet periods and may be present but go undetected when cooler temperatures persist. Only leaves appear to be attacked.

Xanthomonas dieffenbachiae is reported also to be the causal agent of diseases of several species of *Aglaonema* [137] and *Anthurium andraeanum* [68]. On *Anthurium* it causes a serious leaf disease characterized by diffused, water-soaked, firm spots, 1 to 5 millimeters in diameter that are surrounded by a chlorotic halo. New leaves are attacked as they unfold, resulting in a general decline or blight of entire plants. The pathogen is capable of entering both injured and uninjured leaves and is reported to be isolated from vascular elements of petioles and stems of plants exhibiting foliar symptoms.

On *Anthurium, Xanthomonas dieffenbachiae* produces different symptoms, depending on the age of susceptible leaves. On older leaves, angular, pale brown, necrotic spots, 1 to 3 millimeters in size and surrounded by a yellow chlorotic halo are produced, and on the undersurface of these older leaves, dried flakes of bacterial exudate are often present on or around necrotic spots. Infections of younger leaves result in dark brown to black lesions surrounded by a pale chlorotic halo, but evidence of the scaly bacterial exudation is less obvious. Lesions are variable in size, often angular and vein delimited or irregular and extending along the midrib for several centimeters. Blackened lesions on younger leaves often extend from the midrib along and between branched veins, sometimes encompassing all the enclosed leaf area. Severely affected leaves appear torn and distorted. Similar symptoms are observed on the spathe, where black elongated spots extend along branched veins, sometimes filling the entire enclosed areas. No disease symptoms have been observed on stems, petioles, or the spadix.

A bacterial disease of *Syngonium* spp., especially severe on *S. podophyllum* 'Green Gold,' is produced by *Xanthomonas vitians* [223]. First reported as the cause of a leaf and stem rot of lettuce [34], *X. vitians* can cause foliar disease on *Syngonium* that can produce considerable damage. Characteristic symptoms are large, water-soaked lesions along leaf margins and tips often forming elongated areas of diseased tissue extending toward midribs. Lesions initially appear dark green, gradually turn yellow, and later become brown and necrotic. A bright yellow zone often separates lesions from healthy-appearing leaf tissue, and as with *X. dieffenbachiae,* white flakes of dried bacterial exudate are often present on the undersurface of the older lesions. Experimentally, this pathogen has been found to cause a rot and collapse of *Syngonium* propagative units after inoculation. Cuttings taken from vines showing severe leaf infection often rot during propagation, especially under warm to hot, wet environments.

A report [158] in 1977 indicated two species of *Pellionia* and *Pilea cadierei* susceptible to an unnamed species of *Xanthomonas,* with the same bacterial organism found to cause a foliar disease of *Aphelandra squarrosa.* The disease appears restricted to the foliage on all four hosts and can severely affect production. Infections on *Pellionia* result in numerous circular lesions first appearing water soaked, later turning brown, and eventually dropping out of the affected leaf, leaving shot holes. The lesions on *Pilea* and *Aphelandra* begin as greasy, gray, water-soaked areas particularly evident on the lower leaf surfaces; large leaf areas often limited by leaf veins may subsequently become invaded. Infected areas usually turn brown, collapse, and cause abscission of the affected leaves.

An additional member of this bacterial genus, *Xanthomonas vasculorum*, is reported to cause a disease of *Chrysalidocarpus lutescens* [172]. This host planted in locations where royal palms infected with *Xanthomonas vasculorum* were removed developed what was described as a chlorotic condition on the older leaves, and, when examined by transmitted light, affected leaflets had long, faint, yellowish brown veins extending from the dead areas. *Xanthomonas vasculorum* was isolated from the diseased leaflets. The importance of this disease to the foliage industry has yet to be determined.

Diseases Caused by *Pseudomonas* spp.

Members of this bacterial genus have been found on some foliage plants, and a common disease within this group is caused by *P. asplenii* on *Asplenium nidus* [15]. Initial symptoms of infection are small, water-soaked, translucent spots generally found on the upper surface of the frond, which under warm, humid conditions rapidly expand and cover the entire leaf surface. Affected areas become translucent and necrotic, resulting in eventual death of the frond. Necrosis of one or more fronds destroys the symmetrical appearance of the plant and renders it unsalable. The pathogen enters the leaf anywhere on the leaf lamina, but commonly enters via the hydathodes at the apex of fronds.

Pseudomonas cichorii is best known as a pathogen of escarole, cabbage, celery, and chrysanthemum. It was isolated in 1966 from diseased leaves of *Epipremnum* [228], and experimental inoculations of several foliage plants showed that species of *Epipremnum, Aglaonema, Monstera,* and *Philodendron* were susceptible. Species of *Caladium, Syngonium,* and *Anthurium* were found moderately susceptible. *Spathiphyllum* spp. are also listed as host plants [228] of this pathogen.

Natural and experimentally produced lesions on foliage plants caused by *P. cichorii* are usually brownish black and appear 4 to 7 days after infection has taken place, with the lighter and darker zones particularly noticeable on *Epipremnum* (Figure 14-12). In inoculations on *Monstera deliciosa,* a yellow halo around the affected area (Figure 14-13) is particularly prominent [227].

An unnamed species of *Pseudomonas* has caused serious foliar problems on *Dracaena sanderana* [157]. This disease possibly originated on cuttings imported from outside the United States. Symptoms first ap-

Figure 14-12. Leaf spot of *Epipremnum* caused by *Pseudomonas cichorii.*

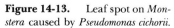

Figure 14-13. Leaf spot on *Monstera* caused by *Pseudomonas cichorii.*

Figure 14-14. Typical leaf blight on *Caryota mitis* caused by *Pseudomonas alboprecipitans.*

pear as circular to irregular water-soaked spots that may form anywhere on the leaf blade, with a thin, reddish brown margin occasionally forming around water-soaked centers and diffuse chlorotic patterns developing around the lesions. The spots continue to enlarge, and affected areas turn papery and dry. Severely infected leaves become brown and necrotic, and the stem or cane tissue does not appear susceptible to attack.

A disease of *Cordyline terminalis* is caused by *Pseudomonas* sp. in Hawaii in out-of-door production areas [218]. The pathogen causes water-soaked, slender, long stripes between veins, and the stripes become darker as the disease progresses, ultimately resulting in the falling out of affected tissue. The extent to which this disease occurs in this host in other tropical foliage production areas is still largely unknown.

The number of actual reported cases of diseases caused by *Pseudomonas* are few in the foliage industry, but they may be more common and go unrecognized.

A severe foliar blight of *Caryota mitis* was discovered in 1977 and found caused by *Pseudomonas alboprecipitans* [110]. The disease appears initially as transluscent, water-soaked areas that surround brown longitudinal lesions. The lesions are varied in length but are mostly parallel to the leaf veins (Figure 14-14). The mature lesions are brown to black, become necrotic, and are often surrounded by a chlorotic margin.

Soil-Borne Fungal Diseases
of Foliage Plants

Soil-borne fungi are the most destructive and prevalent pathogen group affecting tropical foliage plants. Diseases caused by these pathogens are generally most severe in the warm and hot, wet and humid months; in the subtropical and tropical growing regions, the most important members, *Pythium, Phytophthora,* and *Rhizoctonia* spp. can cause disease problems year round.

These pathogens exist in soil, soil water, or in or on infected root, crown, and foliar tissue as actively developing mycelium, spores, or resting structures such as sclerotia or chlamydospores. These structures, especially spores, sclerotia, and chlamydospores, may also exist on tools, equipment, pots, benches, flats, shoes, or other items that may harbor bits of pathogen-infested soil.

Soil-borne fungi may be disseminated to noninfested areas in or on infected plants, by infested items mentioned previously, by infested water employed for irrigation, through infested soil media, and on soil particles displaced from infested outdoor areas during severe wind storms. Pathogenic soil-borne fungi are sometimes moved on the bodies of soil-inhabiting pests.

Soil-borne fungal pathogens normally invade plant tissues at or below the soil line, and disease development is usually well underway before symptoms are noted on plant parts aboveground. Where extended periods of wet foliage, high humidity, crowded plants, and splashing water persist, some of these pathogens (*Rhizoctonia* and *Sclerotium*) are capable of growing up stems and petioles and invading foliar tissue. *Phytophthora* may attack foliar tissue directly where sufficient splashing occurs. Young succulent tissues are most susceptible to soil-borne pathogen attack, with resistance or tolerance to infection increasing usually with host plant maturity.

Cultural and greenhouse management practices are significant factors in the control of soil-borne fungal pathogens. Taking care to employ only pathogen-free pots, benches, tools, plants, and soil media, and growing only in raised benches under permanent cover will help control soil-borne pathogens. Proper greenhouse management and sanitation will minimize the need for excessive use of chemicals in the control of this pathogen group.

Diseases Caused by *Rhizoctonia*

The name of this pathogen comes from Greek and means "death of roots." Its importance as a destructive plant pathogen was clearly described by Baker [21], who stated that "*Rhizoctonia solani* probably causes more different types of diseases to a wider variety of plants, over a larger part of the world and under more diverse environmental conditions than any other plant pathogenic species." *Rhizoctonia* overwinters and survives successfully as thick-walled mycelia and in the form of sclerotia in the soil and on plant debris. It attacks a large number of crop plants in Florida, is considered the most destructive fungus in the state, is statewide in distribution, infests all types of soil, and causes diseases year round. All plant parts are attacked, but generally it does the greatest damage to roots. *Rhizoctonia* root rots are common on *Aglaonema, Aloe, Araucaria,* asparagus fern, *Zygocactus, Coleus, Codiaeum, Dizygotheca, Fatshedera, Sansevieria, Syngonium* [228], *Begonia* [13, 64, 175, 228, 233], *Aphelandra, Caladium, Chamaedorea, Dieffenbachia* [93, 96], *Cordyline* [175, 228], *Dracaena* [175], *Fittonia* [175, 228], *Hedera* [13, 19, 175, 228, 233], *Philodendron* [19, 93, 96, 175, 228], *Platycerium* and *Pleomele* [228], and *Saintpaulia* [13, 228, 233]. *Rhizoctonia* may produce a severe aerial (foliar) web or thread blight during propagation or when plants are crowded in growing areas on *Rumohra* [82], *Nephrolepsis* [83], *Carissa, Dracaena, Epipremnum* (Figure 14-15), *Hoya, Pilea, Syngonium* [228], and *Fittonia* [233]. It also causes stem and tuber decays during propagation, these being especially serious on *Aglaonema* [19, 93, 96, 175], *Dieffenbachia* and *Syngonium* [19, 93, 96], *Aphelandra, Ardisia, Maranta,* and *Pilea* [93, 96], *Scindapsus* [82, 93, 96, 159], *Araucaria* and *Pellionia* [19], *Hoya* [84, 93, 96], *Gynura* [84, 90, 93, 96], *Brassaia, Chamaedorea,* and *Monstera* [93, 96, 228], *Coleus* [228], *Fittonia* [19, 21, 175, 228] *Peperomia* [19, 53, 93, 96, 165, 228], *Philodendron* [19, 82, 93, 96, 175, 228], *Hedera* [13, 19, 175, 228, 233] and *Aechmea, Alsophila, Fatsia,* and *Fatshedera* [228].

Normally, identification of aboveground *Rhizoctonia* infections can

Figure 14-15.   Foliar blight of *Epipremnum* caused by *Rhizoctonia.*

be made in greenhouses or nurseries by growers, since it produces prominent reddish brown mycelium resembling fine threads or webs that may be seen on diseased tissue. Usually, the mycelium or threads can be noted on the soil surface radiating among soil particles in and among areas of infected plants. Infected leaves that rest upon the propagation medium will usually resist lifting when raised slowly, because mycelial threads are firmly attached to the soil and infected leaf surfaces. These threads act as fine ropes holding the leaf to the media. Infected leaves that are close together or on crowded plants will have mycelium evident as webs between the infections, and under severe disease development may tend to mat infected leaves together.

Diseases Caused by *Phytophthora*

This pathogen genus belongs to the phycomycetous group of fungi and its name literally means "plant destroyer." The phycomycetes are commonly referred to as water molds and downy mildews and commonly attack roots, stems, foliage, fruit, flowers, corms, tubers, rhizomes, and seed. *Phytophthora* persists as oospores, chlamydospores, and mycelia in dormant tissues of hosts. Typical symptoms resulting from infection by this pathogen are water-soaked, mushy roots that turn dark brown to black when they dry, usually culminating in complete destruction of affected tissue. Invaded stems exhibit discoloration, sunken areas, and cankers, which cause girdling, wilting, and eventually death. Stem attacks by *Phytophthora palmivora* on dieffenbachias are usually attributed mistakenly to infection by the bacterial agent *Erwinia chrysanthemi* because of the identical appearance of resulting symptoms. Positive diagnosis of either pathogen on this host genus should never be made from symptoms alone and should be reliant upon actual isolation of the pathogen. *Phytophthora*, as discussed, is also extremely destructive as a leaf spot and leaf blight pathogen [214]. *Phytophthora* causes collar rot of *Cereus* [175], crown, leaf, and stem rot of *Peperomia* [14, 92, 198, 228, 233] (Figure 14-16), root and stem rot of *Aloe* [17], root, stem, and foliar blight of *Pilea* [133], stem rot of *Dieffenbachia* [13, 53, 97, 212, 228], damping off of *Fatshedera* [228], crown rot of *Saintpaulia* [13, 228, 233], basal stem and root rot of *Zygocactus* [11, 82, 94, 228], stem rot of *Epipremnum* [228], and root rot of *Hedera* [77, 175, 228]. Control of *Phytophthora* is obtained by careful selection of noninfected stock plants, use of clean equipment and tools, noncrowding of plants, rigid sanitation methods, and steam-pasteurized, well-drained soil mixes. Particular care should be taken not to overwater plants.

Figure 14-16.   Typical stem rot of *Peperomia* cutting caused by *Phytophthora*.

Diseases Caused by *Pythium*

Also a member of the phycomycetes, *Pythium* does not usually attack mature plant tissues as *Phytophthora* does, but tends to cause damping off of immature plant tissues such as seeds and seedlings and/or rotting of young roots and stems. *Pythium* is generally most active under wet, warm conditions, but it is capable of surviving dry, adverse conditions because of its resting structures (oospores). Like other soil-borne fungi, *Pythium* is difficult to eliminate once it becomes established in crop plantings. Serious damping off of seedlings caused by *Pythium* occurs on *Begonia* [175], *Coleus* [13], *Caladium* [93, 96, 182], *Coffea* [50], *Chamaedorea, Aphelandra, Monstera, Ardisia* [93, 96], *Dieffenbachia* [82, 93, 96, 175], *Philodendron* [93, 96, 228], and *Epipremnum* [93, 96, 147]. Stem and root rots caused by *Pythium* are common on *Aglaonema* [93, 96, 150, 228], *Caladium* [182, 228], *Dieffenbachia* [82, 93, 96, 175], *Monstera* [93, 96, 228], *Philodendron* [86, 93, 96], *Epipremnum* [86, 88, 228], *Syngonium* [211, 228, 233], *Aloe* [24, 228], *Begonia* [163, 175], *Saintpaulia* [13, 53, 163, 175, 228, 233], *Aphelandra* and *Ardisia* [93, 96], *Chamaedorea* [192], *Maranta* [93, 96], *Crassula* [233], *Fittonia* [175], *Hedera* and *Hoya* [228], *Peperomia* [64, 93, 96, 165, 228, 233], *Sansevieria* [228], and *Zygocactus* [93, 94, 96, 228]. Control of *Pythium* is best obtained by employing the same practices stated previously for *Phytophthora*. These pathogen groups may be eliminated from propagative material of some plants by placing in hot water dips [19, 24] of 115°F (46°C) for 20 to 30 minutes, allowing to cool, and planting in a clean soil mix.

Diseases Caused by *Sclerotium rolfsii*

Common to the southern United States, Central America, the Caribbean, and South America, this pathogen is well recognized in many other important agricultural areas of the world and has such pathogenic potential that it often causes complete losses in attacks on some ornamentals [18]. Diseases caused by *S. rolfsii* are commonly referred to as "southern blight," "southern wilt," or "southern stem rot." The fungus can attack all parts of plants, though it is more commonly observed as a stem-invading pathogen attacking usually at or near the soil line and is a serious pathogen on propagative stock. It has an extremely wide host range, being known to attack at least 500 species of plants represented by 100 families [18]. It survives between periods of pathogenicity as sclerotia in plant debris, and soil and can remain viable up to 5 years. High soil moisture, acid pH (3.0 to 5.0), optimum temperatures of 25° to 35°C, and adequate aeration favor a high incidence of this fungus. Dissemination occurs by wind, water, infected propagative stock or transplants, and infested plant debris [18]. Symptoms of the disease caused by *S. rolfsii* are wilting of the plant, preceded by water-soaked, usually brown stem lesions at or near the soil line. Lesions are soon colonized with a white, rather coarse mycelium (Figure 14-17), which radiates over the soil and is interspersed with small, round, light tan to dark brown

Figure 14-17. Basal stem infection of *Brassaia* caused by *Sclerotium rolfsii.*

Figure 14-18. Typical blight of *Philodendron scandens oxycardium* cuttings caused by *Sclerotium rolfsii.*

sclerotia that resemble mustard seeds. The affected plant becomes girdled and may collapse and eventually die. The fungus generally rots propagative material, such as cane (stem) pieces, tubers, corms, rhizomes, and bulbs before they can sprout new growth.

Some foliage plants seriously affected by *S. rolfsii* are *Ajuga* [13, 18, 175, 228, 232], *Begonia* [18, 233], *Brassaia* [9, 82, 93, 96, 228], *Caladium* [18, 19, 93, 96, 175, 230, 233], *Chamaedorea, Dieffenbachia, Pilea, Epipremnum* [93, 96], *Chlorophytum, Codiaeum, Fittonia* [228], *Coffea* [221], *Coleus* [173, 220], *Dracaena* [82, 93, 96], *Ficus* [18, 220, 231], *Philodendron* [55] (Figure 14-18), *Peperomia* [10, 82, 93, 96, 228], *Saintpaulia* [13, 146], and *Syngonium* [82, 93, 96, 228].

Careful culture and sanitation is necessary in the control of this pathogen. Infected plant tissue must be removed and destroyed in a manner that does not allow spreading of the resistant and potentially pathogenic sclerotia. Infested soil should be removed or, if reused, adequately steam-pasteurized or treated with chemical fumigants.

Regular scouting for infections should be practiced with this pathogen during wet, hot periods, for if unchecked, small infected areas can spread rapidly and devastate a susceptible crop in propagation or production within a few days.

Figure 14-19. Basal cutting rot of *Dracaena deremensis* 'Warneckii' caused by *Fusarium moniliforme*.

Diseases Caused by *Fusarium*

This pathogenic group contains many species and forms (races, biotypes, pathotypes) within species. Some produce decay on dormant plant organs (bulbs, corms, tubers, and seed), while others are root-rotting and vascular-invading pathogens, causing wilt and eventual death of infected plants [216]. Some invade the cortex, causing preemergence, damping off, root rots, and stem cankers. Leaf spot diseases are more unusual for the fusaria, but do occur on some ornamental hosts and are capable of being a factor of economic importance, particularly with *F. moniliforme*. Symptoms most commonly associated with soil-borne diseases caused by *Fusarium* are root rot, storage dry rots, chlorosis, stunting, vascular discoloration, and wilting. Fusaria are successful inhabitants of the soil, and, after becoming established in soil, they remain indefinitely. *Fusarium* is generally more affected by changes in soil temperatures than soil moisture, with diseases caused by this group more prevalent during warm to hot periods. Dissemination occurs via propagative material, seedling transplants, wind-borne soil, surface drainage water, and contaminated implements and equipment [216]. *Fusarium* has not been proved as the cause of many foliage plant diseases, but does cause root rot, wilt, and damping off of *Coffea* [13, 50], a root rot of asparagus fern (175), decay of *Cactus* [60], cutting rot of *Dracaena* [81, 93, 96] (Figure 14-19), root and stem rot of *Codiaeum, Chamaedorea,* and

Dizygotheca [228], *Saintpaulia* [228, 233], and *Zygocactus* [154, 228], and a tuber rot of *Caladium* [95].

Diseases Caused by *Sclerotinia*

Sclerotinia produces diseases commonly known as cottony rot, which are serious on cultivated plants in cool temperate and subtropical regions of the world. The disease is also known as pink rot, crown rot, stalk rot, and watery soft rot, depending on the host affected. The characteristic feature of this fungus is a prominent mass of white, lacelike mycelium produced on its hosts. It attacks roots, stems, leaves, petioles, flowers, fruits, and storage organs. Sclerotia of this organism persist in the soil, are rather large and easily seen without a hand lens, irregular in shape, and somewhat elongated [186]. They survive and increase in number best within the first 4 inches of soil [1]. Infection of plants occurs as sclerotia germinate, producing mycelium or fruiting structures that produce spores, which are wind borne or splashed onto new hosts [186]. *Sclerotinia* causes cutting rot of *Gardenia, Syngonium,* and *Epipremnum* [82], root and stem rot of *Begonia* [233], leaf rot of *Gynura* [144], cottony blight of *Coleus* [228], and blade and leaf stalk rot of *Adiantum* [13].

Diseases Caused by Miscellaneous Pathogens

Several pathogens are rare in occurrence or have limited foliage plant host range, but do occur and can, on occasion, cause considerable concern.

Aspergillus niger causes a rapid soft decay of *Sansevieria* [56] and can cause decay of unrooted cuttings of *Dracaena,* especially *Dracaena sanderana.*

Ceratocystis fimbriata may cause brown to black, water-soaked rot of roots and stems of *Syngonium* propagative units or growing plants [42]. Infected rooted plants show a characteristic yellowing of foliage, which is usually followed by subsequent death of infected tissues. Heat treatment of hardened propagative vines at 120°F (50°C) for 30 minutes will eliminate the pathogen with minimum injury to plant tissue.

Clitocybe tabescens is a destructive root rot pathogen usually of mature plants that is commonly referred to as mushroom root rot. Its diagnostic presence is noted by a white to cream colored mycelial mat between the cortex and vascular elements of the plant. The mushrooms are honey colored, 4 to 8 inches high (10 to 20 centimeters), and usually in clusters when fruiting on the surface roots or basal stems of plants. This pathogen has been reported on *Coffea* [221] and *Zygocactus* [228].

Virus and Viruslike Diseases of Foliage Plants

Viruses are ultramicroscopic infectious agents of disease capable of reproducing exclusively within living host cells. Fortunately, plant viruses do not infect humans or other vertebrates. Viruses are difficult to characterize because of their exceedingly small size, and much remains to be learned about them, including those infecting foliage plants. The existence of viruses was not known until the latter part of the nineteenth century, and they were not observed until the development of the electron microscope during the 1930s. Nevertheless, some important generalities can be made that will prove helpful to foliage growers in combating virus diseases. Much of this information has been gleaned from research efforts with other types of crops, but it applies equally well to the foliage industry.

Suscepts

The relative youthfulness of the tropical foliage industry, the diversity of plants involved, and the lack of research attention given to this industry by virologists have contributed to the lack of knowledge about specific viral diseases of foliage ornamentals. The paucity of records for viruses of certain foliage plant groups, such as Acanthaceae and Piperaceae, presumably reflect lack of attention rather than immunity of such plants to viruses. Some groups of foliage plants probably are immune to virus infections, particularly botanically primitive ones. Many viruses infect angiosperms, but relatively few are known that infect such plants as ferns, conifers, and cycads.

Agents

Plant viruses vary considerably in size, dimension, and molecular weight. A large majority of viruses consist simply of a core of nucleic acid surrounded by a protective protein shell (Figure 14-20). However, some lack even this protein shell and are referred to as *viroids*.

Another group of pathogens, such as that responsible for aster yellows disease, commonly induce viruslike symptoms in plants. These agents were once thought to be viruses, but are now recognized as cellular organisms called *MPLO*s, or mycoplasmlike organisms. They are more akin to bacteria than viruses and differ significantly from viruses in that the application of certain antibiotics can mask expressions of induced symptoms [132].

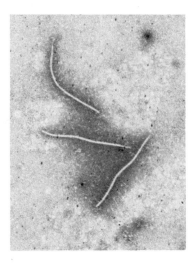

Figure 14-20. Threadlike particles of dasheen mosaic virus. Each particle is about 7,500 angstroms in length and consists of a protective protein coat which envelops a strand of nucleic acid.

Figure 14-21. Infected (a) and healthy (b) leaves of *Dieffenbachia picta* 'Exotica' illustrating the deleterious effect of dasheen mosaic virus on foliage quality.

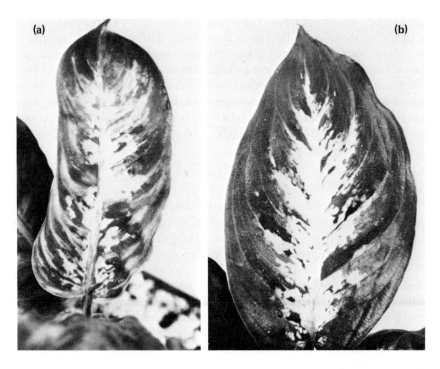

Symptoms Induced by Plant Viruses

Being obligate parasites, viruses require the survival of their hosts for their own procreation; hence it is axiomatic that viruses rarely induce lethal diseases in plants. Viruses typically discolor, deform, or stunt plants rather than induce necrosis or cause their death (Figure 14-21a, b). Necrosis that does occur is usually confined to discrete areas of plants and rarely occurs to such an extent that the entire plant is killed.

Virus particles may permeate the entire plant, but symptoms are normally most evident on the foliage as an uneven pattern of color, such as those induced by nutritional disorders or genetically induced variegations. Such symptoms are often referred to as *mosaic, streak,* or *mottle* symptoms (Figure 14-22a, b, c). Such patterns on floral organs are usually referred to as *color-break* symptoms. Sometimes color patterns are not evident and, in such instances, diseased plants may not be distinguishable from their healthy counterparts, except that vigor and growth rate are reduced. Cactus virus X, for example, induces little or no foliar or floral symptoms in *Zygocactus,* and infected plants frequently pass undetected except by experienced observers. Symptoms are expressed on a seasonal basis in some instances. For example, infected dieffenbachia plants may develop without symptoms throughout most of the year, but may suddenly express conspicuous and damaging symptoms of dasheen mosaic virus at other times, such as in the spring.

Some viruses are erroneously considered beneficial on the basis that virus-induced variegated foliage is not necessarily displeasing in appearance. This concept often is exaggerated, and the belief is expressed that *all* variegated plants are so colored as a result of virus infections. Such is not the case, and foliage growers should recognize that attractive patterns of plants such as caladium, crotons, and pothos are inherited rather than virus induced. The presence of virus symptoms interferes with inherited patterns in most instances and renders infected plants less attractive than their healthy, naturally variegated counterparts. Infected plants grow less vigorously than healthy ones and may serve as "Typhoid Marys" or carriers for other plants in the nursery. The citrus exocortis viroid, for example, was suggested as a means to reduce growth rate of citrus trees and render them more satisfactory for home use as ornamentals. This agent may not induce overt symptoms in certain citrus plants, but this virus is readily transmitted by cutting implements and can infect other plants, such as *Gynura,* inducing damaging symptoms [39, 58, 219].

Further information regarding types of symptoms induced by viruses is available in many university libraries [31].

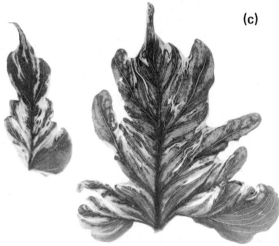

Figure 14-22. Leaves of philodendron infected with dasheen mosaic virus. (a) 'Red Duchess' hybrid showing streak symptoms; (b) *Philodendron scandens subsp. oxycardium* with mosaic pattern; (c) *Philodendron selloum* with mosaic and distortion symptoms.

Virus Diagnosis

Expressed symptoms can be valuable clues for virus identification, but can be easily confused with symptoms induced by other problems, such as nutritional disorders, spray injuries, or certain feeding damage induced by mites or insects. Virus diagnosis is virtually impossible when plant material is received in poor condition, so growers should take special precautions to assure the material to be examined by specialists is forwarded in a fresh condition. Inclusion of specimens from healthy plants in the same nursery for comparison will be helpful. Material suitable for propagation should be forwarded in the event it is necessary for the pathologist to maintain plants under observation over a prolonged period of time. Growers will increase their prospects for receiving an accurate diagnosis of a suspected virus disease by taking these steps.

Elimination of Viruses from Infected Stocks

Unlike vertebrates, plants lack an antibody system that functions to counteract virus infections; thus, they seldom recover from viral infections and remain diseased throughout their lifetimes. Most foliage ornamentals are propagated vegetatively, and infected plants propagated in this manner pass viruses to the progeny perpetually. Certain plants, therefore, have virus infections that are ubiquitous. Viruses cause serious economic damage in some instances, whereas in others losses are not as apparent.

Propagation from seed is nature's way of eliminating viruses from infected stock. Most viruses are not seed borne, and seedlings obtained from infected plants will be free of virus and will remain so until virus is reintroduced into the plants. Studies at the University of Florida [67], for example, suggested that dasheen mosaic virus was uniformly established in certain dieffenbachia cultivars but could be eliminated when plants were propagated from seed rather than by vegetative means. Unfortunately, seedling plants of most foliage ornamentals are not true to varietal type, differing substantially in appearance from the horticulturally superior parental material. Other foliage ornamentals, such as *Philodendron selloum*, are phenotypically similar and thus can be propagated by seed as a practical means of growing plants free of virus.

Plant tissue culture techniques may provide a satisfactory alternative in obtaining plants vegetatively free of virus. This science has expanded rapidly during the last decade, and its application to a wide variety of plant species has been established conclusively [167]. Tissue culture is successful in vegetatively obtaining virus-free plants, because most viruses are unable to invade and survive in actively growing meristematic regions of plants. Meristematic tissue surgically removed from infected plants and transferred to aseptic supportive growth medium often successfully grows into a mature plant. This technique (see Chapter 6] requires a considerable degree of training and expertise to master for the purpose of virus elimination. Acquisition of "meristemmed" stock does not necessarily preclude the possibility that plants are virus infected, however, and proof of virus elimination is contingent upon extensive laboratory and/or greenhouse tests by trained plant pathologists.

Heat therapy has been successful in eliminating virus from certain plants, but it cannot be considered a reliable control measure since the thermal death point of a virus often exceeds that of its host. Heat therapy has been reviewed [171]; it must be considered experimental as applied to foliage plants.

Reducing the Spread of Plant Viruses

Viruses vary considerably in modes of transmission, and specific information regarding transmission properties of each virus of foliage plants is not available. Some generalities are possible to assist growers in taking meaningful steps to minimize or halt the spread of viruses.

Grafting   Few foliage ornamentals are propagated by grafting, but graft transmission is one of the most effective means of virus transmission. The union between stock and scion tissues makes virus transfer inevitable; therefore, growers should take precautions to assure that only healthy, preferably indexed, material is used in making grafts.

Contamination of tools and by handling plants   Many plant viruses can be transmitted by careless handling of healthy plants following contact with infected ones. A considerable degree of variability exists among viruses as to the ease by which they can be transmitted in this manner, and growers should proceed on the assumption that all viruses are readily transmitted by this means. The citrus exocotris viroid is particularly easy to transmit through the use of contaminated tools [58], as are certain orchid viruses. Personnel should wash hands thoroughly and use clean implements between the handling of one group of plants and another. Virus symptoms are not always evident, and these precautions should be practiced whether or not symptoms are apparent.

Cutting implements can be sterilized as an additional precaution by dipping them into formulations containing virus inactivators such as 5 percent household bleach or 2 to 5 percent formaldehyde plus 2 percent sodium hydroxide [59].

Transmission by insects, mites, and nematodes   Viruses differ considerably in their mode of transmission of vectors. Viruses such as cactus virus X have no apparent vector, whereas others are readily transmitted by certain insects, mites, or nematodes. A good pest management program, therefore, is correlated with virus control, particularly within glass or screenhouse operations. Field-grown plants may become infected despite efficient pest control programs because of the entry of vectors from external sources. Unfortunately, virus transmission occurs so rapidly that even the most potent pesticides will not reliably prevent it.

Aphids are by far the most important vectors of viruses among the insects. Whiteflies, leafhoppers, and thrips are also important vectors of specific viruses and should also be controlled. Spider mites are not known to be important vectors, but eriophyid mites have been implicated in transmission of several plant viruses. These and other mites may induce feeding damage to plants that closely resemble virus symptoms. Only a few nematode species have been shown to be virus vectors, and these can be controlled in conjunction with appropriate soil sterilization or nematode control programs.

Weed control   Weeds can serve as sources of virus inoculum or as havens or food plants for potential virus vectors; hence, the merits of a good weed control program are obvious. Some weeds, such as *Commelina* spp., are closely related to certain foliage plants and are likely to serve as reservoirs of inoculum for such viruses as cucumber mosaic virus.

Specific Viral Diseases of Foliage Plants

The following are several viral diseases of foliage plants that have caused concern in Florida.

Dasheen mosaic virus   Originally described in 1970 [238, 240], it appears to be restricted to the family Araceae, including *Aglaonema, Caladium, Dieffenbachia,* and *Philodendron. Syngonium* appears to be nonsusceptible to dasheen mosaic. Like most viruses, dasheen mosaic disfigures and stunts infected plants, but rarely kills them; symptoms vary according to seasons, growth conditions, and the aroid species infected. A mosaic pattern is the most characteristic symptom, although a deformation of foliage, disruption of its symmetry, and impairment of normal genetic color patterns may occur. Infected plants may not have obvious symptoms, but may grow at a reduced rate compared to their virus-free counterparts [235].

Infections of dasheen mosaic are perpetuated by vegetative propagation, although healthy plants are typically infected by means of aphids that have previously had access to infected plants grown nearby. Therefore, a good insect control program is desirable. Heat treatments do not appear effective in eliminating this virus from infected plants. Healthy plants can be obtained through seed propagation, since this virus is apparently not seed borne; however, except for *Philodendron selloum,* plants derived from seedlings may not resemble parental stock [67]. A more practical means of obtaining healthy stock is through tissue culture. This technique is being evaluated extensively for *Dieffenbachia,* and prospects are good for its adaption on an industry-wide basis.

Cucumber mosaic virus   This virus resembles dasheen mosaic in being transmitted by aphids, but differs in having a much broader host range encompassing at least forty dicotyledonous and monocotylendonous families [61]. The widespread ringspotting condition of *Maranta* has been attributed to this virus [70], and cucumber mosaic has been detected infecting such foliage ornamentals as *Aphelandra, Begonia,* and *Dieffenbachia* [229].
   The wide host range includes many common weed species, and its ready means of transmission by aphids accounts for much of its spread. Growers in Florida should take special pains to eradicate weed species of *Commelina* from their operation, especially since other members of the Commelinaceae might be considered as foliage ornamentals and because of the possible susceptibility of these plants to the commelina mosaic, a second virus frequently found in commelinaceous weeds in Florida [162].

Bidens mottle virus   This virus is aphid transmitted and has been incriminated as causing foliar distortion symptoms in *Fittonia* [239]. This virus had previously been described as a pathogen of lettuce and endive and occurs widely in a variety of weeds indigenous to Florida, including Spanish needle, *Bidens pilosa* [177]. A good insect- and weed-control program should be maintained to control spread of this virus. Special efforts should be made to control weeds in the Compositae as well as Mexican pricklepoppy (*Argemone mexicana*) and Virginia pepperweed (*Lepidium virginicum*), which are in other plant families.

Tobacco mosaic virus   Like cucumber mosaic, this virus has a wide host range but differs from previously mentioned viruses in not having a natural insect or nematode vector [237]. This lack of transmissibility by vectors such as aphids is more than compensated, however, by the extreme stability of this virus and its ease in being transmitted by plant to plant contact or through contaminated hands or cutting instruments. This virus is capable of infecting several foliage ornamentals, including *Rhoeo discolor,* in which it induces severe foliar mosaic symptoms [116, 209]. Fortunately, tobacco mosaic virus does not appear to be prevalent in Florida-grown foliage plants, although growers should nevertheless exercise precautions by maintaining strict sanitation practices whenever possible, particularly when handling different batches of plants.

Cactus viruses   Several cactus viruses have been described; cactus virus X is apparently the most common and best characterized [28]. Infected plants may show no macroscopic symptoms, although they may be less vigorous than healthy counterparts. The cactus viruses have no natural vector but are likely to be transmitted readily through propagating tools. The practice of grafting cacti is especially conducive to the spread of these viruses through cultivated cacti. Seedling cacti are likely to be free of virus, since cactus viruses are apparently not seed borne.

Miscellaneous viruslike disorders

Many other foliage ornamentals suffer from diseases presumed to be virus induced, but additional evidence is required before final conclusions can be drawn. Among these include a disease of *Kalanchoe* characterized by foliar mottling, distortion, and, in some instances, floral color break. Whether this condition is due to a single virus or a complex of several viruses remains to be determined. Healthy stock should be selected, although in some instances symptoms of infected plants may not be apparent. Consideration can be given to propagation of these plants from seed, since the condition does not appear to be seed borne.

A spotting of *Dracaena* leaves has also been described, which resembles the early stages of *Fusarium moniliforme* infection. The spots characterizing this condition do not become necrotic, unlike the fungal disease symptoms, vary throughout the season, and frequently diseased plants display no symptoms.

Ringspot conditions of *Brassaia* and *Peperomia* foliage have been attributed to viruses, but further work needs to be conducted before specific control measures can be recommended. Peperomia ringspot is not readily transmitted; therefore, conscientious effort to rogue infected plants would be a promising means to eliminate this disease [40]. Similarly, plants of *Brassaia* may suffer from a foliar disease commonly referred to as a *ghost spot,* possibly caused by one or more viruses [201]. Growing schefflera from seed may be considered as a possible means of controlling this disease.

Members of the Palmae family merit special note as virus suspects because of lethal yellowing disease, which is believed to be incited by a mycoplasmalike agent rather than a true virus. The lethal yellowing agent was originally thought to be restricted to the coconut palm but is now believed to infect other palms, including the fishtail and windmill palms used as foliage ornamentals [208].

Summary

No group of pathogens is more enigmatic than the viruses. They are difficult to handle, impossible to see without an electron microscope, and their effect is not always evident and may be difficult to assess. Viruses can be controlled by careful consideration of their properties and the employment of preventive and/or eradicative control measures. Acquisition of healthy stock, maintaining rigid standards of cleanliness, and taking precautions in handling plants are conducive to controlling viruses effectively with a minimum of expense. These same measures pay added dividends by assisting in the control of other pests and pathogens of foliage plants.

Miscellaneous Diseaselike Problems

Tropical foliage plants may show symptoms typically associated with diseases caused by pathogenic fungi, bacteria, and viruses during production, when evidence of such pathogens is missing. In such cases, causes may be other agents or environmental factors that affect plants adversely and produce diseaselike symptoms. The following discussion presents examples of such problems; others are discussed in other chapters.

Nematode Leaf Spot of *Ficus elastica* 'Decora'

Field plantings of *F. elastica* 'Decora' were found in the 1960s to have leaves with rectangular, yellowish brown streaks occurring between leaf veins. These spots enlarged and coalesced until most of the leaf became affected, causing it to abscise. The spots were first thought to be caused by fungal or bacterial pathogens but have proved to be caused by the nematode *Aphelenchoides besseyi* [119].

A smutgrass weed provides the mechanism for getting the nematode to leaves high up on affected plants [122]. The nematode lives in the soil until the smutgrass starts to grow. It then invades the grass stalk, which grows upward, and populations of *A. besseyi* living between seeds and their glumes are carried up to the underside of *Ficus* leaves. Nematodes then simply move under wet conditions from the grass into the susceptible *Ficus* leaf. Control of this problem can be accomplished by mowing the grass before seed stalks grow to the height of the *Ficus* leaves [125].

Stomatal Leaf Spot of *Philodendron*

Leaves of *Philodendron hastatum* in the Los Angeles area of California in the late 1950s had a leaf spot that was initially thought to be caused by a pathogenic bacterium [166]. The condition is a physiological disorder that can occur on the hastatum and selloum types and is sometimes called *buck shot* by growers.

The spots originate on the undersides of leaves and usually show on the upper sides also. They develop as minute, yellowish spots with exudate and often a necrotic center; where many spots coalesce, the size of the affected area can reach ½ inch in diameter. The exudate associated with the lower leaf surface serves as an excellent medium for the growth of saprophytic bacteria and fungi. The spotting is most serious under warm, moist conditions, with spotting worse between 75° and 85°F (24° and 29°C) and increasing as soil temperatures rise from 60° to 80°F (16° to 27°C).

The problem is somewhat alleviated in susceptible philodendron types by maintaining relatively low soil and air temperatures, a low soluble salts level in the soil, and irrigating in a manner to promote low humidity within growing areas. Fungicide and bactericide applications do not control the condition, but fungicidal sprays may control the development of saprophytic fungi upon the exudate within the spot.

Apical Necrosis of Foliage Plants

Growers of foliage plants in the state of Washington experienced a problem occurring on rooted and unrooted cuttings obtained from southern and tropical sources. The problem was first noted on rooted cuttings of *Monstera deliciosa* [63] that arrived in excellent condition, but shortly after potting, the first newly emerged leaf was blackened and decayed. Cultural isolations revealed no pathogenic fungal or bacterial agents. Experiments with several foliage plants revealed the problem was caused by a rapid rise in temperature when cuttings maintained at about 60°F (16°C) were placed under a temperature of 95°F (35°C) for as little as 48 hours. Plant types found susceptible to this condition under experimental conditions were *M. deliciosa*, *Philodendron hastatum*, *Ficus elastica*, and *Dracaena fragrans massangeana*. *Dracaena deremensis* 'Warnecki' and *Dieffenbachia maculata* were not affected.

Sudden fluctuations from low to high temperatures should be prevented during shipment of susceptible cuttings by packaging in insulated containers. Exposure to high temperatures should be avoided if the shipment is delayed in transit. Cuttage received by wholesalers or growers should be brought slowly to normal culturing temperatures in greenhouses or other structures.

Figure 14-23. Spots on *Ficus elastica* 'Decora' foliage caused by excess boron.

Nutritional Deficiencies Mistaken for Disease

A classic example of a "disease" problem that proved to be a nutrient deficiency was a severe leaf spot on air layers of *Ficus elastica* 'Decora' noted in 1970 on field plantings in south Florida [126]. The problem can be especially severe on leaves of spring and fall air layers shortly before layers are harvested. Early symptoms consist of red, angular interveinal spots 1 to 2 millimeters in diameter on lower leaf surfaces. Lesions enlarge, coalesce to roughly rectangular shapes, and assume a tan coloration as the lower epidermis and mesophyll die. Eventually, some lesions are visible on upper leaf surfaces.

Attempts to isolate pathogenic organisms proved unsuccessful. Greenhouse experiments involving hydroponically grown *F. elastica* 'Decora' revealed the disease problem was diminished by a nutrient solution containing high concentrations of potassium. Additional field studies [127] showed the problem was most severe under a no potassium plus high magnesium treatment. High potassium plus no magnesium resulted in moderate symptom development, whereas high potassium plus high magnesium showed the least symptoms. The ratio providing the best control has 2 potassium (392 kilograms per hectare per year) to 1 magnesium (196 kg/ha/yr).

Another problem that also produces leaf spots on *F. elastica* 'Decora' is boron toxicity (Figure 14-23). These symptoms can result where excess boron exists and can be easily mistaken for disease.

Another deficiency that may be mistaken for disease is boron deficiency of *F. elastica* 'Decora'. With this problem, terminal leaves are stunted and deformed and eventually stop growing (Figure 14-24). Application of a 2 percent borax spray is curative.

Freezing, Chilling, Cold Water, and Lightning

Often injury induced by physical and biotic agents may mistakenly be attributed to diseases, since foliage plant producers forget that agents other than plant pathogens can cause diseaselike symptoms on foliage plants.

Foliage plants grown in the subtropics, though infrequently, are subjected to frost and freezing temperatures, which may be severe enough to kill outdoor plants or may merely damage tissues sufficiently to cause subsequent growth to exhibit distortion (Figure 14-25). Chilling, rather than freezing, may cause yellowing, collapse, and various colored leaf spots in some foliage plants several hours to days after chilling injury

Figure 14-24. Typical symptoms on a new growth of *Ficus elastica* 'Decora' produced by boron deficiency.

Figure 14-25. Various symptoms of frost injury produced on *Ficus elastica* 'Decora'.

Figure 14-26. Typical symptoms caused by chilling of *Sansevieria*.

has occurred. *Sansevieria* leaves develop white blotches when air temperatures remain under 45°F (7°C) for several hours [124] (Figure 14-26). Other plants, such as dieffenbachias, may exhibit foliar yellowing and eventual collapse, starting with older leaves, one to several days after chilling injury.

Leaves of some foliage plants are sensitive to cold water, such as drops of water of condensation or rain that falls from lath, screen, or plastic on cold, foggy, or rainy nights. The spots produced on *Syngonium* spp. and *Philodendron oxycardium* can easily be mistaken for disease caused by fungal or bacterial plant pathogens.

Areas where tropical foliage plants are grown outdoors are often subjected to severe rain storms with accompanying lightning strikes. Lightning damage can be common in fields where various *Ficus* spp. are grown.

Saprophytic Slime Molds

Growers often become concerned about unexpected short, brown, furlike fungal growths that may occur on soil surfaces and sometimes stems and leaves of small plants. The culprit often is one of several slime molds that can appear on easily decomposed, organic components of soil mixes and on plants, usually under warm to hot, wet and humid conditions. Slime molds grow on plant exteriors, do not invade them, and cause harm only if coverage is sufficient to prevent light from reaching the plant's chloroplasts, thus interfering with photosynthesis. Slime molds rarely occur on plants receiving periodic sprays of fungicides.

Disease Control

Diseases only develop when the proper pathogen-host-environment combination occurs. This fact, once understood, will be of enormous value in devising effective systems for disease control.

Growers of tropical foliage plants have traditionally depended upon disease-control chemicals as the primary, if not sole, means for eliminating disease, often overlooking simple reasons why diseases become established, why they continue to develop, and what might be done (other than using chemicals) to control them. Growers should develop a philosophy relative to disease control that employs all possible components found in cultural, chemical, and biological control methods. An integrated and effective disease-control program should make full use of all factors affecting pathogen development and/or host susceptibility.

Cultural Control

Major steps toward disease control often can occur with simple changes in existing cultural methods, such as the employment of more effective irrigation and moisture control systems. Foliar fungal and bacterial pathogens such as *Alternaria, Helminthosporium, Fusarium, Erwinia, Xanthomonas,* and others depend upon splashing water for dispersal and/or spore germination, prior to invasion and infection of host tissue. Water for dispersal is usually provided by rain and/or overhead irrigation practices. Applications of insecticides [47] and ineffective bactericides [87, 111] can provide the mechanism for fungal and bacterial pathogen dispersal, which can abet subsequent disease development if sufficient levels of inoculum exist and the conditions necessary for infection are present. Subsequent spread and development are encouraged when extended foliar wetting is caused by moist, humid weather or by unwise watering practices.

Foliar wetting from rain or overhead irrigation is not necessary for development of the fungal pathogens *Botrytis* and *Cercospora*. These pathogens thrive under warm, sunny days and cool, moist nights, conditions that promote condensation. These conditions aid in their spore dispersal, germination, and subsequent host plant infection. This occurs in late fall and winter to early spring in Florida. The following cultural suggestions will aid in proper management of water or moisture:

1. Grow under permanent (glass, fiberglass) structures.
2. Employ watering systems that do not wet foliage.
3. Decrease watering frequency and water only when needed, and then thoroughly.
4. Water when good drying conditions exist and normally not too early or late in the day.
5. Employ fans, when needed, to move drier air into the greenhouse and around plants to promote foliar drying.
6. Do not crowd plants. This promotes poor drying and extends wet periods by increasing humidity around plants, causing condensation to occur on plant surfaces. Crowding also encourages tissue senescence, which makes it more susceptible to certain fungi such as *Botrytis.*

The source of irrigation water should be considered, since water can be a reservoir for plant pathogens. Species of *Rhizoctonia* [54, 197], *Pythium* [62, 117, 197], and *Phytophthora* [210] have been found to persist in surface bodies of water employed for irrigation. Bacterial pathogens like *Xanthomonas* [202] may also be spread in this manner, although their survival period in water outside host plants is probably shorter than that for fungi. Contaminated water, therefore, can be the pathogen source that could easily undermine an otherwise effective disease-control program. Well water should be employed where possible, and suspicious surface water sources should be assayed for plant pathogens and disinfested if found contaminated.

Employment of effective methods of soil media pasteurization and/or chemical fumigation will eliminate pathogens from infested soil. Steam pasteurization of soil media employed in propagation and growing ornamental plants is commonly accomplished at 180°F (82.5°C) for 30 minutes. Principles, methods, and equipment for heat and chemical treatment of soils have been detailed fully [19]. Pathogen-free soil is a must in any growing operation, and growers who do not treat soil and think they can rely on peat to be pathogen free must readjust their thinking in light of recent findings that show peat can be the source of several soil-borne pathogens, particularly *Pythium* and *Fusarium* spp. [79].

Pots, tools, hands, or other items coming in contact with treated soil medium must be free of plant pathogens. Benches used for propagation and/or potted plants should be raised, washed, and disinfested or steam treated prior to receiving sterilized media or pots. Reintroduction of a pathogen such as *Pythium* to media soon after treatment allows it to proliferate rapidly in this soil environment, because heat or chemical treatments have killed most soil antagonists and competitors of plant pathogens. The first weeks after treatment are especially critical to reinfestation, and safeguards against pathogen reintroduction should be stringent.

Steam and chemical treatments of groundbeds are of questionable effectiveness. Such treatments may reduce the population of pathogens to an insignificant level, but reinfestation occurs rapidly and populations of pathogens begin to climb. Wherever possible, growing plants in the ground, especially out-of-doors, should be discontinued in favor of raised beds under a covered structure.

The major problem in the control of foliage plant pathogens is the unavailability of plant stocks that are known pathogen free. This dilemma is especially important with plants known to be hosts for systemic pathogens, such as *Erwinia chrysanthemi* and dasheen mosaic virus. Hot-water treatment of planting stock for some selected foliage plants can eliminate some plant pathogens [19], but the practice is not always reliable. The development of tissue culture-pathogen indexing methods [102] in the future will probably allow development of known pathogen-free lines of foliage plants and their subsequent multiplication through tissue culture methods [167]. Development and maintenance of known pathogen-free stocks will be the single most important cultural contribution to foliage plant disease control.

Another simple and effective cultural control occurs when soil mixes are adequately aerated, having sufficient noncapillary pore space to allow rapid drainage after irrigation. Soil mixes with adequate aeration have been known [16, 27] to reduce root rots caused by phycomycetes. Reasons for this are not completely clear, but the effect seems to be consistent. Soil mixes that contain high volumes of fine materials tend to have little noncapillary pore space, retain large quantities of moisture, and promote root rots caused by phycomycetes.

Nutrition and its effect upon foliage plant diseases are largely unexplored. Field observations with diseases caused by *Erwinia chrysanthemi* and *E. carotovora* indicate the more rapidly growing, lush plants or propagative pieces are more rapidly decayed than harder, slower-growing cuttings or plants. Adjustments in nutrient levels that promote slower, harder growth will decrease or eliminate *Erwinia* disease development, but will also slow down potential production. One published report [66] on the effects of nutrition on disease development indicates the severity of disease on *Philodendron scandens oxycardium* caused by *Xanthomonas dieffenbachiae* is decreased with increasing levels of nitrogen.

Plant tissue responds to injury in nature by forming wound substances and tissues (suberin, phellogen, and periderm). These often protect plant tissue against invasion by pathogens and thereby prolong the life of tubers, storage roots, and corms of many plant species. Studies with cut, single-node stem pieces of *Dieffenbachia amoena* have shown that suberin forms within 2 days, phellogen within 6 days, and periderm within 9 days at cut surfaces of plant tissues [121]. Optimum conditions for wound tissue formation were 82° to 93°F (28° to 34°C) and 91 to 100 percent humidity. Cane pieces of *Dieffenbachia* spp. or similar foliage plants would probably be more resistant to external pathogen invasion if attention were paid to enhancing production of protective wound tissue layers prior to planting.

Adjusting existing environmental conditions most certainly would have dramatic effects upon disease development, as demonstrated when symptoms decrease or disappear with temperature reductions. This effect is dramatic with the erwinias, *Xanthomonas, Rhizoctonia, Sclerotium rolfsii, Pythium, Phytophthora,* and other warm-weather pathogens, but growth of host plants is so drastically reduced that this type of cultural control is unrealistic. Reduction of soil temperature to control galling of *Ardisia* seedlings is feasible and provides control [185]. High soil temperatures of 86°F (30°C) significantly increased galling at the base of *Ardisia* seedlings when compared to galling produced on comparable seedlings germinated in a soil temperature of 77°F (25°C). Possibly the higher soil temperatures interfered with development of resident symbiotic bacteria known to be necessary for normal development of certain *Ardisia* species.

Chemical Control

There would be little need for chemical control if pathogens could be completely eliminated from propagative material, potting soil, irrigation water, and the growing area and prevented from reentry, and if environmental conditions necessary for spore germination, invasion, and infection were nonexistent. This is not feasible in locations where most foliage plants are normally produced. Reinfestation of steam or chemically treated soil media is common, extended wetting of foliage from overhead irrigation, rain, or condensation generally occurs sometime throughout the production cycle, and finding plants to employ as stock plants that are totally or largely pathogen free is a difficult task. Thus growers should evaluate individual growing operations and determine chemical control needs based upon potential disease problems, but they should guard against overprotection and misuse of materials. Appropriate compounds approved for control of pathogens in question on particular host plants should be employed. Overprotection and misuse of chemicals have been major contributing causes to foliage plant problems, especially where growers fail to read published information on chemical control and directions on labels of chemical control compounds.

Foliar fungicides   The number of fungal pathogens that attack the tops of foliage plants is extensive [228]. The efficacy of fungicides determined by specific studies [5, 12, 83, 104, 105, 120, 128, 143, 155, 179, 185, 226] on the control of several of these disease-pathogen relationships is summarized in Table 14-1, which should be employed only as a guide in selecting foliar fungicides. The pathogens listed are but a few that occur on plants grown in the foliage plant industry, and the host plant listed is only one of possibly many susceptible to the genus of pathogen listed. The table summarizes results obtained under experimental conditions in tests employing specific pathogen-host plant combinations. Certain fungicides, zinc + maneb and chlorothalonil, have consistently provided good to excellent control on a broad spectrum of plant pathogens. Preventative weekly to biweekly sprays with broad-spectrum fungicides to both leaf surfaces will provide adequate protection from foliar fungal invasion. Foliar sprays will leave some residue on the foliage, and this is especially noticeable where stickers are employed to provide better adherence to foliage. Eliminating all over-

TABLE 14-1   Fungicides for foliar fungal pathogen control

Pathogen genus	Host genus	Fungicides exhibiting efficacy in control
Alternaria	*Brassaia*	Zinc + maneb,[a] zineb
Cephalosporium	*Syngonium*	Zinc + maneb, chlorothalonil[b]
Cercospora	*Peperomia*	Zinc + maneb, chlorothalonil
Colletotrichum	*Araucaria*	Zinc + maneb, chlorothalonil
Corynespora	*Aphelandra*	Zinc + maneb, chlorothalonil
Cristulariella	*Ficus*	Zinc + maneb, chlorothalonil, benomyl[c]
Dactylaria	*Philodendron*	Zinc + maneb, chlorothalonil
Fusarium	*Dracaena*	Zinc + maneb, chlorothalonil
Helminthosporium	*Aechmea*	Zinc + maneb, chlorothalonil
Leptosphaeria	*Dieffenbachia*	Zinc + maneb, chlorothalonil
Phytophthora	*Philodendron*	Zinc + maneb, chlorothalonil
Rhizoctonia	*Nephrolepis*	Chlorothalonil, benomyl
Sclerotinia	*Gynura*	Benomyl

[a] Dithane M-45, Fore, Manzate 200.
[b] Daconil.
[c] Benlate.

head watering and growing under permanent glass or fiberglass structures will promote dry foliage and aid in reduction of number of sprays required, thus helping to eliminate residue problems.

Bactericides   More effective bactericides are needed to control bacterial plant pathogens. Major pathogens requiring control are *Erwinia carotovora, E. chrysanthemi, Pseudomonas* spp., *Xanthomonas dieffenbachiae, X. vitians,* and other *Xanthomonas* spp. Little improvement has occurred in recent years in selecting compounds available to growers for control of bacterial diseases. Initial studies employing antibiotics [148] for control of *E. chrysanthemi* on *Philodendron* spp. indicated streptomycin provided beneficial activity in concentrations of 100 to 400 parts per million, with applications of 200 parts per million every 4 days providing optimum control of the pathogen on naturally infected plants. Maximum control occurred if antibiotics were applied 48 hours prior to infection, a difficult determination to make for growers but nonetheless one that could improve control. Streptomycin has been suggested also as a preventive spray for control of *E. carotovora* on *Epipremnum aureum* [106], *Pseudomonas* sp. on *Dracaena sanderana* [157], *X. dieffenbachiae* on *Philodendron scandens oxycardium* [222], *X. poinsettiaecola* on *Euphorbia milii* [156], and *X. vitians* on *Syngonium podophyllum* [225]. Repeated sprays with streptomycin, especially at high concentrations, will promote development of streptomycin-resistant members within the *Xanthomonas* group [87]. This is a common phenomenon where repeated sprays of streptomycin are employed to control *Xanthomonas* spp. For this reason, the compound is basically unacceptable for control of this bacterial pathogen group. Extensive tests [111] employing various bactericides over a 2-year period have shown that a copper-maneb combination can provide good control when used on a regular, preventive basis.

Streptomycin may be used for dips of propagational material, especially where cane and cutting rots resulting from attack by *Erwinia* spp. occur. Dipped cuttings should be allowed to dry before placing them into propagative media. Table 14-2 summarizes the preceding suggestions on bactericides.

Soil fungicides   The largest amount of fungicide applications occurs in the control of soil-borne plant pathogens. Foliage plant growers face the prospect of controlling many different soil-borne plant pathogens, often on the same plant, because of the wide variety of plants grown and the presence of an environment acceptable to development of a wide range of such plant pathogens. Soil fungicides are usually applied as drenches. The volume of drench applied depends largely upon size of container, depth of bed, and amount of organic matter (peat) in soil mixes. Research on the control of soil-borne pathogens of tropical foliage plants has been active in recent years [9, 10, 11, 74, 86, 88, 89, 90, 92, 94, 144], and specific compounds and suggestions for their use in control of specific plant pathogens can be found in Table 14-3. In many cases, fungicides listed have been shown to provide good to excellent activity. Growers should not, however, think of fungicides as their only line of defense against soil-borne pathogens, but rather incor-

TABLE 14-2   Bactericides for bacterial control

Target pathogen	Bactericide and concentration	Comments
Erwinia	Streptomycin, 100–200 ppm	Apply as a spray every 7–14 days; as a dip, never exceed 200 ppm with 1–10 min for leafy units and 10–30 min for cane sections
Xanthomonas	Copper + maneb, 1½ lb each/100 gal	Will provide effective control of leaf infection when applied every 7–14 days
Pseudomonas	Streptomycin, 100–200 ppm	Apply every 7–14 days

Note: With all chemicals listed, add a spreader-sticker.

TABLE 14-3 Soil fungicide drenches for disease control

Soil fungicide (trade names)	Effective concentrations[a] (ounces)	Pathogens controlled	Additional comments
Banrot (Banrot 40 WP[b])	4–12	*Fusarium, Pythium, Rhizoctonia*	May provide *Phytophthora* control outside Florida
Benomyl (Benlate 50 WP)	8–16	*Fusarium, Rhizoctonia, Sclerotinia*	Must be used in conjunction with dexon or ethazol if *Pythium* or *Phytophthora* are also present
Dexon (Dexon 35 WP)	8–16	*Pythium*	May provide *Phytophthora* control outside Florida
Ethazol (Truban 30 WP or Terrazole 35 WP)	8–12	*Pythium*	May provide *Phytophthora* control outside Florida
Ethazol (Truban 25 EC)	4–8	*Pythium*	May provide *Phytophthora* control outside Florida
Ferbam (Fermate 76 WP)	16–24	*Rhizoctonia, Sclerotium rolfsii*	May cause stunting of seedlings and cuttings
PCNB (Terraclor 75 WP)	12–24	*Rhizoctonia, Sclerotinia, Sclerotium rolfsii*	Use only once a year; may cause stunting with some plants

[a] Based on amount of formulated product per 100 gallons of water.
[b] WP, wetable powder.

porate the following fungicide suggestions with the best method of plant culture available.

There are often difficulties encountered when applying soil fungicides that may result in poor control or phytotoxic reactions. One compound, Banrot 40 WP, is currently advertised as a soil fungicide with broad-spectrum activity. This is especially desirable where growers encounter more than one soil-borne pathogen causing a problem they are attempting to correct. Banrot 40 WP may not provide the degree of control desired for disease situations involving *Phytophthora* and *Sclerotium rolfsii* or where disease pressure from *Pythium* is particularly severe. Adjustment must be made to employ compounds providing better control of such pathogens.

Biodegradable, nonionic surfactants may help maintain more uniform moisture conditions within treated soils, which in turn aid in the

TABLE 14-4   Suggestions on drench volume [a] for soil fungicides

Applied to	Needed per square foot of soil surface (pints)
Minipots or shallow flats	$\frac{3}{4}$
Other pots to 4-inch size and propagative beds or units to 4 inches in depth	1
Pots and propagative beds greater than 4 inches diameter or depth	$1\frac{1}{2}$ to 2

[a] If mixes or soils contain less than 50 percent peat moss, never exceed 1 pint per square foot of volume.

fungicide distribution and disease control. Growers should investigate the use of surfactants to determine their relative value to commercial operations.

How much soil fungicide to apply to a bed or pot is often difficult to determine. Table 14-4 provides guidelines and suggestions to help in providing disease control with the least possibility of phytotoxicity.

In addition to the preceding, apply the following rules for soil fungicide drench applications:

1. Do not drench more frequently than every 3 months.
2. Do not apply to plant foliage; if unavoidable, lightly rinse foliage immediately after application.
3. Where drenches are applied to leafy, unrooted cuttings, apply prior to sticking cuttings. Have all workers wear rubber gloves when sticking the leafy, unrooted cuttings to drenched areas.

Foliage Plant Disease in the Future

The list of pathogens affecting foliage plants is numerous [13, 98, 99, 101, 118, 228] and will undoubtedly increase as more plants are introduced into the trade and more plant pathologists become interested in this specialized area of ornamental plant production. The infection potential will continue as long as these plants are grown largely in warm to hot, wet subtropical and tropical regions. In short, there will be no shortage of diseases in tropical foliage plant production in the years to come.

The past emphasis on foliage plant diseases has been placed largely on identification of causal organisms, descriptions of the diseases they cause, and the evaluation and usage of fungicides and bactericides for disease control. More emphasis should be placed upon understanding why diseases occur and what can be done culturally by growers and experimentally by research scientists to develop nonchemical methods of control to augment or even supplant chemical control programs in use today.

Soil Media Preparation and Sterilization

The soil, according to Baker [19], is a major source of plant pathogens; therefore, soil and soil media components present a mechanism by which pathogens gain entrance into plant-growing areas. Most foliage plant production facilities in the past have given little attention to this specific area of foliage plant culture. Where specific soil preparation areas were established, they were often poorly designed and provided inadequate soil media sterilization.

Growers of foliage plants in recent years have realized the importance of providing well-designed soil preparation areas that have adequate storage, mixing, sterilization, and potting capabilities. All growers of quality foliage plants in the future will be required to have modern soil-handling facilities and employ commercially prepared pathogen-free media or treat the media themselves in some manner to rid them of pathogens. Undoubtedly, aerated steam sterilization with its many advantages for soil media treatment [2, 20, 22] will become a common practice, pathologically and economically, and from a safety point of view it is apparently the best method of soil treatment available.

Chemicals for Pathogen Control

Fungicides and bactericides have been the primary tools employed by foliage plant growers for control of plant diseases. Need for chemical controls will probably decrease as scientists learn more about pathogen-plant relationships and as greater emphasis is placed on other methods of plant disease control. Chemical control, however, will continue as an important tool in quality foliage plant production and will never be completely discontinued from commercial production facilities. Chemicals must be employed more judiciously, with use correlated more to times of need instead of overuse as a preventive treatment.

Chemicals for disease control soon will be safer to plants and humans than those presently used. Such chemicals developed will probably either be of the broad-spectrum or the specific type in relation to target pathogens. Also, chemicals will be effective at lower concentrations and will degrade more readily in the environment. Granular, slow-release chemicals will possibly be developed for incorporation into potting media for the control of soil-borne plant pathogens and on long-term crops. These will have the advantage of single applications to eliminate the need for soil drenches, which are labor consuming, wasteful, and have a tendency to pollute.

Cultural Changes and Environmental Adjustment

Foliage growers have become more cognizant of the importance of various cultural and environmental effects upon plant disease initiation and subsequent development, presently employing structures with permanent cover and raised benches to control such effects. Facilities are being developed for watering systems that eliminate foliar wetting or reduce it to minimum duration.

Growers should become increasingly aware of how components of physical and chemical environments affect disease. Research scientists must address themselves to the control of humidity and temperature to eliminate condensation on the foliage in greenhouses, a condition that greatly aids in the development of diseases caused by pathogens such as *Botrytis* and *Cercospora*.

Interactions between light and nutrition upon plant susceptibility to disease are an area of research that should become more important in the future. Effective control and manipulation of these two factors will assist in providing more effective disease control practices.

Soil Media Manipulation and Biological Control

Physical characteristics of soil media have been known to affect the severity of disease caused by soil-borne fungal pathogens. Mixes that provide adequate noncapillary pore space generally assist in better control of root pathogens. Mixes should be designed to provide physical characteristics that are particularly effective in discouraging specific root rots.

Research should attempt the establishment and utilization of microorganisms that compete in a soil medium to the detriment of soil-borne fungal pathogens. Adjustments in media components, pH, nutrients, and other factors will aid in providing a favorable environment for such beneficial organisms, while providing a hostile environment for pathogens. Mixes might be available in the future for purchase that have been seeded with beneficial organisms, containing also specific instructions for subsequent handling to achieve maximum benefit.

Plant Breeding and Disease Resistance

Little attention in tropical foliage plant research has been given to the search for and incorporation of resistance to common plant pathogens of the important plant groups. With increasing emphasis on non-chemical methods of control, benefits in this area resulting from breeding and selection appear likely. The wide range of species within the economically important and large plant groups such as *Aglaonema, Dieffenbachia, Peperomia,* and *Philodendron* probably will provide a broad range of resistance, which should prove useful if such resistance can be successfully transferred to horticulturally acceptable types.

Indexing, Tissue Culture, and Production of Known Pathogen-Free Plants

The greatest problem in disease control in tropical foliage plants is lack of pathogen-free stock plants. This has caused many otherwise effective control programs in foliage nurseries to be ineffective. Growers cannot control systemic plant pathogens, such as *Erwinia chrysanthemi* and dasheen mosaic virus, once the stock is infected because no cultural change, chemical application, or environmental adjustment will rid the stock of these pathogens. Once they have gained entrance, plants and their cuttings usually remain infected.

Methods of detection and indexing for known pathogens of selected foliage plants [102, 240] have been devised that, when coordinated with plant tissue culture propagation [103, 167, 207], will allow for production and increase of plants free of known pathogens. This opens a new concept in the control of systemic plant pathogens of tropical foliage plants. Growers of foliage plants can now approach control of systemic pathogens in a manner similar to the indexing methods developed by Dimock [46, 48] and others [71, 204] in the 1940s to 1950s and utilized today by growers of floricultural crops such as carnations, chrysanthemums, and geraniums. These methods provided the mechanism for developing stocks free of devastating plant pathogens.

Growers of foliage plants will have available sources of certain plant types that have been indexed free of known pathogens and that have been increased in a manner to maintain this freedom from pathogens. Many foliage-producing establishments will develop their own tissue culture facilities for maintenance and increase of improved plant lines. This will provide them with the capability of programming in advance production of indexed plant types without fear of unforeseen losses resulting from systemic plant pathogens.

Epilogue

The future for foliage plant disease control provides many challenging opportunities for commercial growers, research scientists, and extension personnel. The success with which these challenges are met will depend upon the acceptance of an open attitude to change established procedures and methods that contribute to disease development to new practices that will eliminate or deter disease. The tools and information will be available. It will be up to appropriate individuals to utilize them successfully.

REFERENCES

[1] Adams, P. B. 1975. Factors affecting survival of *Sclerotinia sclerotiorum* in soil. *Plant Dis. Reptr.* 59:559–603.

[2] Aldrich, R. A., M. E. Schroeder, R. A. Keppler, and G. H. Diener. 1975. Heating soils, soil mixes and soil substitutes with saturated air. Penna. Agric. Exp. Sta. Bull. 800. 36 pp.

[3] Alfieri, S. A., Jr. 1966. Gray mold disease of *Ficus*. Fla. Dept. Agric., Div. Plant Ind., Plant Pathol. Circ. 45. 2 pp.

[4] ———. 1967. Gardenia canker. Fla. Dept. of Agric., Div. Plant Ind., Plant Pathol. Circ. 54. 2 pp.

[5] ———. 1968. *Cercospora* and edema of peperomia. *Proc. Fla. State Hort. Soc.* 81:388–391.

[6] ———. 1968. Septoria leaf spot of chrysanthemum. Fla. Dept. Agric., Div. Plant Ind., Plant Pathol. Circ. 73. 2 pp.

[7] ———. 1969. The green scurf disease caused by *Cephaleuros virescens*. Fla. Dept. Agric., Div. Plant Ind., Plant Pathol. Circ. 78. 2 pp.

[8] ———. 1970. Spot anthracnose of flowering dogwood. Fla. Dept. Agric. and Cons. Serv., Div. Plant Ind., Plant Pathol. Circ. 98. 2 pp.

[9] ———, and J. F. Knauss. 1970. Southern blight of schefflera. *Proc. Fla. State Hort. Soc.* 83: 432–435.

[10] ———, and J. F. Knauss. 1972. Stem and leaf rot of peperomia incited by *Sclerotium rolfsii*. *Proc. Fla. State Hort. Soc.* 85:352–357.

[11] ———, and J. W. Miller. 1971. Basal stem and root rot of Christmas cactus caused by *Phytophthora parasitica*. *Phytopathology* 61:804–806.

[12] ———, and C. Wehlburg. 1969. Cephalosporium leaf spot of *Syngonium podophyllum* Schott. *Proc. Fla. State Hort. Soc.* 82:366–368.

[13] Anonymous. 1969. *Index of plant diseases in the United States*. USDA Agricultural Handbook 165. 531 pp.

[14] Ark, P. A., and T. A. De Wolfe. 1951. Phytophthora rot of peperomia. *Plant Dis. Reptr.* 35:46–47.

[15] _____, and C. M. Tompkins. 1946. Bacterial leaf blight of bird's nest fern. *Phytopathology* 36:758–761.

[16] Atkinson, G. F. 1895. Damping-off. Cornell Agric. Exp. Sta. Bull. 94. pp. 233–272.

[17] Averre, C. W., and J. E. Reynolds. 1964. Phytophthora root and stem rot of aloe. *Proc. Fla. State Hort. Soc.* 77:438–440.

[18] Aycock, R. 1966. Stem rot and other diseases caused by *Sclerotium rolfsii.* N.C. State Univ., Agric. Exp. Sta. Tech. Bull. 174. 202 pp.

[19] Baker, K. F. (ed.). 1957. The U. C. system for producing healthy container-grown plants. Manual 23, Calif. Agric. Expt. Sta., Berkeley. 332 pp.

[20] _____. 1962. Principles of heat treatment of soil and planting material. *J. Aust. Inst. Agric. Sci.* 28:118–126.

[21] _____. 1970. Types of Rhizoctonia diseases and their occurrence. Pages 125–148 in J. R. Parmeter, Jr., ed., *Rhizoctonia solani,* biology and pathology. Berkeley: University of California Press. 255 pp.

[22] _____. 1971. Soil treatment with steam or chemicals. Pages 72–93 in J. W. Mastalerz, ed., *Geraniums.* Penna. Flower Growers Manual. 2nd ed. 350 pp.

[23] _____, and P. A. Chandler. 1956. Development and production of pathogen-free propagative material of foliage and succulent plants. *Plant Dis. Reptr. Suppl.* 238:88–90.

[24] _____, and K. Cummings. 1943. Control of *Pythium* root rot of *Aloe variegata* by hot water treatment. *Phytopathology* 33:736–738.

[25] _____, and C. M. Olsen. 1960. Aerated steam for soil treatment. *Phytopathology* 50:82 (Abstr.).

[26] _____, N. T. Flentje, C. M. Olsen, and H. M. Stretton. 1967. Effect of antagonists on growth and survival of *Rhizoctonia solani* in soil. *Phytopathology* 57:591–597.

[27] Bary, A. de. 1881. Zur Kentniss der Peronosporeen. *Bot. Zeit.* 39:521–530.

[28] Bercks, R. 1971. Cactus virus X. C.M.I./A.A.B. Description of Plant Viruses. No. 58. Ferry, Kew, Surrey, England: Commonwealth Mycological Institute.

[29] Bessey, E. A. 1968. *Morphology and taxonomy of fungi.* New York: Hafner. 791 pp.

[30] Boeswinkel, H. F. 1975. Bacterial wilt threat. *New Zealand J. Agric.* 130:20–21.

[31] Bos, L. 1970. *Symptoms of virus diseases of plants.* Wageningen, The Netherlands: Centre for Agricultural Publishing and Documentation. 206 pp.

[32] Brown, J. G. 1942. Wind dissemination of angular leaf spot of cotton. *Phytopathology* 32:81–90.

[33] _____, and A. M. Boyle. 1944. Bacterial soft rot of *Sansevieria.* *Phytopathology* 34:350–351.

[34] Brown, N. A. 1918. Some bacterial diseases of lettuce. *J. Agr. Res.* 13:367–388.

[35] Burkholder, W. H., and C. E. F. Guterman. 1932. Synergism in a bacterial disease of *Hedera helix. Phytopathology* 22:781–784.

[36] _____, L. A. McFadden, and A. W. Dimock. 1953. A bacterial blight of chrysanthemums. *Phytopathology* 43: 522–526.

[37] Chupp, C. 1953. *A monograph of the fungus genus Cercospora.* Ithaca, N.Y.: Cornell University Press, 667 pp.

[38] Claflin, L. E., D. L. Stuteville, and D. V. Armbrust. 1973. Wind-blown soil in the epidemiology of bacterial leaf spot of alfalfa and common blight of bean. *Phytopathology* 63:1417–1419.

[39] Cohen, M. 1968. Excortis virus as a possible factor in producing dwarf citrus trees. *Proc. Fla. State Hort. Soc.* 81:115–119.

[40] Corbett, M. K. 1956. Virus ring spot of *Peperomia obtusifolia* and *Peperomia obtusifolia* var. *variegata. Proc. Fla. State Hort. Soc.* 69:357–360.

[41] Crosse, J. E. 1957. The dispersal of bacterial plant pathogens. *In Biological Aspects of the Transmission of Diseases.* Edinburgh and London: Oliver & Boyd. 179 pp.

[42] Davis, L. H. 1953. Black cane rot of *Syngonium auritum. Phytopathology* 43:586.

[43] Davis, S. H., Jr. 1954. Control of *Phomopsis* canker of gardenia in the cutting bench and in mature plants. *Phytopathology* 44:109–110 (Abstr.).

[44] Dawson, J. R., R. A. H. Johnson, P. Adams, and F. T. Last. 1965. Influence of steam/air mixtures, when used for heating soil, on biological and chemical properties that affect seedling growth. *Ann. Appl. Biol.* 56:243–251.

[45] _____, A. A. T. Kilby, M. H. Ebben, and F. T. Last. 1967. The use of steam/air mixtures for partially sterilizing soils infested with cucumber root rot pathogens. *Ann. Appl. Biol.* 60:215–222.

[46] Dimock, A. W. 1941. Disease control. *Florists' Rev.* 87(2252):19.

[47] _____. 1951. The dispersal of viable fungus spores by insecticides. *Phytopathology* 41:152–156.

[48] _____. 1962. Obtaining pathogen-free stock by cultured cutting techniques. *Phytopathology* 52: 1239–1241.

[49] Dye, D. W. 1967. Bacterial spot of ivy caused by *Xanthomonas hederae* (Arnaud) Dowson. *New Zealand J. Sci.* 10:481–485.

[50] Filani, G. A. 1975. The occurrence and prevention of root and stem rot of coffee seedlings in Nigeria. *Plant Dis. Reptr.* 59:137–139.

[51] Fisher, F. E., and R. T. McMillan, Jr. 1972. Chemical control of red algal disease on citrus in Florida. *Phytopathology* 62:11 (Abstr.).

[52] Forsberg, J. L. 1959. Relationship of the bulb mite *Rhizoglyphus echinopus* to bacterial scab of gladiolus. *Phytopathology* 49:538 (Abstr.).

[53] _____. 1963. Diseases of ornamental plants. Champaign, Illinois: Univ. Ill., Coll. Agric. Special Publ. 3. 208 pp.

[54] Freeman, T. E. 1973. Survival of sclerotia of *Rhizoctonia solani* in lake water. *Plant Dis. Reptr.* 57:601–602.

[55] French, A. M., and C. W. Nichols. 1954. *Sclerotium rolfsii* on *Philodendron cordatum* in southern California. *Plant Dis. Reptr.* 38:530.

[56] Garcia, L. A., and M. A. Diaz. 1949. Aspergillus root-stalk rot of sansevieria. *Univ. Puerto Rico J. Agr.* 33(1):45–53.

[57] Garrett, S. D. 1970. *Pathogenic root-infecting fungi.* New York: Cambridge University Press. 294 pp.

[58] Garnsey, S. M., and J. W. Jones. 1967. Mechanical transmission of exocortis virus with contaminated budding tools. *Plant Dis. Reptr.* 51:410–413.

[59] ———, and R. Whidden. 1971. Decontamination treatments to reduce the spread of citrus exocortis virus (CEV) by contaminated tools. *Proc. Fla. State Hort. Soc.* 84:63–67.

[60] Gerlach, W. 1972. Fusarium rot and other fungal diseases of cultivated cacti in Germany. *Phytopath. Z.* 74:197–218.

[61] Gibbs, A. J., and B. D. Harrison. 1970. Cucumber mosaic virus. C.M.I./ A.A.B. Description of Plant Viruses No. 1. Ferry, Kew, Surrey, England: Commonwealth Mycological Institute.

[62] Gill, D. L. 1970. Pathogenic *Pythium* from irrigation ponds. *Plant Dis. Reptr.* 54:1077–1079.

[63] Graham, S. O. 1961. Apical necrosis in ornamental foliage plants caused by rapid temperature changes. *Plant Dis. Reptr.* 45:41.

[64] Gram, E., and A. Weber. 1953. *Plant diseases in orchard, nursery and garden crops.* New York: Philosophical Library. 618 pp.

[65] Hagedorn, D. J., R. E. Rand, and G. L. Ercolani. 1972. Survival of *Pseudomonas syringae* on hairy vetch in relation to epidemiology of bacterial brown spot of bean. *Phytopathology* 62:672.

[66] Harkness, R. W., and R. B. Marlatt. 1970. Effect of nitrogen, phosphorus and potassium on growth and *Xanthomonas* disease of *Philodendron oxycardium. J. Am. Soc. Hort. Sci.* 95:37–41.

[67] Hartman, R. D., F. W. Zettler, J. F. Knauss, and E. M. Hawkins. 1972. Seed propagation of caladium and dieffenbachia. *Proc. Fla. State Hort. Soc.* 85:404–409.

[68] Hayward, A. C. 1972. A bacterial disease of *Anthurium* in Hawaii. *Plant Dis. Reptr.* 56:904–908.

[69] ———. 1974. Latent infections by bacteria. *Ann. Rev. Phytopathology* 12:87–97.

[70] Hearon, S. S. 1979. *Maranta* ringspot caused by cucumber mosaic virus. *Plant Dis. Reptr.* 63:32–36.

[71] Hellmers, E. 1958. Four wilt diseases of perpetual-flowering carnations in Denmark. *Dansk. Bot. Arkiv.* 18:1–200.

[72] Hiremath, P. C., T. B. Anilkumar, and V. V. Sulladmath. 1977. Twig blight in *Pilea microphylla. Indian Phytopathology* 29:89–90.

[73] Hoitink, H. A. J., and G. . Daft. 1972. Bacterial stem rot of poinsettia, a

new disease caused by *Erwinia carotovora* var. *chrysanthemi. Plant Dis. Reptr.* 56:480–484.

[74] Humphrey, W. A., and A. H. McCain. 1973. Pythium root rot of ivy. *Univ. of Calif. Nov. Flower and Nursery Report.* pp. 7–8.

[75] Johnson, J. 1919. The influence of heated soils on seed germination and plant growth. *Soil Sci.* 7:1–103.

[76] Keil, H. L., and T. van der Zwet. 1972. Recovery of *Erwinia amylovora* from symptomless stems and shoots of Jonathan apple and Bartlett pear trees. *Phytopathology* 62:39–42.

[77] Keim, R., G. A. Zentmyer, and L. J. Klure. 1976. *Phytophthora palmivora* on ivy in California and its control with pyroxychlor. *Plant Dis. Reptr.* 60:632–633.

[78] Kelman, A., L. H. Person, and T. T. Hebert. 1957. A bacterial stalk rot of irrigated corn in North Carolina. *Plant Dis. Reptr.* 41:798–807.

[79] Kim, S. H., L. B. Forer, and J. L. Longenecker. 1975. Recovery of plant pathogens from commercial peat products. *Proc. Am. Phytopath. Soc.* 2:124 (Abstr.).

[80] Knauss, J. F. 1970. Ascochyta leaf spot, a new disease of leatherleaf fern, *Polystichum adiantiforme. Proc. Trop. Reg. Am. Soc. Hort. Sci.* 14:272–279.

[81] ———. 1971. Fusarium stem rot, a previously unreported disease of unrooted cuttings of *Dracaena. Proc. Trop. Region Am. Soc. Hort. Sci.* 15:208–215.

[82] ———. 1971. Suggestions for the control of some common diseases of foliage plants. Univ. Fla., Agr. Res. Center, Apopka. Mimeo 71-2. 20 pp.

[83] ———. 1971. Rhizoctonia blight of 'Florida Ruffle' fern and its control. *Plant Dis. Reptr.* 55:614–616.

[84] ———. 1972. Control of Rhizoctonia cutting rot of two ornamental foliage plant species. *Phytopathology* 62:769 (Abstr.).

[85] Knauss, J. F. 1972. Foliar blight of *Dionaea muscipula* incited by *Colletotrichum gloeosporioides. Plant Dis. Reptr.* 56:391–393.

[86] ———. 1972. Description and control of pythium root rot on two foliage plant species. *Plant Dis. Reptr.* 56:211–215.

[87] ———. 1972. Resistance of *Xanthomonas dieffenbachiae* isolates to streptomycin. *Plant Dis. Reptr.* 56:394–397.

[88] ———. 1972. Field evaluation of several soil fungicides for control of *Scindapsus aureus* cutting decay incited by *Pythium splendens. Plant Dis. Reptr.* 56:1074–1077.

[89] ———. 1973. Rhizoctonia blight of syngonium. *Proc. Fla. State Hort. Soc.* 86:421–424.

[90] ———. 1973. Description and control of a cutting decay of two foliage species incited by *Rhizoctonia solani. Plant Dis. Reptr.* 57:222–225.

[91] ———. 1973. Common diseases of tropical foliage plants. *Florists' Rev.* 152(3937):26–27, 55–58.

[92] ———. 1974. Nurelle, a new systemic fungicide for control of Phytophthora crown rot of *Peperomia obtusifolia. Proc. Fla. State Hort. Soc.* 87:552–528.

[93] ———. 1974. Common diseases of tropical foliage plants. III. Soil-borne fungus diseases. *Florists' Rev.* 154(3987):66–67, 114–122.

[94] ———. 1975. Control of basal stem and root rot of Christmas cactus. *Proc. Fla. State Hort. Soc.* 88:567–571.

[95] ———. 1975. Description and control of Fusarium tuber rot of caladium. *Plant Dis. Reptr.* 59:975–979.

[96] ———. 1975. Common diseases of tropical foliage plants. III. Soil-borne fungus diseases. Univ. Fla., Agr. Res. Center, Apopka. Res. Rep. RH 75-8. 10 pp.

[97] ———. 1975. Field evaluations of Nurelle for control of Phytophthora diseases of dieffenbachia and petunia. *Proc. Am. Phytopathol. Soc.* 2:136 (Abstr.).

[98] ———. 1975. Common diseases of tropical foliage plants: Foliar fungal diseases. *Florida Foliage Grower* 12(10):1–5.

[99] ———. 1975. Common diseases of tropical foliage plants: Bacterial diseases. *Florida Foliage Grower* 12(11):1–6.

[100] ———. 1975. Common diseases of tropical foliage plants. I. Foliar fungal diseases. Univ. Fla., Agr. Res. Center, Apopka. Res. Rep. RH 75-6. 9 pp.

[101] ———. 1976. Common diseases of tropical foliage plants: Soil-borne fungus diseases. *Florida Foliage Grower* 13(3):1–8.

[102] ———. 1976. A tissue culture method for producing *Dieffenbachia picta* cv. Perfection free of fungi and bacteria. *Proc. Fla. State Hort. Soc.* 89:293–296.

[103] ———. 1976. A partial tissue culture method for pathogen-free propagation of selected ferns from spores. *Proc. Fla. State Hort. Soc.* 89:363–365.

[104] ———. Unpublished data: *Alternaria* on schefflera—Daconil 1½ lb), Captan (1½ lb), and Kocide 101 (1½ lb) provided control but were phytotoxic. Benlate (½ lb) and Mertect (½ lb) provided no control; Manzate D (1½ lb), Zineb (1 ½ lb) and FORE (1 ½ lb) provided complete control and were nonphytotoxic.

[105] ———, and S. A. Alfieri, Jr. 1970. Dactylaria leaf spot, a new disease of *Philodendron oxycardium* Schott. *Proc. Fla. State Hort. Soc.* 83:441–444.

[106] ———, and J. W. Miller. 1972. Description and control of the rapid decay of *Scindapsus aureus* incited by *Erwinia carotovora. Proc. Fla. State Hort. Soc.* 85:348–352.

[107] ———, and J. W. Miller. 1974. Bacterial blight of *Saintpaulia ionantha* caused by *Erwinia chrysanthemi. Phytopathology* 64:1046–1047.

[108] ———, and J. W. Miller. 1974. Etiological aspects of bacterial blight of *Philodendron selloum* caused by *Erwinia chrysanthemi. Phytopathology* 64:1526–1528.

[109] ———, and C. Wehlburg. 1969. The distribution and pathogenicity of

Erwinia chrysanthemi Burkholder et al. to *Syngonium podophyllum* Schott. *Proc. Fla. State Hort. Soc.* 82:370–373.

[110] _____, J. W. Miller, and R. J. Virgona. 1978. Bacterial blight of fishtail palm, a new disease. *Proc. Fla. State Hort. Soc.* 91:245–246.

[111] _____, W. E. Waters, and R. T. Poole. 1971. The evaluation of bactericides and bactericide combinations for the control of bacterial leaf spot and tip burn of *Philodendron oxycardium* incited by Xanthomonas dieffenbachiae. *Proc. Fla. State Hort. Soc.* 84:423–428.

[112] Lelliott, R. A. 1956. Slow wilt of carnations caused by a species of *Erwinia. Plant Path.* 5:19–23.

[113] Lim, W. H. 1974. The etiology of fruit collapse and bacterial heart rot of pineapple. *MADRI Res. Bull.* 2(2):11–16.

[114] Linn, M. B. 1940. Cephalosporium leaf spot of two aroids. *Phytopathology* 30:968–972.

[115] _____. 1942. Cephalosporium leaf spot of dieffenbachia. *Phytopathology* 32:172–175.

[116] Lockhart, B. E. L., and F. L. Pfleger. 1977. Properties of a strain of tobacco mosaic virus occurring in *Rhoeo discolor* in commercial greenhouses. *Proc. Am. Phytopath. Soc.* 4:126 (Abstr.).

[117] Lumsden, R. D., and F. A. Haasis. 1964. Pythium root and stem diseases of chrysanthemum in North Carolina. North Carolina Agr. Exp. Sta. Tech. Bull. 158. 27 pp.

[118] MacFarlane, H. H. 1968. Plant host-pathogen index to volumes 1–40. *Review of Applied Mycology.* 820 pp.

[119] Marlatt, R. B. 1966. *Ficus elastica,* a host of *Aphelenchoides besseyi* in a subtropical climate. *Plant. Dis. Reptr.* 50:689–691.

[120] _____. 1966. Brown leaf spot of dieffenbachia. *Plant Dis. Reptr.* 50:687–689.

[121] _____. 1970. Suberin and periderm formation in dieffenbachia. *J. Am. Soc. Hort. Sci.* 95:32–33.

[122] _____. 1970. Transmission of *Aphelenchoides besseyi* to *Ficus elastica* leaves via *Sporobolus pioretti* inflorescences. *Phytopathology* 60:543–544.

[123] _____. 1970. Isolation, inoculation, temperature relations and culture of a *Cercospora* pathogenic to *Ficus elastica* 'Decora'. *Plant Dis. Reptr.* 54:199–202.

[124] _____. 1974. Chilling injury in sansevieria. *HortScience* 9:539–540.

[125] _____. 1975. Control of foliar nematode, *Aphelenchoides besseyi,* in *Ficus elastica* 'Decora'. *Plant Dis. Reptr.* 59:287.

[126] _____, and P. G. Orth. 1970. Relationship of potassium to a leaf spot of *Ficus elastica* 'Decora'. *Phytopathology* 60:255–257.

[127] _____, and P. G. Orth. 1973. Field control of a *Ficus elastica* leaf spot by proper potassium : magnesium nutrition. *Phytopathology* 63:1084–1085.

[128] _____, and J. F. Knauss. 1974. A new disease of *Aechmea fasciata* caused by *Helminthosporium rostratum. Plant Dis. Reptr.* 58:445–448.

[129] Martinez, A. P. 1964. Palm leafspot. Fla. Dept. Agric. Div. Plant Ind., Plant Pathol. Circ. 19. 2 pp.

130] _____. 1964. Disease-free production of foliage plants. *Proc. Fla. State Hort. Soc.* 77:484–486.

[131] Mazzucchi, U. 1971. A bacterial stalk rot of Maize (*Zea Mays,* L.) in Emilia. *Phytopath. Medit.* 11:1–5.

[132] McCoy, R. E. 1974. Techniques for treatment of palm trees with antibiotics. *Proc. Fla. State Hort. Soc.* 87:537–540.

[133] _____, D. J. Mitchell, and F. J. Subirats. 1976. A new disease of *Pilea* caused by *Phytophthora parasitica. Plant Dis. Reptr.* 60:680–681.

[134] McCulloch, L., and P. P. Pirone. 1939. Bacterial leaf spot of dieffenbachia. *Phytopathology* 29:956–962.

[135] McFadden, L. A. 1961. Nature, cause and control of diseases of tropical foliage plants. Fla. Agr. Exp. Sta. Ann. Rept. 356 pp.

[136] _____. 1961. Bacterial stem and leaf rot of dieffenbachia in Florida. *Phytopathology* 51:663–668.

[137] _____. 1962. Two bacterial pathogens affecting leaves of *Aglaonema roebelinii. Phytopathology* 52:20 (Abstr.).

[138] _____. 1963. Nature, cause and control of diseases of tropical foliage plants. Fla. Agr. Exp. Sta. Ann. Rept. 344 pp.

[139] _____. 1967. A Xanthomonas infection of *Philodendron oxycardium* leaves. *Phytopathology* 57:343 (Abstr.).

[140] _____. 1969. *Aglaonema pictum,* a new host of *Erwinia chrysanthemi. Plant Dis. Reptr.* 53:253–254.

[141] McKenzie, M. A., L. H. Jones, and C. J. Gilgut. 1940. *Phomopsis gardeniae* in relation to gardenia culture. *Plant Dis. Reptr.* 24:58–62.

[142] McRitchie, J. J. 1976. Stem and frond necrosis of palm. Fla. Dept. Agr., Div. Plant Ind., Plant Pathol. Circ. 173. 2 pp.

[143] _____, and J. W. Miller. 1973. Corynespora leaf spot of zebra plant. *Proc. Fla. State Hort. Soc.* 86:389–390.

[144] _____, and J. W. Miller. 1974. Sclerotinia blight of *Gynura. Proc. Fla. State Hort. Soc.* 87:447–449.

[145] Melhus, I. E., and G. C. Kent. 1939. *Elements of plant pathology.* New York: Macmillan. 493 pp.

[146] Miller, H. N. 1951. Causes and control of diseases of potted plants. Pages 99–100 in Fla. Agr. Exp. Sta. Ann. Rep. for the Fiscal Year Ending June 30, 1951. 277 pp.

[147] _____. 1953. Causes and control of diseases of potted plants. Page 129 in Fla. Agr. Exp. Sta. Ann. Rep. for the Fiscal Year Ending June 30, 1953. 354 pp.

[148] _____. 1955. Investigations with antibiotics for control of bacterial diseases of foliage plants. *Proc. Fla. State Hort. Soc.* 68:354–358.

[149] _____. 1957. An Alternaria leaf spot of *Schefflera actinophylla. Phytopathology* 47:529 (Abstr.).

[150] ———. 1958. Control of Pythium root rot of Chinese evergreen by soil fumigation. *Proc. Fla. State Hort. Soc.* 71:416–418.

[151] ———, and L. A. McFadden. 1961. A bacterial disease of philodendron. *Phytopathology* 51:826–831.

[152] Miller, J. M. 1969. Alternaria leaf spot of schefflera. Fla. Dept. Agr., Div. Plant Ind., Plant Pathol. Circ. 80. 2 pp.

[153] ———. 1971. Tan leaf spot of *Rhoeo discolor* caused by *Curvularia eragrostidis. Plant Dis. Reptr.* 55:38–40.

[154] ———. 1975. Blight and leaf spot of Christmas cactus caused by *Fusarium oxysporum. Proc. Am. Phytopathol. Soc.* 2:62 (Abstr.).

[155] ———, and H. N. Miller. 1975. Leaf spot of black olive caused by *Cristulariella depraedans. Proc. Fla. State Hort. Soc.* 88:571–573.

[156] ———, and C. P. Seymour. 1972. A comparative study of *Corynebacterium poinsettiae* and *Xanthomonas poinsettiaecola* on poinsettia and crown-of-thorns. *Proc. Fla. State Hort. Soc.* 85:344–347.

[157] ———, and C. Wehlburg. 1969. Bacterial leaf spot of *Dracaena sanderana. Proc. Fla. State Hort. Soc.* 82:368–370.

[158] ———, R. J. Virgona, and J. F. Knauss. 1976. Xanthomonas leaf spot on *Pellionia pulchra, P. daveauana,* and *Pilea cadierei. Proc. Am. Phytopath. Soc.* 3:340–341 (Abstr.).

[159] Millikan, D. F., and J. E. Smith, Jr. 1955. Root rot of pothos, a disease caused by *Rhizoctonia. Plant Dis. Reptr.* 39:240–241.

[160] Mitchell, D. J., and L. N. Shaw. 1975. Eradication of plant pathogenic fungi in soil and nursery potting mixtures with a mobile continuous soil pasteurizer. *Plant and Soil* 42:591–600.

[161] Montoya, J., S. Dongo, and A. Osores. 1972. Control de musgos, Algas y liquenes en citricos del valle de Chanchamayo [Control of mosses, algae and lichens in the valley of Chanchamayo (of Peru)]. *Proc. Trop. Region Am. Soc. Hort. Sci.* 16:93–106.

[162] Morales, F. J., and F. W. Zettler. 1977. Characterization and electron microscopy of a potyvirus infecting *Commelina diffusa. Phytopathology* 67:839–843.

[163] Mullin, R. S., and T. A. Kucharek, eds. 1974. Ornamentals and turf. Pages II 1–36 in Florida plant disease control guide. Univ. of Fla. Coop. Ext. Serv.

[164] Munnecke, D. E. 1960. Bacterial stem rot of dieffenbachia. *Phytopathology* 50:696–700.

[165] ———, and P. A. Chandler. 1953. Some diseases of variegated peperomia. *Plant Dis. Reptr.* 37:434–435.

[166] ———, and P. A. Chandler. 1957. A leaf spot of philodendron related to stomatal exudation and to temperature. *Phytopathology* 47:299–303.

[167] Murashige, T. 1974. Plant propagation through tissue cultures. *Ann. Rev. Plant Physiol.* 25:135–136.

[168] Neergaard, P. 1945. *Danish species of Alternaria and Stemphylium: Taxonomy, parasitism, economical significance.* London: Milford. 559 pp.

[169] Nichols, L. P., M. H. Jodon, and B. Scarborough. 1974. Longevity of *Xanthomonas begoniae,* the cause of bacterial leafspot of Rieger begonias. *Plant Dis. Reptr.* 58:814.

[170] Noble, W. E., and S. L. Poe. 1972. Attractancy of several fungi and bacteria for bulb and soil mites frequenting diseased gladiolus corms. *Proc. Fla. State Hort. Soc.* 85:401–404.

[171] Nyland, G., and A. C. Goheen. 1969. Heat therapy of virus diseases of perennial plants. *Ann. Rev. Phytopathol.* 7:331–354.

[172] Orian, G. 1948. Division of plant pathology. *Rept. Dept. Agri. Mauritius* 1947:37–43.

[173] Paintin, R. D. 1928. Notes on the parasitology of *Sclerotium rolfsii. Mycologia* 20:22–26.

[174] Parris, G. K. 1959. A revised host index of Mississippi plant diseases. Miss. State Univ. Misc. Publ. 1. 146 pp.

[175] Pirone, P. P. 1978. *Diseases and pests of ornamental plants,* fifth ed. New York: Ronald Press. 546 pp.

[176] Pitcher, R. S., and J. E. Crosse. 1958. Studies in the relationship of eelworms and bacteria to certain plant diseases. II. Further analysis of the strawberry cauliflower disease complex. *Nematologica* 3:244–256.

[177] Purcifull, D. E., S. R. Christie, and T. A. Zitter. 1976. Bidens mottle virus. C.M.I./A.A.B. Descriptions of Plant Viruses No. 161. Ferry, Kew, Surrey, England: Commonwealth Mycological Institute.

[178] Reynolds, J. E. 1964. Gliocladium disease of palm in Dade County, Florida. *Plant Dis. Reptr.* 48:718–720.

[179] Ridings, W. H. 1973. Collectotrichum needle necrosis of Norfolk Island pine. *Proc. Fla. State Hort. Soc.* 86:418–421.

[180] ———— 1978. A stem rot of cacti. Fla. Dept. Agr., Div. Plant Ind., Plant Pathol. Circ. 191. 2 pp.

[181] ————, and S. A. Alfieri, Jr. 1973. Colletotrichum leaf spot of English ivy. Fla. Dept. Agr., Div. Plant Ind., Plant Pathol. Circ. 80. 2 pp.

[182] ————, and R. D. Hartman. 1976. Pathogenicity of *Pythium myriotylum* and other species of *Pythium* to caladium derived from shoot tip culture. *Phytopathology* 66:704–709.

[183] ————, and J. J. McRitchie. 1974. Phytophthora leaf spot of *Philodendron oxycardium* and related species. *Proc. Fla. State Hort. Soc.* 87:442–447.

[184] ————, and J. J. McRitchie. 1974. Phytophthora leaf spot of philodendron. *Proc. Am. Phytopathol. Soc.* 1:165 (Abstr.).

[185] ————, S. F. Fazli, and J. W. Miller. 1975. Temperature and other factors affecting the frequency of galling in *Ardisia* seedlings. *Proc. Fla. State Hort. Soc.* 88:578–583.

[186] Roberts, D. A., and C. W. Boothroyd. 1972. *Fundamentals of plant pathology.* San Francisco: W. H. Freeman. 402 pp.

[187] Saaltink, G. J., and W. Kamerman. 1971. *Begonia bertinii,* a new host of *Erwinia chrysanthemi. Neth. J. Plant Path.* 77:25–29.

[188] _____, and H. P. Maas Geesteranus. 1964. Een bacterieuerwelkingsziekte by dahlia. *Meded. Landb. Opzoek. Staat Gent.* 39:908–916.

[189] Schaad, N. W., and D. Brenner. 1977. A bacterial wilt and root rot of sweet potato caused by *Erwinia chrysanthemi. Phytopathology* 67:302–308.

[190] Schieber, E. 1972. Leaf blight incited by *Ascochyta coffeae* on coffee in Guatemala. *Plant Dis. Reptr.* 56(9): 753–754.

[191] Schroth, M. N., W. J. Moller, S. V. Thomson, and D. C. Hildebrand. 1974. Epidemiology and control of fire blight. *Ann. Rev. Phytopath.* 12:389–412.

[192] Schulman, J. F. 1971. Etiology of a disease complex in *Chamaedorea elegans.* M.S. thesis, University of Florida.

[193] Schuster, M. L., and D. P. Coyne. 1974. Survival mechanisms of phytopathogenic bacteria. *Ann. Rev. Phytopath.* 12:199–221.

[194] Seymour, C. P. 1974. Phyllosticta leaf spot of *Dracaena. Fla. Foliage Grower* 11(10):4–5.

[195] _____. 1974. Phyllosticta leaf spot of *Dracaena.* Fla. Dept. Agr., Div. Plant Ind., Plant Pathol. Circ. 143. 2 pp.

[196] Shaw, L. N., and D. J. Mitchell. 1978. A continuous soil pasteurizer for organic nursery potting mixtures. *Trans. Am. Soc. Agr. Eng.* 21:33–36.

[197] Shokes, F. M., and S. M. McCarter. 1976. Occurrence of plant pathogens in irrigation ponds in southern Georgia. *Proc. Am. Phytopath. Soc.* 3:342 (Abstr.).

[198] Siradhana, B. S., C. W. Ellett, and A. F. Schmitthenner. 1968. Crown rot of peperomia. *Plant Dis. Reptr.* 52:244.

[199] Sobers, E. K. 1962. Preliminary investigations of a leaf spot of *Kalanchoe* spp. *Proc. Fla. State Hort. Soc.* 75:427–430.

[200] _____, and S. A. Alfieri, Jr. 1972. Species of *Cylindrocladium* and their hosts in Florida and Georgia. *Proc. Fla. State Hort. Soc.* 85:366–369.

[201] Stack, R. W., G. A. Secor, and R. K. Horst. 1978. A proposed viral etiology for schefflera ghost ring. *Phytopathol. News* 12:91 (Abstr.).

[202] Steadman, J. R., C. R. Maier, and H. F. Schwartz. 1975. Implication of bean pathogen contamination of irrigation water. *Ann. Reptr. Bean Improvement Cooperative* 18:75–76.

[203] Stevens, F. L. 1966. *The fungi which cause plant disease.* New York: Macmillan. 754 pp.

[204] Tammen, J., R. R. Baker, and R. E. Skiver. 1959. Control of vascular wilt diseases of carnation by culture-indexing. *Phytopathology* 50:356–360.

[205] _____, P. E. Nelson, and R. S. Dickey. 1964. A carnation disease resembling bacterial slow wilt or stunt. *Phytopathology* 54:610–611.

[206] Tarr, S. A. J. 1972. *Principles of plant pathology.* New York: Winchester Press. 632 pp.

[207] Taylor, M. E., and J. F. Knauss. 1978. Tissue culture multiplication and

subsequent handling of known pathogen-free *Dieffenbachia maculata* 'Perfection'. *Proc. Fla. State Hort. Soc.* 91:233-235.

[208] Thomas, D. L. 1974. Possible link between declining palm species and lethal yellowing of coconut palms. *Proc. Fla. State Hort. Soc.* 87:502-504.

[209] Thompson, S. M., and M. K. Corbett. 1970. A mosaic disease of *Rhoeo discolor* caused by a strain of tobacco mosaic virus. *Phytopathology* 60:1018-1019 (Abstr.).

[210] Thomson, S. V., and R. M. Allen. 1974. Occurrence of *Phytophthora* species and other potential plant pathogens in recycled irrigation water. *Plant Dis. Reptr.* 58:945-949.

[211] Tisdale, W. B., and G. D. Ruehle. 1949. Pythium root rot of aroids and Easter lilies. *Phytopathology* 39:167-170.

[212] Tompkins, C. M., and C. M. Tucker. 1947. Stem rot of *Dieffenbachia picta* caused by *Phytophthora palmivora* and its control. *Phytopathology* 37:868-874.

[213] Towner, D. B., and L. Beraha. 1976. Core rot: A bacterial disease of carrots. *Plant Dis. Reptr.* 60:357-359.

[214] Trujillo, E. E., A. M. Alvarez, and D. N. Swindale. 1975. Phytophthora leaf spot of ti. *Plant Dis. Reptr.* 59:452-453.

[215] Van der Zwet, T., H. L. Keil, and B. C. Smale. 1969. Fire blight in the Magness pear cultivar in north central Arkansas. *Plant Dis. Reptr.* 53:686-689.

[216] Walker, J. C. 1969. *Plant pathology.* third ed. New York: McGraw-Hill. 819 pp.

[217] Waters, W. E., and C. A. Conover. 1969. Chrysanthemum production in Florida. Univ. Florida Agr. Ext. Bull. 730. 64 pp.

[218] Watson, D. P., and W. W. J. Yee. 1973. Hawaiian Ti. Univ. of Hawaii, Agr. Ext. Circ. 481. 14 pp.

[219] Weathers, L. G., and F. C. Greer, Jr. 1968. Additional herbaceous hosts of the exocortis virus of citrus. *Phytopathology* 58:1071 (Abstr.).

[220] Weber, G. F. 1931. Blight of carrots caused by *Sclerotium rolfsii* with geographic distribution and host range of the fungus. *Phytopathology* 21:1129-1140.

[221] ———. 1973. Bacterial and fungal diseases of plants in the tropics. Gainesville: University of Florida Press. 673 pp.

[222] Wehlburg, C. 1968. Bacterial leaf spot and tip burn of *Philodendron oxycardium* caused by *Xanthomonas dieffenbachiae. Proc. Fla. State Hort. Soc.* 81:394-397.

[223] ———. 1969. Bacterial leaf blight of *Syngonium podophyllum. Phytopathology* 59:1056 (Abstr.).

[224] ———. 1969. Two leaf diseases of Spanish bayonet. Fla. Dept. Agr., Div. Plant Ind., Plant Pathol. Circ. 79. 2 pp.

[225] ———. 1970. Bacterial leaf blight of syngonium. Fla. Dept. Agr. and Cons. Serv., Div. Plant Ind., Plant Path. Circ. 91. 2 pp.

[226] _____, and A. P. Martinez. 1967. Leaf spot of *Dracaena marginata* Lam. caused by *Fusarium moniliforme* Sheld. and its control. *Proc. Fla. State Hort. Soc.* 80:454–456.

[227] _____, C. P. Seymour, and R. E. Stall. 1966. Leaf spot of Araceae caused by *Pseudomonas cichorii* (Swingle) Stapp. *Proc. Fla. State Hort. Soc.* 79:433–436.

[228] _____, S. A. Alfieri, Jr., K. R. Langdon, and J. W. Kimbrough. 1975. *Index of plant diseases in Florida.* Fla. Dept. Agr. and Cons. Serv., Div. Plant Ind., Bull. 11. 285 pp.

[229] Welvaert, W., and G. Samyn. 1974. Comparative host range of CMV isolates of different ornamentals in the Ghent region. European Discussion Group Meeting, Ghent, 1974:149–161.

[230] West, E. 1943. Host relations and factors influencing the growth and parasitism of *Sclerotium rolfsii* Sacc. Pages 83–84 in Fla. Agr. Exp. Sta. Ann. Rep. for the Fiscal Year Ending June 30, 1943. 224 pp.

[231] _____. 1947. *Sclerotium rolfsii* Sacc. and its perfect stage on climbing fig. *Phytopathology* 37:67–79.

[232] Westcott, C. 1936. Crown rot of ornamentals in New Jersey. *Plant Dis. Reptr.* 20:198.

[233] _____. 1971. *Plant disease handbook.* New York: Van Nostrand Reinhold. 843 pp.

[234] Wisler, G. C., and W. H. Ridings. 1978. Phytophthora leaf spot of *Brassaia actinophylla. Proc. Fla. State Hort. Soc.* 91:240–242.

[235] _____, F. W. Zettler, R. D. Hartman, and J. J. McRitchie. 1979. Dasheen mosaic virus infections of philodendrons in Florida. *Proc. Fla. State Hort. Soc.* 91:237–240.

[236] Wolf, F. A., and F. T. Wolf. 1969. *The fungi.* New York: Hafner. 438 pp.

[237] Zaitlin, M., and H. W. Israel. 1975. Tobacco mosaic virus (type strain). C.M.I./A.A.B. Description of Plant Viruses. No. 151. Ferry, Kew, Surrey, England: Commonwealth Mycological Institute.

[238] Zettler, F. W., M. J. Foxe, R. D. Hartman, J. R. Edwardson, and R. G. Christie. 1970. Filamentous viruses infecting dasheen and other araceous plants. *Phytopathology* 60:983–987.

[239] _____, J. A. A. Lima, and D. B. Zurawski. 1977. Bidens mottle virus infecting *Fittonia* sp. in Florida. *Proc. Amer. Phytopathol. Soc.* 4:121–122.

[240] _____, M. M. Abo El-Nil, and R. D. Hartman. 1978. Dasheen mosaic virus. C.M.I./A.A.B. Descriptions of Plant Viruses No. 191. Ferry, Kew, Surrey, England: Commonwealth Mycological Institute.

fifteen

R. A. Hamlen
D. W. Dickson
D. E. Short
D. E. Stokes

insects, mites, nematodes, and other pests

Insects, mites, nematodes, and other pests cause economic losses to producers and retailers of tropical foliage plants. Nursery personnel should acquire a working knowledge of the biology of the common pests and methods for their control. Personnel must be able to recognize life stages of pests and understand their feeding habits, development, and behavior. The axiom, prevention is better than a cure, is definitely true for the intensive cultivation of tropical foliage plants. Knowing and following cultural and sanitary procedures required to minimize pest problems, rather than relying on chemical control of established pests, is the best management strategy. Pesticides are necessary when pest populations have reached economic injury levels, and when chemical control is required, a knowledge of pest biology can aid in selecting the correct chemical and the proper method, time, and frequency of application. Basic understanding of concepts involved in the proper use of chemicals for pest control is also necessary.

Pest Control: Theory and Practice

Pests introduced into intensive cropping systems for tropical foliage plant production have an ideal environment for rapid population increases on crops of high commercial value. Applications of pesticides to pest populations when they are initially detected generally will provide acceptable control, providing the pest population is suppresssed before reaching damaging levels. However, in the case where a foliage crop is consistently plagued by a specific pest, a preventative program using pesticides applied at regular intervals may be advantageous. In this instance it may be easier to maintain plants pest free than to eradicate pest populations upon detection. Marginal pest control practices often result in incipient pest populations being passed onto retailers and consumers. This can be avoided by developing and adhering to a sound, integrated pest-management program.

Pests may be introduced into foliage production areas in a variety of ways. Nematodes and certain insects and mites can be spread by mobile materials that carry particles of soil or plant material, such as equipment, containers, propagation material, irrigation or drainage water, and even dust. To limit introductions of new and exotic pests, many countries and states have passed legislation and imposed quarantine measures. Quarantine methods generally include embargoes, inspections at destination, certification at point of origin, and disinfection.

Cultural Control

Cultural and sanitation practices help reduce or eliminate possible sources of infestation inside and outside of growing areas. These practices are essential steps in an effective pest-control program (Table 15-1).

Containers, benches, and equipment should be disinfected regularly to avoid contamination and buildup of pest populations. A surface disinfectant, such as sodium hypochlorite or formaldehyde is effective

TABLE 15-1   Steps for prevention of pest introduction into stock and production areas

1. Use pest-free propagating stock. Planting of contaminated plant material is a common means of initiating an infestation.
2. Plant only in properly sterilized or fumigated growing media.
3. Disinfest plant containers, bins, benches, tools, and other equipment.
4. Use raised benches in stock and production areas as they are easier to maintain pest free, and should infestation occur, control measures are more successful than in ground beds.
5. Use closed structures to exclude entry of pests.
6. Wash hands and disinfest tools frequently when working in planting stock. Do this especially when moving from one area to another.
7. Discard useless plants, plant debris, or plants that have not responded to chemical treatment; eliminate weeds inside and outside growing areas.
8. Do not remove soil, plant material, pots, flats, or other material from infested to uninfested areas. Use color codes to restrict movement.
9. Routinely inspect newly received plant material for infestations. Early detection allows more rapid control.

TABLE 15-2 Surface disinfectants for containers, benches, and equipment

Treatment	Rate
Sodium hypochlorite (5.25% NaOCl)	1 part in 5 parts water
Formaldehyde[a]	1 part in 20 parts water

[a]Caution: Formaldehyde fumes can be phytotoxic.

(Table 15-2). Steam sterilization at 180°F (82°C) for 30 minutes or chemical treatment with methyl bromide or chloropicrin are methods of eliminating pests from soil media.

Chemical Control

Presently, pesticides are generally used to control pests of foliage plants. These chemicals are classified according to the type of pest they control: Insecticides control insects, miticides or acaricides control mites, and nematicides control nematodes. Some chemicals have a broad spectrum of activity and fall into more than one category, such as aldicarb (Temik®), which is an insecticide, miticide, and nematicide.

Insecticides and acaricides may be grouped according to the way they enter the target pest. Stomach poisons such as carbaryl (Sevin®) are applied to foliage that is consumed by the pest. This group also includes bait formulations, such as methiocarb (Mesurol®) for control of slugs and snails. Contact pesticides kill by entry through the insect cuticle, and it is not necessary for the pest to consume the toxicant, only to contact the pesticide-treated areas. Examples of pesticides in this category are Diazinon® and malathion. Pesticides that are classified as fumigants or respiratory poisons include methyl bromide and other chemicals that are applied as vapors, fogs, smokes, or aerosols, which enter the trachea of the target pests. Systemic pesticides when applied on the foliage or to the soil are absorbed by leaves or roots, respectively, and are translocated within the plant. Aldicarb granules or dimethoate solutions applied to the soil are absorbed by plant roots and act as a stomach poison to sucking pests. When systemics such as oxydemetonmethyl (Meta-Systox-R®) or acephate (Orthene®) are sprayed on the foliage, they act as contact insecticides and stomach poisons.

Nematicides are classified as soil fumigants or nonfumigants. Soil fumigants are volatile liquids that diffuse throughout the soil profile in the gaseous state. They are toxic on contact with nematodes that inhabit water films surrounding soil particles. The soil fumigant methyl bromide has a wide spectrum of activity and is effective against nematodes, soil insects, fungal pathogens, many bacteria, and weed seeds. Nonfumigants are nonvolatile nematicides and are further classified as contact or systemic chemicals depending on their mode of action. Fensulfothion (Dasanit®) and ethoprop (Mocap®) are contact nematicides, whereas oxamyl (Vydate®) and aldicarb are systemics. These compounds are generally available as granules or liquids and are applied to the soil surface or drenched into the soil, where the active ingredient dissolves in the soil water and comes into contact with nematodes. Several of these chemicals are also effective in insect and mite control.

Pesticides may be classified also by their chemical structure. Botanical insecticides are "natural" pesticides derived from plants, such as the pyrethrins obtained from *Chrysanthemum cinerariaefolium* and rotenone from *Derris* and *Lonchocarpus* plant species. Synthetic pyrethroids such as allethrin, permethrin, and resmethrin also are available. The inorganic pesticides, which include arsenical or mercurial compounds, act as stomach poisons. Although they were widely used in the past they are generally not used today. Chlorinated hydrocarbon insecticides, DDT, lindane, and chlordane, contain the elements carbon, chlorine, and hydrogen.

DDT, the first pesticide of this group developed, was highly effective and stimulated research that led to the development of many newer insecticides. Most chlorinated hydrocarbons act as contact and stomach poisons; however, lindane also has fumigant activity. Chlorinated hydrocarbons have long residual properties, and, because of their possible role in causing adverse effects on the environment, most have been banned. The halogenated hydrocarbons, such as ethylene dibromide, dichloropropane-dichloropropene and methyl bromide were among the first successful nematicides developed and are volatile liquid soil fumigants. Organophosphates are a large group of pesticides containing phosphorus and often have nematicidal and insecticidal properties. A few examples include parathion, malathion, Diazinon®, dimethoate, fensulfothion, ethoprop, oxydemetonmethyl, and acephate. These pesticides are nonpersistent and may act as contact, stomach, fumigant, or systemic poisons. Organophosphates exert a toxic action through the nervous system by affecting the enzyme cholinesterase. The carbamates are another large class of pesticides, which includes carbaryl, aldicarb, methiocarb, and oxamyl. Carbamates act as contact, stomach, and systemic poisons and, like organophosphates, they interfere with chloinesterase activity.

Insects and mites are affected by specific diseases caused by fungi, bacteria, and viruses. These biological agents may be cultured to produce microbial pesticides. *Bacillus thuringiensis* Berliner, for example, is a bacteria that effectively controls lepidopterous larvae. Insect growth regulators are a relatively new class of chemical compounds being developed for insect control. These compounds, which do not act in the conventional manner, disrupt the normal growth and development cycle of insects so that death or sterility occurs.

Pesticides are available in various formulations designed for specific purposes. Commercial formulations contain a technical grade pesticide, carrier, and other additives. Formulations usually applied as sprays or less frequently, as soil drenches, include solutions (S), emulsifiable concentrates (E, EC), wettable powders (WP,) soluble powders (S, SP), and flowables (F). Dry formulations include dusts (D), granules (G), and baits. Fumigants, as described previously, are liquids at low temperatures or when under pressure that volatilize when released from pressure.

Methods of pesticide application to foliage   The most common method of applying pesticides to foliage plants is with high volume, high pressure sprayers producing 200 to 500 pounds of pressure per square inch (14 to 35 kilograms per square centimeter). Stationary or portable units of several hundred gallons capacity are used in large commercial operations and 2 to 5 gallon (8 to 19 liter) hand sprayers operated at lower pressure are used for spot treating in small ranges. The large sprayers should apply 200 to 500 gallons per acre (1,868 to 4,676 liters per hectare) of the pesticide-water mixture through a nozzle or spray gun that gives a droplet size of 150 microns or greater. Maintenance of good equipment, adequate spray tank pressure, agitation, efficient nozzle systems, proper pesticide concentration, and operation by careful, well-trained personnel are necessary for effective applications. Frequently, an adjuvant or a spreader and/or sticker is added to the pesticide solution to aid in coverage, retention, and persistence of pesticides on foliage. This is especially important when plants are irrigated from overhead.

Low-volume or mist-blower sprayers, although not widely used, are an effective application method, and there are small, gas and electric units for greenhouse use, as well as large units for field applications. These applicators inject the concentrated pesticide-water mixtures into a rapidly moving stream of air or onto spinning discs, which fracture the liquid into small droplets. The liquid-air mixture is rapidly discharged to cover foliage with small, noncoalescing droplets. Low-volume sprays are generally five to ten times more concentrated than high-volume sprays; therefore, application should not be to run off, which would increase the probability of chemical injury to plants.

In addition to applications as sprays, specific chemicals may be released within closed greenhouses as aerosols, thermal fogs, or combustible or vaporized pesticides. Pesticides may be dissolved in a liquified propellent under pressure and applied as aerosols, small droplets of 10 to 50 microns suspended in the air upon release through a nozzle. Droplets of highly volatile materials, such as dichlorvos (Vapona®), evaporate upon release, resulting in fumigation with no residual activity. Particles of nonvolatile materials, for example, resmethrin, settle predominately onto upper leaf surfaces and may be ineffective in controlling pests that develop on the undersides of leaves. Aerosol formulations of volatile pesticides may be discharged toward the fan intake in greenhouses equipped with polyethylene ventilating tubes, so the chemical can be distributed throughout the greenhouse from a single location.

Thermal fogs are aerosol-sized smoke particles usually produced by injecting petroleum oil-insecticide solutions into the hot air of engine exhaust systems. The resulting particles are discharged with the exhaust into the greenhouse until the entire volume is filled. Insecticides used in fogging are specially formulated, and those prepared for spraying or dusting should not be used.

Combustible pesticides that produce smokes of aerosol-sized particles, such as nicotine or sulfotepp (Dithio®), are convenient in small greenhouses. Containers of these materials are placed in the aisles and ignited with sparklers. A limited number of insecticides, including nicotine and naled (Dibrom®), also can be vaporized from steam pipes or pans placed over electric heaters.

To obtain effective treatments with aerosols, fogs, or smokes, greenhouses must be tightly closed for at least 1 to 2 hours after application. Applications are generally made during early mornings or evenings when temperatures are lowest. Foliage must be dry to avoid phytotoxicity and air temperatures should be rising to avoid condensation of moisture on plants. Personnel involved in applications must wear approved gas masks and be properly clothed to protect skin surfaces, and the treated enclosures must be thoroughly ventilated before reentry.

Bare root and soil applications   Various organophosphates (ethoprop, fensulfothion) or carbamates (oxamyl) can be used to control nematodes on bare-rooted plants when used as dip treatments. Soil is washed from roots, which are then placed in nematicidal solutions for an appropriate length of time. Although eradication of nematodes is difficult, some nonfumigant nematicides have reduced nematode populations below detectable levels. Dip treatments involve very close contact between personnel and chemicals that are highly toxic to mammals; therefore, extreme care and use of protective clothing, including rubber gloves, apron, and boots, is necessary.

Multipurpose fumigants (methyl bromide and chloropicrin) are toxic to insects and nematodes on contact, are extremely phytotoxic, and are useful only as preplanting treatments. Methyl bromide is especially effective in control of nematodes, weed seeds, insects, and soil-borne pathogens. Treatment of potting soils and raised or ground beds with methyl bromide is best accomplished by its release as a gas directly under a vapor-proof, polyethylene cover. Other soil fumigants, such as EDB and DD are injected into soil with tractor-mounted applicators; however, structural and irrigation supports restrict movement of large fumigant applicators in most nurseries. Soil should be cultivated in beds or benches prior to fumigation, be at a temperature of 64° to 75°F (18° to 24°C), and contain sufficient moisture for good seed germination to maximize penetration and effectiveness of the fumigant. Nematodes inside undecayed roots are protected from fumigants, and therefore nematode-infected plant material should not be incorporated into soil media. Organic soils require higher fumigant concentrations than mineral soils to compensate for adsorption of the active ingredient on organic matter. Caution must be taken to ensure sufficient aeration of treated soils prior to planting or use.

Pests may be introduced into production areas or may survive preplant treatment; therefore, effective postplant soil treatments are often necessary. Several organophosphate and carbamate contact insecticides and nematicides are effective as postplanting treatments. The systemic carbamates, possessing insecticidal, miticidal, and nematicidal activity, are also effective against foliage-feeding and soil-inhabiting insects, mites, and nematodes. Dimethoate and oxydemetonmethyl are systemics with predominately insecticidal activity. Options for soil treatment include either drench or granular applications, depending on the formulation of the pesticide used. Drench applications to bed or bench areas require that a specific volume of pesticide-water mixture be applied in sufficient water to be evenly distributed over the area to be treated, followed by additional water to wet the soil to a depth of 4 to 6 inches (10 to 15 centimeters). In treating potted plants a specific volume of pesticide-water mixture is applied to each container or sufficient volume is added to completely drench media in containers. Drench application of pesticides to containers should not be followed by additional irrigation. Plants should not receive media drench treatments during moisture stress because root injury might result. Emulsifiable and soluble formulations can be applied with trickle irrigation systems; however, the application of highly toxic solutions by overhead sprinkler irrigation is hazardous and not advised. The highly toxic organophosphate or carbamate pesticides should not be incorporated into soils prior to handling or planting, but applied after root development. Granular formulations should be uniformly distributed over the soil surface of containers, beds, or benches, followed by irrigation with sufficient water to flush chemicals into the root zone. Granules should never be applied to moistened foliage or allowed to remain on foliage because of the possibility of phytotoxicity or injury to personnel who come in contact with treated plants.

The preferred construction of benches for pest control is to have them elevated above the soil surface approximately 30 inches (76 centimeters), as control of soil pests is more successful in aboveground units. Pesticide applications to media in raised benches can reduce some pest species to undetectable levels, but applications to ground beds frequently fail to satisfactorily reduce pest populations. Although regular drench treatments of ground beds can aid in production of quality plants, infestations of pests under quarantine may be difficult, if not impossible, to eradicate.

Pesticide toxicity   Pesticides are toxic substances, and it is essential to understand the basic principles of toxicity. Some pesticides are more toxic than others, and these differences relate to the specific toxicity of the technical chemical, the dose, length of exposure, and the rate of entry or absorption by the body. Toxic effects are determined on laboratory animals under experimental conditions. This toxicity is defined as the LD_{50}, expressed as milligrams of toxicant per kilogram of body weight, and the dose that kills 50 percent of the test animals. Pesticide toxicity is expressed primarily in terms of the oral and dermal LD_{50}, with oral meaning ingestion by mouth and dermal, absorption through the skin. LD_{50} values are only approximate, but the lower the LD_{50} value, the more toxic is the pesticide. For example, the dermal LD_{50} values for resmethrin, oxydemetonmethyl, and aldicarb are 3,000, 250, and 5 milligrams of toxicant per kilogram of body weight of test animals, respectively. Acute dermal toxicity values are usually higher than those for oral toxicity, since more pesticide is required to kill from dermal exposure than from oral ingestion. Dermal toxicity figures are especially important to personnel who handle or apply pesticides, as approximately 90 percent of the pesticides to which the body is subjected during most exposure situations is deposited on the skin.

Phytotoxicity   Pesticides may cause plant damage, which often results in unsalable plants. Phytotoxicity usually is an injury to the foliage exhibited as marginal or tip burn (necrosis), yellowing (chlorosis), blackened or necrotic spotting, or abnormal growth, including stunting or a combination of symptoms. Any portion of the plant may be affected, but new growth is most likely to be damaged. Phytotoxicity may be minimized by applying pesticides early in the morning so the foliage will be dry before temperatures reach 85° to 90°F (29° to 32°C). Rapid drying of foliar spray deposits is important, and chances of injury are increased when spray solutions remain wet on foliage for longer than 1 to 2 hours. Plants to be treated should not be under moisture or other stresses and should be in healthy growing conditions. Almost all aerosols will induce injury if applied closer than 18 to 24 inches (46 to 61 centimeters) from the plant, and aerosols, fogs, or smokes should never be applied to wet foliage or when condensation may occur during treatment. Wettable powders are generally less phytotoxic than emulsifiable concentrates owing to the lack of solvents and emulsifiers that contribute to plant injury, but wettable powders leave objectionable residues on foliage. Phytotoxic effects of pesticide applications may be cumulative. One or two applications may produce no injury, but the third or fourth may result in significant damage. When pesticides recommended as foliar sprays are applied as drenches by using misting heads or overhead sprinklers, excessive amounts of the chemical solution can be trapped in leaf axials, cups, or whorls and increase the probability of phytotoxicity. Such injuries may not appear until several weeks after application when injured, developing leaves begin to expand. Such injuries may not be observed in production but might become visible in retail shops or customers' homes. Combination sprays of several pesticides may produce injury that would not occur if each of the formulations had been applied separately. Labels and compatibility charts should be consulted prior to mixing pesticides. Environmental conditions differ from nursery to nursery, making it necessary to evaluate potential phytotoxic effects of repeated pesticide applications to several plants under actual growing conditions prior to large-scale use. Product labels and other information from state Cooperative Extension Services or Experiment Stations should be consulted for correct dosage rates, applications, information, and phytotoxicity data.

Pesticide regulations   Pesticide labels and provisions resulting from the Federal Insecticide, Fungicide, and Rodenticide Act (FIFRA) of 1947, as amended by the Federal Environmental Pesticide Control Act (FEPCA) of 1972 and the Federal Pesticide Act of 1978, regulate all uses of pesticides, and these regulations must be followed. Labels should be read carefully since they may differ in specific plant and pest listing. Specifics regarding pesticide use and certification of pesticide applicators should be obtained from state extension services.

Insects: Structure and Characteristics

Approximately 1 million described insect species mean this is one of the largest classes of animals. Insects possess bilateral symmetry, a segmented external skeleton, and three pairs of legs and are successful competitors, partly owing to their ability to fly, adaptation to different environments, and small size. Their mouthparts vary from two basic types, with one adapted for piercing and sucking liquids and the other for crushing and chewing of tissue. Insects possess a digestive system, excretory organs, respiratory openings or spiracles along sides of their bodies, circulatory systems with a dorsal heart that moves hemolymph (body fluid) through the hemocoel (body cavity), and a reproductive system. Growth of insects, unlike most animals, is a discontinuous process involving isolated periods of growth separated by ecdyses (molting) of the exoskeleton since the skeleton is external. Old brittle skin is shed in ecdyses to reveal a soft, new cuticle, which is elastic and permits the insect to grow. Individuals undergo morphological changes in addition to ecdyses during development and maturation. This process is called metamorphosis and may include various developmental stages, such as egg, larvae, pupae, and adult.

Insects of Major Importance

Aphids

Aphids are soft bodied, pear shaped, generally less than ⅛ inch (3 millimeters) long, and often are found in greenhouse and field production. Common greenhouse species include the green peach aphid, *Myzus persicae* (Sulzer) (Figure 15-1), spirea aphid, *Aphis citricola*, VanderGoot, and cotton or melon aphid, *Aphis gossypii* Glover. Less prevalent species are *Aphis craccivora* Koch and *Toxoptera aurantii* (Fonsc.).

Aphid populations are either adult or nymphal (immature) females under greenhouse conditions and reproduce parthogenetically (the development of an unfertilized egg). Multiplication rates are enormous and are greatly increased by high temperatures common in greenhouses [42]. Adult females produce about fifty nymphs during their life span, and each nymph begins to reproduce in about 7 days [41]. Generally, aphids are wingless, but when colonies become dense, alate (winged) forms are produced that disperse and establish new infestations. Infestations are often noticed first on plants adjacent to greenhouse vents or evaporative cooling pads where winged migrants gain entry. Winged

Figure 15-1.   Nymphs and wingless female green peach aphids infesting lower leaf surfaces of zebra plant. (Photo by R. W. Henley)

forms caught in air currents are rapidly spread throughout greenhouses.

Aphids feed by piercing-sucking mouthparts on stems and undersides of developing leaves, causing distorted or stunted growth. Alert nursery personnel can detect white skins shed by nymphs on upper leaf surfaces, which are often initial signs of infestations. A by-product of aphid feeding is honeydew, which coats infested foliage and provides medium for growth of black, sooty mold fungi, which further renders affected plants unsightly and unsalable. Tropical foliage plants particularly susceptible to aphid infestation are *Alphelandra, Brassaia, Dieffenbachia, Gynura,* and *Hoya.*

Insecticide sprays, soil drenches, or soil surface applications of systemic granular materials are the best approach in aphid control. Preventative programs are usually unnecessary providing control can be established before populations become damaging. Fumigation, fogging, or applications of insect growth regulators are also effective [66, 105]. Initial sources of infestation may be partly eliminated by strict sanitation outside and inside greenhouses and by making sure newly obtained plants are not infested before introduction into production ranges.

Aphids are vectors of plant viruses, which makes control important to prevent potential virus introduction into stock or production plantings.

Mealybugs

Mealybugs are soft-bodied insects ⅛ to ⅕ inch (3 to 5 millimeters) long covered by flocculent, white, waxy filaments. Common species are long-tailed mealybugs, *Pseudococcus longispinus* (Targ. and Tozz.), solanum mealybugs, *Phenacoccus solani* Ferris, striped mealybugs, *Ferrisia virgata* (Cockerell), and citrus mealybugs, *Planococcus citri* (Risso).

Mealybugs are active throughout their life cycle, and several species, such as *P. citri* and *F. virgata* [36, 63], parthenogenetically produce 100 to 300 eggs enclosed in an egg sac composed of secretions produced by the female. *Pseudococcus longispinus* and *P. solani* are ovoviviparous, however, producing living nymphs that hatch from eggs inside of females [63]. Development time is decreased by high temperatures and humidities found under greenhouse conditions. The incubation period of *P. citri* eggs decreases from 14 to 4 days as temperatures increase from 62°F (17°C) to 90°F (32°C), and nymphal development is rapid with maturation in 18 days at 82°F (28°C) [41].

Mealybugs feed by piercing-sucking mouthparts, and affected foliage is covered with honeydew and sooty molds. Most species infest a wide range of plant species, including *Aphelandra, Ardisia, Asparagus, Crassula, Croton, Cryptanthus, Dieffenbachia, Dizygotheca, Dracaena, Epipremnum, Ficus, Gynura, Hoya, Maranta, Nephrolepsis,* and *Syngonium.*

Reproduction of mealybugs is year round in greenhouses; consequently several thorough coverage sprays of effective insecticides or insect growth regulators at intervals of approximately 14 days should be applied [27, 31, 96]. Adults and nymphs tend to form dense colonies on infested foliage, making it difficult for contact insecticides to penetrate their waxy deposits (Figure 15-2); thus systemic insecticides are more effective than contact types. Initial infestations should be controlled since unsightly waxy deposits that accumulate will remain on foliage even after the insects are controlled.

Root Mealybugs

In addition to foliar mealybugs, several small mealybug species (*Rhizoecus* spp., *Geococcus* sp.) ¹/₂₅ to ⅛ inch (1 to 3 millimeters) long are found below soil surfaces [12, 24, 25, 35, 73]. Certain species of *Rhizoecus* are ovoviviparous, having young born alive [92]. Populations often take 3 to 6 months to become easily visible. A generation from egg to egg for greenhouse colonies of *R. americanus* (Hambleton) requires 42 to 50 days

Figure 15-2. Colony of solanum mealybugs infesting purple passion vine. (Photo by R. W. Henley)

[35], while a generation of *R. pritchardi* McKenzie requires 2 to 4 months [92]. Nymphs are active and may crawl from pot to pot through drainage holes or be spread by irrigation water, with dissemination increased when roots have grown through drainage openings. Infestations were found to be more numerous in loose, well-drained soil consisting of perlite, coarse peat, or wood shavings [73].

These subterranean mealybugs feed on roots and root hair tissues by piercing-sucking mouthparts, and infestations are often overlooked until they are severe enough to cause reduced plant vigor, foliar chlorosis, and slow plant growth. Careful examination of infested roots will reveal white, cottonlike masses that contain eggs and females (Figure 15-3). Greenhouse infestations frequently begin with the purchase of infested plant materials; therefore, samples of newly acquired plants should be removed from containers and the roots inspected before movement into greenhouse areas. Populations may become established in soils beneath infested plants, forming a source of reinfestation to susceptible crops, including *Araucaria, Asparagus,* various Bromeliaceae, *Chamaedorea, Chlorophytum, Chrysalidocarpus, Cordyline, Dieffenbachia, Dizygotheca, Epipremnum, Ficus, Hedera, Hoya, Nephrolepsis, Peperomia, Philodendron, Pilea, Schlumbergera,* and *Syngonium.*

Sterilization of soil, pots, and tools is necessary to eradicate root mealybugs, and destroy infested plants that have not responded to previous insecticide treatments [25, 31, 74]. Drenches are effective and granular insecticides will control root mealybugs provided granules are uniformly applied over soil surfaces and adequately watered in. Placing containers on clean raised benches or plastic sheeting also aids in preventing infestations. The incubation period of *R. americanus* eggs is approximately 9 days [35] and, therefore, drenches applied at approximately 14-day intervals may be useful so that adults and newly hatched individuals are killed.

Scales

Scales are closely related to mealybugs, but have a hard shell rather than waxy filaments and are characteristically sedentary or nonmobile when mature [62]. Scales are usually inconspicuous, and by the time an infestation is noted the population is usually so large the plant is unsalable. Eggs are produced beneath the female shell in a general life cycle and hatch into flat, translucent crawlers about $1/100$ inch (0.3 millimeter) long. Crawlers are the only active stage not covered by a hard covering; they move to newly expanded foliage to settle on or near veins on undersides of leaves or on stems. Plant sap is withdrawn by long stylets during feeding from sieve tubes and phloem parenchyma of hosts [84]. Mated females produce offspring of both sexes, while parthenogenetic female scales produce only females. Mature males are frail, winged individuals and live for only 3 to 4 days.

Figure 15-3. Bromeliad root infested with root mealybug nymphs and cottonlike egg-containing masses.

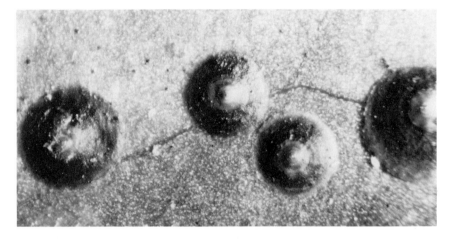

Figure 15-4.   Florida red scale infestation of English ivy.

There are numerous scales of economic importance to ornamental foliage plants, and these species belong to one of two principal groups, the armored (hard-bodied scales) or the unarmored (soft-bodied scales). Armored scales are covered with a hard, nonliving covering composed of secreted material incorporated with castoff skins, and in many species, females can be exposed by lifting this covering. Unarmored types do not possess this hard, separate outer covering. Honeydew is produced during feeding, allowing prolific growth of sooty molds.

Figure 15-5.   Latania scale: Note position of scales adjacent to main leaf veins. (Photo by R. W. Henley)

Figure 15-6.   Fern scale infestation on staghorn fern. The large, dark colored oyster shell shaped structure is the female scale while males are the white, elongated structures.

Principal armored scale pests include Florida red scale, *Chrysomphalus aonidum* (L.) (Figure 15-4), latania scale, *Hemiberlesia lataniae* (Signoret) (Figure 15-5), fern scale, *Pinnaspis aspidistrae* (Signoret) (Figure 15-6), and the false oleander scale, *Pseudaulacaspis cockerelli* (Cooley) (Figure 15-7). Adult female armor for Florida red scale and latania scale is circular, convex, and approximately $^1/_{16}$ to $^1/_{12}$ inch (1.5 to 2 millimeters) in diameter, with the former species reddish and the latter white to gray in color [13, 106]. Adult female cover of fern scale is reddish brown, shaped like an oyster shell, and is $^1/_{16}$ to $^1/_{10}$ inch (1.5 to 2.5 millimeters) long. The fern scale is a polyphagous species, particularly damaging on *Adiantum, Asparagus* sp., *Asplenium nidus* L., *Nephrolepsis exaltata,* and *Platycerium bifurcatum* C. chr. Cover of adult female false oleander scale is pear shaped, white, and about $^1/_{12}$ to $^1/_8$ inch (2 to 3 millimeters) in length [108], and this species frequently infest such hosts as *Chamaedorea* and *Chrysalidocarpus* palms.

Japanese wax scale, *Ceroplastes ceriferus* (Fabricius), is an unarmored scale the adult female of which is $^1/_4$ inch (6.3 millimeters) long, covered with a thick, convex, white to pinkish waxy covering, and parthenogenetically produces approximately 1,000 eggs beneath her body (Figure 15-8). One and one half to two generations occur in greenhouses per year [22]. Wax scales excrete honeydew and the resulting sooty molds may be the first indication of their presence. Heavy infestations may cause leaf drop, and a wide range of ornamentals is susceptible, including the two foliage plants *Ficus* and *Podocarpus*.

Coccus hesperidum L., or brown soft scale, is a widely distributed and

Figure 15-7.   Infestation of false oleander scale on areca palm. The light colored markings radiating from scales are feeding injuries and are a typical symptom of false oleander scale infestation of palms. (Photo by R. W. Henley)

Figure 15-8.   Stem infestation by Japanese wax scale on *Podocarpus*. (Photo by R. W. Henley)

Figure 15-9.   Brown soft scale infesting *Pteris* fern.

persistent greenhouse pest on a vast number of ornamentals [64]. Females are elongate, oval, flat, about ⅛ inch (3 millimeters) long, pale yellow to brown and often flecked with brown spots, and reproduce ovoviviparously (Figure 15-9). The life cycle requires 40 to 60 days at temperatures between 65°F (18°C) and 77°F (25°C), and six to seven overlapping generations occur annually [84]. The number of progeny produced by each female is estimated to range from 80 to 250. Generally, infestation occurs along leaf midribs and production of honeydew allows growth of sooty mold fungi. A related pest, the green scale, *C. viridus* (Green), also is frequently detected on foliage plants [18].

   The hemispherical scale, *Saissetia coffeae* (Walker), is globular, smooth, glossy, hemispherical, brown and ¹/₁₂ to ¹/₆ inch (2 to 4 millimeters) long [16] (Figure 15-10). Reproduction is year round in greenhouses, with overlapping generations. Related species, *S. miranda* (Cockerell and Parrott), the Mexican black scale, and *S. neglecta* De Lotto, the Caribbean black scale, are also serious pests and attack numerous foliage plants, including *Adiantum, Aphelandra, Ardisia, Asplenium, Nephrolepsis, Pteris,* and *Zamia.*

   Chemical control is difficult because of waxy coverings on females, which protects eggs and newly hatched crawlers. Sprays or drenches of systemic insecticides can be effective, and repeated spray applications at 2- to 3-week intervals may be necessary to control established populations [28]. Crawlers will be the only stage affected by contact insecticides, and the interval between applications may need to be decreased to 10 to 14 days. Sprays must be applied to obtain thorough coverage on all plant

Figure 15-10. Hemispherical scale infestation of the lower leaf surface of zebra plant. (Photo by R. W. Henley)

parts, especially lower leaf surfaces. Systemic granules applied to the soil surface may provide long-term protection.

Crawler stages are practically invisible to the unaided eye and difficult to detect on propagation materials, but introductions into production areas usually occur at this stage. Stock plants, therefore, must be maintained scale free. Newly acquired plants should be quarantined to inspect for living scales. Lift the female covering using a knife point to determine whether a scale is alive. Scales firmly attached to leaf or stem surfaces or that reveal a yellow-orange, plump mass beneath the armored cover are alive. Shells easily removed indicate dead scales. Inspect for living scales during all periods of treatment, especially on new foliage. Persistence in treatment and careful observation of results is necessary for successful control. Periodically, dark brown or black circular structures that resemble scales are detected on upper and lower leaf surfaces, but are in fact global deposits from a saprophytic fungus, *Sphaerobolus stellatus* Tode ex Pers., inhabiting soil media [1].

Whiteflies

Trialeurodes vaporariorum (Westwood), the greenhouse whitefly, is a serious pest of poinsettia and bedding plants such as ageratum, fuchsia, and salvia, but is only occasionally important to foliage plants, unless foliage plants are grown in conjunction with major whitefly hosts. Adults are approximately $1/25$ inch (1 millimeter) long, with long wings covered with a white, waxy material and tend to congregate on younger or newly expanded foliage (Figure 15-11). Adults are the most easily detected stage since they fly when disturbed, but quickly settle again on lower leaf surfaces. Females begin laying eggs within 2 days after emerging, and about 100 eggs are produced, usually on the underside of foliage, which hatch in 10 days under greenhouse temperatures. Small scalelike crawlers move about for 1 to 3 days prior to settling near leaf veins. The pupal stage is formed following two nymphal stages that last 3 to 4 days each. Adults emerge in about 6 days at 70° to 80°F (21° to 27°C), with complete life cycles taking 3 weeks at an average 70°F (21°C) [57]. Increased temperatures shorten life cycles [40]. Infestations can begin by introduction of infested plants or migration of adults from other crops or weed hosts inside or outside of greenhouses. All development stages will be present once infestation is established. Adults and nymphs feed with piercing and sucking mouthparts and excrete honeydew. Seriously affected foliage becomes chlorotic, wilted, and covered by sooty molds.

Adults are the most susceptible stage to contact insecticides, while eggs and pupae are the most resistant. Fumigants or aerosols are toxic to adults but have no effect on nymphal stages, but nymphs are susceptible to systemics. Thorough coverage spray applications of insecticides usu-

Figure 15-11.   Adult whiteflies feeding on the lower leaf surface of newly developed foliage.

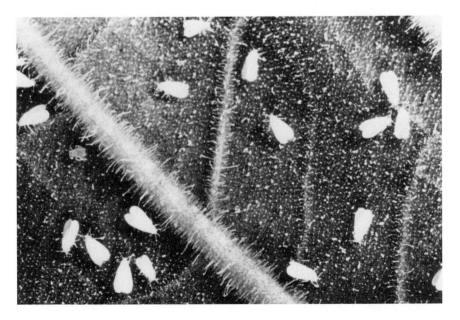

ally are the most effective, but aerosols or fumigants are easiest to use in large commercial greenhouses. Importance of the time interval between aerosol applications and total number of applications has been documented [91]; dichlorvos aerosols applied four times at 10-day intervals reduced *T. vaporariorum* populations by 26.5 percent, while eight applications at 5-day intervals caused a 99.7 percent reduction. Foliar sprays of synthetic pyrethroids also were reported effective [111], but soil drenches of systemic insecticides or soil surface applications of granular systemics might give longer residual activity. Constant inspection and elimination of extraneous host plants inside as well as outside greenhouses [83] are essential to prevent establishment of infestations.

Adults occasionally become infected by entomogenous fungi, such as *Cephalosporium* sp., but this appears of little practical use for biological control since favorable environmental conditions would also encourage plant pathogenic fungi [39]. Interaction between greenhouse whitefly and a small wasp parasite, *Encarsia formosa* Gahan, has been recognized in Europe [6], and control recommendations have been developed for poinsettia production [34].

Thrips

Thrips are slender, $1/25$ to $1/12$ inch (1 to 2 millimeters) in length and include banded greenhouse thrips, *Hercinothrips femoralis* (O. M. Reuter), greenhouse thrips, *Heliothrips haemorrhoidalis* (Bouche), and *Echinothrips americanus* Morgan. Infestations may begin with newly acquired plants or invasion into greenhouses from outside host plants. Their life cycle may require 23 to 31 days under greenhouse conditions and is influenced directly by temperature and humidity [58]. Pupation occurs in the soil or on plant hosts. Larvae are active and adults are able to jump when disturbed.

Adult thrips and larvae feed primarily on young tissue in the bud or shoot apex by sucking sap after rasping surface cells with their mouthparts. Injured tissue dries out, giving a whitish or silver-flecked appearance to affected areas (Figure 15-12). Heavy infestations often result in noticeable deposits of fecal material on infested leaf surfaces. Infestations of vegetative apexes in *Sansevieria* cause necrosis of tissue, which callouses over and disfigures resulting foliage. Other hosts are *Aphelandra, Ardisia, Brassaia, Dieffenbachia, Philodendron,* and *Syngonium.* Cuban laurel thrips, *Gynaikothrips ficorum* (Marchal), produce severe leaf deformation and defoliation of *Ficus nitida* [78, 110].

Aerosols, smokes, and fogs are generally effective in thrip control, but thrips are often protected in shoot apexes or tightly curled leaves, and systemic insecticide sprays or granules are more effective.

Figure 15-12.   Injury due to thrip feeding on *Ardisia*. (Photo by R. W. Henley)

Fungus Gnats

Adults of this pest are ⅛-inch (3-millimeters) long black gnats possessing a delicate pair of wings, a pair of many-segmented antennae, and long dangling legs. They are abundant on soil surfaces or leaves under humid greenhouse conditions. Legless larvae inhabiting soils are slender, white with a black head capsule, and grow to ¼ inch (6 millimeters) long (Figure 15-13). Common dark-winged *Bradysia* spp. are weak fliers and are often observed running over soil surfaces. Adult females live for about 1 week and produce 75 to 200 microscopic eggs in soil crevices. Hatch occurs in 4 to 6 days, and larval development continues for 2 to 3 weeks, followed by a 4- to 6-day pupal stage in soils at 72°F (22°C) [38]. Life-cycle time decreases with increased temperatures, and several generations of flies commonly overlap.

Larvae of many species are saprophagous, feeding on decaying plant tissue, but a few are pests associated with feeding on and decay of plant roots, root hairs, and lower stem tissues. Organic soil of high moisture content appears to enhance infestations, especially in the presence of decaying plant tissue. Feeding may be particularly injurious to rooted cuttings or young plants [70] and larval feeding injury predisposes seedling plants to fungal (*Fusarium* spp.) attack [55].

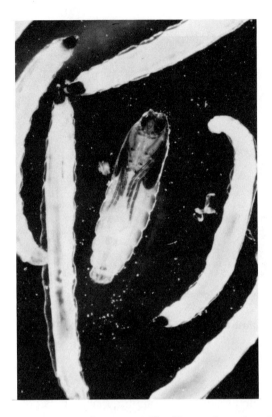

Figure 15-13. Black-headed fungus gnat larvae and pupa (central figure) obtained from invested soil.

Controls are usually directed against larval stages by applications of chemical drenches or sprays to infested soils, and treatment of walk areas and soils beneath benches aid in control. Aerosols or vapor treatments applied against general greenhouse pests reduce infestations providing applications are made every few days over several weeks to eliminate overlapping adult stages. An experimental, nonchemical method of control with potential is the use of entomogenous nematodes that selectively attack and kill larvae and are harmless to plants [37, 75].

Lepidopterous Larvae

Armyworms, loopers, and cutworms are not generally major pests of foliage plants, but infestations can occur when moths fly into greenhouses from outdoor areas. Individuals detected are commonly *Spodoptera* species, including the southern armyworm, *S. eridania* (Cramer), the beet armyworm, *S. exigua* (Hübner), and *S. latifascia* (Walker). Initial infestations are difficult to detect, as newly hatched larvae feed on superficial tissues of lower leaf surfaces. This feeding produces a "window" effect on leaf surfaces, a condition commonly observed with *Brassaia* seedlings and *Peperomia* (Figure 15-14). Large larvae, 1 to 1½ inches (2.5 to 3.8 centimeters) long, begin to skeletonize leaf tissue, dispersing and finally consuming entire leaves. Pupation occurs in protected areas on lower leaf surfaces, leaf axils, or just below the soil surface. Larvae are general feeders, and specific foliage crops infested include *Asparagus, Brassaia, Cissus, Dieffenbachia, Peperomia, Philodendron, Maranta,* and various ornamental Cactaceae and Crassulaceae.

Infestations often begin when moths gain entry to greenhouses from outdoor areas; thus control can be obtained by maintaining structures that exclude adults. Worms are chewing insects, susceptible to contact or stomach poison insecticides, and are usually unaffected by many systemics. Control is easier when infestations are detected early and larvae are small. Preventative sprays may be necessary where constant reinfestation is probable.

An effective and low mammalian toxicity material specific for lepidopterous larvae is the bacterium *Bacillus thuringiensis,* which is not a contact poison; larvae must eat plant parts containing residues of the bacterial spores and crystals for it to be effective. Spray coverage must include both leaf surfaces so that newly hatched larvae consume a lethal dose in initial feedings, and a spreader-sticker should be used to improve coverage and retention on foliage. Feeding is stopped within 1 to 2 hours following consumption of treated foliage and death usually occurs within a week [17, 33]. Repeated applications at 7 to 14 days may be needed to maintain residues on rapidly growing foliage, especially when moths are detected migrating into greenhouses.

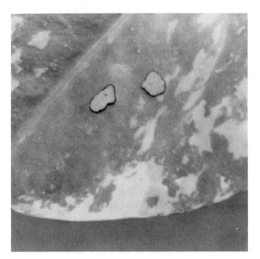

Figure 15-14.   Injury by feeding of small Lepidopterous larvae on lower leaf surface of *Peperomia.* (Photo by R. W. Henley)

Miscellaneous Pests

Collembola

Springtails or collembola are soil-inhabiting insects, usually less than ½ inch (2 millimeters) in length. They are wingless, although most species possess a springing organ that enables them to jump when disturbed; thus they are frequently mistaken for fleas. Springtails are rarely injurious pests, although high populations are often detected in potting soils, especially on surfaces after watering. Damage might occur when seedlings or young plants are attacked, with root hairs destroyed or leaf tissue in contact with infested soil skeletonized [10].

Symphilids

Greenhouse or garden symphilids, *Scutigerella immaculata* (Newport), can be serious pests of greenhouse ornamentals, feeding on fine roots and root hairs. Mature *S. immaculata* are approximately ¼ inch (6 millimeters) long, white with twelve pairs of legs, and resemble small centipedes. Symphilids inhabit moist, highly organic soils and tend to float to soil surfaces following irrigation.

Centipedes

The centipede has a body divided into segments each bearing a pair of legs. They are usually predatory, live in damp places under organic litter or in the soil, and are not harmful to plants.

Millipedes

Millipedes, or thousand-legged worms, are slow moving creatures, live within moist, organic soils, and feed nocturnally primarily on decaying plant tissue. Generally, living plant tissue is not attacked, although seedlings and succulent plants may be injured. The hard-shelled, wormlike body of millipedes has numerous short legs along its sides and tends to form a coil when disturbed.

Sowbugs and Pillbugs

Individuals are ¼ to ⅓ inch (6 to 8 millimeters) long with segmented, shell-like bodies, and roll up into a sphere or migrate to cover when disturbed. They are generally nocturnal, feeding on decomposing organic tissue but occasionally feeding on roots and stems.

The preceding are all soil-inhabiting species and insecticides must be applied to soil for control.

Mite Pests

Mites or *Acarina* lack abdominal segmentation and antennae, are generally small, and, like insects, possess an exoskeletal covering. Plant-feeding mites have needlelike piercing mouthparts. Adults possess four pairs of legs, while the larval stage normally has only three pairs. The major plant-feeding species are Tetranychidae, or spider mites, Tarsonemidae, broad or cyclamen mites, and Tenuipalpidae, false spider mites. A detailed review on mites injurious to economic plants is available [46].

Spider Mites

Mites in the genus *Tetranychus* are the most common and destructive mites on tropical foliage plants (Figure 15-15) and commonly are referred to as two-spotted spider mites, red spider mites, or simply red

Figure 15-15.   Parlor palm leaflets heavily infested by spider mites. Note the mass of mites at the leaflet apex consisting of young female spider mites ready for dispersal. (Photo by R. W. Henley)

spiders. The common green species with two black spots is *T. urticae* Koch, and a reddish carmine spider mite is *T. cinnabarinus* (Boisduval) [2]. The tumid spider mite, *T. gloveri* Banks, is bright red and is occasionally a severe pest of tropical foliage.

Adult *T. urticae* females are about $1/50$ inch (0.5 millimeter) long, eight legged, and hardly visible to the unaided eye. A $10\times$ magnification is needed to see them easily, and populations often become dense before detection. Most alert nursery personnel recognize this pest when it produces webs over the foliage, especially on new leaves. Female *T. urticae* can oviposit an average of 144 eggs over a 19-day period on leaf surfaces or attached to strands of silk [8]. Other reports place the average life duration of females at about 30 days and the number of eggs laid per female at 90 to 200 [46]. Incubation time for eggs is dependent on temperature and varies from 3 days at 90°F (32°C) to 28 days at 50°F (10°C) [41]. Development time from hatch to adult takes about 7 days, but can be reduced by increased temperatures [3, 8], with maximum developmental temperature apparently about 104°F (40°C) [46]. There are eight developmental stages, including the egg, six-legged larva, first quiescent, protonymph, second quiescent, deutonymph, third quiescent, and adult [3, 7]. Unfertilized females produce males and fertilization is needed for production of both sexes [46]. Females have a period of 1 to 2 days following maturation before initiation of egg production [46].

Knowledge of mites' dispersal mechanism is important in understanding the life cycle of this pest. Newly matured females congregate at the apex of plants, typically at the tip of the apical leaf as the infestation and subsequent competition for food increase (Figure 15-15). Individual mites then drop on silken threads, forming a rope of living mites, spreading thus to new areas by air movement, on clothes, by cultural operations, or by dropping from ends of the ropes to disperse along the ground [46]. Severe and irreversible damage has usually occurred by the time of this phase, resulting in an unsalable crop and potential mite introductions into other areas.

Spider mites usually feed on undersides of newly developed leaves by piercing leaf surfaces with their mouthparts and removing the cellular contents. Mites inhabit all plant surfaces in the case of heavy attack. Affected tissues are void of chloroplasts and become grayish or yellowed speckled, a symptom especially prominent when viewing the upper leaf surface. Transpiration is accelerated and photosynthesis is inhibited with severe infestations and leaf injury affecting water balance [46]. These effects result in infested leaves becoming dry, parchmentlike and dropping. Severe defoliation of *T. urticae* infested *Brassaia* has been noted when plants are maintained under low humidity in indoor plantings, which is partly due to mite-induced water stress intensified by low humidity. Toxic or plant growth regulating chemicals are injected in or released on plant tissue during mite feeding, which may be involved in symptom expression [46].

Major foliage plant hosts are *Brassaia, Calathea, Chamaedorea, Chrysalidocarpus, Cissus, Codiaeum, Cordyline, Dieffenbachia, Dracaena, Fatshedera, Fatsia, Hedera, Maranta,* and *Polyscias.*

Best control results for mites often are obtained if preventative miticide sprays are applied at 2- to 4-week intervals. Aerosols, fogs, and smokes may be effective if used in a preventative program, but specific miticides sprayed on upper and lower leaf surfaces a minimum of two times at 5- to 7-day intervals are necessary to control thriving populations. Some miticides are more effective in killing only active stages, and repeated applications are necessary so that adults and active individuals hatching from eggs or arising from quiescent stages are killed.

A major difficulty in continued mite control, especially in greenhouses, is the development of strains resistant to routinely used miticides [14]. This phenomenon is worldwide and occurs with most classes of miticides (Table 15-3). Resistance is the development within mite populations of a strain able to tolerate concentrations of miticides that are lethal to the majority of individuals in such populations. Susceptible species are repeatedly removed from the population, leaving the more tolerant individuals when mite populations are exposed repeatedly to the same chemical. The probability of resistant individuals increasing and becoming established in a population is quite high, while reversion to susceptibility may be slow [69]. Mite populations resistant to one chemical often show various degrees of resistance to other chemically related miticides and even to some nonrelated ones. This has caused difficulties in the development of effective alternative miticides that stay apace with the rise of resistance. Growers should become familiar with chemical classifications of miticides and learn from experience which chemicals, when correctly applied, fail to give satisfactory control and then try nonchemically related products (Table 15-3).

A potentially useful, nonchemical means of controlling *T. urticae* in greenhouses are predaceous mites, *Phytoseiulus persimilis* A.-H. and *P. macropilis* (Banks) [4, 77]. These biological agents are being used in Europe for mite control in greenhouse production of vegetables and ornamentals [15, 45]. However, in production of tropical foliage, supplemental applications of selective miticides may be necessary when *T. urticae* densities reach damaging levels [90]. The predator must be able to survive an integrated control program for an entire pest and disease complex.

TABLE 15-3   Classification of miticides according to chemical structure

Chlorinated hydrocarbons: dicofol (Kelthane®)
Sulfones–sulfonates: tetradifon (Tedion®)
Sulfites: propargite (Omite®)
Cyclic carbonate: oxythioquinox (Morestan®)
Carbamates: aldicarb (Temik®)
Organotin: Plictran®, Vendex®
Pentac®

Tarsonemid Mites

The broad mite, *Polyphagotarsonemus latus* (Banks), and the cyclamen mite, *Steneotarsonemus pallidus* (Banks), are microscopic mites, less than $1/100$ inch (0.25 millimeter) long. Broad mites are translucent to whitish in color, and males carry the female "pupa" prior to copulation, a habit that increases probabilities for dispersal of populations [21]. Individuals may also be spread or vectored by green peach aphids [87]. *Polyphagotarsonemus latus* eggs, on the leaf surface, hatch within 2 to 3 days under greenhouse conditions and nymphs mature in an additional 4 to 6 days [21]. Multiplication of this species can be rapid, with only 4 to 5 days required to complete a generation [46]. Unfertilized females produce only males.

Feeding occurs on lower leaf surfaces of young, tender, and newly expanded foliage of shoot apexes. Toxins are injected into plant tissue during feeding, which cause alteration of normal host tissue development [46]. Feeding is only on living tissue, and infestations cease when susceptible plant tissues die. Webbing, commonly seen with *T. urticae*, is not produced. Initial symptoms of injury are new leaves that are cupped downward, puckered, stunted (Figure 15-16), and have serrated margins. New growth is inhibited during severe infestation (Figure 15-17), and necrosis of the vegetative shoot apex occurs, followed by abscission of affected plant parts (Figure 15-18). Severely affected plants, such as *Aphelandra, Episcia, Fatsia,* and *Hedera,* are stunted with distorted foliage and are unsalable. Infestations often escape detection, particularly in stock areas, thus mites are transferred to propagation and finishing areas before detection occurs.

A minimum of two miticide applications, especially to new growth, at 5- to 7-day intervals will control thriving infestations [26]. Infested cuttings in propagation areas also should be treated or at least receive miticidal sprays immediately following their propagation and movement into production areas. Preventative applications should be applied to stock plants to ensure clean propagation material.

The cyclamen mite, *S. pallidus,* and other *Tarsonemus* spp. fre-

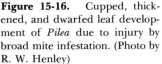

Figure 15-16.   Cupped, thickened, and dwarfed leaf development of *Pilea* due to injury by broad mite infestation. (Photo by R. W. Henley)

quently infest *Begonia, Crassula, Gynura, Pilea,* and *Saintpaulia.* Incubation period for eggs of cyclamen mites is about 4 days at 68°F (20°C), with the life cycle usually requiring 10 to 14 days [41]. Again, males carry female "pupa" until copulation, and high populations occur within unopened buds or between folded leaves [20]. This species also reproduces parthenogenetically [46]. Foliage expanding from cyclamen or *Tarsonemus* mite infested vegetative buds is curled, twisted, and brittle. Toxic substances also are produced in feeding by *S. pallidus* [46]. Cyclamen mites will usually be controlled by measures used to control *P. latus* [88].

Figure   15-17.   Inhibition of leaf expansion due to broad mite infestation of English ivy. (Photo by R. W. Henley)

Figure 15-18.   Necrosis of the shoot apex following severe broad mite infestation of zebra plant. (Photo by R. W. Henley)

False Spider Mites

Several species, including *Brevipalpus californicus* (Banks), *B. obovatus* Donnadieu, *B. phoenicis* (Geijskes), and *B. russulus* (Boisduval), are pests of foliage plants. Reproduction is generally parthenogenetic [60]. Eggs are bright orange red and tightly adhere to leaf surface. Hatch occurs in about 7 days at 77° to 87°F (25° to 31°C); a series of active and quiescent nymphal stages require an additional 10 to 19 days [65]. Female *B. californicus* begin oviposition about 4 days after maturation and lay 1 egg per day for 25 or more days [60]. Adult *Brevipalpus* spp. are more or less sedentary and do not swarm over affected tissue nor produce webs as do spider mites, and individuals are difficult to see as they lie flat against the leaf surface. Infestations are initially indicated by faint brown, scurfy flecks, later merging into bronze or reddish colored areas that may cover an entire upper leaf surface (Figure 15-19). Toxins also may be involved in symptom expression [46]. Adults are reddish and accumulate, as do their discarded skins, which cause, in part, leaf discoloration. Basal leaf areas are affected, vegetative shoot apexes may be killed, and severe leaf drop may occur under heavy infestations. Infestations can be severe on *Aphelandra, Columnea, Hedera, Peperomia,* and various ornamental Cactaceae.

Control consists of two miticidal applications 5 to 7 days apart. Evidence indicates that these species may not be susceptible to the organophosphorus or carbamate chemicals [46].

Infestations are usually detected by the plant injury symptoms rather than by visual observations of the mites themselves because of the

Figure 15-19.   False spider mite injury to basal areas of affected leaves of lipstick plant. (Photo by R. W. Henley)

small size of tarsonemid and tenupalpid mites. Injury is often mistaken as phytotoxicity, disease, or cultural mismanagement. These mites are readily dispersed by brushing infested plants against uninfested ones or by hands or tools during routine cultural operations.

Slugs and Snails

Slugs have soft, unsegmented bodies that exude a slimy mucouslike substance and have the ability to elongate and contract their bodies (Figure 15-20). Snails possess a shell within which the body can be retracted when disturbed. Both are pests in greenhouses. Introductions into production areas may occur in soil or on pots and trays previously stored on the soil, or invasion may occur from outside vegetation. They are omnivorous and voracious feeders, using rasping mouthparts. Immature forms feed on surface tissue and larger individuals eat irregular holes in foliage (Figure 15-21). Feeding is nocturnal, and individuals hide in moist, dark areas, such as under flats or pots during the day, so damage is often attributed to cutworms or other insects. There are numerous species of economic importance. The biology of eleven species of slugs and fourteen species of snails in greenhouses is available [52].

Figure 15-20. Slug inhabiting lower leaf surface of zebra plant.

Figure 15-21. Injury to *Fittonia* from snail feeding. (Photo by R. W. Henley)

Sprays or baits of carbamate insecticide applied to moistened soil around plants, but not directly on foliage, are effective in controlling slugs and snails [50, 51, 89]. Best results are obtained when baits are applied in the afternoon and irrigation avoided until the next day. Feeding is often intermittent and eggs are not affected, making repetitive applications necessary. Good sanitation with removal of extraneous plant material and debris that might shelter these pests aids in control.

Plant Parasitic Nematodes

Plant parasitic nematodes cost producers of tropical foliage plants an unknown but significant sum of money annually. Nematodes affect most major foliage species and cause losses owing to reduced plant yield and quality, as well as marketing losses due to quarantine restrictions. Most producers are familiar with losses due to insects and mites, but often are unaware of actual losses due to nematodes since these pests are hidden from sight; therefore, most damage caused by nematodes goes unreported.

Nematodes: Structure and Characteristics

Plant parasitic nematodes are round worms, generally microscopic, that live in soil or plant tissue. Nematodes are complex in organization, possessing all major physiological systems in higher animals except respiratory and circulatory systems [23]. Plant parasitic nematodes are minute, ranging from $1/100$ to $1/8$ inch (0.25 to 3 millimeters) in length, usually are cylindrical and slender, tapering toward head and tail, and appearing to be worm shaped (vermiform) or threadlike (filiform). Adult females of several horticulturally important species, such as root knot and cyst nematodes, lose their worm shape as they mature and become swollen and saclike or spherical in shape.

Nematodes are nonpigmented, nonsegmented, bilaterally symmetrical, although not related to the common earthworm. External covering of nematodes is a noncellular, multilayered cuticle containing various surface markings important in nematode identification [107]. The cuticle surrounds a cellular layer, the hypodermis, and bands of muscle cells along the length of the nematode. These muscles account for body movement.

Plant parasitic nematodes reproduce primarily by cross fertilization or parthenogenesis [109]. Species in which males and females appear in approximately equal numbers usually produce by cross fertilization, but females predominate in parthenogenetic species. The nematode life cycle consists of specific stages including the egg, four larval stages separated by molts, and the adult. The egg contains an embryo that differentiates to become the first stage larva, which in most species molts inside the egg shell, giving rise to the second stage larva, which hatches. One important aspect in the life cycle of most plant parasitic species is that further development may be retarded until the larva feeds or enters a susceptible host plant [112]. Three additional molts occur, with the nematode finally differentiating into a fully developed adult. Developmental changes, including increased size and maturity, occur between each molt. Females of some species produce one or two eggs per day; others produce 1 to 2,000 during a 30-day period [109]. Species that actually invade and inhabit plant tissue during their life history are referred to as endoparasites and generally deposit eggs within infected tissue as a mass or retain eggs within their body. Nematodes that feed exteriorly on root tissue and complete their life history in the soil are ectoparasitic nematodes, which deposit eggs in soil near or on root surfaces.

Length of the life cycle varies with different nematode species and is affected by environmental factors, such as temperature, moisture, availability of suitable hosts, and soil type [112]. Ectoparasitic nematodes that feed on root exteriors and live totally in the soil and endoparasitic species that invade root tissues, but still have periods of their life cycle in the soil, inhabit soil pore spaces. Nematodes move in water films lining soil particles and are affected by soil types and soil moisture levels. The subject of soil media as an environment for plant parasitic nematodes has been reviewed [49]. Duration of the life cycle and survival under adverse conditions of some nematode species depend on their ability to survive as eggs within the dead female body (cyst nematode) or to persist within infected tissue in a state of cryptobiosis (foliar nematodes) until return of favorable conditions [109].

Nematode feeding is the cause of injury to plants. Anterior ends of nematodes bear a terminal oral opening, usually surrounded by lips, which possess sensory structures referred to as chemoreceptors. These chemoreceptors probably are involved in detection of various chemical or gaseous substances diffusing from plant root tissue and aid in location of food material [9, 53, 56, 109]. The stoma is posterior to the oral opening and contains a stylet used to mechanically rupture plant cell walls, enabling the nematode to invade and/or feed on plant host tissue. Digestive enzymes secreted from esophageal glands are passed through the lumen of the stylet into plant cells [23] to partially digest cellular materials, which are ingested through the stylet into the esophagus and intestine. The salivary secretion of enzymes during feeding often results in abnormal plant cellular growth, including cell enlargement, galls, or distorted foliage or roots. Specific endoparasitic relationships, as with root knot and cyst nematodes, can occur, and specialized feeding sites are developed that provide a constant food source by host tissues.

Detection of Nematode Problems

Nematode effects on ornamental plants are commonly overlooked because they attack generally beneath soil surfaces, and these pests are too small to be seen with the unaided eye. There are several specific plant symptoms useful in diagnosing nematode problems. Symptomology of nematode damage is divided into aboveground or foliar symptoms and below ground or root symptoms. Production personnel should become knowledgeable of these symptoms and be aware that nematode-infected plants will have reduced quality and continue to decline after sale.

Aboveground symptoms are usually due to effects of nematode injuries to root systems. Affected plants may exhibit growth or yield reductions, slow decline, increased wilting even in the presence of adequate soil moisture, nutrient deficiency symptoms, leaf drop, die back, or foliar chlorosis. Infested areas in ground or raised beds typically appear as scattered oval areas of plants exhibiting symptoms that may vary in size and gradually increase in size, resulting from spread of the nematodes by migration or cultivation and irrigation practices. Natural nematode movement in soil is relatively slow; however, rapid spread can occur when infested soil particles, water, plant material, or equipment are moved about [112].

Certain nematodes are not normally soil inhabitants but feed on foliar plant parts. Symptoms of foliar feeding appear as distorted or necrotic leaf and flower buds or leaf galls and, often, angular leaf lesions.

Below ground symptoms of feeding and tissue injury visible on roots include galls, abbreviated or stunted root systems, lesions on roots, and rotting of tissue. A single nematode species may cause one or more of these symptoms. Root galling results as plant host tissues respond to nematode infection by abnormally increasing in size. Galls are often numerous and vary in size from $\frac{1}{8}$ to 1 inch (3 to 25 millimeters) or larger in diameter [107]. Galls induced by nematodes can be distinguished from *Rhizobium* nodules because the latter appear to be produced on the sides of roots and are easily removed from root tissue. Abbreviated root symptoms often result from feeding by ectoparasitic nematodes on root apical meristematic cells. Lesions occurring in surfaces of root tissue are injuries often caused by endoparasitic nematode species that enter plant tissue, migrate through, and damage root tissue during feeding. Many of the symptoms described are similar to those caused by root infections of soil-borne plant pathogens and, therefore, such symptoms do not confirm nematode problems. Nematodes also can interact with soil-borne plant pathogens to further intensify resultant diseases.

Nematode sampling of soil and root samples should be carried out in problems in which nematodes are suspected for confirmation. Specific nematodes and numbers detected are necessary information to determine if nematodes are partially or completely causing the problems. These examinations are necessary in cases where plant symptoms are similar to those encountered with plant diseases. Samples of soil and root tissue can be obtained by using various soil augers or any tool that will remove a 1 to 2 inch (2.5 to 5.1 centimeter) diameter core of soil, 6 to 8 inches (15 to 20 centimeters) in depth from the root rhizosphere. Soils are seldom uniformly infested; thus several samples should be obtained in a systematic manner over the entire suspected area. A composite sample can be formed for each area sampled by mixing all the soil cores and transferring approximately 1 pint (473 milliliters) of soil to a plastic bag. When plants are produced in containers, soil and root samples should be combined from several container-grown plants. Many nematodes are killed when exposed to temperatures in excess of 100°F (38°C); therefore, hold samples at 50° to 60°F (10° to 16°C) until they can be examined.

Nematodes of Major Importance

Numerous genera and species of plant parasitic nematodes have been detected from soil and root samples obtained from commercial tropical foliage plant production facilities. Specific pests, such as root knot, cactus cyst, lesion, burrowing, and foliar nematodes, appear most prominent as economic pests.

Root Knot

Meloidogyne spp. are widely distributed and probably do more damage to foliage plants than any other group of nematodes [71, 85, 94, 103]. Severe damage occurs in temperate areas under greenhouse culture [30, 44], whereas in tropical and subtropical areas injury occurs to greenhouse and field production [80, 101]. There are thirty-five species or subspecies of *Meloidogyne* described, but only *M. javanica* (Treub) Chitwood, *M. incognita* (Kofoid and White) Chitwood, and *M. arenaria* (Neal) Chitwood are recognized as serious pathogens in foliage plant production.

Reproduction in most species of *Meloidogyne* is parthenogenetic; eggs hatch into second-stage larvae that invade root tips from soil, and these migrate through root tissue to the pericycle area where they become sedentary and incapable of further migration [23, 109]. *Meloidogyne* spp. are referred to as sedentary endoparasites because of their permanent positioning within host tissue. *Meloidogyne* spp. exhibit body enlargement in approaching sexual maturity, and during final molt the adult male becomes wormlike while the female remains swollen and about $\frac{1}{50}$ inch (0.5 millimeter) in diameter. Adult females may be completely embedded within root tissue, but most are positioned so that the tail end is near the root surface. Females deposit several hundred eggs in a gelatinous matrix that holds the eggs together in a mass and forms a protective covering (Figure 15-22). The egg mass may be extruded outside the root surface, and root fragments or soil particles may contain numerous eggs or larvae. Individuals disseminate in or on plant material, soil, cultural equipment, and in irrigation water. The egg to egg generation may occur in 20 to 30 days under favorable conditions, but larvae may serve as a survival stage under adverse conditions [109].

Figure 15-22.   Longitudinal section of root-knot nematode infested root tissue illustrating invasion of root tip by second stage larva (A); enlargement of sedentary larvae and syncytia formation in vascular tissue (B); further enlargement of young female (C); spherical form of the adult female (D); deposition of eggs within a gelatinous matrix (E); and development of mature, vermiforme male (F).

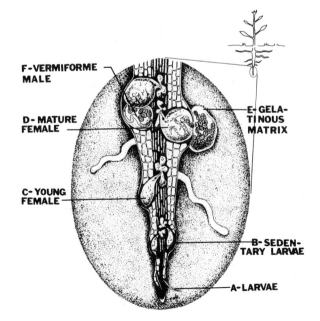

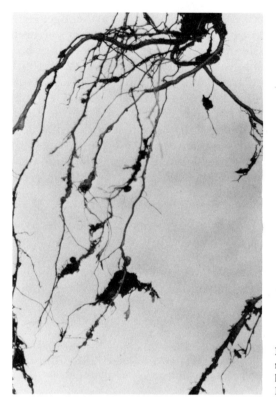

Figure 15-23. Severely galled roots of begonia grown in root-knot infested soil. (Photo by R. W. Henley)

Plant damage begins with the second-stage larval invasion of plant tissue near root tips. Tissues fed upon by developing larvae are affected by nematode salivary secretions, and several cells adjacent to anterior ends of sedentary larvae become abnormally enlarged, multinucleate, and are referred to as syncytia or giant cells [112]. Syncytia functions as a food reservoir throughout the life of the nematode and, owing to their position within vascular tissues, probably interfere with water and nutrient transport from roots to foliar tissue.

Plants infected with *Meloidogyne* spp. commonly exhibit aboveground symptoms such as stunting, chlorosis, wilting, nutrient deficiencies, and sometimes galled foliar tissues [99, 112]. Below ground root galls, which contain developing larvae and/or mature females and egg masses (Figure 15-23), are often readily visible to the unaided eye and serve as a fairly specific identification of a *Meloidogyne* problem. Often where seedlings are transplanted into heavily infested soil, the entire root system may be rapidly destroyed without production of readily visible galled root tissue.

The most important foliage plant species highly susceptible to

Meloidogyne infection include *Ardisia, Asparagus, Brassaia, Caladium, Calathea, Chamaedorea, Dieffenbachia, Maranta,* and *Sansevieria.*

Cactus Cyst Nematode

Heterodera cacti Filipjev and Stekhoven is a serious pest under greenhouse conditions in temperate and semitemperate production areas [29, 54, 59, 68, 93]. A second species, *H. fici* Kirjanova, is injurious to *Ficus elastica,* but the extent of damage by this species is unknown [41].

Little information is available on the life history of *H. cacti;* however, males and females occur and the life cycle of all species of *Heterodera* follows the same general pattern. Second-stage larvae migrate through soil and penetrate roots of susceptible plants just behind the root tip [23], migrate through cortical tissue, and become sedentary near vascular tissue with their heads adjacent to the stele [109]. Further migration is not possible and, like *Meloidogyne,* the *Heterodera* are sedentary endoparasites. Developing larvae of both sexes become swollen, but males ultimately emerge from infected tissue and into the soil, while females continue to enlarge into a spherical shape. Maturing female *H. cacti* are initially white, but later change to cream or yellow and finally to brown. Several hundred eggs are contained within the swollen, lemon-shaped female body, referred to as the cyst (Figure 15-24). Eventually,

Figure 15-24.   Cactus nematode cyst on root of *Schlumbergera.*

the female dies, the cyst hardens, becomes dark brown, and is about $\frac{1}{25}$ inch (1 millimeter) in diameter. Cysts of several *Heterodera* species appear impervious to liquid and gases [107], and eggs within the cyst may remain viable in soil for several years. Dissemination of *H. cacti* occurs through the use of infested media, during irrigation, in performing cultural practices, or in propagation of plant material already infected or contaminated with infested soil under greenhouse production conditions. The histopathological effects on the plant root anatomy are similar to those caused by *Meloidogyne* spp.

Foliar symptoms resulting from infection by *H. cacti* are slow growth, wilting, and a reddish coloration of new phylloclades. The red coloration is not a specific symptom of *H. cacti* infection, but probably a general symptom of injured and dysfunctioning root systems. The presence of cysts (Figure 15-24) on host roots is a characteristic below ground symptom. Root galling, as developed with infections of *Meloidogyne*, does not occur.

Heterodera cacti can cause serious damage to many species of Euphorbiaceae and is the only *Heterodera* detected from Cactaceae. Undetected infestations of *H. cacti* can become limiting in commercial production of *Schlumbergera* [29, 68].

Root Lesion Nematodes

Pratylenchus spp. are worldwide in distribution and are economic pests in field and greenhouse environments [23, 86, 95]. Major species are *P. penetrans* (Cobb) Chitwood and Oteifa, *P. brachyurus* (Godfrey) Goodey, *P. coffeae* (Zimmermann) Goodey, and *P. zeae* Graham [48, 79, 102].

Pratylenchus are migratory endoparasites, and larvae and adults are able to invade susceptible roots from soil and complete their entire life cycle within infected root tissue. Feeding by *Pratylenchus* also may occur ectoparasitically on small rootlets. Feeding within root tissue occurs predominately within the cortex, and as the females mature, eggs are deposited within infected root tissue. Generation time is 4 to 8 weeks but is dependent on the species, host suitability, and environmental factors [109]. Sexual reproduction probably occurs with species where males are abundant, such as *P. penetrans*, while other species may reproduce parthenogenetically.

Symptoms occurring on aboveground plant parts are essentially the same as with other root-feeding nematodes. Roots of infected plants are discolored and contain brown or black colored, longitudinal lesions (Figure 15-25). Necrotic areas may extend throughout cortical tissue in

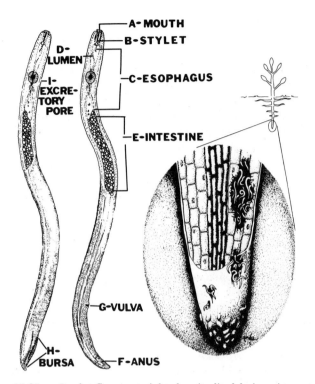

Figure 15-25. In the figure at right, longitudinal lesions in root tissue caused by lesion nematode infection. Center figure shows lateral view of female *Pratylenchus* illustrating the following: (A) mouth, (B) stylet, (C) esophagus, (D) lumen, (E) intestine, (F) anus, and (G) vulva. In the figure at left, male in lateral view with the bursa is shown (H), a structure used in copulation, and the excretory pore (I).

severe infections by *Pratylenchus*. Pathogenic soil-borne organisms invade root lesions, often obscuring the primary cause of the problem. The presence of root lesions is not a positive sign of *Pratylenchus* infections, and an analysis of soil and/or root tissues is required.

Specific plants often affected are *Aglaonema, Ananas comosus, Begonia, Chamaedorea,* and *Rumohra adiantiformis.*

Burrowing Nematode

Radopholus similis (Cobb) Thorne is a serious economic pest in tropical and subtropical areas [43]. Greenhouse infestations of *R. similis* are reported from Europe, Japan, Canada, and Arizona, California, Florida, Louisiana, and Texas in the United States [67]. This nematode causes damage to numerous foliage plant species and is subject to strict quarantine restrictions because of its potential threat to citrus and other subtropical fruits [32, 76].

Radopholus similis is endoparasitic, causing injury to root tissue similar to that attributed to *Pratylenchus*. Its life cycle is completed in approximately 21 days at 75°F (24°C) [76]. Feeding results in production of darkened, necrotic lesions in infected root tissue, formation of cavities within cortical tissue, and eventually destruction of root cortex [107]. Symptoms on aboveground parts, such as reductions in growth or plant decline, result from nematode infection of the host root system.

Infection of the following ornamentals by *R. similis* has been reported: *Calathea, Chamaedorea, Dieffenbachia, Dizygotheca, Maranta, Monstera*, and *Philodendron* [32, 76, 81].

Foliar and Bud Nematodes

Aphelenchoides spp. are commonly called foliar, leaf, or bud infecting nematodes and are found throughout temperate and tropical zones of the world. Species most damaging in foliage plant production are *A. fragariae* (Ritzema Bos) Christie, *A. besseyi* Christie, and *A. ritzemabosi* (Schwartz) Steiner [5].

The life cycle of *Aphelenchoides* is similar to that of most other plant parasitic nematodes, with egg, larval, and adult stages. *Aphelenchoides ritzemabosi* requires about 11 days at 60°F (16°C) for completion of a generation, and approximately 20 to 30 eggs are deposited by a single female within infected tissues [19]. The extremely short life cycle compensates for low fecundity, producing extremely high population levels within infected leaf tissue.

Aphelenchoides feed endoparasitically in the parenchymatous leaf tissues or ectoparasitically in developing flower or leaf buds [107]. These nematodes are not normal soil inhabitants, but occur there when infected plant tissue drops to soil surfaces. *Aphelenchoides* migrate up the surface of stems in a thin film of water and infect leaf tissue through open stomata (Figure 15-26), with lower leaves generally infected first. Spread is enhanced by splashing water, and eliminating overhead irrigation limits dissemination. Propagation of infected cuttings is another means of dissemination. *Aphelenchoides besseyi* can be transmitted to *Ficus elastica* 'Decora' by infected weed hosts in contact with *Ficus* foliage, and weed control will prevent such infection [61]. *Aphelenchoides ritzemabosi* may remain viable in dried, infected tissue for several years, which can serve as sources for reinfestation.

The first noticeable foliar symptoms of *Aphelenchoides* infection are localized chlorotic lesions in leaf tissue, often angular in shape and de-

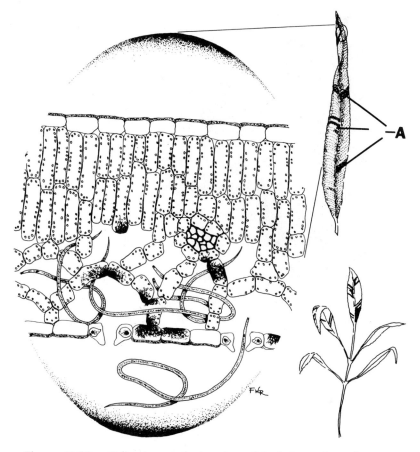

Figure 15-26.   Foliar nematode invasion of leaf tissue through open stomata and intervenous necrosis (A) caused by endoparasitic feeding.

lineated by leaf veins (Figure 15-27). These lesions become necrotic, dark brown or black in color, and symptoms may spread throughout affected leaf areas [97]. Infections of succulent leaves initially appear as water-soaked lesions and later become necrotic, but angular lesions are not formed. Feeding on tissue in buds results in cessation of bud development or in production of deformed flowers or leaves.

Species of *Aphelenchoides* and specific pathogenic organisms have been shown to interact in disease production [11]. *Aphelenchoides ritzemabosi* and *Phytophthora cryptogea* Penthby. and Laff. have been isolated from the same nectoric lesions occurring in leaves of *Sinningia speciosa* Benth. and Hook [100].

Important tropical foliage plants readily injured by *Aphelenchoides*

Figure 15-27.   Foliar nematode injury to fronds of birds-nest fern. (Photo by R. W. Henley)

include *Adiantum, Alsophila, Asplenium, Begonia, Ficus, Nephrolepsis, Pteris,* and *Saintpaulia* [47, 61, 82, 97, 98, 104].

Other Plant Parasitic Nematodes

Genera detected in soil samples obtained from tropical foliage plants include *Belonolaimus, Criconemoides, Dolichodorus, Helicotylenchus, Hemicycliophora, Pratylenchus, Scutellonema, Trichodorus, Tylenchorhynchus,* and *Xiphinema,* but their role in the decline of foliage plants is unknown.

Nematode Control

The problem of freeing plants of nematode infection is difficult. There are highly toxic nematicides available that will suppress established nematode populations for a period of time [72]. Bare root dips of plant material in nematicides are often effective in control of endoparasitic species [102], but some nematodes are so deeply imbedded in root tissue they may be unaffected. Specific nematicides applied to soils around live foliage plants are effective in reducing soil populations of *Meloidogyne, Heterodera, Pratylenchus,* and *R. similis* to low levels and can improve plant growth [29, 30, 32, 68, 81, 101]. Populations will not ordinarily be reduced to undetectable levels, and treatments on a regular basis are necessary to maintain low levels of infestation and allow production of high-quality plants. Higher rates of nematicides applied as a soil drench to heavily infested raised benches will reduce some nematodes species to an undetectable level. However, applications to ground beds will not ordinarily reduce nematodes to an undetectable level, but will provide excellent control. Infestations by *Aphelenchoides* can be controlled by soil drenches of systemic nematicides followed by foliar sprays [47, 82, 104]. Introduction of nematodes into commercial foliage production facilities should be prevented because eradication is very difficult even with nematicidal applications. Avoiding spread of these pests into production areas is extremely difficult once stock plants are infected. Chemicals aid in production of quality plants, but once these plants are in the hands of consumers, chemicals are no longer applied, uncontrolled nematode populations increase, and infected plants will decline and possibly die. Prevention of nematode infestations in commercial production can be successful owing to the slow natural spread of nematodes and the utilization of production practices not conducive to buildup of nematode populations. Production of many foliage plants in containers, production under protective structures, and the short time cropping nature of many foliage ornamentals prevent or reduce nematode incidence. Cultural practices most important to follow are concerned with clean propagation and sanitary maintenance including use of nematode-free propagating material, nematode-free media, and constant sanitation (see Table 15-1).

REFERENCES

[1] Birchfield, W., J. L. Smith, A. Martinez and E. P. Matherly. 1957. Chinese evergreen plants rejected because of glebal masses of *Sphaerobolus stellatus* on foliage. *Plant Dis. Reptr.* 41:537–539.

[2] Boudreaux, H. B. 1956. Revision of the two-spotted spider mite (Acarina, Tetranychidae) complex, *Tetranychus telarius* Linnaeus. *Ann. Entomol. Soc. Am.* 49:43–48.

[3] ———. 1963. Biological aspects of some phytophagous mites. *Annu. Rev. Entomol.* 8:137–154.

[4] Boys, F. E., and P. P. Burbutis. 1972. Influence of *Phytoseiulus persimilis* on populations of *Tetranychus turkestani* at the economic threshold on roses. *J. Econ. Entomol.* 65:114–117.

[5] Brown, E. B. 1959. New host plants of *Aphelenchoides ritzema*-bosi. *Plant Path.* 8:152.

[6] Burnett, T. 1967. Aspects of the interaction between a chalcid parasite and its alurodid host. *Can. J. Zool.* 45:539–578.

[7] Cagle, L. R. 1949. Life history of the two spotted spider mite. Va. Agr. Exp. Sta. Tech. Bull. No. 113. 31 pp.

[8] Chain-ing, T. Shih, Sidney L. Poe, and Harvey L. Cromroy. 1976. Biology, life table, and intrinsic rate of increase of *Tetranychus urticae*. *Ann. Entomol. Soc. Am.* 65:119–123.

[9] Chen, Tseh-an, and A. E. Rich. 1963. Attraction of *Pratylenchus penetrans* to plant roots. *Plant Dis. Reptr.* 47:504–507.

[10] Christiansen, K. 1964. Bionomics of Collembola. *Annu. Rev. Entomol.* 9:147–148.

[11] Crosse, J. E., and R. S. Pitcher. 1952. Studies in the relationship of eelworms and bacteria to certain plant diseases. I. The etiology of strawberry cauliflower disease. *Ann. Appl. Biol.* 39:475–486.

[12] Dekle, G. W. 1965. A root mealybug (*Geococcus coffeae* Green) (Homoptera: Pseudococcidae). Fla. Dept. Ag., Div. Plant Ind., Ent. Circ. No. 43, 2 pp.

[13] ———. 1965. Florida armored scale insects. Fla. Dept. Ag., Div. Plant Ind., *Arthropods of Florida and Neighboring Land Areas,* Vol. 3, 265 pp.

[14] Dittrich, V. 1975. Acaricide resistance in mites. *Z. ang. Ent.* 78:28–45.

[15] Dixon, G. M. 1973. Observations on the use of *Phytoseiulus persimilis* Athias-Henriot to control *Tetranychus urticae* (Koch) on tomatoes. *Plant Path.* 22:134–138.

[16] Essig, E. O. 1915. Injurious and beneficial insects of California. Calif. State Comm. Hort., Supp. Monthly Bull. 541 pp.

[17] Falcon, L. A. 1971. *In* H. D. Burges and N. W. Hussey, eds. *Microbial control of insects and mites.* Chapt. 3, pp. 67–90.

[18] Federick, J. M. 1943. Some preliminary investigations of the green scale, *Coccus viridis,* in South Florida. *Fla. Entomol.* 26:12–15.

[19] French, N.. and R. M. Barraclough. 1961. Observations on the reproduction of *Aphelenchoides ritzema-bosi* (Schwarta). *Nematologica* 6:89–94.

[20] ———, J. D. R. Vernon, and H. C. Woodville. 1968. Cyclamen mites, *Steneotarsonemus pallidus,* on chrysanthemum. *Plant Path.* 12:143.

[21] Gadd, C. H. 1946. Observations on the yellow tea mite, *Hemitarsonemus latus* (Banks) Ewing. *Bull. Entomol. Res.* 37:157–162.

[22] Gimpel, W. F., Jr., D. R. Miller, and J. A. Davidson, 1974. A systematic revision of the wax scales, genus, *Ceroplastes,* in the United States (Homoptera; Coccoidea; Coccidae). Agr. Exp. Sta. Misc. Publ. 841 Univ. of Maryland. 85 pp.

[23] Goodey, T. 1951. *Soil and fresh water nematodes.* New York: Wiley. 544 pp.

[24] Hambleton, E. J. 1973. Florida mealybugs of the genus *Rhizoecus* with description of a new species (Homoptera:Pseudococcidae). *Proc. Entomol. Soc. Wash.* 75:62–71.

[25] Hamlen, R. A. 1974. Control of *Rhizoecus floridanus* Hambleton (Homoptera: Pseudococcidae) on bromeliads. *Proc. Fla. State Hort. Soc.* 87:516–518.

[26] ———. 1974. The broad mite: new and important pest of greenhouse grown Aphelandra. *J. Econ. Entomol.* 67:791–792.

[27] ———. 1975. Insect growth regulator control of longtailed mealybug, hemispherical scale and *Phenacoccus solani* on ornamental foliage plants. *J. Econ. Entomol.* 68:223–226.

[28] ———. 1975. Hemispherical scale control on greenhouse grown Aphelandra. *Fla. Entomol.* 58:187–192.

[29] ———. 1975. Evaluation of nematicides for control of *Heterodera cacti* affecting *Zygocactus truncatus*. *Plant Dis. Reptr.* 59:636–637.

[30] ———. 1976. Efficacy of nematicides for control of *Meloidogyne javanica* in groundbed and container production of *Maranta*. *Plant Dis. Reptr.* 60:872–875.

[31] ———. 1977. Laboratory and greenhouse evaluations of insecticides and insect growth regulators for control of foliar and root infesting mealybugs. *J. Econ. Entomol.* 70:211–214.

[32] ———, and C. A. Conover. 1977. Response of *Radopholus similis* infected *Calathea* spp., container-grown in two soil media, to applications of nematicides. *Plant Dis. Reptr.* 61:532–535.

[33] Heimpel, A. M., and T. A. Angus. 1963. *In* E. A. Steinhaus, ed. *Insect pathology—An advanced treatise.* Vol. 2, pp. 21–73. New York: Academic Press.

[34] Helgesen, R. G., and M. J. Tauber. 1974. Biological control of greenhouse whitefly, *Trialeurodes vaporariorum* (Aleyrodidae:Homoptera), on short-term crops by manipulating biotic and abiotic factors. *Can. Entomol.* 106:1175–1188.

[35] Hermandez-Paz, M. R. 1965. Observations on the biology of the root mealybug, *Rhizoecus americanus* (Hambleton). M.S. thesis. Dept. of Entomology and Nematology, University of Florida, Gainesville, 80 pp.

[36] Highland, H. A. 1956. The biology of *Ferrisiana virgata*, a pest of azaleas. *J. Econ. Entomol.* 49:276–277.

[37] Hudson, K. Elaine. 1974. Regulation of greenhouse sciarid fly populations using *Tetradonema plicans* (Nematoda:Mermithoidea). *J. Invert. Pathol.* 23:85–91.

[38] Hungerford, H. B. 1916. Sciara maggots injurious to potted plants. *J. Econ. Entomol.* 9:538–549.

[39] Hussey, N. W. 1958. Notes on a fungus parasite on greenhouse whitefly *Plant Path.* 7:71–72.

[40] ———, and B. Gurney. 1957. Greenhouse whitefly (*Trialeurodes vaporariorum* Westwood). Ann. Rep. Glass Crops Res. Inst., pp. 134–137.

[41] ———, W. H. Read, and J. J. Hesling. 1969. *The pests of protected cultivation—the biology and control of glasshouse and mushroom pests.* New York: American Elsevier. 404 pp.

[42] Imms, A. D. 1947. *Insect Natural History.* London: Collins. 317 pp.

[43] Ingham, H. R., and S. M. Ayoub. 1972. Tropical plants, susceptible hosts of the burrowing nematode. Calif. Div. Plant Ind. 32 pp.

[44] Iserra, R. N., and J. H. O'Bannon. 1974. Systemic activity of phenamiphos for control of *Meloidogyne arenaria* on *Gardenia jasminoides* and *Ficus carica*. *Plant Dis. Reptr.* 58:1075–1077.

[45] Jackson, G. J., and J. B. Ford. 1973. The feeding behavior of *Phytoseiulus persimilis* (Acarina:Phytoseiidae), particularly as affected by certain pesticides. *Ann. Appl. Biol.* 75:155–164.

[46] Jeppson, L. R., H. H. Keifer, and E. W. Baker. 1975. *Mites injurious to economic plants*. Berkeley: University of California Press. 614 pp.

[47] Johnson, A. W., and D. L. Gill. 1975. Chemical control of foliar nematodes (*Aphelenchoides fragariae*) on 'Fluffy Ruffles' fern. *Plant Dis. Reptr.* 59:772–774.

[48] Johnson, P. W., and R. J. McClanahan. 1974. Nematode control and other effects of soil treatment of greenhouse rose beds with aldicarb and oxamyl. *Plant Dis. Reptr.* 58:730–732.

[49] Jones, F. G. W. 1975. The soil as an environment for plant parasitic nematodes. *Ann. Appl. Biol.* 79:113–119.

[50] Judge, F. D. 1969. Preliminary screening of candidate molluscicides. *J. Econ. Entomol.* 62:1393–1397.

[51] ———, and R. J. Kuhr. 1972. Laboratory and field screening of granular formulations of candidate molluscicides. *J. Econ. Entomol.* 65:242–245.

[52] Karlin, E. J., and J. P. Naegele. 1960. Biology of the Mollusca of greenhouses in New York State. Cornell Univ. Agr. Expt. Sta. Memoir 372. 35 pp.

[53] Klinger, J. 1965. On the orientation of plant nematodes and of some other soil animals. *Nematologica* 11:4–18.

[54] Langdon, K. R., and R. P. Esser. 1969. Cactus cyst nematode, *Heterodera cacti*, in Florida, with host list. *Plant Dis. Reptr.* 53:123–125.

[55] Leath, K. T., and R. C. Newton. 1969. Interaction of a fungus gnat, *Bradysia* sp. (Sciaridae) with *Fusarium* spp. on alfalfa and red clover. *Phytopathology* 59:257–258.

[56] Linford, M. B. 1939. Attractiveness of roots and excised shoot tissue to certain nematodes. *Proc. Helminthol. Soc. Wash., D.C.* 6:11–18.

[57] Lloyd, L. 1922. The control of greenhouse whitefly with notes on its biology. *Ann. Appl. Biol.* 9:1–34.

[58] MacGill, Elsie I. 1927. The biology of Thysanoptera with reference to the cotton plant II.—The relation between temperature and life-cycle in a saturated atmosphere. *Ann. Appl. Biol.* 14:501–512.

[59] Maeseneer, J. D. 1963. New host plant records for the cactus cyst eelworm *Heterodera cacti*, Filipjev and Sch. Stekhoven. *Nematologica* 9:646.

[60] Manglitz, G. R., and E. N. Cory. 1953. Biology and control of *Brevipalpus australis*. *J. Econ. Entomol.* 46:116–119.

[61] Marlatt, R. B. 1975. Control of foliar nematode, *Aphelenchoides besseyi*, in *Ficus elastica* 'Decora'. *Plant Dis. Reptr.* 59:287.

[62] McKenzie, H. L. 1956. *The armored scales of California*. Berkeley: University of California Press. 209 pp.

[63] ———. 1967. *Mealybugs of California with taxonomy, biology and control of North American species*. Berkeley: University of California Press. 525 pp.

[64] Merrill, G. B. 1953. A revision of the scale insects of Florida. Fla. Dept. Agr., State Plant Bd. Bull. 143 pp.

[65] Morishita, F. S. 1954. Biology and control of *Brevipalpus inornatus* (Banks). *J. Econ. Entomol.* 47:449–456.

[66] Nassar, S. G., G. B. Staal, and N. I. Armanious. 1973. Effects of control potential of insect growth regulators with juvenile hormone activity on the greenbug. *J. Econ. Entomol.* 66:847–850.

[67] O'Bannon, J. H. 1977. Worldwide dissemination of *Radopholus similis* and its importance in crop production. *J. Nematol.* 9:16–25.

[68] ———, and R. P. Esser. 1970. Control of *Heterodera cacti* infecting *Zygocactus truncatus*. *Plant Dis. Reptr.* 54:692–694.

[69] Overmeer, W. P. J., A. Q. Van Zon, and W. Helle. 1975. The stability of acaricide resistance in spider mite (*Tetranychus urticae*) populations from rose houses. *Entomol. Exp. and Appl.* 18:68–74.

[70] Parr, W. J., C. Crocker, and E. R. Speyer. 1954. A sciarid fly injurious to seedlings. Rept. Exp. Res. Sta. Cheshunt, 1953, pp. 36–39.

[71] Parris, G. K. 1940. A checklist of fungi, bacteria, nematodes, and viruses occurring in Hawaii, and their hosts: Nematodes. *Plant Dis. Reptr. Supplement,* 121:77–81.

[72] Perry, V. G., and H. N. Miller. 1963. Recommendations for control of nematode infected ornamental foliage plants. *Proc. Fla. State Hort. Soc.* 76:449–454.

[73] Poe, S. L. 1971. Treatment for control of a root mealybug on nursery plants. *J. Econ. Entomol.* 65:241–242.

[74] ———, D. E. Short, and G. W. Dekle. 1973. Control of *Rhizoecus americanus* (Homoptera:Pseudococcidae) on ornamental plants. *J. Ga. Entomol. Soc.* 8:20–26.

[75] Poinar, G. O. 1965. The bionomics and parasite development of *Tripius sciarae* (Bovien) (Sphaerulariidae:Aphelenchoidea), a nematode parasite of sciarid flies (Sciaridae:Diptera). *Parasitology* 55:559–569.

[76] Poucher, C., H. W. Ford, R. F. Wuit, and E. P. DuCharme. 1967. Burrowing nematodes in citrus. Fla. Dept. Agr., Div. Plant Ind. 63 pp.

[77] Prasad, V. 1967. Biology of the predatory mite *Phytoseiulus macropilis* in Hawaii. (Acarina:Phytoseiidae). *Ann. Entomol. Soc. Am.* 60:905–908.

[78] Reinert, J. A. 1973. Cuban laurel thrips: systemic insecticides for control. *J. Econ. Entomol.* 66:1217–1218.

[79] Rhoades, H. L. 1968. Pathogenicity and control of *Pratylenchus penetrans* on leatherleaf fern. *Plant Dis. Reptr.* 52:383–385.

[80] _____, and R. A. Hamlen. 1975. Response of root-knot-infected Caladiums, with and without hot water treatments, to foliar applications of oxamyl and phenamiphos. *Plant Dis. Reptr.* 59:91–93.

[81] _____, and D. B. McConnell. 1972. Control of the burrowing nematode, *Radopholus similis*, on *Philodendron* 'Burgundy'. *Proc. Fla. State Hort. Soc.* 85:358–360.

[82] Riedel, R. M., D. Q. Pierson, and C. C. Powell. 1973. Chemical control of foliar nematodes (*Aphelenchoides fragariae*) on Rieger begonia. *Plant Dis. Reptr.* 57:603–605.

[83] Russell, L. M. 1963. Hosts and distribution of five species of *Trialeurodes* (Homoptera:Aleyrodiadae). *Ann. Entomol. Soc. Am.* 56:149–153.

[84] Saakyan-Baranova, A. A. 1964. On the biology of the soft scale *Coccus hesperidum* L. (Homoptera:Coccidae). *Entomol. Rev.* 43:135–147.

[85] Sasser, J. N. 1977. Worldwide dissemination and importance of the root-knot nematodes, *Meloidogyne* spp. *J. Nematol.* 9:26–29.

[86] Sher, S. A. 1959. Nematodes on ornamentals. *Calif. Agr.* 13:21.

[87] Smith, F. F. 1935. Control experiments on certain *Tarsonemus* mites on ornamentals. *J. Econ. Entomol.* 28:91–98.

[88] _____. 1939. Control of cyclamen and broad mites on gerbera. USDA, Circ. No. 516. 14 pp.

[89] _____, and A. L. Boswell. 1970. New baits and attractants for slugs. *J. Econ. Entomol.* 63:1919–1922.

[90] _____, T. J. Henneberry, and A. L. Boswell. 1963. The pesticide tolerance of *Typhlodromus fallacis* (Garman) and *Phytoseiulus persimilis* A. H. with some observations on the predator efficiency of *P. persimilis*. *J. Econ. Entomol.* 56:274–278.

[91] _____, A. K. Ota, and A. L. Boswell. 1970. Insecticides for control of the greenhouse whitefly. *J. Econ. Entomol.* 63:522–527.

[92] Snetsinger, R. 1966. Biology and control of a root-feeding mealybug on *Saintpaulia*. *J. Econ. Entomol.* 59:1077–1078.

[93] Southey, J. F. 1957. Observations of *Heterodera cacti* Filipjev and Sch. Stekhoven and *Meloidogyne* spp. on imported cactus plants with a list of new host records. *Nematologica* 2:1–6.

[94] _____. 1958. New host records for root-knot eelworms. *Plant Path.* 7:114.

[95] _____. 1959. Some records of root-lesion eelworms *Pratylenchus* spp. in England. *Plant Path.* 8:130–132.

[96] Staal, G. B., S. Nasser, and J. W. Martin. 1973. Control of the citrus mealybug with insect growth regulators with juvenile hormone activity. *J. Econ. Entomol.* 66:851–853.

[97] Stokes, D. E. 1966. Effects of *Aphelenchoides fragariae* on birds-nest fern and azaleas. *Proc. Fla. State Hort. Soc.* 79:436–438.

[98] _____. 1967. Newly reported fern hosts of *Aphelenchoides fragariae* in Florida. *Plant Dis. Reptr.* 51:508.

[99] ———. 1977. Effects of root-knot nematodes on ornamental plants. Fla. Dept. Agr., Div. Plant Ind., Nematology Circ. No. 24. 2 pp.

[100] ———, and S. A. Alfieri, Jr. 1968. A foliar nematode and a *Phytophthora* parasitic to Gloxinia. *Proc. Fla. State Hort. Soc.* 81:376–380.

[101] ———, and R. L. King, Jr. 1972. Control of root-knot nematode in *Sansevieria* groundbeds. *Proc. Fla. State Hort. Soc.* 85:360–362.

[102] ———, and C. W. Laughlin. 1970. Control of *Pratylenchus penetrans* on leatherleaf fern transplants. *Plant Dis. Reptr.* 54:287–288.

[103] Stoyanov, D. 1967. Additions to host records of *Meloidogyne* sp., *Helicotylenchus multicinctus* and *Rotylenchus reniformis. Nematologica* 13:172–173.

[104] Strider, D. L. 1973. Control of *Aphelenchoides fragariae* on Rieger begonias. *Plant Dis. Reptr.* 57:1015–1019.

[105] Rhanassoulopoulos, A. 1974. Some effects of the insect growth regulator, ZR-777 on bean aphid *Aphis fabae* (Scop.). *Z. ang. Ent.* 77:171–175.

[106] Thompson, W. L., and J. T. Griffiths, Jr. 1949. Purple scale and Florida red scale as pests of citrus in Florida. Univ. of Fla. Agr. Expt. Sta. Bull. 462. 40 pp.

[107] Thorne, G. 1961. *Principles of nematology.* New York: McGraw-Hill. 553 pp.

[108] Tippins, H. H. 1968. Observations on *Phenacaspis cockerelli* (Cooley) (Hompotera:Diaspididae), a pest of ornamental plants in Georgia. *J. Ga. Entomol. Soc.* 3:13–15.

[109] Wallace, H. R. 1964. *The biology of plant-parasitic nematodes.* New York: St. Martin's. 280 pp.

[110] Wang, E., and I. W. Hughes. 1975. Indian laurel thrips. *Bermuda Dept. Agr. Fishery Bull.* 45(8):64–66.

[111] Webb, R. E., F. F. Smith, A. L. Boswell, E. S. Fields, and R. M. Waters. 1974. Insecticidal control of the greenhouse whitefly on greenhouse ornamental and vegetable plants. *J. Econ. Entomol.* 67:114–118.

[112] Zuckerman, B. M., W. F. Mai, and R. A. Rohde. 1971. *Plant parasitic nematodes.* Vol. 1. New York: Academic Press. 345 pp.

sixteen

Cecil N. Smith
Elmo F. Scarborough

some economic aspects of producing and marketing foliage plants

Major factors associated with supply and demand for foliage plants are examined in this chapter. Although each item treated has been classified as relating primarily to supply or demand, it is recognized that nearly all also pertain to the other category.

Material covered includes growth and location of the foliage industry, input-output relationships, competition among producing areas, the nature of consumer wants, marketing channels, product mix, transportation, self-help marketing programs, and others. An appendix delineates the economic and statistical data available concerning the foliage industry.

Much of the material covered in the chapter relates only to Florida. The small amount of economic and statistical data pertaining to the foliage industry are much greater in Florida than elsewhere.

Supply Characteristics

Industry Location and Development

As stated in Chapter One, the foliage plant industry in the United States began in the "stove houses," which supplied big estates and conservatories with selections of green plants that had been imported from established dealers in Europe and the tropics. Markets for plants were generally limited to wealthy purchasers who had expensive greenhouses and other production facilities. Most were located in or adjacent to the large urban centers of the East and Midwest.

Development of the foliage plant industry in Florida, now leading the nation in foliage production, resulted from the need for growers to diversify from Boston ferns and other plants. Initial impetus in the Central Florida area did not come from the adoption of "stove house" plants, but rather from personal contact and experience of Floridians with botanical institutions and commercial firms in the St. Louis area. The development in South Florida was based on both native plants and others of tropical origin. Market development activities of the fledgling Florida industry got an assist from floral design schools, and, later, efforts to sell foliage plants in variety and other mass-market stores were successful. Hundreds of cultivars were added to the list of plants grown through the years.

Initially, the foliage industry in California, now second in size, resembled that in the Northeast and Midwest more than that in Florida. Growers responded to the need for "stove house" plants for specialized users and supplied cuttings to other greenhouse operators.

As the Florida foliage industry grew in its earlier years, it for the most part catered to northern greenhouse producers. It largely replaced Puerto Rico in furnishing cuttings to northern greenhouses during World War II. Cuttings for finishing were produced at lower costs in Florida than in the North and were sold to northern operators for further growing and finishing. The advent of lightweight plastic pots and expanded truck service later allowed California, Florida, and Texas operators to market through various wholesale and retail market dealers. Finally, many northern greenhouse operators shifted their emphasis to other phases of related businesses or, with urban expansion encroaching on greenhouse ranges, sold their land and other facilities and went out of business. Many entered the flower or foliage business in California, Florida, North Carolina, or Texas.

Climate and Foliage Industry Development

The relatively mild climate of California, Florida, and Texas is a major factor contributing to the development of the foliage industry in these states. High temperature, humidity, and light conditions generally favor the production of foliage plants in parts of California, Florida, and Texas.

Climatic conditions in these states must be modified in order to achieve the most effective production of foliage plants. Growing areas in all three states have high summer temperatures and the possibility of winter freezing that adversely affect both growing and shipping operations. For instance, the percentages of sunlight reaching growing areas is reduced for most foliage plants by construction of lath, plastic, or glass covers. However, the climates of these states make possible the production of quality foliage plants at lower costs than can be attained in most other areas of the country. Furthermore, improvements in methods of cooling production areas in the summer and heating during the winter, along with advances in packaging and transportation, have tended to accent the advantages of these areas.

Organizational Structure

Most foliage plants are produced by corporations. The majority of operators are organized as individual proprietorships, but there are some partnerships, and at least one cooperative. California and Florida have large conglomerate corporations with integrated production and marketing operations in the foliage business.

Sixty-three percent of the eighty Florida growers interviewed in a 1958 study had either spent their entire working lives in growing foliage plants, had taken over a family business, or had previously grown other nursery or flower crops before producing foliage plants [11]. Many nursery and greenhouse operators transferring to Florida from a northern area were included in this group.

Input-Output Relationships

Resources required in the production and marketing of tropical plants are varied and complex. Land with proper drainage and greenhouses, plastic houses, or other types of covered structures are essential for foliage plant production in most areas of the world. Other needed resources include watering, fertilizing, heating and cooling systems, facilities for sterilizing soil mixes and packing and basic handling, and spraying and other production equipment. Specific lists of equipment would be long and complex and would vary from one nursery to another.

The foliage industry requires a large capital investment per unit of area. Access to capital, technical knowledge, and supplies of stock plants are three minimum essential requirements for entering this industry.

The business analysis studies conducted since 1966 by the University of Florida pertain to input-output relationships in the foliage plant industry [9]. The management information contained in these reports has been utilized for decision-making purposes by many growers. The data released consist of analysis of the costs for the entire foliage enter-

TABLE 16-1   Average costs and returns for fifteen Central Florida foliage nurseries participating in the University of Florida Nursery Business Analysis Program, 1977 (Adapted from [9])

Item	Sales/expenses	
	Dollars	*Percent*
Sales plus inventory change[a]	569,086	100
Expenses		
Wages and salaries	194,507	34
Plants and seeds	77,109	13
Containers, pots, shipping boxes	55,517	10
Production materials and supplies[b]	60,065	11
Other costs[c]	88,666	16
Total variable costs	475,864	84
Fixed costs[d]	58,745	10
Total costs	535,609	94
Net return	33,477	6
Averages		
Production area 3.06 acres		
Employees 26.24		
Capital managed 531,493		

    [a] Includes sales of $543,959 plus adjustment of $25,127 for plant inventory change.
    [b] Includes fuel for heat, potting material, fertilizer, pesticides, and other production material.
    [c] Includes maintenance, equipment operation, travel, entertainment, insurance, telephone, electricity, taxes, licenses, bonds, and advertising costs.
    [d] Includes depreciation on buildings and equipment and interest on capital investment computed at 8%.

prise rather than specific plant products. Similar studies for other states are not available.

Business analysis reports enable growers to compare their relative efficiency with other operators. Such data are useful to potential investors, input suppliers, and credit agencies in estimating input requirements and possible revenue.

Costs and returns   A summary of major cost items for Central Florida foliage plant growers who cooperated in the 1977 business analysis program is shown in Table 16-1. Percentages in the table refer to proportions of total sales plus inventory change. Wages and salaries accounted for 34 percent of the value of sales, with other variable costs such as plants, seeds, containers, and production material making up 50 percent. Fixed costs, including taxes and depreciation, constituted 10 percent of the total, leaving the remaining 6 percent as net return.

TABLE 16-2 Comparative business analysis, with monetary values converted into 1977 constant dollars, for eight foliage plant growers in Central Florida who furnished figures for the years from 1970 through 1977 [9]

Factor	Unit	Average for eight nurseries in:							
		1970	1971	1972	1973	1974	1975	1976	1977
Profit									
Net nursery income[a]	$	55,803	92,293	120,674	170,013	144,235	92,579	145,812	103,321
Return to capital	%	14.0	24.5	30.2	37.1	24.6	12.4	22.1	15.8
Size of business									
Value of own plants sold[a]	$	300,762	344,293	415,806	492,582	589,051	689,032	721,383	702,496
Level of costs									
Costs per $ sales plus plant inventory value change	¢	96.69	88.99	86.87	88.43	93.06	97.34	93.67	96.21
Intensity in use of space									
Plant inventory value turnover annually	%	183	187	201	236	289	364	404	382
Production rate									
Value of own plants sold per square foot total bed and bench space[a]	$	2.13	2.20	2.58	3.01	3.42	4.72	4.20	4.05
Labor efficiency									
Own plants sold per employee	$	16,461	17,612	19,215	20,550	20,482	20,648	22,000	19,481
Efficiency in use of capital									
Owned capital turnover annually	%	127.3	121.7	130.9	136.1	138.9	156.9	151.8	146.0
Growth in sales and inventory									
Increase in sales and plant and inventory value from previous year[a]	$	30,845	91,451	81,246	141,330	174,165	107,574	87,831	43,588
Efficiency in use of space									
Bed and bench space in use	ft²	141,322	157,230	161,120	163,341	171,964	145,968	171,617	173,572
Bed and bench space vacant	%	3.4	2.8	3.0	3.0	2.9	3.6	3.8	3.5

[a] Adjusted by Index of Wholesale Prices (All Commodities) with 1977 = 100 to reflect equivalent values in 1977 dollars.

The 6 percent net return shown in Table 16-1 should not be confused with the different rate of return on investment noted in Table 16-2. Data in Table 16-1 relate to net returns as a percentage of sales and those in Table 16-2 to return on investment. The return to investment on capital of the fifteen growers to which the data in Table 16-1 apply was 15.75 percent in 1977.

Key business analysis factors   Data comparing key business analysis factors for eight Central Florida foliage plant nurseries that furnished figures for eight years from 1970 to 1977 are contained in Table 16-2. The financial figures shown have been transformed into equivalent constant dollars in order to remove much of the effect of inflation on the value of the dollar during the 8-year period considered.[1] These figures show several changes that took place in the business organizations, such as an increase from $301,000 in sales per average firm in 1970 to more than $700,000 in 1977. Percentage of return on capital, which was 14 percent in 1970, rose to 37.1 percent in 1973, but fell to 12.4 percent in 1975. Then, after a sharp rise to 22.1 percent in 1976, it declined to 15.8 percent in 1977. The various shifts are indicative in part of improvements in management skills of operators who participated in the program over the 8-year period. Part of the reason for the decline in the percentage of return on capital was increased supplies and relatively lower prices for foliage, plus inflationary forces driving up prices of production inputs.

An important factor was the cost per dollar of sales plus plant inventory value change. The 96.7 cents cost in 1970 had fallen to 86.9 cents in 1972. However, the figure rose to 97.3 cents in 1975, whereas the 1977 value was 1.2 cents under the 1976 level but 2.5 cents higher than the value a year earlier.

Another indication of efficiency related to intensity in space use. Plant inventory value turned over 1.8 times annually in 1970 and rose continually to 4 times in 1976, indicating that the eight growers had increased their efficiency tremendously. Own plants sold per square foot of total bench space rose from $2.13 in 1970 to $4.72 in 1975, but fell during each of the following years.

Large changes in price level occurred during these years, with the wholesale price level in 1977 having risen 75 percent above the 1970 level. Nevertheless, the vast increases in productivity generally far out-

[1]The adjuster was the Index of Wholesale Prices (All Commodities). It is recognized that many variations exist in the movement of this series and that of foliage prices. Nevertheless, the constant dollar data tend to make year-to-year comparisons more suitable than when actual data are presented.

distanced increases in the price level. Own plants sold per employee were $16,500 in 1970, but were $22,000 in 1976. However, this measure showed declines from 1976 to 1977. Other measures of efficiency are shown in the table.

Financing

In the early years of the foliage industry, operations were financed primarily by growers' savings, active or silent partners, and banking institutions at which growers had equity or, in cases when such loans were made, on the basis of character qualities. Growth was relatively slow, since individuals had to accumulate financial equity and experience to enter the foliage industry.

Much of the substantial growth in the 1940s and 1950s was financed in the same way, but during the late 1960s and in the current decade other sources of financial support have become available. Large national stock corporations and conglomerates have entered the industry, and loans from large financial institutions have become available. National firms became interested because tremendous potential profits in the foliage industry were foreseen by people in various walks of life through business contacts and in articles in national magazines and financial media. Other groups of investors have combined to purchase or begin new foliage operations in various areas of the United States, Central America, and the Caribbean. These include professional people, such as dentists, doctors, and other investors who formerly invested in cattle feeding and other similar operations. However, other than grower savings, most financing is from banks, production credit associations, Federal Land Banks, and similar institutions. The Bank for Cooperatives assisted in the financing of a large Florida firm that sold growing supplies.

Propagating Material

Sources of cuttings   Most growers produce the majority of their own stock plants for propagational purposes despite rapid increases in off-shore production and importation of foliage cuttings. Approximately 65 percent of cuttings utilized by Florida growers in 1975 were home grown [22]. No data are available on such proportions in California and elsewhere. Cuttings for producing salable plants are a major limiting factor in the expansion of foliage operations.

Some 28 percent of the cuttings utilized in Florida foliage production in 1975 came from Latin America [22]. About half were from integrated overseas cuttings operations of U.S. firms and about half were purchased from Latin American sources. Florida growers also purchased 6 percent of their cuttings locally from other growers or from specialists producing foliage plants in the local area. One percent was obtained from other sources, including cuttings from Europe, Africa, the Orient, and other areas.

Imports of cuttings   There has been an expansion in foliage operations in Latin America and the Caribbean during the past 7 or 8 years. Three of the biggest organizations in these areas are Green Thumb, with farms in Guatemala, Costa Rica, Jamaica, and Puerto Rico, United Brands in Honduras, and Far West Botanicals with operations in Honduras, Costa Rica, and Puerto Rico. Other firms producing propagating stock are located in Belize, Costa Rica, Colombia, the Dominican Republic, Guatemala, Puerto Rico, and elsewhere. Many of these operations are integrated units of Florida and other U.S. producing firms. Local operators also have entered the foliage industry to produce cuttings for shipment to California, Florida, Texas, and other U.S. and European markets.

Well over 2,000 acres (810 hectares) are now estimated to be in foliage cuttings in Latin America and the Caribbean, compared to 1,000 acres (405 hectares) in 1976 [14]. The current value of cuttings sold to the United States and Europe from these areas is estimated at more than $25 million.

Advantages to production in these tropical areas include lower costs of labor and land, plus climatic benefits, since most foliage plants are indigenous to those areas. Disadvantages include high transportation costs, difficulties in obtaining specialized supplies, and political risks.

Major sources of tropical foliage cuttings imported into Florida during the past 10 fiscal years are shown in Table 16-3. Shipments from other countries, including Colombia, the Netherlands, Denmark, and Japan, also have increased in the past several years. The Ivory Coast in West Africa has become a large supplier of cuttings to the European foliage industry.

The major genera of foliage plant cuttings imported into the United States from various sources are *Philodendron, Scindapsus, Dracaena, Syngonium, Sansevieria,* and *Codiaeum.*

Competition

From 1968 through 1972 Florida accounted for 50 to 60 percent of the foliage plants sold by growers in the United States, but by 1977 Florida foliage producers marketed only 44 percent of the estimated total value of U.S. output. The value of foliage reported for Florida by

TABLE 16-3 Number of tropical foliage plants (in thousands) imported into Florida, 1968-1969 through 1977-1978 fiscal years [13, 14]

Country or area of origin[a]	Fiscal year			
	1968-1969	1969-1970	1970-1971	1971-1972
Belgium	4	—	b	—
Belize	b	—	—	110
Brazil	—	—	—	—
Colombia	18	27	30	26
Costa Rica	37	20	6	24
Denmark	—	—	—	—
Dominica	—	—	—	—
Dominican Republic	—	—	—	—
Ecuador	—	—	—	—
El Salvador	—	—	—	—
England	—	—	—	—
West Germany	—	—	—	—
Guatemala	315	1,310	2,450	5,315
Honduras	1,974	1,465	6,949	16,730
Jamaica	—	—	—	—
Japan	—	—	—	—
Mexico	—	—	—	4
Netherlands	—	—	1	3
New Zealand	—	—	—	—
Nicaragua	—	—	2	2
Panama	—	—	—	—
Peru	—	—	—	—
Philippines	—	—	—	—
Singapore	—	—	—	—
Surinam	—	—	—	—
Thailand	—	—	—	—
West Africa	—	—	—	—
Other	1	—	3	1
Totals	2,349	2,822	9,441	22,215

[a]Countries listed have shipped at least 10,000 foliage plants to Florida in some year.

[b]Less than 500.

the U.S. Statistical Reporting Service was more than 70 percent higher than the level in California, the next highest state in sales value.

Other states that formerly grew small quantities of foliage reported large increases in foliage production between 1970 and 1978. For example, the percentage change in sales in five leading foliage producing states indicated that Florida's 310 percent increase in production and marketing of this product had the next to the lowest proportionate increase (Table 1-1, page 3). California ranked first, with a rise of 1,141 percent, followed by Texas and Ohio. In fifth place was Pennsylvania.

Of the 2,813 acres (1,139 hectares) or 123 million square feet (11.4

TABLE 16-3 Number of tropical foliage plants (in thousands) imported into Florida, 1968-1969 through 1977-1978 fiscal years [13, 14] (Continued)

		Fiscal year			
1972-1973	1973-1974	1974-1975	1975-1976	1976-1977	1977-1978
2	8	32	40	29	6
48	357	873	827	4,023	4,320
—	28	3	—	b	15
29	37	95	485	722	2,537
76	1,425	4,260	11,780	11,970	12,823
78	103	166	311	133	122
1	30	72	1	—	—
—	126	869	1,360	1,299	1,279
—	1	1	11	b	3
—	—	—	—	—	67
—	—	—	—	59	25
—	—	5	12	360	—
5,861	17,177	28,366	32,341	37,292	44,167
20,354	18,266	18,688	27,963	23,870	25,693
—	1	11,972	31,473	37,119	24,711
—	—	—	111	367	210
—	—	—	43	13	14
10	47	38	436	754	793
—	—	—	—	—	70
—	23	34	51	61	18
—	—	—	—	25	51
—	—	—	—	247	326
—	—	—	—	7	20
—	23	—	8	45	96
—	—	—	—	—	70
—	—	—	—	63	78
—	—	—	26	b	b
1	—	1	72	24	23
26,460	37,652	65,475	107,351	118,482	117,537

million centares) of foliage plants reported in the United States in 1978, approximately 65 percent were in Florida and 18 percent in California. Florida had a lower value of sales per unit of production area, which indicated the more extensive nature of the foliage enterprise there in comparison with other states. Florida growers have large areas, especially in the lower east coast, of plants grown outdoors or under minimum protection. A higher proportion of production area was devoted to stock plants than that in other states. A major market for Florida foliage plants has been out-of-state greenhouse operators.

A comparison of foliage marketings from California and Florida in

TABLE 16-4   Value of foliage plant sales in California, Florida, and the United States (twenty-three) from 1949 to 1978 [23, 24]

| | State | | | | United |
Year	California		Florida		States
	$1,000	*Percent*	*$1,000*	*Percent*	*$1,000*
1949	2,529	20.0	1,844	14.6	12,648[a]
1959	4,391	14.1	12,622	40.9	30,863[a]
1966	3,167	13.2	11,678	48.7	23,988
1967	3,087	11.8	12,265	47.0	26,079
1968	3,028	11.5	14,357	54.4	26,412
1969	3,675	12.6	15,497	53.1	29,158
1970	3,657	13.2	15,938	57.6	27,692
1971	4,634	12.3	23,077	61.4	37,586
1972	6,530	13.5	25,693	53.1	48,428
1973	12,884	19.0	33,807	49.7	67,982
1974	30,552	26.9	48,482	42.7	113,503
1975	45,732	24.4	87,312	46.6	187,183
1976[b]	61,359	25.2	110,656	45.5	243,427
1977[b]	73,231	25.8	119,956	44.1	275,300
1978[b]	86,126	28.8	124,135	41.5	298,998

[a] The proportion of total U.S. production in the twenty-three states for which the U.S. Crop Reporting Board has estimated foliage plant production since 1966 was 96 and 95 percent in 1949 and 1959, respectively.
[b] Sixteen states in 1976, 1977, and 1978.

selected years from 1949 to 1977 is contained in Table 16-4. The $2.5 million of foliage sales in California in 1949 was substantially higher than the $1.8 million figure for Florida. By 1959, however, the value in Florida increased to $13 million compared with a rise to $4 million in California.

Annual data on foliage sales since 1966 have been published by the Crop Reporting Board of the U.S. Department of Agriculture [24]. These data indicate that, during each year, there has been an increase in the sales value in Florida from $13 million in 1966 to $16 million in 1970 and then to $124 million in 1978. California's foliage production exceeded the value of that in Florida in 1949. Despite a rise over the next 10 years, it was only slightly over a third of Florida's value in 1959. Declines in California foliage production were registered through 1968, but rose thereafter, with a takeoff and very rapid growth from $4 million in 1970 to $13 million in 1973, $46 million in 1975, and $86 million in 1978.

California and Florida accounted for only 35 percent of national sales in 1949, but produced 70 percent of the foliage marketed in the

United States in 1978. Since 1968 these two states have provided between two thirds and three fourths of the nation's foliage output.

Data on sales per acre and per square foot in 1970 and 1978 for leading foliage producing states in 1978 are contained in Table 16-5. These ranged from $1.57 in Florida to $3.66 in California and $6.38 in Ohio during 1978. On an equivalent acre basis, the figure for Ohio was $288,000 in comparison with $68,000 in Florida and $173,000 in California. Data in the table are shown in both actual and constant dollars. While there was a 187 percent increase in the value of plants marketed per unit of production area in the United States from 1970 to 1978, the rise, when 1970 sales were converted into terms of constant dollars with 1978 values, had dropped to 52 percent.

Increased demand for foliage plants, generally accompanied by a high degree of profitability for firms producing these products, has contributed to industry growth. Other factors have also been involved, not only in the southern tier of California, Florida, and Texas, but also in other states. One factor has been the trend in the cut flower industry to import larger quantities of carnations and chrysanthemums into the United States from Colombia, Guatemala, and other Latin American

TABLE 16-5   Sales per acre and per square foot of foliage plants in selected states, 1970 and 1978, with 1970 data shown in both actual and adjusted dollars [24]

	Sales per acre[a]			Sales per square foot			Change, 1970 to 1978	
	1970		1978	1970		1978		
	Actual	Adjusted[b]	1978	Actual	Adjusted[b]	1978	Actual	Adjusted[b]
	Dollars						Percent	
Florida	26,000	49,000	68,000	0.59	1.12	1.57	166	40
California	84,000	159,000	173,000	1.93	3.66	3.98	106	9
Texas	34,000	65,000	135,000	0.78	1.48	3.11	299	210
Ohio	146,000	277,000	288,000	3.36	6.38	5.85	74	−8
Pennsylvania	159,000	302,000	258,000	3.64	6.91	5.93	63	−14
Michigan	173,000	328,000	193,000	3.97	7.53	4.43	16	−41
Illinois	374,000	710,000	231,000	8.58	16.28	5.31	−38	−67
Massachusetts	190,000	361,000	234,000	4.37	14.59	5.36	23	−63
New Jersey	112,000	213,000	309,000	2.56	4.86	7.10	177	46
Colorado	—	—	251,000	—	—	5.77	—	—
U.S.[c]	37,000	70,000	106,000	0.85	1.61	2.44	187	52

[a] Rounded to nearest $1,000.
[b] In terms of adjusted (constant) dollars valued at 1978 price level.
[c] Twenty-three states in 1970 and sixteen states in 1978.

TABLE 16-6   Distribution of commercial production, square feet in production, and value of sales, classified by grower size groups, of foliage plants in Florida, 1977 [5]

Value of sales per producer	Firms	Glass or permanent plastic houses and slat houses or temporary plastic	Open area	Total	Net value of sales
Dollars	No.	1,000 ft²			$1,000
10,000–24,999	37	764	111	875	789
25,000–49,999	56	973	756	1,729	1,913
50,000–99,999	72	4,504	737	5,241	5,003
100,000–249,999	98	9,529	2,412	11,941	15,059
250,000–499,999	46	6,684	3,080	9,764	17,867
500,000 and over	69	36,036	14,059	50,095	79,325
Total	378	58,490	21,155	79,645	119,956

Percent distribution,

Percent of total

10,000–24,999	9.8	1.3	0.5	1.1	0.7
25,000–49,999	14.8	1.7	3.6	2.2	1.6
50,000–99,999	19.0	7.7	3.5	6.6	4.2
100,000–249,999	25.9	16.3	11.4	15.0	12.5
250,000–499,999	12.2	11.4	14.6	12.2	14.9
500,000 and over	18.3	61.6	66.4	62.9	66.1
Total	100.0	100.0	100.0	100.0	100.0

sources. Imports now make up in excess of 20 percent of total U.S. sales of these commodities. This resulted in a slow increase in cut flower prices compared with the general price level in recent years. Hence, domestic flower growers have not earned the profits anticipated, and many have turned their resources to tropical foliage plants, flowering potted plants, and bedding plants.

The data on percentage distribution, by grower sales value, of firm numbers, the area in production, and net value of sales in Florida give an indication of the internal organization of the foliage plant industry (Table 16-6). Very large growers account for the highest proportion of production area and the net value of sales in Florida. However, similar data have not been published for other states.

Many former carnation and chrysanthemum growers in California began producing foliage plants. A number of chrysanthemum and gladiolus growers in Florida have shifted into foliage. In both states many woody ornamental wholesale growers and landscape nursery owners, faced with the recession and slowdowns in housing starts, turned their resources into tropical foliage plant production. Other firms grow a combination of flowers or woody ornamentals and foliage plants. Operators in another hard-pressed industry in California, grape bench-grafters, shifted many of their greenhouses and plastic houses into the production of foliage plants in the past few years [16]. Some poultry operators in both California and Florida also found it more profitable to grow foliage plants than to produce broilers or eggs. They have removed tops from their chickenhouses and replaced their roofs with fiberglass for foliage production.

Somewhat the same circumstances were involved in the expansion of the foliage plant enterprise in Texas. Growth in the Midwest and Northeast was largely through the substitution of foliage plants for cut flowers and greenhouse vegetables.

Demand Characteristics

Consumer Demand

There has been an upturn in the demand for foliage plants during the 1970s. No definitive study has been done to delineate causes for the rise in such demand, but probable reasons include (1) the environmental movement with its emphasis on growing green plants, (2) the innate desire of people to possess and grow living things, (3) a rise in population numbers, (4) larger numbers of apartment dwellers, (5) more leisure time, (6) the fuel crunch, encouraging people to stay at home more, (7) the increased availability of foliage plants through new and continuing outlets, (8) the tendency to follow peer group leaders in having plants, and (9) advertising, promotion, and public relations activities on the part of national trade associations, private sales firms, and other groups. The sums spent in advertising and public relations activities by growers and grower organizations have been minimal.

Trends in Consumption

Estimated per capita apparent consumption for foliage plants in the United States in 1949 and 1959 and annually from 1966 through 1978 is shown in Figure 16-1. These figures were generated by dividing the estimated retail value of foliage plant sales by the number of persons in the resident population. The estimated retail sales value was determined by multiplying the value of net sales by 2.5, the approximate ratio of retail sales value to that at the grower level. The consumption figures

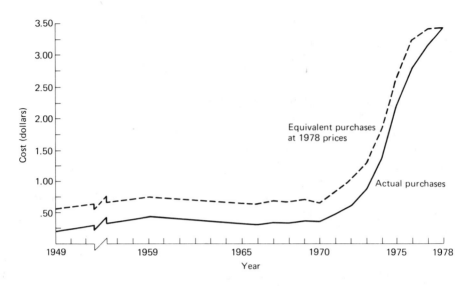

Figure 16-1.   Per capita apparent purchases (valued at retail prices) of foliage plants in the United States during the years 1949, 1959, and annually from 1966 to 1978.

were also adjusted to constant 1978 values by using the Index of Producer Prices (All Commodities) to convert the data.

Consumption figures show vast rises in consumer purchases from 1949 to 1978. A decline in consumption, some portion of which was probably caused by competition from artificial foliage plants, occurred from 1959 to 1966.

Per capita apparent consumption of foliage plants in terms of dollars of 1978 constant value rose from 56 cents in 1949 to 71 cents in 1969, an increase of 27 percent over the 20-year period. The $3.43 per capita U.S. consumption in 1978 represented a 407 percent upward shift over the 1968 level.

A major concern of the foliage plant industry relates to future consumption patterns. With fast expanding production capacity throughout the nation, many growers are worried that supply will outpace demand. Many industry leaders feel that now is the time to develop a series of programs to nourish and expand consumer demand for foliage plants.

Seasonal Shipment Pattern

A barometer of seasonal patterns is the weekly shipment report of 3-inch (7.7-centimeter) pots of all varieties of foliage plants published by the Federal-State Market News Service. A trend during the mid and late

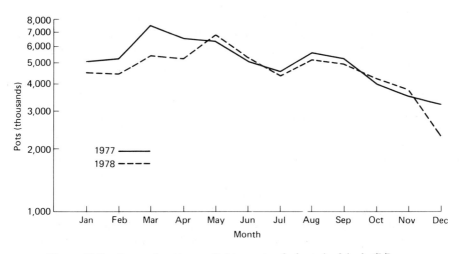

Figure 16-2. Seasonal patterns of shipments of plants in 3-inch (7.7-centimeter) pots from 1977 to 1978 [3].

1970s was an increasing proportion of foliage plants marketed in 5-inch (12.8-centimeter) and larger pots.

Data in Figures 16-2 and 16-3 show the direction of monthly and annual shipments of foliage plants in 3-inch (7.7-centimeter) and 6-inch (15.4-centimeter) pots. The general tendency was for shipments of 3-inch pots to rise in the early portion of the year, drop in the spring, rise

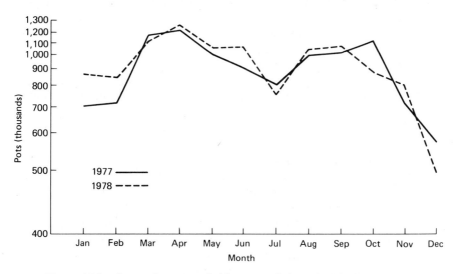

Figure 16-3. Seasonal pattern of shipments of plants in 6-inch (15.4-centimeter) pots from 1977 to 1978 [3].

from July to August, and fall during the last months of the year. Somewhat the same pattern held for plants in 6-inch pots, except that the rise in the early part of the year and the slough off from October to December was more marked.

Marketing Channels

Current channels   Distributors were the major outlet for Florida foliage growers in 1975 [22], with 21 percent of Florida's foliage marketed in this manner (Table 16-7).

Such operators generally warehoused plants for a short time and sold them on truck routes to various retail and wholesale dealers.

The second most important outlet consisted of out-of-state greenhouse operators who used the products for further growing, repotting, and finishing.

Approximately 13 percent of grower sales were marketed through wholesale florists. There is some difficulty in determining the exact shades of distinction between distributors and wholesale florists.

Local growers purchased 9 percent of the foliage plants produced in Florida in 1975. Most were for filling orders when growers themselves did not have the quantities of specific plants necessary.

Eight percent of industry output was sold to grocery stores, 8 percent to variety stores, and 7 percent each to retail florists and department stores. Garden centers bought 4 percent of industry supply in 1975. Plant stores or boutiques appeared on the scene during the 1970s and purchased 2 percent of Florida's 1975 output. Plant stores are organized similar to retail florists, but with specialization in sales of green potted plants without providing design, delivery, and credit services.

Another new outlet consists of "plantscaping" operators who sell or rent plants to residential and commercial clients. Many such firms have been established in large metropolitan areas in the past few years. Plantscaping operators purchased 2 percent of the plants marketed by Florida foliage growers in 1975. Such sales, however, fail to include all purchases by these or other outlets that cater to retail customers, since such outlets also purchase plants from distributors, wholesale florists, and other trade entities.

Eight percent of all foliage sales in 1975 were made through brokers who act as agents in the sale and purchase of plant material. Brokers facilitate and consummate orders between buyers and sellers, then prepare bills of sale. A foliage broker may or may not physically handle the material, but the broker does not take title to the product in the capacity

TABLE 16-7   Market outlets for Florida foliage, 1975 [22]

By area grown

Outlet	Central	South	State
	Percent		
Distributors (jobbers)	27	13	21
Greenhouse operators			
(out of state)	14	30	20
Wholesale florist	12	12	12
Local growers	11	7	9
Grocery stores	8	7	8
Variety stores	10	3	8
Retail florists	8	6	7
Department stores	4	8	6
Garden centers	2	6	4
Plant stores	2	3	2
"Plantscaping" operators	2	3	2

By size of grower

Outlet	Large growers [a]	Medium to small growers [b]	State
	Percent		
Distributors (jobbers)	21	20	21
Greenhouse operators			
(out of state)	18	26	20
Wholesale florists	19	23	12
Local growers	7	20	9
Grocery stores	10	c	8
Variety stores	10	c	8
Retail florists	8	2	7
Department stores	7	c	6
Garden centers	4	3	4
Plant stores	2	2	2
"Plantscaping" operators	2	2	2

[a] Growers with sales of $500,000 or more.
[b] Growers with sales under $500,000.
[c] Less than 0.5 percent.

of a broker. Firms known as brokers may buy and sell to their own accounts in addition to carrying out brokerage operations. Sales made through brokers went to out-of-state greenhouse operators, grocery stores, retail florists, and other outlets. Such sales are included in the totals for each category shown in Table 16-7.

TABLE 16-8 Estimated proportion of sales of Florida foliage plants marketed through various outlets, 1956, 1961, 1967, and 1975 [22]

Outlet	Year			
	1956	1961	1967	1975
	Percent			
Greenhouse operators (out of state)	28	31	29	20
Variety stores	23	25	24	8
Retail florists	7	15	15	7
Grocery stores	8	4	7	8
Local growers	10	7	5	9
Brokers and jobbers (distributors)	22	16	14	21
Retail (place of business)	2	1	—	—
Other	—	1	5	27[a]
Total	100	100	100	100

[a] Includes 12 percent to wholesale florists, 6 percent to department stores, and 4 percent to garden centers. The 8 percent of all sales made through brokers are classified as going to the type of buyers listed under "outlet."

Trends in Market Outlets

Changes have taken place in the relative importance of types of outlets to which foliage plants are sold. Large increases in volume have occurred and new outlets have become important buyers of foliage. Greenhouse operators have consistently been the major outlet to which Florida foliage plants are sold, with the proportion going to this type of outlet being approximately 30 percent in 1956, 1961, and 1967 (Table 16-8). The proportion fell to 20 percent in 1975, but the physical quantity going to these types of outlets in 1975 was larger than in earlier years.

An important outlet prior to 1975 consisted of variety stores, when approximately 25 percent of all marketings went to this type of outlet. The proportion fell to 8 percent by 1975.

Plants going to retail florists rose from 7 percent in 1956 to 15 percent in 1961, remained at the same level in 1967, but dropped to 7 percent in 1975. Retail florists have not developed facilities and merchandising techniques to fill the needs of consumers to the extent that expanding mass markets have done.

Grocery stores accounted for approximately 8 percent of industry sales in 1956 and 1967, with a slightly higher proportion in 1975. Various chain grocery organizations have established buyers in Florida and other foliage supply areas. Local growers have purchased between 5 and 10 percent of the industry's output over the four time periods for which data are available. Much of the output of the industry has been marketed through jobbers and distributors with this outlet accounting for slightly more grower sales in 1975 than out-of-state greenhouse operators. Since classifications in various research studies were changed during the period from 1956 to 1975, comparisons of the trend for brokers, jobbers, and distributors are difficult. Nevertheless, distributors have now become important buyers.

Sales through other outlets have increased in the past several years; that is, 5 percent moved through outlets not otherwise classified in 1967 and 27 percent in 1975. The 27 percent included 12 percent to wholesale florists, 6 percent to department stores, and 4 percent to garden centers.

Sizes of order   The average order size shipped by ten Apopka growers in April 1970 was $270 (Table 16-9). Largest orders averaged $661 and were made to grocery stores; the smallest ($82) in sales were made to brokers.

TABLE 16-9   Average number of plant items per invoice and average value per invoice for sales made to various outlets by growers in the Apopka area, April 1970 [21]

Type outlet	No. Items	Value ($)
Dollars		
Brokers	2.1	82
Distributors (jobbers)	7.3	627
Greenhouse operators (direct)	4.4	312
Greenhouse operators (broker)	4.4	166
Grocery stores (direct)	3.1	100
Grocery stores (jobbers)	1.9	661
Local growers	2.8	125
At retail (place of business)	3.0	97
Retail florists (direct)	4.2	125
Retail florists (broker)	3.4	91
Variety stores	2.8	128
Wholesale florists	4.7	299
Garden centers	4.2	145
Department stores	4.7	99
Other	3.6	96
Average, all sales	4.5	270

Order sizes to distributors and jobbers, greenhouse operators (direct), and wholesale florists were larger than the average. The average order shipped by these ten growers in April 1970 consisted of 4.5 items with the average ranging from 1 item in sales made to grocery stores through brokers to 7.3 in shipments made directly to distributors and jobbers.

Plant Shops

A phenomenon of the 1970s in the United States was the specialized plant shop. These have sprung up in shopping malls, abandoned gasoline service stations, and various other types of buildings and locations. The plant shops were usually started by persons with interest in plants. Unlike many retail florists' shops, which do much of their business by telephone and tend to discourage browsers and shoppers, plant stores desire heavy customer traffic and cater to the mass market.

A study conducted in the summer of 1977, dealing with economic characteristics of plant shops in New York state, indicated that 70 percent of their total sales consisted of foliage plants [8]. The average age of the plant shops was less than 2 years. Average gross sales were $45,000, with 60 percent reporting annual revenues of $20,000 to $39,000. A few large businesses had sales exceeding $100,000 a year.

The average plant store had 2.3 persons—1.7 on a full-time equivalent basis—working in it. Operators generally rented rather than owned their facilities.

The major suppliers of foliage plants to plant shops were local growers. Most suppliers were within 75 miles of the retail business location. Large shops tended by buy from distant sources to a much greater extent than small ones.

Despite many differences in policies on price markups, plants tended to be priced at more than twice their purchase cost. Type and size of plant, season of the year, and competitors' prices were also factors that affected markups.

The Cornell plant shop study indicated that the original form of retail plant shops has changed and that additional changes may be expected. Those most successful in their business operations have generally added additional products and services. This tendency is expected to continue.

Pricing

Prices are determined through interactions of supply and demand. The foliage industry has a complexity of products, packages, and sizes. Thus price-making forces operate with less efficiency than in the marketing of a commodity such as wheat or corn for which market forces interact almost immediately to changes in supply and demand. One indicator in the hands of foliage growers is the Florida market news report, which gives data, on the supply side of the ledger, on weekly shipments of selected types of foliage items.

A grower will generally know that a price is lower than that of the competition, assuming equivalent product quality, if a sharp increase in business occurs. Similarly, business will tend to fall off if prices are higher than the competition.

Foliage growers will remain in business over a period of years only if the return for their products equals or exceeds their costs, both variable and fixed. In this connection, cost studies for individual products may serve a useful purpose in establishing pricing policy. However, such studies are perhaps more helpful in pointing out areas where a firm may improve efficiency and reduce costs than in acting as a guide in setting prices. Certain costs are difficult to assign specifically to individual products; thus these joint costs must be allocated in a arbitrary manner to various products. Such allocations may be done differently in various firms.

A firm might find it advisable to sell its product for any price that exceeds or equals the variable or out-of-pocket costs that are involved in the short run. However, if a firm is to prosper, it cannot afford to sell its output for less than all production costs in the long run.

Pricing in practice   Most foliage firms have price lists that contain some information about their products, especially for material in 6-inch (15.4-centimeter) and larger pot sizes. Such lists usually give plant height and numbers of plants per container and quote prices in case lot orders.

Prices for 5-inch (12.8-centimeter) and smaller pot units of *Philodendron scandens oxycardium (cordatum)* and *Dracaena marginata* in 6-, 8-, 10-, and 14-inch (15.4, 20.5, 25.6 and 35.9 centimeters) containers indicate the value of pot sizes and relationship among sizes. Examples of price ranges are shown in Table 16-10. Prices are FOB shipping point sales to wholesalers unless otherwise stated. Stock reported is of generally good merchantable quality and condition.

Price increases are usually first made by leading marketing firms. Declining prices, when they occur, generally spread almost immediately throughout the industry.

Firms with large volumes are reportedly the price pacesetters in foliage plant marketing with most of them having some of the best quality plants. In Florida, four firms in the Apopka area and three in South Florida are generally mentioned as price setters. A somewhat similar situation holds in California and other foliage-producing areas.

TABLE 16-10   Average wholesale prices received by Florida growers for selected sizes of *Philodendron scandens oxycardium (cordatum)* and *Dracaena marginata*, August 1978 [13]

Type and size of plant	Price ($)
Philodendron scandens oxycardium (*cordatum*)[a]	
3-inch (7.7-cm) plastic pots	0.21–0.34, mostly 0.22–0.28
4-inch (10.3-cm) plastic pots	0.50–0.60, few 0.63–0.75
5-inch (12.8-cm) plastic pots	1.20–1.30
Dracaena Marginata[b]	
6-inch (15.4-cm) metal pots, 1-foot (3.0 dm), 1 cane	1.50–2.00, some best 2.40–2.55, some 1.15–1.25
8-inch (20.5-cm) metal pots, 1 to 2 feet (3.0 to 6.1 dm), 2 to 3 canes	3.40–4.50, few best 4.60–5.00
10-inch (25.7-cm) metal pots, 1, 2 and 3-feet (3.0, 6.1, 9.1 dm), 3 canes	5.00–6.50, some best 6.80–8.00; specimens 8.50–10.00, few 4.50–4.75
14-inch (35.9-cm) metal pots, 2, 3, 4, 5, and 6 feet (6.1, 9.1, 12.1, 15.2, 18.3 dm), 5 canes	13.50–15.00; specimens 20.00–35.00

[a] Including packaging charges.
[b] Excluding packaging charges.

These firms tend to raise prices first, while others usually follow in the next 2 to 3 months. The industry must generally be in a period with good product demand, and cost analyses must show that higher selling prices are needed for favorable profits even for the large organizations to make an upward move in their quotations.

Foliage plants are quite perishable, but prices do not usually fluctuate greatly from month to month. Published price lists tend to place a short-term ceiling on the maximum level at which the industry can sell its product. These lists tend to make prices less volatile and thus contribute to market stability.

Quality   Quality is a relative term in the foliage industry. Although some producers have advocated grades for foliage plants, there are still no industry grade standards. Certain buyers have helped establish unofficial grades and, over the years, have raised their standards for plants purchased. For example, a rule of thumb for specifications of an upright plant such as the schefflera in a 3-inch (7.7-centimeter) pot is that the height of the plant should be two times the width of the pot, or two-thirds plant and one-third pot at time of sale. Roots should penetrate the soil to the side of the pot, the plant should have a natural appearance of good color, leaf shape, and conformation, and it should be clean and free of insects and diseases with no spots on the leaves.

The Florida Foliage Association, a grower organization, in an effort to assist growers in achieving improved standardization, has developed and published specifications for thirty-two indoor decorative plants in pot sizes of 6 inches (15.4 centimeters) and up [5]. A release of additional plant standards is expected in 1979.

Distribution and Transportation

Distribution   Florida foliage plants are distributed from points of production to buyers throughout the United States, with a large quantity also exported. The South, Northeast, and Midwest are the major areas to which shipments are made by Florida growers. The West Coast and mountain states are the primary market for California, Colorado, and Hawaii foliage growers. Nevertheless, these growers, especially operators in California, are shipping an increasing volume into the Midwest, with some specialty products going to eastern and southeastern markets.

The latest information on the distribution pattern for the entire Florida foliage industry was for 1961 [1, 2]. In that year 25 percent of all shipments went to the Northeast, the same proportion to the Southeast, 22 percent to the Midwest and northeastern Rocky Mountain states, and 8 percent to the Southwest. Fourteen percent went to buyers in Florida, and 3 percent each went to the West and for export.

Transportation   Transportation is always a critical factor in marketing. The greater the distance from production area to destination, the more critical the method of shipment because of the added cost.

Foliage plant buyers are usually responsible for transportation charges. Purchasers have received foliage plants by various modes of transit and know which method of shipment is best suited to their needs.

For many years Railway Express was the major method of transporting foliage plants. Approximately half of the foliage plants from Florida moved by Railway Express in 1956, with 28 percent going by air freight and 21 percent by truck [1, 2]. The remaining 2 percent went by various other methods, including parcel post, bus, and growers' trucks. By 1961 trucks were moving 42 percent of Florida foliage, with 30 percent going by Railway Express and 12 percent by air freight. The remaining 16 percent went by growers' trucks.

From 1961 to date, further changes have occurred in the types of transport used for hauling foliage plants. Railway Express services are no longer operating.

TABLE 16-11   Rates per carton[a] in dollars for shipping a 25-pound (11.3-kilogram) carton of foliage plants from the Apopka-Orlando, Florida, area to various destinations, October 1978 [13]

City	Air[b]	Bus[c]	Truck[d]
Atlanta	$ 2.86–4.10	$ 4.41	$ 2.30–2.46
Chicago	5.40–5.75	8.15	2.43–2.69
Cleveland	4.83–5.83	7.73	2.43–2.69
Cincinnati	4.50–5.25	7.73	2.43–2.69
Dallas	5.35–6.36	8.98	2.43–2.46
Denver	7.25–8.55	12.15	N/A
Los Angeles	7.80–9.21	15.48	3.20–3.71
New York City	4.88–5.38	8.98	2.43–2.69
San Francisco	8.50–9.94	15.48	3.58–4.10
Seattle	9.26–11.80	17.75	N/A
St. Louis	4.91–5.13	8.15	2.45–2.53
Washington, D.C.	4.43–5.65	7.15	2.43–2.69
Montreal	6.01–7.68	NA	3.38

[a] Rates converted to the equivalent of a carton containing fifty-six 3-inch (7.7-cm) pots with cubic measurement of 2.53 cubic feet (0.7 ds).

[b] Rates are from the Orlando airport to the destination airport. They do not include pickup or delivery. The first charge is for a 3,000-pound (1360.8-kg) minimum shipment and the second is for a 100-pound (489-kg) minimum. Data shown are the lowest published rates among airlines.

[c] Rate shown is for maximum shipment of three pieces.

[d] Rate is for less than truckload lots, which constitute the bulk of truck movement from the state.

Transportation rates   Currently, rates to different locations by various types of transportation differ substantially. Data on transportation costs from the central Florida area in October 1978 by air, bus, and truck to a series of locations are shown in Table 16-11.

Methods of transportation   Truck, air, and bus are now the main means by which foliage plants are transported from growers to market locations. *Truck* hauling is the major method of shipping foliage plants in the United States. Operators pick up containers of plants at producers' packinghouses and make deliveries to buyers' doors. The cost of truck transportation is low in comparison with air and bus. Three types of truck transportation are utilized: (1) buyers' trucks, (2) producers' trucks, and (3) commercial trucking firms.

Many buyers from consuming market areas have their own vans or large trucks and make on-the-spot purchases of foliage from producers. This type of trading has increased in the past several years. Recent figures show that such shipments now account for about 5 percent of the volume of Florida foliage.

Producers use their trucks for hauling principally to wholesalers, but a few have small 5-ton truck units for hauling and selling merchandise in small lots to retailers within a radius of a journey of 1 or 2 days.

Commercial trucking firms and producers with their own trucks transport an estimated 83 percent of foliage production in Florida. Of the two, the commercial truck hauler is the most important. Commercial carriers haul the bulk of foliage shipments and deliver them along prescribed routes throughout the United States and southern Canada. These routes weave through large cities in which major plant distributor outlets can take deliveries of fifty or more cases.

Trucking firms haul foliage plants, an agricultural exempt commodity, from producing areas and then make backhauls with exempt or nonexempt products. Such trailers used are 40 (12.2 meters) to 45 feet (13.7 meters) in length. Foliage is a bulk item like furniture and weight is not a problem. However, items brought back on return trips may have higher specific gravity.

Smaller lines usually work on a prearranged basis with one or several foliage producers and are generally able to offer certain special services, such as more drops of smaller lots, than larger truck firms.

Airlines account for an estimated 10 percent of the volume shipped from Florida, with Orlando and Miami the two principal airports used. Both cities are near centers of production and have good freight lift capacity owing to the large number of flights. Other airports in the southern part of the state originate a few shipments.

Los Angeles, San Francisco, and San Diego are the major points of air shipments from California. Distribution is to points in the West and Midwest, with some to eastern points.

Florida foliage firms use airlines for small-lot orders distributed throughout the United States, Canada, and Europe. Few air shipments go to southern locations. Shipments to points in the United States and Canada average four to five cartons. Results have been unsatisfactory in moving by air anything larger than 8-inch (20.5-centimeter) pots. Most plant material going to Europe is propagating stock.

Air and bus rates are on a weight basis. Therefore, plants to be shipped these ways are usually watered 2 or 3 days ahead of shipping time to keep down weight during transit. Pots are individually wrapped with newspaper or specially designed sleeves before placing in the carton for insulation against weather changes and for protection against handling damage.

Bus transportation plays a small but important part in distribution of foliage plants. The service is fast and moderately priced for small-lot orders. Approximately 2 percent of the volume from Florida goes by this method. This transportation is used by buyers throughout the United

States, with the largest amount going to southern points and the smallest quantity to populous eastern states. Plants are individually wrapped with newspaper for insulation before placement in cartons in winter months.

Carton specification   The strength of cardboard cartons is a controversial subject among shippers, truck firms, and airlines. Truckers and airlines have contended that the test strength of the 200- to 250-pound (90.7- to 113.4-kilogram) cardboard containers formerly used by most Florida shippers is unsatisfactory since these cartons frequently break down when stacked one on top of another. Claims from broken packages in transit have been high, with resultant increases in transportation charges.

Currently, the most accepted package used in Florida is the minimum 250-pound (113.4-kilogram) test carton with vertical corrugation and waterproof tray.

Foliage Plant Product Mix

The only source of data on the relative production throughout the United States of various types of foliage plants was the 1970 Special Census enumeration. Data on the value of production of ten major foliage plants, as delineated in the census report, are shown in Table 16-12. In the nation, *Philodendron scandens oxycardium (cordatum)* was the leading foliage plant, followed by other types of philodendrons and ferns. Leaders in Florida were the two classes of philodendrons and

TABLE 16-12   Value of sales of various types of finished potted foliage plants in the five leading producing states and the United States, 1970 [23]

Plant	Florida	California	Texas	Ohio	Pennsylvania	U.S.
	($1,000)					
Caladium cv.	44	131	328	46	72	1,292
Dieffenbachia spp.	462	360	65	61	172	1,597
Dracaena spp.	471	336	53	77	65	1,732
Ferns	558	915	117	33	106	2,418
Palms	582	434	103	54	56	1,888
Pandanus spp.	14	118	27	26	30	518
Peperomia spp.	108	417	34	59	61	1,104
Philodendron spp. *cordatum*	1,659	425	65	211	149	3,910
Philodendron spp. other	932	826	75	147	197	3,140
Schefflera spp. *actinophylla*	360	283	55	45	136	1,388
All other	11,595	1,407	923	1,630	930	19,388
Total	16,785	5,652	1,845	2,389	1,974	38,375

TABLE 16-13 Relative importance in percent of various foliage plants in Florida, 1956, 1961, 1967, and 1975 [22]

Plant type	1956	1961	1967	1975
Philodendron oxycardium (cordatum)	34	26	20	14
Dracaena spp.	2	3	4	11
Philodendron spp. (other)	16	18	16	6
Ficus spp.	2	9	6	6
Dieffenbachia spp.	2	5	7	5
Combinations	—	3	11	2
Scindapsus spp. (pothos)	10	11	6	3
Sansevieria spp.	16	8	6	3
Syngonium spp. (nephthytis)	4	2	3	2
Chamaedorea elegans (neanthabella)	2	2	2	2
Peperomia spp.	2	2	2	3
Hoya	—	0.2	1	2
Aglaonema spp.	2	1	1	2
Spathiphyllum spp.	—	1	1	3
Maranta	0.4	1	1	3
Pilea spp.	2	0.3	0.2	0.4
Others	6	8	13	34
Total	100	100	100	100

palms. In California, ferns were first, followed by other philodendrons and palms. The three most important plants in Texas were caladiums, ferns, and palms.

Doubtless many changes have occurred in the mix of plants grown in various states from 1970 to the present. Nevertheless, the 1970 data serve as a benchmark for further comparative analysis.

Product mix in Florida   A series of four studies pertaining to the period from 1956 to 1975 on the product mix of foliage plants in Florida was done by faculty and graduate students at the University of Florida. Unfortunately, other than the 1970 Special Census release, similar studies have not been done elsewhere.

Although composition of the product mix will vary in other states, it is believed that some of the general trends reported in Florida may be applicable elsewhere.

Philodendron scandens oxycardium (cordatum) has been the major item marketed by Florida foliage growers during the years data have been available (Table 16-13). A third of all marketings in 1956 consisted of this plant, but the proportion had dropped to a fourth in 1961 and a fifth in 1967. Fourteen percent of all foliage plants sold in 1975 consisted of *Philodendron scandens oxycardium (cordatum)*.

Dracaena spp. have increased to second in importance in the indus-

TABLE 16-14   Foliage plant product mix in percent in Central and South Florida, 1975 [22]

Product	Area		
	Central	South	All Florida
Philodendron oxycardium (cordatum)	21	2	14
Dracaena spp.	6	20	11
Philodendron spp. (other)	7	5	6
Ficus spp.	2	12	6
Dieffenbachia spp.	6	3	5
Palms	2	9	5
Brassaia actinophylla (schefflera)	2	8	5
Maranta spp.	5	1	3
Scindapsus spp. (pothos)	4	1	3
Totem-pole plants	3	2	3
Ferns	2	4	3
Peperomia spp.	4	1	3
Sansevieria spp.	3	1	3
Syngonium spp. (nephytis)	4	1	2
Combinations	4	a	2
Hanging baskets	2	2	2
Aphelandra spp.	3	1	2
Aglaonema spp.	2	1	2
Chamaedorea elegans (Neanthabella)	2	2	2
Aralias	1	3	2
Hoya spp.	3	a	2
Terrarium plants	2	a	1
Crotons	1	2	1
Cacti	1	2	1
Ardisia spp.	1	a	1
Spathiphyllum spp.	1	1	1
Other	6	14	9
Total	100	100	100

[a] Less than 0.5 percent.

try and accounted for 11 percent of all sales by 1975, compared with 2 percent in 1956, 3 percent in 1961, and 4 percent in 1967.

Other types of philodendron are in third place, but have sustained a substantial relative decline over the period 1967 to 1975.

Ficus spp., in fourth place in 1975, have not changed in relative importance from 1967. *Dieffenbachia* spp. were in fifth place with 4 percent of the total at the same time, and their share represented a decline from higher proportionate levels in 1961 and 1967.

Of sixteen separate groups of plants for which data were available in 1975 and in most other years, many changes took place (Table 16-14). The group classified as "other plants" made up only 6 percent of the total in 1956 but rose to 8 percent in 1961, 13 percent in 1967, and 34 percent in 1975. This indicated the rising importance of plants that contribute large shares to current marketings but that were grown only in relatively small proportions in earlier years.

Packaging   Preparation of foliage plants for shipment and sale is an extremely important phase of the marketing process. Well-grown plants that arrive at their destinations in poor condition do not encourage future purchases by buyers to whom they are shipped.

Many shipment methods are used for transporting foliage plants, but most smaller potted items are packed in containers made of corrugated cardboard. The plants are usually in plastic pots and are generally wrapped in newspaper, kraft paper, or plastic sleeves to protect the foliage and/or totem poles. An increasing amount of 6-inch (15.4-centimeter) and larger pots is now transported to market in bulk form (that is, not in containers) owing to rising costs for cartons.

Rapid changes in the way plants are placed and arranged for shipment in trailer and truck bodies are occurring. Plants are now shipped increasingly in containers set on pallets on racks or loose in pots. Many such trucks are double decked, with plants stacked from the floor to the ceiling. In some cases the plants, mainly 4 inches (10.3 centimeters) and smaller, are placed loose on the racks. Some shippers use returnable trays and collapsible racks in order to utilize most of the trailer space for return hauls. The use of various techniques of rack placement and other innovative loading methods generally results in savings and substantial efficiency.

In 1975, 88 percent of Florida foliage plants, in value terms, were marketed in pots, with 8 percent sold bareroot, 2 percent in totem poles, and 2 percent in other types of containers (see Table 16-15). Similar data are not available for other areas.

A major change in the past 5 years is the large increase in the quantity of plants sold in 6-inch (15.4-centimeter) or larger pots. This proportion in 1975 was 47 percent for Florida, in comparison with only 9 percent in 1970 for the Apopka area (Table 16-15).

The number of all varieties of foliage plants shipped in various containers during 1977 and 1978 is noted in Table 16-16.

Innovative types of packaging and marketing are being tried on operational and experimental bases. One method in use involves placement of large plants in gravel-filled containers with instructions and materials for a liquid feeding program as a part of the sales package. Various sleeves and other packaging materials to minimize the necessity for watering plants while on display in retail outlets are being developed and tested; some show promise of success.

TABLE 16-15   Relative importance in percent of sales (dollar value) of Florida foliage plants in major types of containers, 1970 and 1975 (preliminary estimate) [21, 22]

Type container	Size in inches (cm)	Apopka (1970)[a]	State (1975)[b]
Pots	2¼ (5.8)	6	5
	2½ (6.4)	3	2
	3 (7.7)	37	19
	3½ (9.0)	7	4
	4 (10.3)	18	7
	5 (12.8)	2	4
	6 (15.4)	5	21
	8 (20.5)	4	6
	9 (23.1) and plus	N.D.[c]	20
All pots		82	88
Bareroot		5	8
Totem poles		2	2
Not designated or other		11	2
All sales		100.0	100.0

[a] Data from sales records of ten growers.
[b] Estimates from forty-six growers distributed throughout the state.
[c] No data published.

TABLE 16-16   Number of all varieties of foliage plants shipped in various types of containers from Florida, 1977 and 1978 [4]

Type container	Size in inches (cm)	Number of containers (1,000s)	
		1977	1978
Rooted cuttings		37,766	32,392
Pots	2¼ (5.8) and smaller	10,131	10,416
	3 (7.7)	62,956	58,081
	3½-4 (9.0–10.3)	11,825	12,551
	5 (12.8)	1,837	2,950
	6 (15.4)	11,243	11,366
	8 (20.5)	1,947	1,843
	10 (25.6)	3,205	4,161
	12 (30.8)	400	253
	14 (35.9) and larger	289	343

An indication of the division of foliage plant sales into potted and unpotted (primarily rooted cuttings) for the ten major foliage-producing states in 1970 is noted in Table 16-17. The data show that, while approximately one fourth of all sales in the contiguous United States consisted of unpotted plants in 1949, the proportion had dropped to one fifth in 1959 and to one tenth in 1970. Florida has remained one of the major suppliers of unpotted plants. Nevertheless, less than 15 percent of all Florida foliage plant sales in 1970 were reported to be unpotted plants.

Self-Help Industry Programs

State and federal governments have assisted agricultural industries in various self-help programs for many years. Producers of commodities have expressed problems to legislative representatives, who passed enabling legislation providing for the formation of marketing agreements and orders and for central marketing cooperatives. Such state and federal legislation has been used for developing marketing programs in fruits, vegetables, and other commodities throughout the country, but to date none has been used for ornamental crops.

Marketing agreements and orders   Most marketing agreements and orders are and have been in California, with its plethora of specialty crops. Initiation of most of these agreements was in the 1930s during a time of commodity surpluses. The legislation that permitted growers to organize marketing agreements and orders provided that certain specified activities could be carried on, including size and grade restrictions, and limits on quantities marketed. In the case of state marketing orders, growers could be assessed funds for advertising and promotion. All such legislation necessitates a referendum of growers and handlers with the requirement that a specified minimum proportion vote themselves into any such type of industry program. After this is done the U.S. secretary of agriculture or the commissioner of agriculture or equivalent in state governments is authorized to issue a marketing order. The issuing office becomes legally responsible to assure that all persons in the industry follow the practices stipulated in the marketing agreement.

Most marketing agreements and orders cover broad scopes of activities. However, often only one or two features permissible in the legislation authorizing a marketing agreement are actually put into practice. A committee of growers and handlers is selected to administer any program voted in. Provisions adopted are given the force of law through their promulgation by the government official authorized to issue such regulations. Legislation authorizing market agreements and orders usu-

TABLE 16-17 Distribution of foliage plant sales in thousands of dollars among unpotted plants (rooted cuttings and the like) for growing on and potted plants in ten leading states, 1949, 1959, and 1970 [23]

State	1949			1959			1970		
	Unpotted	Potted	Total	Unpotted	Potted	Total	Unpotted	Potted	total
California	688	1,840	2,528	298	4,093	4,391	192	5,652	5,844
Florida	1,453	391	1,844	5,389	7,233	12,622	2,919	16,786	19,705
Illinois	24	723	747	374	1,183	1,557	a	810	810
Massachusetts	16	380	396	3	908	911	a	860	860
Michigan	59	327	386	42	922	964	6	1,072	1,078
New Jersey	169	706	875	12	1,408	1,420	5	1,106	1,111
New York	89	1,346	1,435	111	1,419	1,530	69	1,438	1,438
Ohio	110	1,136	1,246	53	1,542	1,595	5	2,389	2,394
Pennsylvania	141	1,012	1,153	32	2,004	2,036	12	1,973	1,985
Texas	366	303	669	349	989	1,338	79	1,845	1,924
U.S. (48 states)	3,316	9,842	13,158	6,883	25,607	32,490	3,615	38,376	41,991

[a] No data published.

ally contains provisions for a majority of growers and handlers to vote an end to any agreement and order.

Should a marketing agreement and order program be activated in the foliage industry, many features might be utilized to the industry's advantage. These include advertising and promotion programs, standardization of cartons, plant indexing, the development of programs to maintain disease-free propagating stock, research, and others.

Central marketing cooperatives are provided for under the cooperative laws of Florida and other states. Such organizations have had a great deal of success in the marketing of various agricultural commodities.

Florida foliage plant marketing law   The Florida legislature passed a law in 1961 that authorized a marketing agreement for foliage plants. In response to a request from the requisite number of growers, a referendum was held by the commissioner of agriculture in which approximately 65 percent or more of the producers and handlers, by volume and number, voted to initiate such an agreement. However, many individuals in the industry and the staff of the Florida Department of Agriculture and Consumer Services felt that a sufficient level of support did not exist, and a decision was made not to activate the order.

The Florida Foliage Association convened meetings in four geographic locations of the state during March 1978 to discuss the feasibility of activating a marketing order. There was considerable interest on the part of many growers to develop such a program to foster advertising and research. Straw votes at only one—that on the lower east coast—of the four meetings indicated a desire to work toward collective action by the entire industry. Hence no request for an election was made to the commissioner of agriculture.

Part 2 of Chapter 573 of the Florida Marketing Laws contains the foliage plant marketing law [6]. Its purpose is (1) to enable foliage producers to relate more effectively the marketing of their foliage plants with market demand, (2) to establish and maintain orderly marketing, (3) to provide methods for the maintenance of present markets and the development of newer and larger markets, (4) to provide for uniform grading and proper preparation for market, (5) to eliminate or reduce the economic waste in marketing, and (6) to prevent, modify, or eliminate state barriers that obstruct the free flow of plants to market.

The law contains provisions that would enable the establishment of plans and programs for advertising and sales promotion and for the conduct of research in the production and distribution of foliage plants; it provides for the prohibition of unfair trade practices by allowing for the establishment of the following: (1) grading standards of quality, condition, size, shape, maturity, pack, or other criteria, (2) uniform inspection, grading, and labeling, (3) fixing the size, weight, capacity, and dimensions on back of containers, and (4) provisions for the establishment of surplus, stabilization, or by-product pools for foliage plants and for the equitable distribution among persons participating of net returns derived from sales. The law provides that funds for operation of the marketing order shall be fixed on the volume of foliage plants sold or some other equitable basis.

Further provisions call for the termination of the market order when a referendum called by the Department of Agriculture and Consumer Services finds that 51 percent of the producers who are engaged within the state in the production of foliage plants for market covered by the marketing order, and who produced for market more than 51 percent of the volume of foliage plant produced within that state, are opposed to any marketing order. Such a referendum shall be called when the commission is requested in writing to do so by the number of producers specified in the preceding sentence. The law further provides that the suspension or termination shall not be effective until the expiration of any current marketing season.

Alternative Programs   A variety of marketing devices and programs may be utilized to increase returns to growers and/or expand sales of foliage plants. In addition to marketing agreement programs, these include advertising and promotion, quality control, reduction of container types, and other market-improvement programs.

Individual firms or groups of firms working together in a cooperative or business arrangement, where one firm does the marketing for a group of others, often benefit from improved market situations. With a product of a standard quality, an advertising, promotion, and market-development program can be initiated to the benefit of participants. Many large firms can and have benefited from their own market-development programs, and some have taken steps to differentiate their products through brand-name identification.

Commercial agricultural producers in most areas of the world have organized trade groups to make their collective voice heard more effectively by governments and to work together on insurance, the setting of minimum grade or quality standards, cooperative advertising and promotion, and other endeavors of common interest to members. United States foliage growers have affiliated with two national trade groups, the Society of American Florists and the American Association of Nurserymen. For most of the past three decades foliage growers in Florida were active in the Florida Nurserymen and Growers Association. Foliage growers in other states have also been involved in their state and regional floral and nursery associations. Recently, a separate organization, the Florida Foliage Association, was formed. Similarly, foliage growers in California have formed the Living Plant Growers Association.

On the national level the major advertising programs for flower and foliage plants are done by the Florists Telegraph Delivery Association and the Society of American Florists. The latter group, supported entirely by voluntary contributions, has not received extensive support from foliage growers.

A new organization, Florida Foliage Producers, came into being in 1978 following the lack of interest shown by the majority of Florida foliage growers in activating a marketing agreement program to promote foliage and sponsor research. Thirty-one foliage growers contribute to the organization, which has initiated a public relations and advertising program. The group is developing a labeling program, with labels to be used only on plants of member growers. The program of Florida Foliage Producers provides the consumer with "how-to" information on plant selection, plant care, and decorating with foliage; reaches supermarkets and other retail outlets through personal visits, seminars, brochures, and the like; and counsels architects and designers in selecting quality plant material, ordering plants early to allow acclimatization, and working with interior landscaping in creating designs in which interior foliage will be used.

Appendix

Background Data

Statistical data are necessary tools in making economic analyses of supply, demand, and other economic characteristics of any enterprise. They are relatively sparse in the tropical foliage industry compared with other agricultural enterprises. The first such series of data was the *Special Census of Horticultural Specialties* developed by the Bureau of the Census of the U.S. Department of Commerce [23]. The special census in 1949 provided information by counties throughout the United States of number of plants sold, values of sales, and number of operators growing tropical foliage plants, both potted and unpotted. A similar series of data was contained in the 1959 special census. Another special census done in 1970 provided general information on the entire complex of foliage plants, with detailed data on units produced and value of sales of a limited number of specific plants in producing states.

The U.S. Department of Agriculture, through the Crop Reporting Board of the Economics, Statistics, and Cooperatives Service, releases annual statistics of the value of sales, number of growers, and square feet in production of tropical foliage plants in sixteen states [24]. Actually, the series started in 1966 with data released for twenty-three states, but in the 1976 report (with data for 1975) Delaware and a number of other minor producing states were dropped.

The Federal-State Market News Service has released weekly shipment data on Florida foliage plants since June 1970 [4]. In the earliest reports the information was on specific plants. It then progressed to a tabulation of all varieties of foliage material by pot sizes, as well as rooted cuttings for a number of growers. Beginning in January 1979 a statistical formula was developed to expand the data from cooperating firms to an estimate of total movement of the types of plants included in the market news report. The Federal-State Market News Service publishes an annual summary report at the end of each year. Changes and growth in the foliage industry are documented in the annual summary reports for 1974 through 1978 [3].

Several economic studies have provided information on the foliage industry. Charles A. Nicholls [11, 12] developed data on numbers of growers, value of sales, market outlets, product mix, and other economic characteristics. John R. Brooker [1] obtained data somewhat similar to those in Nicholls's study. Several articles showing results were published [2].

Data from sales invoices collected in 1970 were analyzed [21]. Information was generated on product mix, market outlets, type of shipper, area of distribution, size order, number of plants per order, and other characteristics.

Additional information on the quantities of various types of cuttings imported into the United States has been tabulated from plant quarantine import records by the Federal-State Market News Service at Winter Park, Florida. A tabulation of these data for 1975 through 1978 is contained in the most recent foliage plant summary [3].

One other series of data on business analysis of costs involved by a selected group of foliage plants growers is contained in a series of publications released by the Food and Resource Economics Department at the University of Florida. Annual reports have been published since 1966 [9].

REFERENCES

Note: References [7], [10], [17], [18], [19], and [20] are not quoted in Chapter 16, but are listed here to aid students and researchers.

[1] Brooker, John R. 1963. Recent changes in the market structure of the

Florida foliage plant industry. Unpublished master's thesis, University of Florida.

[2] _____, and Cecil N. Smith. 1962. Changes in the marketing of foliage plants. *Proc. Fla. State Hort. Soc.* 75:439–442.

[3] Federal-State Market News Service. 1970 to 1979. *Marketing Florida ornamental crops: fresh foliage plants, summary 1978.* Orlando and Winter Park, Fla.

[4] _____. 1970 to 1978, weekly. *Ornamental crops—Florida foliage plant report.* Orlando and Winter Park, Fla.

[5] Florida Crop and Livestock Reporting Service. 1978. *Florida specialty crops—flowers and foliage plant report.* Orlando, Fla. 2 pp.

[6] Florida. 1977, 1978. *Official Florida Statutes,* Ch. 573 (Part II, "Foliage Plant Marketing Law" and 1978 Supplement). Tallahassee: Joint Legislative Management Committee.

[7] Gaines, Richard L. 1978. *Guidelines to foliage plant specifications for interior use.* Apopka, FL: Florida Foliage Association. 36 pp.

[8] Goodrich, Dana C., Jr. 1978. *Plant shops: selected economic characteristics.* Cornell Univ. Agr. Exp. Sta. A. E. Res. 78-10. Ithaca, N.Y. 21 pp.

[9] Gunter, Dan L. 1978. *Business analysis of foliage nurseries in Central Florida, 1977* (and earlier reports). Univ. of Fla. IFAS Econ. Info. Rpt. 101. Gainesville: November 1976. 21 pp.

[10] _____, and J. Robert Strain. 1976. Florida wholesale nursery sales and costs, 1971–75, *Proc. Fla. State Hort. Soc.* 89:278–281.

[11] Nicholls, Charles A. 1958. Marketing analysis of the Florida foliage plant industry. Unpublished master's thesis, University of Florida.

[12] _____, Cecil N. Smith, and Donald L. Brooke. 1959. *A survey of the Florida foliage plant industry.* University of Florida Agr. Exp. Sta. Bul. 615. 1978.

[13] Scarborough, Elmo F. 1978. Unpublished data.

[14] _____, and Cecil N. Smith. 1976. Tropical foliage production in Latin America and the Caribbean. *Proc. Tropical Section Am. Soc. Hort. Sci.* 24:455–467.

[15] Smith, Cecil N. 1976. Flower business blossoms. *International Trade Forum* 12(4):4–7, 32–34.

[16] _____. 1976. Increasing competition from California foliage. *Fla. Foliage Horn of Plenty Rept.* 2(3):3–5.

[17] _____. 1976. Some data on the expanding foliage plant industry. *Fla. Foliage Horn of Plenty Rept.* 3(2):34–35.

[18] _____. 1969. Trends in marketing Florida foliage plants. Univ. of Fla. Agr. Exp. Sta. Mimeo. Report EC 70-3. 49 pp.

[19] _____. 1976. Unpublished study.

[20] _____, and Frank A. Dasse. 1976. Tropical foliage marketing trends upward. *Sunshine State Agr. Res. Rept.* 21(1):28–32.

[21] _____, E. F. Scarborough, and Kate F. Gholston. 1973. Product mix and market outlets for Florida foliage plants. *Proc. Fla. State Hort. Soc.* 86:404–408.

[22] ———, and J. Robert Strain. 1976. Market outlets and product mix for Florida foliage plants (Fla. Agr. Exp. Sta. J. Series 239). *Proc. Fla. State Hort. Soc.* 89:274–278.

[23] U.S. Bureau of the Census. 1952, 1962, 1974. *U.S. Census of Agriculture 1949, 1959,* and *1969. Vol. V. Special Reports, Part 1. Horticultural Specialties.* Washington, D.C.: U.S. Government Printing Office.

[24] U.S. Economics, Statistics, and Cooperatives Service. 1969 to 1978. *Flowers and Foliage Plants—Production and Sales in Selected States, 1956-68,* and annually through 1977. U.S. Department of Agriculture Statistical Bulletin No. 442 and related annual reports. Washington, D.C. U.S. Department of Agriculture.

seventeen

C. A. Conover
D. B. McConnell

utilization
of foliage plants

Foliage plants have been used indoors for centuries, but only recently have they become a part of interior living spaces. The opportunities for plant use and availability of different genera are many, but selection of plants for specific locations and care indoors has not been fully understood by many consumers.

Using Plants Indoors

An evaluation of locations where foliage plants will be used must be made before they can serve effectively indoors. Evaluation of interior environments is similar to a site analysis study conducted before plants are installed in exterior landscapes. A complete interior evaluation includes measurements and estimates of year-round light intensity, quality, and duration, high and low temperatures, relative humidity, water quality, expected pedestrian traffic patterns, and location of heating, cooling, or ventilating systems.

The degree and complexity of an interior evaluation depends upon the location, but this information is critical to ensure plant survival and longevity. An individual selecting plants for home use may only need to evaluate a small area, while an interior plantscaper may need to monitor the environment and microenvironments in 100,000 square feet or more of a shopping mall [11].

INTERIOR SITE ANALYSIS CHECKLIST

Name of facility _____ Date _____

Address _____

Contact person _____ Telephone _____

Interior Factors

Room or Floor Level

1) Dimensions – length _____ width _____

2) Pedestrian traffic patterns _____

3) Locations where plants will be used (see sketch on back) _____

    _____

4) Windows: Number _____ Length _____ Width _____

    Windows face   North _____ , East _____ , South _____ , West _____

5) Artificial light: Type of light _____ wattage _____

    Distance from plants _____ Number of hours in use _____

    Spectral distribution (if available) _____

6) Light intensity where plants will be used (see sketch on back)

    Location A: 8 A.M. _____ 12 noon _____ Location B: 8 A.M. _____ 12 noon _____

    Location C: 8 A.M. _____ 12 noon _____ Location D: 8 A.M. _____ 12 noon _____

7) Temperature range (approximate)

    Location A: Winter   (day) _____ (night) _____
    　　　　　　　Summer (day) _____ (night) _____
    Location B: Winter   (day) _____ (night) _____
    　　　　　　　Summer (day) _____ (night) _____
    Location C: Winter   (day) _____ (night) _____
    　　　　　　　Summer (day) _____ (night) _____
    Location D: Winter   (day) _____ (night) _____
    　　　　　　　Summer (day) _____ (night) _____

8) Number of water spigots _____ Location of spigots _____

    Water quality (if analysis of water is available attach here)

    Location of drains: _____

9) Existing Plants:

    Indoor trees _____ Species _____ Condition _____
    　　　　　　　　　　　　　　　 _____ 　　　　　　　 _____
    　　　　　　　　　　　　　　　 _____ 　　　　　　　 _____

    Floor plants _____ Species _____ Condition _____
    　　　　　　　　　　　　　　　 _____ 　　　　　　　 _____
    　　　　　　　　　　　　　　　 _____ 　　　　　　　 _____

    Shelf plants _____ Species _____ Condition _____
    　　　　　　　　　　　　　　　 _____ 　　　　　　　 _____
    　　　　　　　　　　　　　　　 _____ 　　　　　　　 _____

10) Heating, Cooling and Ventilating System (see sketch on back):

Filter system _____

Location of heating ducts _____

Location of air conditioning ducts _____

Location of ventilation ducts _____

11) Relative humidity (approximate):

Summer: _____ Winter: _____

12) Potential problems: _____

_____

Figure 17-1. Example of a checklist used to analyze an interior location for its potential for interiorscaping.

A checklist of important factors can be useful because of the complexity of environmental factors that should be monitored. An example of a site analysis form is found in Figure 17-1, which, when completed, can be used to select plants listed in Table 17-1. This table contains 107 of the best foliage plants available for use indoors and can be used to identify plants with best survival potential.

Plant Selection Determined by Growth Characteristics

Final plant selection can be made after interior environmental conditions are defined and a group of plants selected to survive those conditions by assessing plant growth characteristics, which include form, size, color, and texture.

All foliage plants have a form or outline that is used to describe the geometrical shape the plant most closely resembles. Common forms of interior plants are rounded, spreading, upright, cascading (weeping), oval, and mounded (Figure 17-2). The same foliage plant may be grown in several different ways, for example, as a hanging basket or as a totem pole; therefore, a particular form is not absolute with each plant species used indoors.

A utilitarian classification can be developed for indoor plants based on their potential use. Floor plants usually range in height from 3 to over 20 feet and can be used individually or in groupings with other plants. Table or shelf plants encompass a wide range of plant sizes, but are often defined as an individual or plant grouping small enough to be placed on a table, which includes dish gardens, terrariums, and potted plants in

TABLE 17-1 One hundred and seven foliage plants for interior use

No.	Scientific name	Common name	Light levels [a]			Adaptability for interior use [b]	Suggested interior uses			
			Low	Medium	High		Table plants	Floor plants	Hanging baskets	Totem poles
1.	*Adiantum* sp.	Maidenhair fern		X	X	4	X			
2.	*Aechmea fasciata*	Silver vase		X	X	2	X			
3.	*Aeschynanthus pulcher*	Lipstick vine			X	3	X		X	
4.	*Aglaonema commutatum*	Silver evergreen	X	X	X	1	X			
5.	*Aglaonema commutatum* 'Fransher'	Fransher evergreen	X	X	X	1	X			
6.	*Aglaonema modestum*	Chinese evergreen	X	X	X	1	X			
7.	*Aglaonema commutatum* 'Pseudobracteatum'	Golden evergreen	X	X	X	1	X	X		
8.	*Aglaonema crispum* (*A. roebelinii*)	Pewter evergreen	X		X	1	X	X		
9.	*Aglaonema commutatum* 'Silver King'	Silver king evergreen	X		X	1	X			
10.	*Aglaonema commutatum* 'Silver Queen'	Silver queen evergreen	X		X	2	X			
11.	*Aglaonema commutatum* 'Treubii'	Ribbon evergreen	X		X	2	X			
12.	*Aglaonema costatum*	Costatum evergreen	X	X	X	2	X			
13.	*Ananas comosus*	Pineapple		X	X	3	X			
14.	*Aphelandra squarrosa*	Zebra plant			X	3	X			
15.	*Araucaria heterophylla*	Norfolk Island pine		X	X	3	X	X		
16.	*Ardisia crispa*	Coral ardisia		X	X	3	X			
17.	*Asparagus densiflorus* 'Myersii'	Plume asparagus		X	X	4	X		X	
18.	*Asparagus densiflorus* 'Sprengeri'	Sprengeri asparagus		X	X	3	X		X	

#	Botanical name	Common name				No.			
19.	*Aspidistra elatior*	Cast-iron plant	X	X	X	1	X	X	
20.	*Asplenium nidus*	Bird's-nest fern	X	X	X	3	X	X	
21.	*Beaucarnea recurvata*	Ponytail palm		X	X	4	X	X	
22.	*Begonia rex-cultorum*	Rex begonia		X	X	3	X		
23.	*Brassaia actinophylla*	Schefflera		X	X	2	X	X	
24.	*Brassaia arboricola*	Dwarf schefflera		X	X	3	X	X	
25.	*Calathea insignis*	Rattlesnake plant		X	X	4	X		
26.	*Calathea makoyana*	Peacock plant			X	4	X		
27.	*Carissa grandiflora* 'Bonsai'	Bonsai natal plum			X	3			
28.	*Chamaedorea elegans*	Parlor palm	X	X	X	2	X		
29.	*Chamaedorea erumpens*	Bamboo palm		X	X	3	X	X	
30.	*Chlorophytum comosum* 'Variegatum'	Spider plant		X	X	2	X		X
31.	*Chrysalidocarpus lutescens*	Areca palm		X	X	3	X	X	
32.	*Cissus antarctica*	Kangaroo vine		X	X	2	X		X
33.	*Cissus rhombifolia*	Grape ivy		X	X	2	X		X
34.	*Citrus mitis*	Calamondin			x	4	X	X	
35.	*Codiaeum variegatum* 'Aucubifolium'	Gold dust croton		X	X	4	X	X	
36.	*Coffea arabica*	Arabian coffee			X	4	X	X	
37.	*Cordyline terminalis*	Ti plant		X	X	3	X	X	
38.	*Crassula argentea*	Jade plant	X	X	X	2	X		
39.	*Cryptanthus bivittatus*	Dwarf rosestripe star		X	X	3	X		
40.	*Cryptanthus* 'It'	It earthstar		X	X	3	X		
41.	*Cyanotis kewensis*	Teddy bear vine		X	X	3	X		X
42.	*Cyrtomium falcatum*	Holly fern		X	X	3	X		
43.	*Dieffenbachia amoena*	Giant dumbcane		X	X	2		X	
44.	*Dieffenbachia maculata* 'Exotic Perfection'	Exotic perfection dumbcane		X	X	2	X	X	

(continued)

TABLE 17-1 One hundred and seven foliage plants for interior use (Continued)

No.	Scientific name	Common name	Low	Medium	High	Adaptability for interior use[b]	Table plants	Floor plants	Hanging baskets	Totem poles
45.	Dieffenbachia maculata	Spotted dumbcane		X	X	2	X	X		
46.	Dieffenbachia maculata 'Rudolph Roehrs'	Rudolph Roehrs dumbcane		X	X	2	X	X		
47.	Dieffenbachia 'Tropic Snow'	Tropic snow dumbcane		X		2		X		
48.	Dizygotheca elegantissima	False aralia		X	X	3	X	X		
49.	Dracaena angustifolia honoriae	Yellow dracaena	X	X	X	2	X	X		
50.	Dracaena deremensis 'Janet Craig'	Janet Craig dracaena	X	X	X	1	X	X		
51.	Dracaena deremensis 'Warneckii'	Warneck dracaena	X	X	X	1	X	X		
52.	Dracaena fragrans 'Massangeana'	Corn plant	X	X	X	1		X		
53.	Dracaena surculosa 'Florida Beauty'	Florida beauty	X	X	X	1	X			
54.	Dracaena marginata	Madagascar dragontree	X	X	X	1		X		
55.	Dracaena sanderana	Sander's dracaena	X	X	X	2	X			
56.	Epipremnum aureum	Golden pothos	X	X	X	2	X		X	X
57.	Fatshedera lizei	Botanical wonder		X	X	2	X			
58.	Fatsia japonica	Japanese fatsia		X	X	3		X		
59.	Ficus benjamina	Weeping fig		X	X	2	X	X		
60.	Ficus elastica 'Decora'	India rubbertree		X	X	2	X	X		
61.	Ficus lyrata	Fiddleleaf fig		X	X	3		X		
62.	Ficus retusa	Cuban laurel		X	X	2	X	X		
63.	Fittonia verschaffeltii	Rednerve plant		X	X	4	X			
64.	Fittonia verschaffeltii argyroneura	Silvernerve plant		X	X	4	X			
65.	Gynura aurantiaca 'Purple Passion'	Purple passion vine		X	X	2	X		X	

No.	Scientific name	Common name				#				
66.	*Hedera helix*	English ivy		X	X	2	X		X	
67.	*Howea forsterana*	Kentia palm	X	X	X	1	X	X		
68.	*Hoya carnosa*	Wax plant		X	X	3	X		X	
69.	*Hoya carnosa 'Variegata'*	Variegated wax plant		X	X	3	X		X	
70.	*Maranta leuconeura erythroneura*	Red-veined prayer plant		X	X	2	X			
71.	*Maranta leuconeura kerchoviana*	Prayer plant		X	X	2	X			
72.	*Monstera deliciosa*	Ceriman		X	X	2	X	X		
73.	*Neoregelia carolinae 'Tricolor'*	Striped blushing bromeliad		X	X	2	X			X
74.	*Nephrolepis exaltata 'Bostoniensis'*	Boston swordfern		X	X	2	X	X		
75.	*Nephrolepis exaltata 'Florida Ruffles'*	Florida ruffles		X	X	3	X			
76.	*Peperomia caperata*	Emerald ripple peperomia		X	X	2	X			
77.	*Peperomia obtusifolia*	Oval-leaf peperomia		X	X	2	X			
78.	*Peperomia obtusifolia 'Variegata'*	Variegated oval-leaf peperomia		X	X	2	X			
79.	*Peperomia argyreia*	Watermelon peperomia		X	X	3	X			
80.	*Philodendron 'Emerald Green'*	Emerald green philodendron	X	X	X	1	X			X
81.	*Philodendron 'Florida'*	Florida philodendron	X	X	X	1				X
82.	*Philodendron domesticum*	Elephant ear philodendron		X	X	2				X
83.	*Philodendron scandens scandens*	Velvet-leaf philodendron		X	X	3	X		X	X
84.	*Philodendron scandens oxycardium*	Heart-leaf philodendron	X	X	X	1	X		X	X
85.	*Philodendron bipennifolium*	Fiddle-leaf philodendron		X	X	1	X			X
86.	*Philodendron 'Red Princess'*	Red princess philodendron	X	X	X	1				X
87.	*Philodendron selloum*	Lacy tree philodendron		X	X	2		X		
88.	*Pilea cadierei*	Aluminum plant		X	X	3	X			
89.	*Pilea microphylla*	Artillery plant		X	X	3	X			

(continued)

TABLE 17-1 One hundred and seven foliage plants for interior use (Continued)

No.	Scientific name	Common name	Light levels [a]			Adaptability for interior use [b]	Suggested interior uses			
			Low	Medium	High		Table plants	Floor plants	Hanging baskets	Totem poles
90.	*Pilea* 'Moon Valley'	Moon Valley pilea		X	X	3	X			
91.	*Pittosporum tobira*	Japanese pittosporum		X	X	3	X	X		
92.	*Platycerium bifurcatum*	Staghorn fern		X	X	4	X		X	
93.	*Plectranthus australis*	Swedish ivy		X	X	2	X		X	
94.	*Podocarpus macrophyllus*	Yew pine		X	X	3	X	X		
95.	*Polyscias balfouriana* 'Marginata'	Variegated balfour aralia		X	X	3	X	X		
96.	*Polyscias fruticosa*	Ming aralia		X	X	3	X	X		
97.	*Pteris ensiformis* 'Victoriae'	Victoria table fern		X	X	4	X			
98.	*Sansevieria trifasciata*	Snake plant	X	X	X	1	X	X		
99.	*Sansevieria trifasciata* 'Laurentii'	Goldband sansevieria	X	X	X	1	X	X		

No.	Name	Common name					Maintenance[a][b]		
100.	*Sansevieria trifasciata* 'Hahnii'	Bird's-nest sansevieria	X	X	X		1	X	X
101.	*Scindapsus pictus* 'Argyraeus'	Satin pothos		X	X		3	X	X X
102.	*Schlumbergera bridgesii*	Christmas cactus		X	X X		3	X	
103.	*Spathiphyllum* 'Clevelandii'	Cleveland peace lily	X	X	X X		2	X	
104.	*Spathiphyllum* 'Mauna Loa'	Mauna Loa peace lily	X	X	X		2	X	X
105.	*Syngonium podophyllum*	Nephthytis		X	X		2	X	X
106.	*Yucca elephantipes*	Spineless yucca		X	X X		3	X	
107.	*Zebrina pendula*	Wandering Jew		X	X		2	X	X

[a] Low light, 25 to 75 footcandles; medium light, 75 to 150 footcandles; high light, 150 to 1,000 footcandles.

[b] 1, minimal care, tolerates low light, low humidity, and has low maintenance; 2, average care, requires low to medium light and humidity, and requires some maintenance; 3, above average care, requires medium light and humidity or higher, and has maintenance needs; 4, special care, requires medium to high light and humidity, and has high maintenance needs.

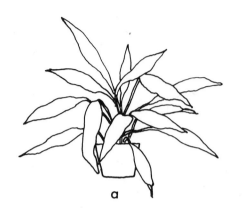

a

b

c

d

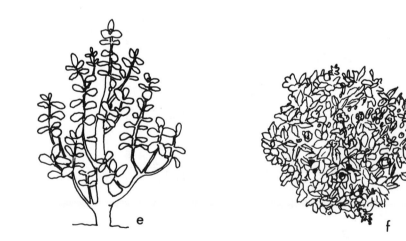

e

f

Figure 17-2.   Common forms of interior plants: (a) spreading; (b) upright; (c) cascading; (d) mounded; (e) oval; and (f) rounded.

containers up to about 6 inches in size. Another general grouping is hanging baskets, which includes vines and plants that have a trailing, weeping, or cascading growth habit. The last generalized group of plants are totem poles, which includes interior plants that form aerial adventitious roots that enable them to grow on a support made of bark, wood, or sphagnum moss.

A fairly broad color selection is available with foliage plants, including shades of green, silver, white, purple, red, and yellow. Several commonly used interior plants such as *Spathiphyllum* and bromeliads are used both for foliage color and occasional flowers. The deep green color of many interior plants is often used as a background for flowering plants that are rotated as their blooms decline.

Plant texture varies from coarse to fine and refers to the tactile surface qualities of leaves and stems. Large leaves and rough bark of fiddle-leaf fig make it a coarse-textured plant, while small leaves and short internodes make artillery plant a fine-textured plant. Textural coordination in limited spaces assumes greater importance than when plants are used in large spacious mall-like settings.

Plant Selection

Only the best quality plants should be selected, and these should be purchased close to desired size since interior environmental conditions are often marginal for plant growth. This requires some familiarity and knowledge of each plant species under consideration. To assist plant buyers and growers in determining what constitutes quality plants, the Florida Foliage Association has published specifications of forty-three foliage plants [12] and the Florists' Transworld Delivery Association has published the *Professional Guide to Green Plants* [14].

When considering plants not described in the specification list, there are general guidelines that can be used to select plants of a particular species.

Color

Select foliage plants with medium to dark green foliage unless leaves are supposed to be light green or another color. Light green leaves may indicate mineral deficiences or that plants were grown under excessively high light. Leaves of such plants will often turn yellow and abscise after placement indoors. Another indication that plants have been grown under excessively high light is short internode length or dense foliage. Plants grown under recommended light levels have longer internodes and more widely spaced leaves than those grown under higher light intensities.

Examine root systems of plants being considered for purchase by removing the container from the soil ball. If only a few roots are visible and the soil ball breaks apart easily, the plant probably does not have an adequate root system and will wilt easily in a dry interior environment unless it was grown in a translucent pot. Conversely, if a thick layer of roots has grown over the outside of the soil ball, the plant is root bound and only a limited amount of new growth may occur unless it is repotted.

Soluble salts levels of potting media should be checked since research has shown that levels over 1,000 parts per million result in premature leaf abscission. This service is often offered free or at a small charge by local agricultural agents' offices. If soluble salts levels are over 1,000 parts per million, the soil should be leached with an amount of water equal to one half the container capacity to lower the soluble salts level and reduce the possibility of root injury [7].

Culture

Aesthetically and culturally interior plants arranged in groupings are more attractive and easier to maintain (Figure 17-3) than single specimens. Grouping simplifies cultural care, such as watering, and other maintenance practices can be performed in one area, thus minimizing skipped waterings or fertilizations.

Large groupings of foliage plants in shopping centers, airport terminals, and hotel lobbies are usually maintained by nursery firms or others specializing in interior plant maintenance. Plants that become unattractive owing to carbohydrate depletion, leaf abcission, or pest infestation can be returned to a greenhouse or other favorable growing environment and a new plant substituted in the arrangement. This procedure can also be used by an individual maintaining interior plants if a greenhouse or other growing area is available.

Maintenance and growth of foliage plants indoors is a specialized skill and requires an understanding of how plants respond to environmental conditions found inside structures. Some of the most important factors include acclimatization, light, temperature, humidity, watering, and fertilization. Many of these factors are interdependent, and thus changes in one factor influence the level of other factors, such as the relationship of reduced light intensity on lowered fertilizer requirement [5, 8, 16]. A brief discussion of each factor influencing the culture of interior plants follows.

Acclimatization   According to Webster, acclimatization is the climatic adaptation of an organism, especially a plant, that has been

Figure 17-3.   Plant groupings reduce maintenance time and are aesthetically more pleasant.

moved to a new environment. The basic objective of acclimatization as applied to foliage plants is to prepare them for a life indoors, rather than for continued growth in a nursery or in their native habitat. Changes in environment during acclimatization influence plant anatomy and physiology [4].

Foliage plants grown under excessively high light intensities have smaller, thicker leaves that are closer together than those grown in reduced light. Such leaves are better adapted to drought and are not damaged when grown in full sun because their anatomy (thicker cell walls and cuticle and multiple epidermal layers) reduces light energy reaching the interior of the cell. Thus, this survival mechanism aids the plant in a high light environment, but works to its detriment in an interior location where light energy is low. Leaves on a shade-grown plant will be larger (often one to two times), thinner, and more widely spaced to make maximum use of limited light energy. Such leaves also have thinner cell walls and usually only a single epidermal layer of cells at the surface.

Several complex physiological changes can occur within cells that allow conversion of a plant adapted to bright light to low light intensities. These include increase in number of chloroplasts, reorientation of chloroplasts within cells, and reorientation of grana within chloroplasts.

Under high light intensities, chloroplasts tend to vertical orientation as a protective mechanism from heating due to excessive light. Within chloroplasts, grana also tend toward vertical orientation rather than the open-stack arrangement found in low light. Not only is chlorophyll destroyed in excessive light, but chloroplast and grana orientation is aimed toward minimizing heating effects; thus, plants grown in high light are inefficient when placed under low light interior environments. Figure 17-4 provides an indication of how the compensation point, that point at which the plant is neither growing, accumulating, nor consuming reserves, is influenced by type of leaf. For example, at a light intensity of 50 footcandles a plant with sun leaves would be consuming stored carbohydrate reserves, while one with shade leaves would be manufacturing enough to grow. Recent research [15] has shown that

Figure 17-4. Comparison of a foliage plant with shade leaves (upper line) with one with sun leaves (lower line). A shade-grown plant under an interior light intensity of 50 footcandles would be above the light compensation point while one with sun leaves would not.

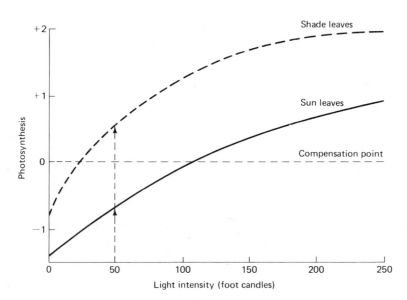

level of acclimatization is more important than stored carbohydrate reserves at the time a plant is moved into an interior environment.

Chloroplasts and grana can reorientate themselves to low light conditions, but this process can take up to 6 weeks. Acclimatization also affects respiration rate [10], and as a plant becomes fully acclimatized, respiration rate declines dramatically, which reduces carbohydrate requirements. This process is probably responsible for conservation of carbohydrate reserves that are present, although in small quantities, in shade-grown plants.

Additional physiological changes continue to occur upon placement of an acclimatized plant in the interior environment. Therefore, it is important during the first 1 to 2 months that plants receive sufficient light to remain at or above their compensation point. This can be assured by providing light levels equivalent to the higher range of suggested light intensity shown in Table 17-1. After this adaptation period, the plant can then be placed under any light level within the suggested range.

Light   Light is the most important factor influencing interior plant maintenance. Without sufficient light—above the plant's compensation point for several hours or more a day—food produced by photosynthesis will be inadequate for maintenance and growth. If this occurs over a long period of time, food reserves will be consumed and the plant will die. Three aspects of light need to be discussed, since all influence plant quality.

Light intensity, or the brightness of light, is usually measured in footcandles or lux in interior locations. This system is inaccurate, because such meters measure the light seen by the human eye rather than photosynthetically active light utilized by plants, but the equipment needed is low cost and, in most cases, serves adequately. Each plant has a compensation point for light intensity; thus a minimum level of light is required to provide the energy for food production. Generally, the higher the light intensity is, the better a plant will grow as long as it does not exceed its suggested production light intensity (Chapter 10). Higher light intensity increases photosynthetic rate, and thus food production, as long as other factors such as fertilizer, temperature, and water do not become limiting. To aid in plant selection, interior light levels can be divided into three intensity levels: (1) low light, 25 to 75 footcandles, (2) medium light, 75 to 150 footcandles, and (3) high light, 150 to 1,000 footcandles, as listed in Table 17-1.

Light duration, or the length of time a plant receives light in a 24-hour period, is almost as important as intensity, since the correct intensity received for too short a period will result in insufficient food

TABLE 17-2 Effects of various artificial light sources on growth of foliage plants under interior environments [1]

Lamp	Plant responses
Fluorescent: Cool white (CW) and warm white (WW)	Green foliage that expands parallel to surface of the lamp Stems elongate slowly Multiple side shoots develop Flowering occurs over a long period of time
Fluorescent Gro Lux (GL) and Plant Light	Deep green foliage that expands, often larger than on plants grown under CW or WW Stems elongate very slowly; extra thick stems develop Multiple side shoots develop Flowering occurs late; flower stalks do not elongate
Fluorescent: Gro-Lux-WS (GL-WS), Vita-lite (VITA), Agro-lite (AGRO), and wide spectrum lamps	Light green foliage that tends to ascend toward the lamp Stems elongate rapidly; considerable distance between leaves Suppresses development of multiple side shoots Flowering occurs soon; flower stalks elongate; plants mature and age rapidly
High intensity discharge: deluxe mercury (HG) or metal halide (MH)	Similar to CW and WW fluorescent lamps compared on equal energy basis Green foliage that expands Stems elongate slowly Multiple side shoots develop Flowering occurs over a long period of time
High intensity discharge: high-pressure sodium (HPS)	Similar to Gro-Lux and other color-improved fluorescent compared on equal energy basis Deep green foliage that expands; often larger than on plants grown under HG and MH Stems elongate very slowly; extra thick stems develop Multiple side shoots develop Flowering occurs late; flower stalks do not elongate
Low-pressure sodium (LPS)	Extra deep green foliage, bigger and thicker than on plants grown under other light sources Stem elongation is slowed; very thick stems develop Multiple side shoots develop even on secondary shoots Flowering occurs; flower stalks do not elongate *Exceptions:* Saintpaulias, lettuce, and impatiens must have supplemental sunlight or incandescent to ensure development of chlorophyll and reduction of stem elongation
Incandescent (INC) and incandescent-mercury	Paling of foliage; thinner and longer than on plants grown under other light sources

(continued)

TABLE 17-2   Effects of various artificial light sources on growth of foliage plants under interior environments [1] (Continued)

Lamp	Plant responses
(INC-HG)	Stem elongation is excessive; eventually becomes spindly and breaks easily Side shoot development is suppressed; plants expand only in height Flowering occurs rapidly; the plants mature and senesce *Exceptions:* Rosette and thick-leaved plants such as *Sansevieria* may maintain themselves for many months; the new leaves that eventually develop will elongate and will not have the typical characteristics of the species

being produced. Plants must receive 8 to 12 hours of light a day when intensity is near or slightly above the compensation point [3]. If light levels are considerably above the compensation point, 6 to 8 hours duration may be sufficient. Continuous light or durations of 18 hours or more have been used in some malls and office buildings, but recent data [9] indicate severe quality reductions of some plants when this practice is followed.

Light quality, the wavelengths of light received by a plant, can have a strong effect on its growth habits [1]. Natural light (sunlight) provides wavelengths of the visible spectrum, from which the plants absorb energy in the blue and red ranges, which correspond to photosynthetic requirements. Thus, one would suspect that the same light supplied indoors would result in similar growth habits. However, foliage plants of high quality can be grown under fluorescent lamps that provide primarily blue but also some red light. The best fluorescent lamps are cool white and warm white, which are most energy efficient. Tables 17-2 to 17-5 provide data on some of the differences between artificial light sources and their selection for interior environments.

Temperature   Although very important to plant growth indoors, temperature is rarely regulated to suit plants. The best range for plants, considering photosynthesis and respiration during the day and respiration during the night, is 70° to 80°F day and 65° to 70°F night. Night temperatures below 65°F will stop most plant growth, while those above 70°F at night increase utilization of energy. Care should be taken during winter months to protect plants placed near doors from cold drafts and from the possibility of thermostats being turned to 55°F or below on weekends or other periods.

TABLE 17-3 Efficiency and useful life of various artificial light sources [1]

Lamp	Total lumens per watt	Visible radiation, percent	Nonvisible radiation conduction and convection ballast loss, percent	Average useful life of lamp hours (1000's)	Time 12 hr/day (months)
Fluorescent (F)					
Cool white CW	70	20	80	8-10	12-24
Warm white WW	71	20	80	8-10	12-24
Gro Lux-Plant Light (GL-PL)	20	13	87	4-5	6-12
Gro Lux-WS (GL-WS)	37	15	85	4-5	6-12
Agro-lite (AGRO)	41	15	85	4-5	6-12
Vita-lite (VITA)	47	18	82	8-10	12-24
Discharge					
Mercury deluxe (HG)	50	13	87	15-20	24-36
Metal halide (MH)	75	20	80	10-15	12-18
High-pressure sodium (HPS)	100	25	75	15-20	24-36
Low-pressure sodium (LPS)	143	27	73	12-18	15-20
Incandescent (INC)	17	07	93	1-3	2-6
Incandescent-mercury (INC-HG)	18-25	—	—	8-10	12-24

TABLE 17-4 Influence of artificial light source for interior plants on color rendering of plants, people, and furnishings [1]

Lamp		General appearance on a neutral wall or surface	Complexion (the actual appearance of skin)	Atmosphere (effect or general feeling of room)	Flower colors (improved or strengthened)	Grayed (undesirable)
Fluorescent						
Cool white	CW	White	Pale pink	Neutral to cool	Blue, yellow, orange	Red
Warm white	WW	Yellowish	Sallow	Yellow to warm	Yellow, orange	Blue, green, red
Gro Lux–Plant Light	GRO-PL	Pink white	Reddish	Purple to pink	Blue, red	Green, yellow
Gro Lux–WS	GRO-WS	Light pink white	Pink	Warm	Blue, yellow, red	Green
Agro-lite	AGRO	White	Pink	Neutral to warm	Blue, yellow, red	Green
Vita-lite	VITA	White	Pink	Neutral to cool	Blue, yellow, red	Green
Discharge						
Mercury (all types)	HG	Purplish white	Ruddy	Cool	Blue, green, yellow	Red
Metal halide	MH	Greenish white	Grayed	Cool green	Blue, green, yellow	Red
High-pressure sodium	HPS	Yellowish	Yellowish	Warm	Green, yellow, orange	Blue, red
Low-pressure sodium	LPS	Yellow	Grayed	Warm	Yellow	All except yellow
Incandescent	INC	Yellowish white	Ruddy	Warm	Yellow, orange, red	Blue
Incandescent-mercury	INC-HG	Yellowish white	Ruddy	Warm	Yellow, orange, red	Blue

TABLE 17-5 Approximate distance plants should be placed from artificial lighting lamps to provide equal energy for growing plants [1]

Lamp		Approximate		
		Equal energy, equal radiant energy (visible) (footcandles)	Lamp wattage	Equal growth, lamp distance from plants (inches)
Fluorescent				
Cool white	CW	300	40	15
Warm white	WW	300	40	15
Gro Lux–Plant Light	GRO–PL	140	40	10
Gro-Lux–WS	GRO–WS	200	40	13
Agro-lite	AGRO	225	40	13
Vita-lite	VITA	240	40	13.5
Discharge				(feet)
Mercury	HG	325	400	5
Metal halide	MH	260	400	7
High-pressure sodium	HPS	260	400	8
Low-pressure sodium	LPS	400	180	4.8
Incandescent	INC	100	150	3.5
Incandescent-mercury	INC-HG	150	450	7
Sunlight		160	N/A	N/A

Watering   Watering indoors presents problems for those not experienced with indoor plants, since they often overwater. This results in saturated potting media, which excludes oxygen from the medium and often results in root death. Most foliage plants, except cacti, are adapted to regions where the soil is moist, but they cannot tolerate continually saturated soils. The best practice is never to allow the potting medium to become completely dry, but when watering supply a sufficient amount to thoroughly wet the entire root ball.

A number of self-watering containers have appeared on the market in recent years and use capillary action to move water from a reservoir to the potting medium. Plants already established in such containers usually grow well in the home provided the water reservoir is refilled once every 2 to 4 weeks, or as needed. However, because plants in these containers have a different type of root, conversion of soil-grown plants to the rock, gravel, or clay granule culture common to many self-watering containers is not recommended. When watering containers with drainage holes, the plant should be placed in a saucer to catch excess drainage and allowed to remain there for about 30 minutes before pouring off excess water. This allows reabsorption of water should the root ball have shrunk during the drying process and allowed water to run down the inside of the container.

Plants grown in containers without drainage holes are easily over-watered. Several methods to prevent this include use of a gravel layer in the bottom of the container to act as an excess water reservoir, placement of a hollow tube in the potting medium to allow use of a dipstick to measure water level, and, if neither of these systems can be used, placement of the container on its side after watering to allow excess water to run out.

Humidity   Humidity control is often lacking in building interiors and can become extremely low during the winter heating season. Most foliage plants can tolerate relative humidities of 50 percent without damage, but relative humidities of 10 percent or lower have been recorded in building interiors, and plant damage has been observed. Most plant injury resulting from low relative humidity occurs as marginal browning of foliage, which seriously detracts from overall appearance.

The best way to raise relative humidity is to install a humidifier on the heating system. Where this is not possible, particularly susceptible plants can be placed on a pebble tray filled with water in an area of a mall (around a water feature) or in the home (kitchen or bathroom) where higher relative humidity exists. Healthy plants with strong root systems are better able to tolerate low humidity than those with poor roots or poor food reserves.

Fertilization   Fertilizing needs of indoor plants have a direct correlation with the light level received and subsequent growth rate. Plants in low light situations may only need to be fertilized once or twice a year with a small amount, while those under high light need higher levels applied more often [2, 6, 8].

Most commercial house plant fertilizers that can be purchased off the shelf provide higher than required levels of macronutrients if applied at recommended rates and often have unacceptable ratios of N, P, and K [13]. In some instances, rates listed on containers are higher than rates suggested for commercial production; thus, in the low light environment of interior locations injury to plants occurs through build-up of excess soluble salts. Tables 17-6 and 17-7 provide an indication of fertilizer needs of the most important plant types.

Fertilizer levels suggested for interior use are generally one fifth to one tenth of the production rate unless the plants are under high or very high light levels. As in production areas, fertilizer ratios of 3-1-2 are suggested since they supply needed levels of N-P-K with minimal salts buildup. Weak and spindly plants most frequently result from low light levels; under these conditions, addition of fertilizer rarely improves the appearance of such plants and may even cause soluble salts damage [13].

TABLE 17-6   Fertilization (grams of nitrogen per square foot per year) of indoor foliage plants under various light intensities for 8 to 12 hours per day[a]

Plant	Light intensity (footcandles)			
	Low, 50–75	Medium, 75–150	High, 150–250	Very high, 250–500
Aglaonema [b]	0.60	1.20	2.00	3.00
Brassaia (schefflera)	1.00	2.00	3.00	4.50
Calathea	0.50	1.00	1.50	2.50
Cordyline	0.60	1.20	2.00	3.00
Dieffenbachia	0.80	1.50	2.50	4.00
Dracaena	0.50	1.00	1.50	2.50
Ferns	0.30	0.60	1.00	1.60
Ficus	1.00	2.00	3.00	4.50
Palms	0.75	1.50	2.00	3.00
Peperomia	0.30	0.60	1.00	1.50
Philodendron	0.75	1.50	2.00	3.00
Scindapsus	0.75	1.50	2.00	3.00
Syngonium	0.60	1.20	1.80	2.50

[a]This figure is the base used to calculate the amount of any fertilizer analyses to apply.

[b]Example: You desire to fertilize *Aglaonema* under medium light in a 6-inch pot with a 18-6-12 analysis fertilizer as the nutrient source.

1. Use nitrogen portion (the first number in the analyses) of your fertilizer for calculation. In our example, 18.

2. Divide 100 by 18 to obtain the grams of fertilizer (18-6-12) that contain one gram of nitrogen.

$$\frac{100}{18} = 5.56$$

3. Multiply 5.56 times base figure for *Aglaonema* under medium light (1.2 g to obtain grams of 18-6-12 required per square foot per year).

$$5.56 \times 1.20 \text{ g} = 6.67 \text{ g } 18\text{-}6\text{-}12/\text{ft}^2/\text{yr}$$

4. See Table 17-7 to determine approximate number of pots of a specific size found in a square foot (in this case a 6-inch pot).

5. Divide 6.67 g by 5 (there are five 6-inch pots to a square foot).

$$\frac{6.67}{5} = 1.33 \text{ g/6-in. pot/yr}$$

6. Fertilizer should be divided into three applications a year: February, June, and September. Divide 1.33 by 3.

$$\frac{1.33}{3} = 0.44 \text{ g}$$

7. Each teaspoon contains approximately 5 g, so divide 0.55 g by 5 to determine portion of a teaspoon to use per pot per application.

$$\frac{0.44}{5} = 0.09 \text{ or about 1/10 teaspoon per application}$$

TABLE 17-7 Approximate number of pots of various sizes
required to equal a square foot of surface area

Pot size (inches)	No. pots per square foot
3	16
4	9
5	7
6	5
8	3
10	2
12	1.3
14	1

Insect Control

Insects and mites can become serious plant pests in interior environments. Newly acquired plants should be carefully examined and isolated in a separate holding area for at least a month before they are placed with other foliage plants. During this time period, plants can be closely observed and any pest infestation found eradicated before serious damage occurs. Pasteurized soils should be used for plants repotted after purchase to prevent infestations of soil pests such as nematodes, springtails, and fungus gnats.

Isolation of new plants helps prevent insect infestations, although many insects can become established on plants in other ways. Aphids sometimes enter through open windows and doors, and mites are often brought indoors on clothing.

Plants should be inspected weekly to detect initial infestations before they cause extensive damage. All parts of the plant should be carefully inspected for insects and mites, but especially both leaf surfaces should be examined, as insect and mite infestations usually start on the lower surface. The leaf axil is another location where pest problems can be detected before spreading to other parts of the plant. Tender new growth is preferred by many sucking insects, and growing points should be examined to detect pests before distortion or stunting occurs. Scales are often found on stems, petioles, and undersurfaces of leaves. Any brown, yellow, or similarly discolored leaves should be examined for possible insect damage. The soil surface should also be carefully examined for soil insects before and after watering. When insect pests become a problem, it is easier and safer to move plants to an area where insecticides can be safely used. The most common pests on interior foliage plants are mealybugs, mites, aphids, scales, whiteflies, fungus gnat maggots, psocids, springtails, and symphlids. Detailed descriptions of mite and insect pests are found in Chapter 15. A small hand lens makes insect detection much easier.

Disease Control

Few foliage plant diseases commonly occur under most interior conditions because conditions are not favorable for disease development. Using a pasteurized soil mix and observing good cultural care will usually prevent most diseases.

A number of different organisms may cause roots to rapidly decay, turn soft, and pull apart easily. Infected roots do not function normally, often causing plants to wilt even when the soil is moist. This is often the first indication that plants are diseased. Root rots usually are the result of overwatering, poor drainage, and using a soil mix that does not provide enough aeration.

Other common diseases indoors include crown rot and damping off, which results from organisms similar to those that cause root rots. Crown rots usually occur on acaulescent plants that have a rosette growth habitat. Plant parts closest to the soil line become soft and slimy, and leaves will be wilted even when the soil is moist. Crown rots often occur when the top layer of the soil is not allowed to dry sufficiently between waterings. Damping off affects germinating seeds and seedlings when the stem emerges from the soil medium.

Since leaves of foliage plants rarely have free moisture on them indoors, there is little possibility that fungal or bacterial diseases will present any foliar problems. Detailed description of disease pests are found in Chapter 14.

REFERENCES

[1] Cathey, H. M., and E. C. Lowell. 1978. Zero based budgeting for lighting plants. *Foliage Digest* 1(3):10–13.

[2] Conover, C. A. 1974. Don't blame it on the plants. *Florist* 8(2):28–31.

[3] _____. 1975. Handling foliage plants in the retail shop. *Am. Florist* 7(12):6–7.

[4] _____. 1975. Acclimatization of tropical foliage plants. *Am. Nurseryman* 142(5):64, 65, 68–71.

[5] _____, and R. T. Poole. 1975. Acclimatization of tropical trees. *HortScience* 10(6):600–601.

[6] _____, and R. T. Poole. 1977. Fertilization of indoor foliage plants. Proc. 1977 National Foliage Short Course, Orlando, Fla.

[7] _____, and R. T. Poole. 1977. Influence of fertilizer and watering on acclimatization of *Aphelandra squarrosa* Nees cv. Dania. *HortScience* 12(6):569–570.

[8] _____, and R. T. Poole, 1978. Influence of light intensity on fertilizer requirements of acclimatized foliage plants maintained under an interior environment. *HortScience* 13:363.

[9] _____, and R. T. Poole. 1978. Unpublished data, University of Florida Agr. Res. Ctr. Apopka, Fla.

[10] Fonteno, W. C., and E. L. McWilliams. 1978. Light compensation points and acclimatization of four tropical foliage plants. *J. Am. Soc. Hort. Sci.* 103(1):52–56.

[11] Gaines, R. L. 1977. *Interior plantscaping.* New York: Architectural Record. 182 pp.

[12] _____. 1978. Guidelines for foliage plant specifications for interior use. *Florida Foliage* 4(1):Special Supplement. 36 pp.

[13] Henley, R. W. 1978. House plant fertilizers—a closer look. Proc. 1978 National Tropical Foliage Short Course, Orlando, Fla.

[14] McConnell, D. B., C. A. Conover, and R. W. Henley. 1976. *Professional guide to green plants.* Chicago: Florists' Transworld Delivery Assoc. 96 pp.

[15] Milks, R. A., J. N. Joiner, L. A. Garrard, C. A. Conover, and B. O. Tjia. 1979. Effects of shade, fertilizer and media on production and acclimatization of *Ficus benjamina* L. *J. Am. Soc. Hort. Sci.* 104:410–413

[16] Poole, R. T., and C. A. Conover. 1975. Light requirements for foliage plants. *Florists' Rev.* 155(4024):44, 45, 94–96.

eighteen

D. B. McConnell
R. W. Henley
R. L. Biamonte

commercial foliage plants

Adiantum: Family Polypodiaceae

A popular genus of fern, *Adiantum* comprises over 200 fern species from tropical America, with a few representatives from temperate North America and Eastern Asia. Adiantums are collectively referred to as maidenhair ferns; most cultivated species and cultivars have fronds divided into numerous thin, fan-shaped pinnules. Spores are organized in distinctive patterns in sori located along the under margin of fertile fronds. The stipe or petiole of most types is shiny and very dark. Maidenhair ferns are not among the most durable foliage plants, but they grow well in medium light and high relative humidity if the growing medium does not dry excessively. These ferns can be used as small potted plants and in terrariums and hanging baskets.

   Culture. Commercially, maidenhair fern is propagated easily from spores, which develop rapidly following germination. Large specimens can be propagated by crown divisions. Plants should be planted in well-drained mixes and irrigated frequently enough to keep them moist, since wilting usually causes severe and permanent frond dieback. A few species are reported grown best if soils are adjusted to pH 7.0 or slightly above. Light levels of 1,200 to 1,800 footcandles (fc) or 12 to 18 kilolux (klux) and 800 to 1,000 pounds per acre per year (lb/A/yr) or 900 to 1,125 kilograms per hectare per year (kg/ha/yr) of N-P$_2$O5-K$_2$O is suitable for production. Greenhouse night temperatures should remain at 60° to 65°F (16° to 18°C).

Diseases. Leaf spots caused by *Corynespora cassiicola, Glomerella* sp., and *Mycosphaerella* sp. have been reported [3].

Insects and related pests. Scales, mealybugs, and mites are serious pests.

Species and cultivars. *Adiantum hispidulum, A. peruvianum,* and *A. raddianum.*

Aechmea: Family Bromeliaceae

The *Aechmea* genus consists of over 160 species of mostly epiphytic bromeliads distributed from Mexico to Argentina. Commercially grown species have attractively marked leaves arranged in a rosette and are grown for interior use as table or small floor plants. Although the foliage is attractive, they are usually sold after inflorescence formation has been induced. Flowers are short lived, but the bracts remain colorful for a month or so, followed by colorful berries.

Culture. Aechmeas grow best if greenhouse night temperatures are kept above 60°F (16°C). They are propagated by severing offshoots from the parent plant, by tissue culture, or by seed. Commercially grown plants are epiphytes; therefore, well-aerated soil mixes should be used. Commercially, they are grown in light levels of 3,000 to 4,000 fc (30 to 40 klux) and are fertilized with 900 to 1,200 lb/A/yr (1,005 to 1,345 kg/ha/yr) of $N-P_2O_5-K_2O$.

Diseases. Reported diseases include anthracnose (*Collectotrichum gloeosporioides*), basal rot (*Phytophthora* sp., *Rhizoctonia solani*), and leaf spot (*Phyllosticta* sp.) [3].

Insects and related pests. Scales and mites are serious pests.

Species and cultivars. *Aechmea chantinii, A. fasciata.*

Aeschynanthus: Family Gesneriaceae

The *Aeschynanthus* genus consists of over 100 species of epiphytic vines or shrub forms native to tropical regions in Asia. All have opposite or whorled, usually simple leaves and, often, attractive flowers. They are used in hanging baskets or as pedestal plants.

Culture. *Aeschynanthus* species require warm greenhouses with night temperatures of 60°F (16° to 18°C) for best growth. They may be propagated from tip and stem cuttings with intermittent mist and bottom heat, but some growers use high-humidity chambers and no mist to avoid foliar diseases. They are commercially grown under light intensities of 1,500 to 2,000 fc (15 to 20 klux) and fertilized with 1,200 lb/A/yr of (1,345 kg/ha/yr) of N-P_2O_5-K_2O. Well-aerated soil mixes should be used.

Diseases. Reported diseases include leaf blight (*Rhizoctonia solani* and *Myrothecium* sp.), leaf spot (*Alternaria* sp., *Cercospora* sp., and *Corynespora cassiicola*), and stem canker (*Plenodomus* sp.) (3).

Insects and related pests. Mites, nematodes, and scales are common pests.

Species and cultivars. *Aeschynanthus pulcher, A. speciosus.*

Agave: Family Agavaceae

All 300 species in the *Agave* genus are native to North America or northern South America, where they grow in semiarid regions. They are monocarpic, flowering once and dying, and are often called century plants because they take a decade or longer to flower. However, they produce offsets before the flowering plant dies. Agaves have fleshy, thick leaves arranged in rosettes; the leaves of many species are harvested for fiber content or fermented for alcoholic beverages (tequila). A number of species are grown outdoors as ornamentals in succulent gardens, and several tolerate low light levels characteristic of building interiors. Small specimens are used indoors as table plants; larger ones are used as floor plants.

Culture. In commercial foliage production, agaves are grown in 4,000 to 5,000 fc (40 to 50 klux) and fertilized with 800 to 1,000 lb/A/yr (900 to 1,125 kg/ha/yr) of N-P_2O_5-K_2O. They are propagated by offshoots or seed. Plants require well-drained media and minimum temperatures of 60°F (16°C).

Diseases. Reported diseases include anthracnose (*Colletotrichum* sp. and *Glomerella cingulata*), leaf spots (*Coniothyrium concentricum* and *Gloeosporium* sp.), and bacterial soft rot (*Erwinia carotovora*) [3].

Insects and related pests. Mealybugs and scales may be troublesome.

Species and cultivar. *Agave americana, Agave angustifolia marginata,* and *Agave victoriae-reginae.*

Aglaonema: Family Araceae

The thirty or so known species of aglaonemas are native to tropical Asia and consist of herbaceous plants usually under 3 feet (0.9 meter) in height. Most have deep green foliage highlighted with silver or white markings, and their ability to grow in low light indoors makes them popular foliage plants. Aglaonemas are used as small specimen plants or massed in interiorscape planters, as most species produce multiple stems.

Culture. Stock plants are grown in raised or ground beds and are usually propagated from tip or cane cuttings. Some aglaonemas are propagated from seed, and *A. costatum* is propagated by division. Light intensities for stock and finishing production should be about 2,000 fc (20 klux). Higher light levels cause the foliage to point upward rather than horizontally. Greenhouse night temperatures should remain above 65°F (18°C) for best growth. Fertilization rates of 1,200 lb/A/yr (1,345 kg/ha/yr) of $N-P_2O_5-K_2O$ produce acclimatized plants [2].

Diseases. Reported diseases include anthracnose (*Colletotrichum* sp., *Glomerella cingulata*), bacterial leaf spot (*Corynebacterium* sp. and *Xanthomonas dieffenbachiae*), bacterial soft rot (*Erwinia carotovora* and *E. dieffenbachiae*), bacterial spot (*Pseudomonas cichorii*), bacterial leaf blight (*Xanthomonas vitians*), root rot (*Pythium splendens* and *Rhizoctonia solani*), and southern blight (*Sclerotium rolfsii*) [3].

Insects and related pests. Mealybugs and mites may become troublesome.

Species and cultivars. *Aglaonema commutatum maculatum, A. commutatum elegans, A. commutatum* 'Fransher,' *A. commutatum* 'Pseudobracteatum,' *A. commutatum* 'Malay Beauty,' *A. commutatum* 'Snow Queen,' *A. commutatum* 'Silver King,' *A. commutatum* 'Silver Queen,' *A. commutatum* 'Treubii,' *A. costatum, A. crispum,* and *A. modestum.*

Alocasia: Family Araceae

This is a genus of about seventy species of tropical herbaceous plants native to moist, humid regions of Asia. They have short internodes, long petioles, and usually large peltate to sagittate soft leathery leaves, which may be solid green or highly colored. Most hybrids have unusual leaf patterns, and many are grown as landscape ornamentals in subtropical and tropical regions or as collector's items in greenhouses. A few are occasionally used in building interiors for their distinctive forms. A high relative humidity is required to keep plants looking attractive.

Culture. Alocasias are propagated by tuber division, cane (stem pieces), or seed. Greenhouse night temperatures should remain above 60°F (16°C) to maintain growth. Commercially, light intensities of 2,000 to 3,000 fc (20 to 30 klux) should be used with fertilization rates varying from 1,000 to 1,200 lb/A/yr (1,125 to 1,345 kg/ha/yr) of $N-P_2O_5-K_2O$. Alocasias grow best in soil mixes with over 50 percent organic matter.

Diseases. Reported diseases include bacterial soft rot (*Erwinia carotovora*) [3].

Insect and related pests. Mealybugs and chewing insects are often serious pests.

Species and cultivars. *Alocasia macrorrhiza, A. macrorrhiza* 'Variegata,' and *A. plumbea* or *A. indica metallica.*

Aloe: Family Liliaceae

Aloe is a genus of succulent herbs, shrubs, and trees containing about 255 species native to arid regions of Africa and Asia. Many species are grown as landscape plants in frost-free regions and several small species are grown indoors. Thick, succulent leaves are arranged in rosettes, and many plants are acaulescent.

Culture. Aloes are propagated from suckers, seeds, and occasionally tip cuttings. Light intensities of 5,000 to 6,000 fc (50 to 60 klux) are used for production as foliage plants with fertilization at 900 lb/A/yr (1,008 kg/ha/yr) of N-P_{25}-K_2O. Minimum night temperatures of 55°F (13°C) are suggested for best growth.

Diseases. Reported diseases include leaf spot (*Alternaria* sp., *Cercosporidium* sp., *Coniothyrium concentricum, Gloeosporium* sp., and *Leptosphaeria nigrans*), leaf blight (*Fusarium* sp.), root rot (*Rhizoctonia solani*), and stem rot (*Pythium ultimum*) [3].

Insects and related pests. Mealybugs and scales may be troublesome.

Species and cultivars. *Aloe barbadenis* and *A. variegata.*

Ananas: Family Bromeliaceae

All nine species in the *Ananas* genus are terrestrial bromeliads with relatively stiff armed leaves arranged in a rosette. The pineapple species is native to tropical regions in the Americas and is grown throughout the tropics. Most species grown for interior use are used as novelty plants.

Culture. Plants are propagated from offshoots and grown in a porous, well-aerated soil mix. Stock plants may be grown in full sun, but acclimated plants are commercially grown under 2,500 to 3,500 fc (25 to 35 klux) and fertilized with 900 lb/A/yr (1,008 kg/ha/yr) of N-P_2O_5-K_2O. Greenhouse night temperatures should remain at or above 65°F (18°C), and floral development is often induced with growth regulators that contain or release ethylene.

Diseases. Reported diseases include anthracnose (*Colletotrichum gloeosporioides*), leaf spot (*Phyllosticta* sp.), and root rot (*Rhizoctonia* sp.) [3].

Insects and related pests. Scales and mites may be troublesome.
Species and cultivars. *Ananas bracteatus* and *A. comosus.*

Anthurium: Family Araceae

This is a large genus of about 600 species native to tropical regions of the
Americas. Anthuriums are epiphytes or terrestrials, and the widest
grown types produce a showy spathe subtending the spadix. Most have a
plain inflorescence and are grown for their large, leathery, arrow-
shaped, green, or attractively marked leaves. Some anthuriums look
similar to large-leaved philodendrons, but can be identified by a swell-
ing on the petiole base. Large-leaved anthuriums are used in large
plantings in airports and hotels, and those with showy foliage or inflorescences are grown as specimen plants.

    Culture. Anthuriums are propagated from cuttings, division, and
fresh seed. Commercially, they are grown under light intensities of 1,500
to 2,500 fc (15 to 25 klux) and fertilized with 1,200 lb/A/yr (1,345 kg/ha/
yr) of N-P_2O_5-K_2O. Terrestrial anthuriums grow well in standard foliage
plant mixes, but epiphytes require extremely porous soil mixes similar to
those recommended for bromeliads. Greenhouse night temperatures
should remain at or above 65°F (18°C).

    Diseases. Reported diseases include algal leaf spot (*Cephaleuros
virescens*), anthracnose (*Colletotrichum* sp.), bacterial soft rot (*Erwinia
carotovora*), bacterial leaf spot (*Xanthomonas* sp.), leaf spot (*Cercospora
richardiaecola, Gloeosporium* sp., *Phyllosticta* sp., and *Septoria* sp.), root rot
(*Pythium* sp. and *Rhizoctonia solani*), and dasheen mosaic virus (*Mosaic*)
[3].

    Insects and related pests. Thrips, spider mites, scale, and
mealybugs.

    Species and cultivars. *Anthurium andraeanum, A. clarinervium, A.
cordifolium* or *A. caribaeum, A. cubense, A. harrisii,* and *A. scherzerianum.*

Aphelandra: Family Acanthaceae

The *Aphelandra* genus contains over eighty species native to tropical
America, where most grow as semiwoody plants with attractive opposite
leaves. Both terminal and axillary inflorescences usually have short-lived
flowers but persistent colorful bracts. Most aphelandras are used indoors
as small container plants.

    Culture. The most common grown commercial species, *A. squar-
rosa,* is grown in 95 percent shade to keep plants vegetative, and cuttings
are taken as needed to produce split node propagative units. Cuttings

are rooted under intermittent mist and grown in 1,000 to 2,000 fc (10 to 20 klux) and fertilized with 1,500 lb/A/yr (1,680 kg/ha/yr) of N-P_2O_5-K_2O [2]. Greenhouse night temperatures should not drop below 65°F (18°C) to maintain growth rate.

Diseases. Reported diseases include bacterial soft rot (*Erwinia carotovora*), leaf blight (*Botrytis cinerea*), leaf spot (*Corynespora cassiicola*), stem rot (*Rhizoctonia solani*), and tip dieback (*Pseudomonas* sp.) [3].

Insects and related pests. Mites, aphids, mealybugs, and scale may become troublesome on aphelandra.

Species and cultivars. *A. squarrosa.*

Araucaria: Family Araucariaceae

Araucaria is a small genus with about fifteen species of coniferous trees occurring in wide areas over the southern hemisphere. Whorled branches and stiff needlelike leaves are typical of this genus. Most species grow to heights over 100 feet (30 meters), but their symmetrical evergreen foliage and slow growth in containers makes them popular as indoor trees.

Culture. Araucarias are propagated from seed, although a few are grown from terminal cuttings. Lateral branches will root and grow, but continued growth is lateral, never producing typical terminal growth. Acclimatized plants can be grown in 5,000 to 6,000 fc (50 to 60 klux) and are fertilized with 1,500 lb/A/yr (1,680 kg/ha/yr) of N-P_2O_5-K_2O [2]. Araucarias will tolerate cooler temperatures than many foliage plants, but minimum night temperatures should not drop below 45° to 50°F (8° to 10°C) for continued growth. Some needles may turn brown and abcise when plants are subjected to abrupt environmental changes.

Diseases. Reported diseases include leaf spot (*Pestalotia* sp.), needle browning (*Colletotrichum* sp., *Gloeosporium* sp.), needle blight (*Macrophoma* sp. and *Phyllosticta araucariae*), needle and stem blight (*Leptosphaeria* sp.), root rot (*Rhizoctonia solani*), and twig dieback (*Cercospora thujina*) [3].

Insects and related pests. Mealybugs, scale, and thrips are common pests.

Species and cultivars. *Araucaria bidwillii* and *A. heterphylla.*

Ardisia: Family Myrsinaceae

Ardisia is a genus of about 250 species of woody shrubs and trees native to warm temperate subtropical and tropical countries. Cultivated species are grown primarily as landscape subjects, but one species, *Ardisia cre-*

nulata or coralberry, is commonly grown as a foliage plant for use as a specimen pot plant with fruit or as a small filler plant in dish gardens or terrariums.

Culture. Coralberry is propagated commercially from seeds, but cuttings or air layering can be used. Light intensities from 3,500 to 4,500 fc (35 to 45 klux) are used by many growers, with a fertilization rate of about 1,200 lb/A/yr (1,345 kg/ha/yr) of $N-P_2O_5-K_2O$. Minimum greenhouse night temperature of 55°F (13°C) are required to maintain growth.

Diseases. Reported diseases include crown gall (*Agrobacterium tumefaciens*), algal leaf spot (*Cephaleuros virescens*), leaf spot (*Cercospora* sp., *Hysterostomella floridana,* and *Phyllosticta* sp.), leaf rot (*Rhizoctonia solani*), and root rot (*Pythium* sp.) [3].

Insects and related pests. Scale, mites, and nematodes may be troublesome.

Species and cultivars. *Ardisia crenulata.*

Asparagus: Family Liliaceae

Asparagus is a genus containing herbs, woody vines, and shrub forms. There is taxonomic uncertainty, and the genus may contain as few as 100 species or as many as 300, all native to Old World countries [1]. Excluding the edible asparagus, *A. officinalis,* cultivated members are grown as ornamentals, cut foliage, landscape plants, or as interior plants. None has true leaves, and what appear to be their leaves are modified branches called cladodes. Depending on growth habit, asparagus species are used as pedestal plants, hanging baskets, indoor vines, and table and floor plants in well-lighted interiors.

Culture. *Asparagus* species are usually propagated by division or seed. Commercially, they are grown with 3,500 to 4,500 fc (35 to 45 klux) and fertilized with 900 lb/A/yr (1,008 kg/ha/yr) of $N-P_2O_5-K_2O$ [2]. Greenhouse night temperatures should be kept above 55°F (13°C) to maintain growth.

Diseases. Common diseases include blighted stem canker (*Ascochytula asparagina*), crown gall (*Agrobacterium tumefaciens*), anthracnose (*Colletotrichum* sp.), canker (*Phoma asparagi, Fusarium oxysporum,* and *Helminthosporium* sp.), root rot (*Fusarium* sp.), rust (*Puccinia asparagi*), root, stem, and leaf rot (*Rhizoctonia solani*), and stem diseases (*Hendersonia asparagi* and *Leptosphaeria asparagina*) [3].

Insects and related pests. Mealybugs, scale, nematodes, aphids, mites, and thrips may be troublesome.

Species and cultivars. *Asparagus densiflorus, A. setaceus,* or *Asparagus plumosa.*

Aspidistra: Family Liliaceae

Aspidistra is a small genus of about eight species of herbaceous plants native to Asia and surrounding islands. Of these, *A. elatior* or cast-iron plant is widely used as a landscape and an indoor plant.

Culture. Cast-iron plant is propagated by division of thick underground stems. Commercially, plants are grown under 3,000 to 5,000 fc (30 to 50 klux) and fertilized with 900 to 1,200 lb/A/yr (1,008 to 1,345 kg/ha/yr) of $N-P_2O_5-K_2O$. Cast-iron plant tolerates below freezing temperatures, but greenhouse night temperatures should be kept above 50°F (10°C) for best growth. Aspidistra is sensitive to fluoride injury. Water quality should be checked and soil amendments adjusted to increase soil pH to 6.9 to eliminate fluoride damage.

Diseases. Reported diseases include bacterial soft rot (*Erwinia carotovora*) and leaf spot (*Ascochyta aspidistrae*, *Cercospora* sp., *Colletotrichum omnivorum*, and *Gloeosporium* sp.) [3].

Insects and related pests. Scale is the only common insect pest.

Species and cultivars. *Aspidistra elatior*.

Asplenium: Family Polypodiaceae

The genus *Asplenium* includes approximately 700 species of fern, most of which have evergreen foliage that may be entire, deeply cut, or compound.

Culture. Most types are propagated from spores or vegetative bulblets or plantlets that form on fronds of parent plants. Species that have spreading crowns are divided. Light intensities of 1,500 to 2,000 fc (15 to 20 klux) and fertilizer applied at 600 to 1,000 lb/A/yr (672 to 1,125 kg/ha/yr) of $N-P_2O_5-K_2O$ will produce high-quality plants. Soil mixtures should be rich in organic matter, well drained, and kept moist. Night temperatures of 60°F (16°C) should be provided if continued growth is desired.

Diseases. Reported diseases include leaf spot (*Cercospora asplenii*) and bacterial leaf spot (*Pseudomonas asplenii*).

Insects and related pests. Scale, mealybugs, foliar nematodes, and slugs may be troublesome.

Species and cultivars. *Asplenium bulbiferum* and *A. nidus*.

Beaucarnea: Family Agavaceae

Beaucarnea comprises a genus of about six species, all eventually assuming treelike proportions in their native habitat of Texas and Mexico where they are used in landscape plantings. *Beaucarnea recurvata* or ponytail is also widely grown as a foliage plant since it is extremely slow growing. Seedlings make unusual container plants that stay small enough for desk or table tops for years before becoming large enough for use as a floor plant.

Culture. Ponytails are commercially grown under 4,000 to 6,000 fc (40 to 60 klux) and fertilized with 900 to 1,200 lb/A/yr (1,008 to 1,345 kg/ha/yr) of N-P$_2$O$_5$-K$_2$O. Plants are propagated from seed, and seedlings grow well in a variety of well-drained soil mixes. Greenhouse temperatures should remain above 55°F (13°C) for continued plant growth.

Diseases. Reported diseases include bacterial soft rot (*Erwinia carotovora*), stem rot (*Fusarium* sp.), root rot (*Fusarium* and *Pythium* spp.), and leaf spot (*Phyllosticta* sp.) [3].

Insects and related pests. Common pests include mites, mealybugs, and scale.

Species and cultivars. *Beaucarnea recurvata.*

Begonia: Family Begoniaceae

The *Begonia* genus contains over 1,000 species native to tropical and subtropical regions. Plants vary from 2 inches (5 centimeters) to over 6 feet (1.8 meters) and are herbs or semiwoody shrubs with root stocks that may be fibrous, bulbous, rhizomatous, or tuberous. The asymmetrical leaves are petioled and alternate. Begonias are extensively cultivated, and over 10,000 hybrids have been developed [1]. Most plants are used as bedding plants, flowering pot plants, or foliage plants. They are usually divided into three groups: fibrous-rooted, rhizomatous, and tuberous forms. Only fibrous-rooted and rhizomatous forms are commonly used indoors.

Culture. Rhizomatous begonias are propagated from leaf or stem cuttings and leaf vein sections, and fibrous-rooted begonias from seed and stem or tip cuttings. Commercially, plants are grown under 2,000 to 3,000 fc (20 to 30 klux) and fertilized with 900 to 1,200 lb/A/yr (1,008 to 1,345 kg/ha/yr) of N-P$_2$O$_5$-K$_2$O. Greenhouse night temperatures should be 60°F (16°C) or above for best growth.

Diseases. Reported diseases include anthracnose (*Colletotrichum* sp., *Gloeosporium* sp., and *Glomerella cingulata*), bacterial soft rot (*Erwinia carotovora*), crown gall (*Agrobacterium tumefaciens*), leaf spot (*Alternaria* sp., *Cercospora begoniae*, *Corynespora cassiicola*, *Myrothecium roridum*, *Macrophoma* sp., and *Phyllosticta* sp.), gray mold (*Botrytis cinerea*), powdery mildew (*Erysiphe cichoracearum* and *Oidium* sp.), and leaf rot (*Rhizoctonia solani*) [3].

Insects and related pests. Mites and scale are the most common pests.

Species and cultivars. *Begonia masoniana* and *Begonia* × *rex-cultorum.*

Blechnum: Family Polypodiaceae

The genus *Blechnum* consists of over 200 species native primarily to the Southern Hemisphere. Fronds are singly pinnate or nearly pinnate. A few species are cultivated as ornamentals outdoors and indoors. One species, *B. occidentale* or hammock fern, is commonly grown for interior use.

Culture. Hammock fern is primarily grown from spores, but can be divided and is tolerant of a wide range of soil mixes with adequate moisture. Plants should be grown with approximately 2,000 to 3,000 fc (20 to 30 klux) and 800 to 1,200 lb/A/yr (900 to 1,345 kg/ha/yr) of $N-P_2O_5-K_2O$.

Diseases. Diseaselike leaf spots are occasionally noted, but specific pathogens have not been reported on this species.

Insects and related pests. Scale and mealybugs are infrequent pests.

Species and cultivars. *Blechnum occidentale.*

Brassaia: Family Araliaceae

Brassaia is a genus of about forty species of trees and shrubs native to tropical and subtropical areas of Asia and the South Sea Islands. Mature leaves are palmately compound with long petioles. Small plants are used as low floor plants, while seedlings of *Brassaia actinophylla* are used in dish gardens.

Culture. *Brassaia* spp. are propagated from fresh seeds, air layers, and cuttings. Acclimatized plants should be grown in 5,000 to 6,000 fc (50 to 60 klux) and fertilized with 1,800 lb/A/yr (2,017 kg/ha/yr) of $N-P_2O_5-K_2O$ [3]. *Brassaia* spp. tolerate cool temperatures, but greenhouse night temperatures should be kept at 60°F (15°C) or higher to maintain productive growth.

Diseases. Reported diseases include anthracnose (*Colletotrichum* sp. and *Gloeosporium* sp.), algal leaf spot (*Cephaleuros virescens*), leaf spot (*Alternaria* sp., *Cercospora* sp., *Coniothyrium* sp., and *Corynespora* sp.), root rot (*Pythium* sp.), stem rot (*Rhizoctonia solani*), and southern blight (*Sclerotium rolfsii*) [3].

Insects and related pests. Mites and scale are common pests, and thrips, nematodes, and leaf miners are occasional problems.

Species and cultivars. *Brassaia actinophylla* and *B. arboricola.*

Calathea: Family Marantaceae

Calathea is a genus with about 100 species of herbaceous plants native to tropical America. Most have short underground stems with attractively marked leathery leaves arranged compactly near the soil surface. Most cultivated species are produced for interior use as container specimens in terrariums and dish gardens or occasionally are grown as landscape ground covers. They grow well indoors if relative humidity levels are kept above 25 percent.

Culture. Calatheas are usually propagated by division, although cuttings from mature plants with aboveground shoots are sometimes used. Calathea requires greenhouse temperatures over 55°F (13°C) for continued growth. Recommended light intensities for production of acclimatized foliage plants are 1,500 to 2,000 fc (15 to 20 klux), with fertilization rates of 1,200 lb/A/yr (1,345 kg/ha/yr) of N-P_2O_5-K_2O [2]. Calatheas are moderately sensitive to fluoride soil levels, and fluoride sources should be eliminated from potting mixes. Plants grow best in well-aerated soils of high organic matter.

Diseases. The only reported disease is leaf spot (*Phyllosticta* sp.) [3].

Insects and related pests. Spidermites, scale, nematodes, and slugs are common pests.

Species and cultivars. *Calathea picturata, C. insignis* or *C. landifolia, C. makoyana,* and *Calathea roseopicta.*

Carissa: Family Apocynaceae

About thirty species of *Carissa* are native to tropical regions of Asia and Africa, consisting primarily of small shrubs and trees. Many are used for landscape plantings, and some cultivars of *Carissa grandiflora* are sold as interior plants, usually as small potted plants for tables or desks. These are often grown as indoor bonsai.

Culture. Carissa cultivars are propagated from stem or tip cuttings. Commercial foliage plants are produced with light levels of 5,000 to 6,000 fc (50 to 60 klux) and fertilized with 1,200 lb/A/yr (1,345 kg/ha/yr) of N-P_2O_5-K_2O.

Diseases. Reported diseases include algal leaf spots (*Cephaleuros virescens*), leaf spots (*Cercospora* sp., *Colletotrichum gloeosporioides, Phyllos-*

ticta sp.), twig dieback (*Diplodia natalensis*), dieback (*Physalospora obtusa, P. rhodina, Rhizoctonia ramicola, R. solani*), stem canker (*Dothiorella* sp.), stem gall (*Sphaeropsis tumefaciens*), and root rot (*Phytophthora parasitica* and *Pythium* sp.) [3].

Insects and related pests. Aphids, scale, and thrips may be trouble-some.

Species and cultivars. *Carissa grandiflora.*

Cereus: Family Cactaceae

This genus contains about thirty-six species of erect treelike branching cacti; most are native to the West Indies and eastern South America. They are used in warm climates as landscape plants, but some species tolerate low interior light and are often used in hot, dry interior locations.

Culture. *Cereus* is propagated by seeds or cuttings, but cuttings should be allowed to heal before sticking. Commercially, plants are grown under 6,000 to 8,000 fc (60 to 80 klux) and fertilized with 600 to 900 lb/a/yr (672 to 1,008 kg/ha/yr) of N-P_2O_5-K_2O. The growth rate of greenhouse *Cereus* is reduced if temperatures drop below 55°F (13°C).

Diseases. Reported diseases include anthracnose (*Colletrotrichum cerei, C. gloeosporioides,* and *Gloeosporium lunatum*), bacterial soft rot (*Erwinia aroideae* and *E. carotovora*), root and stem rot (*Fusarium oxysporum, Phytophthora parasitica, Rhizoctonia solani*), and stem blight (*Cercosporidium* sp.).

Insects and related pests. Scale is the only major problem.

Species and cultivars. *Cereus peruvianus.*

Ceropegia: Family Asclepiadaceae

Ceropegia is a genus of about 150 species of succulent twining herbs or subshrubs. Almost all have xerophytic adaptations, thick, leafless, swollen stems, or enlarged water-storing leaves. Most commercially grown species are vinelike and are grown as hanging baskets or pedestal plants.

Culture. *Ceropegia* is propagated from cuttings, and *C. woodii* is also propagated from tubers that form at nodes. Commercially, *C. woodii* is grown under 3,000 to 4,000 fc (30 to 40 klux) and fertilized with 900 lb/A/yr (1,008 kg/ha/yr) of N-P_2O_5-K_2O. Greenhouse night temperatures should be kept at or above 55°F (13°C) to maintain growth.

Diseases. Growers report leaf spot and root rot create problems.

Insects and related pests. Mealybugs and scale are common pests.

Species and cultivars. *Ceropegia woodii.*

Chlorophytum: Family Liliaceae

Chlorophytum is a genus composed of 200 or more species of acaulescent, herbaceous plants native to subtropical and tropical areas, excluding North America and Europe. Sessile leaves are arranged in basal rosettes that grow from fleshy rootstocks. *Chlorophytum* develop a long pedicel and, after flowering, plantlets develop on the pedicels. This makes plants especially useful as hanging basket and pedestal plants.

Culture. Chlorophytums are propagated by crown division or from plantlets developing on the inflorescence. They are commercially grown under 3,000 to 4,000 fc (30 to 40 klux) and fertilized with 1,200 lb/A/yr (1,345 kg/ha/yr) of N-P_2O_5-K_2O. Chlorophytums will tolerate chilling temperatures, but require minimum night temperatures of 55°F (13°C) for best growth. Soil mixes, fertilizers, and irrigation water should be fluoride free to prevent fluoride injury.

Diseases. Reported diseases include bacterial soft rot (*Erwinia carotovora*), root rot (*Pythium* sp.), and southern blight (*Sclerotium rolfsii*) [3].

Insects and related pests. Scale and whitefly are common insect pests.

Species and cultivars. *Chlorophytum bichetti* and *Chlorophytum comosum*.

Cissus: Family Vitaceae

The *Cissus* genus consists of about 350 species of vines and shrubs native to tropical and subtropical regions through the world. Leaves are alternate and may be simple or palmately compound, with vining *Cissus* often climbing by tendrils. Several vining *Cissus* species are grown as foliage plants and often used for hanging baskets, pedestal plants, or trained as totems.

Culture. Commercially, they are grown under 2,000 to 3,000 fc (20 to 30 klux) and fertilized with 1,200 lb/A/yr (1,345 kg/ha/yr) of N-P_2O_5-K_2O. Plants are normally propagated from leaf-bud cuttings under intermittent mist.

Diseases. Reported diseases include leaf spot (*Cercospora* sp.), root rot (*Rhizoctonia solani*), rust (*Endophyllum circumscriptum*), and smut (*Mykosyrinx cissi* and *Ustilago cissi*) [3].

Insects and related pests. Broad mites, mealybugs, spider mites, and scale may occasionally cause problems.

Species and cultivars. *Cissus antarctica*, *C. discolor*, *C. rhombifolia*, and *C. rotundifolia*.

Clusia: Family Guttiferae

The genus *Clusia* contains about 145 species of trees and shrubs native to tropical and subtropical tree regions of America, but only one, *C. rosea* or autograph tree, is commonly grown as a foliage plant. It is used as a floor plant or indoor tree where coarse-textured foliage is required.

Culture. Autograph tree is usually propagated by air layering, but occasionally seeds are used. It is commercially grown as a foliage plant under light intensities of 3,000 to 3,500 fc (30 to 35 klux) and fertilized with 1,200 lb/A/yr (1,345 kg/ha/yr) of N-P$_2$O$_5$-K$_2$O. *Clusia rosea* tolerates occasional temperatures of 40°F (5°C), but minimum greenhouse night temperatures of 55°F (13°C) are needed to maintain growth rate.

Diseases. The only reported disease is leaf spot (*Ascochyta* sp.) [3].

Insects and related pests. Scale is the only common pest.

Species and cultivars. *Clusia rosea.*

Codiaeum: Family Euphorbiaceae

Codiaeum is a small genus of six species of woody shrubs and trees native to the South Sea Islands and the Malay Peninsula. One variable species, *C. variegatum*, is cultivated as a landscape shrub in tropical countries, and selected cultivars are grown as interior foliage plants.

Culture. *Codiaeum* is usually propagated by cuttings in a propagation bed with temperatures maintained around 80°F (27°C). Occasionally, air layers are used commercially as seedlings vary and are not used for cultivar propagation. Acclimatized foliage plants can be grown under 7,000 to 8,000 fc (70 to 80 klux) and fertilized with 1,800 lb/A/yr (2,017 kg/ha/yr) of N-P$_2$O5-K$_2$O [2]. Greenhouse night temperatures should not go below 55°F (13°C) for desired growth, since crotons may drop their leaves if subjected to temperatures below 40°F (5°C). Only shade-grown plants should be considered for use indoors, even though the color patterns are not as intense as those plants grown in full sun.

Diseases. Reported diseases include anthracnose (*Colletotrichum gloeosporioides* and *Gloeosporium* sp.), crown gall (*Agrobacterium tumefaciens*), leaf spot (*Cercospora stevensonii, Helminthosporium* sp., *Macrophoma* sp., *Phomopsis* sp., *Phyllosticta* sp.), stem canker (*Coniothyrium* sp., *Leptosphaeria* sp.), root and stem rot (*Fusarium* sp.), stem gall (*Nectria* sp.), root rot (*Phytophthora* sp., *Rhizoctonia solani*), rust (*Puccinia crotonia*), southern blight (*Sclerotium rolfsii*), and scab (*Sphaceloma venezuelanus*).

Insects and related pests. Reported pests include mealybugs, mites, scale, and thrips.

Species and cultivars. *Codiaeum variegatum.*

Coffea: Family Rubiaceae

The genus *Coffea* is composed of about forty species of trees or shrubs native to tropical regions of Africa and Asia. All have opposite, simple leaves and whitish flowers. Several species are grown for coffee in subtropical and tropical regions around the world, but species grown as foliage plants are usually used as seedlings or novelty indoor trees.

Culture. Minimum night temperatures of 60°F (16°C) should be maintained. Coffee trees are propagated from freshly sown seed or terminal cuttings. Coffee is grown as a foliage plant in 4,000 fc (40 klux) and fertilized with 1,200 lb/A/yr (1,345 kg/ha/yr) of N-P$_2$O$_5$-K$_2$O. It has a high rate of transpiration, and in building interiors, potting media should not dry out as leaves will desiccate.

Diseases. Diseases include anthracnose (*Colletotrichum coffeanum*), damping off (*Rhizoctonia solani*), leaf spot (*Cercospora coffeicola* and *Glomerella cingulata*), neck rot (*Fusarium* sp.), and pink mold (*Trichothecium roseum*) [3].

Insects and related pests. Mealybugs, scale, and whitefly.

Species and cultivars. *Coffea arabica.*

Coleus: Family Labiatae

The genus *Coleus* is native to tropical regions of Asia and Africa and has about 150 species of mostly succulent herbs. Several species grown for their colorful foliage have been hybridized to produce new cultivars. *Coleus* cultivars are often grown outdoors as bedding plants and used indoors as table plants. They can be trained as standards with a supporting stake for the trunk.

Culture. *Coleus* hybrids can be propagated from cuttings, which root in 2 to 3 weeks under intermittent mist. Seeds of many cultivars are also available. Light intensities of 4,000 to 5,000 fc (40 to 50 klux) with fertilization rate of 1,500 lb/A/yr (1,680 kg/ha/yr) of N-P$_2$O$_5$-K$_2$O will produce high-quality plants. Minimum greenhouse night temperatures of 60°F (16°C) are required for continued growth.

Diseases. Reported diseases include canker (*Volutella* sp.), damping off (*Rhizoctonia solani*), cottony blight (*Sclerotinia sclerotiorum*), leaf spot (*Stemphylium* sp.), and root and stem rot (*Rhizoctonia solani*) [3].

Insects and related pests. Common pests include caterpillars, mealybugs, mites, nematodes, scale, slugs, and whitefly.

Species and cultivars. *Coleux × hybridus.*

Cordyline: Family Agavaceae

Most of the twenty species of *Cordyline* are native to tropical and subtropical regions of Asia and Australia. In their native habitat they eventually assume treelike proportions, but when grown as foliage plants they are used as floor plants, desk or table top plants, or as focal points in dish gardens. Indoors they develop willowy stems topped by colorful leaves.

Culture. Commercial propagation is by tip cuttings, stem sections, seed, and root cuttings. Light intensities of 3,000 to 3,500 fc (30 to 35 klux) are suitable for stock and finishing plants. Fertilization rates of 1,200 lb/A/yr (1,345 kg/ha/yr) of N-P_2O_5-K_2O are recommended for stock production and container plants [2]. Soluble fluoride in water, fertilizer, or potting media will cause necrotic spots on the foliage. Greenhouse night temperatures should remain above 55°F (13°C) to maintain optimum growth rate.

Diseases. Reported diseases include leaf spot (*Cercospora cordylines, Cladosporium dracaenatum, Fusarium moniliforme,* and *Phyllosticta dracaenae*), anthracnose (*Colletotrichium* sp. and *Glomerella cingulata*), bacterial soft rot (*Erwinia carotovora*), crown rot (*Phytophthora* sp.), and root rot (*Rhizoctonia solani*) [3].

Insects and related pests. Mites, root mealybugs, mealybugs, and scale can become troublesome.

Species and cultivars. *Cordyline australis* and *C. terminalis.*

Cryptanthus: Family Bromeliaceae

The *Cryptanthus* genera contains about twenty species of terrestial bromeliads native to Eastern Brazil, and numerous hybrids have been developed. Species are relatively small, with an appressed rosette of flat, stiff leaves with toothed margins. The foliage may be plain or variously striped or patterned depending on the species. Whitish flowers develop in terminal heads. *Cryptanthus* sp. are used as small table or window plants or as part of a xerophytic dish garden or terrarium.

Culture. Plants are propagated by offsets removed from between leaves of stock plants that have finished flowering. Commercially, plants are grown in 3,500 to 4,500 fc (35 to 45 klux) and fertilized with 900 to 1,200 lb/A/yr (1,008 to 1,345 kg/ha/yr) of N-P_2O_5-K_2O. Night greenhouse temperatures should be kept at or above 60°F (18°C) for best growth.

Diseases. Reported diseases include anthracnose (*Colletotrichum gloeosporioides*), gray mold (*Botrytis cinerea*), leaf spot (*Phyllosticta* sp.), stem rot (*Cephalosporium* sp.), and wilt (*Verticillium* sp.) [3].

Insects and related pests. Mealybugs and scale may be trouble-some.

Species and cultivars. *Cryptanthus bivittatus* or *C. bivettatus minor.*

Cyanotis: Family Commelinaceae

Cyanotis is a genus of approximately fifty species of herbaceous creeping ground covers native to tropical Africa and Asia. All have sessile leaves with sheathing leaf bases that cover most of the internode sections and varying amounts of pubescence on stems and leaves. Commercially grown species have small leaves and are used in hanging baskets, ter-rariums, or as ground covers with other plantings.

Culture. *Cyanotis* is usually propagated from tip cuttings and rooted under intermittent mist, but they may also be divided or started from seed. Commercially, they are grown under 2,500 to 3,500 fc (25 to 35 klux) and fertilized with 1,200 lb/A/yr (1,345 kg/ha/yr) of N-P_2O_5-K_2O. Minimum night temperatures should be 55°F (13°C) to main-tain plant growth.

Diseases. No diseases are reported in the standard listings, but growers report leaf spots and leaf blight.

Insects and related pests. Mealybugs and scale may become troublesome.

Species and cultivars. *Cyanotis kewensis* or *C. somaliensis.*

Cycas: Family Cycadaceae

Cycas is a genus of about twenty species of slow-growing plants with stout trunks capped by pinnate palmlike, very stiff fronds. This genus and other cycad genera are ancient plants, and fossil remains show they existed millions of years before angiosperms evolved. Existing species are native to tropical areas around the world, excluding the Americas. Their distinctive and unusual shapes are used as focal points in subtropi-cal and tropical landscape plantings. *Cycas revoluta* is used as a distinctive container subject or as a conservatory plant.

Culture. *Cycas* species are propagated from seed or suckers from male plants. Commercially, cycads for interior use are grown under 4,000 to 5,000 fc (40 to 50 klux) and fertilized with 900 lb/A/yr (1,008 kg/ha/yr) of N-P_2O_5-K_2O. The species commonly grown for interior use, *C. revoluta,* tolerates temperatures below freezing, but greenhouse night temperatures should be above 55°F (13°C) to maintain growth.

Diseases. Reported diseases include leaf spot (*Alternaria* sp., *Col-*

letotrichum sp., *Coniothyrium* sp., *Dendrophoma clypeata*, *Fusarium oxysporum*, *Gloeosporium* sp., *Pestalotia cycadis*, *Phoma* sp., *Phomopsis cycadina*, and *Phyllosticta* sp.), butt rot (*Ganoderma* sp.), and mushroom root rot (*Clitocybe tabescens*) [3].

Insects and related pests. Scale is the most common pest.

Species and cultivars. *Cycas revoluta.*

Cyperus: Family Cyperaceae

Cyperus is a large genus of about 600 herbaceous plants native to tropical and subtropical areas throughout the world, usually growing in or next to water. Many species produce large photosynthesizing bracts subtending inflorescences that function as leaves; others may have no sheathing leaves. Several species are grown indoors as novelty plants.

Culture. *Cyperus* is propagated by division, and some are propagated by cutting off stems with intact bracts and inserting these in sand under intermittent mist. Commercially grown interior plants are grown under 4,000 to 6,000 fc (40 to 60 klux) and fertilized with 600 to 900 lb/A/yr (672 to 1,008 kg/ha/yr) of $N-P_2O_5-K_2O$. Greenhouse night temperatures should remain above 55°F (13°C) for best growth.

Diseases. Reported diseases include black choke (*Balansia cyperacearum*), inflorescence smut (*Cintractia limitata*), leaf spot (*Cercospora* sp. and *Septoria cyperi*), rust (*Puccinia angustata, P. canaliculata, P. cyperi, P. cyperitagetiformis,* and *Uredo nociviola*), root and culm rot (*Rhizoctonia solani*), stem blight (*Scirrhia* sp.), tar spot (*Phyllacora cyperi*), and thread blight (*Corticium vagum*) [3].

Insects and related pests. Common pests include mealy bugs, scale, thrips, and whitefly.

Species and cultivars. *Cyperus albostriatus* and *Cyperus alternifolius.*

Cyrtomium: Family Polypodiaceae

The genus *Cyrtomium* consists of ten or more species of ferns with singly, pinnate fronds, which are generally coarse, leathery, and persistent. Members of *Cyrtomium* are native to tropical and semitropical areas of the Old World. Fronds develop from a single erect rhizome. Plants do well in the landscape in regions where they are hardy and are excellent indoor specimens or interiorscape ground covers under medium to bright light levels.

Culture. Plants are propagated from spores, which are germinated and grown on with ease. Production light levels of 1,800 to 2,400 fc (18 to 24 klux) and fertilizer rates of 800 to 1,200 lb/A/yr (900 to 1,345 kg/ha/hr) of N-P_2O_5-K_2O are suggested. Moist but well-drained soils rich in organic matter are best for this genus.

Diseases. Producers rarely mention diseaselike problems.

Insects and related pests. Scale and mealybugs are occasionally serious pests.

Species and cultivars. *Crytomium falcatum, C. falcatum* 'Rochfordianum,' and *C. falcatum* 'Mayi.'

Davallia: Family Polypodiaceae

Davallia comprises approximately thirty-five species of fern from the Old World, most of which are epiphytic and tolerate tropical or subtropical climates. Several species and cultivars from this group are cherished for their finely divided lacy fronds and relatively coarse rhizomes covered with hairlike scales. Plants are frequently grown in hanging baskets or on fern bark slabs, but also do well as potted plants if rhizomes are not permitted to cascade excessively.

Culture. Extremely well-drained, highly organic soil mixes are a must for *Davallia* culture since most are epiphytes. Plants can be started from spores, rhizome divisions, or tissue-cultured plantlets. Rhizome pieces must be placed at the soil surface, which should be kept moist without disturbing rhizomes until they are rooted. Light intensities from 2,000 to 2,500 fc (20 to 25 klux) and fertilization rates of 800 to 1,000 lb/A/yr (900 to 1,108 kg/ha/yr) of N-P_2O_5-K_2O will produce high-quality plants. Temperatures should not drop below 65°F (18°C) for continued growth.

Diseases. Gray mold (*Botrytis cinerea*), leaf spot (*Cercospora phyllitidis*), and leaf blight (*Rhizoctonia solani*) have been reported on *Davallia* [3].

Insects and related pests. Scale and mealybugs are the most frequently observed pests.

Species and cultivars. *Davallia fejeensis, D. pentaphylla,* and *D. trichomanoides.*

Dichorisandra: Family Commelinaceae

Dichorisandra is a genus of about thirty species of erect, herbaceous plants native to tropical America. All have alternate sheathing leaves and succulent stems. Cultivated species are grown in tropical outdoor gardens and indoors, usually in groupings with other plants requiring high humidity.

Culture. Plants are propagated from cuttings and rooted under intermittent mist. Commercially, plants are grown under light intensities of 3,500 to 4,500 fc (35 to 45 klux) and fertilized with 1,200 lb/A/yr (1,345 kg/ha/yr) of N-P$_2$O$_5$-K$_2$. Greenhouse night temperatures should be kept above 50°F (10°C) to maintain good growth.

Diseases. Reported diseases are leaf spots (*Cercospora* sp. and *Cylindrocladium* sp.) [3].

Insects and related pests. Mealybugs and scale are common pests.

Species and cultivars. *Dichorisandra reginae.*

Dieffenbachia: Family Araceae

The genus *Dieffenbachia* contains about thirty species of herbaceous plants native to Central and South America. Ultimate plant height depends on the species and ranges from 2 feet (70 centimeters) or less to 10 feet (3 meters) or more. Usually, plants have an unbranched, thick, succulent stem that may develop a thin, corky layer with maturity. The alternate leaves may be variously colored or patterned depending on the species, but all are broadly elliptic in shape. Many species tolerate interior conditions well, and small species are used in dish gardens or as small potted plants, while large plants may be used as floor plants.

Culture. *Dieffenbachia* or dumbcane stock is commonly grown in ground or raised beds, and tip cuttings are the most widely used method of propagation. Cane can also be used for propagative purposes. Light intensities for stock production can be as high as 4,000 fc (40 klux) with light intensities of 3,000 fc (30 klux) for finishing plants. Greenhouse night temperatures should not drop below 65° to 70°F (18° to 21°C), as cooler temperatures may reduce plant growth and rooting of tip cuttings. Suggested fertilization rates for container-grown plants are 1,200 lb/A/yr (1,345 kg/ha/yr) of N-P$_2$O$_5$-K$_2$O [2].

Diseases. Reported diseases include anthracnose (*Colletotrichum gloeosporioides, Glomerella cingulata*), bacterial leaf spot (*Xanthomonas dieffenbachiae*), brown leaf spot (*Phaeosphaeria eustoma*), leaf margin blight (*Fusarium moniliforme*), leaf spot (*Cephalosporium* sp., *Cercospora* sp., *Gloeosporium Leptosphaeria eustoma, Myrothecium roridum, Phyllosticta* sp., and *Volutella* sp.), root and cane rot (*Rhizoctonia solani*), stem and bud rot (*Fusarium* sp.), stem and leaf rot (*Erwinia dieffenbachiae*), stem rot (*Pythium splendens, Phytophthora palmivora*), and southern blight (*Sclerotium rolfsii*) [3].

Insects and related pests. Mites are most troublesome, although mealybugs and thrips may cause injury.

Species and cultivars. *Dieffenbachia amoena, D. amoena* 'Tropic

Snow,' *D.* 'Bausei,' *D.* 'Exotica,' *D. oerstedii, D. oerstedii* 'Variegata,' *D.* 'Perfection Compacta,' *D.* 'Exotic Perfection,' *D.* 'Memoria-corsii,' and *D. maculata* (*D. picta*).

Dizygotheca: Family Araliaceae

Fifteen species of shrubs and trees native to the islands of New Caledonia and Polynesia comprise the genus *Dizygotheca*. All have palmately compound leaves with leaflets that become progressively broader and longer as they mature. Seedlings are grown as desk plants, while larger specimens are used as indoor trees. Frequently, several plants are potted together when multiple trunks are desired.

Culture. Plants are normally propagated from fresh seed, but cuttings and air layers are sometimes used. Acclimatized *Dizygotheca* require light intensities of 5,000 to 6,000 fc (50 to 60 klux) and 1,200 lb/A/yr (1,345 kg/ha/yr) of $N-P_2O_5-K_2O$ [2]. Greenhouse night temperatures should be kept at or above 65°F (18°C) for continued growth.

Diseases. Reported diseases include leaf spot (*Cercospora* sp.), root rot (*Fusarium oxysporum* and *Rhizoctonia solani*), and spot anthracnose (*Sphaceloma araliae*) [3].

Insects and related pests. Mealybugs, spider mites, root mealybugs, and scale are common pests.

Species and cultivars. *Dizygotheca elegantissima.*

Dracaena: Family Agavaceae

The genus *Dracaena* encompasses approximately forty species native to tropical regions of Asia and Africa. They vary in size from under 3 feet (1 meter) to large tree forms exceeding 30 feet (9 meters). A number of species are grown commercially because they are excellent interior plants, with small specimens often used in dish gardens or terrariums and larger ones as low floor plants or tree forms.

Culture. Most dracaenas are propagated by tip cuttings or cane, and a few species are sometimes propagated from seed. Stock plants can be grown in full sun but growth rate is faster if grown under 6,000 fc (60 klux). Rooted cuttings of *D. marginata* should be grown in 4,500 fc (45 klux), while other *Dracaena* species require 2,700 to 3,700 fc (27 to 37 klux) to produce best quality plants for interior utilization [2]. Fertilizer levels of 1,800 lb/A/yr (1,345 kg/ha/yr) of $N-P_2O_5-K_2O$ are recommended for *Draceana* species [2].

Diseases. Reported diseases include bacterial leaf spot

(*Pseudomonas* sp.), bacterial soft rot (*Erwinia carotovora*), leaf spot (*Colletotrichum dracaenae, Corynespora cassiicola, Fusarium moniliforme, Gloeosporium polymorphum, G. thuemenii, Helminthosporium* sp., *Phyllosticta dracaenae*), stem and leaf rot (*Phytophthora* sp.), southern blight (*Sclerotium rolfsii*), and web blight (*Rhizoctonia microsclerotia*) [3].

Insects and related pests. Mites, mealybugs, and thrips are the most common pests.

Species and cultivars. *Dracaena angustifolia honoriae* or *Pleomele angustifolia honoriae, D. arborea, D. deremensis, D. draco, D. fragrans, D. goldieana, D. marginata, D. reflexa, D. sanderana, D. sanderana borinquensis, D. surcolosa,* and *D. thalioides.*

Epipremnum: Family Araceae

Epipremnum contains about ten species; most were formerly classified as *Scindapsus* [1]. They are root-climbing vines, native to tropical areas in Southeast Asia, and often have entire leaves when immature and large pinnatified leaves as they mature. Their growth habit makes them useful as pedestal plants, terrariums, totems, hanging baskets, ground covers, and in dish gardens.

Culture. Cuttings are taken from stock plants as needed and propagated from tip cuttings and single- or double-eye cuttings under intermittent mist. Acclimatized plants can be grown under 3,500 to 4,500 fc (35 to 45 klux) and fertilized with 1,500 lb/A/yr (1,681 kg/ha/yr) of N-P_2O_5-K_2O [2]. Greenhouse night temperatures should be above 60°F (15°C) to maintain productive growth rates.

Diseases. Reported diseases include anthracnose (*Glomerella cingulata*), bacterial soft rot (*Erwinia aroideae* and *E. carotovora*), bacterial leaf spot (*Pseudomonas cichorii*), gray mold (*Botrytis cinerea*), leaf spot (Cercospora richardiaecola), leaf rot (*Colletotrichum* sp.), leaf spot (*Phyllosticta* sp.), root rot (*Phytophthora* sp., *Pythium splendens,* and *Sclerotium rolfsii*), and stem rot (*Rhizoctonia solani*).

Insects and related pests. Mealybugs, root mealybugs, scale, and thrips are common pests.

Species and cultivars. *Epipremnum aureum* or *Scindapsus aureus.*

Episcia: Family Gesneriaceae

This is a small genus of about ten species of herbaceous ground covers native to tropical America. They have fleshy, opposite, usually colorful leaves and solitary axillary flowers, and may be used as ground covers or in hanging baskets.

Culture. Episcias are usually propagated by cuttings or leaves and are usually grown under 2,000 to 2,500 fc (20 to 25 klux) and fertilized with 1,200 lb/A/yr (1,345 kg/ha/yr) of N-P_2O_5-K_2O. Episcias are extremely cold sensitive, and night temperatures must be kept at 60°F (13°C) to prevent growth distortions and leaf abscissions. Only water at or slightly higher than room temperature should be used to prevent cold-water damage to leaves.

Diseases. Episcias are not listed in standard plant disease compilations, but growers report troubles with root rot.

Insects and related pests. Mealybugs, mites, and nematodes may create problems.

Species and cultivars. *Episcia cupreata.*

Euphorbia: Family Euphorbiaceae

This large genus consists of over 1,600 species of herbs, shrubs, and trees; many have succulent properties and milky sap. Many species have short-lived, deciduous leaves and stems resembling cacti. Several are grown outdoors in warm climates with other xerophytic plants, and some make good interior plants.

Culture. *Euphorbia* is propaged from cuttings, usually over bottom heat. Most species can be grown in full sun, but those grown for interiors should be grown under 3,000 to 5,000 fc (30 to 50 klux) and fertilized with 900 to 1,200 lb/A/yr (1,008 to 1,345 kg/ha) of N-P_2O_5-K_2O. Greenhouse night temperatures should be kept above 55°F (13°C) to maintain growth.

Diseases. Reported diseases include anthracnose (*Colletotrichum* sp.), gray mold (*Botrytis cinerea*), leaf spot (*Cephalosporium* sp., *Cercospora* sp., *Corynebacterium poinsettiae*, *Gloeosporium* sp., *Helminthosporium* sp., and *Phyllosticta* sp.), bacterial leaf spot (*Xanthomonas poinsettiaecola*), twig dieback (*Diplodia natalensis*), stem rot (*Fusarium* sp.), powdery mildew (*Microsphaera euphorbiae* and *Oidium* sp.), downy mildew (*Peronospora* sp.), stem rot (*Phytophthora* sp. and *Sclerotinia sclerotiorum*), and rust (*Puccinia panici* and *Uromyces* sp.) [3].

Insects and related pests. Scale and aphids may become troublesome.

Species and cultivars. *Euphorbia lactea, E. milii, E. tirucalli,* and *Euphorbia trigona.*

Fatshedera: Family Araliaceae

This genus is composed of one species, *Fatshedera lizei*, a bigeneric hybrid developed by crossing *Fatsia japonica* with *Hedera helix*. Small plants are used as desk plants; larger ones are used as low floor plants. *Fatshedera* is a good choice for drafty areas since it is tolerant of chilling temperatures.

Culture. *Fatshedera* is propagated from stem or tip cuttings as needed. Commercially, *Fatshedera* is grown under 4,000 to 6,000 fc (40 to 60 klux) and fertilized with 1,500 lb/A/yr (1,681 kg/ha/yr) of N-P_2O_5-K_2O. Minimum greenhouse night temperatures should remain above 50°F (10°C) to maintain growth.

Diseases. Reported diseases include algal leaf spot (*Cephaleuros virescens*), anthracnose (*Colletotrichum* sp.), damping off (*Phytophthora parasitica*), leaf spot (*Cercospora* sp., *Corynespora cassiicola, Gloeosporium* sp., *Glomerella cingulata,* and *Phyllosticta concentrica*), and root and stem rot (*Rhizoctonia solani*) [3].

Insects and related pests. Scale, mites, and mealybugs are the more common pests.

Species and cultivars. *Fatshedera lizei.*

Fatsia: Family Araliaceae

Fatsia is a genus composed of one species, a large shrub *F. japonica,* native to Japan. Its size curtails use as a desk plant, but it makes an ideal floor plant; larger specimens are used as indoor trees. It tolerates chilling temperatures, and can be used in cooler locations than many foliage plants.

Culture. *Fatsia japonica* is propagated from seed, tip, stem, or root cuttings. Commercially, *Fatsia* is grown under 4,000 to 6,000 fc (40 to 60 klux) and fertilized with 1,500 lb/A/yr (1,680 kg/ha/yr) of N-P_2O_5-K_2O. *Fatsia* tolerates cool temperatures and can be grown with greenhouse minimum night temperatures of 50°F (10°C).

Diseases. Reported diseases include anthracnose (*Colletotrichum* sp.), basal stem rot (*Phytophthora parasitica*), leaf spot (*Alternaria* sp., *Cercospora* sp., and *Phyllosticta* sp.), and root and stem rot (*Rhizoctonia solani*) [3].

Insects and related pests. Mealybugs, scale, and thrips are common pests.

Species and cultivars. *Fatsia japonica.*

Ficus: Family Moraceae

The genus *Ficus* has about 800 species of trees, shrubs, and woody vines native to the world's tropical regions. Figs are widely planted in warm areas of the world for fruit, shade, and ornamentals. Several species are useful as indoor foliage plants for their attractive leaves and ability to tolerate interior light and relative humidities. Most *Ficus* grown indoors are tree forms or large floor plants, but some vining forms are used in hanging baskets or terrariums.

Culture. Large-leaved, tree-form *Ficus* is usually propagated by air layering, and small-leaved ones by terminal cuttings or simple layering. Vining forms may be propagated by division. Optimum light intensities for production of potted acclimatized plants vary with individual species and range from 3,500 to 8,000 fc (35 to 80 klux) [2]. However, 4,000 to 5,000 fc (40 to 50 klux) is commonly used unless otherwise stated in individual species descriptions. Some *Ficus* intended for interior use are initially grown in full sun to increase stem caliper and then moved into shade houses for acclimatization. Fertilization rates for suggested light intensities are 1,800 lb/A/yr (2,017 kg/ha/yr) of N-P_2O_5-K_2O [2].

Diseases. A rather extensive list is reported to occur in *Ficus* sp., but many of these diseases occur in outdoor plantings rather than in greenhouse situations [3].

Insects and related pests. Insects and related pests include scale, mealybugs, whitefly, chewing insects, and thrips.

Species and cultivars. *Ficus benjamina, F. deltoides, F. elastica, F. lyrata, F. pumila, F. retusa, F. retusa nida, F. sagittata, F. sagittata* 'Variegata,' and *F. triangularis.*

Fittonia: Family Acanthaceae

Fittonia is a genus having two species; only one is of major horticultural importance, *Fittonia verschaffeltii* or nerve plant. It is native to moist humid regions of Colombia and Peru and is commonly grown for use in terrariums, hanging baskets, and dish gardens.

Culture. *Fittonia* is easily propagated from tip or stem cuttings in a media of peat and perlite, where cuttings root in 3 weeks. Stock plants are often grown in containers or in raised greenhouse beds. Light intensities for stock or container production should be between 2,000 to 3,000 fc (20 to 30 klux), with fertilizer requirements of 1,200 lb/A/yr (1,345 kg/ha/yr) of N-P$_2$O$_5$-K$_2$O. Night temperatures should remain above 60°F (15°C) for a productive growth rate.

Diseases. Reported diseases include crown and root rot (*Rhizoctonia solani*) and southern blight (*Sclerotium rolfsii*) [3].

Insects and related pests. Mealybugs and mites are the most common insect pests.

Species and cultivars. *Fittonia verschaffeltii, F. vershaffeltii argyroneura, F. verschaffeltii argyroneura* 'Minima,' and *F. verschaffeltii pearcei.*

Gynura: Family Compositae

Gynura is a genus with approximately 100 species of herbs and small shrubs native to tropical regions of Africa and Asia. Cultivated species have attractive foliage in shades of green and purple and are grown as ground covers or as hanging baskets.

Culture. Gynuras are propagated from stem or tip cuttings. Commercially, plants are grown under 5,000 to 6,000 fc (50 to 60 klux) and fertilized with 1,500 lb/A/yr (1,680 kg/ha) of N-P$_2$O$_5$-K$_2$O. Night greenhouse temperatures should remain above 55°F (13°C) to maintain growth rate.

Diseases. Reported diseases include anthracnose (*Colletotrichum gloeosporioides*), leaf and stem blight (*Botrytis cinerea*), leaf rot (*Phytophthora* sp.), and root and stem rot (*Fusarium oxysporum* and *Rhizoctonia solani*) [3].

Insects and related pests. Scale and mealybugs are common pests.

Species and cultivars. *Gynura aurantiaca* or *Gynura samentosa.*

Haemaria: Family Orchidaceae

Haemaria is a genus limited to one species, *Haemaria discolor,* a terrestrial orchid native to tropical Asia. It is one of the few orchids with foliage attractive enough to merit classification as a foliage plant.

Culture. For a terrestrial plant, fewer cultural problems are experienced if *H. discolor* is grown in a porous soil mix suitable for epiphytes. Commercially, plants are grown under 2,000 to 2,500 fc (20 to 25 klux) and fertilized with 1,200 lb/A/yr (1,345 kg/ha/yr) of N-P$_2$O$_5$-K$_2$O. Greenhouse night temperatures should not drop below 60°F (16°C) for best growth. Plants are propagated by division of stock plants or meristeming.

Diseases. No diseases are reported specifically for *Haemaria;* however, growers report various leaf spots and stem and root rots as problems.

Insects and related pests. Common pests include aphids, mealybugs, mites, and scale.

Species and cultivars. *Haemaria discolor* and *H. discolor downsoniana.*

Hedera: Family Araliaceae

Hedera is a genus comprised of about fifteen species of root-climbing vines native to North Africa, Asia, and southern Europe. They have juvenile and adult foliage similar to other plants in the Aralia family. Many cultivated species are used for wall coverings or ground covers in subtropical and temperate regions. They are grown as hanging baskets, totems, topiary plants, and ground covers with other plantings.

Culture. *Hedera* is usually propagated from stem cuttings. Commercially, as foliage plants, they are grown under 4,000 to 6,000 fc (40 to 60 klux) and fertilized with 1,200 lb/A/yr (1,345 kg/ha/yr) of N-P_2O_5-K_2O. *Hedera* tolerates cool temperatures, and minimum greenhouse night temperatures can be set at 55°F (13°C).

Diseases. Reported diseases include algal leaf spot (*Cephaleuros virescens*), anthracnose (*Colletotrichum* sp. and *Gloeosporium* sp.), bacterial leaf spot (*Xanthomonas hederae*), leaf spot (*Cercospora hederae, Coniothyrium* sp., *Corynespora* sp., and *Phyllosticta concentrica*), root rot (*Phytophthora* sp., *Pythium* sp., and *Rhizoctonia solani*), and stem gall (*Nectria* sp. and *Volutella* sp.).

Insects and related pests. Broad mites, spider mites, and scale may become serious pests.

Species and cultivars. *Hedera helix.*

Hemigraphis: Family Acanthaceae

Over sixty species of *Hemigraphis* are native to moist shaded areas in Asia, but only one species and its cultivars are commonly grown as foliage plants. Their maximum height of 6 inches (15 centimeters) makes them useful for hanging baskets, terrariums, and dish gardens.

Culture. Plants root readily from tip or stem cuttings. Stock plants may be grown in ground or raised beds or cuttings taken from plants in the finishing area. Light intensities for stock and container production may be between 3,000 to 4,500 fc (30 to 45 klux), with fertilization rates of 900 to 1,200 lb/A/yr (1,008 to 1,345 kg/ha/yr) of N-P$_2$O$_5$-K$_2$O for stock or container-plant production. Night temperatures should be kept above 60°F (16°C) to maintain growth.

Diseases. No diseases are listed in standard disease compilations, but growers report occasional root rotting diseases.

Insects and related pests. Aphids, mites, and mealybugs are common greenhouse pests.

Species and cultivars. *Hemigraphis exotica* and *H. exotica* 'Colorata.'

Hoya: Family Asclepiadaceae

Hoya is a relatively large genus containing over 200 species of vines and vining shrubs. Most are native to areas of China and India, where they climb up supports via adventitious roots or twist around a support. Hoyas have alternate leaves, and most produce attractive clusters of colorful waxlike flowers. Each cluster develops on spurs that produce subsequent inflorescences year after year.

Culture. Hoyas are propagated from semihardened stem cuttings or by layering. Commercially, they are grown under 3,000 to 4,000 fc (30 to 40 klux) and fertilized with 1,200 lb/A/yr (1,345 kg/ha/yr) of N-P$_2$O$_5$-K$_2$O. Greenhouse night temperatures should be maintained at 55°F (13°C) for continued growth.

Diseases. Reported diseases include anthracnose (*Colletotrichum gloeosporioides*), leaf spot (*Cercospora* sp., *Corynespora* sp., and *Gloeosporium*), leaf blight (*Rhizoctonia solani*), and ring spot virus [3].

Insects and related pests. Common pests include scale and mealybugs.

Species and cultivars. *Hoya carnosa* and *H. purpurea-fusca.*

Hypoestes: Family Acanthaceae

Over forty species of *Hypoestes* are native to South Africa, Madagascar, and Southern Asia, but only one, *Hypoestes phyllostachya* (synonym, *H. sanguinolenta*) or freckle face, is commonly grown as a foliage plant.

Culture. Tip and stem cuttings are taken from stock plants as needed for propagative purposes, or plants may be grown from seed. Cuttings are rooted under intermittent mist, potted, and finished under 3,000 to 4,000 fc (30 to 40 klux) and grown with 900 to 1,200 lb/A/yr

(1,008 to 1,345 kg/ha/yr) of N-P$_2$O$_5$-K$_2$O with night temperatures above 55°F (13°C).

Diseases. Standard complications do not list *Hypoestes.*

Insects and related pests. Chewing insects, mites, and scale are common pests.

Species and cultivars. *H. phyllostachya.*

Iresine: Family Amaranthaceae

Iresine is a genus of about seventy species of herbaceous and semiwoody plants native to tropical regions around the world. They have opposite leaves, with most cultivated species having colorful foliage that makes them useful as bedding plants in tropical areas.

Culture. Plants are propagated from tip or stem cuttings. Light intensities of 5,000 to 6,000 fc (50 to 60 klux) are adequate for stock and finishing plants, with fertilization rates of 1,200 lb/A/yr (1,345 kg/ha/yr) of N-P$_2$O$_5$-K$_2$O. Greenhouse night temperatures should be 55°F (13°C) or higher to maintain growth.

Diseases. Reported diseases include leaf spot (*Septoria iresines*) and root rot (*Rhizoctonia solani*) [4].

Insects and related pests. Scale and aphids are common insect problems.

Species and cultivars. *Iresine herbstii* and *I. herbstii* 'Aureoreticulata.'

Maranta: Family Marantaceae

Maranta is a genus composed of about twenty species of herbaceous plants native to tropical America. Although caulescent, the stems are pendant and plants grow in clumps, root at nodes, and spread from underground tuberous roots. Most cultivated species are grown as interior foliage plants for their thin, attractively patterned leaves. Their growth habit makes them suitable as pedestal plants, hanging baskets, or in terrariums or dish gardens. Their ability to "fold" or close their leaves at night resulted in the common name prayer plant. If relative humidity is kept above 25 percent, prayer plants are excellent interior plants.

Culture. *Maranta* is propagated by division or by tip cuttings rooted under intermittent mist. Recommended light intensities are from 2,000 to 2,500 fc (20 to 25 klux), with fertilization rates of 900 lb/A/yr (1,008 kg/ha/yr) of N-P$_2$O$_5$-K$_2$O for potted, acclimatized foliage plant production [2]. Minimum greenhouse night temperatures should be above 55°F (13°C).

Diseases. Reported diseases include leaf spot (*Alternaria* sp. and *Helminthosporium* sp.), soft rot (*Erwinia carotovora*), rust (*Puccinia cannae*), root rot (*Pythium* sp. and *Rhizoctonia solani*), and stem rot *Rhizoctonia solani*) [3].

Insects and related pests. Caterpillars, mites, mealybugs, scale, nematodes, and slugs are common pests.

Species and cultivars. *Maranta leuconeura, M. leuconeura erythroneura, M. leuconeura leuconeura,* and *M. leuconeura* 'Minima.'

Mikania: Family Compositae

This is a diverse genus of about 150 species of shrubs and vining herbs native to North and South America. A few species are used as ground covers or for naturalizing; only *M. ternata* is commonly grown as an interior plant, usually as a hanging basket.

Culture. Members of the *Mikania* genus are propagated by tip or stem cuttings. Plants for building interiors are grown under 4,000 to 6,000 fc and fertilized with 1,500 lb/A/yr (1,700 kg/ha/yr) of N-P_2O_5-K_2O. Greenhouse night temperatures should remain above 55°F (13°C) to maintain growth.

Diseases. Reported diseases include rust (*Puccinia spegazzinii*) [3].

Species and cultivars. *Mikania ternata.*

Monstera: Family Araceae

Monstera is a genus of approximately twenty-five species of epiphytic vines native to tropical America, which climb by adventitious stem roots. Many species have small, simple entire leaves during juvenile growth phases and large fenestrate leaves when mature.

Culture. Plants are propagated from tip and stem cuttings taken from stock plants. Light intensities of 3,500 to 4,500 fc (35 to 45 klux) are recommended for production of acclimatized foliage plants, and fertilization rates of 1,500 lb/A/yr (1,700 kg/ha/yr) of N-P_2O_5-K_2O produce high-quality plants.

Diseases. Diseases include anthracnose (*Glomerella cingulata*), bacterial soft rot (*Erwinia carotovora*), black leaf spot (*Pseudomonas cichorii*), leaf spot (*Macrophoma philodendri, Phyllosticta* sp., and *Phytophthora* sp.), necrotic leaf spot (*Leptosphaeria* sp.), root rot (*Pythium splendens*), and stem and root rot (*Rhizoctonia solani*) [3].

Insects and related pests. Mealybugs, mites, scale, and thrips are common pests.

Species and cultivars. *Monstera deliciosa, M. deliciosa borsigiana,* and *M. friedrichsthalii.*

Nautilocalyx: Family Gesneriaceae

Nautilocalyx is a genus of about twelve species of herbaceous plants native to tropical America. All have opposite large leaves, usually with erect succulent stems. These plants grow best with relative humidities of 50 percent or more and are grown in groupings with other plants or in conservatories where marked color contrast in plantings is desired.

Culture. *Nautilocalyx* is propagated by cuttings and rooted under intermittent mist with bottom heat. Commercially, plants are grown under 2,000 to 2,500 fc (20 to 25 klux) and fertilized with 1,200 lb/A/yr (1,345 kg/ha/yr) of $N-P_2O_5-K_2O$. Greenhouse night temperatures should be above 55°F (13°C) to maintain growth.

Diseases. *Nautilocalyx* is not listed in disease complications, but growers report root rot, leaf spot, and stem rot as occasional problems.

Insects and related pests. Mites, scale, and nematodes can create problems.

Species and cultivars. *Nautilocalyx lynchii* or *Alloplectus lynchii.*

Nephrolepis: Family Polypodiaceae

The sword ferns of the genus *Nephrolepis* include approximately thirty species in tropical and subtropical areas of the New and Old World. Fronds of most species are long, narrow, singly pinnate, often pinnatified toward the tip, and arise from short upright rhizomes that develop along surface stolons. Representatives of this genus constitute some of the original commercial foliage plants produced in the United States. Many *Nephrolepis* are durable and versatile as interior plants; they are used also as ground covers in indoor gardens, hanging baskets, pedestal plants, terrarium plants (dwarf types only), and large floor plants (upright types).

Culture. Plants are normally propagated from small rooted rhizomes with several fronds attached, which are easily removed from stolons on the soil surface. Some specialists in southern production areas grow large beds or benches of stock from which plantlets are harvested periodically. Other producers obtain propagation material from finished baskets or large pots prior to sale. Care should be taken in selecting propagules as some cultivars produce variants that are not true to type. *Nephrolepis* cultivars can be propagated rapidly through tissue-culture techniques. Growers are cautioned to purchase tissue-cultured plants only from reputable propagators who, through experience, know which cultivars they can maintain true to type.

Plants grow well under light levels of 2,500 to 3,000 fc (25 to 30 klux) and fertilizer rates of 1,200 to 1,500 lb/A/yr (1,345 to 1,700 kg/ha/yr) of N-P_2O_5-K_2O [2]. A moist, well-drained soil mixture rich in organic matter is recommended. Greenhouse night temperature should be above 60°F (18°C) for continued growth.

Diseases. Reported diseases include leaf spots (*Cercospora phyllitidis, Cylindrocladium pteridis,* and *Phyllosticta* sp.) and damping off (*Rhizoctonia solani*) [3].

Insects and related pests. Caterpillars, scale, mealybugs, and nematodes can be problems.

Species and cultivars. *Nephrolepis biserrata* 'Furcans,' *N. biserrata, N. exaltata, N. exaltata* 'Bostoniensis,' *N. exaltata* 'Bostoniensis Compacta,' *N. exaltata* 'Fluffy Ruffles,' *N. exaltata* 'Verona,' and *N. exaltata* 'Bostoniensis Aurea.'

Opuntia: Family Cactaceae

The genus *Opuntia* includes almost 300 species dispersed throughout North and South America. Many species are characterized by distinct flattened stem segments, resembling pads, while others have round stems. Their aeroles may have spines and glochids or just glochids. Several species are used outdoors in succulent gardens, and smaller species are used indoors as individual plants or in dish gardens or terrariums with other xerophytic plants.

Culture. Opuntias are propagated by joint or stem cuttings that have been allowed to heal for several days. Commercially, plants are grown under 6,000 to 8,000 fc (60 to 80 klux) and fertilized with 900 to 1,200 lb/A/yr (1,008 to 1,345 kg/ha/yr) of N-P_2O_5-K_2O. Greenhouse night temperatures should be kept above 55°F (13°C) to maintain growth.

Diseases. Reported diseases include anthracnose (*Colletotrichum* sp., *Gloeosporium* sp.), bacterial soft rot (*Erwinia* sp.), and root and stem rot (*Phytophthora* sp. and *Rhizoctonia solani*).

Insects and related pests. Mites and scale are common pests.

Species and cultivars. *Opuntia falcata, O. microdasys,* and *O. vilis.*

Palms: Family Palmaceae

The palm family includes over 200 genera and about 2,800 species of vines and shrublike or treelike plants native primarily to subtropical and tropical areas of the world. Many of these are grown as landscape ornamentals and a few, the African oil palm, coconut palm, and date palm, are important economic plants. In addition to small mature palms, many seedling and juvenile palms can also be grown indoors.

Palms can be divided into two broad groups, the feather palms, which have compound leaves with pinnae (leaflets) arranged along the rachis, and fan palms, which have simple or nearly simple leaves.

Culture. Many commercially grown palms are started from seed, but the clump-forming ones can be propagated by division. Landscape palms may be grown in full sun, but acclimatized plants for interior use should be grown under recommended light intensities for acclimatized plant production, ranging from 2,500 to 6,000 fc (25 to 60 klux), and fertilized with rates from 1,200 to 1,500 lb/A/yr (1,345 to 1,680 kg/ha/yr) of N-P_2O_5-K_2O [2]. Palms are tropical plants and should be grown with minimum greenhouse night temperatures of 60°F (15°C).

Diseases. Diseases that have been reported on *Arenga engleri, Caryota mitis, Chamaerops humilis, Chrysalidocarpus lutescens, Howea forsteriana, Licuala grandis, Livistona chinensis, Phoenix roebelenii, Ptychosperma elegans, Rhapis excelsa,* and *Veitchia merrillii* include anthracnose (*Colletotrichum gloeosporioides, Gloeosporium* sp., *Glomerella cingulata*), black spot (*Catacauma palmicola*), bud rot (*Cytospora palmarum, Fusarium* sp., *Phytophthora palmivora*), false smut, (*Graphiola phoenicis*), leaf spot (*Alternaria* sp., *Cercospora* sp., *Curvularia lunata, Cylindrocladium scoparium, Cytospora* sp., *Didymella phacidiomorpha, Didymopleella* sp., *Diplodia* sp., *Exosporium palmivorum, Gloeosporium* sp., *Helminthosporium* sp., *Monilochaetes* sp., *Pestalotia palmarum, Phomopsis* sp., *Phyllosticta* sp., *Physalospora rhodina,* and *Stigmina palmivora*), mushroom root rot (*Clitocybe tabescens*), mushroom rot (*Ganoderma sulcatum*), rachis spot (*Leptothyrium* sp. and *Phomopsis* sp.), root rot (*Ceratocystis paradoxa, Endoconidiophora paradoxa, Pythium* sp., *Rhizoctonia solani*), tar spot (*Phyllachora* sp.), and wood rot (*Ganoderma* spp.) [3]. Lethal yellowing (causal agent is a microplasma) is a serious disease of many landscape palms but has not been known to occur on palms that are routinely sprayed for insect control.

Insects and related pests. Common pests of palms include scale, mites, nematodes, saddleback caterpillars, mealybugs and chewing beetles, leaf skeletonizer, thrips, and seed weevils.

Pandanus: Family Pandanaceae

The *Pandanus* genus consists of over 600 species of shrubs and trees native to tropical regions of Asia, Africa, and India. All have their sessile leaves spirally arranged on leaf scarred stems. Rooted *Pandanus* suckers are often used in combination foliage plantings; larger plants are used as indoor trees or focal points in mall or airport plantings.

Culture. *Pandanus* is propagated from suckers around the base or fresh seed. It is recommended that seeds be soaked for 24 hours prior to planting. Plants for interior use are usually grown under 4,000 to 5,000 fc (40 to 50 klux) and fertilized with 900 lb/A/yr (1,008 kg/ha/yr) of $N-P_2O_5-K_2O$. Suggested greenhouse night temperature for best growth is 65°F (16°C).

Diseases. Anthracnose (*Colletotrichum gloeosporioides*) and leaf spots (*Diplodia theobromae, Macrophoma pandani, Melanconium pandani, Pestalotia palmarum, Phoma coryphae,* and *Phyllosticta* sp.).

Insects and related pests. Mealy bugs, spider mites, and scale are common pests.

Species and cultivars. *Pandanus utilis, P. veitchii,* and *P. veitchii* 'Nelsoni.'

Pellaea: Family Polypodiaceae

The genus *Pellaea* is comprised of approximately eighty species indigenous to temperate regions of the New World. Plants have fronds ranging from singly pinnate to those that are four times pinnate. Collectively called cliff brake, members of *Pellaea* can be used indoors if high light levels exist. They are used as potted plants, and a few types with pendulous fronds make good hanging baskets.

Culture. Commercial propagation of *Pellaea* is from spores, but crowns of older, container-bound plants can be divided. Production light intensities of 2,000 to 3,000 fc (20 to 30 klux) and fertilization at the rate of 1,000 to 1,200 lb/A/yr (1,125 to 1,345 kg/ha/yr) of $N-P_2O_5-K_2O$ are suggested. Well-drained but moist soil mixes are desired, and 60°F (15°C) temperatures are required for continuous growth.

Diseases. Diseases do not seem to be serious with this group.

Insects and related pests. Scale and mealybugs can be serious pests.

Species and cultivars. *Pellaea rotundifolia, P. viridis* or *P. hastata,* and *P. viridis* var. *macrophylla.*

Pellionia: Family Urticaceae

Pellionia is a genus of approximately fifty species of herbaceous and woody plants native to tropical and subtropical regions of Asia. Two of these species, *P. daveauana* and *P. pulchra,* are grown as foliage plants. Both are used as ground covers in groupings with other foliage plants, as hanging plants, and in terrariums and dish gardens.

Culture. Tip or stem cuttings are taken from stock plants. After rooting, plants are grown under light intensities of 2,000 to 3,000 fc (20 to 30 klux) with fertilization rates of 600 to 750 lb/A/yr (672 to 1,008 kg/ha/yr) of N-P_2O_5-K_2O.

Diseases. Grower communications indicate root and stem rot can be expected.

Insects and related pests. Mites and scale are common pests.

Species and cultivars. *Pellionia daveauana* and *P. pulchra.*

Peperomia: Family Piperaceae

Peperomia is a large genus of over 1,000 species of small herbaceous plants native to tropical and subtropical regions around the world. Many species are grown as individual container plants or in dish gardens or terrariums.

Culture. Peperomias are propagated from cuttings and leaf or stem sections taken from stock plants maintained in beds or large containers. Peperomias for indoor use should be grown under light intensities of 3,000 to 3,500 fc (30 to 35 klux) and fertilized with 1,500 lb/A/yr (1,681 kg/ha/yr) of N-P_2O_5-K_2O [2].

Diseases. Reported diseases include algal leaf spot (*Cephaleuros virescens*), edema (*Cercospora* sp.), gray mold (*Botrytis cinerea*), leaf spot (*Corynespora* sp.), leaf and stem rot (*Phytophthora parasitica* and *Pythium* sp.), necrotic ring spot virus (ring spot), and stem and leaf blight (*Sclerotium rolfsii*) [3]. Leaf and stem rot are often serious diseases if the soil mix is kept excessively wet.

Insects and related pests. Cyclamen and broad mites, thrips, and mealybugs can cause problems.

Species and cultivars. *Peperomia bicolor, P. argyreia, P. caperata, P. galabella* 'Variegata,' *P. incana, P. metallica, P. obtusifolia, P. scandens* or *P. serpens,* and *P. verschaffeltii.*

Philodendron: Family Araceae

The *Philodendron* genus consists of about 200 species native to tropical America. Basically, they can be divided into two groups, vining philodendrons and self-heading ones, which have short internodes, do not climb, and eventually produce self-supporting stems or trunks. Among species, leaves exhibit great variation in size, types of margins or pinnatified margins, and leaf color.

Culture. Philodendrons may be propagated by fresh seed, tip cuttings, single- and double-eye cuttings, and air layering. Generally, vining philodendrons are used in hanging baskets, totems, pedestal plants, and as ground covers in plant combinations; small-leaf forms are used in terrariums and dish gardens. Self-heading philodendrons are used as desk or shelf plants; larger types are used as floor plants.

Light intensities used for most commercial species are between 2,500 and 3,500 fc (25 to 35 klux), with fertilization rates of 1,500 lb/A/yr (1,680 kg/ha/yr) of N-P_2O_5-K_2O recommended for acclimatized plant production [2]. Stock beds of vining philodendrons are usually maintained for cuttings; self-heading philodendrons are propagated from seed.

Diseases. Anthracnose (*Colletotrichum philodendri*), bacterial leaf rot (*Erwinia chrysanthemi*), bacterial soft rot (*Erwinia carotovora*), bacterial leaf rot (*Erwinia aroideae, Pseudomonas cichorii,* and *Xanthomonas dieffenbachiae*), basal stem rot (*Rhizoctonia solani*), gray mold (*Botrytis cinerea*), leaf spot (*Cephalosporium cinnamomeum, Cercospora* sp., *Dactylaria humicola, Gloeosporium* sp., *Glomerella cingulata,* and *Phyllosticta* sp.), brown leaf spot (*Phytophthora nicotianae*), root rot (*Pythium* sp.), southern blight (*Sclerotium rolfsii*), and virus (*mosaic*) [3].

Insects and related pests. Mealybugs, mites, scale, and thrips.

Species and cultivars. *Philodendron domesticum* or *P. hastatum, P.* 'Emerald Queen,' *P. bipennifolium* or *P. panduraeforme, P.* 'Florida,' *P.* 'Majesty,' *P.* 'Prince Dubonnet,' *P.* 'Red Princess,' *P. scandens* or *P. micans, P. scandens oxycardium* or *P. oxycardium* and *P. cordatum,* and *P. selloum.*

Phyllitis: Family Polypodiaceae

Phyllitis consists of eight fern species of temperate areas through the tropics. Fronds are simple and straplike. This genus was formerly listed as *Scolopendrium* [1].

Culture. Commercial propagation is primarily from spores, although some cultivars produce spores that are not reliably true to type. Amateurs have propagated plants from basal stripe sections. Plants are used primarily as potted plants in interiors with medium light levels. Plants are produced successfully under light intensities of 800 to 1,000 fc (8 to 10 klux) with 800 to 1,200 lb/A/yr (896 to 1,345 kg/ha/yr) of

N-P$_2$O$_5$-K$_2$O. Plants are reported to do best if the soil is slightly basic, and approximately 60°F (15°C) minimum is suggested for continued growth.

Diseases. *Phyllitis* is not indexed in standard disease compilations.

Insects and related pests. Scale and mealybugs are frequent pests of *Phyllitis* sp.

Species and cultivars. *Phyllitis scolopendrium.*

Pilea: Family Urticaceae

Pilea is a genus of about 200 herbaceous species native to tropical and subtropical regions throughout the world. They grow upright or trail along the ground. Upright species are used as desk and table plants or in dish gardens as focal points; trailing species are used in hanging baskets, terrariums, or as ground covers in combination plantings.

Culture. They are propagated by stem and tip cuttings and rooted under intermittent mist. Recommended light intensities are 2,000 to 3,000 fc (20 to 30 klux) and fertilization rates of 600 lb/A/yr (672 kg/ha/yr) of N-P$_2$O$_5$-K$_2$O [2].

Diseases. Reported diseases include gray mold (*Botrytis cinerea*), leaf spot (*Rhizoctonia solani*), leaf spot (*Cercospora pileae*), powdery mildew (*Erysiphe cichoracearum*), and southern blight (*Sclerotium rolfsii*).

Insects and related pests. Growers report few problems with this plant.

Species and cultivars. *Pilea cadierei, P. involucrata, P. microphylla, P.* 'Moon Valley,' *P. nummulariifolia, P. repens, P.* 'Silver Tree,' and *P. spruceana.*

Pittosporum: Family Pittosporaceae

Pittosporum is a genus of approximately 100 species of trees and shrubs native to warm temperate, subtropical, and tropical regions of Asia, Africa, and India. Most are grown as landscape ornamentals in warmer parts of the world, with *Pittosporum tobira* often grown as a foliage plant, primarily as a floor plant.

Culture. Plants are propagated from fresh seed or stem cuttings [1]. Commercially, plants are grown under 5,000 to 6,000 fc and fertilized with 1,200 lb/A/yr (1,345 kg/ha/yr) of N-P$_2$O$_5$-K$_2$O. Greenhouse night temperatures above 55°F (13°C) will maintain continued growth, but *Pittosporum tobira* withstands freezing temperatures.

Diseases. Reported diseases include angular leaf spot (*Cercospora pittospori*), crown gall (*Agrobacterium tumefaciens*), dieback (*Physalospora* *rhodina*), foot rot (*Diplodia* sp.), limb blight (*Corticium salmonicolor*), leaf spot (*Alternaria tenuissima* and *Gloeosporium* sp.), stem gall (*Leptosphaeria* sp., *Nectria* sp., and *Volutella* sp.), mushroom root rot (*Clitocybe tabescens*), stem canker (*Diaporthe* sp.), twig dieback (*Coniothyrium* sp.), thread blight (*Pellicularia koleroga* and *Rhizoctonia ramicola*), root rot (*Pythium* sp. and *Rhizoctonia solani*), southern blight (*Sclerotium rolfsii*), and rough bark virus [3].

Insects and related pests. Scale, mealybugs, and bud mites are common pests.

Species and cultivars. *Pittosporum tobira.*

Plectranthus: Family Labiatae

The genus *Plectranthus* includes about 250 species of herbs and shrubs native to tropical regions of Asia, Africa, and Australia. Most *Plectranthus* grown as foliage plants are creeping ground covers and, consequently, are commonly used in hanging baskets or as pedestal plants.

Culture. *Plectranthus* is usually propagated from stem cuttings or tip cuttings, although sometimes propagated by seeds. It is usually grown under 3,000 to 4,000 fc and fertilized with 1,200 to 1,500 lb/A/yr (1,345 to 1,700 kg/ha/yr) of N-P_2O_5-K_2O. Even though some species of *Plectranthus* tolerate freezing temperatures, they require minimum night greenhouse temperatures of 55°F (13°C) for best growth.

Diseases. No reported diseases are listed.

Insects and related pests. Mealybugs, nematodes, and whitefly may become troublesome.

Species and cultivars. *Plectranthus australis* and *P. coleoides.*

Podocarpus: Family Podocarpaceae

Podocarpus is a genus of dioecious, coniferous trees and shrubs native to mountainous areas in the southern hemisphere. Most of the seventy-five species are characterized by flat, needlelike, spirally arranged leaves. They are widely used as landscape plants, but several tolerate interior building conditions, with seedlings used in dish gardens and terrariums and large specimens used as indoor trees. Unlike many foliage plants, they tolerate chilling temperatures of 32°F to 50°F (0°C to 10°C).

Culture. *Podocarpus* is propagated from freshly sown seed or tip cuttings and grown under light intensities of 4,000 to 5,000 fc (40 to 50 klux). Fertilization rates of 900 to 1,200 lb/A/yr (1,008 to 1,345 kg/ha/yr) of N-P_2O_5-K_2O are adequate for stock plants or container-grown plants.

Diseases. Reported disease include dieback (*Botryosphaeria* sp., *Dip-*

lodia sp.), anthracnose (*Colletotrichum gloeosporioides*), leaf spot (*Cylindrocladium* sp., *Heterosporium* sp., *Macrophoma* sp., and *Phyllosticta* sp.), mushroom root rot (*Clitocybe tabescens*), leaf blight (*Fusarium* sp.), and root rot (*Pythium* sp. and *Rhizoctonia solani*) [3].

Insects and related pests. Aphids, mealybugs, mites, and scale may be troublesome.

Species and cultivars. *Podocarpus macrophyllus.*

Polypodium: Family Polypodiaceae

The genus *Polypodium* is a large genus, which may be subdivided into as many as twenty different genera. Most plants in *Polypodium* are tropical and epiphytic, with creeping rhizomes and fronds simple to once divided. Some large types are reserved primarily for conservatories or private collectors with sizable greenhouses. Medium and small forms are suitable as potted plants and hanging baskets indoors under bright light levels. Plants can be displayed effectively in pots, hanging baskets, and in ground plantings in large interiorscapes.

Culture. Plants in this genus do best in well-drained soils of high organic matter content that are kept moist but not wet. Light levels of 1,200 to 1,800 fc (12 to 18 klux) and fertilization rates of 800 to 1,200 lb/A/yr (900 to 1,345 kg/ha/yr) of $N-P_2O_5-K_2O$ will produce high-quality plants. Propagation is by spores or rhizome divisions.

Diseases. Diseases include leaf spot (*Cercospora phyllitidis*) [3].

Insects and related pests. Scale and mealybugs are frequent pests of several species of *Polypodium.*

Species and cultivars. *Polypodium aureum* and *P. punctatum* or *P. polycarpon.*

Polyscias: Family Araliaceae

This genus of eighty species of small trees and shrubs is mostly native to South Sea islands and tropical Asia. Leaves are usually compound and often exhibit considerable variations, especially between juvenile and mature wood. Stems and branches are usually slender and flexible, and new growth is characterized by conspicuous lenticels. Plants in the genus are widely used as landscape specimens and hedge plants in tropical areas. A number of species are used indoors as indoor trees and floor and desk plants, and several cultivars are grown as bonsai subjects.

Culture. *Polyscias* is usually propagated from tip or stem cuttings from field-grown or container-grown stock plants, and some plants can be propagated from root cuttings. Plants for interior use are grown commercially under 4,000 to 6,000 fc (40 to 60 klux) and fertilized with 1,200 lb/A/yr (1,345 kg/ha/yr) of N-P$_2$O$_5$-K$_2$O. *Polyscias* often react to sudden changes in relative humidity, light intensity, and temperature by dropping their leaves. Consequently, greenhouse environments should remain relatively constant for optimum growth, and night temperatures should be at or above 55°F (13°C).

Diseases. Reported diseases include leaf spot (*Alternaria* sp., *Cercospora* sp., and *Colletotrichum peregrinum*) and leaf, stem, and petiole rot (*Rhizoctonia solani*) [3].

Insects and related pests. Mites, scale, and mealybugs are common pests.

Species and cultivars. *Polyscias balfouriana, P. filicifolia, P. fruticosa,* and *P. guilfoylei.*

Rhoeo: Family Commelinaceae

Rhoeo is a small genus consisting of one species, *R. spathacea,* native to moist areas in the West Indies, Mexico, and Guatemala. It is widely used as a ground cover in exterior plantings and as a container plant or ground cover in interiors.

Culture. *Rhoeo* is commercially propagated from cuttings, although division can be used on established plants. Commercially, it is grown under light intensities of 4,000 to 6,000 fc (40 to 60 klux) and fertilized with 1,200 lb/A/yr (1,345 kg/ha/yr) of N-P$_2$O$_5$-K$_2$O. Native to tropical areas, greenhouse night temperatures should not fall below 55°F (13°C) to maintain continued growth.

Diseases. Reported diseases include anthracnose (*Colletotrichum* sp.), leaf spot (*Curvularia eragrostidis*), and stem rot (*Pythium* sp.) [3].

Insects and related pests. Mealybugs and mites may become serious pests.

Species and cultivars. *Rhoeo spathacea.*

Rhoicissus: Family Vitaceae

This genus has about ten species of vines or shrubs native to tropical and southern Africa. Plants closely resemble *Cissus* species, but differ in floral structure.

Culture. *Rhoicissus* is propagated from leaf bud cuttings taken from stock plants as needed. They are finished after rooting in light intensities of 3,000 to 4,000 fc (30 to 40 klux) and fertilized with 1,200 lb/A/yr (1,345 kg/ha/yr) of N-P$_2$O$_5$-K$_2$O.

Diseases. Reported diseases include leaf spot (*Cercospora* sp.), root rot (*Rhizoctonia solani*), rust (*Endophyllum circumscriptum*), and smut (*Mykosyrinx cissi* and *Ustilago cissi*) [3].

Insects and related pests. Broad mites, mealybugs, spider mites, and scale may occasionally cause problems.

Species and cultivars. *Rhoicissus capensis.*

Ruellia: Family Acanthaceae

Most of the 250 species in the *Ruellia* genus are native to tropical America, Africa, and Asia. Most of the cultivated species are grown for flowers; only the species *Ruellia makoyana* is commonly grown as a foliage plant.

Culture. Plants root readily from stem or tip cuttings in a peat-perlite mixture under intermittent mist. Light intensities for both stock and finishing plants are between 2,000 to 3,000 fc (20 to 30 klux). Fertilization rates of 900 to 1,200 lb/A/yr (1,008 to 1,345 kg/ha/yr) of N-P_2O_5-K_2O would be suitable for stock or container plant production. Greenhouse night temperatures should be kept above 60°F (16°C) to maintain growth.

Diseases. Reported diseases include bacterial leaf spot (*Pseudomonas cichorii*), leaf spot (*Cercospora consociata*), root and stem rot (*Rhizoctonia solani*), and rust (*Puccinia ruelliae*) [3].

Insects and related pests. Mites and mealybugs are common insect pests.

Species and cultivars. *Ruellia makoyana.*

Sansevieria: Family Agavaceae

All sixty species found in the *Sansevieria* genus are native to Africa, Arabia, and India, where many are cultivated for their leaf fiber. Several species are grown as foliage plants as they tolerate low light, infrequent waterings, and low relative humidities. Most plants are sold as container plants, but they are often used as focal points in dish gardens.

Culture. Stock beds of *Sansevieria* are usually grown in open fields or under 40 to 60 percent shade in shade house or greenhouse ground beds. Three-leaved divisions are removed every 2 to 3 months for potting or shipment as unrooted divisions. Small plants of the nonvariegated cultivars may be propagated from 2 to 6 inches (5 to 15 centimeters) leaf sections. *Sansevieria* is sensitive to chilling damage, and lesions develop on leaves when exposed to chilling temperatures (32° to 50°F or 0°

to 10°C). Potted acclimatized foliage plants should be grown in 3,500 to 4,500 fc (35 to 45 klux) with 600 to 900 lb/A/yr (672 to 1,008 kg/ha/yr) of N-P$_2$O$_5$-K$_2$O. Greenhouse night temperatures should be kept at or above 60°F (15°C) to maintain growth.

Diseases. Reported diseases include algal leaf spot (*Cephaleuros virescens*), anthracnose (*Colletotrichum* sp.), bacterial soft rot (*Erwinia* sp.), gray mold (*Botrytis cinerea*), leaf blight (*Pythium* sp.), and root and stem rot (*Rhizoctonia solani*) [3].

Insects and related pests. Thrips and root knot nematodes may become serious pests.

Species and cultivars. *Sansevieria trifasciata* and *S. trifasciata* 'Golden Hahnii' and 'Silver Hahnii'.

Saxifraga: Family Saxifragaceae

A varied genus of 300 or so species, many are native to cool, rocky regions of Europe, Asia, Africa, and North and South America. Of these 300 species, only *Saxifraga stolonifera* is grown as a foliage plant.

Culture. Commercially, plants are propagated by severing the stolon and propagating the plantlets. It is grown in 3,000 to 5,000 fc (30 to 50 klux), with fertilization rates of 900 to 1,200 lb/A/yr (1,008 to 1,345 kg/ha/yr) of N-P$_2$O$_5$-K$_2$O.

Diseases. Reported diseases include gray mold (*Botrytis cinerea*), leaf spots (*Cercosporella saxifraga, Phyllosticta saxifragarum, Septoria albicans, Ramularia* sp.), powdery mildew (*Sphaerotheca macularis*), and rust (*Melampsora artica, Puccinia leucherae, Puccinia pazschkii*) [4].

Insects and related pests. Mealybugs and whitefly may become troublesome.

Species and cultivars. *Saxifraga stolonifera (S. sarmentosa).*

Schlumbergera: Family Cactaceae

Schlumbergera is a genus of epiphytic cacti containing three species all native to Brazil. They have flattened, photosynthetic, branching, green, jointed stems. Cultivated species are usually grown as container plants for their interesting cascading stems and attractive flowers.

Culture. *Schlumbergera* is usually propagated in peat moss using two jointed stem cuttings. Acclimatized plants are produced under 3,000 to 4,000 fc (30 to 40 klux) and fertilized with 1,200 lb/A/yr (1,345 kg/ha/yr) of N-P$_2$O$_5$-K$_2$O [2]. Commercially, plants are brought to flower with 7 weeks of short days. Plants tolerate temperatures near freezing, but greenhouse night temperatures should remain above 55°F (13°C) for continued growth.

Diseases. Stem blight (*Cercosporidium* sp.), anthracnose (*Gloeosporium* and *Colletotrichum* sp.), bacterial soft rot (*Erwinia* sp.), root and stem rot (*Fusarium oxysporum*), stem rot (*Helminthosporium* sp.), and root and stem rot (*Phytophthora* sp., *Pythium* sp., *Rhizoctonia solani*) [3].

Insects and related pests. Mites, scale, and mealybugs are common pests.

Species and cultivars. *Schlumbergera bridgesii* and *S. truncata* (*Zygocactus truncatus*).

Scindapsus: Family Araceae

Scindapsus is a genus of about twenty species of vining, root-climbing plants with simple leaves native to the Malay Archipelago. Golden pothos is now classified as *Epipremnum aureum*. *Scindapsus pictus* is the only one commonly grown as a foliage plant; because of its vining characteristics, it is used as a totem, hanging basket, ground cover in large planters, pedestal plant, and, occasionally, in dish gardens.

Culture. Six-node or larger cuttings are taken from stock plants as needed and cut into single- or double-eye cuttings propagated under intermittent mist. To produce acclimatized plants, *S. pictus* should be grown under 3,500 to 4,500 fc (35 to 45 klux) and fertilized with 1,500 lb/A/yr (1,700 kg/ha/yr) of N-P$_2$O$_5$-K$_2$O [2]. *Scindapus pictus* is chill sensitive, and greenhouse night temperatures should be kept at a minimum of 60°F (15°C).

Diseases. *Scindapus pictus* is not listed individually in disease listings, but growers report problems with bacterial soft rot, leaf spot, and root rot.

Insects and related pests. Mealybugs, root mealybugs, and scale are among the common insect pests.

Species and cultivars. *Scindapsus pictus*.

Sedum: Family Crassulaceae

Sedum is a genus of about 600 species of shrubs and herbs native to temperate zones in the northern hemisphere. Many *Sedum* species resemble *Crassula* species, but they usually can be distinguished by having alternate rather than opposite leaves. Sedums are commonly grown in temperate succulent gardens, and a number of the smaller species are grown as interior plants, where they do best in high light areas.

Culture. *Sedum* is propagated from leaf or tip cuttings, and plants are usually grown under 5,000 to 6,000 fc (50 to 60 klux) and fertilized with 1,200 lb/A/yr (1,345 kg/ha/yr) of N-P$_2$O$_5$-K$_2$O. Soil mixes should be well drained, and plants should not be overwatered. Sedums grow better when greenhouse night temperatures do not go lower than 55°F (13°C).

Diseases. Reported diseases include leaf spots (*Cercospora* sp., *Septoria* sp., and *Stemphylium bolicki*) [3].

Insects and related pests. Mealybugs and scale are the most troublesome.

Species and cultivars. *Sedum morganianum.*

Senecio: Family Compositae

The 2,000 to 3,000 species in the genus *Senecio* place it among the largest genera. This large number of plants includes annuals, perennials, herbs, vines, shrubs, and even treelike plants. Cultivated species are grown for their flowers, foliage, or xerophytic properties. Usually, those grown as interior plants are vines used in hanging baskets or as totems.

Culture. *Senecio* can be propagated by stem or tip cuttings. Commercially, senecios are grown under light intensities varying from 4,000 to 6,000 fc (40 to 60 klux) depending on the species, and fertilization rates varying with species from 900 to 1,500 lb/A/yr (1,008 to 1,700 kg/ha/yr) of $N-P_2O_5-K_2O$. Senecios tolerate cool temperatures, but greenhouse night temperatures should be kept at 55°F (13°C) or higher for continued growth.

Diseases. Reported diseases include black scab (*Systremma* sp.), leaf spot (*Alternaria senecionis, Cercospora senecionis, Stemphylium* sp.), root rot (*Rhizoctonia solani*), stem rot (*Sclerotinia sclerotiorum*), and southern blight (*Sclerotium rolfsii*).

Insects and related pests. Scale and mealybugs are the most common pests.

Species and cultivars. *Senecio herreianus* and *S. macroglossus.*

Soleirolia: Family Urticaceae

Soleirolia is a small genus confined to a single species, *S. soleirolii,* native to the Mediterranean area. It was formerly classified as *Helxine* [1].

Culture. This plant is propagated from stem or tip cuttings as needed from stock plants. Light intensities of 2,000 to 2,500 fc (20 to 25 klux) are suitable for stock and finishing production areas, with fertilization rates of 600 lb/A/yr (672 kg/ha/yr) of $N-P_2O_5-K_2O$. Greenhouse temperatures should remain above 55°F (13°C) for continued growth.

Diseases. Standard disease compilations do not list *Soleirolia* sp.

Insects and related pests. Mealybugs and scale are common insect pests.

Species and cultivars. *Soleirolia soleirolii.*

Sonerila: Family Melastomataceae

About 100 species of herbs and semiwoody shrubs native to tropical Asia comprise the genus *Sonerila.* Many have attractive, puckered, pearl-spotted leaf blades, but require warm temperatures and high humidity to remain attractive. Plants in the genus are used for terrariums, dish gardens, and plant collections.

Culture. It is propagated by cuttings and freshly sown seed and grown under 1,500 to 2,000 fc (15 to 20 klux). Fertilization rates of 1,200 lb/A/yr (1,345 kg/ha/yr) of N-P_2O_5-K_2O produce quality plants.

Diseases. Growers report leaf spot and root rot as occasional problems.

Insects and related pests. Scale and nematodes may cause problems.

Species and cultivars. *Sonerila margaritacea.*

Sphaeropteris: Family Cyatheaceae

This genus has around 120 species of tree ferns; many are native to tropical regions in Australia and New Zealand. Several species are grown as landscape ornamentals in warm climates, and some are used as interior plants in plant groupings or as a specimen plant in conservatories where high relative humidity can be maintained. Poor growth in building interiors is usually associated with low humidity and trunk drying.

Culture. Tree ferns are propagated from spores, with several years required to produce a sizable plant. Commercially, plants for interiors are grown under 3,000 to 5,000 fc (30 to 50 klux) and fertilized with 1,200 lb/A/yr (1,345 kg/ha/yr) of N-P_2O_5-K_2O. Greenhouse night temperatures should be maintained at 55°F (13°C) or above to maintain productive growth.

Diseases. Reported diseases include leaf spot (*Cercospora* sp.) and stem rot (*Rhizoctonia solani*) [3].

Insects and related pests. Scale and mealybugs are the most common pests of these plants.

Species and cultivars. *Sphaeropteris cooperi* or *Alsophila cooperi* or *Alsophila australis.*

Spathiphyllum: Family Araceae

The genus *Spathiphyllum* has about thirty-five species of tropical, perennial, herbaceous plants. The sheathing leaves normally arise in clusters from a stem so short that they appear acaulescent. Although some species and cultivars occasionally are grown outdoors in tropical countries, most are grown as interior foliage plants for their ability to tolerate low light levels and produce occasional white inflorescences. Small spathiphyllums as indoor plants are usually grown as shelf or table plants; larger specimens are grown as low floor plants, often as facing plants for groupings of other plants.

Culture. *Spathiphyllum* is propagated by division of mature plants or from seeds or by tissue culture techniques. To produce acclimatized indoor plants, suggested light intensities are 1,500 to 2,500 (15 to 25 klux); fertilize with 1,200 lb/A/yr (1,345 kg/ha/yr) of N-P_2O_5-K_2O [2]. Greenhouse night temperatures should be kept above 55°F (13°C).

Diseases. Reported diseases include anthracnose (*Colletotrichum* sp.), bacterial leaf spot (*Pseudomonas cichorii*), green scurf (*Cephaleuros virescens*), leaf blight (*Phytophthora* sp.), and leaf spot (*Cercospora* sp.).

Insects and related pests. Common pests include mites, mealybugs, and scale.

Species and cultivars. *Spathiphyllum cannifolium, S.* 'Clevelandii,' *S. floribundum, S.* 'Mauna Loa,' *S. phryniifolium,* and *S.* 'Wallissi.'

Strobilanthes: Family Acanthaceae

More than 200 species of *Strobilanthes* are native to tropical Asia, but only a few are grown as foliage plants. They are herbaceous or shrublike plants with opposite leaves.

Culture. Stem and tip cuttings root readily in 3 to 4 weeks. Light intensities for stock production and finishing plants are from 3,000 to 4,000 fc (30 to 40 klux), and fertilization rates of 900 to 1,200 lb/A/yr (1,008 to 1,345 kg/ha/yr) of N-P_2O_5-K_2O would be suitable for stock or container plant production. Greenhouse night temperatures should be 60°F (15°C) or higher for continued growth.

Insects and related pests. Mites and mealybugs are common problems.

Diseases. *Strobilanthes* is not listed in standard disease compilations, but growers report occasional trouble with leaf-spotting diseases.

Species and cultivars. *Strobilanthes dyerianus.*

Syngonium: Family Araceae

This genus is comprised of about twenty species of climbing vines native to South America. Leaves of young plants are usually arrow shaped and simple, but as plants mature, leaves become compound, with three to thirteen segments depending on plant leaf maturity. Their vining growth habit makes them ideal for totems and hanging baskets, but rooted cuttings are often used in dish gardens and terrariums.

Culture. *Syngonium* is propagated from single-eye cuttings taken as needed from stock plants. Stock plants should be grown under the most sanitary conditions possible to minimize disease losses during propagation. Acclimatized plants should be grown under 2,500 to 3,500 fc (25 to 30 klux) and fertilized with 1,500 lb/A/yr (1,700 kg/ha/yr) of N-P_2O_5-K_2O [2]. Greenhouse night temperatures should be kept at 65°F (18°C) or higher to maintain growth rate.

Diseases. Reported diseases include bacterial soft rot (*Erwinia* spp.), bacterial leaf blight (*Xanthomonas vitians*), bacterial leaf spot (*Xanthomonas dieffenbachiae*), leaf spot (*Cephalosporium cinnamomeum* and *Cercospora* sp.), leaf blight (*Colletotrichum* sp.), leaf margin blight (*Pseudomonas* sp.), root rot (*Pythium splendens*), root and stem rot (*Rhizoctonia solani*), rust (*Uromyces* sp.), and stem rot of cuttings (*Sclerotium rolfsii*).

Insects and related pests. Mealybugs, scale, and thrips are common pests.

Species and cultivars. *Syngonium podophyllum* and *S. wendlandii*.

Tolmiea: Family Saxifragaceae

The *Tolmiea* genus is limited to one species native to western North America, *T. menziesii*.

Culture. Commercially, the plants are grown in 3,500 to 4,000 fc (35 to 40 klux) shade and fertilized with 900 to 1,200 lb/A/yr (1,008 to 1,345 kg/ha/yr) of N-P_2O_5-K_2O.

Diseases. *Tolmiea* is not listed in standard disease compilations, but growers indicate root rot can be troublesome, especially during hot weather.

Insects and related pests. Mealybugs, whitefly, and mites are the most common pests.

Species and cultivars. *Tolmiea menziesii*.

Tradescantia: Family Commelinaceae

Tradescantia is a genus of a little over twenty species native to North and South America. Hardiness varies, and some species survive outdoors in temperate zones. Growth habit varies from erect to trailing plants.

Cultivated species are grown outdoors as flowering perennials or as ground covers. Those grown indoors are trailing species with colorful foliage and are often used in hanging baskets or as pedestal plants.

Culture. *Tradescantia* is propagated by cuttings taken as needed from stock plants and rooted under intermittent mist. Commercially, they are grown under 3,500 to 4,500 fc (35 to 45 klux) and fertilized with 1,200 to 1,500 lb/A/yr (1,008 to 1,345 kg/ha/yr of $N-P_2O_5-K_2O$. Greenhouse night temperatures should not drop below 50°F (13°C) for best growth rate.

Diseases. Reported diseases include bacterial soft rot (*Erwinia* sp.), bacterial leaf spot (*Pseudomonas woodsii*), and leaf blight (*Rhizoctonia* sp.) [3].

Insects and related pests. Mealybugs, scale, and nematodes are reported as common pests.

Species and cultivars. *Tradescantia albiflora* and *T. fluminensis.*

Yucca: Family Agavaceae

All forty species of *Yucca* are native to North America, where they grow on semiarid or well-drained soils. Over half the species eventually attain heights over 30 feet (9 meters) with a rosette of leaves on top of a bare, woody stem. The other yuccas are acaulescent. Stem-forming yuccas may be propagated by cane cuttings, terminal cuttings, or seed. Most yuccas have extremely sharp spines on the tip of their sessile leaves and, for this reason, are seldom grown for interior use. However, some species have spineless leaves and can be used in interiors.

Culture. Cut cane of *Y. elephantipes* plants is propagated in beds or directly in containers filled with a well-drained soil mix. Light intensities for potted plants are 3,500 to 4,000 fc (35 to 45 klux), with fertilization rates of 1,200 lb/A/yr (1,345 kg/ha/yr) of $N-P_2O_5-K_2O$.

Diseases. Reported diseases include leaf spots (*Alternaria* sp., *Cercospora* sp., *Coniothyrium concentricum, Diplodia circinans, Fusarium lateritium, Septoria yuccae, Sphaerodothis pringlei,* and *Stagonospora gigantea*), leaf necrosis (*Cytosporina* sp.), tip dieback (*Hendersonia*), leaf blight (*Kellermannia anomala*), and southern blight (*Sclerotium rolfsii*) [3]. Although a lengthy list, diseases are not a major production problem.

Insects and related pests. Root mealybugs and scale may become troublesome.

Species and cultivars. *Yucca elephantipes.*

Zebrina: Family Commelinaceae

Zebrina is a small genus of two species native to Mexico and Guatemala. Stems grow upright, but lack sufficient strength to attain heights over 1 foot (30 centimeters) or so before cascading over and becoming prostrate, rooting at the nodes where they touch the soil surface. They are grown as outdoor ground covers in subtropical and tropical regions, and also make attractive interior plants where they are usually grown as hanging baskets or pedestal plants.

Culture. *Zebrina* is propagated from tip cuttings taken as needed from stock plants. Commercially, zebrinas grown for interiors are grown under light intensities of 3,500 to 4,500 fc (35 to 45 klux) and fertilized with 1,200 to 1,500 lb/A/yr (1,008 to 1,345 kg/ha/yr) of $N-P_2O_5-K_2O$. Greenhouse night temperatures should not drop below 50°F (13°C) to maintain growth.

Diseases. Leaf spot (*Cercospora zebrina* and *Chaetoseptoria* sp.) and rust (*Uromyces commelinae*) [3].

Insects and related pests. Mealybugs, scale, and nematodes are reported as common pests.

Species and cultivars. *Zebrina pendula.*

REFERENCES

[1] Bailey, L. H., and E. Z. Bailey. 1976. *Hortus III.* New York: Macmillan.

[2] Conover, C. A., R. T. Poole, and R. W. Henley. 1975. Growing acclimatized foliage plants. *Florida Foliage Grower* 12(9):1–7.

[3] Wehlburg, C., S. A. Alfieri, Jr., K. R. Langdon, and J. W. Kimbrough. 1975. *Index of Plant Diseases in Florida.* Bulletin 11. Florida Dept. of Agriculture and Consumer Services.

[4] Wescott, C. 1971. *Plant Disease Handbook.* New York: Van Nostrand Reinhold.

index